T0318479

Enterprise Operations Management

HANDBOOK

2ND EDITION

OTHER AUERBACH PUBLICATIONS

A Standard for Auditing Computer Applications, Martin Krist,
ISBN: 0-8493-9983-1

Analyzing Business Information Systems, Shouhong Wang,
ISBN: 0-8493-9240-3

Broadband Networking, James Trulove, Editor, ISBN: 0-8493-9821-5

Communications Systems Management Handbook, 6th Edition,
Anura Gurugé and Lisa M. Lindgren, Editors, 0-8493-9826-6

Computer Telephony Integration, William Yarberry, Jr.,
ISBN: 0-8493-9995-5

Data Management Handbook, 3rd Edition, Sanjiv Purba, Editor,
ISBN: 0-8493-9832-0

Electronic Messaging, Nancy Cox, Editor, ISBN: 0-8493-9825-8

Enterprise Systems Architectures, Andersen Consulting, 0-8493-9836-3

Enterprise Systems Integration, John Wyzalek, Editor, ISBN: 0-8493-9837-1

Healthcare Information Systems, Phillip L. Davidson, Editor, ISBN: 0-8493-9963-7

Information Security Architecture, Jan Killmeyer, ISBN: 0-8493-9988-2

Information Security Management Handbook, 4th Edition,
Harold F. Tipton and Micki Krause, Editors, ISBN: 0-8493-9829-0

IS Management Handbook, 7th Edition, Carol V. Brown, Editor,
ISBN: 0-8493-9820-7

Information Technology Control and Audit, Frederick Gallegos, Sandra Allen-Senft,
and Daniel P. Manson, ISBN: 0-8493-9994-7

Internet Management, Jessica Keyes, Editor,
ISBN: 0-8493-9987-4

Local Area Network Handbook, 6th Edition, John P. Slone, Editor,
ISBN: 0-8493-9838-X

Multi-Operating System Networking: Living with UNIX, NetWare, and NT,
Raj Rajagopal, Editor, ISBN: 0-8493-9831-2

Network Manager's Handbook, 3rd Edition, John Lusa, Editor,
ISBN: 0-8493-9841-X

Project Management, Paul C. Tinnirello, Editor, ISBN: 0-8493-9998-X

Effective Use of Teams in IT Audits, Martin Krist,
ISBN: 0-8493-9828-2

Systems Development Handbook, 4th Edition, Paul C. Tinnirello, Editor,
ISBN: 0-8493-9822-3

AUERBACH PUBLICATIONS

www.auerbach-publications.com
TO Order: Call: 1-800-272-7737 • Fax: 1-800-374-3401
E-mail: orders@crcpress.com

Enterprise
Operations
Management

HANDBOOK

2ND EDITION

Steven F. Blanding

EDITOR

CRC Press
Taylor & Francis Group
Boca Raton London New York

CRC Press is an imprint of the
Taylor & Francis Group, an **informa** business

AN AUERBACH BOOK

CRC Press
Taylor & Francis Group
6000 Broken Sound Parkway NW, Suite 300
Boca Raton, FL 33487-2742

First issued in paperback 2019

© 1999 by Taylor & Francis Group, LLC
CRC Press is an imprint of Taylor & Francis Group, an Informa business

No claim to original U.S. Government works

ISBN-13: 978-0-8493-9824-7 (hbk)
ISBN-13: 978-0-367-39936-8 (pbk)

Library of Congress Cataloging-in-Publication Data

Enterprise Operations Management Handbook / edited by Steven F. Blanding.—2nd ed.
  p. cm.
Includes index.
ISBN 0-8493-9824-X (alk. paper)
    1. Information Technology—Management. 2. Client/server computer—Management 3. Business enterprises—Computer networks—Management. 4. Electronic data processing departments—Management.
I. Blanding, Steven F.
HD30.2.H364 1999
658'.05—dc21

99-39628
CIP

Library of Congress Card Number 99-39628

Visit the Taylor & Francis Web site at
http://www.taylorandfrancis.com

and the CRC Press Web site at
http://www.crcpress.com

Contributors

ANN S. ANGEL, *President, Technologies Training of the Triad, Inc., Winston-Salem and Greensboro, NC*

JOE AUER, *Founder and President, International Computer Negotiations, Inc., Winter Park, FL*

C. WARREN AXELROD, *Senior Vice President, Corporate Information Systems, Carroll McEntee & McGinley, Inc., New York, NY*

LAYNE C. BRADLEY, *Vice President, Technology Management Group, Computer Sciences Corporation, Fort Worth, TX*

CHARLES V. BREAKFIELD, *Senior Engineer, Symposium Professional Services, Nortel, Dallas, TX*

JOE R. BRIONES, *Manager of Computer Services, Computer Sciences Corporation, Ft. Worth, TX*

THOMAS A. BROWDY, *Director, Center for the Application of Information Technology, Washington University, St. Louis, MO*

ROXANNE BURKEY, *Senior Consultant Designer, Symposium Professional Services, Nortel, Dallas, TX*

VISHAL DESAI, *President, Savli Group, Silver Spring, MD*

EDWARD S. DEVLIN, *Independent Consultant, Westchester, PA*

S. ANN EARON, *Director, Telemanagement Resources International, Inc., Skillman, NJ*

COLE H. EMERSON, *President, Cole Emerson & Associates, Fair Oaks, CA*

JOHN FISKE, *Independent Writer, Prides Crossing, PA*

MICHAEL L. GIBSON, *Professor of Management, Auburn University, Auburn, AL*

CARL STEPHEN GUYNES, *Professor, College of Business Administration, University of North Texas, Denton, TX*

RON HALE, *Senior Manager, Deloitte & Touche LLP, Chicago, IL*

IAN S. HAYES, *Principal, Clarity Consulting, Salem, MA*

ROBERT L. HECKMAN, *Assistant Professor, School of Information Studies, Syracuse University, Syracuse, NY*

GILBERT HELD, *Director, 4-Degree Consulting, Macon, GA*

LUKE HOHMANN, *Vice President of Engineering, SmartPatents, Inc., Mountain View, CA*

KEITH A. JONES, *Certified Quality Analyst and Senior Data Services Consultant, Dun & Bradstreet, Palm Harbor, FL*

LEON A. KAPPELMAN, *Department of Business Computer Information Systems, University of North Texas, Denton, TX*

RANDY KECK, *Technology Manager, Operations Control Systems, Palo Alto, CA*

CAROL L. LARSON, *Freelance Desktop Publisher, Beaverton, OR*

JAMES A. LARSON, *Senior Software Engineer, Intel Architecture Lab, Hillsboro, OR*

ANDRES LLANA, JR., *Telecommunications Consultant, Vermont Studies Group, Inc., King of Prussia, PA*

MARTIN F. MEDEIROS II, *Manager, Technology Procurement, United States Fidelity and Guarantee Co., Baltimore, MD*

STEWART S. MILLER, *President and Owner, Executive Information Services, Carlsbad, CA*

NANCY BLUMENSTALK MINGUS, *President, Mingus Associates, Inc., Williamsville, NY*

NATHAN J. MULLER, *Independent Consultant, Huntsville, AL*

WILLIAM HUGH MURRAY, *Executive Consultant, Information Systems Security, Deloitte & Touche, New Canaan, CT*

JEFF MURRELL, *Manager, Enterprise Computing Operations, Information Systems and Services Division, Texas Instruments, Inc., Plano, TX*

KATE NASSER, *President, CAS, Inc., Somerville, NJ*

PAUL NISENBAUM, *Software Engineer, Candle Corp., Santa Monica, CA*

RAJ RAJAGOPAL, *Principal Scientist, MITRE Corp., McLean, VA*

CHRIS ROOKE, *Director of Product Marketing, Tandem Computers, Inc., Cupertino, CA*

SALVATORE SALAMONE, *News Editor, Byte Magazine, New York, NY*

TARI SCHREIDER, *Director of Research, Contingency Planning Research, Inc., White Plains, NY*

GREG SCILEPPI, *Executive Director, RHI Consulting, Menlo Park, CA*

DUANE E. SHARP, *President, SharpTech Associates, Mississauga, Ontario, Canada*

ROBERT E. UMBAUGH, *Principal, Carlisle Consulting, Carlisle, PA*

MICHAEL E. WHITMAN, *Assistant Professor, Department of Computer Science and Information Systems, Kennesaw State University, Kennesaw, GA*

STEVEN M. WILLIFORD, *President, Franklin Services Group, Inc., Columbus, OH*

JOHN WINDSOR, *Interim Chairman, IS Department, University of North Texas, Denton, TX*

LEO A. WROBEL, JR., *President and Chief Executive Officer, Premiere Network Services, Inc., DeSoto, TX*

Contents

Contents

Contents

Introduction

IN TODAY'S CORPORATE ENVIRONMENT, enterprise technology operations extend well beyond the traditional boundaries of the data center to touch virtually every aspect of the organization's business. Nearly every business need is supported in some way by information technology. As IT operations professionals, you must be in a position to deploy and support the best IT solutions across a broad range of technologies to effectively contribute to your company's competitive advantage.

To respond to your ever-expanding and growing needs as IT operations professionals, this year's edition of the *Enterprise Operations Management Handbook* has been expanded to include four new sections:

- Applications Infrastructure and Operations.
- Desktop Computing.
- Equipment Asset Management.
- Customer Support Operations.

In these new sections, you will be introduced to the latest technology developments that are shaping the industry. Also, this year's edition of the handbook contains completely new material — no chapters from last year's edition have been repeated. This will provide you with a totally fresh perspective of each area of the handbook.

The **Applications Infrastructure and Operations** section is designed to help IT managers deal with these challenges by providing methodologies and solutions for integrating new applications into existing, complex, multiple-platform computing processing environments. The explosion of new client/server application technology has forced the IT operations manager to be more closely involved with the integration of these systems. The IT manager must be capable of analyzing and evaluating the impact of new applications on existing enterprise operations. Because more than 70 percent of all major application systems are still running as legacy systems on mainframe platforms, IT managers are presented with critical challenges in how to integrate both internally developed and purchased client/server applications with these systems.

Another new topic is **Desktop Computing**. IT operations managers must understand the users' desktop configurations in order to effectively provide

1

enterprise-wide computing services to all PCs connected to central computers through local area and wide area networks. In addition, IT managers are typically responsible for centrally managing user desktop software configurations through network management tools. In this section, you will be introduced to a wide range of desktop computing technology solutions that will help manage this important investment.

Also added to this year's handbook is a section on **Equipment Asset Management**. IT operations managers are responsible for the acquisition and maintenance of the assets under their control. These assets include both IT hardware and software, ranging from PCs and printers to mainframes and large enterprise-wide purchased applications. To remain competitive, organizations must acquire and use information technology resources effectively. With the introduction of new decision-support and systems development tools, including prototyping methods, and end users' growing computer literacy and independence, serious attention must be given to not only receiving financial return on investment, but also to acquiring quality products from multiple vendors who are reliable.

The responsibility for providing customer support for the use of technology deployed by the organization's IT department has grown dramatically over the last ten years. Within most organizations, this responsibility is typically placed directly on the shoulders of IT operations management. **Customer Support Operations**, another new section, addresses the issues IT managers face in providing end users this valuable service. To meet this challenge, IT departments are establishing customer-support help desks; providing liaisons into the organization's user departments; assisting end users with their development of client/server applications; providing consultation through user-feedback sessions; and delegating access and control of systems directly to end-user groups. The IT operations manager must understand the best practices in providing these highly visible and critical services.

This year's edition of the *Enterprise Operations Management Handbook* also reinforces the themes introduced in last year's edition. These themes center around the continuing shift of IT services deeper into the day-to-day operations of the enterprise. Your ability to manage these IT services has, in turn, become more critical to business success as technology becomes more embedded in the services provided to clients and customers. As a result, enterprise IT operations managers must broaden their skills to meet this challenge. This includes not only managing the traditional IT infrastructure, but also enabling end users to more effectively use technology to deliver business products and services.

As your job continues to change in support of the delivery of critical business services, your skills as IT operations professionals must also change. Traditional mainframe and mid-range systems coexist today with LANs (local area networks) and WANs (wide area networks) that connect users' PCs to each other and to these larger systems. Applications systems operate on all these IT platforms and within a complex interconnected environment, all of which you must manage and support. In addition, the Internet has introduced new opportunities to increase business growth through direct communication connectivity solutions with vendors, suppliers, and customers. IT must develop and support the infrastructure for these complex business connectivity solutions by connecting internal LANs and WANs to the Internet and, in some instances, directly to internal networks of business partners and customers.

In this edition of the handbook, we provide a broader range of technology-operations knowledge to help meet the information needs of today's IT professional. The information is presented with a practical orientation so that it can be readily applied to your environment. Areas of coverage include:

- IT Management.
- Data Center Management.
- Application Infrastructure and Operations.
- Enterprise Network Management.
- Desktop Computing.
- Equipment Asset Management.
- Customer Support Operations.
- Quality Control & Computer Security.
- Contingency Planning.

Within the sections that existed in last year's edition, more emphasis has been added to network communications, end-user support operations, computer security, and contingency planning. These areas require increasing attention from IT operations personnel. The material focuses not only on the technology, but also on methodologies for decision making. Knowing how to apply the knowledge in this handbook is critical to your success as an IT operations management professional.

ADDRESSING ENTERPRISE BUSINESS SUPPORT

In the area of network communications, the handbook includes the topics which reflect the explosion of new technologies now emerging in the marketplace. Networking has always been a vital part of the overall IT operations solution; these emerging technologies provide new opportunities for competitive advantage, delivering high-speed, reliable service in support of network-based applications.

The help desk industry is one of the fastest growing areas in the IT operations area today. End users are requiring growing levels of support as they become more empowered to deliver technology-based services to customers and to meet the demands of business partners and vendors. The help desk is an extremely important IT investment and must constantly adapt to be responsive to ongoing technology changes, including changes in how technology is used by end users. This handbook addresses these issues and provides the IT operations manager with solutions to effectively manage this area.

As technology is pushed deeper into mainstream business operations, computer security, quality assurance, and contingency planning become increasingly important. Loss or failure of technology service operations can have a disastrous impact on business operations. This edition of the handbook, once again, provides important guidance on how the IT operations manager should protect this critical investment. IT management should work closely with senior management to properly address these areas within the appropriate business context.

THE FUTURE OF ENTERPRISE COMPUTING

As business organizations continue to increase their investment in technology to deliver business products and services more cost-effectively, proper management of the technology infrastructure becomes more critical to the success of the organization. Even as traditional IT operations become more and more automated, new opportunities for IT investment and increasing changes in the IT industry require organizations to react more quickly to remain competitive. Business will always be dependent on technology and, as a result, on someone to effectively manage IT operations. As we move into the next century, this handbook will continue to be a valuable source of information to IT operations management, providing important answers to increasingly complex IT issues.

Steve Blanding
Houston, TX
April, 1999

Section I
IT Management

IT MANAGEMENT MUST CONTINUALLY CONFRONT a wide range of important technology issues. You are required to possess multiple skills to meet these diverse and pervasive challenges. This section of the handbook provides insight on how management issues are addressed and solved within the IT profession. To effectively manage the IT environment, management must be constantly focused on strategic planning, while maintaining communications skills, analytic skills, and budget control.

Chapter 1, "Strategic Planning: Business and Technology Issues," describes the business and technology issues that must be considered when preparing a strategic business plan. The plan must be developed in accordance with organizational goals and ever-changing technology needs. IT management must continually focus on seeking ways to more tightly integrate technology with the organization's overall business plan. This chapter relates the barriers and shortcomings most organizations face today in achieving the benefits of effective strategic planning.

Another challenge facing IT management today is the effectiveness in negotiation with senior business management for appropriate levels of IT support and services. Chapter 2, "The Corporate Information and Communications Hierarchy: Technological Management in Modern Enterprises," presents various case studies of how the technology infrastructure can most effectively be positioned within the organization as a result of a three-way negotiation between the CIO, middle management, and senior management. The author demonstrates in this chapter how this three-party struggle contributes to the overall effectiveness of the enterprise.

Staffing an IT organization with highly technical individuals has been the traditional requirement in mainframe application legacy environments. Today, however, IT managers must hire individuals with a blend of technical and interpersonal skills. IT personnel are increasingly having to interact with users on more levels than before, due to the dramatic shift toward client/server application environments. Chapter 3, "Developing People Skills: A New IT Priority," addresses the important issue of interpersonal skill development within the IT organization.

In some instances, you may need to hire professional consultants to provide the organization with an expert perspective for a particular field of technology. Chapter 4, "Professional Consulting: The Analysis Methodology," provides a road map to determining the appropriate expectation level when using professional consultants. This chapter describes the difficulty in relying on the expertise of someone who is not on the payroll, and is of unknown loyalty to the organization. The author describes the process IT management should pursue to establish a realistic expectation level regarding the performance and deliverables of consultants. Using a case-study approach to illustrate this point, a description of the steps necessary to determine the type of thoroughness and in-depth analysis required when using professional consultants is drawn out.

IT management is also responsible for maintaining an efficient, cost-effective technology environment. Demonstrating this in a complex network environment is a challenging task. Chapter 5, "Pricing Methods Across Linked Networks," shows you how to implement a strategy to recover costs across linked networks and how to communicate to senior management that the data center is more than a service bureau — it can be a profit center, as well.

Chapter 1
Strategic Planning: Business and Technology Issues

Layne C. Bradley

IN A RECENT SURVEY CONDUCTED BY A CHANGE MANAGEMENT CONSULTING ORGANIZATION, 1500 chief executive officers indicated their second most-pressing problem was the integration of technology into their companies. (Their number-one problem was government regulation.)

The pace of technology development today is far ahead of most organizations' ability to implement it effectively. There are several reasons for this situation:

- Most organizations today are not structured to realize the true benefits of technology and still cling to rigid management hierarchies that make implementing organizationwide technologies very difficult. There is often too much focus on departmental issues and goals rather than organizationwide goals.
- Even with the rapid growth of computer technology in the past few years, many workers today are still intimidated by it. Whereas they may understand how to do a few basic tasks at the computer — which they are often forced to learn to keep their jobs — they have no real understanding of the technology, how it benefits them and the organization, and how to use it to become even more productive.
- Lack of focus, understanding, and senior management support of long-term technology projects often hampers the effective implementation of new technology. The cost, both in time and money, often deters senior management from making the kinds of investment commitments that are required. Also, many senior managers consider computer technology to be a tool only for the organization's workers rather than for themselves in running the company. Consequently, they often delegate

the implementation of new technology to the information systems group without enough of their own personal involvement.

- Finally, the lack of skilled systems professionals to plan, implement, and maintain technology is becoming a significant problem. As the demand for new technology grows, the demand for systems professionals is beginning to outstrip the supply. As we enter the twenty-first century, however, it is becoming increasingly clear that business and technology are beginning to merge into a single discipline. Rather than merely being a part of the business, technology may very well become the business. Given the increasing global nature of business, the use of technology may become the only way a company can compete and survive.

All of these issues have a direct impact on the data center manager. The data center still serves as the focal point of merging technologies. Knowing how to manage these technologies from a business perspective may become the single determining factor governing the data center manager's career success.

FACTORS EFFECTING CHANGE

Historically, the data center's daily operations have been fast-moving, labor-intensive, and highly focused. In the early days of business data processing, the data center produced reports for the organization's functional department in a batch environment. The introduction of online systems has made life in the data center more demanding. Data centers must now make several hours of online processing available to users and still produce the required batch reports.

The data center environment has changed even more dramatically with the introduction of local area networks (LANs), telecommunications, relational databases, and microcomputers. The third-party software industry has helped improve the situation by providing systems that automate a great deal of the manual work. Production control and scheduling; tape and disk management; operator responses; network management; and restart-rerun operations are routinely automated. The logical and technical extension of this approach is the concept of lights-out or unattended operations — that is, a data center that functions with few, if any personnel, much like the automated automobile factory.

The data center, however, is becoming much more than the central point where daily production systems processing is conducted. Rather, it is rapidly becoming the hub of technology for the organization it serves. The data center manager must become a business person whose skills involve managing technology for business effectiveness rather than merely a technical manager.

BUSINESS ISSUES

Industry journals, newspapers, and magazines frequently report on the business of data processing. These articles address not only the financial aspects of data centers (e.g., cost centers versus profit centers and return on investment), but also career issues, such as how data center managers can become chief information officers (CIOs) and how CIOs can eventually become chief executive officers (CEOs).

Discussions about the business of data processing have gone on for many years, yet the issue is more relevant today than ever before. Because of the introduction of new technology, new management techniques, global competition, and increasing cost pressures, senior management must look closely at MIS's role in the organization as it seeks ways to tightly integrate these operations into the business.

Clearly, data center managers face the challenge of managing the data center as a business, not merely as a cost center. In fact, many organizations are actually turning their MIS capabilities and resources into separate businesses by offering services to outside customers. Even organizations that continue to provide services only for internal users are seeking ways to turn MIS into a profit center. Efforts to make the MIS department more like a functional line of business have a clear and definite strategic impact on the data center itself. If data center managers are to run the data center as a business and more effectively integrate it into the organization, they must keep abreast of several important business issues.

The Organization's Goals

One of the most important, if not critical, changes data center managers must make is in how they are seen in the organization. They simply cannot continue to operate, or be perceived as, a purely technical manager. Senior management usually does not have the time or the inclination to become highly knowledgeable of technology. Therefore, data center managers must invest the effort to become knowledgeable business people who can effectively communicate with senior management on their terms. Only in this way can data center managers come to be perceived as an integral part of the organization's business management and, therefore, able to participate directly in setting the organization's goals. Then, they can set the data center's goals in harmony with the organization.

Becoming a skilled business person may be a challenging task for the data center manager. It is no longer optional, however. In addition to learning the organization's specific business, it may be necessary to obtain a great deal of basic business training through seminars, workshops, or enrollment in college courses — perhaps even obtaining a degree in business. The task must be accomplished by whatever means necessary if the data center manager is to become an effective part of the organization's management team.

Businesses become successful because they set and reach goals. Goals provide direction, help identify obstacles and opportunities, and allow for the efficient allocation of available resources. The data center must follow this same goal-setting process for its own operations. The real key to managing the data center as a business, however, is knowing the organization's goals and understanding how the data center can help the organization to attain them.

Unfortunately, this task is still often quite difficult because a communications gulf exists between senior management and data center management — neither side effectively understands the other side. Although this situation is beginning to change, it is a slow process. Data center managers must take the lead in bridging this gap by proposing ways for the data center to be included in the organization's goal-setting process. If the data center and its operations are to become a key business function of the organization as well as assume a greater role in using technology to drive the business, this goal-setting process must take place.

Expectations for the Data Center

Another major challenge for the data center manager is getting senior managers to define their expectations for the data center. Most senior managers do not understand the real role of the data center, and, therefore, their expectations for the data center are far different than the data center manager's. In fact, most data center managers would be startled by what they would hear if they were to ask their senior managers to define their expectations for the data center. No matter how difficult this expectation-defining process is, however, it must take place so data center managers know what is expected of them and which direction the data center should take. Becoming perceived as a business manager and becoming part of the organization's management team helps this process greatly.

Profit Center vs. Cost Center

The idea of making the data center a profit center is not new, but it is gaining much more credibility as a real option. A cost center recognizes expenses used for conducting operations. It usually falls into the overhead category of the corporate budget and its costs are in some way allocated across all user departments. A profit center, however, recognizes revenue for its services, as well as expenses, and attempts to show a profit. A data center manager can take one of three approaches to accomplish this goal.

The first is to accept only internal revenue. The data center charges service fees to all the organization's internal users. These fees can be structured in a variety of ways depending on the organization's goals. At times, these fees may be strictly arbitrary, though more organizations are directing their data center to charge true market rates. Data center managers are then held responsible for managing data center operations to produce a profit. Many times this approach results in the downsizing and streamlining of data center operations, which allows data center managers to eliminate a great deal of the expenses that limit their center's profit margin.

The second approach is for data center managers to consider providing services to users outside the organization on a contractual basis. In this case, the data center, which is usually part of the larger MIS department, becomes a true business. This approach is feasible if there is sufficient demand for services and the data center has the processing resources, personnel, and management talent to implement such a business. Contracting for business can be a risky proposition, though some organizations have created successful information systems subsidiaries.

The third approach combines the first two approaches. The data center provides services on a for-profit basis for both internal and outside customers.

Outsourcing

Some organizations are selecting outsourcing as an option for their MIS operations. Under this arrangement, the organization signs a contract with a third-party vendor to take over responsibility for running the MIS operation. Usually, only the actual computer operations are involved, but there have been instances of organizations that have outsourced the management of their network and even their applications development. The organization's employees usually become employees of the third-party vendor.

This new approach could have a major impact on data center managers. In some cases, organizations obtain bids from outsourcing vendors and, at the same time, ask their data center managers to write a bid for providing computer services. In other words, data center managers must justify the cost-effectiveness of continuing the operation in-house. This situation is purely a business one — senior management is looking for the best return on its data processing dollar, and outsourcing must be considered an option.

Outsourcing is controversial. However, a large number of organizations have pursued it, with varying results. Nonetheless, it is a business issue that data center managers must be aware of when preparing a strategic plan for the data center.

TECHNOLOGY ISSUES

It has been said that the only constant is change, and that observation rings true in the MIS field. Since its beginning, MIS has been in a constant state of flux brought about by new hardware and software developments. Identifying, planning for, acquiring, and integrating technology is part of the data center manager's function — and it must be accomplished as cost-effectively as possible and perhaps even on a profit basis. Although the MIS department has never been afforded free spending, it is being scrutinized as never before by senior management. The primary goal today, then, is to decide the best way to use technology so it enhances the organization's operations, improves its competitive position, and increases its profit margins. Gaining greater economic leverage is, after all, the reason for creating a business-oriented data center.

Deciding what technology is appropriate and how best to use it is the real challenge for data center managers. Because very few organizations have the financial resources or the need to incorporate all current technology, data center managers must look at what makes sense for their organizations. Strategic planning involves recognizing current needs as well as future requirements. Identifying the need for more central processing unit power, disk storage, and terminals is clearly part of a strategic plan, but capacity planning alone is not enough.

For example, an organization has a centralized manufacturing facility that is served by a centralized data center. In an effort to expand and remain competitive, the organization is considering creating several smaller manufacturing facilities that will produce the product locally and get it to the market faster. Adding more CPU power centrally may not be the appropriate solution. Instead, a distributed network of smaller, fault-tolerant systems may be needed. This is a strategic issue because it represents a major change from the current approach and commits the organization to an entirely new long-term direction.

This example illustrates how business and technology issues demand that the data center manager be very knowledgeable — not only about the data center's capabilities and goals, but also about the direction in which the organization itself is heading, and its management philosophies and goals. To effectively support the organization's changed business strategy, data center managers must know the business issues — for example, how the change will affect the organization's goals and the projected time frame for the change. For the organization to be successful, from the technology point of view, data center managers may have to plan for and implement a technology entirely new to the organization. Failure to introduce new technology has seriously hurt or even eliminated organizations over the years.

Strategic planning in the data center is intended to be a process whereby data center managers can be involved as early as possible in the organization's long-term goals and know how current technology relates to those goals and what new technology will be required in the future to make it all happen. Some of the information technologies data center managers should consider when developing a strategic plan include:

- Supercomputers, mainframes, minicomputers, microcomputers, workstations, and portable computers.
- Optical storage.
- Fault-tolerant systems.
- LANs.
- Integrated services digital networks.
- Fiber-optics.
- T1 networks.
- Vector processes.
- Artificial intelligence and expert system.
- Databases (relational and object oriented).
- Fourth-generation languages.
- Computer-aided software engineering (CASE) development environment.
- Operating systems.
- X-terminals.
- Image processing.
- Executive information systems.
- Voice response systems.
- Videoconferencing.
- Cellular technologies.
- Wireless communications.

The data center's strategic plan must also address organizational issues. Personal computing, departmental computing, and distributed processing have changed the way work is processed in the organization. Likewise, business issues are going to affect how work is performed in the data center. Major business organizational issues about which the data center manager must stay informed include: outsourcing; downsizing; mergers and acquisitions; union contracts; unattended operations; telecommuting; and reporting structures.

THE BUSINESS PLAN

In the language of business today, the strategic plan is more commonly referred to as the business plan. Most successful organizations operate from a business plan. Depending on the organization's size and management philosophy, such plans can be very informal or extremely complex and may cover as little as one year or many years. To succeed in the long term, an organization must have a directive as to where it is going, how long it will take to get there, and how it must allocate its resources. If data centers are to be run as businesses, they must also have such a plan. The business plan is where the data center manager combines the business issues and the technology issues discussed in this chapter.

There are as many types and formats for business plans as there are businesses. Each organization has its own style. There are, however, some common elements that all data center managers should include in their business plans:

- A statement of purpose.
- An executive summary.
- Goals.
- Objectives.
- Strategies.
- A cost/benefit analysis.
- A description of the hardware and software configuration.
- A description of the network configuration.
- Organizational charts and staffing plan.
- Budgets.
- Milestones and target dates.

When preparing the business plan, data center managers must remember that they are not simply preparing a budget for the coming year. Rather, they are attempting to present the data center as a business that can be run efficiently and cost effectively. Creating a data center business plan is actually a straightforward process that begins by answering the following questions:

- What are the business goals that senior management wants to achieve?
- Are there enough resources to achieve these goals?
- What is the best way to allocate available resources to achieve these goals?
- What are the steps involved?
- What is the projected time frame for the goals to be achieved?
- Who is responsible for this task?
- What are the costs involved?
- What is the projected return on investment?

RECOMMENDED COURSE OF ACTION

Planning of any kind is always difficult when dealing with unknown factors, some of which managers control to only a small degree. Long-range or strategic planning is extremely difficult because the longer the planning horizon, the more uncertainty exists. Today more than ever, data center managers are required to do long-range business planning for the data center. To do this effectively, data center managers must:

- Know the organization's business thoroughly.
- Find out the organization's business goals.
- Know and understand the trends in technology.
- Understand what technology would most benefit the organization in reaching its goals.
- Know senior management's specific goals and expectations for the data center.
- Develop a business plan that effectively combines business goals and technologies issues.
- Become a member of the organization's business management team.

Although change may be constant, it can be managed. Making strategic planning for the data center a priority can give data center managers much more control over their environments and goes a long way toward enhancing their careers as they become full partners in the organization's business plan.

Chapter 2

The Corporate Information and Communications Hierarchy: Technological Management in Modern Enterprises

Thomas A. Browdy

TODAY THE TRADITIONAL DP MANAGER, with his or her one-size-fits-all approach, has become almost a relic. It is no longer a single technology that needs to be managed for process efficiency gains, but multiple technologies that could be critical for business survival or growth. The chief information officer (CIO), or perhaps a team of decentralized Information Systems (IS) directors, has replaced the traditional DP manager and, in some cases, provides a new way for leadership to interact.

Telecommunications networks, data exchange, satellites, microwave, LANs, WANs, switches, fiber optics, twisted pair, PBXs, cellular communications, trans-border information automation, and a variety of telecommunications standards and proposed standards have been thrown into a multiplicity of computing environments creating a mixture that requires a whole new management orientation.

The new technological management orientation should include ways for planning, assessing, and deploying technology within and across enterprises. CIOs or IS leadership teams need to balance technological capability with enterprise capability to become or stay a modern organization that has a chance of survival. Survivability consists of not merely staying competitive in existing markets, but learning to adjust quickly to dynamic markets with changes founded in unclear global business opportunities and processes, as well as technological innovations.

A power struggle ensues. Computing is pushed down the line until every department has a computing resource to manage, but little experience in managing it. Here the CIO or IS leadership team steps in to bring particular rationality to situations that often become irrational (incompatibility of computing devices, networks that do not talk to one another, etc.)

ENTERPRISE EFFECTIVENESS

Results of this three-party struggle will contribute to the enterprise's effectiveness. If any one role constantly wins, they all lose. If top leadership wins the case for controlled stable growth, the next technological paradigm shift will be missed and a competitor quickly will sweep by. (Airline reservation systems were not a part of a stable growth strategy by many now defunct airlines.) Most incumbents in existing markets miss innovation-based paradigm shifts and usually suffer the consequences of losing all or significant pieces of their businesses.

If middle-level business management always wins there will be a constant changing of direction and technology learning will be stifled. Learning never will be able to reach a maturity level, which could spell the difference between enterprisewide effectiveness and point solutions that seldom contribute to the mission. If the CIO always wins there will be a sophisticated technological infrastructure that no one uses. When one of these positions is weakened by organizational design, private power struggles, or ignorance, then the enterprise becomes less effective and even could threaten survival (Exhibit 2.1). A balanced power struggle is healthy.

Managing telecommunication within an enterprise is a formidable task. The swirl of technology coupled with the ever-changing business context creates a situation that demands high creativity and sharp intellectual acuity. Along with these characteristics the individual manager also is expected to get something done. Being creative and smart is just not enough.

This chapter presents frameworks that should sharpen one's intellectual capability about managing telecommunication, but more than that, through usage of five case examples shows how these frameworks can be applied creatively to get something done. The frameworks are provided as a way to understand the parameters of effective technological management.

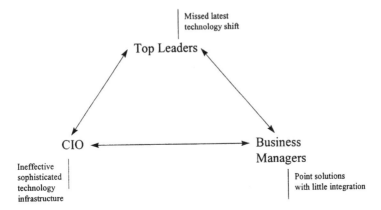

Exhibit 2.1. Leadership imbalance results.

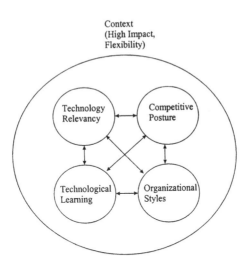

Exhibit 2.2. Parameters for technological management.

These parameters include technology context (high expectations of impact and extreme flexibility), technology relevancy, competitive posture, technological learning, and organizational styles (Exhibit 2.2). The effective technological manager quickly can assess the values these parameters take on and see how they interact to create a unique but understandable technological environment.

CASE EXAMPLES

Not all enterprises are created equally. This is illustrated by briefly describing five institutions. These institutions will be used throughout the chapter to highlight technological and organizational issues.

MasterCard International

At MasterCard International a group of potential customers are escorted through the machine room and given a presentation on how networks are managed to ensure fast and efficient processing of information. Pride clearly is intoned by the head network administrator as he comments on how often they identify wide area network problems of commercial carriers before the carriers themselves know. MasterCard's expertise about networking has grown since the very beginning of their business. The technology used to keep the network functioning in a reliable manner is aging quickly, and there have been various projects to replace the equipment.

Movement around the halls is fast and furious. People are coming and going to various meetings and conferences. Human resources has just posted jobs for all varieties of IS positions, and a new management team tries to create a portfolio of projects that will keep the enterprise up-to-date. Some of these projects are large and aggressive. Even though similar projects have failed in the past, still there is a penchant to strive for success in large projects. Large projects have been international in scope due to purchasing behavioral differences of cardholders between countries. Internet initiatives have become a serious endeavor, but exactly how to handle this new technology is still an open issue.

The customers for MasterCard are primarily banks, and cardholders are customers of the banks. MasterCard International adds value to its customers by supplying various information products, network services, and advertising. They are owned and operated by their customers — a group of banking and other financial card-issuing institutions.

SMooth Ride Trucking (SMRT)

SMRT, a small- to medium-sized trucking firm nestled in the heart of mid-America, is run by a former driver. As tours are given to existing and potential customers, oohs and aahs can be heard in the plush balcony that overlooks a gymnasium-size war room located behind a one-way glass window. People, quietly seated behind the glass in the hush of semidarkness, overlook the dispatchers' war room. The war room is a beehive of activity and with its sophisticated information displays, reminds one of the movie "War Games." The room contains an impressive array of 15 square-foot video-projected images showing summary load distributions, individual truck locations, and weather conditions across North America.

The war room is both functional for dispatchers and a marketing device for potential customers. Building on the tradition of transporting soda bottles without breakage, this enterprise continues to move all sorts of delicate cargo. Specially equipped trailers and attention to driver care for cargo has remained a part of their tradition. SMRT handles delicate loads with routes that primarily go north and south to Canada and Mexico. For the southern routes trailers usually are dropped off just over the border and drivers from Mexico take the cargo to its final destination. After losing equipment through various pilfering schemes, contracts were negotiated with the Mexican trucking firms on penalties for lost goods (including cargo, trailers, and trailer equipment).

One of the competitive edges the enterprise has is accurate and efficient dispatching. Trucks across the United States and parts of Mexico and Canada are monitored constantly to make sure few of them are without loads between destinations. It is not good business to have empty trailers traveling too far without a load. Ideally, for every load that is dropped off the trailer is refilled for a new destination. Each dispatcher has earned his or her stripes behind the wheel. The owner/president, being a former driver, maintains the rule that dispatchers have to know how drivers are thinking to make the drivers' jobs efficient.

Coupled with dispatcher expertise is a set of medium-sized computers that supports war room activities. Drivers are given cellular phones for official and private use. Each truck also has a telecommunication device that provides positioning information to dispatchers. The sophistication that has provided a competitive advantage now is becoming available to small independent trucking enterprises. This company feels compelled to take on the next network or computing challenge to maintain its market position. They hear the competition on their heels.

Big Auto Leasing (BIGAL)

From humble beginnings in a small dealership to one of the largest available fleets in the world, BIGAL competes aggressively on renting, selling, and leasing autos. It is a privately held company that has experienced exponential growth. BIGAL is within the top ten companies who buy and move autos from manufacturing to ownership.

Local offices are opened with assistant managers learning their craft by washing autos — it often is heard on the lots that this is a company where "everyone starts from the bottom." An army of drivers, mostly part-time workers, constantly are moving autos from one location to another — sometimes to fulfill customer demands, sometimes in anticipation of demand (a large convention), and other times to level out the fleet across geographic locations (multiple states could be involved in any of these).

One of the biggest problems they face is knowing vehicle location. Each branch office has a significant number of vehicles. Operational decisions need to balance an ever-aging fleet (moving out older models) against individual and dealership customers who may want to buy, rent, or lease. An individual dealership purchase of a fleet of program cars from BIGAL is a critical part of their business.

BIGAL has one of the largest medium-sized computer environments in the world (housing a multitude of medium-sized computers in one location). Their communication technology is primarily satellite-based microwave. Using this communication capability each office reports its activities during the day to aid decision making about their multitude of vehicles.

Washington University (WU)

While strolling the WU campus, gothic architecture and the appearance of students and professors elicit a vision of great minds at work. WU is a private research- and education-based institution of higher learning located in St. Louis, MO. Freshman students make decisions about attending WU versus other institutions such as Yale, Stanford, Princeton, Cornell, Northwestern, and Carnegie-Mellon. Along with high value comes a high cost. However, each of these institutions has endowments that support scholarships for those whose qualifications add quality to each admitted class. Students are housed in campus dorms and in various individually leased or rented apartments located nearby.

The University includes schools of Arts and Sciences, Engineering and Applied Science, Medicine, Business, Social Work, Law, Fine Arts, and Architecture. There is also a first-class library and supporting libraries in most of the schools. Departments of Computer Science and Information Management are housed in the Engineering school.

The University is operated in a decentralized fashion with each school responsible for its own budget, academic viability, and services. Some services are provided through central administration including development, physical plant, accounting/finance, human resources, and computing. Each school also has its own small version of the central services including computing. Schools have their own computing lab environments that may attach to central administration services. Some departments even run their own computer labs. The central administration is also responsible for an electronic network and communication including one of the first major Internet sites. Dorms and offices are wired for network communications.

The dean of the library holds the Chief Information Officer position for the University. Administrative systems are very old (most written in the 1970s) and there has been little interest in investing in such systems.

Both full- and part-time students make up the University community. Part-time students take courses in the evening usually taught by adjunct faculty. Distance learning has been discussed, but the strategy is to maintain a classroom environment with classes taught by highly qualified faculty.

Amazon.com

This Internet-based business is one of the most popular examples cited for E-commerce. The quick and almost immediate success of Amazon has been both exciting to E-commerce entrepreneurs and feared by many traditional businesses. Started just a few years ago, this business provides a specialized link between book purchaser and publisher.

As Amazon is able to establish partnerships with publishers and book warehouses, they are able to offer a tremendous variety of books from a single source, which can be accessed at any time and almost from anywhere. Although they have no actual storage of books, the ability to present a book to a potential customer, along with ancillary services such as reviews and titles of similar books, has created a very powerful business. Special services are provided in terms of preference searches, as well as searches by author, topic, and title. Links to other services such as chat rooms also are provided.

Because of its success and the potential of E-commerce, Amazon has become a well-known brand name for book stores — even though it has no frontal footage in any mall or along any street. It has given "book store" a new meaning. One might say its telecommunications environment is its real business, along with adequate compute power to service Internet requests. Amazon.com also must pay attention to traditional front and back office information systems to carry out its business.

Defining Characteristics

Each enterprise possesses a set of defining characteristics including people, business/market, location, size, structure, culture, and technology. The combination of these characteristics creates a unique enterprise not to be replicated anywhere. It is easy to forget this principle of uniqueness when common measures such as financial performance, market share, and service performance are used for comparison purposes. These comparisons can lead to actions that mimic those taken by another company in an attempt to achieve a similar outcome.

But what MasterCard does to be successful will not be the same as SMRT, nor the same as BIGAL, nor the same as WU. What is common among

Future Relevance

		Low	High
Present Relevance	Low	Support	Transitioning
	High	Sustaining	Strategic

Exhibit 2.3. Telecommunication relevancy grid.

enterprises is not as great as what is different. Yet, one can speak in generalities about enterprises to understand how to manage them. Technology
relevance is one of these generalities.

TECHNOLOGY RELEVANCY AND COMPETITIVE POSTURE

Network managers are expected to provide key insights on telecommunication technology investment for their enterprises. One way to gain insight
into telecommunication investment is to consider the current versus
future enterprise relevancy of telecommunication technology. The importance of telecommunication technology varies according to type of industry, how an individual enterprise competes in that industry, and the impact
of industry changes. A given level of telecommunication usage may or may
not be appropriate for where an enterprise is now. The same can be said
about the future. If future events are envisioned that require additional
telecommunication capability, then these kinds of projects need to be considered today. Exhibit 2.3 shows a relevancy grid for telecommunication
technology. Determining where one is positioned on this grid may spell the
difference between future success or failure.

Industries, in general, may be placed on the relevancy grid. This gives
one a place to start when considering an individual company (Exhibit 2.4).

Because each enterprise competes in a unique way, blindly assigning an
enterprise to a position on the relevancy grid, strictly on the grounds of
industry type, may be unwise. Traditional market competitive analysis
says an enterprise can compete on cost, differentiation, or niche. The combination of industry technology relevancy, competitive posture, plus available expertise provides guidance for where a particular enterprise falls on
the grid. Exhibit 2.5 depicts where the five case examples fall.

The example cases are completely predictable by industry type according to Exhibit 2.5. However, with a little more detail on one of the cases one

Future Relevance

		Low	High
		Low	High
Present Relevance	Low	Universities	Trucking
	High	Auto Leasing	Financial

Exhibit 2.4.   Industry specific telecommunication orientations.

can see how it could change positions. Suppose it was decided at WU to initiate distance learning and begin recruiting freshmen through the Internet or multimedia and initiate research consortia through electronic sharing of research results that may include nontext-based medical diagnostic documents. The ability for multiple researchers at multiple locations to share information quickly is assumed to create the synergy to drive the research toward early conclusions and perhaps more funding.

At WU, future telecommunication technology capability will play a key role. Hence, the relevancy moves from support to transitioning. Relevancy should be coupled with a competitive posture to make clearer what, in particular, needs to be planned. Coupling relevance with competitive posture permits one to see what technology may be applicable. For example, if WU is a low-cost provider, then telecommunication technology can be used to increase volume. If WU is competing by differentiation, then one way to apply technology would be to use the Internet to increase the quality of the freshman class (Exhibit 2.6).

Support relevance suggests there is little need for planning significant changes to the telecommunication infrastructure. Sustaining indicates the current level of investment must continue, and the network manager needs to ensure contributions to the business remain visible so they may continue. A transitioning enterprise means the network manager will be required to identify projects and gather resources to raise the telecommunications environment to a new plane. For strategic, the current investment needs to remain visible, and future investment opportunities need to be identified and planned (Exhibit 2.7).

The big challenge looming before the business world is to be able to choose between learning businesses as they continually evolve, which implies looking for competitive advantage through technology, or responding

Future Relevance

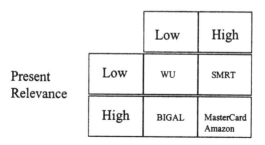

	Low	High
Low	WU	SMRT
High	BIGAL	MasterCard Amazon

Present Relevance

Exhibit 2.5.   Telecommunication relevancy for case examples.

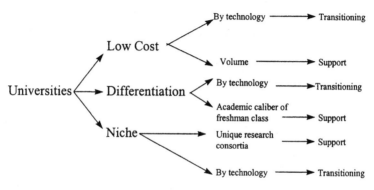

Exhibit 2.6.   Telecommunication relevancy for WU.

to transmutations of business segments, which implies using technology to create and compete in dynamic markets.

Due to globalization of businesses, including production and market implications, and innovative connectivity technologies such as the Internet, markets have become much more dynamic in this decade and will continue well into the next. One of the general goals of many companies has been to strive for a competitive advantage using technology. Now, since markets have become so dynamic, this goal may need to be replaced with one that utilizes technology to create and participate in dynamic markets. To illustrate this point consider Amazon Books and *Encyclopaedia Britannica.*

With Amazon, what was a very traditional market became much more dynamic with the use of the Internet to sell books. One needs only to access Amazon on the Internet at any time from anywhere, use a provided search mechanism, order a book or books, wait a few days, and it/they

Exhibit 2.7. Investment posture by telecommunications relevancy.

Telecommunication Relevancy	Investment Posture
Support	Keep budget
Sustaining	Keep attention focused on current contribution
Transitioning	Plan new telecommunication portfolio
Strategic	Balance between current and future portfolios

arrive at one's doorstep. Responses by Barnes and Noble and others are on the way, bringing their own new added dimensions to selling books. This has become a changing market.

The ease of customers choosing between companies/products, customers that may visit at any time from almost anywhere, along with integrative services, contributes to this new era of dynamic markets. These three characteristics present demands on those who expect to compete. First, the new ease that customers have to choose between companies means brand identity of the company will become more important and seen in new ways that open cross-selling approaches (i.e., buying music CDs as well as books at Amazon). Second, customers visiting at any time from almost anywhere means there has to be a sustainable connectivity and responsiveness capability. Third, integrative services means bringing together in one place responses to direct as well as tangential customer needs and interests (e.g., getting a loan from the same place one purchased an auto).

Britannica did not consider the three demands of customer ease of choice, potential ubiquitous access, and integrated services resulting in them getting driven from the market by a lower quality product partnered with a personal computer-operating system (e.g., Encarta and Windows). They had brand identity, but failed to understand the interests of customers to look up information with ease and the ability to integrate that information with other things (i.e., use it while writing a term paper). These new demands require a leadership that can think about future possibilities as well as an appropriate technology infrastructure. Although there are other considerations in analyzing the negative outcome of Britannica, failure to realize the dynamic nature of their market contributed significantly to a disaster from which they may never recover.

OVERALL TECHNOLOGY IMPACT

Modern planning practices have shifted from reducing everything to their lowest level of control toward understanding which containing whole or context the enterprise is a part of. To this end, consider what technology sea an enterprise finds itself afloat on. Two important context issues are stability/flexibility of the environment and technological synergistic effects.

Regardless of an enterprise's position on the relevancy grid, almost every enterprise will have to deal with telecommunication technology in some form. What has been experienced and will be experienced for some time is the impact of technological component synergy. Technological component synergy occurs when mutually dependent, yet independently developed, technologies come together in a way that creates something new.

The DC 3 aircraft is a prime example of commercial aviation. Independent development of retractable landing gear, flaps, wing structure, powerful engines, and a desire from the public to travel at faster rates from coast to coast came together in the DC 3. The importance of component interdependencies was not realized until the idea of commercial air travel became a problem someone thought was solvable.

The personal computer was also a result of technological component synergy. The combination of computer on a chip, display devices, electrical printers, word processing, and eventually spreadsheet software, along with an increasing demand in office environments, led to a computing sea change.

Technological component synergy also is driving telecommunication technology. Components that are a part of this synergistic effect are fast switches, installed communication links, standards, communications interfaces (e.g., the Navigator browser from Netscape), and an Internet feeding frenzy by the general public. Few enterprises will be immune from the effects of this new technological component synergy. This means not just understanding where one is now technologically speaking, but where he or she wants to be in the future.

The new imperative of modern enterprises is flexibility within constraints of intense competition. To become a low-cost producer means acquiring that capability usually through repeated trial and error refinements (continuous process improvement as an example). But to continue to improve the processes that are in place means to entrench the enterprise further into what is now important. Enterprise flexibility requires a focus on the future and could result in changing the way of doing business — the business product(s), the target customers, suppliers, who the workers are, geographic location, etc. To compete by differentiation, flexibility means finding new ways to make product(s) different. Flexibility for a niche strategy could mean making or finding a new niche to compete within.

Constant exploration of what can be done and creative solutions to problems of work-force integration coupled with the wisdom of controlled expansion characterize modern organizations. The new era of flexibility requires that telecommunication technology be managed to achieve the connectivity necessary to compete and remain agile. In fact, the agility of

Exhibit 2.8. Learning curve attention.

	Learning Phases			
	Phase I **Initiation**	**Phase II** **Expansion**	**Phase III** **Control**	**Phase IV** **Assimilation**
Strategic	High	High	High	High
Transitioning	High	High	High	Low
Sustaining	High	High	Low	Low
Supporting	High	Low	Low	Low

many enterprises will be their ability to establish a multiplicity of communication modes, although in others it will be a more narrowly focused telecommunication approach.

TECHNOLOGY LEARNING

Every significant technology goes through a learning process. If one can decide where he or she fits on a technology learning curve, then actions can be taken to move to a more mature usage of the technology. The learning curve has four distinct phases (flex points on the curve): Phase I is an initial exposure of the technology to a select group; Phase II is expanded usage with contagious effects within and across enterprises. In Phase III there is a recognition that the uncontrolled nature of experiences needs to be controlled so standards for usage are put into place, and Phase IV is widespread assimilation. How much attention one pays to enterprise-leaning issues depends upon how relevant the technology is to the enterprise.

Exhibit 2.8 relates technology relevancy to effort expended within each phase. Phase I needs to be traversed no matter the relevancy position, although high effort for Phase IV is suggested for only the strategic relevancy condition.

Exhibit 2.9 shows how managerial actions differ by what phase of learning an organization is in with respect to telecommunication technology. Management's job will shift as the enterprise becomes more and more aware of how telecommunication technology will affect them. There is little doubt that everyone eventually will go through Phases I and II. Phases III and IV should be traversed by those who see telecommunication technology as becoming critical for their enterprise.

ORGANIZATIONAL STYLE

Where telecommunication technology fits in the enterprise depends on the current organization style and what enterprise contribution telecommunication will have in the future. Organizational style may be characterized as organic or mechanistic. Mechanistic organizations are command/control centric, hierarchically run, concerned with production efficiency (both service

Exhibit 2.9. Managerial action examples.

	Organic Style		Mechanistic Style	
	Phase I Initiation	**Phase II Expansion**	**Phase III Control**	**Phase IV Assimilation**
Projects	Experimental projects (some fail)	Establish connections with various users	Connected LANs. Client/server projects	Inter-organizational systems
	Example: Provide connections to Internet Information exploration projects	Example: Home pages on Internet Online catalogs with phone numbers and e-mail responses	Example: Implementa-tion of intranets	Example: Knowledge sharing among professionals Integrated supplier/ buyer chain
Key Decisions	Initiate a special project team	Hire telecomm. expertise	Develop network mgmt. function	Provide a secure telecomm. environment — both physically and logically
	Educate small group	Negotiate WAN capability	Become a telecomm.-enabled buyer (EDI)	
	Outsource LAN install (learn)	Install additional LANs		
	Secure WAN connectivity			

or product), structured planning and control techniques, and monolithic in how projects are approached (not given to an experimental/ research orientation). Organic organizations are loosely controlled, group/team-oriented, flat chain of command, and concerned with intra- and interenterprise boundary spanning.

Mechanistic enterprises are very good at continuous process improvement (usually leading to low cost) because they can enact the standards that come with operational efficiencies. Telecommunication technology can enable mechanistic organizations to behave in flexible ways contributing to long-term survival. Cross-functional networked teams can reach into the heart of an enterprise and provide a new view of what could be done and is being done. Such teams have been used to initiate new businesses, to attack immediate problems, as well as to seek out new ways in which a business can reintegrate itself internally among divisions, departments, and staff as well as externally with markets, customers, and other institutions.

This is using telecommunication to enable an organic overlay on a mechanistic organization to keep it competitive.

Changes are incremental by nature within mechanistic enterprises, hence, planning is a critical issue. Plans should be of two varieties: one dealing with infrastructure and the other with penetration of the effect of telecommunication on the enterprise's products and services. (This is a telecommunication relevancy issue as discussed above.) Managing telecommunication in such an environment means providing official mechanisms by which telecommunication capabilities are installed, maintained, and supported. For the network manager it means trying to stay ahead of the demand curve both in volume and sophistication.

This may be done with official surveys (not terribly popular with participants), help facilities (resource laden), sponsorship of events depicting the next wave of telecommunication capability during which individuals discover a viable usage for the technology, or initiating projects that may seem risky due to complexity of the technology involved.

Projects that use sophisticated technology do not lend themselves to planning, but may be a necessary organic overlay to sustain a competitive posture. Organic overlays for the mechanistic structure of MasterCard are critical moves to keep their telecommunication technology relevant. Their overlays include running large projects with fairly loose controls.

Organic organizations, due to their nature, often need to provide a control overlay so technology can mature beyond Phase II of learning. Organic organizations, although flat, usually have a residual hierarchy that serves to integrate teams/groups and provide a communication mechanism for top leadership, owners, or a board of directors. Teams/groups are enabled by a participant from the team/group representing them to the residual hierarchy. A committee made up of these representatives, when required to meet regularly, can function as a mechanistic overlay to the organic organization. One of the functions of this committee is to provide a control point for technological decisions.

For network managers this committee is critical. Otherwise, each team/group may enact its own standards and technology infrastructure sometimes serving to disintegrate activities that, through telecommunication technology, could be integrated for the good of the enterprise. The issue is not to remake an organic organization into a mechanistic one, but to engage the enterprise in control activities that mature telecommunication to Phase IV. Phases III and IV are critical for organizations with telecommunication technology that is transitioning the technology or is of strategic relevance.

WU requires a committee, appointed by deans of its respective schools, to make sure there is telecommunication compatibility that reaches within the schools. Although students have majors in each school and departments within schools all support particular programs, the push for across-school eclectic experiences by students is very real. Also, departments are sharing intellectual resources to conduct research and secure research funding. For the organic WU enterprise this committee provides a mechanistic overlay that reinforces the mission of education and research.

For an enterprise such as BIGAL that is experiencing phenomenal growth, the organization style is moving from organic to mechanistic. To survive, a more mechanistic structure is needed to control the vast numbers of people and resources. Telecommunication projects are critical because information needs to be consolidated and used for effective decision making. Telecommunication decision making, as well as other decision making, becomes more centralized in keeping with the move toward a more mechanistic structure. Hence, planning for telecommunication has been a part of the core planning process for the business.

SUMMARY

The parameters of technology context (expected impact and flexibility), technology relevance, competitive posture, technological learning, and organizational styles each have values they take on. For instance, one could be managing telecommunication technology with a transitioning relevancy, a differentiation posture, in a flexible and high-technological impact context, at an expansion phase (Phase II) of learning, within a mechanistic organization. Given these values, one manages differently in terms of planning and control, kinds of projects initiated, and how much relative attention to spend in a particular phase of learning.

There are over 300 possible "solutions spaces" given these parameters and their respective values. One cannot learn them all (and some parameters are undoubtedly missing), but one can develop the agility to manage according to what the possibilities are. It will take high creativity and sharp intellectual acuity, along with the energy to get something done (Exhibit 2.10).

The new reality for technological managers involves flexibility while remaining competitive. This calls for a flexible style of organization, led either directly or indirectly through overlays, by a powerful technological management. The new breed of technology managers should be able to think abstractly through such frameworks as presented in this chapter and others. The new breed of technology managers can participate to effect a balance between technology, its application, and resources within an enterprise. Also, they ought to understand implications for various technologies, take up

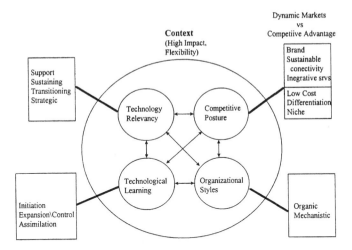

Exhibit 2.10.   Parameters and values for technological management.

---

the slack for novice management of other computing resources, be advocates for particular technological solutions, and generally be held accountable for how technology affects the enterprise. The DP manager of yesterday has been and is being replaced with multitalented executives who step out and lead their enterprises technologically.

Chapter 3
Developing People Skills: A New IT Priority

Greg Scileppi

IN THE PAST FEW YEARS, hiring managers have been actively seeking a certain breed of IT experts — those with a mixture of technical and interpersonal skills. The current move toward client/server environments is bringing IT staff, including data center personnel, network administrators, LAN specialists, and others — in closer contact with end users. Consequently, possessing strong people skills is one of the leading ingredients for success as a computer professional today.

According to a nationwide survey developed by RHI Consulting, nearly three out of four executives believe that IT professionals with effective interpersonal and communications skills are scarce. To fill this void and become the type of employee or consultant that managers need, data center professionals should consider taking stock of their skills, making adjustments when needed. They should not, however, approach the task of self-evaluation in a haphazard manner. Effective change, especially if the goal is to achieve long-term results, requires careful thought and persistent effort.

TAKING STOCK: UNDERSTANDING BUSINESS ISSUES

One of the best places to start a personal evaluation is with corporate knowledge. In the past, data center professionals may have been able to argue that understanding their company's business had only an indirect impact, at best, on their job responsibilities. Today, however, with the growing importance placed on information, the onus clearly rests on individual data center staff members and the technology they recommend and support to provide the company's working foundation. If they do not know the business well, their effectiveness in formulating solutions is severely limited. They may also err when dealing with colleagues and management, leading to diminished professional credibility within the organization.

When evaluating the strength of business knowledge, the individual should consider the following "big picture" questions:

- How much does he or she really know about the employer's business?
- What types of products or services does the company sell?
- Who are its target customers?
- How does the company stack up against the competition?
- Is the company's industry relatively flat or constantly evolving?
- What role does each department, or division, play in its success?
- How do these groups typically interact?

Increasing the Knowledge of the Business

There are some immediate steps data center professionals can take to learn more about a company's products and goals. For example, one of the most valuable publications a public company has to offer is its annual report. Some firms make sure that every employee receives a report, especially if employee stock options are offered. If the company is a privately held organization, an annual report probably is not available. In that case, data center staff should ask for a copy of the company's backgrounder, a document that describes the company's goals, accomplishments, key products, and other related information. If nothing else is available, the company's marketing materials give a helpful overview.

At the very least, data center professionals should know their employers' mission statements. If they do not understand the strategy, they can seek help from their manager; employees' interest in the organization is almost always viewed positively. When data center managers are able to relate their companies' missions to their jobs, they are more likely to perform at their best, because that understanding gives greater perspective to the work and its implications. Managers also find it invaluable when checking that they are operating in a manner that supports their companies' goals.

BUILDING BRIDGES THROUGH COMMUNICATION

Once data center managers have increased their company knowledge and feel comfortable supporting the company mission, they are prepared to break through the stereotype that IT professionals do not spend much time interacting with others. In today's client/server environment, strong interpersonal skills in addition to technical acumen are more important than ever.

Although the data center employees speak with people every day, the truth is that they may need to develop some new skills and techniques to improve their effectiveness. Contrary to what many believe, being a "people" person is not easy, and it does not come naturally to everyone. Like programming languages, networking topologies, or any other computer-based discipline, working with people is a skill that can be learned, practiced, and improved.

Earning End Users' Respect

One of the most important accomplishments is to earn the respect of end users. Many data center professionals may argue that their technical expertise automatically earns them respect. In reality, this is not true. Users may be in awe of their knowledge, but they do not respect data center personnel as people simply because they know technology. In fact, showing off an understanding of bits, bytes, and other technical tidbits may earn mistrust instead, because people are often afraid of what they do not know. To help users become comfortable with technology — and with data center personnel — there are several steps data center managers can take:

- Listening.
- Validation.
- Availability.
- Tact and honesty.

Listening. In dealing with end users' concerns, listening can be the greatest bridge builder. A seemingly simple skill, listening is often the most difficult interpersonal task to master; it is also one of the most desired traits. Data center managers should consider their most recent conversation with a user. How many times did they interrupt the user to ask questions or make comments? How much time did they spend listening intently to what the user had to say? How often did they let their mind wander? If they are like most people, staying on track has not been easy.

One of the most useful ways to begin to listen more effectively is to remain silent — but to signal attentiveness with a few nods of the head — until asked a question. Admittedly, this requires a great deal of discipline, and the listener is likely to feel uncomfortable. However, this cold-turkey approach will assist in breaking poor listening habits. As this rule is enforced, listening will begin to feel more comfortable over time. This approach, however, should not be adopted as a permanent solution; it should, rather, be used as an experiment to evaluate listening skills and to develop new ones. For instance, after focusing on listening for a few weeks, the individual can better gauge when it is appropriate to ask questions or interject with comments.

Validation. The next step, once listening skills have been honed, is to offer the user some validation. Sometimes all people want, when they have a problem, is for someone to affirm their feelings. For instance, if users go to their data center grumbling that the network is too slow and they cannot get their work done fast enough, the data center manager should not take a defensive stance. Instead, he can agree that this could be a problem. Then, if he has a solution, he can offer it. If not, the steps that will be taken to investigate the problem should be explained and a promise made to contact the users by a certain point in time with a plan of action.

Availability. Another useful tool in improving interpersonal skills is to increase data center personnel availability. When the network goes down or a printer is jammed, users tend to quickly lose patience if they have to search the building for help. Because data center professionals are typically on the go, this is an ongoing problem. If the company has a paging system, this can help. In many cases, though, paging systems do not reach all areas of a building. Instead, the data center manager can consider carrying a cellular phone or a pager, so that users can get in touch whenever a major problem occurs.

Tact and honesty. When dealing with end users, it pays to tread carefully. First, when users show up with a problem, the data center manager should never, never make them feel inadequate. This immediately makes the data center and its staff the enemy. Another communications faux pas is claiming to know more than is the reality. There is no faster way to lose face — and respect — when users find out that they have been given misinformation. Data center staff are better off admitting that they do not have an answer but will find one and deliver it. This not only makes data center staff appear more human, but it also saves them later embarrassment.

WINNING TOP MANAGEMENT SUPPORT

By now, areas in which the manager excels and those that need some improvement have been determined. These skills, however, are only part of the picture. To further enhance performance, data center managers also need to learn how to communicate effectively with top management. This is where many data center professionals have an excellent opportunity to demonstrate their value to the company. In fact, by implementing the appropriate communications tactics, data center professionals can easily win the respect and trust of top management.

First, however, understanding how management thinks is important. Typically, their number-one concern is the bottom line. In other words, they want to know how the company revenue is affected or what happens to the company's ability to deliver and sell products. The data center's actions, like everyone else's within the company, are seen through this filter; therefore, gauging communications accordingly is critical. For instance, data center personnel should never make promises they cannot keep. If they say that the new sales system will be ready in six months, they must make sure that they have looked at all aspects of the project to ensure they will meet this deadline. Management may have predicted upcoming revenue based on data center promises. Also, if the data center misses a deadline, sales people may temporarily be without a system, causing confusion and slowdowns in productivity. The same holds true for project budgets. Make sure that numbers are checked and double-checked. Overages will not endear anyone to management.

Obtaining Hands-Down Approval

If charged with obtaining management's approval on a project, data center managers must detail benefits in real terms, such as productivity improvements and cost. If none of these benefits exist, data center managers may need to reevaluate their reasons for the project. Also, when management attempts to impose a project deadline that is not realistic, data center manager should not say, "That is impossible." Instead, they must show management that they know what they are talking about by presenting management with data and time lines to support their positions. Always, without fail, data center managers must incorporate milestones and checkpoints into project schedules to avoid delivering past deadline or over budget.

By taking these few simple steps, the data center manager can begin to earn the trust of management. Also, he or she may find that he or she has more job security and potential for career growth.

COMMUNICATING TECHNICAL MESSAGES

Perhaps one of the most difficult tasks that data center professionals face is communicating technical information to non-technical people. Several ways have proven to make this process less frustrating — and more successful.

First, whatever the message is, data center managers must keep it simple. No one should go overboard defining technical details. Users are looking for an explanation of just enough to get them going — but not so much that they become confused or overwhelmed. When data center staff members deliver their messages in person, they have a fairly easy time telling by listeners' facial expressions when they have gone too far. The same holds true for management. When making a presentation, data center managers should provide them with a technical overview and let them know that additional technical details are available; they should not go any further except at management's request.

In addition, although it's tempting, data center professionals must never use their technical expertise to show off. They will only bore people or, worse, put them off entirely about of what they are saying. In fact, the best way to explain a complex topic is to eliminate as many acronyms and buzzwords as possible. Instead, analogies simplify technical details, and diagrams can also help to clarify concepts. Users and management appreciate this approach as long as the data center manager is careful not to be condescending.

Finally, the message should be reinforced whenever possible. For instance, when users are introduced to a new system, they should be provided with an easy-to-read handout for later referral. This saves time in answering endless questions and aids users in helping themselves. Formal presentations to management should provide them with materials, including current situation, solution, benefits, cost, schedules, and diagrams, for later referral. In addition, presentation speakers should always invite questions — after ensuring that there is time to answer them properly.

WORKLOAD JUGGLING

Data center professionals are often short on time and long on responsibility. Finding a balance between the two is no easy task. Effective interpersonal communications can help gain the edge when dealing with end users. When a user asks for help and the data center staff member is in the middle of something else, the staff member should simply ask the user if he or she can wait. This forces the user to stop and think for a moment. Often, after some consideration, the answer is yes. Data center professionals often overlook this simple tactic and miss the opportunity to maintain some control over their work schedule.

There are times, however, when other tasks take priority, and data center personnel may have to say no — at least temporarily. They should be careful how they do this, though, so they do not offend the user's sensibilities. Data center personnel should also remember to never say no without first knowing the reason behind the request. It may be that the assignment that has come up is a top priority. If the project does have to wait, the best way to handle the situation is to explain why immediate assistance cannot be offered and to be clear about when assistance will become available. An alternate solution should be offered, if one exists.

In some cases, users can learn how to solve problems on their own. For instance, reloading the plotter with paper is not an intuitive task, but if the data center staff were to take the time to show people how this is done, they could permanently cross this job off their list. In fact, many users prefer doing tasks on their own, so they don't have to spend time tracking down an IT person.

RECOMMENDED COURSE OF ACTION

For the individual serious about revamping his or her interpersonal skills, plenty of additional help is available. First, the individual should let his or her manager know that he or she is interested in improving communications skills. Most managers, if money and time allow, are willing to send their staff to workshops or seminars. Also, plenty of books and tapes that address interpersonal communications are on the market. Networking with others in the same field, through, for example, users' groups, conferences, or chat rooms on the Internet, is also helpful.

At the beginning of the process of improving communications skills, the individual may feel awkward and frustrated, but this will pass as new skills are practiced. Meanwhile, what is gained far outweighs any discomfort the individual may experience. Without even realizing it, data center personnel will begin to garner the respect and trust of users and management and will also have a keener sense of their own purpose and direction. Although change is not easy, a job becomes more satisfying if the individual knows how to work with people effectively.

There is no doubt, with the narrowing of the gap between users and data center staff, that many professionals will need to develop additional skills to fit into this new environment, so they should not wait to hone their interpersonal communications skills. The investment of time and energy can lend to tremendous personal and professional rewards.

Chapter 4

Professional Consulting: The Analysis Methodology

Charles V. Breakfield
Roxanne E. Burkey

THIS CHAPTER DEFINES THE ROLES AND RESPONSIBILITIES of the contract consultant in relationship to the firm utilizing this type of resource. To provide the outline for this role definition, a methodology to capture a computer telephony integration (CTI) system migration analysis and the detailed steps throughout the process are provided. It is prudent to verify the background of the firm and the actual representative contracted for a particular activity. The background verification should include known expertise in the technology required, as well as a reputation to stand by the final work product.

CONSULTANT REQUIREMENTS

The contracted firm, as a whole, should possess some level of expertise with the hardware and software currently in place in the business environment. For a CTI system migration analysis effort, the demonstrated knowledge should include the following items:

1. An understanding of basic switch architecture
2. A working knowledge of the data components from a variety of platforms and networking architecture issues
3. The interoperating issues presented with this system integration

The consultant expertise should include the following verifiable items. It would not be inappropriate to require a resume from the firm in advance of the person performing the activity required.

1. A functional understanding of business operations even particular to an industry. This would include potential identification and clarification of the interaction between department's roles as defined within a particular business.
2. Asking relevant questions of the appropriate client support person to assemble a correct picture of the call center with a focus on the technology and business interaction. This involves discussions with several levels of call center staff and peripheral support departments.
3. Listening to the answers spoken and implied to integrate isolated but relevant data into the final picture of the call center puzzle.
4. Writing a summary of the piece parts of the on-site investigation into a functioning document. This summary should map out the necessary steps for completing the actual migration activity by internal or external technicians.

SCOPE OF WORK

The request for consultant services should include an itemization of the goals and accomplishments expected of the consultant firm. The primary components are the system review process, interviewing interested parties, and a report of findings. Contracting for consulting support is not a passive service request. It requires the ongoing interaction between the firm and the consultant to ensure that the activity requested is on target and moving in the required direction. The contracted consultant and the firm each have a role to fulfill during the process. Results of the analysis can be invalid if both parties do not actively participate.

CONSULTANT APPROACH

The scope of work outlines the requirements for a CTI system migration analysis defining the timeframes and deliverables from the client perspective. Each migration analysis, however, is different due to the complexity variance of a call center, but the methodology used to approach each one is the same. Upon receipt of an authorized request for services, the contracted firm typically assigns the consultant with the background most aligned to the requested services. Time in an industry or with a specific technology will often dictate that the experience level of the assigned consultant is broader than what was contracted to ensure meeting the overall client needs. Having the broader background may seem more expensive, but the results are generally of a higher quality and more in line with the overall objectives.

The typical model that the consultant will interact with in the telecom world is one of distributors and end users. Manufacturers of telecommunications gear usually sell to the end users through distribution channels. It is through the distribution channels that the consultant will be engaged for services. The consultant begins the process with introductions to the purchaser (distributor) of the service. In some cases, the distributor is different from the actual consumer (client) of the system analysis. Formal introductions to the distributor are done primarily to understand the role and expectations of the distributor. Much information about the end user is available and gathered from the distributor. The initial meeting, either in person or via phone, with the distributor should be held without the end user present. This sets the tone and ensures that all parties with a vested interest in the process are included in future discussions.

It is during this phase that distributor tactics and overall strategy are agreed to before going to the client site. The existing relationship between the client and distributor are discussed so that any politically sensitive issues are clarified prior to introductions to the end user. This initial meeting further sets the expectation levels of the distributor and in turn the end user. Success or failure in managing the distributor begins with the first meetings. Any misunderstandings or unrealistic expectations are dealt with before going on to the subsequent stages. A good indication of the caliber of the consultant is his or her ability to validate and verify each step of the process by obtaining sign-off and approval for milestones.

Key Contacts/Interviewees

The consultant should diligently determine the names, titles, and roles of all the players during the initial phases of discovery discussions. The key issues targeted here are information players versus authority players from both the distributor layer and the client layer. The sphere of influence that each of these players has is instrumental in the analysis process.

Typically, the consultant will find that the authority figures do not have the technical knowledge to answer key questions about the underlying technical infrastructure. Conversely, the technical personnel are not in a position to approve the overall process and must have the authority figure complete the project sign-off. The consultant will most likely find this duality at both the client level and the distributor level. Roles and responsibilities are defined up front at these first meetings so the players can be approached at the right time with the right request or question. All of these players share a significant role in the process steps.

The consultant should look for the following personnel at each of the levels listed on the next page (see Exhibit 4.1). Acquiring their name, title, and contact information is essential. In some cases, the availability of various personnel can determine the analysis approach.

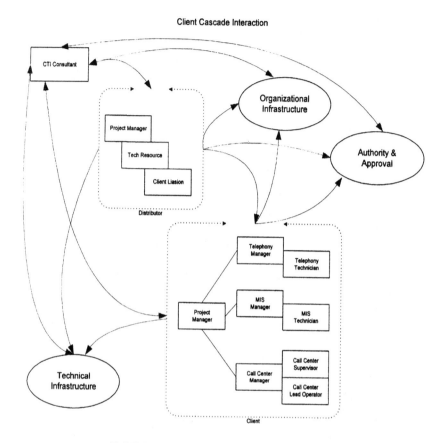

Client Cascade Interaction

Exhibit 4.1.   Client cascade interaction.

- Distributor
  - Project manager/coordinator
  - Client intermediary
  - Technical resources
- Client
  - Telephone support manager
  - Telephone support switch technician
  - MIS manager
  - MIS support technician(s)
  - Call center manager
  - Call center supervisor(s)
  - Call center lead operator(s)
  - Client project manager/signing authority

Customer Background

Good consultants are interested in learning about the underlying business of the client during the interview process. The consultant's enthusiasm for learning about the client's business has several positive effects on the discovery process. This learning or fact-finding process is not restricted to just the client; the distributor's business should also be discovered. The art of listening and asking questions based on what is heard is extensively exercised during this stage. At times, it may seem the consultant is out of scope with the request, but any technology change — especially to a call center — impacts other areas, even if it is only a subtle impact. There are three primary benefits to the consultant who actively cultivates this activity.

The first benefit is building the relationship between the consultant and those interviewed. The consultant can uncover not just technical issues, but also begin learning the hidden profile of each of the players, which is built upon throughout the on-site visit. This lays the foundation of trust between the consultant and the distributor/client.

The second benefit to learning about the client's business is that this information will help to establish how the client got to where it currently is, and why the client believes that what it is purchasing or is thinking about implementing will solve the problems. The consultant must learn how the client feels and what the client is thinking from these preliminary interviews and client history. The client's history and background information will help the consultant to ask the right question and to appropriately direct it to sources with the knowledge.

The third benefit is for the consultant to begin thinking like the client in the current situation. A high identification with the client makes questioning processes easier and allows the client to begin trusting the consultant with information that might not be forthcoming otherwise. The internal politics of the client's organization become more easily discussed at this stage. The internal politics of any firm drive decisions and changes to the roles and responsibilities of the staff. The staff of an organization not supportive of any system change can and often does cause the system integration to fail.

Current Call Center Environment

Once the client background has been explored, the consultant is now in a position to delve into the current call center environment. The methodology of asking questions and listening to answers is again key to the process.

The consultant has the option to begin either at the point where the call enters the PBX switch or at the desktop. If beginning at the PBX switch, then the consultant would follow the technology down the call process to the desktop. If beginning at the desktop, then the consultant would follow the technology up the call process to the PBX switch. Often, the complexity of the environment or the internal politics will warrant a review in each direction using multiple sources for the information.

If the process is started at the switch, the consultant will need to know not only how the switch is configured, but also why. Again, asking questions may uncover potential problems for connecting "downstream" technology. At each stage of call processing, the consultant looks for and asks questions about how and why something is done to a call. This is done to determine the critical areas from a management and user perspective. Without knowing why something is in place, the consultant could recommend a change that negatively disrupts the organization.

The following is a list of technical components that a call center might have or is considering installing. A thorough consultant will learn as many aspects of these as are needed to provide clear and concise recommendations.

1. The PBX (telephone switch) and all pertinent configuration information (contents) about it. This would include version, remote access, and technical support staff.
2. What add-on components (monitoring facilities, mail systems, etc.) are installed and all detailed information about how they are configured.
3. Any reader board technology that might be installed and how it is currently working.
4. If there is an IVR (interactive voice response) installed and all there is to know about it. This includes the manufacturer and the current scripts that are being used.
5. Are there any special applications currently operating in the environment that depend on switch application links? Need any and all specifics.
6. Are there any CTI (computer telephony integration) middleware servers in the environment? What are the specific roles and interactions of the CTI middleware servers with other existing call center technology?
7. What does the LAN/WAN environment look like? What topology is being used in the call center environment? What protocols are being used? What network operating system is employed?
8. Does the call center use static addressing or DHCP (Dynamic Host Configuration Protocol) to support TCP/IP in its environment?
9. What is the agent/supervisor desktop operating system of choice running in the call center? How much disk space, RAM, and processing power do the agent/supervisor PCs have?
10. What is the customer care or help desk application being used in the call center? Is it currently or is it destined to be "screen-popped"?

What type of ODBC hooks does the help desk application support? Does the customer care/help desk application reside on a host mainframe? How is access to the host mainframe application accomplished?

11. Are there any custom applications residing in the call center that must be accounted for?

12. Is Web/Internet accessing a part of the call center or is it intended for the near future?

13. Is outbound predictive dialing technology being used or being planned?

14. Is the call center "front-ended" by a carrier's network and perhaps their voice mail menu, or are the calls coming straight into the call center and being handled in-house? Are there other sites that are routing calls to this site? Are there other sites receiving calls from this site?

Current Call Flows

The consultant's next target is to understand to what level the call flows have evolved. A call center should be considered a dynamic organism and as such so should its call flows. It is important to understand that although the call center is designed to "take calls from the outside," it functions on many levels depending on who is being asked, "how do callers get service?"

The switch technician is the resource to understand how calls come in from the "network cloud" and are routed to the ACD queue or to a CDN. The data network people know about the network operating system, the LAN/WAN topology, and the customer care application. The call center manager knows about the service-level agreement, the average speed of answer, and the required staffing levels. The call center supervisors know about the call center group dynamics, individual performance issues, and weekly call center statistics. The senior call center agent knows how to answer the phone, use a PC keyboard, and get an order processed. None of them know all of the call flow process; they usually only know their small part.

The consultant must be able to meet with each key player as identified above and discuss with them at their own level of expertise to extract the interrelated parts of the call center's call flow puzzle. Often, educating the players on the interaction of call center dynamics highlights cause-and-effect relationships that were previously unknown and, as a result, secures great respect from the end user. This is the very heart of the consultant's role in the CTI system migration analysis.

Disaster Recovery Methodology

It is assumed that the consultant was brought into the call center to do the analysis because of the strategic significance of the center. It follows then that there should be plans in place for the call center to always be operational and be able to quickly recover from an unforeseen disaster. Important clues as to how the call center would recover or remain operational in the event of a technical failure on site, a technical failure outside the site, or a natural disaster affecting the site should be covered in an internal client specific disaster recovery document.

The consultant should be permitted to review the document (assuming one exists) and make notes as to how the procedures will need to be changed once new call center technology is introduced or existing technology is altered. It is also important to know who would be responsible for implementing and maintaining the disaster recovery procedures after the consultant has finished the assignment. Some firms do not have recovery plans in place. In these cases, short discussions and future documentation may help a client formulate the foundation, at least for a critical operational area such as a call center.

Customer Care/Help Desk Application

The consultant requires a good understanding of the customer care/help desk application (CC/HD). Typically, the client has integrated or wants to integrate the CC/HD application with the incoming call to produce a CTI screen pop. Whether or not screen pops are already functioning in the call center, the CC/HD application must be understood properly. The technology available to permit integration of the telephony event with the data integration of the caller is the basis for high-end quality customer service functionality in many call centers.

If the call center is already doing screen pops, then any new technology being introduced cannot disturb that existing functionality. If the call center does not have screen pop technology, then the consultant should include the proper implementation procedures to allow for its installation. The important issues for the consultant to capture are the supported ODBC hooks to get to the CC/HD application, the database engine supporting the CC/HD application, the database location (local or remote), and whether it is client/server technology or legacy host system technology.

Customer Goals

The ultimate objective of the CTI system migration analysis is to identify where the client is and to correctly map where the client wants to go. The consultant is to be considered the mapmaker in this process. By identifying the existing technology that is currently in place, and then listening to what the client says about what it wants, a chart of how to do what and when formulates.

The client goal is the final destination — the arrival point of how the call center should function. This is the "what" portion of the migration analysis. Here is what the client said that it wants to do. These customer goals should correctly mirror what is being said by all the players identified at the beginning of this process. Any misunderstanding of what the client wants at this point will cause the consultant and the CTI system migration analysis to map in the wrong direction. Again, the key here is to listen closely to what the client is saying.

ANALYSIS REPORT

The report provided by the consultant firm usually follows the site visit by one to two weeks. It is delivered to the distributor with copies made available for the end user. If the distributor takes exception to a point contained within the report, they can alter or modify the report. Main components of the final report include a recap of the interviewees, company background, goals with respect to the technology changes under consideration, and the changes required. Other elements, depending on the complexity of the call center or contracted deliverables, can include the following items:

Functional Diagram

The consultant can vastly improve what is being communicated and what is being understood by creating functional diagrams for the migration analysis. Two functional diagrams are minimally provided: the currently installed technology and the proposed technology. These before-and-after pictures should employ enough detail to correctly capture and convey all that is known about the current environment and what it will look like after the migration. From these, the client can readily confirm or deny the facts and the stated direction to the consultant. The goal is to intercept any misconceptions and stay on target with what the client is expecting. Exhibit 4.2 is an example of a call center.

Technical Issues Reviewed

Technical issues are outlined with an itemization of any deficiencies, incompatibilities, necessary upgrades, necessary additions, or lost functionality that the client can expect if the implementation project is undertaken. The "gap analysis" produced here includes all the research done by the consultant on each of the call center components. In some areas, a work-around for a particular gap is recommended based on a goal or requirement of the client.

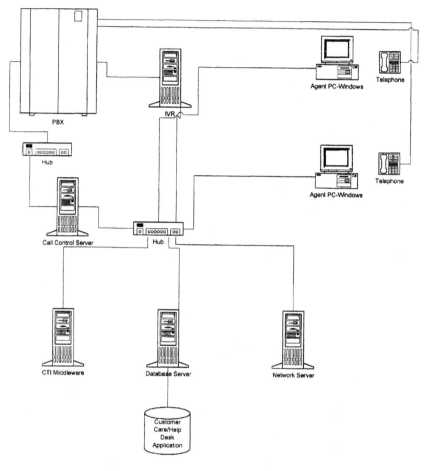

Call Center Components

Exhibit 4.2.   Call center.

The integration process and any interoperability issues are discussed in this area. Any custom coding (programming) required for full functionality is in this area for review. The consultant recounts all technical aspects of the call center in this section — even those not directly changed by the proposed technology. From this, the client has a picture of the environment at hand for future modifications, as new technologies become available.

Observations and Recommendations

The consultant charts the technical process in this section. All technical concepts, processes that need to be evolved, and any technical disconnects are explored. It is in this area that the consultant will try to map the client's needs and wants to the proposed technology under consideration. In this section, the consultant will either confirm or deny the appropriateness of the chosen technology for the call center. A recommendation not to integrate a specific technology with the correct arguments usually means the consultant truly understands that all available technologies do not fit all environments.

Additionally, the consultant would point out any overlooked areas of the system migration process not addressed by the new technology. Any missing technical components or any functionality not addressed by the technology under consideration is accounted for in this area. Sometimes, a technology benefit is sold to the end user but the ramifications or other pieces were missed. The consultant, from the in-depth interviews and overall understanding of the business goals and internal processes, can recognize the departments or functions that would benefit if also utilizing the technology. The importance of this area of the report cannot be overlooked.

Finally, the consultant should try to comment on future technology that might impact the call center. Any relevant and pending call center technology that might benefit the client should be noted in this section. While this type of information might delay an implementation or even preclude a sale, good consulting efforts are built on the delivery of all the known facts relevant to the client's situation at that point in time. The consulting process must be impartial and technically accurate.

IMPLEMENTATION PROCESS DESIGN

The final result in the system migration analysis is the actual process of implementation. This portion is often not included in the system migration report, but as an after-report review effort. The end user needs time to digest the initial report and address the gaps contained within the report. If the result of the review involves the end user going forward with the system integration, the consulting firm completes a plan for implementation.

The consultant creates a step-by-step methodology for the implementing engineer. At this point, all the knowledge of the proposed technology, the existing technology, and any deficiencies have been chronicled, and, typically, no portion of the implementation process is unknown. The consultant or any other technically qualified engineer should be able to pick up the migration analysis and implementation process design to integrate the system technology.

The implementation methodology places, in chronological order, all the necessary implementation steps, approximate time duration of each stage during the process, any task dependencies, and also the skill set necessary to complete each phase. A timeline project is an excellent addition to this section. If the consultant has done a thorough job on the migration analysis, there are usually no delays during the implementation and no surprises. The end user and distributor should approve the approach for implementation and provide any additional resources recommended. The client should designate an internal staff member to include throughout the implementation process to ensure proper care and feeding of the technology when the consulting firm is finished.

CONCLUSION

Contracting with a consultant can prove invaluable to a firm because of the rapid release of technology and the need for business to remain competitive. Outlining the requirements of, selection of, and integration with the consultant are critical factors. The final success or failure of a given project, however, is typically in the hands of the consultant firm, based on its approach and dedication to the needs of the client. It is very difficult for a firm to allow the consultant to perform his role if the consultant is always required to sponsor only the products backed by the firm. The mark of a good consulting firm is the willingness to lose a potential sale by allowing the consultant to recommend the right technology to the end user.

It is the responsibility of the end user to know that if the recommendations made during the various stages are not followed, the system integration will probably fail. Wanting any system integration because of a need to have all the newest toys is not always the prudent course for the business. Whatever the system integration benefits appear to be, they must meet the overall requirements of the organization with regard to increased competitiveness or profitability. Anything less is not acceptable.

Chapter 5
Pricing Methods Across Linked Networks

Keith A. Jones

DATA CENTERS, WHEN UNDER EFFICIENT MANAGEMENT, provide services to a business enterprise that are recovered by a cost allocation system that distributes these costs to customer business units. Operational expenses can be allocated across data communications network infrastructures along the lines of chargeback systems established for the host processing environments.

Most data center managers are already very much aware of all the host system resources that must be charged back to their users. This includes the most common direct system use charge categories (e.g., host central processing unit, system printer, Direct Access Storage Device storage, and tape drive units) as well as indirect resource costs that must be billed (e.g., space, utilities, and technical support services).

Many data center managers may not be as well aware of the resources that must be charged to recover costs across host-linked enterprisewide information networks — or of the impact that such networks can have on their host resource costs. Use of these networks can result in new categories of host data center costs that must be recovered through more complex pricing methods. Although data center managers can readily accommodate any of the more conventional unexpected changes in data center operating expense (e.g., a rise in utility or paper costs) by using an industry-standard strategy that adjusts availability of host access to match available capacity, they are often uncomfortable at the prospect of charge-out across their host network links. This is primarily because they are not as aware of their options for recovering unexpected changes in costs of supporting an enterprisewide data network.

CHARGEABLE RESOURCES

At first, it is easier for a data center manager to focus on effects to support chargeback of direct network costs on services involving equipment with very short paybacks and high plug compatibility. The ideal initial resources are modems, terminals, printers, and if already in place, a central help desk telephone line to contact vendors.

The ideal arrangement is to leverage the volume-purchasing power of the central-site data center to obtain the lowest possible direct cost for the business users. In addition to increasing economies of scale in purchase of hardware, software, and supplies, the data center can offer a central focal point for vendor contacts, negotiations, and coordination of maintenance services — at lower pass-through costs than can be obtained by independent arrangements.

Data center managers should begin viewing their function as more than just a service bureau for data processing services. The network-linked host data center provides expanded opportunities to offer an enterprisewide range of business information management support services (e.g., computer systems hardware and software purchasing, inventory control, financial analysis, and physical plant engineering).

Especially if existing departments within the organization already offer such basic services, the data center does not have to provide these services directly. Instead, data center management should increasingly position and present its overall operation as a ready and effective conduit to help enable each business enterprise client to tap into — and leverage — existing packets of expertise within the organization. Data center managers are in a unique position to identify common areas of operational business needs and present both internal and external sources as options to help pool costs.

Regardless of the source of the resources that make up the information enterprise network and host system costs that are to be allocated across the client service base, the primary consideration of the data center manager must be that of defining the categories of use that are to be charged. The chargeable resource categories must be easily understood by the customers who are to be billed and must be measurable by use statistics that can be readily accumulated for the review of customers in their billing statement. This is true regardless of whether the costs are to be allocated according to direct line item unit measure charges or indirect fee assignments.

As with the host chargeback system, it is first of all necessary to be able to identify — and track — all possible network services and resources. Once there is a reasonable assurance that a system of resource accounting procedures has been established that does not allow any network cost or any contingent host system cost to escape unaccounted for, data center managers can consolidate individual categories of network services and resource costs into network cost pools suitable for use in pricing out network chargeback billings.

The definition of these cost pools must be sufficiently detailed to support future strategy for directing patterns of desirable network use in a manner that is predictable and compatible to host cost-efficiency and cost-containment procedures. In other words, categories of resource that are identified to network customers for cost allocation purposes must serve to increase customer awareness of the types of expenses involved in managing the network, regardless of how much is to be billed to recover costs of each resource type.

NETWORK RESOURCE CATEGORIES

The chargeable resources for enterprisewide network cost allocation can absorb some of the data center resources (e.g., printing, database use, data media, and data center operational services), as well as the resources required for the network. The most important network resource categories are discussed in the following sections:

Cable. The costs of cabling to connect enterprisewide network devices can easily be the largest and most complicated category of all network management expenses. Among the available options are:

- *Coaxial cable.* An example is the cable used in IBM 3270 terminals. It is expensive, but extremely reliable and compatible with most of the existing network methods. It is often kept in stock by data centers.
- *Unshielded twisted-pair cable.* Also known as telephone wire, this is inexpensive, but subject to interference; it often causes host-linkage error.
- *Shielded twisted-pair cable.* Although similar to the unshielded telephone wire, this is wrapped like coaxial cable. It is moderately expensive and moderately dependable.
- *Fiber-optic cable.* This has the widest possible range of applications, and it is the most reliable cable option.
- *Wireless networks.* These are increasingly feasible options, especially when rapid installation is desired and the physical layout of the business enterprise facility is suitable.

Linkages. In network terms, these are interconnectors, or plug-compatible interfaces, between networks and host lines. Linkage components include:

- *Plugs.* These include cable connectors and data switches, splitter and sharing devices, wire ribbons, and all other interface linkage hardware. This is typically the most overhead-intensive cost category in network management, because it requires inventory control and planning to have every possible plug type on hand.
- *Modems.* Modems and all other dial-up line management devices, as well as communications line multiplexing hardware are most critical to line-speed costs.
- *Wire boxes.* These involve all the business enterprise physical plant or facility-determined access hardware and management.

Workstations. This category includes microcomputer configurations that are connected at each local network node or station. The components are:

- *Terminals.* These can include intelligent workstations through gateway servers.
- *Storage.* Storage elements can include the fixed hard disk (if available at the workstation node), diskettes, and any dedicated tape or CD-ROM storage devices.
- *Personal printer.* This is included if a dedicated printer is attached.

Servers. This category always comprises an intelligent workstation with the minimum central processing unit and storage required by the particular network control methods used. It includes:

- *File-server hardware.* This includes the file-server workstation and all network boards that it controls, including LAN boards and host gateway link boards, as well as fax boards and other specialized hardware.
- *File-server software.* This includes the network file management control software and shared applications.

Storage. High-volume mass storage is frequently needed for backup and archival purposes, which may involve technical support and specialized hardware or software well beyond the usual range of support for LAN administrators. This may include optical memory, imaging, CD-ROM jukeboxes, or other advanced technology with many gigabytes of storage capacity. The need for this technology is increasingly likely if the client network involves graphics, engineering, or any other application requiring intensive backup cycles and complicated version control. The use of high-volume mass storage is usually controlled from a dedicated server that automatically manages files and application software. The client-server may be a minicomputer that functions as a front-end processor to manage enterprise network message requests for real-time access to host programming functions or a back-end processor to manage online access to a host database.

Communications. This is by far the most cost-intensive network resource. Telecommunications can make or break the network chargeback system, and unfortunately it is an area in which a data center may have limited options. Much can be learned about network billing from a local telecommunications company, often at great expense.

LAN Administration Support. This can include the salaries of the local LAN administrator and the LAN help desk personnel, the costs of training, and the costs of host-based support of LAN inventory, purchasing, billing or any other service provided by the data center. It can also involve both short-term and long-term leasing of network hardware or software, diagnostics, or user training. This category can be large or small, depending on the client. In some cases, clients may prefer to provide some of the LAN technical support; in others, a data center may provide it all.

Internet Gateway Access

Whether the data center network is System Network Architecture or TCP/IP dictates whether it is an option to establish the enterprise's own Internet gateway, which can cost as much as ten intelligent workstations. That gateway, however, can be cost justified if the enterprise organization does any kind of business on the Internet.

Typically, business on the Internet takes one or more of three forms: e-mail, user news groups, or a home page on the World Wide Web (WWW, or just the Web). A dedicated gateway requires substantial UNIX-related technical expertise to establish and maintain. A more viable option is a dedicated line to an online service account, which normally costs no more than a single workstation, and internal enterprise customers can still be supported in the three major functional business support areas.

Both a dedicated gateway and a dedicated line can usually be financed using long-term methods. If Internet access is a legitimate enterprise business need, it can be more than easily justified. If not, until the demand (and real need) for Internet access can be precisely predicted, it is often feasible to simply pass through direct charge billing of departmental accounts on online services with Internet access, such as Compuserve, Prodigy, or America Online.

EXPENSE CATEGORIES

The next step in developing an enterprisewide network cost-allocation system is to assign all expenses into a manageable number of non-overlapping categories. Most data center managers can develop a matrix of network resource categories that has a direct correspondence to their host data center resource assignment matrix. If there is no existing host data center expense matrix to use as a model for defining the network cost allocation

Exhibit 5.1. Sample enterprisewide network expense matrix.

Expenses	Resources				
	Stations	Servers	Linkages	Storage	Telecom
Fixed Costs Equipment Facilities Insurance Interest Maintenance Salary					
Variable Costs Consultants Database Support Help Desk LAN Support Paper Supplies Telecom Support Vendors					
Surcharges Diagnostics Disaster Recovery Documentation Planning Prevention Tuning Training					
TOTAL COSTS					

expense matrix, the data center manager can begin by grouping the basic categories of network expenses. Exhibit 5.1 shows a basic network expense assignment matrix.

There are two important considerations. First, each of the categories in the expense matrix must correspond to budget line items that will be forecasted and tracked by a business enterprise financial controller or accountants assigned to audit network costs. Second, expense line items must be defined so they are clearly separated from all other items and so there is limited opportunity to assign expenses to the wrong category or, even worse, duplicate direct and indirect costs.

Although the data center manager should consult with the financial controllers who audit the network before preparing the network cost assignment matrix, the data center manager must usually define how the resource allocation procedures are to be administered, which includes assumptions about the methods for measurement and assignment of enterprisewide network resource use and billing obligations. The proposed network resource cost allocation matrix should also be reviewed with the prospective network customers. In addition, the anticipated categories of host-lined data network expenses should be reviewed by the business enterprise organizational management before any pricing strategy or rate structure is determined for the enterprisewide network cost chargeout.

RATE DETERMINATION

To expand enterprisewide business information services and allocate host system costs across interconnected distributed networks, data center managers must change their fundamental view from a centralized focus to a decentralized one. This change in focus must include a reorientation to accommodate market-driven, as well as demand-driven operations planning.

Data center managers are increasingly in a position of competition with alternative outside-vendor sources for every product and service that has traditionally been a vital part of their exclusive business organizational domain. It is therefore necessary for data centers to begin defining their pricing structure on not only what chargeable resources there are, but also how each of the resources is charged, to help achieve strategic market advantage over the competition.

Data centers can no longer simply apply a straight distribution formula to recover costs, they must also factor in potential future costs associated with the risk that new technology will be available at a lower cost and that business enterprise users may bypass the data center. Unless the data center manager is also an expert in both financial management and risk management, this usually means an increasing emphasis on leasing or subcontracting most new services and resources at short-term premium rates, until a sufficient economy of scale can be achieved by bundling enterprisewide data network resource demands to reduce risks, as well as costs.

In some cases, host-linked network domains may be large enough to quickly achieve the break-even economies of scale, especially if sufficiently large proprietary data stores are involved. In most cases, however, the process will be more like a traditional tactical penetration to achieve a dominant share of mature, nongrowth market segments, also known as buyer's markets. The management of the central site host data center must go to the business enterprise customer, rather than the other way around.

If a data center cannot package centralized services as superior to the competition, not all costs may be recovered. Furthermore, the ultimate determination of what constitutes a chargeable resource is not simply a data center expense that must be recovered, but is now also an information network service or resource that a business enterprise customer must want to buy.

The manner of rate determination is directly determined by the network resource allocation strategy and chargeback system cost-control objectives. The most basic consideration determining the rate structure is whether data center management has decided to fully recover network costs on the basis of actual use or to distribute indirect costs of a network resource pool evenly among all of its users. This consideration applies to each network resource category, as well as to each category of network customer.

As a basic rule of thumb, the decision to recover costs on the basis of actual use or to distribute costs evenly among business enterprise users is largely determined by the extent to which a resource is equally available for shared, concurrent use or is reserved exclusively for use by an individual network user. If the resource is shared, the rate structure is based on forecasted patterns of use, with sufficient margin to absorb potential error in the forecasted demand, as well as the potential probability of drop-off in demand for network services. On the other hand, rate structures can be based on underwriting network capital equipment or financing service-level agreements, which provide greater security for full recovery of all costs from an individual business enterprise customer on the basis of annualized use charges, with provisions for additional setup fees and disconnection fees to recover unforeseen and marginal costs.

As a matter of practical reality, the decision on which of the two methods of rate determination to use must also take into account the availability of dependable enterprisewide network use measurements to support direct line charges. It is also critical to first determine whether the costs that must be recovered will vary depending on the level of use (e.g., the pass-through costs of data transmission over a public telecommunications carrier line) or will be fairly well fixed regardless of whether they are fully used at all times when they are available (e.g., the on-call network technical support cost of labor). It is also important to attempt to define all assumptions on which each resource cost recovery strategy is based; this identifies all the conditions that would necessitate a change in the rate structure and exactly how each cost would be recovered in the event of major changes in enterprise information network use or underlying rate-strategy assumptions.

The degree to which the enterprisewide network chargeback pricing can be easily understood by the customer largely determines how effectively all costs are recovered. It is also critical that business enterprise clients be aware of the goals of each rate decision. Depending on how responsibly they use the network, each individual enterprise network customer can help or hurt overall efficiency of the LAN, as well as all interconnected LANs and the host.

RECOMMENDED COURSE OF ACTION

Opportunities exist to broaden the data center's customer base through identifying and establishing chargeback methods for host-linked enterprisewide information networks. These new categories, however, require more complicated pricing methods. Increasing economies of scale make network chargeout a valuable strategy for the data center manager and staff. Data center operations managers should:

- Initially focus on services based on equipment with short paybacks and high compatibility, such as modems, terminals, printers, and a help desk phone line to vendors.
- Begin viewing their function as more than a service bureau for data processing. Instead, the data center manager should position the data center as a resource where expertise can be found in the organization.
- Identify and track all network services and resources, including cable, linkages, workstations, servers, storage, communications, and LAN administration support.
- Establish, if possible, the organization's own Internet gateway.
- Develop a matrix for defining network cost allocation expenses, to assign all expenses into non-overlapping categories.

Chapter 6
Enterprise Modeling for Strategic Support

Michael E. Whitman
Michael L. Gibson

SUCCESSFUL STRATEGIC BUSINESS ENGINEERING, whether a reactive effort to gain competitive advantage or a proactive effort to maintain and improve performance, depends on an organization's ability to accurately and methodically analyze its internal and external environments, people, processes, organizational structure, information uses, and technology. Enterprise modeling (EM) greatly enhances strategic business engineering by providing a structured, diagrammatic framework for depicting the myriad interconnected and changing components addressed in large-scale change. Its representative models of the organization serve as baseline against which all subsequent change is measured and provide a basis for strategic planning. Using EM as a forecasting tool fosters a more effective and efficient planning process that dramatically increases the probabilities of success.

IS professionals are uniquely situated to apply enterprise modeling technology to overall business change. Enterprise modeling originated in data processing departments as a software development tool and plays a critical role in computer-aided systems engineering, allowing systems designers to map current and proposed information systems as a predecessor to development. IS professionals have direct access to the organizational information and the discipline necessary to support information flow. It is, therefore, a logical extension for the IS function to aid business engineering strategists achieve the revisions inherent in strategic business engineering.

ENTERPRISE MODELING

Enterprise modeling has been described by E. Aranow as "a combination of diagrammatic, tabular, or other visual structures, which represent the key components of the business that need to be understood." More simply put, enterprise modeling consists of representing complex objects in an easy-to-understand diagram. Complex modeling tools facilitate EM, but the

0-8493-9824-X/00/$0.00+$.50
© 2000 by CRC Press LLC

basis for understanding a large, complex organization relates to the ability to represent it in a series of elementary graphs that allow modelers to view components individually without losing the contextual overview of the entire organization.

Enterprise modeling is referred to as one of many qualitative models that can be used to represent quantitative measures of particular facets of an organization in a higher level of abstraction that represents the organization in a more holistic manner. Qualitative modeling allows the modelers to view the organization synergistic existence as a whole entity vs. the sum of its parts, in supporting the organizational mission, objectives, and functions. This systems view provides critical analysis of the organization as a preparation for strategic business engineering, as organizational modelers must encapsulate the interaction of the components of the organization depicted as part of the conceptual view of the organization.

The enterprise model itself can be decomposed into two functional models, a business model and a systems, or information, model (Exhibit 6.1). The business model depicts business functions, events, and activities, and organizational structures, geographic locations, and interrelationships. The information systems model comprises the information needed, produced, and used by business functions.

Enterprise Modeling Constructs

Business models are concerned with what processes are needed to run a selected business area, how processes interact, and what data are needed. Systems models present a high-level overview of the enterprise—its functions, data, and information needs. Whereas the business model represents a view of the entire business, the information systems model represents that portion of the business targeted for computer support.

Modeling an organization begins at the strategic or corporate level and progresses through decomposition of corporate-level objects, activities, and associations down to the tactical and operational levels. Objects (business) are those things internal and external to the business for which it is important that the business retain information. Activities (enterprise) represent what the enterprise does in terms of major functions, processes, and procedures. Associations are relationships, dependencies, shared characteristics, or other connections between organizational objects and activities.

As shown in Exhibit 6.2, a top-down, comprehensive approach to modeling the business divides the conceptual (i.e., strategic objects, activities, and associations) into greater and greater detail. In the intermediate levels, these objects, activities, and associations are logical (e.g., functional), at the lowest level they are physical (e.g., operational). This process spans

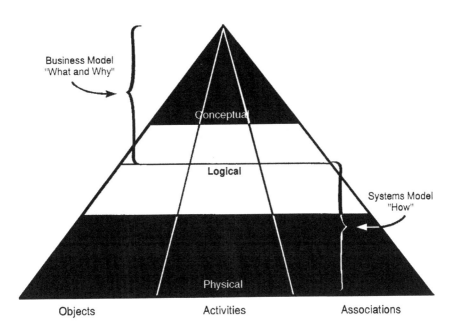

Source: M.L. Gibson and C.A. Snyder, "Computer Aided Software Engineering: Facilitating the Path for True Software Knowledge Engineering," International Journal of Software Engineering and Knowledge Engineering (January 1991).

Exhibit 6.1. Functional models of the enterprise model.

the business life cycle, continuing down through the layers of organization until they are at a primitive level and need no further decomposition to be clearly understood. At this lowest level, the objects, activities, and associations inform and are used by employees (who are also some of the business objects) in conducting the daily activities of the business.

The concept of organizational analysis resembles the business evaluation techniques presented in most current management literature. Just as a formalized structure for collecting and representing environmental scanning data, in organizational analysis, modeling methodologists responsible for modeling the enterprise must use a structured framework to facilitate accurate and precise analysis. The resulting models should accurately represent what the business is, does, and uses, and with whom it interacts.

A CASE tool that has high degrees of graphic and text (dictionary and repository) support often helps the modeler show how things are related (associated). A good CASE tool should have some type of intelligence. Modeling with case tools imposes formality on all phases of the methodology

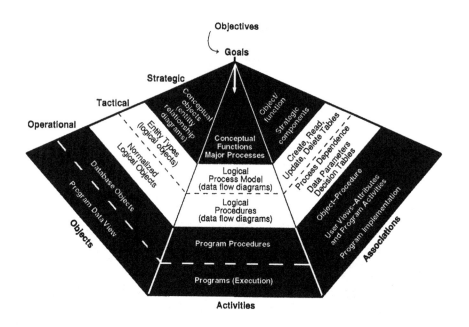

Exhibit 6.2. Enterprise modeling paradigm.

and provides repositories and extensive capabilities for cross-checking and storing data.

The Enterprise Modeling Methodologist

As the CIO of a large oil company has said, "The business line managers within the organization must be the individuals responsible for any change effort and for reengineering, specifically." For any intervention strategy to succeed, the managers and employees within an organization targeted for strategic business engineering must become an integral part of the effort and continually be informed and educated regarding the process. In fact, for a successful strategic business engineering (SBE) effort, managers and employees must be the individuals actually performing the change, empowered by their supervisor to use their personal innovation and ingenuity to achieve desired improvements.

The complexity of EM, however, necessitates that a methodologist trained in EM techniques must instruct managers and employees in the EM process, if not actually conduct the modeling. Using a methodologist does not detract power or responsibility from the business personnel for the end project, it provides them with an experienced knowledge base from which to draw ideas and suggestions on overall design improvements.

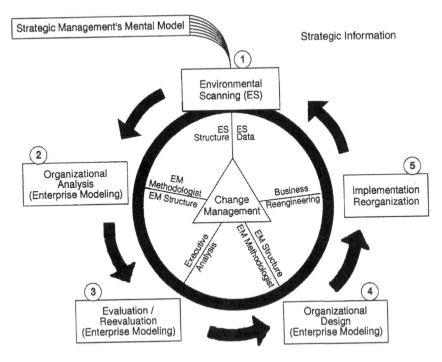

Exhibit 6.3. Contextual paradigm of strategic business engineering.

Enterprise Modeling in SBE

As depicted in a contextual SBE model (Exhibit 6.3), enterprise modeling plays a significant role in supporting the various processes of a typical engineering effort. The model begins with the strategic planner's mental model of the organization: a conceptual image of what the organization is, how it operates, and how it interacts with its environment. The mental models of executives are ever-striving attempts to match the physical with the logical that drives the organizational restructuring and change management evident in today's organization.

- *Environmental scanning.* Selectively retrieving information from the organization's internal and external environments to support the development of an organization's strategy.
- *Enterprise modeling.* Accurately reflecting the current processes and information usage within an organization and mapping out the desired end result of the SBE effort.
- *Evaluation and reevaluation of the enterprise model.* Developing a blueprint of the organization as it currently exists to allow strategic planners

to compare the model of what the organization is to their conceptual models.

- *Blueprinting the new and improved organization.* Creating a revised organizational design that models what should be instead of what currently exists.

The final stages of the SBE paradigm involve implementing the revised enterprise model and continuously monitoring and revising the previous processes. The central controlling factor of the entire SBE process embodies the structured change management principles that lie in the center of the model. Current practices in organizational development and organizational behavior theory are extremely useful in SBE. In fact, some projects undertaken by IS professionals fail because due attention is not given to the change intervention strategies proposed by organizational development professionals.

Once the first iteration of the engineering process is completed, the next one begins. As an organization becomes committed to the kinds of revolutionary changes and improvements resulting from successful SBE, it must continue to practice the constructs and lessons learned, or else again begin to stagnate and fall behind in the competitive race.

ENTERPRISE MODELING, REENGINEERING, AND STRATEGIC PLANNING

The true value of an enterprise model lies in its ability to support a conceptual understanding of the present situation of an enterprise and to aid in mapping out a strategy for the future developments. Enterprise modeling is, thus, a dynamic strategic tool that allows a strategic planner to assess the organization's position before establishing the means to accomplish organizational goals and objectives. A strategic planning life cycle that incorporates enterprise modeling and strategic business engineering encompasses the following several steps:

Goal Development. Directly related to the business profile analysis is the identification and evaluation of business opportunities and threats present in the company's external environments. These opportunities and threats help develop strategic goals and objectives. Business engineering, as a logical extension of the change process, should be a cornerstone for strategy development. The enterprise models created should be used to supplement the goals developed within this process.

Strategy Formulation. The second step in a typical strategic planning life cycle is the development of specific strategies for the organization, as well as a single context-level strategy that addresses the focus and mission of the organization. As strategy emerges, a key component is the continuous process of evaluation and engineering. Again, enterprise modeling provides a useful tool in evaluating the organization to determine the feasibility of the various alternative strategies.

Strategy Implementation. The next phase of the strategy life cycle involves implementing the developed strategy, focusing on achieving results, and relying heavily on change management, organizational behavior analysis, and performance measures. SBE during implementation concentrates on organizational structure, relationships, and processes, and on the behavior of the firm's top leadership. Modeling the structures and associations within the organization coupled with an aggressive implementation strategy provides a fundamental blueprint for a successful implementation.

Strategy Assessment. During the implementation stage, the simultaneous evaluation of strategy development and strategy implementation directly affect final strategies. The engineering phase of implementation and reorganization is ideally suited to support the integration of the strategy into the business environment. As the strategy is implemented, the engineering constructs are regained in the process, creating an atmosphere conducive to the ongoing change that characterizes reengineering and strategy implementation.

Strategy Control and Maintenance. Success in strategic planning is a relative concept. Reengineering does not ensure the success or failure of a strategy; rather, it serves to report the state of the organization as it responds to the planning process. Strategy maintenance is a continuous looping process whereby the organization continues existing strategies and develops new ones throughout the strategy life cycle. The continuing analysis, design, and implementation steps in enterprise modeling and engineering facilitate strategy maintenance. The relationship between SBE and strategic planning is symbiotic — the constructs behind each support the other.

The following example illustrates the application of enterprise modeling:

Enterprise Modeling at State University

State University (a pseudonym) is a major public university in the Southeast with an enrollment of approximately 25,000 students. As a land grant university, State pursues its charter missions of research, instruction, and extension. The university currently manages it financial operations through a single functional division, known as the Business and Finance Division. The department within the business office primarily responsible for the information systems and financial reporting procedures supporting the university is known as Financial Information Systems (FIS). The director of FIS contacted an enterprise modeling group to develop a series of models of FIS operations in preparation for business process redesign efforts.

History of Computing in the Business Office. The administrative computing function at State University was originally part of the Business Office (now known as the Business and Finance Division). In the mid 1970s, administrative computing was supported by an IBM 370 mainframe located in the basement of the administration building. Around the same time, the Division of University Computing (DUC) was formed and the function of administrative computing support was moved to it. The office of Financial Information Systems was formed primarily as the Business Office's central data entry office.

After the departure of the administrative computing function from the university's administration building, the Division of University Computing set up a remote batch station to handle the transmission of the data that was key punched by FIS. The remote batch station also printed output generated by administrative mainframe. At the time, FIS consisted of four data-entry clerks, a production supervisor, and the director. The responsibility for the remote batch station was taken over by FIS in 1981. The batch station operator was then transferred to FIS. In 1982, FIS purchased an IBM System/38 to meet the growing demand for business office computing support. Within two years the network grew to over 150 users, requiring that FIS upgrade the System/38 to the most current and largest model available.

From 1981 to 1986, the director handled all mainframe ad hoc programming requests. The director also handled the coordination of projects involving the installation and upgrade of mainframe-based systems used by the Business Office. In 1988, the System/38 was replaced by an IBM AS/400 B60, which in turn was replaced by an AS/400 model E60 providing 120 megabytes of main memory and approximately 20 gigabytes of direct-access storage devices. At the time of the study, FIS offered administrative support computing services on the IBM AS/400. The system supports two high-speed printers and more that 260 local and remote terminals, personal computers, and printers located in administrative offices around campus. The primary operations of FIS are presented in Exhibit 6.4; an organizational chart is presented in Exhibit 6.5.

Existing Strategic Plans. The existing plan of FIS centered around directives from the office of the vice-president of Business and Finance that attempted to integrate the university's long-range goals with this office. The strategic planning and implementation process was, at best, ad hoc and informal. At the time of the study, the university and the business office were undergoing a change in administration and organizational structure,

1. Provide computing and technical support to the various departments within the Business Office.
2. Act as computing liaison between the Business Office and the Division of University Computing for mainframe computer application problems.
3. Coordinate the purchase of computing equipment and software.
4. Coordinate the maintenance and repair of computer equipment.
5. Maintain computer data communications network between offices within the Business Office and between the AS/400 and the campus network.
6. Coordinate the installation of new mainframe-based systems or upgrades of existing systems.
7. Coordinate the scheduling of all production program runs.
8. Print and distribute reports generated by production systems.
9. Provide training to end users of new systems or applications.
10. Coordinate the requesting of new reports or applications with DUC; this includes establishing programming priorities for all outstanding requests at DUC that belong to the Business Office.
11. Develop new department AS/400-based applications when requested by departments.

Exhibit 6.4.   FIS operations.

---

which resulted in less emphasis on long-range planning in the area of information.

Objective of the Enterprise Model. Creating an enterprise model for FIS and the university's central computer center would allow the university to formulate a long-term plan for decentralizing the activities that FIS currently performs and making constituent groups self-sufficient. This includes examining activities and replacing them with AS/400 applications and client/server processing, integrated with PC networks. Modeling FIS supported a structure analysis of the functions and processes that can be redesigned with an overall IT focus. The underlying objective of this goal set was to lessen the load on FIS to create a more efficient operation that still meets the financial reporting needs of the constituent groups.

The FIS director and his staff would use the enterprise model for the long-term strategic planning process and as a blueprint for processes redesign. By shedding additional light on the operations and expertise of FIS, the models would also allow the office of Business and Finance and the office of the vice-president of Academic Affairs to support their long-range planning.

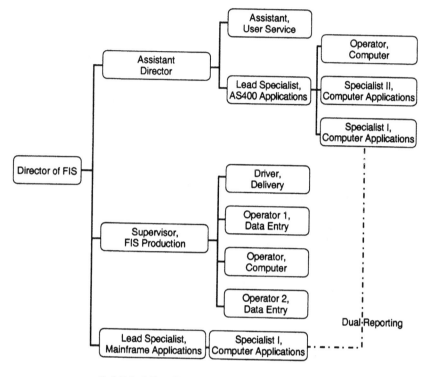

Exhibit 6.5. Organizational chart for FIS.

The various constituency groups served by FIS are also affected by the project. These include the bursar's office, the bookstore, the police department, risk management and insurance functions, and property control functions of the university.

Methodology. The first step in developing the model was to delineate the scope of the study. FIS has three primary functions:

- To provide computer support to various other departments of the university.
- To provide mail services within the university.
- To administer the department.

Clearly, the main focus of FIS is in the provision of computing support. The development team was fortunate to have the director of FIS as a member of the team. As director for more than ten years, he was intimately acquainted with operations and organization. His input was invaluable in accurately modeling this portion of the enterprise.

The enterprise modeling itself was performed on a PC running Knowledgeware's Information Engineering Workbench (IEW), a planning workstation software formulated on James Martin's information engineering modeling methodologies. Although the IEW software is no longer available, other software packages and CASE tools are fully capable of performing similar functions. Knowledgeware itself has evolved into a tool called ADW; other possibilities for developing the requisite diagrams, matrices, and charts include Systems Architect, Oracle CASE/Designer 2000, and even the graphic program Visio. The tools used simply serve to reinforce the methodology applied without which any application will fail to deliver the desired outcome.

Procedure. Four aspects of FIS were entered into the project encyclopedia and decomposed in diagrams. These were organizational units, functions, goals, and critical success factors. Decomposition proceeded in a top-down fashion. Units were decomposed into subunits and in some cases, into individual employees. Functions were decomposed into subfunctions down to the highest level of processes. Goals were decomposed into subgoals. Through an iterative sequence of interviews, the top two goals and their corresponding subgoals were identified (Exhibit 6.6).

The functional decomposition was examined for responsibility and correspondence with the organizational goals. Then, the corresponding subfunctions were identified and their subfunctions, and so on down the line until major processes were identified. Exhibit 6.7 presents one path of the provide-computer-support function.

Once the functions and goals were identified, the critical success factors (CSFs) were identified and associated with functions and goals. Examples of CSFs for FIS are presented in Exhibit 6.8.

Next, association matrices were created. These matrices relate three aspects to one another: functions to organizational units, goals to organizational units, and functions to goals. The purpose of doing this is to see which organizational units and subunits and which functions and subfunctions support which goals. At this point, factors critical to the success (CSFs) of FIS were entered into a series of matrices to determine which activities of FIS supported the achievement of success for the department.

Data model (entity-relationship) diagrams were created for each subfunction. These depict the various entities tracked by the organization, and the relationship between them. Thus, for example, the first diagram clearly shows what entities are involved in establishing priorities to guide the installation of applications on the university's mainframe computer. Also shown on this diagram are the ways in which the entities relate to one another in the course of establishing these priorities. The encyclopedia tracks these relationships to facilitate analysis of which entities support which subfunctions and processes of FIS.

1. Goal: To Increase Computing Self-Sufficiency

   Subgoals:
   - Maximize end-user services.
   - Decentralize computing on the State University campus.
   - Improve operational quality.

2. Goal: To shift all users on the campus away from mainframe computing toward computing on mini- and microcomputers

   Subgoals:
   - Install additional microcomputers where appropriate.
   - Increase promotional materials for user of micromachines.
   - Enforce a policy to promote the use of microcomputers.
   - Provide application training for all related computer areas.
   - Outsource training for all related computer areas.
   - Decrease dependence on the mainframe by
     - Shifting toward mini applications from mainframe applications where feasible.
     - Streamlining ad hoc reporting.
     - Streamlining output generation.
   - Decrease dependence on minicomputers by
     - Increasing dependence on network usage across campus.
     - Reviewing minicomputer use.

Exhibit 6.6.   FIS goals and subgoals.

The resulting matrix of entities and business functions was augmented by showing the involvement of the entities that have responsibilities for the functions. The classification included: direct management responsibility, executive or policy-making authority, functional involvement, technical expertise, and actual execution of the work. The association matrices resulted in the following comparisons (the order of mention is vertical axis, then horizontal axis):

- Subject area supports goal.
- Goal is cited by organizational unit.
- Entity type is responsibility of organizational unit.
- Function is responsibility of organizational unit.
- Function supports goal.
- Critical success factor is cited by organizational unit.
- Function supports critical success factor.
- Goal is affected by critical success factor.

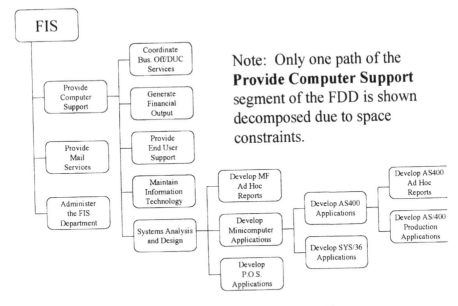

Exhibit 6.7. FIS functional decomposition diagram.

1. Attract, train, and retain high-quality IS personnel.
2. Communicate service quality and reliability to top management.
3. Continually align IS priorities with university goals.
4. Deliver reliable, high-quality IS service.
5. Effectively use current technology.
6. Maintain professional IS operating performance.
7. Maintain close contact with all users, especially those in top management.
8. Maintain effective IS planning and leadership.

Exhibit 6.8. Critical success factors for FIS.

Following the creation of these matrices, a collection of property matrices was developed based on the entity type (either fundamental, associative, or attributive); organizational units; critical success factors; and goals.

Through the modeling process, several interactive sessions were conducted to integrate the director of FIS and selected staff into the development of the models. The director acknowledged that he really hadn't comprehended the department's complexity until it was laid out in the models. Integrating various members of the modeling team and end users resulted in a much more comprehensive analysis of the business operations. These interactive sessions are better known as joint strategic planning (JSP) sessions.

Joint Strategic Planning

JSP sessions involve end users in collaborative strategy development and planning sessions. IE methodology is used to provide an overview enterprise model of the organization, including its strategies and plans. CASE systems, particularly an upper-case system, may be used to support interactive and more productive sessions. During these sessions, executive and top-level systems personnel interact to develop or modify strategies and plans and subsequently develop the enterprise model for the functional activities of the organization. These sessions can also be used to determine how to use information technology strategically.

The earlier stages (statement of objectives, development of user requirements, and logical design) of the traditional systems development life cycle are the most important for user participation. From the IE perspective, these stages correspond roughly to the strategy, planning, analysis, and design stages.

There are three compelling reasons for stressing user participation during these phase/stages: first, when CASE is employed, the use of JSP sessions followed by joint application development sessions permits strategic specifications to be integrated with analysis and design specifications. Second, during the early stages, the users' experience and contributions are strongest and the IS professionals' are weakest. Third, the potential cost associated with detecting and correcting errors in the later stages of the systems development of complete and accurate user requirements.

JSP may require many participants. To be most effective, each participant (both user and IS professional) must have the authority to make decisions concerning user requirements that will not later be overruled by high-level management. For this reason, it is important that participants be experts in the areas they represent.

During sessions with the modeling team, the director of FIS helped evaluate and define the functional relationships incorporated into the CASE-driven enterprise model. The JSP sessions employed by this project enabled the business modeler to fully and quickly engage the director in the accurate description and subsequent modeling of the business. As the director of FIS was able to see the model being built interactively, he was able to suggest changes from previous sessions, thus deriving a better model in the earlier stages. The Information Engineering Workbench (IEW) software enabled interactive changes to be made in the model that automatically made subsequent changes in all related parts of the model. Use of JSP improves requirements analysis and subsequent results in more effective systems that enable and enact the strategic plans of the organization.

CONCLUSION

The ideals of enterprise modeling as an integrated component of strategic business engineering provide a competitive alternative to the continual decline of businesses and organizations. Organizations continually focus their attention on reducing existing cost structures and resources in a vain attempt to counteract the increasing gap between mature organizations and newer, more innovative organizations. Only by fundamentally changing not only how business is performed, but also how business is defined, can businesses expect to survive and adapt in the new information age.

Since this study was completed, FIS has implemented many of the proposed changes. It has completed consolidation of university financial applications into the AS/400 environment allowing increased centralized control, code standardization, and security. The results of the study were incorporated into the strategic planning for FIS, the Division of University Computing, and the university as a whole. The changes presented stabilized, allowing additional emphasis on integrating IT strategic planning with overall strategy and an improved focus on technology. The university has made the advancement and development of technology one of its strategic goals, to support administrative and academic computing and has begun a university-wide enterprise modeling project. The results of this subsequent analysis should serve to provide the basis for requests for additional funding for technology and technology-related materials and personnel. The president of the university is optimistic about the implementation of new technologies that will provide increased quality in education, both locally and through distributed education programs.

Section II
Data Center Management

IN THIS SECTION, WE WILL TRANSITION TO MANAGEMENT ISSUES regarding the data center. Centralized data centers remain a vital portion of the overall enterprise IT environment. We will focus on management of technologies and processes within the data center and its impact on the organization.

The first chapter in this section, "Reverting to Centralized Data Center Management," describes how management of the data center has recently shifted from a decentralized approach back to a centralized approach. This recent shift has, however, has resulted in the virtual data center, where distributed systems are now managed centrally by sophisticated management tools. Centralized control of these resources must be in an efficient, cost-effective manner.

Another area of focus for data center managers is uninterruptable power supply (UPS) systems. These were originally designed to provide battery backup in the event primary utility-provided power was lost. In Chapter 8, "Acquiring and Using a UPS System," the author explains that modern UPS systems go far beyond simple battery backup to include regulating raw power from the local utility company, providing power over long periods of time, and diminishing transfer times. This chapter outlines these systems and recommends a selection process for data center managers to use in evaluating the criteria for acquiring the proper UPS system to support the organization's needs.

Other areas of computer operations include production job scheduling; data management; report distribution; incident reporting; problem resolution; and production data backup and recovery. As described in Chapter 9, "Providing Quality Information Services to the Customer," the data center manager must ensure user satisfaction from the efficient execution of these services. This chapter describes how data center managers must focus on maintaining a high level of integrity between the end user and the computer operations department. Production job scheduling systems are of particular importance because of the potential cost savings that can be realized with more efficient operations. Chapter 10, "Evaluating a Job

Scheduler in the Open Systems Arena," considers the aspect of justifying the purchase of a job scheduler. This chapter provides an analysis methodology that data center managers can use to evaluate job schedulers.

Enterprise operations data center managers must also be concerned with how user support activities are efficiently and effectively performed, through the implementation of supporting technologies. Chapter 11, "Help Desk Technology," discusses how new technologies, including remote access and interactive computer communications, are presenting opportunities for increasing efficiency and productivity in the help-desk environment. Also discussed are help-desk features, capabilities, and charges, as well as options such as outsourcing and commercial services available to create a cost-efficient and productive help desk. Chapter 12, "Call Center Computer Telephony Integration: A Case Study," also discusses productivity enhancements for the help desk through the implementation of computer telephony integration (CTI) technology. Data center managers will learn how this technology can be leveraged to significantly improve end user support, permitting faster response to customer requests, while allowing business to use existing data warehoused information in very effective ways.

Chapter 7
Reverting to Centralized Data Center Management

C. Warren Axelrod

COULD IT BE THAT THE PENDULUM IS SWINGING BACK to more centralized forms of managing computer and network resources? Since the mid-1980s, management has followed technology into a more distributed environment. As creating smaller centers of computing power linked via local-area and wide-area networks (LANs and WANs) became more feasible, business units found it practical to control their own destinies insofar as developing applications and running computer systems were concerned. No sooner, however, had computing power and expertise been distributed across many segments of the organization than the needs evolved toward a more integrated use of information and systems expertise.

Such concepts as data warehousing have turned attention to the need to have some form of central controlling function to ensure completeness and integrity of data and the repositories of information. The popularity of object-oriented programming, too, is giving rise to the centralization of libraries of software modules.

At the same time, remote sites are often finding that the benefits of being totally in control of their own destinies does not, in fact, outweigh the headaches of being responsible for maintaining their own systems. Fortunately, technological developments include the emergence of tools that allow for the centralized management of remote facilities and networks. These tools make management of computer and network resources largely independent from their physical location.

This chapter examines the technological and managerial trends that led to distributed computing, including the movement from mainframes to timesharing, from minicomputers to departmental computers, to microcomputers and LANs. Also examined are trends contributing to a reversion to centralized computer and network resource. The chapter also introduces the concept of the "virtual data center" and examines future implications. In addition, concluding sections discuss tools that are evolving to support this emerging environment.

TECHNOLOGICAL HISTORY AND TRENDS

Any history of computers in business must begin with the mainframe. Computers really hit the business scene in a big way in the 1960s with the introduction of the IBM 360 series, perhaps the single-most significant component in the popularizing enterprise computing. Until that time, practically every so-called computing machine was different from the others in design, structure, and software — even IBM had several different incompatible product lines. With the 360 series, however, IBM offered a wide range of computer power, with each machine in the series able to run the full complement of available software.

Minicomputers

The 1970s saw minicomputers begin to encroach on the mainframe's arena. Minicomputers were more cost effective than mainframes — usually by a multiple of several times. This was achieved through simpler engineering architectures than the mainframe had, and low-overhead operating software. Minicomputer architecture was also characterized by more flexible data communications capabilities.

Yet, to a large extent, minicomputers still maintained the mainframe paradigm of a central processor supporting many user terminals. Being smaller and cheaper, however, they migrated from being front-end appendages on mainframes to standalone, smaller business and departmental machines.

Microcomputers

Microprocessor-based personal computers (PCs), workstations, and servers evolved in the 1980s. Initially introduced as standalone desktop machines, they have increasingly become interconnected on LANs and WANs, both communicating with each other and interacting with central servers. These computers represented a major divergence from the traditional, centralized model. This change was induced by the price-performance of microprocessors, which far outweighed that of mainframes and even minicomputers — often by an order of magnitude.

The Rise of Client/Server Computing

The price-performance of microprocessors continued to improve in the 1990s, and an increasing number of very powerful, moderately-priced servers that frequently contain several processor are being manufactured. A product category has emerged that consists of massively-parallel computers containing large numbers of microprocessors; this type of machine is used primarily for scientific applications. By incorporating high-powered profiles into central servers, these machines are competing in power with mainframes and minicomputers and are available in considerably less expensive form factors. In fact, in many situations, mainframes are being redefined as large enterprise servers.

Ironically, the very technology that caused the dispersion of computer power to the desktop is today leading to the regrouping of computing power into central servers. This does not mean that the desktop power is in any immediate danger of being drawn back to the data center; the explosion in desktop (and, increasingly, laptop) computing power is still increasing unabated for personal applications.

Networks

The revolution coming in the late 1990s is anticipated to be in the area of global networks. Many large players, such as IBM, Microsoft, AT&T, MCI, Sprint, and EDS are expected to form alliances internationally with foreign telephone companies in their bids for control and profits. The whole structure of networking both within organizations and among companies and individuals is in a state of flux, as is the impact on data center management.

The main revolution is in the software, as the processors and circuitry are largely in place. Nevertheless, an increasing interest is in cable modems that provide high-bandwidth access from the home or office, as well as in services over regular telephone circuits, such as Integrated Services Digital Network, which also offer increased bandwidth.

Research in video servers, wireless communications, and other means of providing new services over the Internet and private and public networks is proceeding apace, and new offerings will likely appear with increasing frequency.

THE ORGANIZATIONAL RESPONSE

Mainframe computers, by their nature, required large staffs of experts to install, maintain, and support them. Often teams of elite individuals handled system software (e.g., the operating system and utilities), computer performance measurement, and management and technical support. Because early mainframes were continually failing — it was not unusual for some component, hardware or software, to crash several times a week as late as the mid 1970s — substantial operations staffs were needed, often working three shifts, seven days a week. Whereas system-management and performance-measurement tools were on the market, they tended to run on individual machines. This meant that management of systems was also people intensive.

Later, as database technology became more prevalent, the data-implementation, data management, and data-tuning functions were built up. Such groups of staff required proportionally large managerial and supervisory staff. As a result, mainframe data centers tended to be heavily populated.

The large staffs tended toward centralization. Systems programmers, for example, were and continue to be very expensive, and it did not pay to have pockets of such expertise scattered throughout an organization. Also, each department contained individuals with specific specialized knowledge and experience. Again, this was something that would have been expensive to duplicate — even if the individuals could be found.

Minicomputers

Minicomputers were not only introduced as machines available as smaller units and demonstrating a much-improved price-performance ratio, they were also touted as needing much less in the way of human intervention and support. Part of the reason for this was that they were introduced, for the most part, as single-function machines, often running real-time applications, both of which reduced support needs. Much of mainframe support focused on multiprocessing of real-time applications and complex, multi-thread, batch stream processing.

The slimmed-down operating systems were often supported by a single individual who usually covered other areas, such as those categorized as technical support in the mainframe arena. As a result, distributing minicomputers throughout a large organization and managing them locally was much more feasible than before.

Microprocessors

To a large extent, the initial support of PCs was left to the user. After all, most early applications — such as word processing and spreadsheet programs — were standalone. Once inside the obscure world of DOS on the IBM PC, few general users could navigate the cryptic codes and messages; however, for the most part, support was somewhat casual, with self-appointed gurus providing assistance. When use became more complex, particularly with the requirement for communications between one desktop PC and other PCs or mainframes — a more in-depth technical knowledge was required.

Over time, centralized PC support groups developed within companies and, as the job became increasingly overwhelming, a more structured organization was formed, including a "help desk," which fielded calls, solved simple matters (i.e., plug in the monitor), and directed callers to the appropriate technical staff (e.g., equipment, software, and communications).

Client/Server Systems Support

The support of client/server systems is, to some degree, an extension of PC support. In most cases, client/server systems support requires the same support group, but with a few added skills, particularly in the area of LAN technology, which includes equipment; cabling; operating software; network management software; and computer operating systems and utilities, including UNIX, IBM's OS/2 and Microsoft's Windows NT.

From an organizational perspective, there is a much greater chance that the client/server support function will more likely reside within the central technical group, rather than exist as an independent group, as is more common for regular PC support.

Networks

In many organizations, the implementation and support of voice and data communications have been separate from data processing management. Often, too, voice and data are handled by different departments.

Increasingly, voice and data communications management are becoming integrated, especially as voice technology is moving away from the traditional analog to digital. More recently, there has been even greater cooperation between communications and data processing areas, as processing and information flows become more distributed in their architectures.

MANAGEMENT TRENDS

In the early years of mainframe computing, there was little option other than to centralize the physical equipment, as well as the staff who managed and supported that equipment and related software. Even though remote facilities existed early in computer development, they were used mostly for inputting programs and data, usually in the form of Hollerith punched cards, and for receiving printed reports as output.

Later, as remote facilities acquired processing capabilities, largely due to the introduction of minicomputers, management and support functions were built to support these facilities on a local basis. Whereas the amount of support for minicomputers is generally significantly less than that required for mainframes, it still follows the centralized model — although support for minicomputers acts independently. This form of management can perhaps be called distributed centralized management, as the basic control mechanisms did not change.

The next major change was the data center management's loss of control of proliferating PCs. Frequently hidden in the company's budget as office equipment, PCs sprouted up all over organizations, often without the knowledge of headquarters' technology staff. Early adopters of PCs were usually technologically savvy and tended to support themselves and deal directly with vendors. As the use of PCs extended to non-technical end users, however, the need for formal support increased. At first, pockets of expertise formed; these pockets then coalesced into PC-support departments, including help desks. As support demands became more technical, many firms turned to their central IS departments to provide the necessary support.

When client/server systems became popular, it quickly became apparent that support could not be assigned just to individuals, as with PC support, because a high level of sophisticated technical knowledge was needed. One person could not be expected to be knowledgeable in all aspects of support. To some degree, client/server support follows the minicomputer paradigm, with local support groups dominating. Here also, there appears to be a move toward more centralized management of client/server systems, especially as enterprisewide client/server systems and data warehouses are pointing to a single source of support.

As the move toward network-based systems gains momentum — particularly public networks not under an organization's direct control — little is being done to actually manage the systems' environments. The issues of network security and integrity are foremost in data center managers' minds when contemplating venturing onto the Internet, for example, or onto any public network. To a large extent, organizations are depending on such standard software approaches as passwords or encryption, but it is clear from the industry press that these methods are less than satisfactory. This area is very much in a state of flux, but it is clear that eventually some central body will have to take control before organizations will rely on out-of-house network management.

PHYSICAL VS. LOGICAL CENTRALIZATION AND DECENTRALIZATION

As described earlier, the management of computer and network systems flows back and forth between centralized and decentralized forms along with changes in technological structures. However, the physical realization of such management can mask a different form of logical management. For example, a centralized network management function controls logically dispersed circuits and equipment. On the other hand, a series of locally-managed computer sites may be configured as a single logical system performing one function.

Exhibit 7.1. Characteristics of various forms of centralization and decentralization.

	Primary Characteristics	Advantages	Disadvantages	Methods Used for Implementation
Physical Centralization	Groups work as one.	High level of communication and control.	Relatively high administrative overhead.	Physical proximity or very extensive telecommunications linkages.
Logical Centralization	Disparate groups optimize globally.	High level of communication and control.	Some measure of additional overhead.	Management control through procedures, such as goal setting, standards, and chargebacks.
Physical Decentralization	Different cultures.	Can reduce friction with headquarters.	Likelihood of suboptimizing; lack of control.	Intentional absence of communications; independent profit and loss reporting.
Logical Decentralization	Autonomous management optimizing locally.	Relatively low overhead.	Possibility of suboptimizing for overall organization; reduction in control.	Independent management with few linkages to central body; local profit and loss accountability and central reporting.

Exhibit 7.1 lists the different forms of physical and logical centralization and decentralization and identifies their advantages, disadvantages, and primary characteristics. Clearly, to understand the differentiation between these different forms, terms should be carefully defined.

Physical Centralization

With advances in communications technologies, the definition *of physical centralization* has changed dramatically in recent years. Traditionally, *physical centralization* meant that individuals worked at the same location under the same management. Today, instant communications are facilitated by e-mail, fax transmissions, beepers, voice mail, telecommuting, and video-conferencing, and are being increasingly augmented with two-way beepers, mobile computers, and groupware. The actual physical location of an employee is becoming less relevant to centralized management.

For this chapter's purposes, *physical centralization* indicates a combination of organizational structure, physical proximity, and communications technology that operates as if everyone were part of a single department. The primary characteristic of physical centralization is that the group works as if it were one.

Logical Centralization

Logical centralization is largely procedural. Individuals may be physically located in the same building but not necessarily be logically related. The primary characteristic of logical centralization is that disparate groups working independently operate so that they optimize globally. The procedural structure is such that each subunit is indirectly encouraged to act to the benefit of the entire organization. This can be achieved, for example, through such methods as establishing interdivisional chargebacks or cross-divisional goals.

Physical Decentralization

To a very large extent, physical decentralization is a meaningless concept due to the communications advances described above. It is often argued that it is economically preferable to locate individuals in low-labor-cost areas or close to users or customers, but today that no longer need isolate the groups, even if they are in foreign countries.

The only relevant situation is when cultures, either national or organizational, are so different that physical proximity might be considered counterproductive.

Logical Decentralization

Logical decentralization is also procedural in that a determination is made — whether consciously or not — that the management and control of dispersed computer and communications resources should be handled locally without regard to central standards, methods, and procedures. The argument is often that the cost of overhead for administering logically centralized organizations outweighs the benefits of such features as standardization and central negotiation of vendor contracts.

The primary characteristic of logical decentralization is that management of satellite computer operations is autonomous for each unit.

THE IMPACT OF TECHNOLOGY

The major influence of technology over the past decade has been the increasing practicality of creating distributed applications. Although new application development is still a difficult task, the software and communications tools have improved dramatically. The main deficiencies are the lack of experienced designers and builders and an underinvestment by management, often leading to unsatisfactory results. Nevertheless, the juggernaut of distributed processing and data warehousing is plowing forward — increasing numbers of organizations are building client/server and network-based systems. These in turn call for new forms of management and control.

Distributed Design

The design of systems is increasingly being farmed out to designers located in many parts of the world — a situation that results from both the availability of highly educated and well-trained technicians in many countries and vastly improved communications. This type of outsourcing can work as long as the interfaces among the various components are carefully defined and well communicated to all involved parties.

Multilocational Development

Increasingly, especially in multinational organizations, the development of applications is taking place in multiple locations throughout the world. In addition, companies find that they can outsource system development to countries such as India, the Philippines, and Israel, and obtain good-quality development at a fraction of the domestic cost. Often, such systems are enterprisewide applications in which several development centers work together to produce a unified system. In other instances, the existence of specific local expertise is exploited.

Remote Control and Operation

Whereas in the past, computer systems control and operation from afar were impractical — after all, someone had to be on location to view the operator consoles, mount tapes, and feed the printers paper — two areas of change have encouraged remote control and operation:

Remote Control. The innovations that have promoted remote control of computer systems are sophisticated management software and wideband communications networks. Sophisticated management software allows an operator, sitting at a workstation, to monitor and manage many computer systems distributed over a number of separate geographical locations, as well as manage the communications networks themselves. High-capacity communications lines allow for the transmission of sufficient volumes of data from remote systems and networks to provide the necessary real-time monitoring capabilities.

Remote Operation. The movement from dominance of batch jobs on early mainframe computers to today's predominantly online environment has made it much more feasible to run entire systems "lights out," with minimal operator intervention, a change made especially feasible due to the reduced need for extensive use of tape-based data files and for large volumes of central printing. Even if archival data has to be accessed, there are now automated means of retrieving tape cartridges and loading them automatically under software control. Also, with the falling cost of disk capacity, it is reasonable to carry much more data online. Many applications enable users to obtain most necessary output from PC and workstation screens and to occasionally print using low-volume local printers.

CONCLUSION

As technology has cycled through centralized and distributed forms, so has data center management; however, the most recent cycle broke from tradition. Whereas there is an increasing tendency to broadly disperse computer power and applications, with the advent of sophisticated management tools, there is increasing capability to control these distributed systems from a centralized management function. This has resulted in the virtual data center, which carries forward into today's distributed and networked world many of the management models of the physically centralized data center.

Chapter 8
Acquiring and Using a UPS System
Gilbert Held

THE DATA CENTER MANAGER MUST BE FAMILIAR WITH THE OPERATION AND USE of various types of equipment to operate the data center effectively and efficiently. Possibly the most important type of equipment, however, is an uninterruptible power supply (UPS) system. Originally designed to provide battery backup in the event primary utility-provided power was lost, today's modern UPS system performs additional functions beyond the scope of the traditional UPS. The acquisition of a UPS system, therefore, involves the consideration of a number of features beyond battery backup time.

First, the data center manager must understand the various power problems, their effects on data processing, and how UPS systems can be used to alleviate those problems. This information serves as a base for developing a checklist, which facilitates the equipment-acquisition process.

After the type of UPS system has been chosen, the data center manager must perform a second, critical step: correctly size the system to support the organization's data center environment. Otherwise, the manager may not have an appropriate amount of time to correctly bring down a mainframe or minicomputer system during a power failure outage or be able to continue operations if the battery of the UPS system is connected to a local motor generator.

This chapter focuses on the power-protection features incorporated into many modern UPS systems, as well as computational methods to determine the capacity of such systems to satisfy the operational environment. Highlighted are the power-protection features that should be evaluated during the UPS selection process, as well as the methods used to obtain a system with sufficient capacity to satisfy the data center's operational requirements.

Exhibit 8.1. Common electrical power problems.

Power Problem	Typical Cause	Potential Effect
Brownout or Sag	Start-up power consumption of electrical motors or voltage reduction by electric utility	Reduction in the life of electrical equipment
Blackout	"Act of God" or accident	Loss of data being processed; possible disk crash
Spike	Lightning or resumption of power after a power failure	Damage to hardware, loss of data
Surge	Completion of an electrical motor cycle, such as an air conditioner	Stresses to equipment's electrical components, resulting in premature failure of a service
Noise	Electromagnetic interference caused by equipment, lightning, or radio interference	Data corruption

POWER PROBLEMS

Inhabitants of the northeast U.S. are familiar with the effects of a summer heat wave — when the local electric utility company lowers the voltage level during peak electrical consumption periods. Dimmer lights, television screens, and computer monitors and slightly lower operating rates of motor-driven elevators are but a few of the effects of brownouts. Also known as voltage sags, this situation results from the start-up power demands of different types of electrical motors. Brownouts can adversely affect computer systems, causing electrical devices to fail as a result of repetitive occurrences. Although brownouts and sags are common, they are not the only electrical power problem the data center manager can expect to encounter.

Exhibit 8.1 lists five of the most common electrical power problems, including the previously discussed brownout or sag power problem. Although most, if not all, managers should be familiar with the term *black-out,* which represents the total loss of electrical utility power, the remaining events in the exhibit may require a degree of elaboration.

A spike represents an instantaneous increase in voltage level resulting from lightning or when utility power is restored after an electrical outage. The effect of a voltage spike can literally fry computer equipment, causing the destruction of hardware, as well as the loss of any data stored on the hardware, both in memory and on disk.

A power surge represents a short-term increase in voltage that over a period of time stresses electrical equipment until a point of failure is reached. The most common cause of a power surge is the cycling of equipment, such as air conditioners, refrigerators, and similar machinery for which motors are turned on and off on a periodic basis. When such equipment is turned off, extra voltage that was flowing to operate the equipment is dissipated through the power lines in the office or home.

The last power problem listed in Exhibit 8.1, noise, represents electromagnetic interference (EMI) and radio frequency interference (RFI). Both EMI and RFI result in noise that disturbs the smooth, alternating sine wave generated by the electrical power utility. Depending on the amount of noise, the effects range from no adverse effect on equipment and data to the corruption of data when noise reaches a level that precludes equipment from operating correctly.

An appreciation for the types of power problems is critical before understanding how UPS systems operate. The description of UPS operation in the next section provides information that can, in turn, be used to evaluate UPSs during the equipment-acquisition process.

UPS OPERATION

Early UPS systems were developed as backup power sources and simply consisted of a battery charger, battery, and inverter. The inverter converts direct current (DC) to alternating current (AC) and is commonly referred to as a DC-to-AC converter.

A UPS can be used in an online-without-bypass mode of operation, in which it always provides power to equipment, or in a standby mode, in which a transfer switch is used to provide UPS power in the event utility power fails. Exhibit 8.2 illustrates the configuration of UPS systems used in an online-without-bypass mode of operation and in a standby online mode of operation.

When used in an online-without-bypass mode of operation, the UPS accepts and uses raw electric utility power to charge its battery. In actuality, the battery illustrated in each example in Exhibit 8.2 represents a bank of batteries whose number and charge capacity vary. The number and capacity are based on the amount of electrical power required by the organization, both in the event that primary power fails, and for the duration for which battery backup power must be furnished during that failure. Because raw electrical power is first used to charge the battery, the effect of any surge, spike, or brownout is isolated from equipment that obtains power from the online UPS system shown in Exhibit 8.2.

In the standby mode of operation, raw electrical utility power is directly output through the transfer switch to equipment when utility power is present. Only when power fails does the transfer switch sense the loss of power and switch the connection to battery-supplied power. The key problem associated with this UPS configuration is that it does not

Online-without-Bypass Mode of Operation

Input Utility Power

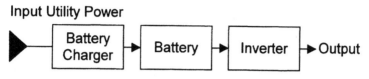

Standby Mode of Operation

Input Utility Power

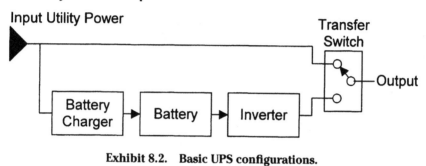

Exhibit 8.2.   Basic UPS configurations.

provide protection to equipment from dirty electric power, corrupted through utility company-induced brownouts, natural causes, or manmade problems.

Because of this deficiency, the standby mode has been supplemented by the use of separate surge protectors and power line filters. The surge protector is used to block or chop off peak voltage spikes and to smooth out reduced voltage surges, while the power line filter is used to reshape the power sine wave, eliminating the effect of sags and noise. Some UPS manufacturers are incorporating surge-suppression and power line-filtering capabilities into their products, resulting in the surge suppressor and power-line filter operating on raw electrical power that bypasses the UPS when electrical utility power is operational. Exhibit 8.3 illustrates a general-purpose UPS system configuration that protects equipment from utility power irregularities, as well as provides a redundant backup power source.

COMMON VARIATIONS

The general-purpose UPS configuration illustrated in Exhibit 8.3 forms the foundation for all modern UPS equipment. Batteries used to store electrical power for use when primary power fails are both bulky and costly; therefore,

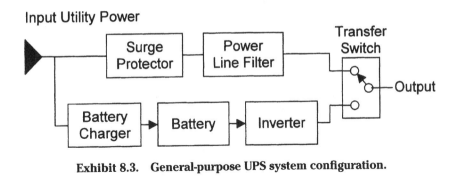

Exhibit 8.3. General-purpose UPS system configuration.

by itself, a typical UPS is sized to provide no more than 30 minutes to one hour of backup power, typically a sufficient duration to provide an orderly shutdown of a mainframe or minicomputer in the event primary power fails. Recognizing that many organizations need to continue computer operations for prolonged periods of time once primary power fails, a common technique used to meet this need is a diesel generator to supply power to the UPS when primary power fails. This can be accomplished by a transfer switch, which changes the UPS battery charger power source from the utility company to the diesel generator. Then, once diesel-generated power flows into the UPS system, the battery backup capability is only limited by the organization's ability to keep the generator operational.

SIZING A UPS SYSTEM

Sizing a UPS system is the process by which the data center manager determines the battery capacity required to operate equipment for a desired period of time after primary power is lost.

To size a UPS, the manager first makes a list of all computer equipment, as well as lights, air conditioners, and other equipment required for continuity of operations. Next, the manager determines the voltage and amperage requirements for each device and other equipment, such as interior lighting that may be on the circuit that the UPS is to protect. Multiplying voltage times amperage determines the volt amps (VA) requirement for each device. (Some types of equipment specify their power consumption in watts (W); that number can be converted to volt amps VA units by multiplying watts by 1.4.) The sum of the VA requirements for all resources requiring power is the minimum volt amps capacity required in a UPS.

The VA rating measures only the power load, however, and does not consider the duration for which battery power at that load level must be supplied. Therefore, the data center manager must determine the period of time during which the organization will require battery backup power. For

Evaluation Parameter	Requirement	Vendor A	Vendor B
Maximum Line Current			
Capacity in VA	_____	_____	_____
Load Power Duration	_____	_____	_____
Recharge Time	_____	_____	_____
50 percent	_____	_____	_____
100 percent	_____	_____	_____
Operating Environment			
Operating Temperature	_____	_____	_____
Relative Humidity	_____	_____	_____
Dimension	_____	_____	_____
Weight	_____	_____	_____
Transfer Time	_____	_____	_____
(Milliseconds)			
Surge Response Time	_____	_____	_____
(Milliseconds)			
Noise Suppression (dB)	_____	_____	_____
Warranty	_____	_____	_____
Cost	_____	_____	_____

Exhibit 8.4. UPS operational parameters worksheet.

many organizations, this normally equals the time required to perform an orderly computer shutdown, plus a small margin of safety time. For example, some IBM mainframes require 20 minutes for an orderly shutdown; in this case, a 30-minute battery backup at peak load is usually sufficient. Because total power provided by a UPS battery backup is measured in volt-ampere hours, the VA requirements are multiplied by .5 to determine the volt-ampere hours (VAH) capacity the battery backup must provide.

UPS EVALUATION

Although it is important to ensure that a UPS is correctly sized to satisfy organizational operational requirements, it is equally important to examine other UPS operational parameters. For example, a product from one vendor may provide a higher level of protection from dirty electric utility power than a competitive product, may offer a longer warranty, or have another feature which can satisfy organizational requirements in a more cost-effective manner.

To facilitate the UPS evaluation process, Exhibit 8.4 contains a checklist of UPS operational parameters for consideration. Although several of the entries in the exhibit were previously discussed or are self-explanatory, some entries require a degree of elaboration.

The recharge time contains two entries, 50 percent and 100 percent. Although not a common occurrence, power does sometimes fail, is restored, then fails again; in this case, the ability to obtain a quick partial recharge of UPS batteries can be more important than determining the time required to obtain a complete battery recharge.

The operating environment entries refer to parameters that govern where the UPS system can be located. Some organizations construct a separate building or an annex to an existing building to house a large-capacity UPS system. Other organizations either use an existing location within a building or modify the location to support the installation and operation of the UPS. Due to the weight of lead acid batteries normally used by UPS manufacturers, the floor-load capacity of the intended location of the batteries should be checked. This is especially important when considering the use of battery shelf housing, since the weight of a large number of batteries mounted in a vertical shelf concentrated over a relatively small area of floor space can result in sagging floors or, worse, the collapse of the floor.

The transfer time entry refers to the time required to place an offline UPS system online when utility power fails. If a load-sharing UPS system is installed that is always active, the transfer time is quoted as zero; however, there is always a small delay until battery backup power reaches the level required by equipment and lighting connected to the UPS. Thus, many times the term *transfer time* is replaced by *transfer to peak time*, which is a better indication of the time required to fully support the backup power requirements. As might be expected, the quicker this occurs the better, and better-performing equipment requires the least amount of time. Similarly, the quicker the built-in surge suppressor operates, the better. Thus, a UPS requiring a low amount of time to respond to a power surge condition is favorable.

The last entry in Exhibit 8.4, noise suppression, indicates the UPS system's ability to filter out EMF and EMI. Noise suppression capability is measured in decibel (dB), and a larger dB rating indicates an enhanced ability to remove unwanted noise.

RECOMMENDED COURSE OF ACTION

Dependence on raw electric power can result in a number of problems ranging in scope from brownouts and blackouts to spikes, surges, and noise. Since the investment of funds used to acquire data processing equipment can be considerable, the acquisition of a UPS system can save an organization many times its cost simply by protecting equipment from harm. In addition, the ability to continue operations by using battery backup power provided directly from the UPS system or indirectly from a diesel motor generator can be invaluable for many organizations. Because there can be considerable differences between vendor products, the data center manager should carefully evaluate the features of different UPS systems. By doing so and installing a UPS system correctly sized to satisfy the organizational requirements, the data center manager may avoid equipment failures that result from power problems, as well as permit continuity of operations on an orderly computer shutdown in the event of a blackout.

Chapter 9
Providing Quality Information Services to the Customer

Joe R. Briones

THE DATA CENTER'S PRIMARY OBJECTIVE should always be to provide the customer with state-of-the-art information processing capabilities. To meet this objective successfully, data center managers must have a clear understanding of the customers' requirements. More often than not, data center managers make assumptions about customer requirements. Process improvements are generally based on what the data center management believes the customer needs or on historical customer requirements. Open communications with the customer, however, should be the foundation for ensuring overall customer satisfaction.

The data center's ability to monitor and gauge its performance against customer expectations is a critical part of ensuring customer satisfaction. Data centers should establish what is generally referred to as service-level agreements. These agreements document the level of service that the data center provides; they also identify the commitments that the customer makes to ensure that the information processing objectives are met. The fundamental concept of service-level commitments is that there is a two-way level of commitment. The customer, as well as the information processing organization, must put forth the effort to achieve their objectives. For the most part, however, it is the responsibility of the data center management team to drive the establishment and implementation of these service-level commitments.

Data center management is responsible for ensuring that state-of-the-art processing techniques are used in the processing of the customer information. Processes such as report distribution, production turnover, and online viewing of reports are just a few of the processes that can be improved by incorporating the most advanced processing enhancements.

0-8493-9824-X/00/$0.00+$.50
© 2000 by CRC Press LLC

This chapter discusses these processes and also the production software that is currently available on the market to achieve the processing improvements required to ensure that customer requirements are being met at the highest level of customer satisfaction.

DEFINING USER REQUIREMENTS

The data center manager can best determine user requirements by analyzing and understanding the user's obligation to the organization. Regardless of the customer's organizational structure, information processing is vital to the continued operations of the following functional areas:

- Finance.
- Manufacturing.
- Marketing.
- Materials.
- Human Resources.

Because user requirements usually change suddenly and frequently, the data center manager must ensure some degree of flexibility in the production processing environment. Last-minute changes in the scheduling of computer resources and movement of development program modules from development libraries into production controlled libraries are just a few of the changes that require quick and immediate support. The data center must have procedures in place to handle such situations.

Tracking and evaluating job scheduling on a daily basis enables the data center to adjust to sudden changes. Changes to the processing cycle typically occur late in the production week. Therefore, particular consideration must be placed on Thursday scheduling reports to determine whether extended weekend processing is required to meet user requirements. Another important factor to consider in supporting unplanned extended computer scheduling is the effect that it may have on hardware and software mainframe maintenance.

The data center manager must be aware of the customer's closing schedules (i.e., the obligations that the customers have to their suppliers, financial institutions, and government agencies). The customer depends on its computer processing support for the reports they require to prepare the documents that are required for their compliance with both private and government agencies.

Year-end processing creates an especially high degree of activity for the data center. Income statements and other federal and state documents are just a few of the documents that are produced during the year-end closing period. A clear understanding of the customer's year-end requirements helps ensure the successful and timely completion of the customer's processing requirements.

The success of the data center is strongly dependent on how well the data center manager understands customer requirements; this should be the number-one priority of the data center manager.

ESTABLISHING STANDARDS AND MEASURING PERFORMANCE

Data center managers must ensure that the information processing services provided by their organizations address and support user requirements. A service-level agreement between the user organization and the information processing organization establishes the standards by which the data center's responsiveness and quality of work can be defined.

Development of a service-level agreement requires a statement of the user's workload requirements and a commitment to the standards of performance. The data center manager must keep in mind that service-level commitments are basically an understanding between the user and the information processing organization that each will do their part in achieving the overall objective of quality performance.

It is known that the user and the information processing organization establish from service-level agreements what are sometimes referred to as incentive performance objectives. Incentive performance objectives have direct costs associated with them. If the data center successfully meets the predefined incentive performance objectives, the data center is rewarded with some predefined monetary compensation. If, however, the data center fails to meet the incentive objective successfully, it is subject to penalties that are paid to the customer organization.

Service-level agreements and incentive performance objectives should be negotiated at least annually. These agreements should be coordinated by representatives of the customer organization (some customer organizations have what is referred to as information resource organizations, or Information Resource Management). The information processing organization is generally represented by the account manager, who is responsible for that customer's account. In some cases, however, the financial department of the information processing organization represents the data center in these negotiations. Service-level agreements should incorporate system availability, online response times, batch turnaround, and report deliverability.

CHANGES TO SERVICE-LEVEL AGREEMENTS

Although service-level agreements are generally negotiated annually during the customer contract negotiation period, changes to the service-level commitments must be incorporated as necessary. Some of the factors that drive a change in the service-level agreement cannot be postponed until the annual contract negotiation period. Any changes in a customer's workload or service requirements or changes in the data center's ability to provide the services and support required by the customer within the funding provided by the customer are reflected in writing by incorporating such changes into the service agreement revision.

Circumstances that could initiate revisions to service-level agreements include:

- Authorization for a new development project or the completion or cancellation of an existing project.
- Changes to authorized spending levels or revisions to capital or lease authorizations.
- Changes to computer hardware equipment configurations (including telecommunications lines and terminals) or operating system software.
- Changes to customer departments or department functions that result in the need for changes to the data center support and performance levels.

Changes should be incorporated into the service agreement as soon as reasonably possible following the mutual recognition and assessment of the impact of the change. An effective change date should be established mutually between the data center and the data center customer.

OPERATIONAL PERFORMANCE OBJECTIVES AND MEASUREMENTS

To ensure that the data center is successfully meeting the information processing requirements of the customer, the data center must establish operational performance objectives, as well as a method or process by which these operational performance objectives can be measured and reported. Operational performance data is generally prepared and reported on a monthly basis and is used as a management tool to resolve current and prevent potential problems.

It is imperative that the data center manager define, document, monitor, and maintain standards and procedures to ensure that quality computer processing services are provided to the user community. Some of the operational performance objectives that may be established may include the following:

- *Online systems availability.* Maintaining database management availability at 98 percent or higher is imperative. These systems include IMS, dB2, and CICS.

- *Mainframe systems availability.* This means ensuring that mainframe computer hardware and software is up and running 98 percent of the time or more.
- *Time-shared option (TSO) availability.* This means ensuring that TSO response time is at 90 percent less than two seconds.
- *Production abends.* This means ensuring control of production processing to see that production abends are less then 0.26 percent of the scheduled production workload.
- *Production reruns.* This means maintaining control of production reruns to ensure that production reruns are less than 0.38 percent of the scheduled production workload.
- *Report deliverability.* This means ensuring that batch report delivery is at 99 percent or higher. (The percentages for production abends and reruns should be confirmed, however, by checking the existing service-level agreements.)

Depending on the computer-processing installation and the specific requirements of the customer, additional performance objectives may be required.

OPERATIONAL IMPROVEMENTS

The data center manager must put forth an effort to improve the operational capabilities of the data center. Within the processing environment of a data center, several unique operational functions play key roles in producing customer deliverable products. This section presents the key functional processing elements within a data center. These functions are made up of both hardware and software components.

The operational elements focused on are:

- Turnover of programs from development staging areas into production-controlled libraries.
- Report distribution.
- Incident reporting and problem resolution.
- Online viewing of production reports.
- Scheduling of production applications.
- Backup and recovery of production data.
- Contingency planning to ensure the recovery of customer-critical applications.
- Retention of customer data.

Program Turnover from Development to Production

The data center manager must ensure that procedures are in place to secure the accuracy and quality of the programs being moved into production. Also associated with the turnover of programs is the turnover of the job control statements that drive the processing of the program application.

There are two important factors associated with the turnover of programs and job control statements. First is the validation of the application code and the integrity and accuracy of the job control statements. In addition, the data center manager must secure and restrict access to the libraries that store both the application programs and the job control statements. The objective of restricting access to the production libraries is to ensure the integrity of the application modules in production. Any modifications made to the program code must be made in the application development areas. Once the application module has been modified, movement of the module into the production library must be processed through the turnover process. This not only ensures the integrity of the module, but also provides an audit trail of the changes made, why the change was required, and who made the change.

Report Distribution

The data center manager must assume full responsibility for providing customers with the output reports they require within the agreed-upon delivery schedule. To ensure that this commitment is successfully completed, the data center manager must have a system that tracks the delivery time of the production reports. Although the delivery of non-production reports is important, data center managers must focus their attention on the delivery of production reports. This is because the service-level agreement commitments are directed at production reports and are not open-shop-level reports.

There are several software products on the market that provide data center managers with this tracking capability. Most of these products are online systems. Once installed in the production environment, they are easy to use and maintain. One such product, called Express Delivery, is marketed by Legent, Inc.

Incident Reporting and Problem Resolution

The data center manager must establish adequate procedures for reporting and analyzing both hardware and software production failures. The information captured at the time of the failure is critical to the timely recovery of the failed process. The accurate recording of facts and sequences of events contributes directly to the quality of the corrective action process.

The data center manager must do whatever is required to ensure that the failure will not recur. To make this happen, the technical staff must identify the root cause of the problem. This is often referred to as the RCA analysis process. To perform a successful RCA analysis, accurate information relative to the failed incident is required. The incident report information log must include such information as device address, failure time, vendor contact time, and any other pertinent information that would assist in identifying the cause of the failure. An RCA analysis should also be conducted if there is an application failure. As in the case of hardware failures, the information obtained at the time of the failure is also vital in identifying the root cause of the failure. The information required to support the resolution of application failures should include the time of the failure, abend code, history of most recent program modifications, or job control modification.

The importance of incident reporting and application abend reports cannot be overemphasized. The time spent in preparing an incident report or an application abend failure report can prove instrumental in preventing the problem from recurring.

Problem Review Meetings

Regardless of the size of the computer installation, the quality and service-ability of the hardware and software depend on the level of support provided by the vendors and the data center's technical support organization. That is why the lines of communication between the data center operations organization and its support groups are critical. Problem review meetings provide an excellent means of informing the support organization of the problems and also provide the vendor or the technical support staff with a tool by which they can keep the data center's management informed on the corrective actions being taken to resolve the problems at hand.

Online Viewing of Production Reports

Data center processes are subject to continual changes in processing technology. For this reason, the data center management team must always ensure that the organization keeps up with current technology. Improvements in the computing labs, such as the use of state-of-the-art hardware, must always be pursued. This is especially true in the area of Direct Access Storage Device and tape unit devices. Although in today's environment, hard-copy printing is not as critical as it was in the late 1970s and early 1980s, the need to produce high-quality, hard-copy output is still a customer requirement. Therefore, the data center should secure a high-quality laser printer, as well as state-of-the-art, roll-paper units that can feed the laser printers continually for an eight-hour period without having to stop the printer. These roll-paper units provide a 57 percent improvement in turnaround time.

Data center managers must acquire both hardware and software that will allow them, when possible, the capability of providing their customers with cost-effective production of computer-generated, paperless reports. Products being marketed today that provide for online viewing of production data include IBM's Report Management Distribution System (RMDS) and Legent's Sysout Archival and Retrieval (SAR) system.

Online viewing of production data eliminates or greatly reduces the costs associated with producing and handling hard-copy reports. Online viewing of production data also ensures that the customers have immediate access to their reports. In most cases, hard-copy reports arrive at the customer site an average of three hours after the data is produced. By eliminating unneeded paper, the organization saves filing space, computer processing time, and handling time. The faster a data center can process information, produce reports, and develop successful systems, the more competitive and prosperous the organization will be.

Scheduling of Production Applications

As technological advances and operational improvements, and their impact on the data center, are identified and discussed, the scheduling of production jobs should be of major importance to the data center manager. Data centers today process on an average 30,000 to 80,000 jobs per month. Of all the jobs the data center may process per month, only a small percentage are what could be classified as self-contained, jobs that create their own data files, use their own files, and neither pass nor receive data. The largest percentage of jobs processed by a data center today are what could be classified as successor- and predecessor-type jobs. In other words, the data files created by these jobs are passed on as input to other jobs. For this reason, the data center manager must provide a scheduling software package that automatically monitors the creation of input data files and submits the production jobs into the system when all required dependencies are met. In some cases, the job requirement may not be a data file, but rather, a specific time of day. Due to the magnitude of the jobs being processed and their specific requirements, the manual scheduling of production jobs in today's data centers is highly discouraged.

There are several scheduling software packages available on the market today. Data center managers should first identify their specific requirements and then purchase or lease a scheduling package that meets their requirements. Computer Associates and 4th Dimension are just two of the vendors which can provide this type of software.

Backup and Recovery of Production Data

The data center is responsible for ensuring the integrity of customer data. This level of accountability, however, also extends to protecting the data. To ensure that production data is secured, the data center manager must have documented backup and recovery procedures. The process for backing up data may vary from data center to data center, and the complexity of the recovery process depends on the amount of data being backed up.

Regardless of the complexity level of backing up the data, data center managers must understand and take the appropriate measures to safeguard the data put in their trust.

Most data centers ensure the integrity of the data by performing what is generally referred to as standalone backup maintenance. Standalone backup maintenance means that the backup of all Direct Access Storage Device volumes is performed when there is nothing else processing on the system. This type of backup ensures that the data being backed up is accurate to the point of the backup. There are ways to streamline the backup process, and improved processes should be discussed with the data center's storage management group or with the center's production control organization.

Off-Site Vaulting of Backup Data

As part of the production data backup process, the data center manager must ensure that the data center has the ability to store its critical production data in an off-site tape vault. The distance from the data center of the off-site tape vault facility is not of major importance. The key objective is to have the off-site facility away from the main processing lab and away from the production tape library. It should be noted that the primary emphasis of an off-site tape library is to support the recovery of the data center in the event of a major system outage. System restorations of this magnitude are generally supported by a disaster-recovery hot-site data center. (The aspects of contingency planning and disaster recovery are discussed in more detail in the following section.) The primary emphasis of an off-site tape vaulting procedure, however, is to secure recovery of data in the event of a long-term system outage. Day-to-day recovery of data files should be provided by using the backup files that reside within the computing area tape library. To help ensure this level of recovery, the current version of the production backups should be kept in the computing tape library for immediate access. The –1 generation of the backup files should be stored at the off-site tape vault. The data center must work together with the storage management group and the customer to help determine and establish a suitable off-site vaulting tape rotation process.

The data center manager must also establish a process to audit the off-site tape vaulting process. This audit must focus on the support provided by the off-site tape storage vendor and the internal rotation process with the data center. The audit should be conducted at least on a quarterly basis.

Contingency Planning/Disaster Recovery

Assuming the role of data custodian for the data center customer incorporates the assurance that during periods of extended outages, customers are still provided with the capability of accessing their data, as well as the assurance that their critical applications will be processed as close to normal schedule as possible.

To ensure that the customer is provided with this level of support, the data center manager must provide a contingency planning/disaster recovery plan. A workable disaster recovery plan must incorporate the following key components:

- A disaster recovery manual must be established. This manual must address the detail level of the recovery process. This manual can be viewed as a how-to manual that not only identifies specific processes, but the supporting parties, as well.
- Critical applications must be identified by the customer. The data center manager should never assume responsibility for identifying the critical applications. Defined as applications vital to the continued success of the customer's organization, these critical points are usually tied to financial or contractual requirements. The data center manager can assist the customer in identifying the critical applications, but the final selection should be in the hands of the customer.
- The data center must select and subscribe to a disaster recovery hot site. The hot site is used to process the critical applications identified by the customer. The hot site recovery center provides the following:
  — Network communications hardware and technical support.
  — Mainframe hardware as required to support the critical workload.
  — DASD and tape resources.
  — Printing capabilities.

The recovery plan must be tested at least annually. Operational objectives should be established. The recovery test should support the accomplishment of the stated objectives.

Retention of Customer Data

Under normal processing standards, deletion of data files is generally controlled by system-controlled parameters. Simple data sets are generally marked for deletion by system-defined and system-controlled expiration dates. Generation data groups (GDGs) are controlled by system-defined catalog indexes. Deletion of data files within GDG groups is managed by deleting the oldest data file in the index. The best approach overall in managing and controlling data files is to let the system manage the retention and deleting of files.

There are, however, times when operations personnel must override the system-defined controls. The data center manager must take every precaution possible to ensure that the customer data is protected. This is why manual overrides that delete a data file must be coordinated with the customer.

The simplest method of ensuring that the customer concurs with the deletion of data files is to request that the customer's representative sign the deletion request that is submitted to the operations organization. By no means should data files be deleted on a verbal request. All data file deletion requests must be in writing. It is suggested that the data center manager establish a data file deletion request form to incorporate and require data owner approval.

RECOMMENDED COURSE OF ACTION

Data center managers should carefully analyze the effectiveness of their organizations. All of the activities performed within the data center should have one primary objective: to achieve total customer satisfaction at the lowest cost possible. The data center manager must establish and implement policies and procedures to ensure that customer objectives are achieved. The customer and the data center must have a clear understanding of the commitments that each must make to achieve a successful long-term partnership. Once these commitments are established and understood, a service-level agreement should be developed to support the mutually agreed-upon commitments and deliverables.

The data center manager should then implement a procedure by which operational performance metrics can be obtained and monitored. The primary objective of these is to confirm the data center's ability to meet customer requirements, but it will also identify shortfalls within the customer's commitments to the data center.

Data center managers must realize that customer satisfaction can be secured only by providing the customer with state-of-the-art processing at a minimal cost. If the data center cannot achieve this, the customer will be forced to move its data center processing to a vendor which will meet its technological and cost targets.

Chapter 10
Evaluating a Job Scheduler in the Open Systems Arena

Randy Keck

THERE ARE TWO FUNDAMENTAL BENEFITS THAT DATA CENTER MANAGERS look to achieve when acquiring a production job scheduler. The first benefit is personnel-related cost savings that result from the automatic execution of a company's daily, monthly, and year-end processing requirements. The second is the business-related savings that are produced by the consistency, accuracy, and timeliness of a job scheduler's automatic activity. Because the degree of value that a company derives from a job scheduler is in direct proportion to the degree of automation that it can deliver, the cost justification of a job scheduler is inherently tied to the level of automation that its features and functions can produce.

Despite the automation benefits that personnel may receive from a production job scheduler, the expected cost savings can be seriously diluted by the degree of complexity involved in implementing production workloads into a job scheduler. This is especially true in the open systems environment, in which the heterogeneous nature of production jobs and the potential involvement of end users result in an enterprise quickly complicated by multiple platforms, client/server technologies, and significant networking topologies. Considering that one of the primary objectives associated with a job scheduler is to meet production timelines, the requirement for a job scheduler to shield its users from their environments needs to be viewed as a major factor in evaluating an open-systems-based job scheduler. Therefore, whereas the cost-saving benefits that can be derived from the features and functions of a production job scheduler need to be measured according to its degree of automation, the same degree of emphasis must also be placed on time-to-production benefits derived from potential ease of use and transparency factors.

0-8493-9824-X/00/$0.00+$.50
© 2000 by CRC Press LLC

CLASSIFYING COST-SAVING OPPORTUNITIES

To justify the acquisition of an automated scheduler, costs must be assigned to production activities, and potential savings need to be associated with the purchase of a job scheduler. To evaluate the cost-saving factors of a job scheduler, the following three categories need to be examined:

Cost of Implementation. This uncovers the costs associated with implementing the job scheduler into production. These costs go beyond the cost of the software to include training, installation time, and the conversion of existing jobs created through manual or primitive operating system commands. The objective is to create the fastest path possible to support the production environment.

Recurring Savings. These savings are associated with automating production job schedules and increasing the accuracy and timeliness of job executions on an ongoing basis.

Environmental Support. This addresses how the scheduler fits into an existing enterprise, including integration into existing system management frameworks and meeting centralized and decentralized requirements with job-scheduling architectures.

These categories are the underlying crux of a job-scheduling evaluation, regardless of the mix of platforms that will be associated with the scheduler. The features and functions that comprise the recurring cost-savings category result in the highest return on investment (ROI) from the purchase of a job scheduler. This is due to the high degree of redundancy and automation associated with a job scheduler during its production usage.

An example of how these categories relate to an evaluation of a job scheduler is shown in Exhibit 10.1, which shows a sample job scheduler cost-justification worksheet. Because environmental issues are often independent of cost savings, they are not assigned an ROI value.

RECURRING COST SAVINGS

The features and functions of a job scheduler that comprise recurring cost-savings can be sorted into three categories: automated schedule administration, ease-of-use considerations, and automated operations. Because these areas promise the highest degree of cost savings, they are highlighted here:

Automated Schedule Administration

This is the process that must take place to organize jobs into their scheduled runs, and includes:

Cost of Initial Implementation	
Cost of Job Scheduler Acquisition (First Copy)	$
Installation (Effort): Number of Hours * Hourly Pay	$
Cost of Training:	$
___ People *___ Days Number of Hours * Hourly Pay	
Pilot Program (Potential Vendor Assistance)	$
Conversion of Current Schedules	$
Total Costs	$

Recurring Cost Savings Estimated Man-Hour Savings				
	Daily Savings	Current Hours/Day	Number of Personnel	Estimated Savings/Day
Automated Schedule				
Administration				
• Production Scheduling	90%			
• Job/Application Preparation	100%			
Output Distribution	80%			
Ease of Use				
• Increase Productivity	33%			
• Increased Accuracy/Consistency	75%			
Automated Operations				
• Operator Processing	40%			
• Coordinating User Requirements	75%			
• Job Management	90%			
Total Daily Hours				
Total Monthly Hours (21 Work Days/Month)				
Total Man-Hour Dollar Savings Per Month			$	
			(per month)	

Payback/Return on Investment	
$_____ (Implementation Costs)/_____ Savings	_____ Months

Exhibit 10.1.   Job scheduler cost-justification worksheet.

- Production scheduling.
- Job/application preparation.
- Output distribution.

Production scheduling and job/application preparation include setting up the different business calendars and defining workload requirements. Calendaring is considered the heart of any production job scheduler, and calendaring options must be reviewed to ensure that a job scheduler can easily handle simplified versions of one-time runs, as well as recurring schedules involving complicated yearly runs. Options must also be carefully reviewed for on-demand scheduling requirements, in which the scheduled dates are unknown, but environment variables, runtime parameters, and alert handling need to be predefined. In either case, the objective is to reduce duplication of effort and ensure that application requirements and system resources are accurately assigned to jobs.

Output distribution involves accurate and controlled distribution of appropriate reports. Interestingly, many of the platforms that have come to the forefront of today's information technology do not offer the degree of sophistication that has come to be expected of mature platforms. The overall queuing process and its association with self-defining selection processes is a prime example of an expected luxury with operating systems such as MVS, whereas job schedulers have had to offset serious problems with operating systems such as UNIX.

On the other hand, mature platforms may not always take advantage of today's networked and integration topologies, including multi-CPU and multiplatform workload balancing, external processing integration, SNMP-based alerts, and even e-mail processing. Open-systems-based job schedulers must, therefore, provide an appropriate set of features and functions to offset a subset of operating system deficiencies while also delivering the same standard set of scheduling benefits that customers have come to expect from a production job scheduler. The magnitude of cost savings that customers can receive from open systems automated administration can be in excess of 90 percent.

Ease-of-use characteristics significantly influence recurring cost savings when new technologies are introduced to meet users' production needs. This is especially apparent in the open systems arena, in which new technologies are often the underlying base of an enterprise. In the open systems arena, a job scheduler must eliminate the need to know the individual platforms and provide features that reduce the time required to meet job-scheduling requirements. This allows the data center staff to more efficiently perform their tasks and drastically reduces the costs often incurred with retraining. In addition, the automation of processes and procedures incorporates consistency and accuracy into the way day-to-day job scheduling tasks are carried out. This is mostly noted in job scheduling with respect to the chain of events that are supposed to occur when an unexpected or temporary change occurs to the scheduling criteria. Personnel-related savings in this area are often as high as 33 percent, depending on turnover, newness of platforms, and complexity of environment. Business-related savings are often as high as 75 percent and are mostly dependent on the mission-critical nature or size — or both — of the workload.

Automated operations defines the last set of recurring cost savings and encompasses the degree of notification and control that is operationally required to manage enterprise-wide workload schedules. Receiving information on an exception basis is vital to properly resolving issues and to better plan production processing in the future. This information is key not only to central processing, but also to a decentralized environment, in which end users may wish to receive direct information on their workloads. With GUI-based production status windows that cover past, current, and future status information, along with exception-based filters and alert-processing options, a job scheduler can provide immediate cost-saving values to a company. When a job scheduler provides flexible layouts and an audit log for increased granularity and end-user focus, productivity gains result, in terms of excellent responses to unexpected errors within an application's program. Similar benefits are also realized with unexpected scheduling changes. By offering provisions for temporary changes to a workload's schedule (e.g., "Quickly add this job to Saturday's schedule!") and automatically handling changes to a workload's runtime requirements (e.g., the Sputnik system is no longer available and recovery jobs need to be run), a production job scheduler can average a 70 percent cost savings by expediting and handling problem resolutions.

Exhibit 10.2 is an example of an evaluation checklist that further illustrates the one-time factors and recurring cost savings that can be used when evaluating an open-systems-based production job scheduler.

ENVIRONMENTAL SUPPORT

Environmental support relates directly to the level of integration that a job scheduler provides to a company's environment. Even though this level of support is not assigned with a cost-savings value, it must be addressed during the evaluation process to determine its fit with the company's environment. To evaluate a job scheduler's integration into an environment, answers to the following issues should be examined:

- Will job scheduling administration be centralized or decentralized?
- Will job scheduling operations be centralized or decentralized?
- Will users benefit from client/server operations?
- Will job scheduling operations integrate with other third-party software? If so, will networking protocol standards such as SNMP be required?

Meeting Centralized or Decentralized Requirements

The architecture of a job scheduler must provide the flexibility to meet centralized or decentralized requirements. The primary component of an open-systems-based job scheduler is the master schedule, which contains all

Exhibit 10.2. One-time factors and recurring cost savings.

Feature/Function/Benefit	Weight	Job Scheduler	Manual
Cost of Implementation (one-time factors) • Installation in under 60 minutes. • No Kernel modifications required. • Workloads created from primitive tools are upgradable (e.g., UNIX at, batch, and crontab workloads). • No hidden or third-party software required to implement (i.e., the product will not tie the organization to a third-party runtime database license). • Usable and easy-to-learn interface.	10		
Recurring Cost Savings			
Automated Schedule Administration (savings of 90 percent) • Production Scheduling (savings of 90 percent) — Flexible calendars capable of handling complex relationships (i.e., if Sunday is holiday, run on Monday; otherwise, run on Saturday; workday relationships to days, week, month, and yearly schedules are centrally created; hard-coded dates are not required. There is no need to reset calendars annually). — Intra-day executions (e.g., repetitive status inquiries and posting jobs). — Time, date, job, file, and external processing dependencies. — Dependencies related to job-scheduling status and application status. — Multiplatform executions not restricted by naming and usage conventions. — Centralized and user-based scheduling supported. — Ability to set exceptions (e.g., maximum run times) and to place predefined actions at workload and system level. — All functionality available through all interfaces. — Workload balancing and support. • Job/Application Preparation (savings of 100 percent) — Supports parameter passing. — Supports setting of environmental variables. — Supports binary or shell scripts. — Application independence. — Supports multiple business calendars. • Output Distribution (savings of 80 percent) — Provides e-mail and other options for output handling. — Output transferable to external processes. — Supports the setup of exception-handling conditions.	9		

Exhibit 10.2 (continued). One-time factors and recurring cost savings.

Feature/Function/Benefit	Weight	Job Scheduler	Manual
Ease of Use (savings of 54 percent) • Increased productivity (savings of 33 percent) — Offers client interfaces to meet end-user requirements (e.g., Motif, PC Windows, command-line interface). — Functions entered through the Graphical User Interface. — Truly a Windows-based application (i.e., the scheduler has pick lists, is mouse-driven, and does not have a syntax-driven interface). • Increased accuracy and consistency (savings of 75 percent) — Ad hoc jobs predocumented and added to the schedule at any point. — Changes automatically reflected in the schedule. — Changes to the calendar automatically reflected in the schedule. — Pick lists provided in the setup of jobs.	5.4		
Automated Operations (savings of 50 percent) • Operator processing (savings of 40 percent) — Current, historical, and future workload activity shown in production status window. — Ability to easily determine workload and production status. — Issues isolated by color-coded highlights and filters. — Centralized or distributed support. • Coordinating user requirements (savings of 75 percent) — Ad-hoc/on-demand jobs vs. regularly-scheduled. — Supports workload priorities and processing limits. — Central or distributed administration. — Supports the modification of specific job occurrences. — Security options to restrict user-based access and control of scheduling functions and workloads. • Job management (savings of 90 percent) — Allows temporary and permanent scheduling changes. — Actions restricted to specific users or scheduling functions. — Alert management at workload and system levels. — Job selection controllable by job and queue priorities. — Queues customizable and easy to set up. — Concurrency of jobs able to be set through dependencies or queues.	5		

rules created during the job-preparation step to meet production scheduling and output distribution requirements. The machines which act as candidates for actually processing workloads are called agents. The platforms which support a master schedule should be able to connect to any supported agent platform, and job schedulers which provide true client/server architectures maintain transparency between the different platforms for the end user. The client interfaces remain independent of the master/agent installation procedures and can centrally connect to any of the master schedules. Because the master schedules maintain all scheduling information for each of their respective agents, the clients can centrally or decentrally control all enterprise scheduling activity.

The Master/Agent Architecture

When administration tasks must be centrally controlled, the master/agent architecture provides a convenient alternative, in which all scheduling tasks can be performed centrally on a single master schedule while workloads are automatically distributed out to agent machines. To place control on the possible destinations of a workload, the job scheduler should make provisions to isolate machines into specific host lists, without restrictions for the same host to appear in more than one list. Each host list can then be assigned to a workload within the master schedule.

At the time of launch, the host lists are scanned for machine availability. Therefore, unavailable agents will not affect the scheduling of workloads when at least one agent in a host list is still available. Additionally, when a workload balancing option is available, job schedules can be balanced across the various machines contained within a host list.

Even though the master/agent architecture is susceptible to master and network outages, the effect of these outages can be minimized with store-and-forward intelligence on each agent. When an outage occurs across the network, for example, workloads that are currently executing on an agent continue to completion and workload status is stored in an agent database. When the network becomes available again, all status information is automatically forwarded from the agent to the master.

Multiple or Networked Masters

In an environment in which administration must be decentralized or the degree of fault tolerance must be increased to meet service level agreement, job scheduling options should be reviewed to increase the number of master schedules. With additional master schedules, workloads can be decentralized and the effects of outages can be reduced. Workloads within the networks may still need to be networked to resolve minimal dependencies between the schedules.

Some job-scheduler architectures limit networking options to a master/agent architecture. Others place temporary data sets on remote machines in an effort to create an illusion of networked masters. Only by installing fully functional master schedules on each machine, with provisions to network the masters, can true master-to-master operations be maintained and connectivity formed between multiple master/agent architectures.

The Benefits to the End User

The degree of flexibility that a job scheduler can lend to end users in managing their schedules can be heavily influenced by the availability of a client/server architecture. With a client/server architecture, a job scheduler's client services enables end-user control over scheduling activity to remain independent of its server's master scheduling services. This allows users to have a single point of control over the operational aspects of their schedules, regardless of the location, platforms, or number of machines that must be controlled.

Given the independence of client/server technologies, the complexity of the environment can be transparent to the end users, allowing them to focus on their job-scheduling tasks. Fault tolerance can also be a plus with a client/server technology, because outages incurred by any single master schedule do not affect the end users' access to operations related to other master schedules. A PC client, for example, who has access to multiple UNIX master schedule servers, each of which contains a variety of Microsoft NT, IBM MVS, and UNIX agents, remains unaffected by any server outages.

Determining Third-Party Integration

Open integration with other systems software, especially console-management products, should also be taken into consideration when reviewing environmental issues. With the number of platforms and product-sensitive data that can result from an open systems enterprise, status data must be filtered on an exception basis. Open systems management strategies include such offerings as NetView by IBM, OpenView by HP, and Command Post and Ensign by Boole & Babbage. These solutions offer a single point of control for any number of systems software point solutions.

By using protocol standards, such as SNMP, and command line interfaces, a job-scheduling solution can send workload-based and systems-based alerts to a central control point. With an appropriate set of alerts and usage of protocol standards, a job scheduler can highlight issues, call pagers, send e-mails, or resolve problems automatically, either directly or through the single point of control provided by an open-systems management product.

An example of a checklist containing the environmental features and functions that should be reviewed when evaluating a job scheduler are shown in Exhibit 10.3. This checklist can serve as an addendum to the one-time and recurring cost savings evaluation checklist discussed earlier.

Exhibit 10.3.   Environmental features and functions.

Feature/Function/Benefit	Weight	Job Scheduler	Manual
Environmental Support • Supports master/agent architecture. • True client/server architecture. • Masters able to be networked for intermachine dependencies. • True client/server-based architecture. • Adheres to operating system-based security. • Agents able to tolerate network and master faults. • Agent destinations able to be controlled through host lists. • Agents able to help balance workloads. • Supports distributed or centralized administration and support. • Integrates with console managers (OpenView, NetView).	N/A		

CONCLUSION

When reviewing a job scheduler for an open-systems environment, evaluators must combine their knowledge of job-scheduling basics while responding to a whole new set of platform-independent criteria. Many of the features and functions that have been sought in the past remain fundamental requirements in the open-systems arena. Yet the need to offset many of the luxuries that companies have come to expect from their more mature systems are not necessarily available in platforms which have also moved to the forefront of production processing.

Primitive operating-system tools cannot provide the level of sophistication and environmental transparency required to meet today's job scheduling needs, and the same is true of job schedulers initially developed for single-platform environments and then transported to the open-systems arena. Built upon a single-platform philosophy, such products have inherent limitations in key areas such as client/server technology and networking topologies.

Open systems-based job schedulers must, therefore, move in a direction that accommodates the ongoing scheduling requirements of most customers, while also incorporating the necessary technologies needed to schedule workloads in an open-systems enterprise. Client/server architectures, networked topologies, multiplatform scheduling, and open-systems-based alert management exemplify the types of features that are needed from today's new breed of job schedulers. Additionally, the evaluator must always keep in mind that the array of features and functions can have little value unless the job scheduler can provide the ease-of-use and transparency characteristics required to align the mix of new technologies likely to be associated with an open-systems environment with the end users' knowledge base.

Chapter 11
Help Desk Technology
Nathan J. Muller

ANY USER WHO HAS EVER PLACED A CALL TO IN-HOUSE SUPPORT PERSONNEL knows how frustrating it can be to explain a problem over the telephone. Novice users have a particularly hard time determining what information — and how much — to provide. On the other end of the phone line, technical support professionals are often equally handicapped. Unable to see what is happening at users' terminals, they struggle to solve problems blindly. Today, however, technology has gone far in resolving this situation, and more sophisticated tools and services are available.

REMOTE CONTROL ACCESS

Although help desk personnel can solve most problems over the phone with the aid of databases, another tool they can draw on is remote control software that allows them to view the computer screens of callers to determine the source of a problem and take control of their machines to provide a solution. These problems can be overcome with software products that provide help desk operators with the ability to access remote computer systems, allowing support staff to monitor users' terminals as if they were there in person. If necessary, the support person can even guide the user through the problem by entering appropriate keyboard input. This provides an effective vehicle for quick and efficient troubleshooting and lets organizations centralize their end-user support functions. This means technical support people no longer have to run from location to location to fix problems.

Remote control software is most useful to help desk staff who support LAN users at the applications level. As much as 80 percent of all trouble calls are applications related rather than hardware related. With this percentage of problems now solvable by the help desk operator, technicians do not have to waste time diagnosing hardware for problems they will end up not being able to fix anyway. About a dozen remote control application packages are currently available to provide bidirectional remote support over the local-area network (LAN). These products differ in capabilities, features, and pricing. Generally, they offer a set of remote support and diagnostic tools that enable help desk operators and other support people use their time more productively.

A number of capabilities, such as screen echo, in particular, are especially useful to help desk operators. Screen echo allows a help desk operator to initiate a session to view the user's workstation screen. By viewing the end user's screen or witnessing keystrokes as they occur, the help desk operator can often determine the exact cause of the problem.

Another useful capability is remote run, which allows the help desk operator to take over a workstation and operate it remotely from his or her own keyboard, thus locking out the user. This capability is often used when problems cannot be detected simply by watching remote video activity. The help desk operator can even join applications in mid-session.

With an integral capability, help desk operators can compose, send, save, and recall window-type messages from a message library and direct them to any or all workstations. This feature, for example, permits important status messages to be sent quickly to individual users as required, or general-interest messages to be broadcast to all workstations in the local or target cluster or to workstations at remote nodes.

Help desk operators can communicate interactively with select workstation users in conversation mode, allowing both ends of the connection to converse via keystrokes displayed in separate message windows. The conversation mode is toggled on and off by the help desk operator, who can continue the questioning or instructions to the user as appropriate until the problem is solved.

Often, verification of certain system services, such as a print spooler, at a remote site is necessary. A partition status function permits the help desk operator to review the memory allocation of the target workstation, without disrupting the user. In addition, this function allows the help desk operator to confirm operating system levels installed, services currently installed in memory, and other vital information to ensure the proper operation of various services.

A reboot workstation function allows the help desk operator to reboot local cluster workstations or remote workstations and resume the testing of target locations once network communications are restored.

If a workstation user is going to be working on a sensitive task such as payroll processing, the user can toggle off the remote control software functions to prevent help desk access to that application. Upon completion of the task, the remote control software functions can be toggled back on.

Remote Access Security

In the hands of unauthorized users, such remote control functions can be misused to wreak havoc on the LAN, as well as invade the privacy of individual workstation operators. To protect the user privacy and user data integrity, most remote control software includes security mechanisms.

First, only those capabilities required by the help desk operator can be made available to that operator. Also, individual workstation users can selectively enable or disable any or all target functions that the help desk operator can perform on their workstations. This can also be done on a cluster-wide basis. Second, when a help desk operator dials into a remote workstation, cluster, or LAN, the proper node-level password must be entered to gain access. Third, workstation users are alerted by an audio and a visual notification when a remote control session is initiated by the help desk operator. The workstation users can retrieve identification of the node location and, with a single keystroke combination, the ID of the user initiating the remote session. If there is no match to an authorized help desk operator, the workstation user can terminate the session with a single keystroke combination.

OUTSIDE SUPPORT

An alternative to internally staffed help desks is to subscribe to a commercial service or to use one of the many such services offered by computer manufacturers.

Commercial Services

With a commercial service, subscribers typically call an 800 number to get help in the use of DOS-based microcomputers, software programs, and peripherals, for example. A variety of pricing schemes are available. An annual subscription, for instance, may entitle the company to unlimited advice and consultation. Per-call pricing is also available. The cost of basic services is between $11 to $15 per call, depending on call volume. Depending on the service provider, calls are usually limited to 15 or 20 minutes. If the problem cannot be resolved within that time, the provider may even waive the charge for the call.

Resolution can be anything from talking the caller through a system reboot to helping the user to ascertain that a micro-to-mainframe link is out of order and what must be done to get it back into service. Callers can also obtain solutions to common software problems, including recovering an erased file, importing files from one package to another, and modifying CONFIG.SYS and AUTOEXEC.BAT files when adding new applications packages or hardware.

Some hotline services even offer advice on the selection of software and hardware products, provide software installation support, and guide users through maintenance and troubleshooting procedures. Other service providers specialize in LANs.

Because many callers are not familiar with the configuration details of their hardware and software, this information is compiled into a subscriber profile for easy access by online technicians. With configuration information readily available, the time spent with any single caller is greatly reduced. This helps to keep the cost per call low, which is what attracts new customers. The cost of a customer profile varies greatly, depending on the size of the database that must be compiled. It may be based on the number of potential callers or may entail a flat yearly charge for the entire organization.

Databases. The operations of some service providers can be quite sophisticated. To service their clients, staff may, for example, access a shared knowledge base residing on a minicomputer that contains tens of thousands of questions and answers.

Sometimes called expert system, the initial database is compiled by technical experts in their respective fields. As online technicians encounter new problems and devise solutions, this information is added to the database for shared usage when the same problem is encountered at a later time.

Help Lines. Even users with access to vendors' free help-line services can benefit from a third-party help line. This is because the third-party service may cover situations in which more than one application or hardware platform is being used, whereas vendor help-line services provide assistance covering only their products. Moreover, most users rarely bother to phone the vendors because of constantly busy lines. So rather than supplanting vendor services and in-house support desks (which may be overburdened), third-party services may be used to complement them.

In addition to delivering a variety of help services, for an extra charge, third-party service providers can issue call-tracking and accounting reports to help clients keep a lid on expenses for this kind of service and allocate expenses appropriately among departments and other internal cost centers.

Vendor-Provided Services

Many computer vendors offer help desk services for the distributed computing environment. Such services go beyond the subscriber's network to monitor and control the individual endpoints — the workstations, servers, and hubs.

Using remote control software on a dial-up or dedicated link, workstations and servers are monitored periodically for such events as errors, operational anomalies, and resource usage. Upon receiving a report of such an occurrence, the vendor's technical staff respond within the contract-specified time frame to resolve the problem.

The specific services provided by the vendor may include one or more of the following:

- *Local event management.* This service accepts events created by application and systems software and filters these events according to user-defined criteria.
- *Integrated event monitoring.* This service enables the vendor's centralized technical staff to monitor events received from remote managed sites. Each technician can have a specific "view" into the event database, allowing for different functional areas of responsibility.
- *Remote access.* This service enables the vendor's technical and management center staff to review or control any remote workstation or server, as well as any memory partition on a workstation or server. The target screen is viewed in a window on the technician's monitor and the commands work as if they were input locally.
- *Software distribution.* This service provides controlled electronic distribution and installation of system and application software at remote sites. License management also may be included in this type of service.
- *Asset management.* This service keeps a complete inventory of the subscriber's hardware and software. This is accomplished via periodic scans of workstation and server configuration files. Moves, adds, and changes are tracked, as well, to keep the inventory current.

NMS-INTEGRATED HELP DESKS

One of the newest trends is to integrate help desk and trouble-ticketing functions within network management systems (NMS). Such integration allows network managers to coordinate all activities on the network, from problem detection to resolution, on a single computer screen.

When an alarm is generated by the NMS, alerting the network manager of the status of any device on the network, a device identification code is passed to an element management system (EMS), which locates and displays the physical connectivity. After the information is collected by the NMS and Electronic Meeting System, the help desk software produces a trouble ticket listing the problem's symptoms and its probable causes. Recommended actions are also detailed on the trouble ticket.

In addition to inventory information, a circuit trace can be added to the trouble ticket, which provides a map of all the connections to an ailing LAN segment. The trouble ticket also lets help desk personnel log user complaints, automatically assigns priority to complaints that have not been resolved, and keeps a history of recurrent problems.

This comprehensive management solution improves the information-gathering process used by network managers to make critical decisions, eliminating duplication of effort and allowing different components of the network to be managed as a single enterprise. The solution also allows for the integration of problem history, planning, and resource-management functions under one platform. This, in turn, improves the user's ability to keep vital network devices efficiently up and running.

STANDARDIZATION EFFORTS

The Help Desk Institute, a 32,000-member international networking forum for help desk professionals, has developed the Helpdesk Expert Automation Tool (HEAT), a hypertext-driven, LAN-based help desk expert system. HEAT is designed to replace mainframe-based help desk systems, which are often expensive and cumbersome to use. The objective of HEAT is to assist help desk personnel by speeding up their response time and increasing their expertise in running the help desk.

HEAT requires companies to define caller profiles, which contain background information about callers and their system configurations. Thus, when a call comes in, the help desk operator can key in the caller's name or terminal identifier and immediately view a history file containing the caller's title and office location, as well as a record of previous help desk calls. The file also includes the caller's hardware and software configuration, by manufacturer's name and serial number.

HEAT also allows companies to define the types of problems that could arise in their organizations, to assign them priority for response, and to list who is qualified to resolve them. The system prompts the help desk operator with questions to ask callers and leads them through the three-structured database until the correct solution is found.

Help desk operators can set alarms as a reminder to check back with a caller or technician to determine the status of efforts to resolve the problem. HEAT can suggest alarm times based on the type and priority of the call and, if action is not taken to resolve problems by a certain time, can escalate alarms to the supervisor or manager of a technician.

A Windows-based interface lets HEAT users hot-key into a graphics library that includes images of proper switch settings on hardware, system configuration diagrams, specification charts, and floor maps.

Other features of HEAT permit help desk operators to:

- Use multiple variables to search through call records for a problem similar to the one currently being worked on.
- Establish a single file to record multiple calls caused by a major system failure.
- Audit changes made to call records.
- Automatically dial phone numbers.

CONCLUSION

Although a help desk costs money, it can pay for itself in many ways that, unfortunately, can be hard to quantify. The fact is, most companies have millions of dollars invested in computer and communication systems that support complex applications. They also have millions of dollars invested in people whose productivity is dependent on the proper functioning of these assets.

To ensure that both people and technology are utilized to optimal advantage there must be an entity in place that is capable of solving the many and varied problems that inevitably arise. For most companies that entity is the help desk, which can go a long way toward easing the burden of managing information-processing resources by eliminating many of the routine problems that occur on a daily basis.

Chapter 12
Call Center Computer Telephony Integration: A Case Study

Charles V. Breakfield
Roxanne E. Burkey

SALES LEADERS IN ANY GIVEN INDUSTRY need to carry performance through from product development, marketing, and customer service to maintain industry leadership. It is essential for a firm selling product, perched on the leading edge of technology, to provide the same level of performance for state-of-the-art customer support. This demonstrated company aggressiveness toward maintaining industry leadership is essential from a customer support level, especially in a competitive field such as wireless communications. Even with technological advancement, high-tech support methods to ensure customer satisfaction are primary forces for industry leaders.

Telecommunication consumers demand high levels of immediate support. Consequently, when servicing this type of customer using a low-end call center with old technology to support a leading-edge product, the deficiency is extremely apparent. The immediate features required as part of the high-tech call center included the ability to stand up to the anticipated high growth of the industry, increase caller response by 50 percent, and automate repetitive tasks, thereby freeing representatives' time. The overall benefits of the latter were expected to result in a reduction in support staff training, as well as minimization to meet these business objectives.

CALL CENTER MANAGEMENT PROBLEM DEFINITION

The call center support group as it existed prior to relocation was totally inadequate to the expected customer requirements. The phone instruments were 15 years old, the environment noise levels were deafening, and the database access was unresponsive and tedious. The size of the building limited the number of representatives, growth was not an option, and all

0-8493-9824-X/00/$0.00+$.50
© 2000 by CRC Press LLC

processes had reached the limits of effectiveness. The decision to incorporate computer telephony integration (CTI) technology into the planned state-of-the-art call center was mandated by call center management as a part of the move and necessary call center improvements.

The representatives' desktop was experiencing "application creep." The PC needed more RAM and faster CPUs to accommodate the new, improved applications at the desktop. Additionally, the primary database used to support the customer look-ups was consuming too much bandwidth. Overall, wide area network (WAN) traffic was being impacted at the same time more functionality was needed at the desktop. CTI functionality would therefore require implementation into an evolving data/telecom environment reengineered during relocation. In addition, staff from both IS and telecom sides of the house would need to demonstrate newly recognized complementing skillsets to finalize the CTI system implementation.

CURRENT CALL CENTER SITUATION

The current call center operation divides staff into focus areas, resulting in staff groups versed in the service requirements of one to two designated areas. This allows the development of representatives to meet specific customer needs. In turn, the representatives can offer optimum support to customers for specific problems and issues and provide immediate solutions. Follow-up with customers or crafting outbound call campaigns are suited to this type of compartmentalized operation.

The staff responsible for an area are experienced and offer an extensive knowledge pool of the products and services available. The processes are in place for staff to learn multiple product areas and integrate with other groups to service fully the diversified needs of the customer. The new call center provides a quiet, yet open area for staff to work. This atmosphere is conducive to friendly, helpful, outgoing customer service. The space is open for discussion of issues with other staff, yet quiet. The staff is pleased with the working environment and that attitude clearly was reflected in the methods for handling customers. Any changes introduced to the area will impact the representatives' effectiveness. Therefore, planning the implementation of all changes to the call center with an understanding of the potential impact is critical to success and minimal operations disruption.

CURRENT IS OPERATIONS

The IS staff supports all network, desktop, and implementation of operation's software changes for the entire organization. The local on-site staff is made up of specific technical expertise and supported by remote IS staff qualified to deploy changes rapidly and effectively to any member or specific groups within the organization. The processes are documented and rules are in place to ensure an orderly approach to system access, usage, and change throughout the organization. The internal staff works closely with the shared services corporate IS staff to ensure good technology integration within the defined rules.

With these rules and processes in place, it is important to seek approval from IS management for any implementation plan that affects the desktop or operations center. All implementation plans must consider the equipment requirements, processes effected, changes needed, testing required, and maintenance anticipated. For CTI integration, the impact on the IS organization, much like operations staff, is a major consideration. The potential increases to staff workload during the implementation and for ongoing maintenance are strong factors in determining the methods to approach CTI changes.

The IS group voiced concerns of ongoing manageability of the CTI software, especially with remote locations. Several small satellite offices exist, as well, and any deployment, whether it is local or remote, must lend itself to being distributed using automated software distribution techniques. Currently, the call center is using Systems Management Server (SMS) from Microsoft to do software "push" distributions to the PC desktop. The IS management requires use of this method for technology distribution to reduce costs at the desktop PC level.

CALL CENTER OVERALL PROJECT GOALS

The phenomenal growth promised in the wireless industry will stress-test the support infrastructure of the company. Southwestern Bell Wireless's management determined that, without a robust after-sales support structure, they would suffer a reduced customer retention rate, resulting in higher cost for support per customer. The overall objective of management and, thus, the operational mandate of the IS/Telecom group is to handle and increase volume of calls quicker and more efficiently by automating tasks at the desktop. More simply put, widespread use of CTI technology is necessary to save time and reduce additional labor requirements.

The CTI-specific project goal was to use all the advantages of third-party call control and associated middleware to reduce the amount of time spent handling each call. At the current call levels, if 30 seconds are cut from the total talk time of each call, the company can save almost $900,000 per year. It is assumed that delivering the call and all the appropriate account information to the representative and desktop simultaneously will permit a more expeditious handling of the call and promote greater customer satisfaction with the wireless phone purchase/service. The conventional wisdom is that it is harder to lose a customer to a competitor if the customer is pleased with the technology (products purchased) and responsive after-sale support.

The decision was made to front-end the entire call center with interactive voice response (IVR). Calls route through the IVR call flow via a script that supports common questions or, if necessary, forwards a call quickly to an appropriate representative to assist in the customer problem/solution. As part of the routing process, the IVR prompts the caller for account number and other bits of information deemed significant are collected and attached to the call. This data is used to look up legacy database information and then route simultaneously to the PC desktop along with the phone call delivery. Once the account information is determined, it is returned to the PC desktop via a "screen-pop." Optimally, the representative greets the caller by name and is able to verify the accuracy of the information displayed on the screen.

PROJECT ORGANIZATION

CTI implementation for the call center consisted of four separate stages. The specific aspects of each stage and the delineation of responsibilities were documented for all involved parties. All tasks checked at various points to ensure end-to-end CTI functionality. The definition of each stage and the technology implemented were provided to internal operations and IS staff to promote cooperative support for this leading-edge technology integration.

Stage 1 of the CTI integration was the TAPI server installation within the call center's network environment. It was necessary to complete the TAPI server installation and then install the Remote TAPI service for the representative desktops. This permits third-party call control within the call center environment.

Stage 2 of the CTI integration is to establish connectivity between the TAPI server and the interactive voice response (IVR). As a result, the data pieces requested of and given by the customer during IVR, the call flow scripting is routed effectively to the desktop via the TAPI server. This is the first area for significant savings of staff time and the main point for evaluating increased call efficiency.

Stage 3 of the CTI integration is coupled with skills-based call routing to the call center representative. This technology implementation was scheduled for late 1998 and provides additional reporting/call monitoring capabilities along with skills-based call routing. This stage will provide additional staff efficiency in the call center and increased customer satisfaction in faster response to issues from the most experienced staff.

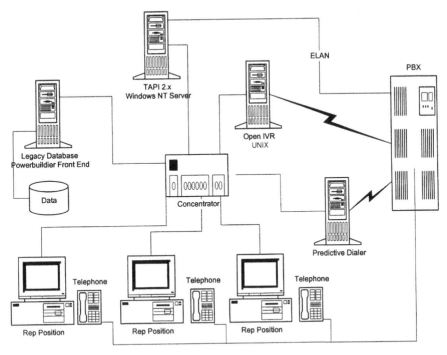

Exhibit 12.1. CTI integration design.

Stage 4 of the CTI integration is the screen-pop presenting the representative with caller account information available in the existing corporate database. The recommended screen pop was for a Microsoft TAPI-compliant developer software. The selected developer effectively gleans account information from legacy databases for current account information presented in a PC readable format based upon a screen scrape approach. This portion of the CTI solution uses the interaction between the PBX, TAPI/CTI server, Open IVR, and desktop application to provide customer data information with the call presentation.

The call center is also in the process of implementation of a predictive dialer to provide outbound calling campaigns geared toward specified criteria. They intend to integrate the predictive dialer with the CTI solution for a more blended environment in the near future. This effort will result in more efficient, effective representatives coupled with more satisfied customers.

The initial design of the CTI integration (Exhibit 12.1) involves Open IVR, TAPI server, and desktop functionality with the third-party software. The architecture requirements for the hardware integration was provided in advance for IS approval and equipment installation.

During the design phase of the project, several problems existed due to the leading-edge technology selected. The first problem was determining the correct version of software products for the functionality expected by the client. The TAPI software required for the call to pass IVR attached data was close to final release. Therefore, a special release form was obtained before delivery to the client. Typically a firm can field test a product to rate the effectiveness, gaining additional support from the vendor in the process. This additional attention from the vendor is designed to prevent major interruptions in the production environment. The prerelease product performed extremely well within the client environment.

The second problem encountered was how to determine adequately the size of the TAPI server for a call center this large. No actual sizing requirement information existed from Microsoft, so a projected server size based on estimated call volumes was specified. In determining the size of the server, the expected growth over the first two years of operation was considered. The server houses the specifics of the phone instrument and associated desktop information for synchronization of calls and customer presentation information. The volume of information monitored by the server was expected to be in direct proportion to the size of the call center.

The third problem was scheduling and coordinating technical resources to arrive and work through the implementation process. The finish of construction at the facility complicated this resource coordination. Resources required for the implementation included staff with switch expertise, IVR technicians, network administrators, and application testers.

The fourth problem was created from a new method for internal communications between management and staff on site. Network administrators changed the access rights of the installer, and everything ceased to function. As it turned out, the necessary staff were not briefed on the CTI installation and requirements for ongoing processing. Additionally, internal processes caused functionality interruptions for the software applications.

The fifth problem encountered was that the third-party screen pop application required a service patch to bring it up to the proper version level. Additional problems were encountered with the software load order of Windows NT service pack #3, TAPI desktop, and the screen pop application software. These problems were resolved in the on-site lab/testing area.

The last problem encountered was working with the customer's PBX dialing plan and the IVR attached data offered to the TAPI server. An unexpected design limitation was defeated with a quick application patch to the IVR server. Once that change was effected, data attached screen pops were delivered regularly.

Leading-edge technology often requires changes when used within an actual environment. During design and testing phases of hardware or software integration, every conceivable configuration cannot be created and tested. The fine tuning of technology implementation within the actual environment is expected and the method used to respond to and handle these issues marks the integrity of the firms involved dedicated to providing high levels of on-site support.

Objectives

The initial project objective was to prove that the technology existed and could be deployed in a complex call center/data network environment and provide the cost justification for outfitting not only the 300 existing agent machines, but also call center agents in other markets around the country. Additionally, the deployment of the desktop software applications required to increase effectiveness demanded use of centralized, controlled push technology to keep the cost of desktop maintenance from rising.

Evaluation

The project began with the entire CTI infrastructure in place but operating on only 20 workstations. This control group of users was the proof of concept evaluation that would confirm or deny the ultimate deployment of the technology. A separate controlled route point was created in the PBX, and the control group logged in there for inbound calls. The IVR script was modified to accommodate the CTI-enabled control group.

Work Products

The original 20 CTI-enabled representatives in the control group used all of the CTI solution products. The calls were received by the PBX and given IVR treatment. The caller was given the option to enter in their account number and then was routed via a special CDN to CTI-enabled representatives ready to receive calls. The IVR passed the attached data to the TAPI server that then supported the presentation of appropriate customer information to the active desktop. The CTI-enabled PC sensed the telephony event, the rules-based application looked for the caller attached data, passed the attached data to a database application running in a WinFrame type of session at the desktop, and the application returned the appropriate account information for presentation. The screen pop was accomplished with subsecond response times.

PROCESS REQUIREMENTS

As the CTI-enabled technology was confirmed by the control group, processes for use, as well as deployment were discussed. The call center staff was given modest usage training at the point of application installation.

This individual contact and tech transfer at the point of installation was timely and provided immediate feedback to the CTI installation team. Input and comments from the staff impacted the 300-representative deployment process. A concern was the direct interaction immediately at the point of application installation to ensure rapid functionality with the new screen pop technology. An unexpected side benefit occurred by being on the floor doing the actual installation. The activity of the installation team and the enthusiasm of the CTI-enabled representatives created spontaneous requests for staff outside the control group wanting to receive the same functionality. As a result, the roll out of the CTI-enabling technology had greater buy-in by the call center managers and representatives. This issue required attention for the push technology for mass distribution.

THE IS RELATIONSHIPS CHANGES

As the control group implementation drew to a close, the IS group was faced with not just supporting a limited control group of CTI-enabled representatives and the support infrastructure, but deploying to 300 workstations with full support. As the support issues and the demands on the IS seemed to escalate, additional support with automated software push deployment of the CTI-enabling software was done. This provided the ability of no technician intervention and use of the existing SMS push technology available within Microsoft-networked systems.

Because CTI technology depends heavily on desktop and server computers, the support of the CTI products ultimately would fall to the IS group. The original CTI-enabling order was initiated from the telecom side of the organization rather than the IS side. No additional staff for the technical staff in either area was planned for the technology implementation. Maintenance issues and permanent process changes require review potentially at the sixth and twelfth month mark of the system implementation. The CTI deployment process in the call center requires regular review of associated activities to improve efficiency and customer satisfaction.

CONCLUSION

Any form of system change offers a positive and negative impact on the organization. The capability of staff throughout the organization to respond to the change in a positive manner speaks well of an entire organization. Management must support the staff through all of the ups and downs of technology change. In the case of call center CTI integration efforts, the expected gains in effectiveness and ability to move forward more effectively based on technology implementation demonstrate the risk-taking ability of an organization competing in a chaotic industry. The foundation is in place not only to continue with integrating technological changes into their environment, but also to take advantage of the offer of streamlining and a competitive edge in their industry.

All of the vendors involved were dedicated to the success of the show-case call center. This effort provides the pattern for demonstrated risk required to compete effectively with anyone for customers in this industry. The results of the implementation showed the expected payback numbers, but it is expected already that within the first year the savings on staff train-ing and customer retention will be higher than projected. The staff involved in the project all work from a company edict to serve the needs of their customers along with a personal commitment to customer satisfaction.

Section III
Applications Infrastructure and Operations

As CLIENT/SERVER-BASED SYSTEMS CONTINUE TO GROW IN USE, IT managers face the challenge of integrating these new systems with existing applications. In this year's edition of the handbook, we will focus on this important area in a new section — Application Infrastructure and Operations. This new section is designed to help IT managers deal with these challenges by providing methodologies and solutions for integrating new applications into existing, complex, multiple-platform computing-processing environments. The IT manager must be capable of analyzing and evaluating the impact of new applications on existing enterprise operations. Because more than 70 percent of all major application systems are still running as legacy systems on mainframe platforms, IT managers are presented with critical challenges on how to integrate both internally developed and purchased client/server applications with these systems. To be successful, you must be able to select the right integration tools and the right implementation partners to attain the best combination of functionality and support.

The first chapter in this section, "Maintaining Data In Mainframe and Network Environments," describes the issues associated with managing application data across multiple processing platforms. The process by which organizations manage application information has significantly changed with the gradual migration from single mainframe systems to larger numbers of mid-range computer systems and PCs. The purpose of this chapter is to describe the evolution of the database environments — from single mainframe to multiple PCs — and the impact this has had on data proliferation, availability, accessibility, and integrity. As a result of the continuing dramatic increase in desktop computer power and storage capacity, the IT manager must address the issues of decentralized storage-management operations and procedures.

Chapter 14, "Managing Data Storage and Distribution," offers suggestions for maintaining and controlling data in distributed and mainframe environments. Technology and business end users view current data handling practices of storing, updating, and accessing databases as both a problem and a significant strategic advantage. This chapter's purpose is to compare the database environments — from single mainframe computers to multiple minicomputers, micro-computers, and networked PCs — to identify the lessons learned, and look to the future for improved database handling.

Imaging systems is another fast-growing area of application system processing with a major impact on the IT operations infrastructure. As discussed in Chapter 15, "The Data Center Manager's Guide to Networked Imaging Systems," organizations of all types and sizes are reaping efficiency improvements and productivity increases by implementing document-imaging systems. LANs and WANs facilitate the exchange of image files between local processing points and remote locations, thus eliminating the delay inherent in traditional paper-based systems. In combination with workflow software, the LAN and WAN make possible an efficient assembly-line approach to document processing whereby each workstation operator processes a portion of the information contained in the document before passing it on. This chapter introduces IT managers to the issues associated with networked imaging systems.

Also dependent upon a strong network infrastructure are applications involving various forms of collaboration. Chapter 16, "Collaborative Applications," describes how organizations are implementing these types of applications and how they are impacting the technology infrastructure. IT managers must address concerns such as developing a network infrastructure capable of handling multimedia communications, utilizing compelling applications accessible from the desktop, and maintaining open standards and interoperability to ensure compatibility and ease of use for the end user. This chapter presents an overview of the current state of collaborative applications, which are very much works in progress that most companies, if not all, will have to have to implement in some form in the near future. These applications hold great promise for geographically diverse and virtual organizations if well developed and implemented.

Chapter 13
Maintaining Data in Mainframe and Network Environments

Roxanne E. Burkey

THE TRANSITION FROM SINGLE MAINFRAME COMPUTERS to multitudes of minicomputers, microcomputers, and network environments has significantly altered the manner by which businesses manage their information. Rapidly improving technology, coupled with multiple hardware choices, have contributed to a decentralized processing environment that can benefit or cripple every aspect of an organization. The dramatic increase in desktop computer power and storage capacity, at a decreasing cost, will continue to decentralize functions that previously required central mainframes or minicomputers.

In addition to the dramatic hardware and telecommunication expansion over recent years, computer end users have become much more adept at accessing, handling, and creating information. Unfortunately, their use — and abuse — of database information have also brought an entire new set of problems to the database environment, including how and where data is updated. The proper methods of handling database information in a decentralized environment are still under development, and requirements are changing far too rapidly for the data center manager to spend the time necessary to develop the proper long-term methods.

Information systems are a resource critical to the operation of almost any business. What was previously considered a burdensome overhead has rapidly become a strategic and competitive asset for businesses, especially those in the international arena. The sheer volume of data currently available to businesses requires data center managers to pay additional attention to database information management. The proper management of database information primarily concerns businesses' confidence in the data integrity and immediate database access. Most organizations recognize the redundant elements present within their database structures and the impact this has on end-user accessibility and overall data reliability.

EVOLUTION OF THE DATABASE

Mainframe systems, historically, were the main electronic repositories for company information. The database was stored in a centralized system, and users could request information in formats to meet most of their financial needs. As information was centralized, the data center manager determined the methods for updating the data stored and then maintained a certain amount of control over access to the database for updates.

This discipline was developed to ensure data security and integrity. The systems developed for mainframe data storage limited direct user access to the source information, much of which was financial in nature. The role of the data center manager eventually came to be viewed as a barrier that prevented or limited the business from meeting its information needs. Further, data center managers often could not meet the reporting demands of business, especially as the information requirements began to explode. They could neither restructure the databases fast enough nor provide timely reports to meet the ever-increasing business strategic needs without significant cost increases.

Personal computers (PCs) really began the end-user access to subsets of a database and provided the flexibility to structure data to quickly fit specific business project needs. Initially, the limited amount of software available in the PC environment required data structuring methods similar to those found in the mainframe environment. End users quickly determined where the basic data elements required were available on the mainframe and developed methods to transfer or download the data to their personal environment. Free to modify the structure and adapt the data to fit their specific needs, end users understood the business information requirements, as well as the need to rapidly expand and access these multiple data elements.

In the meantime, data center managers developed methods to upload the information created on the PC to the mainframe database. They simply replicated the hierarchical database structure already present on the mainframe for the PC. This batch-like update allowed data flexibility and yet provided current data updates to the mainframe system, an important consideration, as business still relied on the mainframe as the centralized information repository. With this structure in place for both environments, the business felt that overall database integrity and consistency was provided.

The end users dictated the elements required from their information systems, and these specifications were rapidly expanding. To meet these specifications and specific business issues, data elements were added to databases and became part of the information repository. These new data elements, however, were not part of that centralized information repository, because most of the information in the mainframe was financial- and statistical-based. From this grew multiple databases containing many redundant pieces of data, often without regard to reviewing data structure and data element relationships. Without a centralized repository from which to view the information, this proliferation process remained unchecked and uncontrolled.

DATA CONTROL

Data control in the mainframe environment once meant maintaining and accounting for data elements within the system process. The organizational structure and ownership of the data origin generally determined where the information was updated. As data needs expanded and organizational structure was modified, the responsibility of the data updates commonly was passed from one operating unit within the organization to another. With the expansion of telecommunications, mainframe users began to access data more frequently from outside the mainframe location. This, in turn, caused the data point of origin to be more widely diffused than before.

The control of data changes was often kept within the realm of corporate responsibility. As businesses evolved to include more prevalent remote locations, the need to update data information from multiple locations was also increased. More data to meet regional business needs was being downloaded and manipulated at remote locations, which then accepted a certain responsibility to maintain their data, but did not always update it to the corporate level. To rectify this situation, more databases were created to assist with gathering the information to the centralized repository; the structuring of these additional databases, however, was not always compatible with the existing ones. Businesses allowed operating units that proved profitable to basically dictate the data information requirements needed to continue their success.

PCs continued to play a part in the decentralization of database information. Operating units purchased PCs for exclusive use by their staff; many of these systems were not even required to have the data center manager's approval. The equipment, therefore, did not necessarily meet the standards of corporate data processing policies, nor did anyone envision the effects these PCs would have on database control.

For example, end users were not particular about the kind of software used, as long as it met the reporting requirements they faced. Data elements were named according to a user's whim, without regard to how someone else might reference it. In addition, staff believed that their database knowledge would protect their jobs; the more they made the database confusing to others, the more secure were their places within the organization.

Staff turnover in many organizations during the late 1970s also contributed to the massive amount of uncontrolled database information. Staff replacements were not left with clear guidelines on where a database resided or what it was called. Consequently, to meet reporting needs, the new users began their own databases. They often extracted information from the mainframe databases and made modifications to conform to their comfort levels. Operating units within a business organization were too busy meeting reporting needs to document every process required to maintain all the database information on a continual basis. This lack of control over the data caused the information to become scattered over many localized PCs with many unclear data elements and unclear processes in place.

DATA REDUNDANCY

Mainframe systems initially limited the amount of redundancy present in a database, because programmers reporting to the data center manager structured and controlled these systems. The redundancy factor was not a big issue until information outside of financial data was found to be useful when processed by the computer. In most cases, organizations added to the existing database structure to meet the minor increased needs of the business. Even at this point, however, controls on access to the information and updating remained very stringent.

Data redundancy began to proliferate in the mainframe environment when programming languages became more sophisticated, and the data was structured to perform within that environment. Programming staffs were increased to create systems in the new languages, often under very tight time frames. The mainframe process moved toward replacing existing data structures with new ones. During these development processes, minor databases were created to work with existing systems and the implementation of the new system. Users, however, often found their old systems were still required for specific processes that were not incorporated into the new system.

PCs contained within the network environments became the link to continued development of massive amounts of redundant databases. Typically, these began as subsets of the primary database, which may have originally been on the mainframe. Each person continued development of his database files and structures without regard to what may have already been developed within the organization. This created many subsets of redundant, and often outdated, data used by the business to make decisions. The validation and control of the database was essentially not in the forefront when the focus was meeting reporting deadlines.

One example of the problems caused by redundant information is the case of a major advertising agency in New York, which presented analysis information on the direction a customer should take for its advertising. Unfortunately, the market-analysis information contained an unrealized amount of replicated data, resulting in an inflated proportion of the population being identified as the correct target market. As a result, the advertiser spent thousands of dollars in repackaging goods to hit that inflated target, all because there were no checks and balances to ensure the merging of multiple databases, maintained by different operating units.

Redundant information, unknown and uncontrolled, threatens the very integrity of the data files. A more careful review of databases within the network environment is of concern to network staff and users alike. Software vendors (e.g., Lotus and Oracle) are responding to data-validation needs with programs targeted at element redundancy factor identification.

The traditional problem with databases in both the mainframe and PC environments is the database file approach. Data center personnel using the flat file approach collect and maintain data within an organization in a manner that does not truly share the information. The resulting situation is one of growing inefficiency and complexity. Those with a general knowledge about the files and software are not always knowledgeable about the data's history. Knowledge about the source of the data, who maintained it, and its current validity are the main requirements. As the process of using unvalidated data continues over a number of years, the firm becomes tied in database knots of its own creation — regardless of the computing environment. The business may be saddled with multiple programs and databases in multiple environments with no one on staff who knows what these databases do, what data elements they use, the definitions of the data elements, or who is responsible for maintaining them.

DATA INTEGRITY

The continued automation of business operations substantially increased communications needs between users and information systems people. Globalization will only add to the massive needs for the international transfer of data. The consolidation of worldwide sales, service, manufacturing, and operations into a cohesive entity, while remaining physically separated, requires effective and dependable data.

Business increasingly relies on quality data for strategic planning purposes. Sometimes the fact that one piece of information is easily accessible to one particular person can make or break a deal. Whether the database resides on a mainframe, a desktop, or is networked, handling that data must be controlled. A case in point is the Geographic Information System, which contains data stored and maintained at the federal, state, and private levels, with updates from all locations.

Recently, geographic information system (GIS) database information became subject to question when a Dallas University database depicted population information overlaid on geographic information that turned out to be more than 50 years old. This old information, taken down in notebooks and backed up by photo representations, was found to be out of date with the current physical location. This caused inaccurate representations of the area and the problems faced from an ecological-risk standpoint. Decisions to send federal aid to the project were delayed until accurate information could be obtained, recorded, and presented.

In the 1970s and early 1980s, as the data processing departments expanded in response to increased demand and as software allowed for more flexibility, companies had programmers working independently on projects. If the controls were not in place to centralize the information, multiple programs and multiple databases were created. The responsibilities for the information updating were not always clearly defined; however, the current PC and network environment provide even less clearly defined roles.

Current network environments are fighting to restore database reliability. The relational, or logical, database is a step in the right direction. The current trend is to ensure that information users ask first where any required data might be available in the organization. A general rule is that some part of an organization can always be found embedded in its information systems. An organization must coordinate work through a structured, formal set of standard operation procedures. Without these in place, the integrity of the data is difficult to ensure.

The goal of effective relational database design is to eliminate data redundancy through well-defined tables, and the key to definition is understanding element relationships. For example, one-to-many relationships may be defined by adding a column in the definition indicating the association. For many-to-many relationships, a third table is often constructed to hold each instance of the database relationships.

Database design should be continually refined by checking the table against data normalization rules, such as ensuring that the intersection of a row and column contains only a single value. This information then needs to be shared with the user community to provide a view of what data elements can be accessed and their points of origin.

That is not to say that because one database has a problem that all of an organization's databases are subject to question. Those which have maintained controls over content, access, and update, and have clearly defined responsibilities are sound. Before requesting structure changes, database managers must provide end users with knowledge — or end users must actively seek it out — as to who is responsible for the data and what it contains.

QUALITY ASSURANCE

Quality assurance for mainframe database structuring was initially designated as the data processing manager's responsibility. With these responsibilities clearly defined, controls for database handling where firmly placed within system processes. The data processing manager was to ensure that reports generated from the company databases were current and up to date. End-user expectations were that data would be valid and usable.

Updates were commonly performed in a batch environment, on a regularly scheduled basis. Checks and balances on the changed data were maintained. The end users were provided with custom reports to meet their specific needs. Changes to these reports, however, were often not available on demand. Requesting the changes also proved to be difficult if the user's communication level was not in synchronization with the programmer. Purging old information was typically performed on a regularly scheduled basis. In the case of the financial information, for example, this was easily scheduled based on period close dates. The variable information stored in databases today is subject to different purge requirements based on the type of information and how subject it is to change.

Again, the PC environment has had to develop database controls to meet the high volume of databases being maintained. The popular method for effective maintenance is through a database management specialist (DBMS), who is responsible for coordinating data throughout the entire organization, for approving database changes, and for ensuring data quality. The DBMS position usually resides outside a specific operating unit and is functional at all levels of the organization. Responsibilities include:

- Backing up data and restoring it when necessary.
- Coordinating all data needs of end users, management staff, and strategic groups within the organization.
- Within the network environment, controlling access to data changes. That is, end users can still extract subsets of information for specific use, but they know the full information is contained within the network environment.
- Purging information, which is based upon how subject it is to change. The DBMS also must outline and include purging in the processes.

Current end users have more responsibility than ever to help ensure the database housekeeping functions. Whether the mainframe or microcomputer environment is the home of the database, the user must communicate as much information as is available regarding the impact to the database. The channels for this communication need to be part of the business rules of the organization. The DBMS should also maintain high communication with the users regarding anything affecting the database contents. Many organizations have focus groups, made up of representatives from the user community across the organization, who communicate their needs and desires with regard to the database. These groups have been extremely successful at increasing the information flow.

CONCLUSION

Data control is the most essential element for successful database maintenance. It is the responsibility of the end user, whether in the network or mainframe environment, to ensure that the proper controls for data handling are established. The controls, previously within the mainframe environment, are a good foundation for the personal computer to build upon. Data redundancy causes the database to grow out of control and become inaccessible by users. The trail of the information available is often lost. The multiplicity factors, coupled with no clear lines of database responsibility, reduce the overall effectiveness of the database.

A business cannot survive with inaccurate or incomplete database information. Decisions made today by business — for direction and approach tomorrow — are often made based on the database information at hand. Unreliable information, acted upon by a business, can cause the business to fail; therefore, it is critical for the process controls to be in place to maintain and ensure database integrity.

Chapter 14
Managing Data Storage and Distribution

Roxanne E. Burkey

THE MAINFRAME AND NETWORK ENVIRONMENTS have the ability to distribute data to the locations closest to the origin. The advantages of distributed data, which provides for the database to be present in multiple locations, are in the ease of updates and user frequency of access. Software, such as Lotus Notes, actually replicates the databases to many locations and synchronizes the information. In case of a catastrophic disaster in one location, the information can be easily recovered from another location, reducing downtime.

The efficient resource management of multiprocessor architectures depends on the efficiency level of the data structure management that defines the state of the system. The consistency requirements of strict data structures introduce serialization of update operations that can result in performance bottlenecks. However, the approach that employs weakened structure specifications to allow simultaneous update by many processors is not necessarily an advantage. Concurrent updates of databases still require the initial sound structure of the database. This should not be compromised for increased user performance. Acceptable avenues for solving this problem include timing when updates are performed and determining how to actually distribute the database.

This methodology is particularly important to a critical database shared by a company with many locations. The information is typically critical to everyday operations; without access, business essentially halts. With recent advances in telecommunication technology, the information systems group's ability to provide access is extremely fast. Data transfer rates between systems and platforms can be presently accomplished without affecting the user as the distributed data is well planned.

The same rules apply to updating and modifying the database structure as previously discussed, but user access is generally faster, and the most current information is available to all at least on a daily basis. With software applications, such as Lotus Notes, the current information can travel across a network on a more concurrent basis, but can have a negative impact on system performance.

DATA STORAGE

The mainframe provided a vast amount of storage capacity compared with that of personal computers (PCs) as first introduced. The ability to store large databases was best served in the mainframe environment. The end user could use subsets of the database effectively, but most personal computer programs were not capable of processing large quantities of data efficiently.

PCs over the last five years have turned megabyte storage capacities into gigabyte, with increased capacity on an annual basis. Data compression routines also allow larger data storage than mainframes of the 1970s and 1980s. The PC processing capability has also significantly increased, allowing a faster method for processing the data, including complex calculations and formulations previously reserved for the mainframe environment. PCs are rapidly meeting the capacity of the mainframes of old.

However, the technology used to increase the microcomputer capacity and power has also been used by mainframe computers to increase their power. The power behind a mainframe dealing with a large database is still superior to the microcomputer environment.

Managing storage across a decentralized, distributed computing system involves several major challenges, including optimizing data accessibility and system performance, while keeping costs down. The labor cost of maintaining storage on a network may be as much as eight times the cost of the physical storage media, but implementing storage management does not necessarily involve a conflict between the users and information systems staff. Hierarchical Storage Management is a design effort to make the best use of available media while minimizing human intervention. It is closer to the concept of a disk cache than an extension of backup routines. It keeps the most frequently accessed information located close to the user and stores the least frequently accessed with remote pointer routines. Files are then migrated between primary and secondary storage according to the access rates.

Storage may also take place in tape or CD-ROM methods. These data storage methods, suited for specific data types, frequently reduce the time required to access the data, but do require a more scheduled purge routine.

Some companies, moving from a mainframe to a network environment, have found an alternate data-storage source in the mainframe. Whereas limitations for storage are based on the business system configuration, the accessible space available in the network environment meets and exceeds single mainframe capacity. Considerations when determining where to store data include the timely access to the information and the type of data. In the 1970s and 1980s, the majority of the database information used was text; today, users employ graphic representations and make data comparisons — all of which use significantly more storage space. Graphics also eat up space because they introduce the need for system compatibility for software and memory to properly — and quickly — access the information. Helping to ease the storage binds are various methods of data compression.

END-USER ACCESS

In the mainframe environment, end-user data access was established on a need-to-know basis. Specific access to the information was part of the entire control process; the data processing manager controlled all security access to the database. The database manager coordinated the rights to access with the operating units responsible for information retrieval. Database design was left to the interpretation of the programmer's understanding of the operational unit's needs.

The end user was then provided with the minimum documentation necessary to maintain and use their portion of the database. As databases proliferated in the mainframe environment, the amount and distribution of documentation accessed was significantly reduced. End users had a tendency to make notes, photocopies, and supplemental cheat sheets to help ensure their accuracy in database handling. As a consequence, with employee turnover, backup documentation was sometimes unavailable.

On the other hand, within the PC environment, the end users control all the databases, which they have created either as subsets of other databases or as their initial database. They control which fields are updated and the scheduling of those updates. Frequently, there are very few controls over the process for maintaining the database. The uploading of the altered data still remains under the control of the information systems support or the database management specialist (DBMS). As business needs change, data requirements are quickly altered to meet the reporting needs, through restructuring databases or creating additional subsets. The typical end user frequently leaves multiple fragmented databases, many of which are not documented, within their working environment. The main control for this database proliferation is space limitation or information staff review, but the end users control with whom they share the data, and many tend to be possessive of it.

The end user currently has access to more information than ever before. The control of how and when the database is updated is left up to the user. Continuity issues have caused problems with data reliability for the business, which might be best served to maintain tighter controls over databases while allowing the user the freedom to create. Standards for documenting information and providing a trail of database evolution would also provide the end users with more confidence in their databases.

END-USER EXPERTISE

The end users experienced in the mainframe environment rarely varied from the existing procedures and processes known to them. The devices used primarily as input or access screens were usually dumb terminals. If end users did not have a programming background — in particular, access to the unpiled code — they were unable to effect tremendous change, and their ability to modify either the programs or databases was limited. The logical programming structures within the mainframe environment are complex and often require special training. End users' main requirement was simply to read documents and screens, replicating what they saw.

In addition, the role definitions of programmer, user, and report reviewer were very specific. Very rarely did an end user, for example, become an expert in the mainframe systems.

The experienced end user in the PC environment, however, frequently understands how the database is structured, knows how to change the structure and report definition, and has the basic programming skills sufficient for the applications used. The logical sequences of most PC programming are replaced with improved programming documentation and simple English commands. The ability to program in user-friendly languages allows the end users the freedom to create their own information, and affords them greater control over the database, in or out of the network environment.

Another factor driving the rise of the sophisticated end user is the overall increased level of education of the work force. In the early 1970s, 15 percent of the work force were college graduates; by the late 1980s, that figure rose to upward of 50 percent. The competition within the work force is also driving the high achievers to do more. Today's end users are more solution-oriented and proactive — questioning their environments — than the old-style mainframe work force. Today's users can discuss a wide range of issues regarding their databases; however, they lack the skills provided within a structured environment such as the old-style mainframe shops.

DATA PROCESSING SUPPORT

Support for the mainframe users came primarily from programming and the data center. End users and data processing departments frequently clashed on the database priorities and the needs of the business. Each group considered its point of view the most important. When this proved to be a poor method of communication, some mainframe operations hired staff to coordinate between the two groups. Even with these efforts, the mainframe environment, for the most part, was considered a barrier to the business's future needs. PCs provided the mechanism for the change from the mainframe environment.

Support in the PC and network environments comes from many sources, including software documentation written to the novice-user level. The primary software vendors also provide user-support hotlines during regular business hours throughout the continental United States. Information systems staff within organizations typically provide a variety of support for programming expertise, database management, and the extensive user access to information. In-house end users have a variety of skills, including experience with the multiple software available in the marketplace. These end users frequently work with one another to solve the various problems they face in using their databases. Businesses today understand their dependency on effective software use, so they are more disposed to supplement employees' knowledge with training courses in the application software used. Many companies also want to be on the leading edge of technological developments in order to meet their strategic needs. This requires their employees to become experts very quickly in the newest database application programs.

IMPROVED COMMUNICATIONS

The mainframe environment under the jurisdiction of the data center manager was reputed to contain less-than-effective communicators. For example, programmers were viewed as silent types best suited for limited contact with the end-user community. This lack of communication was typically exhibited throughout the entire data center staff. The restructuring and downfall of many large mainframe shops can be attributed to poor communications and poor understanding of the business.

The end users in today's environment are much more attuned to the volumes of information available and have more abilities to manipulate this information to present their viewpoints completely. The business, in an effort to sift through the information and gather what is important to its objectives, employs the expertise of its users. The technical expertise an end user may lack can frequently be supplemented with other experienced staff. There are significantly improved discussions on data storage and handling methodology. More publications are available that outline specific problems and solutions to the database needs of the organization. Each year, the gap is closing between technical discussions and business discussions.

COST DIFFERENCES

To establish a mainframe was, and continues to be, a large capital investment for a company. Profits in the early years of mainframe systems allowed these expensive purchases with limited pay-back analysis required. Mainframe vendors' responsiveness to expand and upgrade organizations' systems provided the comfortable growth and expansion level businesses required. The long-term cost of centralized database handling was readily offset by both staff reductions resulting from process automation and the security of the business records. The automation process was viewed as a way to improve profitability by looking at information in a more timely manner than manual processes could provide. Businesses, however, did not realize their profitability would require more immediate access to more information.

Establishing users on PCs required a very low initial cost. By purchasing a little wire, a PC, and some software, an operations unit was off and running. As budgets allowed, PCs and software could be added by the hundreds. The investment was limited, frequently not approved by the data processing department. As the technology improved, coupled with the immediate access to the databases, the operation's units determined it more effective to link PCs together by networking, which added only insignificantly to the cost. The increased dependence on the information availability increased the participation by business in PC expansion.

The PC began competing with large mainframes. Vendor advertising started focusing on independent work groups, shared database information, and reduced mainframe requirements. The nature of business dramatically changed, and organizations left it to their staff to establish the business rules for systems operation. For their part, most business leaders did not understand the technology, but knew they required information for planning purposes.

Increases in technology met the demands, but the costs were not inexpensive. The increase in local and wide area networks, outdated PCs, and system caretakers began to have an effect on the system budget estimates. Costs to achieve the type and frequency of database information quickly matched, and in some cases, exceeded the costs of the mainframe. In some cases, extensive systems were installed — after poor planning — that did not function as expected or did not provide the database information required. Once a business has changed the processing environment, it is very expensive to switch back.

INTERNET ACCESS

The newest factor to affect the database environment is the Internet, a means of access to even more information. The Internet provides for information access on most subjects discussed by businesses today. Internet users can access and download a variety of information in formats that can provide supplemental links to their existing databases. The primary impact on the business systems will come from the increased requirements for data storage. Additionally, the Internet affects security because of the increase in overall business communications with outside sources; the possibility of virus transfers poses risks, as do outside sources, which could gain access to company information though the Internet gateway. Once any access between two systems is allowed, there is always the risk of someone gaining database information from the user.

The Internet itself cannot exceed an organization's system capacity, as it is merely the link between multiple systems. The individual user could, however, exceed his or her capacity by downloading too much information. Novice Internet users may not even realize the volume of data being received or consciously think of the impact to the system. The PC, as the window to the Internet, may quickly exceed its capacity. Most information systems staffs typically do not allow a user to download to the server or core database areas. Based on historical approaches, it seems likely that business will tap into the information highway to gain access to more data to guide business decisions. The database information gathered and presented with the goal of increased profitability will continue to focus business direction.

CONCLUSION

The evolution from the mainframe to network environment has altered the way organizations do their business. The need for information to place a business strategically in the forefront will continue to increase, and the database is the mainstay of business information.

Data control is the most essential element for successful database maintenance. It is the responsibility of the end user, whether in the network or mainframe environment, to ensure that the proper controls are established for data handling. The controls, previously within the mainframe environment, are a good foundation for the personal computer to build upon. Data redundancy causes the database to grow out of control and become inaccessible by users. The trail of the information available is often lost. The multiplicity factors, coupled with no clear lines of database responsibility, reduce the overall effectiveness of the database.

A business cannot survive with inaccurate or incomplete database information. Decisions made today by businesses for direction tomorrow are often made based on the database information at hand. Unreliable information, acted upon by a business, can cause the business to fail. It is critical for the process controls to be in place to ensure database integrity. Maintaining the most current database information is the responsibility of the user community. This includes the purging of outdated information so it cannot be inadvertently used to make decisions.

The distribution of the database information throughout the organization is necessary to increase efficiency. Again, however, the process controls need to be in place, documented, and adhered to by the user community as a corporate policy. To help ensure that the end user appreciates the serious nature of the proper care and handling of the database, companies need to establish policies reflecting their concern.

Today's end users are much more experienced than their predecessors. Their expertise is limited to their knowledge of the software applications currently in vogue. Their ability to effectively communicate with other users, system support staff, and the business's strategic planners is required. This effective communication, however, works in all directions. It is just as important for the information-systems staff to communicate their needs, as it is for the strategic direction of the business to be known and understood by those developing the databases. Valid database information is very profitable to an organization. The access to the database information by the end user is proper when based on their level of system expertise and proper use of their rights to access it. The volume of information available is useful only if it is incorporated in a logical manner. The need for the user to maintain clean database environments is necessary.

Data storage is very expensive for an organization. The plan for what data is stored, where it is stored, and how it is accessed should reduce the cost for the storage. Planning the database environment includes considering its security, volume, and growth. The plan should cover the individual requirements of each organization, rather than be dependent upon the current trends.

Mainframe procedural controls for a database and an effective communication method within the organization are the two areas where networks and mainframes can, and must, come together for overall database integrity. Without stringent process controls, the integrity of the database information can be likened to the threat upon the blood supply when AIDS was identified. The problem exists and is recognized by many, but the solution is difficult to implement.

Chapter 15
The Data Center Manager's Guide to Networked Imaging Systems

Nathan J. Muller

COMPUTERIZED DOCUMENT IMAGING SYSTEMS allow businesses and government agencies to automate paper-based workflow processes by scanning documents into digital form and storing them in massive image databases for instant access. When implemented over a LAN storing documents on an image server can solve many of the problems commonly experienced with paper files, including that of multiple access. The digitized document images can be retrieved and processed in sequence by multiple workstation operators, until the entire transaction is complete.

The automation of document workflow can be compared to an assembly line whereby repetitive, paper-intensive tasks are performed at image-enabled workstations. There, resource allocation can be monitored and productivity improved through automatic document distribution and routing. Special workflow management software controls the flow of documents from station to station, typically eliminating many intervening document processing stages and streamlining others. Some imaging systems even allow the documents to be updated by different users, whereupon the updated document is filed in order of last update first. That way, a complete history can be maintained in an electronic case file.

When the WAN is used to connect geographically separate LANs, the benefits of imaging can be extended throughout the entire enterprise. The size of image files versus other types of traffic normally traversing LANs and WANs, however, can affect existing networks in terms of slowing access and response time unless such networks are upgraded or optimized to handle the increased load.

A full-time image application involving document scanning and distribution, file retrieval and annotation, and case file assembly and transfer, can easily dominate a LAN and possibly overwhelm it. For this reason, many companies will need to modify their networks to accommodate imaging applications.

Network upgrades can be accomplished in a number of ways, including the addition of higher performance equipment and transmission media to build higher-speed backbone networks, the use of file compression and forms reduction software, or subscription to carrier-provided digital services. Understanding the impact of imaging on existing networks and carefully evaluating the available alternatives will permit maximum levels of efficiency and economy to result from the imaging application, while ensuring the highest levels of availability and performance for the entire corporate network.

PROCESSING REQUIREMENTS

The success of document imaging often hinges on how well the system's implementors understand business processes and workflows. For them, the most obvious task is to learn how employees execute their responsibilities and to solicit employee input on how things can be improved. The participants should settle procedural problems early so that workflows can be properly scripted for automation and documents routed to the appropriate workstation operators. Mapping existing departmental procedures usually reveals processes that duplicate effort, employees working at cross-purposes, and unnecessary paperwork and filing requirements.

The key planning undertaking is an evaluation of document processing needs. At minimum, this should include the following:

- Listing all documents that are currently being processed in the course of business.
- Determining how many of each type of document arrive at each business location daily, weekly, monthly, and yearly.
- Finding out who provides the data in the documents, the purpose of the data, and what information systems or applications currently use the data provided in the documents.
- Establishing which information in each document is most frequently used.
- Determining appropriate index fields for each type of document.
- Preparing a flowchart for each type of document that shows the path it follows when it is received in the office: the stops it makes, what happens at each stop, and what alternative paths exist.

Company structures adapt to changing customer needs and market directions. Imaging tasks, to be implemented effectively, should be critiqued against the same standards. Automating an inefficient process only wastes corporate resources. The best applications for imaging technology are:

- Those whose contribution to the company's core business function is widely understood and those whose need for improved quality and timeliness is readily apparent.
- Those whose workflows involve repetitive tasks, which lend themselves to automation.
- Those in which the time spent in paper handling can be dramatically reduced.
- Those for which a significant positive return on investment is likely.
- Those in which early implementation mistakes will not jeopardize mission-critical functions and place the company at risk.

Merely overlaying imaging technology on an existing workflow will almost always produce the smallest benefit. There are several levels of technology implementation that merit consideration, categorized by increasing levels of process reorganization:

- *Pilot projects.* These are created for limited use at one location. Instead of fostering commitment, they often promote a wait-and-see attitude that more often than not guarantees failure.
- *Internal integration.* Using imaging to transfer information between processes may yield significant benefits. If existing processes are not made more efficient first, long-term gains will be limited and return on investment prolonged.
- *Process redesign.* An entire organization or discrete departmental process can be restructured to take advantage of imaging technology. Although this method can produce noteworthy improvements in efficiency, it can also be difficult and time-consuming to execute.
- *Network engineering.* Extends the reorganization process to locations outside the company's main location. This method can produce enterprisewide benefits, but is more difficult to implement.

To properly implement a technology at the right level of process reorganization requires that companies strive to understand their business processes, which is not as easy as it sounds because it involves a commitment of staff, effort, and time. If many corporate managers have a stake in preserving the status quo, this complicates matters. Having an outside consultant evaluate various business processes and workflows may render a more objective and accurate assessment. This, in turn, helps ensure that the investment in corporate resources can be targeted wisely. Internal evaluations of business processes and workflows can be performed, with third-party assistance or third-party review to validate, or invalidate, the conclusions. The high cost of imaging system implementation justifies these extended measures.

LAN CONSIDERATIONS

The most popular LAN types are Ethernet and Token-Ring, and although most companies already have LANs by the time they are ready to add image applications, they often have a choice between Ethernet and Token-Ring because both are available among various workgroups and departments. The question is not which LAN to build, but which one to extend to accommodate the imaging application. Additionally, there are several standards to choose from when building high-speed backbones that are used to interconnect multiple LANs or high-performance workstations, or both. These standards include FDDI 100Base-T Fast Ethernet, and VG-AnyLAN — all of which offer a data rate of 100M bps.

Depending on the existing traffic load, adding an imaging application may require the legacy LAN to be reconfigured or upgraded to maintain an acceptable level of performance for all the applications. If the imaging application involves continuous use of the LAN for large files, a dedicated LAN may be required. Alternatively, the workgroup running image applications may be partitioned from the rest of the LAN, so as not to affect the performance of other applications.

Ethernet

If the bus network remains fairly static, traffic is uniform over time, and users can tolerate some delay from retransmissions caused by collisions, an existing Ethernet may be an economical choice for supporting imaging applications. Networks have a tendency to grow, however, as organizational needs become more varied and sophisticated. As the number of workstations increases and the volume of traffic grows on the Ethernet, so does the possibility of collisions, which slow down the network with retransmission attempts.

Performance Tuning. Using LAN management systems, analysis tools, and utilities, the network manager can accurately measure performance and take immediate steps to make improvements, such as segmenting the network into subnets, caching images, using file compression, and adding higher-performance peripherals. Since performance demands may vary on a daily basis, the ability to respond quickly constitutes a key benefit of LAN-based imaging systems over mainframe-based systems.

Performance on the main imaging network can be maintained by putting resource-intensive services, such as scanning, printing, and faxing, on sub-networks. These subnets can be selectively isolated from the rest of the network using bridges or routers. This allows a large accounts-payable department, for example, to scan 10,000 invoices a day without bogging down the main network where users are trying to retrieve data. Scanned images are stored on disk and registered in the image system index using a batch process. Similarly, when a large image print job is scheduled, the data can be dumped off to a subnet for printing, instead of tying up the main network.

For those who want to integrate standard data and images on the same Ethernet, there are several issues that must be addressed: among them, packet size. The maximum packet size for the IEEE 802.3 standard is about 1500 bytes. Larger packet sizes allow an 802.3 network to approach the theoretical maximum throughput of the network, which is 10M bps. This is because larger packet sizes decrease the likelihood of information-destroying packet collisions.

It is possible to implement networks with packet sizes that exceed the 802.3 standard to improve LAN performance during image transfers. Implementing non-standard packet sizes has several implications, however. Larger packet sizes violate the 802.3 standard, so steps must be taken to ensure that this violation does not negatively affect network hardware and software designed to the standard. This can be accomplished by ensuring that network interface boards on all network stations have enough buffer memory to support nonstandard packets. Such interface boards are usually more expensive, however. If adjacent networks are not configured to support larger packet sizes, internetworking can become more complex. This is because a packet-restructuring function must exist at network interface points and, due to the increased processing that must be done, network performance may degrade.

Shared vs. Dedicated Networks. Image planning becomes quite difficult when there are other types of data flowing on the network, so it becomes necessary to consider whether a dedicated imaging network or a shared network is better. The main issues are the predictability of the traffic pattern and the performance required. Transmitting mixed data types across a network does not necessarily cause problems. If, however, problems occur, performance optimization becomes a requirement, and this may entail compromises that affect all users.

Although due consideration should be given to all users in the mixed-usage network, image-intensive production environments, such as an insurance claims-processing application, are likely to require dedicated networks. In these instances, network parameters can be more easily tuned to optimize performance for predictable traffic patterns. To be on the safe side, a pilot image network can be segmented from the production network to test all of the assumptions about LAN performance under varying load conditions.

The Impact of Protocols. Protocols, too, have an impact on LAN performance. Deterministic protocols, characteristic of Token-Ring, provide a more predictable worst-case response time if many stations have information to send. In low-traffic situations, however, deterministic protocols also impart a fixed-delay overhead. Contention media-access protocols, characteristic of Ethernet, provide immediate access to the transmission medium when there are few stations with information to send, or when a station infrequently sends information. The performance of a contention medium-access protocol degrades significantly if there are many stations attempting to generate traffic at the same time.

If delay proves to be a persistent problem, consideration should be given to putting the image application on its own LAN. This can be accomplished very economically over the same type of unshielded twisted-pair that already connects telephones to the corporate PBX. Enough excess wiring exists in most offices so that usually no additional installation is required. The reliability of telephone wire for LANs has been improved with the adoption of the 10Base-T standard.

Among the advantages of 10Base-T is that it does not require existing Ethernet installations to be retrofitted with special adapters at the wall and wire closet; it works with standard IEEE 802.3 Ethernet interfaces and the eight-pin modular jacks typically found on most business telephones. Centralized 10Base-T hubs can be created to compress and route image traffic, provide network management capabilities, and provide access to the WAN via optional bridge router modules.

Token-Ring

Among the advantages of Token-Ring over Ethernet for imaging applications is that access is not contention-based, but is deterministic, meaning that each station has, in turn, guaranteed access to the ring network. Therefore, a higher throughput rate is possible on the Token-Ring in heavily loaded situations, even when image transfers are factored into the equation.

Overall, Token-Ring has a lot to recommend it for image applications. At 16M bps, it exceeds Ethernet performance by 63 percent and overcomes the distance limitations of Ethernet, about 2.5 miles, through token regeneration at each station. Unlike Ethernet, Token-Ring provides every station with guaranteed access to the network instead of making each station wait for access until the network is idle, as in Ethernet. Token-Ring traffic can even be ranked according to priority, so that workstations can swap document images, for example, before other types of applications can use the network.

Fiber Distributed Data Interface

Legacy LANs may not have enough bandwidth capacity and growth potential to meet an organization's long-term imaging needs, especially with the addition of image applications. FDDI is a 100M bps fiber optic LAN that addresses the bandwidth distance, and fault-recovery issues that limit conventional LANs. FDDI provides the needed capacity and added throughput by a deterministic token-passing access method, which makes for a high level of network availability.

FDDI uses a timed token-passing access protocol for passing frame as large as 4500 bytes. The standard permits support of up to 1000 connections over a fiber path of 200 km in length. Each station regenerates and repeats frames sent to it, which also serves as the means for identifying newly attached devices on the network. FDDI includes built-in management capabilities that detect failures and reconfigure the network automatically.

Although FDDI boards for connecting microcomputer and workstations to the backbone have been available for several years, they are still too expensive to allow most organizations to exploit FDDI fully as a super Token-Ring LAN. Currently, the most economical use of FDDI is as a backbone between hubs through which LANs may be interconnected in a campus environment.

100Base-T Fast Ethernet

100Base-T is a 100M bps version of 10Base-T, the dominant LAN technology in the industry. It provides ten times the performance of 10Base-T for less than twice the price. Like 10Base-T, 100Base-T is being standardized by the IEEE 802.3 committee, the group responsible for all Ethernet standards. 100Base-T uses the same media access-control method, contention with collision detection, that is used on all Ethernet products.

In addition, Fast Ethernet allows the use of the same unshielded twisted-pair wiring that is already installed for 10Base-T networks and is implemented using the same star topology as a 10Base-T network. This allows Fast Ethernet to leverage proven Ethernet technology, as well as the existing base of Ethernet hardware and software products. Many hub vendors support both 100Base-T and 10Base-T, providing users with a smooth migration path to higher-speed networking in accordance with application needs.

One difference between Ethernet and Fast Ethernet is that the maximum network diameter of a 100M bps Fast Ethernet network is roughly 210 meters, whereas the maximum network diameter in a 10M bps Ethernet network can be up to 500 meters. This may appear to be somewhat restrictive. However, distance is rarely a limiting factor in today's collapsed backbone networks implemented by intelligent wiring hubs, with interconnections accomplished by bridges and routers. This makes Fast Ethernet easy to implement for large-scale enterprise networks in support of heavy-duty imaging applications.

VG-AnyLAN

The other 100M bps standard is 100VG-AnyLAN. Like 100Base-T, 100VG-AnyLAN uses the Ethernet-frame format, which means that compatibility between 10M bps and 100M bps networks can be achieved with a speed-matching bridge between the networks. The key difference between the two 100M bps networks is that Fast Ethernet preserves Ethernet's CSMA/CD mechanism, whereas VG-AnyLAN dispenses with it entirely. In using a collisionless access method, VG-AnyLAN is able to consistently deliver 95 percent of the available bandwidth to users, assuming a large packet size. The collisionless protocol ensures fairness by not permitting bandwidth hogging and offers strong performance in very heavy loading situations, making it very suitable for document imaging.

100VG-AnyLAN supports a variety of media, including four-pair category 3, 4, and 5 cable. It can support a mix of voice and data on each pair. VG-AnyLAN also supports two-pair shielded twisted-pair and optical fiber. VG-AnyLAN provides more robust signaling than 100Base-T, making it virtually insensitive to cable quality. These characteristics make VG-AnyLAN worthy of consideration for upgrading legacy LANs for document image transfers.

Asynchronous Transfer Mode

With document imaging and multimedia applications consuming an ever-larger portion of the available bandwidth on legacy LANs, the performance of all applications diminishes accordingly. ATM technology promises to address this and other problems by providing:

- *Increased bandwidth.* ATM goes considerably beyond the 10M bps and 16M bps offered by legacy Ethernet and Token-Ring LANs. To date, there are ATM standards for transmission at 25M bps, 52M bps, 100M bps, 155M bps, and 622M bps.
- *Low delay.* Because ATM uses very short fixed-length packets that can be switched in hardware (instead of software), there is very little delay in transmission.
- *Improved network availability.* With ATM's increased bandwidth and low delay, the network is always available to run applications on demand. Control mechanisms at various levels in the network ensure that congestion does not become a problem.
- *Scalability.* ATM is easily scalable, meaning that the amount of bandwidth can be tailored to the needs of expanding application complexity and faster host processors without adversely impacting the performance of other applications and hosts on the network.
- *Overcoming limits on cable length.* ATM overcomes the distance limitations of Ethernet and Token-Ring. In fact, there is no practical limit on the distance of ATM transmission links.

For these reasons, ATM may emerge as the technology of choice for LAN backbones in the not-too-distant future. Both 100Base-T and 100VG-Any-LAN offer a migration path to ATM. In addition, ATM is also used on the WAN, so LANs can be seamlessly internetworked over great distances. The problem with ATM, however, is that a totally new infrastructure must be overlayed onto the existing network. This is still too expensive for most companies, as well as for the carriers.

Wireless Transmission

To convey document images between buildings, laser-optic infrared technology can be used to connect Ethernet or Token-Ring segments in each building, when laying fiber lines or leasing private lines is impractical due to cost or physical barriers. The wireless transceivers attach to a hub, switch, or router at one building and transmit the document images to a similar setup at a second building.

The wireless link derives its speed from the device to which the infrared transceivers are connected. An ATM switching hub, for example, could transmit data at 155M bps. The distance between the transceivers varies according to the data rate. When running at standard Token-Ring or Ethernet speeds, for example, the transceivers can be spaced about 3300 feet apart. When attached to an ATM hub running at 155M bps, the transceivers can be only 900 feet apart.

Normally, laser-optic transmission is subject to signal interference from environmental factors. Vendors are employing new techniques, such as using a wider transmitting beam and a larger receiving lens, to provide more immunity to signal interference, which results in more reliable transmission. To gain this increased reliability, however, users of these products must be prepared to sacrifice transmission distance, which is usually limited to 1000 feet.

STORAGE CONSIDERATIONS

After documents have been scanned and indexed, they must be moved to a storage facility, where they can be retrieved as needed by multiple users. Image files must be moved from the scanning station's own hard disk to a server on the network, where higher-capacity magnetic or optical storage is available. In a small office, the "server" may be just another PC or workstation configured with a high-capacity hard disk. In a large IBM host-based environment, however, this arrangement may be inadequate, and DASD would be used instead. For longer-term storage, there are several optical disk types, including WORM drives, and equipment configurations to choose from, as well as tape drive and library systems.

Optimization Techniques

Although the source of performance bottlenecks can be any one of the many system components, in an imaging system, the I/O devices are usually the culprits. Of these, an optical disk jukebox's robotics and disk spin-up and spin-down time can constitute a serious bottleneck. The situation worsens when a few large documents, stored across multiple optical platters, are requested at the same time.

There are several ways to alleviate this type of problem. The first entails prefetching the images through workflow software. This allows the system to batch-retrieve images overnight, when the system is used the least. The images are moved from the server's optical media, where images are permanently stored, to local magnetic media, which provides a faster access time for workflow operations. Cache is implemented based on an understanding of which images are likely to be required next. This technique is effective in workflow applications, where there are queues of images to be worked on. The vendors' storage-management utilities are used to implement image caching.

A second solution is to employ an optical-storage manager that writes all the images that belong to one folder to a single optical disk. This prevents the folder from being fragmented over multiple optical disks, in case it grows.

Another method is to implement a hierarchical data-storage scheme. This involves understanding the use and life cycle of a document. When a document is in the active part of its life cycle, for example, it is stored on magnetic storage, which has fast retrieval capabilities. When the document becomes inactive, it should be automatically moved to optical media in a jukebox. When the document is archived, it should be moved to an archive medium, such as helical scan tape. A document should be able to move back and forth through this hierarchy.

The Role of Data Compression

Image documents are much larger than ordinary text or binary files, so most vendors' imaging systems support one or more compression schemes, including their own proprietary method. Compression allows images to be stored on the PC's hard drive until the increasing volume justifies moving to more expensive optical WORM units or tape storage systems. Compression ratios of 25:1 are common for most types of document images. For graphics and photos, the compression ratios are as high as 50:1 without a noticeable loss of image quality. The latest algorithms promise compression ratios of up to 300:1.

Compression is typically a function of software, which is usually bundled with the imaging software. Compression may also involve the addition of a compression board to offload the extra processing from the workstation's main CPU and provide a substantial performance boost. Document images and text are stored in compressed form and transparently restored when accessed. A service is said to be "transparent" when it is provided without an explicit request from the user, operating in the background and having no noticeable effect on the requesting program or any other application, including the operating system.

Compression typically works as follows:

- The data is examined to identify patterns.
- To each identified pattern, a unique code is assigned, which consists of significantly fewer bytes.
- The unique codes are substituted for the corresponding patterns.
- The data is then stored in its new format.
- Upon retrieval, the encoded data is replaced with the original strings of data, completely restoring the image.

A process called forms removal can improve compression ratios, no matter which algorithm is used. When scanning forms, the data, rather than the form itself, is important. In eliminating the repetitive forms and saving only the data, compression ratios can be vastly improved.

A dental claim form, for example, scanned at 300 dots per inch (dpi) and compressed according to the international Group 4 standard, typically uses 73K bytes of disk storage. When the form is removed, the same image file occupies only 13K bytes in compressed form. When the form is called up for display on a workstation monitor, the data is overlayed on an image of an empty form. The file containing the empty form can be stored locally, while the data can be retrieved from a database server.

WAN CONSIDERATIONS

To transfer image files to remote corporate locations, carrier-provided services or private backbone facilities can be used to interconnect LANs. However, because of the huge size of image files and the need to support myriad other applications, not just any carrier service or backbone facility will do, even if the image files are compressed before transmission.

Dialup and Analog Leased Lines

For occasional image transfers to remote locations, modems operating at up to 28.8K bps over dialup or leased analog transmission lines may suffice. However, if image transfers are frequent or continuous, the use of analog lines, dialup or leased, is fraught with problems. In addition to creating intolerable transmission bottlenecks, analog lines are commonly affected by voice frequency impairments that can corrupt data. This means modem transmissions can fall back to 14.4K bps or lower until line quality improves, or the connection can drop altogether, forcing a new connection to be established and the imaged documents to be retransmitted.

To minimize the effects of line impairments on analog leased lines, extra-cost line conditioning may be requested from the carrier. No performance guarantees come with line conditioning, however; the carrier promises higher quality lines on a best-effort basis. The low-speed and uncertain line quality of dialup and analog leased lines renders them unreliable for carrying any type of LAN traffic, let alone image traffic.

Packet Switched Services

Packet switched networks thrived in the 1970s and 1980s as a way for asynchronous terminals to access remote computers over noisy dialup and analog leased lines. The driving force behind the acceptance of packet switching networks was the adoption of the international X.25 standard. However, carrier-provided packet data services based on the X.25 standard have been limited to 56K bps, mostly because of the X.25 protocol's overhead burden that, among other things, provides error checking and correction at every network node to ensure error-free transmission.

If a receiving node detects a transmission error, it requests a retransmission from the sending node. While this is valuable for point-of-sale applications requiring the accurate transmission of credit card and other financial information, it is a cumbersome and unnecessary process when image traffic is concerned, especially when large image files are being transferred. Consideration must, therefore, be given to more reliable digital services, starting with Digital Data Services (DDS).

Digital Data Services

DDS offers a range of speeds, from 2.4K bps to 56K bps. DDS does not require a modem, but requires a digital termination device called a Digital Service Unit. The appeal of DDS for data is the higher quality of digital vs. analog transmission. At one time, DDS at 56K bps was considered a good way to connect LANs via remote bridges. Today, the 56K bps line rate is viewed as a bottleneck to LANs that operate from 10M bps to 16M bps.

Fractional T1

FT1 entails the provision and use of bandwidth in 56/64K bps increments without paying for an entire T1 facility. FT1 allows users to order only the amount of bandwidth needed to support the image application. This saves the user the expense of leasing a full T1 line for partial use, while easing the WAN bottleneck between LANs, which is a problem with DDS and X.25 at 56K bps. FT1 is widely available among local and interexchange carriers, so there is less of a back-haul problem to contend with, as in DDS, and because it is derived from a T1 facility, FT1 offers high reliability and availability.

To avoid the cost of leased lines when the amount of image traffic is relatively low, an inverse multiplexer or bandwidth controller can be used to dial up as many 56/64K bps channels as needed. The inverse multiplexer aggregates multiple channels to achieve a single higher-speed channel. Upon completion of the transmission, the channels are taken down. Instead of incurring a fixed monthly charge for an underutilized leased line, the user is billed for the dialup channels on a usage basis, which can be more economical.

Integrated Services Digital Network

Primary rate ISDN (23B+D) is another wide-area internetworking option that may be used to support image applications. ISDN is a carrier-provided switched digital service that is billed for on a time-and-distance basis, just like an ordinary phone call. ISDN channels are available in bandwidth increments of 56/64K bps, 384K bps, and 1.536M bps.

The billing method is both an advantage and a liability, depending on how many hours a month the ISDN channels are used to support the image application. When used continuously, ISDN channels in the U.S. are considerably more expensive than using the bandwidth equivalents offered over dedicated leased lines (FT1/T1), which entail fixed monthly charges determined by distance, no matter how long the line is used. However, if the ISDN channels are used only 20 hours a month for image transfers, ISDN can be more economical than paying for full-time leased lines.

Dedicated T1 Lines

T1 digital lines are an ideal medium for interconnecting LANs from point to point, especially LANs carrying high-volume image traffic. They offer excellent reliability and availability, in addition to high capacity. An increasing number of bridges and routers offer T1 interfaces to facilitate LAN-to-WAN connectivity.

With imaging applications already putting a strain on today's Ethernet and Token-Ring LANs, however, running image applications over T1 lines may not be an adequate long-term strategy. Complementary LAN interconnection strategies may be called for, such as frame relay, which make more efficient use of the available bandwidth.

Frame Relay

To prevent the network from becoming the bottleneck, it is advisable to avoid protocols that feature a high degree of error-checking overhead and acknowledgments and instead seek protocols that feature no acknowledgments at all, or offer multiple-packet receipt acknowledgment. Of the former, frame relay is a good example.

The technical concept behind frame relay is simple: to eliminate protocol overhead and unnecessary processing to speed up network throughput. Error correction and flow control already exist at the upper layers of most modern computer communication protocol stacks, and thus may be relegated to the "edges" of the network rather than performed at every node within the network, as in X.25. Frame relay eliminates 75 percent of the protocol overhead of X.25, including error correction.

Because frame relay operates over high-quality digital facilities, there is no need for error correction. This function can be relegated to customer-premises equipment. Frame relay also offers greater efficiency, since an application can momentarily seize the entire amount of allocated bandwidth to transmit information in bursts. Upon completion of a duty cycle, it relinquishes the bandwidth to other applications.

T3 Services

T3 service is typically offered over fiber facilities. The applications touted by T3 advocates include LAN interconnection, multiple T1 line replacement, and high-speed backbones that integrate voice, data, video, and image traffic.

T3 service entails special construction of access lines from the customer's premises to the carrier's serving office. Special construction costs at each end differ widely from region to region, from a low of approximately $8000 to a high of approximately $150,000. These costs are almost never factored into the crossover comparisons with T1, so the true cost of T3 makes it difficult for even the largest companies to justify.

In the absence of optical standards for T3, proprietary interfaces have proliferated which, in turn, restrict the ability of users to mix and match different manufacturers' equipment end-to-end. T3 services, such as AT&T's T45, require the customer to negotiate the type of optical interfaces to be placed in the various serving offices of the interexchange carriers.

Some carriers are capitalizing on the appeal of Fractional T1 by extending the "fractional" concept to T3. Under this concept, the user can order bandwidth in T1 increments up to the full T3 rate of 44.736M bps. This service is designed for users who need more than the 1.544M bps offered by T1, but less than the full bandwidth offered by T3, to support the interconnection of Token-Ring or Ethernet LANs carrying image traffic. A bridge is used to connect each LAN to the public network. From the user's point of view, the public network appears as an extension of the LAN.

Current FT3 offerings are not intended as a migration path to more advanced broadband services, such as Broadband ISDN, which will be based on Synchronous Optical Network (SONET) and Asynchronous Transfer Mode (ATM) technologies.

Switched Multimegabit Data Service (SMDS)

SMDS ultimately may offer a better solution than frame relay for linking LANs in a metropolitan area so that corporate locations can share image files. SMDS is a high-speed data service, offering customers the economic benefits of shared transmission facilities, combined with the equivalent privacy and control of dedicated networks.

Access to SMDS is provided via dedicated lines. On each access line, the required customer-premises equipment consists of a router with an SMDS interface and a CSU/DSU (channel service unit/data service unit) with an SMDS interface. A DXI provides standardized connectivity between the two devices, while a LMI permits the CSU/DSU to pass performance information to the router so it can be sent to a SNMP-based management workstation.

Carrier-Based ATM Services

Only a handful of carriers offer ATM services. The carriers that do, provide only PVC. These are ATM connections that are set up between a sending and receiving station on the network. They are set up by a network administrator and remain up until torn down manually. Another type of ATM connection, which will be offered in the future, is called the Switched Virtual Circuit. This type of connection is set up and torn down by the ATM network on demand without manual intervention.

PVC connections are more reliable for certain types of applications, such as document imaging, whereas SVC connections are intended for routine types of applications. SVCs can time out and tear down after a brief period without traffic between resources. When a replacement connection is requested, the network may not be able to provide the same guaranteed bandwidth it had previously allocated to that application. PVCs stay in place, even if there is no traffic for a prolonged period of time.

SUPPORT ISSUES

A variety of support issues deserve attention with a LAN-based document imaging system. Among them are systems reliability, systems integration, and training.

System Reliability

When documents critical to a business's operation are committed to imaging technology, the systems and networks involved must be reliable and stable. Specifically, these systems and the networks they run on must be protected against failure. The possible solutions include, but are not limited to:

- Uninterruptible Power Supply.
- Redundant components and subsystems.
- Alternate WAN routes between corporate locations and bypass circuitry between LAN hubs and major subsystems.
- Arrangements for local service and support from vendors to minimize system downtime.

A determination must be made as to what protective measures are already available and to what extent they can be applied to the imaging system. If new protective measures are needed, such considerations must be entered into the planning process and factored into the purchase price of the imaging system.

Systems Integration

When an imaging system is being designed from scratch and is composed of products from different vendors, the task becomes one of tying together these diverse elements to provide users with transparent access to every other element on the network. Only rarely do in-house staff have the expertise to accomplish this alone. Systems integrators can help.

A systems integrator's qualifications can include the following:

- Specialized industry knowledge, awareness of technology trends, and experiences gained from a broad customer base.
- Knowledge of specific protocols, interfaces, and cabling requirements.
- A reputation for fast, high-quality work.
- The ability to train existing systems staff to take over responsibility for ongoing management, administration, and control.
- The need for an outside party to act as a catalyst in implementing change and to validate (or fine tune) in-house plans.

Integration firms provide several services, some of which are listed here. No single firm can provide all of these services, which is why they frequently form working partnerships to propose a total solution. In-house data center professionals may also have experience in one or more of these areas:

- *Design and development.* This area includes such activities as network design; facilities engineering; equipment installation and customization; hardware, software, network integration; acceptance testing; and network management.
- *Consulting.* This area includes business planning; systems and network architecture; technology assessment; feasibility studies; request-for-proposal development; vendor evaluation and product

selection; quality assurance; security auditing; disaster recovery planning; and project management.

- *Systems implementation.* This area includes procurement, documentation, configuration management, contract management, and program management.
- *Facilities management.* This area includes operations, technical support, hot-line services, change management, and trouble-ticket administration.
- *Systems reengineering.* This area includes maintenance; systems and network optimization; remote monitoring and diagnostics; and the application of automated design tools.
- *Training.* This area includes hands-on user training; technical and management courses; executive briefings; and seminars that address industry trends.

Training

A LAN-based imaging system can be quite complex, especially when configured for workflow applications; therefore, extensive operator and supervisor training may be required. A reputable imaging system vendor will offer a full line of instruction about its products and technology and offer dedicated training staff and facilities.

Many times, formal classroom training at the vendor's facilities is not sufficient, especially if the imaging system requires a high degree of customization. In this case, the vendor or systems integrator should be willing and capable of offering on-site training at the customer's location. During the planning phases, extra costs, if any, of additional training for new employees hired after the original training period, as well as the cost of follow-up training to fine tune user skills, should be identified.

It is always a good idea to ask about the experience and qualifications of the trainers. The vendor should not simply send technicians to provide training; generally, technicians lack a user's point of view and do not always make effective instructors, unless they have been specifically trained for that responsibility.

The nature and scope of training can usually be ascertained by reviewing copies of the training materials before committing to a specific imaging system vendor. The materials should provide clear and comprehensive learning objectives supported by well-organized lesson structures and descriptions which can be used as reference material after the training sessions. If the vendor does not provide this kind of depth in its training package, the customer may be getting less out of the capital investment than anticipated at the time of purchase.

CONCLUSION

Despite the large investments companies have made in office technologies over the years, productivity gains have been hampered by the huge quantity of paper these technologies have tended to produce. Now that LAN-based imaging has arrived to address the problems of paper overload and workflow, planning and implementing such systems can provide significant opportunities for reengineering work processes and streamlining management structures within organizations.

With proper planning, the benefits of implementing LAN-based imaging systems include better document control, faster retrieval of vital information, and multiuser access. These benefits can improve the quality and timeliness of customer service, a strategic goal in many businesses, and are likely to have a substantial impact on the data center. Data center managers can benefit themselves and their companies by applying their experience and expertise to helping departmental managers in evaluating, planning for, and implementing this relatively new technology.

Chapter 16
Collaborative Applications

S. Ann Earon

COLLABORATION MEANS WORKING TOGETHER. In the context of networks and remote workers, it means almost anything from e-mail to groupware to real-time conferencing. Collaboration, as it relates to teleconferencing, refers to the combination of voice communications (point-to-point and multipoint) with PC-oriented graphics, document sharing, and data. The voice portion of the communication takes place over ordinary telephone lines (POTS), and the data portion may occur over a variety of networks such as LANS, WANS, ISDN, ATM, the Internet, and POTS. The result is an enhanced teleconference in which images are created, exchanged, shared, and discussed.

Group collaboration provides the ability for two or more individuals to gather around a virtual conference table to observe and work on documents, even though the individuals are at a distance. Regardless of geographic location or computer operating system, conference participants deploy an array of software- and hardware-based tools to simulate being together. Collaboration eases the burden of having to prepare documentation to be shared during a teleconference. Before collaboration, those sharing data needed to be concerned with font size, pagination, and the type of information being discussed to ensure that those at distant sites would be able to see the information clearly. Additionally, prior to a meeting, individuals had to exchange faxes, overnight materials, or send e-mail messages to communicate information they needed to share during the meeting. With the advent of collaborative conferencing, attendees can collect information, focus on issues, and store ideas and results as the meeting takes place.

BACKGROUND

Standards for collaborative conferencing (also known as data, document, and multimedia conferencing) are relatively new. The transmission protocols for multimedia data, also known as T.120, were approved by the ITU-T

0-8493-9824-X/00/$0.00+$.50
© 2000 by CRC Press LLC

(International Telecommunications Union's Telecommunications Standardization Sector), first quarter, 1996. The recommendation contains a conceptual description of the T.120 series of recommendations that define multipoint transport of multimedia data in a conferencing environment. The T.120 standard still is evolving, although manufacturers have developed interoperable products around elements of the recommendation that are complete. The ITU-T plans to extend the T.120 recommendation to include remote camera and microphone control, standardized reservation protocols, and management of the quality of service (QoS) delivered by transmission systems.

HOW COLLABORATION HAPPENS

Generally, work is accomplished with people talking about documents (proposals, contracts, spreadsheets, etc.). Although video has its place, the need to see someone throughout the work process is less important than the ability to interact with the person verbally while reviewing the supporting documentation. When someone makes a suggestion regarding a proposal or contract, all meeting attendees need to hear the person speaking and view the proposal or contract. Actually seeing the person making the proposal is less important than evaluating the issue and reaching a decision. For most meeting scenarios, the real value of collaboration is in audio and data interaction.

When only using audio, meeting participants at a distance cannot interact easily with the documents and presentations around which traditional meetings usually revolve. Although information can be faxed, mailed, or e-mailed ahead of time, there is no way to control the information that meeting participants are viewing. Nor can new visual information be introduced or interactive exchanges be captured. Participating in a collaborative conference solves the problem. Most users now have access to desktop computers equipped with Web browsers or to network connections and software packages that allow them to share files. With the advent of the Internet, engaging in collaborative conferences on an enterprise scale has become as simple as surfing the Web. Now users who want the convenience of managing both audio and data from their desktops can get quality connections by using a PC for data and a handset or headset for audio. By leveraging the Web browser as a user interface, users easily can tie realtime data collaboration with audio bridging for group meetings.

Here is how a collaborative conferencing session might work. The salesperson and the client talk on the telephone while simultaneously using a second telephone line to connect their personal computers. Both computers are equipped with communications software that understands T.120. The salesperson calls up a draft of a document from his hard drive. The first page of the document appears immediately on his screen and very quickly thereafter on the client's screen. Each user has control of a cursor and a keyboard. Thus, the salesperson could be changing $7,000 to $70,000 on the second line — with the change seen on both screens — while the client is correcting a misspelling on line 17. In effect, the document becomes a whiteboard with chalk and an eraser handed to each participant. While this is going on, the computer modems stay connected and the remaining ten pages of the document in discussion are sent unobtrusively between the computers. The document scrolls down instantaneously on both screens because the file is available in computer memory at both sites. Either participant can store the file on both hard drives.

A number of vendors are developing products to meet this need. Collaborative application examples include coordinating product development activities, managing product review sessions, conducting desktop-to-desktop corporate training, collaborating on medical cases, reviewing new applicant files, and discussing quarterly marketing and sales projections with field offices. Following are examples of collaborative applications that have benefited a variety of organizations in differing industries:

Collaborative Applications

An aerospace company has 75 percent of their work force located in the field. They use 1,200 subcontractor companies to build their products. They are using collaborative technology to share timely data in an engineering environment. Individuals and groups dial an audio call and make a separate computer data connection. Files and drawings are shared between sites with each site having annotation capability and the ability to print modifications. Using these collaborative tools has allowed projects to be completed in a much shorter timeframe, thus saving millions of dollars.

A financial institution is initiating a program to improve communication with 5,000 commercial customers. They are using collaborative software to share documents with their customers. Using the technology allows them to respond more quickly online without the need for fax, e-mail, or express mail. Customers are able to obtain immediate response to their requests and receive a printed document confirming their conversations. The financial institution is able to process requests more quickly, thus making better use of their funds.

A high-tech company with offices around the United States, serving clients in 42 countries, has found that the use of collaboration tools helps promote less costly sharing of information. The firm is a virtual organization where teams often are pulled together from different offices to engage in particular projects. Most conferees use collaboration for conventional activities, such as sharing images on electronic whiteboards. A few do more advanced collaboration, such as sharing a spreadsheet. All find the technology not only easy to use, but a time saver.

Another high-tech company has launched a virtual university to provide courses to their employees scattered around the globe. Students and teachers are joined together over the company's intranet and share documents and data via the intranet and voice via an audio bridge. The virtual university allows this firm to get to people in a timely basis without the typical costs associated with travel. The Internet is used for prerequisite work. Students download the information they need and work on it in their own time. Students are able to learn in bite-size modules and have the opportunity to apply what they learned before "returning to class." Students retain and record everything that is being done in the course of delivering the sessions.

A university is using collaboration tools to gather information for grant proposals. Everyone can work on the proposal together and download the final submission. Because universities often apply for grants right up to the deadline, the technology allows everyone, regardless of their location, to be involved up to the last minute.

Another university is using collaboration tools for continuing education and other programs where students are not always able to attend in person. In this way they are able to offer courses to students scattered across the country.

A secondary school finds collaboration allows students to participate in courses not offered in their local environment. In some instances, this can mean the difference between being able to take a particular course needed for graduation or having to travel to find the course elsewhere. Additionally, where face-to-face sessions may not have enough interested students to warrant offering a course, with collaboration tools, students can be scattered and get the information they need to fulfill a requirement.

SUMMARY

The development of collaborative applications is still in its infancy and is dependent on the evolution of standards, the development of applications, and a behavioral change in the way people work. It requires discipline to be involved in a collaborative meeting and not be interrupted by other activities or individuals who think users are just working on a personal computer. It requires a culture where management supports an environment of people working or taking courses without interruption.

User acceptance still is limited. People do not realize how much work can be done using collaboration tools online. Many are not used to audioconferencing and videoconferencing and have had minimal experience with dataconferencing, which in its basic form resembles chat. To many, chat has a reputation as a time waster, not a business tool.

Organizations still are trialing the use of collaborative applications. Widespread adoption is the exception rather than the rule. However, there are enough trials taking place to cause others to begin investigating what will prove to be a cost-effective and valuable communications tool.

If the market for collaborative communications is to develop, at least three elements must be in place:

1. A network infrastructure capable of handling multimedia communications;
2. Compelling applications accessible from the desktop, the conference room, the home, and the road; and
3. Open standards and interoperability to ensure compatibility and ease of use for the end user.

As these issues are resolved, collaborative applications will become the norm, rather than the exception.

In the future, the market for realtime collaboration will take on many innovative forms. Internet-based collaboration will continue to be an effective tool when tied to POTS audioconferencing. Additionally, a large number of Internet-based audio- and videoconferencing products will become available to end users. This will be especially true as bandwidth is increased within organizations and the power of intranets and the global Internet is realized.

Chapter 17
Supporting Legacy Systems
Nancy Blumenstalk Mingus

LEGACY SYSTEMS CONTINUE TO BE USED because they still add value to the business and because they are so expensive to replace. Yet staff members responsible for supporting and maintaining 10-to 20-year-old mission-critical systems may feel they are being denied a chance to acquire new skills. IS managers can protect staff morale in their departments by conveying the business reasons for using legacy systems to the staff assigned the job of maintaining and supporting them. This chapter outlines various ways to minimize apathy among support staff, with tips for helping maintenance employees keep the job fresh.

RECOGNIZING LEGACY SYSTEMS

Any of the following conditions may be true of a legacy system:

- It was programmed by someone who left the company 10 years ago.
- It was patched for Year 2000 compliance.
- It uses data base technology or a programming language rooted in the 1970s.
- It was translated from one language or operating system to another by an automated translating utility.
- It has been modified so many times, the code looks like spaghetti; there are pages of variable names that are never referenced and whole sections never executed.
- It is so old the source code is missing.

Although physical age and old technology are hallmarks of a legacy system, another equally important identifier is that a company still uses the system in production. If the system is a purchasing, order entry, inventory, human resources, or even an executive information system, odds are the company still trains or supports the user and maintains or enhances these systems even though they are past their prime.

Many companies call their older systems legacy systems. Legacy is a nicer name than dinosaur, though the idea is basically the same. More specifically, however, legacy systems are usually financial or human resources systems left over from the 1970s or 1980s. Most legacy systems are mainframe-based, but they need not be. A ten-year old dBASE II, Lotus 1-2-3, or client/server application can also be a legacy system, especially if the corporate standards for PC software packages, networks, or operating systems have changed.

Why Legacy Systems Linger On

These systems got to be legacy systems in a variety of ways. Here are just a few:

- They were state-of-the-art when implemented. Many of the systems still running today were ahead of their time when they were written. They used the latest technology, and in ways the product developers never intended.
- The systems were passed from person to person, until finally ending up with the one or two employees who know them now. Unfortunately, the documentation never made it past the third or fourth handoff.
- They were already Year 2000 compliant or have not yet been patched to be Year 2000 compliant.
- The systems continued to be patched instead of redesigned as corporate conditions changed.

Many systems that became legacy for these reasons continue to be used for similar reasons. The most common rationale is: if it's not broken, why fix it?

BUSINESS AND FINANCIAL REASONS

Even though code is patched, often several layers thick, the system continues to serve its function. A company may be leery about investing time in a redesign of something that still works. What companies often fail to realize, however, is that in many cases, when these systems do break, they might not be fixable. This is especially true of those systems with hard-coded date routines that will not be able to handle the Year 2000.

Another reason why these systems linger on is that they meet a need no preprogrammed package can meet, even today. Legacy systems are almost universally in-house written and fit the organization so well that no one wants to change procedures so they can upgrade the system.

In addition, other high-priority jobs continue to push legacy systems rewrites to the back burner. This reasoning ties in with the first one: as long as these systems continue to perform their function, a company may determine that it is better to invest in systems that can save money or make money.

Converting legacy systems to new technology is costly in terms of redesigning and recoding the software, as well as purchasing new hardware. Furthermore, current staff may not have the required skill sets for recoding the systems, so new controllers, mainframes generally used with the existing systems are paid for. Networks and PCs require additional capital.

The company's legacy systems were often the first automated systems, so they usually contain sensitive corporate financial, personnel, and product data. Some companies maintain that rewriting the systems could jeopardize data confidentiality and potentially affect data integrity and for this reason opt to keep their legacy systems.

OBJECTIVELY EVALUATING LEGACY SYSTEMS

Drawbacks of Legacy Maintenance

The drawbacks to maintaining existing systems are fairly obvious. IS professional confront them daily. Some of the major drawbacks are that:

- *Only a few people know the system, so they end up doing all the training, support, and maintenance.* This deprives the staff of time to learn new systems, which virtually every employee would rather be doing.
- *These systems were installed before data entry validity checks were popular, so bad data is often entered.* It takes extra support time to fix errors, extra maintenance time to fix the system, and extra training time to tell people how to enter data correctly. Furthermore, these systems are often used in departments with high turnover, which adds to the problem of training and support.
- *Training generally must be designed and delivered in-house.* Because the systems are not standard packages, there are no canned or vendor-delivered courses available. Even if they were generally written in a standard, supported product, the product may be so old that it is difficult to find anyone who teaches courses on it anymore.
- *Every time operating systems, file structures, or other support programs change, the existing systems might not work.* This often requires significant support time to get them running again, if they will run at all.
- *Systems are not Year 2000 compliant.* This means they need to be analyzed and updated.

Benefits of Legacy Maintenance

There are some benefits to providing quality training, support, and maintenance on existing systems. Among them:

- *Maintenance can add another five or more years to their life.* Although this strategy often makes the technology of the legacy system even further removed from state-of-the-art, it also buys time for the company as it makes plans to migrate to newer strategic systems and downsized platforms.
- *Proper maintenance minimizes system errors.* Because legacy systems are often complicated to use, it is easy to create errors and difficult to correct them. Proper training and support minimize the chance of operator error.
- *Unlike off-the-shelf PC or mainframe packages, legacy systems do not change significantly.* The benefit in this case is that there is no need to update training materials or support procedures every time the vendor introduces a change.

Minimizing Apathy Toward Legacy Systems

Burnout is probably the number-one problem where maintenance staff is concerned. IS managers attentive to the morale of their departments can encourage IS maintenance personnel to regain interest in their work in several ways.

Maintenance staff should be encouraged to dig through the fossil record. For example, one method is to allow the people responsible for legacy systems to investigate the history of the systems, to find out who wrote them, and what particular design or programming problems they overcame. This information can give the staff new respect for the systems. By compiling a list of the ages of the various production systems, the people charged with these systems may also be surprised to find that these systems are not as old as some others.

It helps to explain to staff members doing legacy maintenance assignments why the systems are still being used. There is a strong inclination to want to scrap systems simply because they are old. This thinking obscures the real reasons that management and users may be reluctant to bury their existing information systems. It also erodes the sense of purpose maintenance staff members need to remain motivated.

IS managers can take several measures to keep systems and their remaining business value in perspective. At the same time, these practices will help to minimize low morale among employees responsible for legacy systems maintenance.

Do not give responsibility for legacy systems as a punishment. If IS employees have had problems adjusting to new systems, the manager's first urge might be to pull them off that assignment and relegate them to the job of providing maintenance or support for existing systems. This action will always be seen as punishment. In many companies, junior-level people with limited experience or senior-level people nearing retirement are also saddled with older systems. Whether this decision is intentional, this action is generally viewed as a punishment, too. IS managers may be inviting trouble if they give legacy maintenance assignments as a punishment.

Consider adding a GUI front end. Adding a graphical user interface (GUI) to an existing system is a common first step in migrating to new platforms. Customers (i.e., Users) reap the benefits of a consistent look and feel; at the same time, the GUI front end gives maintenance staff a taste of new technology, trainers new screens to work with, and support people fewer data entry errors to contend with.

Suggest that trainers change the exercises in the training course. This simple suggestion takes less time to implement than developing a completely new course, yet it will make the course feel new and give trainers a chance to propose new ideas.

Allow staff to find an undocumented feature of the system and publicize it.
This is like uncovering a new type of dinosaur bone. It can stimulate more interest in the whole system and give the department some additional visibility.

Encourage people to train others as backup. For maintenance staff, backup usually comes from a colleague, but for trainers and support staff, backup might come from an end user who favors the system, a colleague, or even a consultant. Regardless of the source, having a backup gives the regular maintenance, training, and support staff room to breathe.

Converting the training material to an online delivery method. Because staff turnover is usually a problem in user areas, converting the training material to an online medium (traditional CBT, or Web-based multi-media) may be beneficial. It gives users on-demand training and because legacy systems do not change frequently, the materials stay current. Converting also give the training and support staff a chance to learn new training media.

Perform a full systems analysis on existing systems. The purpose is to find out why the system is still in use. A full systems analysis usually reveals that the documentation for the company's legacy system is missing, dated, or incomplete. That is why only one or two people know the system. A full systems analysis will provide documentation to bring it up to date.

A full systems analysis that includes a cost/benefit section for replacing the existing system can be used to explain to the staff why management has decided to keep and maintain the existing system. Conversely, a cost/benefit analysis may convince management that the benefit of keeping the system are overstated and that it is time to retire the system, thus paving the way for redeploying current training, support, and maintenance personnel to learn new systems.

Allow training, support, and maintenance people to learn a new system.
They often will find that returning to their dinosaurs is like coming home to more comfortable and familiar surroundings.

Give the entire staff time to keep up with new technology. Rather than have everyone read all the literature, though, let each person pick a topic they would like to keep abreast of, then have each of them summarize the latest developments at weekly staff meetings.

Encourage more business knowledge. If IS personnel are working on accounting systems, for example, suggest that they take an accounting course so they can better understand how their system fits in the overall business scheme.

Outsourcing the training, support, and maintenance of existing systems.
Although in-house people might view legacy assignments as punishment or dead-end jobs, consultants tend to view them simply as work. Outsiders taking over existing maintenance also are likely to lend a fresh perspective to uncovering opportunities to improve efficiency.

CONCLUSION

Even companies committed to downsizing need people to provide training, support, and maintenance for their existing systems that keep the business functioning. But that does not have to mean a step backward for the IS staff involved. By viewing legacy systems objectively, and helping employees do what they can to keep their job fresh, IS managers can help their employees avoid becoming dinosaurs themselves.

Chapter 18
Client/Server Architecture and Implementation

Nathan J. Muller

THE CLIENT/SERVER ARCHITECTURE came about out of the need to bring computing power, information, and decision-making down to the user, so business could respond faster to customer needs, competitive pressures, and market dynamics. This was a welcome alternative to the overly bureaucratic mainframe environment where departments, workgroups, and individuals typically had to put in written requests for the information they needed.

THE CLIENT/SERVER MODEL

In the client/server model, an application program is broken out into two parts on the network. The client portion of the program, or front end, is run by individual users at their desktops and performs such tasks as querying a database, producing a printed report, or entering a new record. These functions are carried out through structured query language (SQL), which operates in conjunction with existing applications. The front-end part of the program executes on the user's workstation.

The server portion of the program, or back end, resides on a computer configured to support multiple clients, offering them shared access to a variety of application programs as well as to printers, file storage, database management, communications, and other resources. The server must not only handle simultaneous requests from multiple clients, but perform such administrative tasks as transaction management, security, logging, database creation and updating, concurrency management, and maintaining the data dictionary. The data dictionary standardizes terminology so database records can be maintained across a broad base of users.

0-8493-9824-X/00/$0.00+$.50
© 2000 by CRC Press LLC

DISTRIBUTED NETWORKS

The migration from central to distributed computing has produced two types of networks involving server: the traditional hierarchical architecture employed by mainframe vendors and the distributed architecture employed by LANs. The hierarchical approach uses layers of servers that are subordinate to a central server. In this case, PCs and workstations are connected to servers that are connected to remote server or servers. This server contains extensive files of addresses of individuals, databases and programs, as well as a corporate SQL database or a file of common read-only information (e.g., a data dictionary). A terminal on a LAN making a request for data not on the LAN has it request routed to the central server. The server adds any pertinent information from its own database and sends the combined message to the end user as a unit. To the end user it appears to be a single, integrated request. Also, the local LAN server passes database updates to the central server, where the most recent files reside.

This type of server network maintains the hierarchical relationship of mainframe communications architectures (e.g., IBM Corp.'s SNA), thereby simplifying software development. An added benefit is that more programming expertise is available here than in distributed environment. The disadvantage is in the vulnerability of the hierarchical network to congestion or failure of the central server, unless standby links and redundant server subsystems are employed at considerable expense.

In contrast, the distributed server architecture maintains the peer-to-peer relationship employed in LANs. Each workstation on the LAN can connect to multiple specialized servers as needed, regardless of where the servers are located. Local servers enable such services as databases, user authentication, facsimile, and electronic mail, among others. There are also servers responsible for managing connections to servers outside the LAN. The workstation merges data from the server with its own local data and presents the data as a composite whole to the requesting user.

The distributed client/server architecture is more difficult to implement than the hierarchical server architecture because the software is magnitudinally more complex. After all, the workstations need to know where to find each necessary service, be configured with appropriate access privileges, and have the applications software to access the required data. When the data is finally accessed, it must be current data. Keeping the network and computing process transparent to end users is another challenge. And of course, everyone has come to expect a graphically rich user interface.

The network also consists of the transmission medium and communications protocol used between clients and servers. The transmission medium used is no different from that found in any other computing environment.

Among the commonly used media for LANs is coaxial cable (thick and thin), twisted-pair wiring (shielded and unshielded), and optical fiber (single- and multimode). Emerging media include infrared and radio signals for wireless transmission.

A medium-access protocol is used to grant user access to the transmission facility. For Ethernet and Token Ring network, the medium-access protocols are Carrier Sense Multiple Access with Collision Detection (CSMA/CD) and token passing, respectively. When linking client/server computing environments over long distances, other communications protocols come into play that are used over private facilities such as point-to-point T1 links, which provide a transmission rate of up to 1.544M bps. Frame relay and Asynchronous Transfer Mode (ATM) are among the latest technologies for carrying LAN traffic over wide-area networks (WAN), while Transmission Control Protocol/Internet Protocol (TCP/IP) networks are the oldest. Of these, more companies seem to be turning to TCP/IP-based networks for mainstream business applications. Corporate intranets and global Internet, in essence, are large-scale client/server networks. Gateways are used to join the two for such applications as electronic commerce and remote access, while firewalls protect corporate assets from unauthorized access.

The choice of media and protocols will hinge on high performance and reliability factors weighed against the requirements of the applications. More often than not, no single solution will meet all the diverse needs of an organization. This adds to the complexity of developing client/server applications.

OBSTACLES AND IMPLEMENTATION

Although many organizations have embraced the concepts behind client/server, many are still wary about entrusting their mission-critical applications to the new architecture. Despite all the vendor hoopla, today's client/server environment is still burdened by the lack of diagnostic and applications development tools, which are readily available for the mainframe environment. In particular, such troubleshooting tools as debuggers and other diagnostic programs, although more powerful than they were several years ago, are still less robust than those found in the mainframe world.

Another important concern is the inability to centrally control client/server networks linked to one another and to a larger host machine. For the most part, the tools used locally on the LANs to diagnose, correct, and troubleshoot problems cannot be used remotely or across different platforms. The lack of such tools as autobackup and autorecovery in current client/server configurations is a big concern for many organizations, as is the lack of integrated data dictionaries and development tools.

Because PC-based networks can be unstable, the hardware platform should be thoroughly tested before it is entrusted with mission-critical applications. Isolating a problem on the LAN can be a very time-consuming task because of the difficulty in tracking it down, whereas on a mainframe, the cause of a problem is often immediately apparent.

Although management tools are emerging for the client/server environment, they are still few and far between. Therefore, it is important to have knowledgeable staff who understand the nut-and-bolts of the operating system, the interrelationships of the applications, and the networking environment. The reason for this is disaster recovery. Many companies do not fully appreciate or understand how they are going to manage distributed data on multiple servers that may be scattered all over the country. When disaster strikes, it is important to have a recovery plan already in place so that vital data does not get lost. An effective disaster recovery plan will not only be thoroughly scripted to correspond with various disaster scenarios, but be tested periodically and refined, if necessary.

INTEGRATION ISSUES

Even where development and diagnostic tools do exist, users often find they must wrestle with complex integration issues, as well as learn a whole new language. Until there is more collaboration among mainframe and microcomputer vendors to make integration easier, users may want to consider a systems integrator to facilitate the transition to client/server and use them for knowledge transfer.

Integrators can play a key role in managing the complex relationships and problems — both technical and administrative — that arise in a multi-vendor environment. They not only help to integrate products from many different vendors, but smooth out incompatibilities between communications protocols. Integrators also lend valuable assistance in negotiating service and support contracts.

When choosing a systems integrator, it is important that it shares the organization's vision. One area in which shared vision is particularly important is that of technological innovation. If the organization wants to implement leading-edge solutions, the integrator must be willing and capable of supporting that vision with investments in emerging technologies and cutting-edge concepts.

Most integrators are concerned with the problem at hand so they can get on with solving the next problem. They generally do not help clients articulate a vision that will provide essential guideposts into the future. An integrator that can provide business process reengineering services for select applications, for example, is a better choice than a vendor that provides basic service only.

Until corporate management sees the client/server platform providing equivalent stability, performance, consistency, and reliability to the mainframe, they will not be comfortable moving mission-critical applications. Pilot programs can help organizations evaluate the client/server platform in terms of performance, reliability, and disaster recovery. The time to initiate a pilot program and try new techniques is when new programs must be developed. Small, manageable applications allow time for staff to get through the learning curve, which can greatly facilitate the transmission to client/server.

NETWORK SUPPORT

Those who have taken the plunge into client/server applications have noted that their organizations are becoming increasingly dependent on enterprise networks.

Behind the growth in expenditures for network support is the confusing array of communications challenges that is confronting managers, from evaluating new internetworking technologies needed to create enterprise networks to maintaining, managing, and leveraging far-flung corporate databases. The hope of saving money by using client/server applications may be dashed once managers realize that the cost required to make each program work remains the same. Although it does make end users more productive, by itself, the client/server approach does not really save money. For faster applications development and cost savings, the client/server approach may have to be coupled with computer assisted software engineering (CASE) or object-oriented programming (OOP).

Companies spend $20 million annually in network support. Of that amount, it is estimated that one-third goes to the management of the client/server computing environment.

THE CASE FOR OBJECTS

The basic premise of object-oriented programming is that business functions and applications can be broken up into classes of objects that can be reused. This greatly reduces the application development time, simplifies maintenance, and increases reliability. This is also the idea behind Java, a relatively new object-oriented programming language that is expected to play an increasing role in transaction processing over the Internet, particularly in electronic commerce applications such as Electronic Data Exchange (EDI).

Objects provide functionality by tightly coupling the traditionally separate domains of programming and code data. As separate domains, it is difficult to maintain systems over time. Eventually the point is reached when the entire business system must be scrapped and a new one put into place at great expense and disruption to the business processes. In the object-oriented approach, data structures are more closely coupled with the code, which is allowed to modify that structure. This permits more frequent enhancements of applications, while resulting in less disruption to the end users' work habits. In the case of Java, only the code on the server is updated. Because the applications or applets are downloaded from the server only when needed and never take up permanent residence on the client machines, software maintenance is greatly simplified.

With each object viewed as a separate functional entity, reliability is improved because there is less chance that a change will produce new bugs in previously stable sections of code. The object-oriented approach also improves the productivity of programmers in that the various objects are reusable. Each instance of an object draws on the same piece of error-free code, resulting in less applications-development time. Once the object method of programming is learned, developers can bring applications and enhancements to users more quickly, thus realizing the full potential of client/server networks. This approach also makes it easier to maintain program integrity with changes in personnel.

CASE tools, fourth-generation languages (4GLs), and various code generators have been used over the years to help improve applications development, but they have yet to offer the breakthrough improvements demanded by an increasingly competitive business environment. In fact, although these tools have been around for years, the applications development backlog has not diminished appreciably.

This is because many CASE tools are too confining, forcing programmers to build applications in one structured way. This can result in redesign efforts often falling behind schedule and over budget. In addition, CASE tools are not typically compatible with each other. This would require a CASE framework with widely disclosed integration interfaces. Complicating matters is the growing number of government and industry standards organizations that are offering proposals that supersede and overlap one another.

Object-oriented technologies, however, are starting to deliver on the breakthrough promise. In some instances, OOP technology has brought an order of magnitude improvement in productivity and systems development time over that of CASE tools — it is not unheard of for some IS staff to compress five or six months of applications development time to only five or six weeks. Few technologies available to the applications development community hold as much promise as object orientation.

TRANSITIONING TO OBJECTS

Several concrete steps can be taken to ensure the successful transition to object technology in the applications development environment. The success of any large-scale project hinges on the support and financial commitment of senior management, who must be made aware of the benefits, as well as the return on investment. Fortunately, this is not hard to do with object-oriented technology.

To demonstrate the potential advantages of object-oriented technology, IS managers should seize the opportunity to apply it to a new project. Projects that lend themselves to object-oriented technology include any applications that are being downsized from the mainframe to the client/server environment, because the applications will have to be rewritten anyway.

It is a wise idea to prepare for object-oriented technology now by determining the availability of training and consulting services and reference materials. If senior management wants to know about object-oriented technology and its potential advantages, IS managers will elicit more trust and confidence by demonstrating immediate knowledge and understanding of the topic rather than begging off until they can become more informed.

Like the move from mainframes to client/server, the skills mix necessary in object-oriented technology differs from that in conventional methods of applications development, if only because the shift in activities is toward the front end of the applications development cycle.

This means that there is more emphasis on such things as needs assessment and understanding the workflow processes in various workgroups and departments. This affects the design of the applications in terms of the modularity and reusability of various objects.

New incentives may be needed to encourage systems analysts and programmers to learn and adhere to object-oriented analysis and design methods, and to reward those who create and implement reusable code. The object-oriented paradigm signals a fundamental shift in the way networks, applications, databases, and operating systems are put together, as well as how they are used, upgraded, and managed. The ability to create new objects from existing objects, change them to suit specific needs, and otherwise reuse them across different applications promises compelling new efficiencies and economies, especially in the client/server environment.

STAFFING

A potential obstacle that may hinder the smooth migration to client/server is the apparent lack of skills among programmers outside the traditional mainframe or standalone personal computer environments. Those with PC experience typically have never worked in an IS shop and are not familiar with the control procedures and testing rigor that a formal shop expects in mission-critical applications development. Alternatively, moving from the mainframe to client/server environment require knowledge of multiple platforms, rapid applications development tools, relational database design, and, ultimately, the principles of object-oriented programming.

One difference for many mainframe operators switching to client/server environments is the heavier involvement with users. This often means reconciling system wants and needs among end users. Also, IS managers usually have more contact with senior management who want to know how the new technology can benefit the company and what to anticipate in terms of investment.

TRAINING

The shortage of skilled object-oriented programmers is perhaps the biggest obstacle to speedy implementation. Object-oriented methods require that programmers think about things differently, and thinking in terms of objects as opposed to lines of code is certainly different. Even with the three to four months needed to train staff members in the object-oriented approach, once programming staff are up to speed they can develop applications faster and more efficiently.

The client/server environment tends to require more staff experts, because no one person typically understands all the pieces. As if to underscore this point, there seems to be more trial and error in developing applications for client/server than on older, well-understood legacy mainframe systems.

One of the trends driving training is the whole information technology arena undergoing a paradigm shift — from mainframe to client/server systems. This means a major retooling of organizations around the country, requiring substantial increases in training dollars.

Only two possibilities exist for obtaining the necessary skill base required for moving from a mainframe orientation to a client/server orientation. One is to fire everyone and start over, which is not viewed by many companies as even remotely feasible. The other is to work with existing professionals to upgrade their skill base with training. Within the context of most companies, training is the best solution because the people already have the underlying knowledge base. The object of training is to apply an existing knowledge base in a new direction.

Staff members need not wait to be told that they need training. They should start now to get acquainted with the departmental systems and managers in their organizations who are currently developing or looking into LAN technologies and discuss the chances of working on their projects. Beyond that, they should try to become familiar with pertinent operating systems and applications development tools through such channels as vendors or industry shows. In preparing for internal opportunities, motivated staff members will be better positioned to survive organizational shakeouts that may occur in the future.

Consideration should also be given to purchasing visual development tool that promise rapid application development. For programmers already versed in C/C++ and derivative languages, these tools can shorten the learning curve, enabling them to become immediately productive, particularly with regard to Java. There is JavaBeans — pre-built, platform-independent components — that developers can use to create their own applications without having to waste time reinventing the wheel.

Managers should endeavor to become as well versed in client/server issues as they are about mainframe issues. Such people will be greater assets to companies making the transition to smaller, diverse platforms. The person most valuable is somebody who has the desire to learn the client/server environment and has the flexibility to go back and do work on the mainframe when it is appropriate.

Outside consultants can be brought in to provide the necessary training, but programmers and systems analysts must learn more than just the details of how products and software work. Working closely with senior management doing strategic planning and getting hands-on experience with how applications are being used can be equally important.

CLIENT/AGENT/SERVER PARADIGM

Client/server applications have been dependent on the reliable, high-speed networks used within the corporation. However, these networks are not available to the growing base of mobile users who must rely on expensive low-speed wireless services to access corporate information. Compounding the problem is that wireless networks disconnect or fade in and out of coverage regularly, neither of which is tolerated by the connection-oriented nature of client/server applications.

Agents — software that allows sophisticated messaging between clients and servers — can insulate mobile users from the complexities of establishing and maintaining connections to corporate resources (Exhibit 18.1).

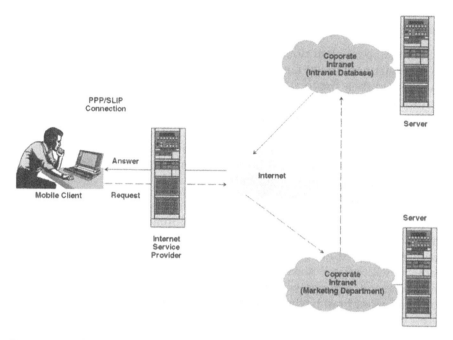

Exhibit 18.1. Path of request message by mobile client and answer message from agent.

The following scenarios provide a few examples of agents and how they serve their mobile clients:

In Exhibit 18.1, a request message is issued by the mobile user and an agent is dispatched to find the information. The collected information is returned to the mobile user in the form of a message. If the user is not online to receive the message, it is held in queue and delivered the next time the user logs on to the network.

- An order-status performs standard query, insert, and update capabilities against a database to manage sales orders. This agent also regularly checks all open orders against inventory levels to alert field representatives and inventory managers on increased demand or shortages. Even if the remote user has not accessed the order system in days, he or she can be notified of data changes impacting their orders.
- A support-call tracking agent manages call entry and update for field support engineers. Additionally, the agent identifies all priority customer problems as they occur and automatically forwards the details along an escalation path for problem resolution. The agent can also automatically send the customer contact Internet e-mail updates with

the call's status and individuals working on the problem's resolution as this data changes.

- A stock portfolio manager allows users to access real-time stock quotes, as well as the current value of their personal portfolios from their mobile computer. In addition, for any stock, buy and sell limits can be placed to either alert the user to points of interest, or to automatically execute trades via online trading gateways.

Several companies offer mobile agents that work over wireless, as well as wireline networks. The mobile agents offered by Racotek and Oracle provide a useful illustration of their capabilities, as does IBM's experimental aglet technology.

KeyWare uses agent-like distributed processes, called service providers, to perform work on behalf of the application client and report the results. KeyWare service providers reside in the mobile workgroup server and mobile client servers and are designed to provide specific application services and message exchange services. This design free application allows clients to perform application-specific tasks.

KeyWare Data Exchange Service facilitates transmission of data packets of up to 32K in size across a variety of wireless data networks. This frees the application software from having to repackage data to match the differing protocol and packet size requirements of each wireless network. Messages larger than 32K in size may be handled as file transfers. The Data Exchange Service uses agent technology. It can insert different requests into a single transmission. KeyWare looks inside message envelopes and directs data or procedures to the appropriate application client and/or server.

KeyWare provides data compression and data bundling to enable efficient network utilization. If compression is used, KeyWare will automatically analyze messages and perform compression on only those messages that the compression algorithm will actually reduce in size. If messages held by the KeyWare Server can be sent more efficiently together rather than separately, they are automatically bundled by the KeyWare server. However, the server will only bundle message if it will increase network efficiency.

The KeyWare Systemwide Synchronization Service provides a single, consistent time reference between host and portable computers, and ensures proper event sequencing by determining the duration and scheduling of activities.

KeyWare can run with any host, operating system, network topology, database (e.g., Oracle, Sybase, Microsoft SQL Server, IBM OS/400), or application. In addition to running over remote dialup wireline connections, KeyWare operates over ARDIS, CDPD, NORCOM, RAM, and specialized mobile radio (SMR) wireless networks.

Racotek also offers KeyScript Toolkit, an authoring tool for the rapid development of mobile applications that are automatically enabled for wireless processing. Since KeyWare services provide a single logical interface to multiple wireless networks, developers can build applications independent of the wireless networks that will ultimately be used.

ORACLE MOBILE AGENT

Oracle Mobile Agents enable remote users to access corporate information from a variety of data sources. Employing agents that work on the user's behalf to locate information, Oracle Mobile Agents can access relational or flat databases, electronic mail interfaces, fax services or other Unix services via wireless networks, LANs, or phone lines. This gives remote users many choices for accessing their information: wireless while in the field, dialup from a hotel, or LAN from the office.

Clients communicate with agents via messages, causing the agent to execute work on behalf of the client. The result of the agent's work are bundled into a single message, which is sent back to the client application where the results can be displayed. Overall transaction performance is enhanced by minimizing use of the mobile client's wireless communications link and taking advantage of the high-speed link between the agent and the server. This results in the fastest possible performance to the mobile client, regardless of the complexity of the task. In addition, automatic data compression reduces message size and increases throughput.

Users interact with Oracle Mobile Agents using either an OLE 2.0 (Object Linking and Embedding) object or a window DLL (Dynamic Link Library). Any Windows tool that can act as an OLE 2.0 client or a call Windows DLL can be used to write Oracle Mobile Agents applications, including: Microsoft C/Visual C++, Microsoft Visual Basic, Microsoft Excel, Powersoft Powerbuilder, and Gupta SQL Windows.

A message manager receives messages from all client applications and delivers them over the available communications link. The message manager resides with the client applications on the laptop or mobile device. Client messages are sent from the message manager to the message gateway to be forwarded to the appropriate agent. The message gateway has several roles:

- Forwards messages between mobile users and their agents.
- Queues messages intended for clients or agents that are out of coverage, turned off, or otherwise unavailable.
- Contains configuration information about all system-level components. All components are self-configuring, minimizing the risk of installation or user errors.

- Applies all system security through user password, encryption, and message authentication.

The message gateway and the message manager work together to guarantee that the data sent over the radio link or phone line is sent successfully, securely, and with the integrity of the contents intact.

Messages are forwarded from the message gateway to application-specific agents. Agents programs consists of two components:

- The agent event manager: Oracle software on a server that is responsible for communicating with the message gateway to send and receive messages determine what action a message should initiate.
- Customer-written handler: the specific code required to interpret a message, perform some action based on its contents, and return a response. One handler is required for each transaction the client applications can initiate.

Agents can be written using native applications environments. For example, on UNIX server this will most commonly be the C programming language, while for Windows, any of the tools mentioned earlier could be used to write an agent.

While agents will often execute database servers, such as Oracle 7, they can also use files or file servers, or online services such as electronic mail or online information services as their data sources. The system is as open on the server side as it is on the client side. Agents access servers using the best available native interface. For example, an Oracle 7 database is accessed using the Oracle PRO*C or OCI interface on UNIX, while on Windows these same interfaces, as well as Oracle Glue or OBBC, are available.

An SNMP agent can be used to manage and monitor the Message Gateway and Agent Event Manager components of a system. Dynamically configurable logging provides an audit of system activities, while statistics information provides trend capabilities. Additionally, a remote administration tool for user, service, and message administration can be used from a LAN, dialup, or wireless connection.

IBM'S AGLET TECHNOLOGY

Corporate intranets represent a vast repository of information scattered among hundreds of databases worldwide. Extranets are even larger because they allow the resources of many different organizations to be interconnected. A mobile user might have to spend hours logged on to these nets to find a key piece of information that would help close a sale or solve a customer's problem, for example. But being mobile means that time is limited and more efficient means must be employed to find and gather the desired information.

An agent can be dispatched to roam the net and report its findings when the user logs on again. While this approach can be effective for simple tasks, the problem is that the agent's functionality is rather limited. There are more complicated tasks than database access that can be handled by agents. IBM has introduced a more flexible and functional approach to building and implementing mobile agents, called the aglet, which is capable of very complex operations.

It is expected that the aglet will be commonly used for database access. In this scenario, a client creates an aglet to gather information from several databases. The client provides the aglet with an itinerary and sends it off to the first database server. The itinerary controls the routing of the aglet and is able to handle exceptional conditions. For example, if a server is not responding, the aglet will go on to the other servers first and then return to that server later. On each database server, the aglet can be engaged in heavy data retrieval without suffering from network latency, since the database is accessed locally at a very high bandwidth. The possibly mobile client can be disconnected from the network while the information gathering takes place. The aglet will return when the client is eventually reconnected. Aglets can also be put to work as web-site monitors. In this scenario, a web browser can dispatch an aglet to a web site. The aglet can perform a local high-bandwidth search among the documents on the site or it can monitor specific documents for updates. When a document is updated, the aglet can either send an e-mail to its owner or return to its origin. The client can search and monitor the Web even while it is disconnected, and monitoring of web sites does not require a continuous network connection. For web sites, it means that interested readers are automatically and instantaneously notified of important updates. A web-crawling aglet can move among web sites to perform high-bandwidth local searching or index building.

Aglets can also be used to help with scheduling meetings. In this scenario, an aglet is dispatched by a client to other locations to arrange a meeting. The agent will use an itinerary to visit other hosts (meeting participants) in order to negotiate an acceptable meeting schedule. At each host, the aglet will accommodate the host's calendar system. When negotiating has finished, the aglet will notify all participants of the meeting time and place. The meeting scheduling takes place in a truly heterogeneous and distributed fashion with no central calendar system. Multiple mobile clients can have meetings arranged this way, since not all participants need to be connected to the network at the same time. The meeting scheduling aglet acts like an electronic secretary.

Aglets also have electronic commerce applications. In an auction scenario, for example, a client can dispatch an aglet that offers an item for sale. Other clients can dispatch aglets that are in search of specific items. When such aglets meet, they can bargain. "Smart" aglets may make a good bargain and less clever aglets may make bad bargains. There is no central auction or marketplace server. Commerce aglets may meet on any host. There is no fixed algorithm for accepting or rejecting a bid. The transaction is left up to the individually programmed aglets.

Aglets are Java objects that can move from one host on the net to another, taking their program code along with state information. This autonomy lets an aglet execute on one host, halt execution, and go to another host where execution resumes. When the aglet moves, it takes along its program code, as well as its data. Once started, aglets decide where they will go and what they will do independent of any external request. They also can receive requests from external sources, such as other aglets, but each individual aglet decides whether or not to comply with them. Aglets can even collaborate with each other and exchange information. Aglets also can copy themselves and dispatch the clones to other network locations to carry out tasks.

The term aglets is a play on words between agents and applets. The Java aglet extends the model of network-mobile code made possible by Java applets. Like an applet, the class files for an aglet can migrate across a network. But unlike applets, when an aglet migrates, it also carries its state. While applets move across a network from a server to a client, an aglet is a running Java program (code and state) that can move from one host to another on a network. In addition, because an aglet carries its state wherever it goes, it can travel sequentially to many destinations on a net, including eventually returning back to its original host.

A Java aglet is similar to an applet in that it runs as thread (or multiple threads) inside the context of a host Java application. To run applets, a web browser launches a Java application to host any applets it may encounter as the user browses from page to page. That application installs a security manager to enforce restrictions on the activities of any untrusted applets. To download an applet's class files, the application creates class loader that know how to request class files from a Web server.

Likewise, an aglet requires a host Java application — an aglet host — to be running on a computer before it can visit that computer. When aglets travel across a network, they migrate from one aglet host to another. Each aglet host installs a security manager to enforce restrictions on the activities of untrusted aglets. Hosts upload aglets through class loaders that know how to retrieve the class files and state of an aglet from a remote aglet host.

IBM offers its Aglet Workbench to assist developers in creating Java-based mobile agent applications. Java makes an ideal language for developing aglets due to its network centricity, sandbox security model, and platform independence. The Aglet Workbench defines its own Java agent

API — which has been submitted to the Object Management Group (OMG) for consideration as a standard — and provides a set of tools and samples for getting started. Because aglets work only on aglet-enabled hosts, they are more suited for running on corporate intranets and extranets where that level of control resides. It may take many years before aglet technology migrates to other sites on the public Internet.

ASSESSMENT OF CLIENT/SERVER TECHNOLOGY

The promise of client/server has not yet been realized. Because client/server systems are distributed, costs become nearly impossible to track, and administration and management difficulties are multiplied.

The Gartner Group of Stanford, CT has estimated that the total cost of owning a client/server system is about three to six times greater than it is for a comparable mainframe system, and the software tools for managing and administering client/server cost two-and-a-half times more than mainframe tools. Other studies have found that less than 20% of IS managers say their client/server projects were on time and on budget and that only about 40% of companies view the client/server architecture as a worthwhile investment.

Client/server computing is undergoing a resurgence with the growing popularity of corporate intranets and the Internet, and the advancement of network-centric computing. Although these technologies are becoming the new focus of many corporate IS departments, others now view client/server as a stepping stone to network-centric computing.

Internet-based computing provides new opportunities for integration and synthesis among networks and applications inside the company and those that are outside the company. With proper security precautions, intranets can easily be set up to reach international divisions, customers, suppliers, distributors, and strategic partners. The greater Internet is used for worldwide connectivity among distributed intranets. Companies are also banding together through so called extranets to access each other's resources for a common purpose, such as research and development, joint marketing, and EDI.

The greatest potential of corporate intranets may be making client/server truly open. The average desktop PC today has seven to 15 applications — 50 to 100 software components — each of which has different versions. With the single universal web client likely to be Java-enabled, IS managers do not have to worry about configuring hundreds or thousands of desktops with appropriate drivers.

However, the web-based client/server approach is not without problems of its own. For example, the Hypertext Transfer Protocol (HTTP) and gateway interfaces are not designed to support high-performance, high-volume applications. This means that the Web is not a panacea and that many companies might have to settle for blending Web and client/server applications. This can be done by moving applications logic to the client browser in the form of Java applets.

Web-based technology is certainly less costly. A business does not need to standardize desktops and operating systems for Internet technology to work. An existing client/server infrastructure can serve as the backbone of the Internet. Also, with free or low-cost applications development tools available on the Internet, the creation of distributed systems and applications is much cheaper than in the client/server environment, allowing IS managers to get more within available budgets while preserving existing investments in legacy and client/server systems and applications. A web browser provides a single window to all data, regardless of location.

CONCLUSION

Many experts believe that the rise of the global economy has force business to improve their operating efficiency, customer-satisfaction levels, and the product-to-market implementation cycle to a degree rarely seen before. This has contributed to widespread acceptance of client/server technology as the most practical solution for distributing applications and sharing information.

The trouble is that most companies are too heavily focused on the technical issues and ill-prepared to deal with equally important management and budgetary issues. Failure to consider such management issues as support requirements, the skills mix of staff, and training needs can sidetrack the best-laid technical plans for making the transition to the client/server environment. Attention must also be paid to the cost of client/server implementation, which tends to be high. Even on the technical side, attention must be paid to the availability of diagnostic and applications development tools, as well as the opportunities presented by such complementary technologies as object-oriented programming, so that the full potential of client/server networks is realized.

An alternative for many companies is to look at how the Internet and corporate intranets can achieve the same objectives, or even complement existing legacy and client/server investments. The openness of the Internet and its continued growth in terms of universal connectivity ensures compatibility among all components, which not only greatly reduces the cost of implementing corporate intranets but also enables businesses to transcend time and distance, lowering boundaries between markets, cultures, and individuals.

Section IV
Enterprise Network Management

NETWORK MANAGEMENT continues to be one of the most critical areas for success in the operation of computer systems. In fact, when you speak of computing technology, you also speak of networking technology — that is, your network is your computer. So many aspects of network technology are changing at such a rapid pace, that IT managers are finding it difficult to keep up. In this section of the handbook, we will provide you with the latest changes and newest developments in the field of enterprise networking.

Chapter 19, "TCP/IP Network Management: A Case Study," leads off this section with a comprehensive case study of a large organization's experience in establishing a new TCP/IP inter-network supporting both satellite and terrestrial-based transmission. This chapter looks at such major considerations as avoiding downtime; reducing implementation risk and cost; training and developing the implementation team; and the facilitation of incorporating ensuing software upgrades. These all represent key areas that IT managers must address when building a complex network. This case study discusses the implementation path decided upon, the platform and software chosen, and the new operations-workflow model that resulted within the organization.

The most recent technological developments in the communications field are explored in Chapter 20, "Trends in Data Communications Services." Data communications plays an important and growing role in the operations of today's data center, and technological advances in this field continue at a breakneck pace. Not only have new offerings, such as frame relay and switched multi-megabit data services demonstrated their value, but older services, such as X.25, T1/T3, and integrated digital services digital network (ISDN) are also being revitalized. This chapter helps enterprise IT managers keep current with trends in data communications by examining recent developments in carrier-provided technologies for communicating data.

The most recent advancement in the communications industry is the dramatic increase in the use of Digital Subscriber Line (DSL) technology.

This has been prompted by an expanding group of Internet users who wish to be connected with high-speed access at an affordable cost. Chapter 21, "The Emerging Advantage of xDSL Technology," provides advice to IT managers as to how they should evaluate the need for this new technology in their organizations. Many telecom service providers today are positioning DSL technology as the broadband solution for the masses; however, the need for this high-speed bandwidth, as some vendors would like for you to believe, may not be necessary.

Managing the LAN printing environment is another area IT managers must address. Although the price of laser printers has significantly declined over the past decade, network printing remains an important service supported by LANs. As a result, it is important for the IT manager to understand the different options available for installing network printers, as well as the advantages and disadvantages associated with each option. Chapter 22, "LAN Printing Techniques," explains the different options available for installing network printers, as well as their advantages and disadvantages, so IT managers can satisfy organizational network printing requirements in a cost-efficient and secure manner.

As usage of the Internet gains popularity within corporate America, organizations are trying to establish ways to connect to the information superhighway at speeds that make economic sense. Chapter 23, "Preparing For Cable Modems," describes the operation of cable modems, devices which provide high-speed connectivity and enable the organization to take advantage of transmission rates of up to tens of millions of bits per second. Cabling infrastructure — that is, the cabling within buildings — is another key component defined and discussed, and will introduce the IT manager to a rapidly evolving new technology that can help keep the organization competitive.

Chapter 19
TCP/IP Network Management: A Case Study

Vishal Desai

ONE LARGE ORGANIZATION is currently setting up a new TCP/IP internetwork supporting satellite and terrestrial-based data transmission. It intends to process collected data at two separate locations and to distribute that data to 15 remote sites; therefore, the organization is designing the network to support a high volume of data transfer, initially supported by a DS3 backbone with an eventual migration to an Asynchronous Transfer Mode (ATM) OC3 backbone. Aggregate network data rates are expected to range from 200M bps to 300M bps. Data types include administrative, historical, and time-sensitive, real-time data.

Initially, the network will be comprised of 30 routers supplied jointly by Cisco and 3Com vendors, and 20 to 30 Ethernet and FDDI hubs from Cabletron Inc. and InterPhase Inc. Twenty DS3 CSU/DSUs, and about five DS1 multiplexers from Digital Link corporations are also included. As the network grows, additional routers will be deployed to handle increasing traffic requirements. The network is expected to grow exponentially over the next five years.

MISSION-CRITICAL AND FAULT-TOLERANT REQUIREMENTS

The data is considered mission critical and needs to be protected accordingly in the event of network failure. Because data transfer rates are high, a huge buffering capability is required to preserve captured data in the event of even a brief period of network downtime. As a result, one of the organization's primary goals is to avoid downtime at all costs. Accordingly, the organization is designing the network in a highly fault-tolerant manner. This includes provisions for redundant cabling; dual uninterruptible power supplies for all routers and hubs; and an out-of-band network connectivity.

0-8493-9824-X/00/$0.00+$.50
© 2000 by CRC Press LLC

The transport system must have its own restoral capabilities, allowing the network itself to take care of as many problems as possible before the Network Management System (NMS) must step in. In addition, to accommodate the stringent mean-time-to-restore requirements of 1 min. restoral, the organization has decided to maintain an inventory at each node. This inventory will, at a minimum, include spare interface cards, chassis, cables, connectors, and test equipment. This will allow technicians to swap parts quickly and perform detailed diagnostics off line. The organization has also given careful consideration to equipment room design and equipment placement, ensuring such things as proper bottom-to-top airflow, placement of equipment with reference to ceiling water sprinklers, and easy access to the backs of routers and other devices.

NETWORK MANAGEMENT SYSTEM IMPLEMENTATION STRATEGY

The organization researched leading industry surveys and reports and concluded that large undertakings such as its implementation project are highly susceptible to cost overruns and schedule extensions and often fail to deliver the promised functionality. Accordingly, management developed a phased implementation strategy based on the philosophy, "Bite off only what you can chew." Limiting middleware integration in the initial phase was deemed to be critical to the eventual success of the project.

As such, the company analyzed and listed all functions that comprise an enterprise management solution and selected the absolutely essential functions for its phase-one implementation, which included:

- An SNMP-based platform.
- Trouble-ticketing software.
- A physical management application.
- RMON capability.
- Report-generation tools.

The organization decided to evaluate additional value-added functions, such as event correlation, integration with legacy systems, and modeling software, on a per-need basis in successive phases. The organization believes that such an implementation path greatly reduces its implementation risk and cost and allows it to train and develop an implementation team of manageable size instead of an army of operators and technicians. Finally, this strategy allows the organization to easily incorporate software upgrades as part of subsequent delivery.

Another area that the organization considered vital to the success of its system was early integration of its business processes with the underlying management technology. As such, in each phase, during the system design and development, the managers decided to define and closely couple their operations concepts with the network management system. This ensured that issues pertaining to maintenance philosophies; remote-sites; operator roles and responsibilities; and handling and parsing of trouble tickets were probed in-depth during the system design-and-implementation cycle. Such an approach guaranteed that the implementation engineers would weigh and consider the operational needs early in the development cycle. Not only did this provide the organization with a "complete workable solution," but also greatly reduced system changes after it became operational.

The SNMP Platform-Evaluation Criteria

Before selecting a network management platform, the organization tested several systems in its development lab. Between 1992 and 1994, the systems tested in the labs included Cabletron Spectrum, SunNet Manager, HP OpenView (HPOV), NetLab's DiMONS, and IBM NetView. The organization made its selection carefully, as the decision entails a 15-year commitment to the network management infrastructure. The organization was initially impressed by the NetLab's product, particularly its ability to perform alarm correlation using its Nerve Center application. However, the organization took into consideration NetLabs' precarious market position and chose to select a larger, established player.

The organization decided against Cabletron Spectrum for two reasons. First, the managers were concerned about Spectrum's ability to fully manage competing vendors' hub products. Second, the organization wanted to customize Spectrum's filtering and network modeling capabilities and, after extensive testing, concluded that detailed customization would entail immense up-front development.

SunNet Manager was ruled out because the organization found the user interface to be too archaic, and Sun's higher-end Enterprise Manager was not yet ready for shipment. Finally, IBM NetView, although it offered high product stability and advanced features, was not selected because of its DOS/OS-2-centric hardware dependency. Such dependency, according to the organization's existing skill base, would require retraining of its operators, who were familiar with Sun and HP workstations.

The organization then chose HP OpenView (HPOV), primarily because the product offered a flexible and industry-pervasive management platform that facilitated the integration of third-party applications and because it appeared to pose the least risk in terms of product longevity. Additionally, the Network Node Manager (NNM), HP's SNMP manager, adequately provided the basic management functions without requiring significant up-front configuration or development investment.

The NMS Middleware

In addition to selecting HPOV as the SNMP-based network management application, the organization selected the following third-party, value-added applications to develop an enterprise-level network management system:

- Remedy Corporation's Action Request System (ARS), as the event-tracking software for generating, tracking, and documenting trouble tickets.
- A Relational Database Management System from Sybase Inc., which works with the ARS to store and distribute event tickets and reports.
- A performance-analysis application from SAS Inc., which integrates with HPOV to access Management Information Base (MIB) data to maintain historical data, produce summaries, perform statistical analyses, and generate network reports.
- Isicad Corp's Command 5000, as the physical and asset management software to obtain a graphical representation of the physical location of devices on the network to track network assets and device-to-device connectivity.
- Frontier's NETScout Remote MONitoring probes, to collect networking data on remote LANs and forward selected information to the network management system.
- A redundancy application from Qualix Group to monitor all of the network management applications running on the primary and secondary NOC workstations.

The organization carefully considered including additional types of value-added applications, but in maintaining a phased system-implementation approach, it chose instead to initially roll out a suite consisting of the barest minimum needed to manage the network effectively.

The Enterprise Network Management System

Physically, the NMS comprises four SunSPARC 20 workstations (WS) that are situated at the NOC. The primary workstation and redundant secondary workstations (e.g., the WS1 and WS2) are connected to the TCP/IP network by an Ethernet local area network (LAN). These workstations collectively run HPOV NNM, ARS clients, and Sybase clients. Two additional workstations, WS3 and WS4, support the NMS. WS3 houses the SAS application, as well as the ARS clients and Sybase servers. WS4 hosts Isicad's physical management software. WS4 is also used as an X-Terminal.

The four NMS workstations are connected internally to each other by an Ethernet LAN, which is also used for printer connectivity. Each workstation on this LAN supports Ethernet and FDDI interfaces and is also connected to high-speed, secured modems through the RS232 port to perform out-of-band management. A standalone 486 PC hosts the capability to manage the modems that are used for the out-of-band network access.

The SNMP-Based Management Platform

Hewlett Packard's OpenView Network Node Manager 3.3.1 (NNM) is used to monitor and control the network and provides the necessary platform to integrate middleware applications to maximize data sharing and processing. The NNM:

- Automatically discovers the devices on the TCP/IP networks and monitors the status of these devices.
- Automatically draws the topology of the network based on the discovered information and creates appropriate map views. A map is a graphical and hierarchical representation of the network.
- Collects performance information from the device's MIB, stores it for trend analysis, and graphs the collected data.
- Defines event thresholds for MIB objects remotely.
- Takes specific actions upon receipt of specific SNMP traps.
- Diagnoses and displays network faults and performance problems.
- Allows integration with the popular third-party applications to enhance the system's management capabilities.

HPOV IMPLEMENTATION

Two copies of NNM are deployed on NOC workstations WS1 and WS2. WS1 houses the primary NNM, whereas WS2 hosts the secondary copy. Each copy is configured and customized in an identical manner. Database synchronization between these copies is maintained by scripts that are automatically initiated on a periodic basis.

Each NNM is configured at various levels. The map views of each are customized to easily view and isolate faulty devices. Each NNM's alarm and event handling is configured to notify operators in real time using a combination of beeps, pop-up windows, and e-mail messages. The map and event color schemes are carefully defined to quickly determine fault criticality (e.g., red implies critical failure; yellow is minor; blue is unmanageable). The capability to obtain real-time performance graphs for selected backbone links is also implemented for quick status reports. Finally, to ensure that sufficient Management Information Base data is collected for performance, fault, and accounting purposes, selected MIB variables, with associated collection frequency, are identified for all network devices. Applicable threshold checks are also instilled.

SAS Reporting Software

The SAS Corporation offers a suite of products capable of integrating with HPOV NNM to perform data processing, analysis, and report generation. These products collectively allow the users to import data from NNM MIB files into its proprietary database, reduce the collected data, and perform statistical analysis on this data to generate strategic and performance baseline reports. These reports are used by the NOC operators, managers, and sustaining engineers to jointly perform network trend and capacity-planning analysis.

By using the SAS product suite, the organization is able to parse information and reduce the amount of storage needed without compromising on disaster-recovery requirements; also, SAS provides the ability to more easily summarize network performance data and generate reports on circuit utilization, LAN utilization, and device performance.

Trouble-Ticketing Software

The organization has developed a help-desk call process model with the goal of handling the user's problem on the first call. To that end, the organization will people the help desk on a 24 x 7 basis with a mix of operators and operations support personnel. These NOC personnel interface with the remote node personnel using a combination of commercially available trouble-ticketing packages, secured telephone lines, facsimiles, and e-mail to resolve problems in a timely manner.

Remedy Corporation's Action Request System (ARS) 2.0 was selected as the centerpiece for the organization's help desk. The ARS generates trouble tickets and tracks network events in a customizable work-flow process. The ARS uses an interactive process similar to e-mail to track network events with repair personnel. To accomplish this, the ARS provides the capability using a Graphical User Interface to customize the following:

- Defining information to be passed among repair personnel.
- Defining automatic processes to assist operator data entry on event tickets.
- Notification and communication of defined information among repair personnel.
- Define work flow rules, such as escalation procedures.
- Provide statistical analysis and reporting capabilities.

Using these ARS features, the NMS design engineers defined three primary trouble-ticket schemas. The event-ticket schema specifies the date, time, and severity of the problem, as well as suggested problem-resolution steps. The node-contact schema provides information about repair personnel (e.g., phone number and other contact information). The common-carrier schema provides information about the transport circuits, and carrier-contact data. All schemas adhere to a predefined escalation process that ensures automatic notification to management of unresolved or forgotten event tickets.

Along with tracking events and communicating information, the help desk designers have coupled ARS with Sybase database transparently to automatically retain a database of problem-solving experience. This problem-solving information can be used by the NOC operator or nodal technician as a trouble-shooting aid and to provide statistics. Trouble-shooting assistance is achieved by querying for solutions from previous similar problems. Furthermore, storing all previous event tickets allows the ARS to provide, for example, statistical analysis concerning the length of outages, the frequency of outages, most frequent cause of events, and the amount of time spent by individual repair personnel. Also coupled with this functionality is the capability to generate reports for statistical results, event ticket summaries, complete event tickets, and other information as needed.

Preparing for the next release of the help desk, the organization is considering listing these reports, as well as the status of all trouble tickets on a secured server that is accessible by either a Web or e-mail interface. Such a capability would allow network users to investigate, and obtain and track, status of reported problems without calling the help desk. This, the organization believes, will allow its NOC operators to spend more time resolving network problems.

HPOV-ARS INTEGRATION

Rather than have a standalone help desk that has no insight into the network status information collected and presented by the SNMP manager, the organization decided to integrate its ARS with HPOV. The coupling with HPOV relies on a combination of menu-bar integration, along with the in-house-developed scripts that automatically filled in specified data fields upon opening a trouble ticket. This reduces the amount of information that NOC operators must fill in for each trouble ticket. As the dynamics of the network behavior is captured, analyzed, and understood by the engineers, the organization plans to build upon the existing HPOV integration to include the SNMP trap — ARS event-mapping lists to automatically generate trouble tickets for selected network traps and events.

Redundancy Application

Due to the mission-critical nature of the network, system reliability and redundancy required careful handling. For the NMS, several software components are used together to provide the required system reliability. The Online Disk Suite (ODS) is used to perform disk mirroring to provide redundancy for all of the data and applications used by the primary and secondary NMS workstations (WS1 and WS2).

The Qualix Group's First Watch software monitors all of the applications running on the primary workstation, and sends a heartbeat between the primary and secondary workstations. In the event of some type of fault or failure, the First Watch maintains a log and notifies the NOC operator and, if needed, will shut down the primary workstation and initiate the secondary workstation.

Physical Configuration Application

Isicad Corporation's Command software resides on WS4. It provides a graphical representation of the physical location of devices on the network to track network assets and device-to-device connectivity to perform fault isolation. It also documents such useful information as circuit identification numbers, cable type, and personal identification numbers. It is used to locate the exactness of the reported fault. Although it can be integrated with HPOV NNM and Remedy's ARS, the NMS will initially use it as a standalone application.

Frontier NETScout

NETScout probes are installed on FDDI LANs at selected sites. These probes function to collect networking data on remote LANs and forward selected information to the network management system. Besides providing standard RMON information, the probes allow the network management system to maintain traffic accountability for individual users at the LAN level. This is extremely important to avoid congestion on the organization's WAN backbone links. NETScout was chosen above other competitors' products for its ability to collect FDDI, as well as Ethernet data and because of its close integration with the HPOV platform.

Customized Scripts

To date, the organization has written about a half-dozen scripts that integrate the Remedy AR, SAS, and NETScout into the OpenView NNM environment. These scripts assist in customizing the interdependency among multiple applications and underlying UNIX processes. As an example, the SAS integration with HPOV NNM requires a script that will ensure SAS's ability to access data files created by HPOV NNM. These scripts, in most instances, are no longer than few lines, but they provide the necessary "glue" to implement an integrated network management solution.

Operations Work-Flow Model

Simultaneously with the design and implementation of the NMS, the organization began to develop operations concepts. This model addressed issues pertaining to operations roles and responsibilities, equipment sharing, problem diagnostic procedures, and an external interface from NOC perspective. Once these concepts and philosophies were sufficiently developed, an operations work-flow process was developed.

216

In the work-flow process, a network event is typically reported to the NOC, either by the user or by the HPOV through its map or event windows. For the initial deployment of the ARS, an NOC operator opens event tickets to document a network event. Associated severity levels are noted along with a brief problem description. Once the event information is entered, the ARS is assigned and forwarded, electronically, to the appropriate repair personnel or circuit carrier for investigation of the condition.

At the repair site, the technicians receive the assigned trouble ticket and begin the required fault isolation and resolution process. To accommodate the stringent mean-time-to-restore requirements, the organization has decided to maintain an inventory at each node, which allows the technicians to swap parts quickly and perform detailed diagnostics off line. A summary of such actions is entered in the Restoral Action and Problem Found fields of the opened trouble ticket. Future releases will require the operator to input the trouble-ticket equipment-sparing loads at each site to track and maintain the sparing profile. Upon problem resolution, the trouble ticket is assigned back to the NOC operators in order for them to perform the verification process.

For specific faults, such as outage in carrier-provided circuits, the NOC operator monitors and records the action taken by the carrier to restore the circuit. Associated durations are entered as time tags, and this information is eventually used as metrics to gauge the service-level agreement with the WAN carriers. A similar information base is maintained for individual operators and technicians who are assigned trouble tickets. For the future, the organization is considering incorporating the service desk of its router vendor to leverage the operators' expertise in real time by involving them in the help desk process.

As an aid to the current work-flow process, rules, as well as responsibilities, are defined to ensure the timely processing for each event. This allows the implementation of escalation procedures to guarantee timely tracking of event conditions. The organization has developed an escalation process that involves three levels and leverages on the skill mix of myriad people. Level-one escalation relies on NOC operators who, in conjunction with technicians, resolve failures. Level two includes an NOC manager, whose skill mix allows him or her to make system-level decisions to resolve problems in real time. Levels three and beyond are the domain of design engineers, as well as vendor support. At these levels, the problem usually requires expert handling.

SYSTEM DEPLOYMENT AND SUSTAINING ENGINEERING

The organization anticipates a four-to-six-month field test of the network. During the field test and thereafter, the network design team will take on the new role of sustaining systems engineering and support. In their sustaining engineering role, they will integrate and test third-party applications, perform trend analyses on collected data, and provide recommendations on operations strategies. They will also be an integral part of the organization's problem-escalation process.

NMS Status

To date, the organization has deployed this NMS to monitor and manage its TCP/IP network resources. It has also developed an in-house structured training/certification program to ensure that the proper skill mix is maintained on the NOC floor. During the initial months, the NOC will house two operators on a 24x7 basis, with an NOC manager for the day shift. A maintenance contract with a private company will provide technicians at remote sites. Eventually, as the network grows, additional operators and managers will be hired.

Based on the initial feedback from the NOC floor, the design engineers have incorporated minor changes — especially in the areas of data collection and report formats and contents. Currently, these design engineers are completing the as-built documentation suite, as well as finalizing the operations concept and procedure guidelines. They are also beginning to evaluate the middleware to be incorporated in phase II.

From a high-level corporate perspective, the phased implementation approach has resulted in immense dividends. It has kept the initial hardware/software costs in check, as well as minimized the up-front implementation risk. As the understanding of the NMS processes and the network dynamics increases, the organization will find itself in a better position to deploy additional software packages in future releases. Finally, such a phased and structured approach has allowed the organization to gradually hire the proper skill mix, and at the same time, retrain its existing operations staff.

Chapter 20
Trends in Data Communications Services

Nathan J. Muller

THE PAST FEW YEARS HAVE BEEN MARKED by unprecedented technological innovation in the communications field. Not only have new offerings such as frame relay and SMDS demonstrated their value, but older services such as X.25, T1/T3, and Integrated Services Digital Network are being revitalized. Making their debut are several new technologies that leverage the carrier's existing local loop infrastructure in support of high-speed data, including asymmetric digital subscriber line (ADSL) and high-bit-rate digital subscriber line (HDSL). Also being deployed are new wireless technologies, including Cellular Digital Packet Data, that connect mobile computer users to each other as well as to the data center. In addition, the country's entire communications infrastructure is poised for advancement with Synchronous Optical NETwork and Asynchronous Transfer Mode technologies for transmission and switching at multigigabit speeds. Long term, the combination of SONET and ATM paves the way for broadband ISDN (BISDN).

Communications at the customer premises is also undergoing rapid advancement. Fiber to the desktop and between LAN hubs is now a reality with the Fiber Distributed Data Interface, which offers transmission speeds of up to 100M bps. Several economical, albeit limited-distance, alternatives are offered over ubiquitous twisted-pair wiring, including 100Base-T and 100VG-AnyLAN. LAN hubs are also available that offer high-speed ATM switching enterprisewide. Another type of device, the bandwidth controller, is available for assembling low-speed 56K or 64K bps channels into economical high-speed pipes to support high-bandwidth applications over the public network.

Communications already plays an important role in the data center, and recent developments in this area will strengthen its role there. To aid the data center operations manager in keeping up with rapidly changing technologies,

0-8493-9824-X/00/$0.00+$.50
© 2000 by CRC Press LLC

this chapter examines the key advances in communications in the context of corporate networking and applications requirements. In particular, this chapter examines developments in:

- Optical fiber (e.g., line technologies, such as asymmetric and high-bit-rate digital subscriber line).
- Cellular digital packet data.
- T1 and T3.
- X.25 frame relay.
- Integrated services digital network.
- Switched multimegabit data services.
- Asynchronous transfer mode.
- Synchronous optical network.
- Fiber distributed data interface.

OPTICAL FIBER

More computer and telephony applications are being developed that require the bandwidth that can only be provided by optical fiber. Carriers have been installing fiber-optic cable when it can be provided at a cost that is comparable to other transport modes, such as copper, or when competition from alternative access providers forces them to take counter measures. Thus, the carriers are committed to providing a fiber backbone as close to the point of service as is cost effective.

However, if the telephone companies are to offer advanced services in support of such bandwidth-intensive applications as multimedia, document imaging, and videoconferencing, they must increase as much as possible the transmission capacity of existing twisted-pair wiring in the local loop — and do so without further delay. Fiber to the customer premises would be best, but replacing existing arrangements could cost billions of dollars and will likely take 25 years to complete.

Asymmetric Digital Subscriber Line. One of the most promising local-loop upgrade technologies is asymmetric digital subscriber line (ADSL). This technology allows for the transmission of more than 6M bps over existing twisted-pair copper wiring. ADSL carves up the local loop bandwidth into several independent channels suitable for any combination of services, including LAN to LAN data transfers, ISDN, and plain old telephone service (POTS). The electronics at both ends of the ADSL compensate for line impairments, increasing the reliability of high-speed transmissions.

High-Bit-Rate Digital Subscriber Line. An alternative to ADSL is high bit-rate digital subscriber line technology (HDSL), which uses two full duplex pairs, each operating at 784K bps. This technology is an electronic technology for conditioning lines for heavy data usage without the use of repeaters over distances of up to 12,000 feet from the central office. Because approximately 85 percent of the local loops nationwide are within this distance, HDSL promises to have a significant impact on the embedded copper network. With the addition of a "doubler" technology, transmission distances can be increased even more, enabling HDSL to be used in all local loops and further easing the bottlenecks from fiber facilities.

Although HDSL was invented to solve telephone companies' T1 provisioning problems in the local loop, it is being extensively used in private networks, as well. Universities, military bases, hospitals, corporate complexes, local governments, and other campus environments where multiple buildings require connections over relatively short distances, are ideal for HDSL solutions. Previously, campus applications, such as LAN-to-LAN, videoconferencing, CAD/CAM, and PBX networks were often restricted to 56K bps, due to cost and technical limitations.

CELLULAR DIGITAL PACKET DATA

Cellular digital packet data (CDPD) is a data-over-cellular standard for providing a LAN-like service over today's cellular voice networks. The CDPD infrastructure uses existing cellular systems to access a backbone router network, which uses the internet protocol (IP) to transport user data. PDAs, palmtops, and laptops running applications that use IP can connect to the CDPD service and gain access to other mobile computer users or to corporate computing resources that rely on wireline connections.

Because CDPD leverages the existing $20 billion investment in the cellular infrastructure, carriers can economically support data applications and avoid the cost of implementing a completely new network, as most competing technologies would require. CDPD also offers a transmission rate that is four times faster than most competing wide-area wireless services, many of which are limited to 4.8K bps or less.

In addition to supporting enhanced messaging services, including multicast, cellular paging, and national short-text messaging, CDPD extends client/server-based applications from the LAN environment into the wireless environment in support of mobile computer users. This extension can be used for such applications as database updates, schedule management, and field service support. However, the ultimate success of CDPD is closely tied to industry efforts to standardize its implementation. Using a universal standard for cellular packet data would allow users to roam and would simplify the introduction of wireless data services.

T1 AND T3

Traditional T1, which operates at 1.544M bps, is also undergoing innovation. For example, local exchanges are now being equipped to support switched T1 for on-demand (e.g., dial-up) service. Setup takes less than two seconds, providing a fast, efficient, and economical alternative to dedicated lines, which entail fixed monthly charges regardless of how little they are used. Some local-exchange carriers offer switched fractional T1, operating at 384K bps.

Some interexchange carriers offer fractional T3, in which a number of T1-equivalent pipes can be selected by customers to meet the bandwidth requirements of bandwidth-intensive applications without having to oversubscribe.

Nx64. A related innovation is Nx64 service, available from all major carriers. This allows users to build switched data pipes in bandwidth increments of 64K bps to support such applications as videoconferencing, CAD/CAM, or LAN interconnection. Channels of 64K bps can be added or dropped as necessary to support an application.

Inverse Multiplexer. A relatively new type of T1 device is the inverse multiplexer or bandwidth controller. Inverse multiplexing is an economical way to access the switched digital services of interexchange carriers because it provides bandwidth on demand, without having to subscribe to ISDN, which by comparison is more expensive and more complicated to configure.

Users dial up the appropriate increment of bandwidth needed to support a given application and pay for the number of 56K bps local-access channels needed. Channels can even be added or dropped during the transmission if bandwidth requirements change. Once transmission is completed, the channels are taken down. This eliminates the need for private leased lines to support temporary applications.

Fractional T3

T3 represents the equivalent of 28 T1 lines operating at the DS3 rate of 44.736M bps. With T3, users gain the additional bandwidth needed for a new generation of bandwidth-intensive applications, as well as traditional LAN-to-LAN and host-to-host interconnection. The absence of an optical standard for DS3 restricts the user's ability to mix and match equipment from different manufacturers. Customers must negotiate the types of optical interfaces to be placed in the interexchange carrier's serving office. In contrast to the more widely available T1 lines, T3 requires special construction for the local channel, from CPE to POP. Thus, T3 local-access lines are provided on an individual basis and usually entail high installation costs.

To broaden the appeal of T3, some carriers are offering fractional T3. With fractional T3, users can order bandwidth in T1 increments up to the full T3 rate of 44.736M bps. This service is designed for users who need more than the 1.544M-bps rate offered by T1, but less than the full bandwidth offered by

T3 to support the interconnection of Token-Ring or Ethernet LANs. This enables corporate locations to share such high-bandwidth applications as document imaging, CAD/CAM, and bulk file transfers between LANs or hosts. In the case of LANs, a bridge or router is used for interconnection through the public network. The public network appears as an extension of the LAN.

X.25

X.25 was developed before digital switching and transmission technology became available. Because networks suffered at that time from interference from noise, X.25 relied on a store-and-forward method of data communication to ensure error-free transmission. When errors arrive at a network node, a request for retransmission is sent to the originating node, which retains a copy of the packets until they are acknowledged. This process is repeated at each network node until the data is delivered to its destination.

Although X.25 is highly reliable, today's digital networks have rendered unnecessary its stringent error-correction and other overhead functions. Network throughput can be greatly increased by leaving out these processing-intensive functions and relegating them to the customer premises equipment, as is done with frame relay. Despite the advances made with frame relay technology, the popularity of X.25 remains high.

Because frame relay is often compared to X.25, managers have become more informed about X.25 and its role in supporting value-added and dial-up applications, data entry, short file transfers, and financial and point-of-sale transactions. X.25's error correction is particularly useful for data communications to international locations where high-quality digital facilities still are largely unavailable. Although X.25 has been eclipsed by frame relay and switched multimegabit data services (SMDS), there have been advances in X.25.

Most X.25 networks operate at 56K bps, but some vendors have increased the transmission speed of their X.25 offerings to T1 rates and faster, making them more effective for LAN interconnection. Speeds as high as 6M bps performance are supported by some packet switches. Currently available are integrated switches that support both circuit and packet switching — the most appropriate switching method is selected in real time according to applications requirements. Also available are X.25 gateways to frame relay, SMDS, and other data services.

FRAME RELAY

Frame relay is a packet technology that offers performance advantages over X.25 while allowing users to more easily interconnect high-speed LANs over the WAN.

The concept behind frame relay is simple: protocol sensitivity, unnecessary overhead functions, and associated processing at each network node — all characteristic of X.25 — are eliminated to obtain higher transmission rates. The reliability of digital links enables frame relay service, because error correction and flow control already exist at the network and transport layers of most computer communication protocol stacks. Because these functions have been relegated to the edges of the network rather than placed at every node along a path, as in X.25, bad frames are simply discarded. Upon error detection, customer premises equipment at each end of the path requests and implements retransmissions.

Frame relay is optimized to transmit traffic in bursts, which is the way applications traverse the LAN. Therefore, when interconnecting geographically separate LANs, organizations should consider frame relay service. It is often cost-justified for sites only 750 miles apart, roughly the distance between New York City and Chicago. Frame relay also allows a variable frame size to make the most efficient use of available bandwidth. Frame relay's variable-length frames also mesh well with the variable-length packets used in TCP/IP, OSI, and DECnet.

Today's frame relay services are based on permanent virtual connections (PVCs) that correspond to the organization's network nodes. Node addresses are stored in each switching point on the network so that frames can be routed accordingly. For each PVC, the customer chooses a committed information rate (CIR) that supports the application, and the carrier bills for it accordingly. In frame relay, a 256K bps virtual connection can handle bursts of up to 1M bps. However, too many users exceeding their CIRs at the same time creates the possibility of the network becoming congested and of frames being discarded. Fortunately, carriers overprovision their frame relay networks to guard against this situation.

As companies continue to move from the host-centric data center to the distributed computing environment, the major carriers are starting to offer managed services that address the specific needs of System Network Architecture users. The advantages of frame relay over leased lines are clear-cut, especially for SNA users with many remote locations that must be tied into one or more hosts. Among them are the following:

- Frame relay PVCs replace expensive SDLC and BSC multidrop networks between the host and branch offices.
- Consolidating connections through frame relay eliminates costly serial line interface coupler (SLIC) ports on FEPs while increasing performance.
- WAN access extends the useful lives of SDLC/BSC controllers and 3270 terminals.

- The availability of systems network architecture (SNA) connections is increased by allowing controllers to take advantage of WAN connections with multiple host paths.

A managed frame relay service includes the frame relay access devices (FRADs) — leased or purchased — that transport SNA traffic over the PVCs. FRADs are more adept than routers at congestion control and ranking traffic according to priority. Some FRADs multiplex multiple SNA/SDLC devices onto a single PVC, instead of requiring a separate PVC for each attached device, resulting in even greater cost savings.

For a legacy SNA shop that does not have the expertise or resources, a carrier-managed frame relay service is a viable option, especially because frame relay networks are much more difficult to configure, administer, and troubleshoot than private lines. All of this activity can be outsourced to the carrier. The frame relay services themselves are priced attractively. On average, the frame relay service costs about 25 percent less than the equivalent private network. In some cases, discounts of up 40 percent are possible.

INTEGRATED SERVICES DIGITAL NETWORK

Services built around the Integrated Services Digital Network (ISDN) primary rate interface (PRI) rely on switched T1 facilities. Of the 24 64K bps channels, 23 are bearer channels used for voice or data applications, and the twenty-fourth — the D channel — supports call-management functions.

ISDN has enabled early users to eliminate modem and infrequently used dedicated lines and to economically back up dedicated lines. The ISDN automatic number identification feature has also enabled some users to build new applications that integrate the traditionally separate domains of computer databases and voice communications. In this type of application, customer data is retrieved from a database and displayed at a terminal as the call is routed to a customer service representative. This arrangement improves customer response and employee productivity.

Another innovative use of ISDN comes in the form of improved call routing. Without actually connecting the call, ISDN's signaling channel first determines whether a PBX or automated call distributor (ACD) can handle it. If not, the call is forwarded to a PBX or ACD at another location that can take the call. This arrangement is useful for businesses spread across different time zones in that they can extend normal business hours. It also provides failure protection, so that if one location experiences an outage, another location can take the calls.

After a slow start, ISDN PRI is finally gaining user acceptance for such practical applications as network restoral, performance control, and peak traffic handling. The ISDN basic rate interface (BRI), which offers two bearer channels of 64K bps each and one 16K bps signaling channel, also is undergoing a resurgence, supporting such high-demand applications as computer-telephony integration (CTI), telecommuting, and Internet access. Many communications servers on the LAN now support ISDN, as do communications controllers in the host environment. Because ISDN service uses digital lines, users benefit from improved reliability, as well as from faster call setup time.

SWITCHED MULTIMEGABIT DATA SERVICES

Switched Multimegabit Data Services (SMDS) is a high-speed, connectionless, cell-based service offered by the regional telephone companies. It is used primarily for linking LANs within a metropolitan area. It offers customers the economic benefits of shared transmission facilities, combined with the equivalent privacy and control of dedicated networks. SMDS is much easier to provision and manage than frame relay and, over short distances, SMDS can be more economical than frame relay.

Despite its advantages, however, SMDS has not fared well against frame relay. One reason for frame relay's popularity is that it became available nationwide at a very early stage, whereas SMDS was promoted as a regional service. Only recently has SMDS become available from long-distance providers. This may alleviate user concerns about being able to link far-flung corporate sites using SMDS. Another sticking point for SMDS has been that access was not available at speeds lower than T1. Now SMDS is routinely offered by the regional telephone companies at access speeds between 56K bps and 34M bps. With these improvements, the demand for SMDS should grow at a much faster clip in the foreseeable future.

ASYNCHRONOUS TRANSFER MODE

Asynchronous Transfer Mode (ATM), also known as cell relay, is a general-purpose switching method for multimedia (e.g., voice, data, image, and video). Whereas frame relay and SMDS use variable-length frames, the cell size used by ATM is fixed at 53 bytes. This fixed size facilitates the switching of cells by hardware-based routing mechanisms, enabling operation at extremely high speeds. ATM speeds are scalable and can exceed 2.5G bps over optical fiber.

Despite the need to break larger variable-rate frames into fixed-size cells, the latency of ATM is orders-of-magnitude less than frame relay alone. For example, on a five-node network spanning 700 miles, ATM exhibits 0.3m-second latency vs. 60m-second latency for frame relay at T1 speeds. (At T3, the latency of ATM is only 0.15m seconds.) Thus, ATM makes for fast, reliable switching and eliminates the potential congestion problems of frame relay networks.

A non-blocking switching method, ATM virtually eliminates the buildup of congestion that can hamper the performance of campus LANs and inter-campus backbones. ATM hubs also allow networks to grow smoothly. Only switching capacity needs be added to handle increases in traffic; the user interfaces are not changed. ATM hubs are star-wired with direct links to every attached device. This configuration not only minimizes network management overhead but facilitates the collection of statistics for fault isolation, accounting, administration, and network planning.

ATM provides the features necessary for successful multimedia applications. Specifically, it has the ability to define different traffic types, with each traffic type delivering a different quality of service based on the unique properties associated with it. The traffic type that supports multimedia applications is called constant bit rate (CBR) service. CBR supplies a fixed-bandwidth virtual circuit, which addresses the special handling needs of delay-sensitive multimedia applications — those that contain real-time video and voice, for example. The quality of service is negotiated with the network. The applications themselves can do the negotiation through native ATM interface, or such interfaces as LAN emulation, an ATM Forum standard, and classic IP can perform the negotiation for the applications over ATM.

When the quality of service is negotiated with the network, there are performance guarantees that go along with it: maximum cell rate, available cell rate, cell transfer delay, and cell loss ratio. The network reserves the full bandwidth requested by the connection. There is no data rate limit for CBR connections, nor is there a limit on how long a connection can transmit at the maximum cell rate, otherwise known as the peak cell rate (PCR). The PCR is the maximum data rate that the connection can support without risking data loss. Any traffic above the specified rate risks being dropped by the network, whereas traffic below the specified rate will fail to satisfy the needs of the application.

These and the other advantages of ATM — including low latency, high throughput, and scalability — will one day make it the network of choice for supporting new, high-bandwidth multimedia applications, as well as legacy LAN and TCP/IP traffic. Meanwhile, ATM has been slow to take off because of the start-up costs of implementation. On the WAN side, carriers must invest in a new overlay infrastructure — something they have been slow in doing. Likewise, on the LAN side, companies must invest in new hubs, server interfaces, and workstation adapters. In some cases, new cabling may also be required.

SYNCHRONOUS OPTICAL NETWORK

Synchronous Optical Network (SONET) technology allows the full potential of the fiber-optic transmission medium to be realized. SONET standards specify transmission rates that start at 51.84M bps and reach to 2.488G bps and make provisions for transmission rates of 13G bps. Throughout this decade and beyond, SONET will gradually replace the proprietary T3 asynchronous networks of today.

With the same fiber cable that supports asynchronous networks, transmission capacity can be increased one-thousandfold by using end-to-end SONET equipment. SONET also supports a variety of current and emerging carrier services, including ATM, SMDS, and BISDN, increasing their reliability through embedded management functions.

Most of the activity in SONET deployment has been in building fiber rings that offer customers fail-safe data communications in major metropolitan areas. SONET equipment can reroute traffic instantly if a section of the network fails or becomes disabled. This level of reliability is increasingly becoming a critical requirement for businesses whose networks are becoming more data intensive with each passing year.

Today's self-healing SONET ring networks are capable of operating at 622M bps. Within 50m-seconds of a cable cut, customer traffic running over the primary path is automatically routed along the backup path, with no loss of data. This recovery process is implemented by the SONET Add-Drop Multiplexer (ADM), which duplicates and sends the data in opposite directions over the dual paths. When the signals reach a common point on the network, they are compared, then one set is discarded, while the other is delivered to the destination. If the primary path is disrupted, the data on the backup path is passed on to the destination.

Although the carriers have been installing SONET rings in major metropolitan areas at a pace that has been keeping up with customer demand, they are expected to step up their deployments of SONET. For many telcos, the cost-benefit threshold has been crossed; that is, the financial incentives of SONET deployment now exceed the costs of new installations.

FIBER DISTRIBUTED DATA INTERFACE

There is no question that traditional Ethernet and Token-Ring LANs are beginning to get bogged down by the added bandwidth requirements of CAD/CAM, document imaging, collaborative computing, and multimedia applications. Fiber Distributed Data Interface (FDDI) backbones offer 100M bps of bandwidth that can alleviate potential bottlenecks. FDDI uses a token-passing scheme similar to Token-Ring and a dual-ring fault protection scheme similar to SONET.

Normally considered a private networking solution for office environments, FDDI is now being offered as a wide-area network service by some carriers. Bell Atlantic, for example, provides a service to extend 100M-bps FDDI LANs across WANs. The service, called Full FDDI, is a response to requests from financial firms that wanted to use this kind of service together with a similar one offered by New York Telephone. The financial companies wanted to interconnect offices in New York City with data centers in New Jersey. The only difference between the two services is that Bell Atlantic places FDDI concentrators on customers' premises, while under New York Telephone's service, called Enterprise Service FDDI, concentrators are located at the carrier's central office.

Optical fiber equipment and adapters are still too expensive for FDDI deployment throughout the enterprise. An economical alternative to FDDI in the office environment is the twisted-pair distributed data interface (TPDDI). TPDDI offers the same speed as FDDI over ordinary twisted-pair wiring at distances of up to 100 meters (328 feet) from station to hub, which is enough to accommodate the wiring schemes of most office environments. TPDDI is designed to help users make an easy transition to 100M-bps transmission at the workstation level, in support of bandwidth-intensive data applications.

For companies with large investments in Ethernet, other 100M-bps technologies worth considering are 100Base-T, also known as Fast Ethernet, and 100VG-AnyLAN, a non-standard Ethernet extension technology. The major difference between the two is that 100Base-T preserves the contention access scheme of pure Ethernet, while 100VG-AnyLAN dispenses with it.

CONCLUSION

Data center managers are under increasing pressure to get all the value possible out of communications equipment and services, as well as to control the cost of networks. Despite these pressures, companies continue to make investments in applications and technologies out of a desire to gain competitive advantage. In implementing new applications and running them over various combinations of services, media and equipment, a balance of efficiency and economy can be achieved to obtain or sustain that advantage.

Telephone companies and interexchange carriers recognize that their financial futures hinge on their ability to provide data communications services that can support new and emerging applications. With data traffic already surpassing voice traffic on many corporate networks, the arrival of efficient and economical data communications services, such as frame relay and SMDS, is welcome and timely.

At the same time, digital communications over fiber-optic networks is becoming more available and cost justifiable. Such older forms of data communication as X.25, ISDN, and T-carrier have also undergone innovation in recent years. Data communications already play a major role in data center operations, and developments in this field will strengthen this role.

Chapter 21
The Emerging Advantage of xDSL Technology

Andres Llana, Jr.

SOME OF THE FLAVORS OF XDSL TECHNOLOGY have been around for awhile but sold under a different label. However, for the most part, end users just do not care what it is called, so long as it provides more bandwidth at less cost than before. Currently, Digital Subscriber Line (DSL) technology comes in several popular flavors: asymmetrical DSL (ADSL), high bit rate DSL (HDSL), symmetric DSL (SDSL), or very high speed DSL (VDSL). There is also rate adaptive ADSL (RADSL). All of these are collectively referred to as xDSL, where x is the designator for the service.

In the proper setting, xDSL is capable of supporting any specific user bandwidth requirement given the local availability of copper. This is fine as long as one is the local exchange carrier (LEC), and one owns the copper. (See Exhibit 21.1.)

As a result of earlier initiatives by state and federal agencies to deregulate the "local loop," a new group of end users has emerged to benefit from this largesse. This emerging group of digital subscriber line (DSL) service users has now become accustomed to the "always connected" convenience of high-speed access to the Internet. These charter users, joined by an expanding group of Internet users, continue to want "more for less."

While these initiatives have not been well received by the incumbent local exchange carrier (ILEC) and the Regional Bell Operating Companies (RBOCs), these changes have altered forever the provisioning of copper local loops.

Because the RBOCs and their LECs have been slow to deploy DSL services, a new breed of aggressive service provider has come on the local scene. With little in the way of traditional organizational structures to get

Exhibit 21.1. xDSL.

---

xDSL technology is potentially a lower-cost replacement for dedicated 56Kbps local loops used to tie into a Frame Relay service. Enterprise network owners should investigate the availability of dry copper within their serving Central Office as one alternative to the more-expensive dedicated service. In addition, enterprise network architects might also negotiate with their competitive local exchange carriers (CLECs). Some enterprise network operators have been able to greatly improve their network access arrangements using lower-cost xDSL links to their Frame Relay service provider's POP. In addition, where there was a requirement for Internet access or a shadow network to back up the primary network, xDSL links provided full-time online access at less cost. Some network operators found that they could deploy a DSLAM behind their DMARC and use dry copper to link LANs or desk top terminals to the Internet for an "always on" connection.

---

in the way, Competitive Local Exchange Carriers (CLECs) and Internet Service Providers (ISPs) are charging ahead to get new local loop business at reduced prices.

Thus far, they have been able to provide local loop access on an unbundled basis, utilizing the local embedded copper. These CLECs and ISPs, deploying xDSL technology, have been able to provide their customers with a very cost-effective, high-speed data service.

WHAT HAS CHANGED

The original Digital Subscriber Line (DSL) service was introduced as ISDN in the 1980s. This technology compressed 160Kbps into an 80KHz bandwidth of the local loop. ISDN utilized a four-level PAM modulation (2 Binary, 1 Quaternary) "2b1Q" to reach the range of 18,000 feet.

High Bit Rate Digital Subscriber Line (HDSL) came along in the early 1990s and used the same 2 Binary, 1 Quaternary (2b1Q) line coding to support T1 services. HDSL made it possible to provision loops of up to 12,000 feet long using 24 AWG. Some vendors are offering equipment that can extend this reach to 18,000 feet.

HDSL is more robust than the old T1 service, which required repeaters every few hundred yards. More advanced HDSL equipment, on the other hand, has eliminated many of the problems associated with provisioning T1 service, which resulted in much lower rates for local T1 access.

SOME OTHER FLAVORS OF DSL

Asymmetrical Digital Subscriber Line (ADSL) service came about in the 1992/1993 timeframe as a vehicle for offering video services to the home. Another DSL technology, Rate Adaptive Digital Subscriber Line (ADSL), came along as a means of allowing a transceiver to automatically adjust line speed to attain the highest level of speed over a given loop.

ADSL and RADSL promise to deliver rates of about 7Mb downstream with upstream links of about 1Mb; and while ADSL and RADSL are supposed to run up to 18,000 feet, to get the promised 7Mb downstream, the user would have to be very close to the serving central office (CO). While all of this technology sounds great, one needs to focus on the real-life application of technology for thousands of end users. Today, the majority of domestic use is focused on the World Wide Web; however, there are a growing number of Small Office Home Office (SOHO) users that require multi-network access as a means of directly or indirectly earning a living. Therefore, it is ADSL/RADSL service that ultimately offers a solution to the needs of the SOHO user.

Today, business applications have grown to stress higher speed access to public and private network infrastructures. The real-life issue is providing access to the corporate or public network without spending large amounts of money for local loop access.

Initially, HDSL technology reduced the cost for provisioning T1 services because it eliminated the need for extensive engineering, expensive repeaters, and the huge labor costs associated with deploying traditional copper wire T1 services. The adoption of HDSL technology allowed the LECs to make use of their copper infrastructure to offer more competitive T1 local loops without the burden of high provisioning costs.

Symmetrical Digital Subscriber Line (SDSL) is similar to HDSL in that vendor equipment supports the same line encoding scheme: 2 Binary, 1 Quaternary (2b1Q), which avoids any conflict when installed on the LECs' local copper. In addition, depending on vendor equipment and desired line speed, SDSL differs from HDSL in that the loop reach for an SDSL line has the potential of being somewhat greater than HDSL.

Like its predecessor, SDSL technology has become an enabler for high-speed services at a much more affordable price. This is due to that fact that the application of SDSL technology, like HDSL, causes no change in services and uses the same embedded copper infrastructure as HDSL. Potentially, SDSL technology, where applicable, provides lower install and monthly recurring costs for the installation of a circuit capable of supporting up to 1.5Mb of service.

Perhaps the largest demand for service has come from the Internet community of users and their access to the World Wide Web for the conduct of their business. Today, access to the Web has become the medium of choice for the dissemination of information to business associates and customers alike.

SDSL ENABLES ISP SERVICES

Historically, the gateway to any network — either private or public — was through a local copper loop that connected the end user to the network through the Central Office. The service providers or networks contracted with the serving utility to provide connectivity at the edge of their network. The end user or customer paid a high price for connectivity to the network, with the monthly price being determined by the available bandwidth of the line. The arrival of SDSL equipment, together with enabling legislation that supports competition at the local level, has changed the service arrangements at the local level. Because SDSL equipment requires a physical connection to the local loop, an ISP must locate a Digital Subscriber Line Access Multiplexer (DSLAM) within 12,000 to 18,000 feet of a subscriber. The ISP can do this by locating a DSLAM adjacent to the Central Office. Unconditioned "dry copper" is ordered from the LEC to connect the subscriber's location through the Central Office to the ISP's DSLAM adjacent to the central office.[1] T1, multiple T1, or T3 facilities connect the DSLAM to the ISP central hub. This arrangement gives the end user a direct link to the Internet at speeds of from 64Kbps through to 1.5Mb depending on the distance from the DSLAM. (See Exhibit 21.2.)

Another variation is the location of a DSLAM on the premises of an industrial park or campus. Located at a central location (usually the facility's demarcation point [DEMARC]), DSL lines are extended to users around the industrial park or campus area. (See Exhibit 21.3.) The DSLAM serves to concentrate all of the DSL lines and provide high-speed access to the Internet via T1/T3 access to a central ISP hub. In a multitenant industrial park, it is estimated that at least 200 or more users would be required to make this business model a success, although fewer tenants would work where higher-speed access is required. On the other hand, enterprise network operators have found that the application of dry copper can be used to support the connection of local offices or remote buildings that are served by the same Central Offices. They have also used dry copper and a local DSLAM as a more cost-effective method for concentrating a number of LANs or desktop terminals into the Internet.

Until the advent of more advanced xDSL technology, local loop lengths were limited to end users located within a 2.5-mile radius of the Central Office. However, the newer SDSL equipment utilizing proprietary technology can potentially lengthen the reach of a dry copper circuit's effectiveness to 30,000 feet at a lower bandwidth of 64Kbps. However, with incremental speed increases to 1Mb, the circuit length conversely would get shorter. For example, Bellcore, the former research arm of the Regional Bell Operating Companies, has conducted SDSL tests with single pair service, which was extended out to 24,700 feet at 192Kbps. These extensions are possible through continual advances in SDSL technology. For example,

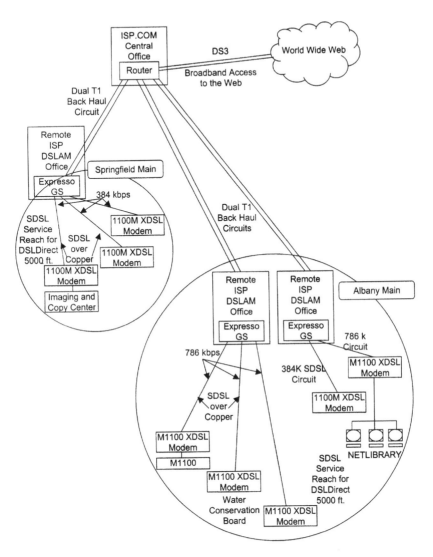

Exhibit 21.2. ISP.COM application of TUT systems expresso SDLAM.

TUT Systems of Pleasant Hill, CA, deploys a patented process called Fast-Copper™ technology that removes ambient electronic noise and other distortions in the environment where copper pairs are used. The focus of this technology is aimed at noise reduction circuits, analog and digital signal processing circuits, and digital modulation. This technology makes possible the deployment of dry circuits to within a radius of five to six miles, rather than the more limiting factor of one to two miles. An extension in the Central Office service range provides support for increased bandwidth for

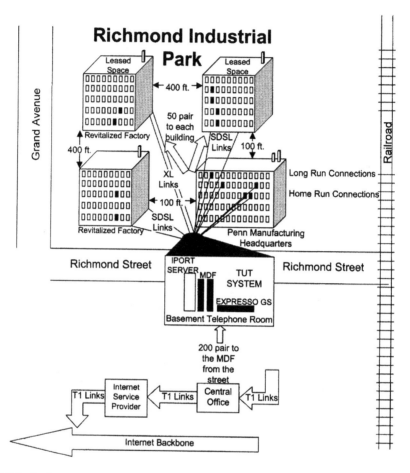

Exhibit 21.3. Richmond Industrial Park redeploying copper lines using DSL technology.

private metropolitan networks as well as access to the Internet at high speeds for power users.

DSLDirect AND ISP.COM

ISP.COM is an Eastern Internet Service Provider, serving eastern businesses with high-speed Internet access. ISP.COM provides direct support to a number of downtown office buildings in several eastern cities. At present, these internal connections are brought to an Ethernet switch at the DEMARC and then in turn brought back to a TUT Systems Expresso DSLAM that is connected to the ISP.COM DS3 central hub via a fiber link. (See Exhibit 21.2.)

236

DSLDirect

ISP has recently introduced DSLDirect for direct high-speed Internet service for small and medium-sized Albany and Springfield businesses. The DSLDirect service utilizes TUT Systems Expresso DSLAM units to provide direct access via dry copper, which is a more cost-effective solution than previous provisioning methods. Using these low-cost copper circuits, the ISP is able to provide 384Kbps and 768Kbps Internet connection speeds in direct competition with other larger service providers. The ISP service is not a bridged connection, as is the local RBOC service offering. All of the ISP DSLDirect end-user packets are shipped directly to the Internet, without being routed over several switches to the designated Internet switch.

With ISP DSLDirect service, the customer is linked directly to ISP Expresso DSLAM, which, in turn, is linked via multiple T1 links back to the ISP hub and their DS3 connection to the Internet. This in effect provides customers with their own dedicated circuit into the Internet.

The Expresso DSLAM, when first put on a dry copper pair, will adjust its speed depending on the line condition. When it finds its level, the speed remains constant. This has been a very helpful feature because customers can order a 384Kbps line but get a slightly better level of service. Because the level of service on the Expresso DSLAM is software adjustable from 64Kbps through to 1.2Mb in 64Kbps increments, ISP has a great deal of flexibility in serving the needs of its customers using SDSL technology. To use this service, the customer must purchase or lease a TUT Systems 1100M DSL modem/router for about $495, or $30 per month. There is also an ISP charge of about $175 (384Kbps), $275 (786Kbps), or $375 (1.2Mb per month) for the desired level of Internet service. These charges can vary from one region of the country to another.

Presently, DSLDirect is available to businesses located in the immediate vicinity of the Albany Main and Springfield Main (Central Office) locations. Additional Central Office sites will be added to the DSLDirect service offering in the future. (See Exhibit 21.2.)

ANOTHER SERVICE MARKET

Just about every service provider and equipment manufacturer is expanding into the enhanced multiple dwelling units (MDU) Internet service provisioning market. This market is comprised of over 40,000 office buildings, 3.5 million hotels, and as many up-market apartment complexes whose tenants have two or more PCs. Companies like Copper Mountain, Paradyne, and TUT Systems have organized special marketing efforts to support the multiple-dwelling market.

For example, TUT Systems has put together an integrated support service through a network of value-added resellers (VARs) that will provide the hotel or a multiple-dwelling property owner like a real estate trust (REIT), with a turnkey operation. This turnkey solution utilizes the TUT Systems HomeRun™[2] technology together with an IPORT™ Internet Access System premium Content Billing Platform System to provide an integrated solution called the Connected Community. This is a complete service package sold by local VARs that provides a full package of services.

The advantage of the Connected Community package to the property owner is the fact that there is nothing for the property owner to do. The VAR handles all the arrangements for Internet access with the local CLEC/ISP service provider. All arrangements for equipment configuration and installation are arranged by the VAR. In addition, the equipment can be configured and priced based on the property owner's immediate requirements. Therefore, costs for equipment can be based on present need. As the property owner's end-user requirements expand, additional equipment can be purchased as needed. Another cost-saving feature is the ability of the TUT Systems HomeRun™ technology to use existing standard telephone lines to deliver service without affecting the existing voice service. This solution eliminates much of the cost associated with rewiring a hotel or MDU for data transmission and Internet access.

MORE THAN JUST SPEED

The xDSL market focus until recently has been on speed and low-cost access. While DSL is a very compelling technology, it is worth mentioning that there are other competitors that offer other products and services. For example, a growing number of companies offer cable modems and Internet appliances that will support delivery of competing services over cable.

Recognizing the requirement for something more than bandwidth, service providers like GTE, U.S. West, Bell Atlantic, and others have announced an ADSL product. With over 700 million phone lines worldwide, service providers can take advantage of this technology to offer an extensive number of voice and data services.

ADSL offers great promise as an alternative to cable because it supports voice and data over the same twisted pair. Further, advanced xDSL line coding algorithms allow for the effective division of the frequency spectrum on copper telephone wire to support voice and data. (See Exhibit 21.4.) With the voice spectrum confined to the 4KHz baseband, the upstream and downstream channels can be dedicated to data. This allows the service provider to offer multimegabit data service while leaving voice

Exhibit 21.4.   SDSL technology at risk.

Not all of the RBOCs have been happy with the rush by the CLECs and ISPs to take advantage of dry copper tariffs. For example, hearings were held before the utility commissions in some western states in an effort to drop the dry copper tariff, as it is known. While Nebraska allowed the discontinuance of the dry copper tariff, Colorado did not allow this measure to take place. Other states are considering the matter. Utility commissioners in other jurisdictions throughout the United States should be mindful of this because the Telecommunications Act of 1996 did specifically provide for competition at the local level. SDSL offers a number of opportunities for Competitive Local Exchange Carriers (CLEC), Independent Telephone Operating Companies (ITOCs), Internet Service Providers (ISPs), and enterprise network owners to deploy dry copper circuits to the advantage of the subscribing end user. For this reason, one should protect the embedded base of dry copper that forms much of the basic infrastructure of the U.S. communications system. This is a resource that has long been paid for by subscribers and should really be declared part of the public domain.

service intact. Thus, ADSL connects two different entities — voice and data — all over the same physical wire pair. Recently, the International Telecom Union (ITU) has determined G-lite (G.992.2) to be the standard for ADSL-based service products. Many of the DSLAM manufacturers and service providers have settled on this standard so as to support interoperability. This will greatly simplify the acquisition of CPE (customer premise equipment) and the cross-integration of services across the country and internationally.

THE NEXT FRONTIER

As the ADSL G-lite services begin to take hold among the service providers, a new segment of the networking marketplace is poised for rapid deployment. Networks in the home represent the next window of opportunity for all service providers because ADSL splitterless services make it possible to support the delivery of service over a single pair of telephone cables.

To address this market, AT&T Wireless, AMD Networking, Hewlett-Packard, IBM, Lucent Technologies, Rockwell, and TUT Systems have come together to establish the Home Phoneline Networking Alliance (Home-PNA). This alliance was formed to develop the specifications for interoperability for all home network devices.

Subsequently, TUT Systems, who had announced their HomeRun™ technology early in 1998, licensed this technology to Lucent Technologies. As a result, the other members of the HomePNA group adopted HomeRun™ technology as the first specification for home networking. This move will serve to greatly facilitate the introduction of more than just bandwidth to the consumer market. HomeRun™ provides support for splitterless 1Mbps Ethernet transmission over existing telephone lines already in the home. When the proper customer premise equipment (CPE) is deployed, the consumer can establish a home-based local area network (LAN). In this operating environment, multiple applications can be run in the home with "always on" access to the Internet where there may be access to specific databases.

Notes

1. An ISP DSLAM can only be used to transport the subscriber to the Internet. It cannot be used to switch traffic at the CO.
2. The HomeRun™ technology has been adopted by the Home Phoneline Network Alliance as the standard home network LAN technology.

Chapter 22
LAN Printing Techniques

Gilbert Held

DURING THE EARLY DEVELOPMENT STAGE of local area networking technology, the sharing of expensive laser printers was one of the primary reasons cited for using that relatively new technology. Although the price of laser printers has significantly declined over the past decade, network printing remains an important application supported by LANs. Thus, it is important to understand the different options available for installing network printers, as well as the advantages and disadvantages associated with each option. Doing so will provide data center managers with information necessary to satisfy organizational network printing requirements in a cost-efficient manner, while considering such key issues as the effect of printing on other network operations, as well as network security.

CONNECTION METHOD

There are four basic methods that can be used to connect a printer to a local area network. Those methods are:

- File server connection
- Print server connection
- Remote printer via PC connection
- Direct connection

They are presented in the order that network printing technology developed and do not represent an order of preference. The remainder of this chapter examines each connection method in detail to understand the advantages and disadvantages associated with each method.

File Server Connection

The first series of network operating systems that were developed provided support for network printing via the attachment of printers to the serial or parallel ports of file servers. Although this option limits the num-

0-8493-9824-X/00/$0.00+$.50
© 2000 by CRC Press LLC

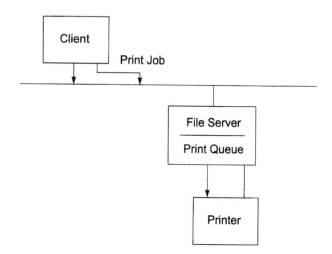

Exhibit 22.1. File server print connection data flow.

ber of network printers that can be used prior to purchasing a license to operate another file server, it minimizes network traffic, which can be an important consideration when a network has a high level of activity. To understand why a file server connection minimizes network print traffic in comparison to other network printing options requires a review of the flow of print job traffic.

PRINT JOB TRAFFIC

In a client/server environment, all network traffic originated by client workstations first flows to a server to include print jobs. When a print job flows to a file server, it is first placed into a print queue from which it will be serviced. Thus, the attachment of a printer directly to a file server results in a print job flowing from the client to the file server, as illustrated in Exhibit 22.1. Note that every byte in the print job only flows once on the network. As will be noted later in this chapter, each of the other network printing options results in every byte in a print job flowing twice on the network, in effect doubling the print job workload in terms of its impact on network traffic.

FILE SERVER ATTACHMENT PROBLEMS

Although the direct attachment of network printers to a file server minimizes the effect of print job traffic on a network, its use in this manner has a number of disadvantages. Those disadvantages include potential file server performance problems and printer access constraints.

When a file server supports directly connected printers, data leaves the server's print queues at the serial or parallel port interface speed, which is typically a fraction of the network operating rate. Because the file server must use interrupts to service print jobs exiting its print queues, the server will perform a periodic series of interrupt servicing operations for a longer period of time than if the print job was directed onto the network. This in turn adversely affects the ability of the server to perform other network-related functions. Based on a series of performance measurements conducted by the author of this chapter, a NetWare 3.1X or 4.X server operating on an Intel 486 50-MHz or lower performance processor will be adversely affected by at least 10% through the use of two or more directly connected printers when 20 or more pages of network printing occur per hour. Although such printing will adversely affect the performance of a file server operating on an Intel Pentium processor, the actual decrease in the level of performance was found to be so slight that it was difficult to measure, varying between 1% and 2%. Thus, if a 75-MHz or higher Pentium processor is used as the platform for an organization's file server, the file server's level of performance when printers are directly connected should be considered to be equivalent to other network printing methods that relocate network printers to other areas on the network.

A second, and for many users a more serious, problem associated with the direct attachment of printers to a file server is printer access. Most organizations consider their file servers to represent repositories of important data they wish to secure. Thus, it is quite natural for file servers to be located in access-controlled areas within a building, such as the corporate data center, a technical control center, or a similarly controlled access location. Because one of the goals of network printing is to provide convenient access to shared printers, many organizations prefer to maintain security for their file servers and eliminate this printing option from consideration. Other organizations, such as small departments where access for all employees is already controlled, may install a server in an empty office. For such organizations, the direct connection of printers to a departmental file server may represent a viable network option, especially if they are using NetWare on an Intel Pentium processor-based computer.

PRINT SERVER CONNECTION

A print server is a computer that runs network software developed to extract print jobs from print queues residing on a file server. Through the use of a print server, network printers can be located at any location where the print server can be connected to a network. Thus, the use of a print server removes the controlled access problem associated with the direct connection of printers to a file server.

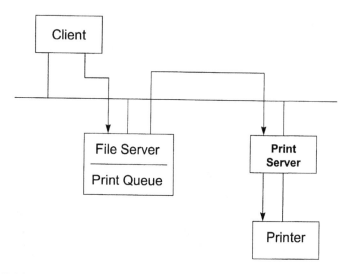

Exhibit 22.2. Print job data flow when a printer server is used.

Exhibit 22.2 illustrates the data flow for a print job when printers are connected to a print server. In a client/server environment, the print job first flows to the file server, where it is placed into a print queue. The print server operates software that communicates with the file server, and the two servers negotiate the transmission of the print job from the print queue in the file server to the print server, where it is directed to an attached printer. Thus, the print job must flow twice on the network, first from the client workstation to the file server, and then from the file server to the print server.

If the network has a high level of utilization, a significant amount of printing can result in a degradation of network performance, especially when using graphics embedded in documents directed to the network printer. Thus, for many network managers and administrators, the choice between connecting network printers to a file server or to a print server represents one of printing convenience and security versus a degradation of network performance.

REMOTE PRINTING ON A PC

Remote printing represents a network printing technique that turns a workstation into a limited-function print server. The major differences between remote printing and a print server concern the ability of each device to perform other operations and the number of printers that can be supported. A remote printer capability is established by loading a terminate and stay resident (TSR) program on a PC connected to a network. The TSR program works in a manner similar to print server software, establishing communications with a file server and extracting jobs from print queues associated with the remote printer. The TSR program works in the background on the host PC, enabling foreground operations to continue. This enables a PC user to use his or her computer for both local and network-related operations, while network printing is performed on a printer connected to the computer. In comparison, a print server is dedicated to servicing attached printers and cannot be used for other operations.

A second difference between a remote printing TSR program operating on a PC and a dedicated print server concerns the number of printers that can be supported by each computer. Remote printing on a PC is normally limited to one per computer. In comparison, a print server is only limited by the number of serial and parallel ports that can be installed in the server.

One of the key advantages associated with the use of remote printing is its simplicity, because the installation of the TSR program can be performed in under a minute. Another advantage associated with this network printing method is the fact that many organizations have large quantities of obsolete Intel 286-, 386-, and 486-based computers. Because the remote printing processes are not processor intensive, just about any computer platform can be used to obtain a remote printing capability. This means remote printing PCs can be located within several areas of an organization to better distribute print jobs to areas where users work. In comparison, a print server that is normally used to support multiple printers does not provide the level of location flexibility typically associated with the use of remote printing PCs.

Disadvantages associated with the use of remote printing include the doubling of print job traffic and the possibility that the PC user whose computer is operating the TSR program may automatically power down his or her workstation at the end of the day, precluding the ability of other network users to use one or more printers attached to that computer. Concerning the latter, for this reason most organizations now set up a remote printer capability on unattended workstations that are left on continuously. This alleviates the problems associated with the tendency of computer users to power off their computers when they leave the office. In addition, if the organization has an inventory of older Intel 286-, 386-, or 486-based computers, those computers can be used as remote printer workstation platforms to distribute a network printing capability throughout the organization.

Exhibit 22.3 illustrates an example of the use of print server and remote printer-printer connections. In this example, it was assumed that engineering department employees were grouped in a small area and those employees had a sufficient amount of network printing to justify the use of three

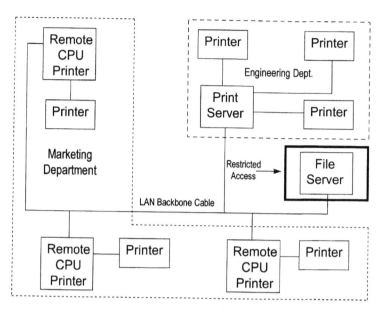

Exhibit 22.3.   Using print server and remote printer-printer connections.

network printers. Thus, rather than install three separate remote printer-based computers, one computer was installed operating print server software, which enabled that computer to support the attachment of three network printers. The marketing department, which occupies the remainder of the floor shown in Exhibit 22.3, has employees spread out over an extended area of floor space. Based on an assumption that there are three convenient areas where network printing jobs could be delivered for pickup by marketing personnel, three remote printing computers were installed to service the requirements of that department. Thus, mixing the use of print servers and remote printer-based computers, allows for a degree of flexibility in satisfying the network printing requirements of organizational employees. In addition, note that access is restricted to the file server shown in Exhibit 22.3, precluding its use for convenient pickup of network printing jobs. Thus, no printers are shown as being attached to the file server. If access to the file server was not restricted, an alternative approach that could be considered would be the use of the file server for network printing to support the engineering department. However, if the file server is not located within a 15-foot radius of the location where the engineering department wants to locate network printers, the file server would have to be relocated, which may not be an easy task. The 15-foot radius limitation is based on the common use of 15-foot parallel printer cable. If serial printers are used, the radius of support can be extended to

Exhibit 22.4.   Comparing LAN printer connection methods.

Effect on Network and End-User Operations	LAN Printer Connection Method			
	File Server Connection	**Print Server Connection**	**Remote Printer**	**Direct Connection**
Minimize network traffic	Yes	No	No	No
Typical printer support	Up to 4	Up to 4	1 or 2	1
Effect on file server performance	10% when non-Pentium system is used	None	None	None
Printer access	Usually restricted	More flexible	Very flexible	Extremely flexible
Requires dedicated computer	Yes	Yes	No	N/A

approximately 50 feet, which represents the maximum standardized drive distance for serial connections when an RS-232 interface is used.

DIRECT CONNECTION

The fourth method for supporting network printing is via the direct connection of a printer to the network. To do so, the printer must have a network adapter and ROM code that convert the printer into a mini remote printer. This method of connection was introduced by Hewlett-Packard in 1995, and provides users with a great deal of flexibility in supporting user network printing requirements because the necessity for having a separate printer is eliminated. Thus, this network printing method minimizes the amount of desk space required to support network printing. The disadvantages of this network printing method concern its printer support and network traffic. Because the LAN adapter and ROM code are physically inserted into a printer, support is limited to one printer. Concerning network traffic, print jobs first flow to the file server, and then from the file server to the card in the printer, doubling network traffic. Exhibit 22.4 compares the four LAN printer connection methods with respect to their effect on network and end-user operations.

RECOMMENDED COURSE OF ACTION

As indicated in this chapter, there are significant differences associated with the use of different methods for supporting network printing. Some network printing methods provide more flexibility in locating printers than other methods, while the use of a file server minimizes the effect of print jobs on network traffic. In developing a network printing solution to satisfy organizational requirements, it is important to understand the advantages and disadvantages associated with each method, as well as the volume of print traffic and desired printer locations. In many situations, a mixture of network printing methods may be more suitable for satisfying user requirements than the use of a single method. Thus, in attempting to match the characteristics of different network printing methods against organizational requirements, the data center operations manager should consider implementing several methods rather than a single method.

Chapter 23
Preparing for Cable Modems

Gilbert Held

DURING 1995, THE USE OF THE INTERNET EXPANDED CONSIDERABLY, with tens of thousands of corporations, universities, government agencies, and individuals creating home pages on servers, while tens of millions of users surfed the World Wide Web. As corporations began to recognize the value of the Internet for building software applications, promoting products and services, and locating as well as disseminating information, the addition of graphics to World Wide Web home pages literally slowed Web surfing operations to a crawl, adversely affecting user productivity. Whereas the replacement of 14.4K bps modem by state-of-the-art 28.8K bps devices has assisted many users in speeding up their Internet search operations, even at that operating rate the display of a typical Web page containing one or two graphic images can result in a delay of 10 to 15 seconds as the picture is "painted" on a monitor.

Recognizing the operating limitations associated with transmissions via the public switched-telephone network, as well as looking for an additional source of revenue, several cable television (CATV) companies initiated broadband access trials to the Internet during 1995. Each of these trials involved the use of cable modems, which enable a personal computer (PC) to access the Internet via a common CATV coaxial cable at operating rates up to tens of millions of bits per second. Although cable modems are in their infancy, both independent market research organizations and many cable operators predict that within a few years, the installed base of this new type of communications device will rapidly grow to over 10 million modems.

Due to the advantages associated with obtaining high-speed Internet access, as well as the potential economics associated with the use of cable modems to obtain such access, data center managers should consider preparing their facility for the infrastructure required to use cable modems.

This chapter discusses the nature of cable modems and describes their operation. The scope of the discussion also includes the cabling infrastructure being developed to provide a megabit transmission facility to residences and businesses. The chapter outlines the cabling requirements for installation within buildings, requirements that are necessary to access this new high-speed information highway via the use of cable modems. The data center manager should have a background of knowledge concerning a rapidly evolving new technology and be able to support its use when corporate policy begins to include Internet issues.

MODEM FUNDAMENTALS

The ability to appreciate why cable modems are able to provide a transmission capability that is an order of magnitude or more than conventional modems used for transmission on the switched telephone network, requires knowledge of certain transmission concepts, including the Nyquist theorem. This section concentrates on the operation of conventional analog modems that are used on the switched telephone network. This can provide the data center manager with an understanding of why analog modems' operating rate is limited and how they may be able to overcome that operating rate limitation.

A conventional analog modem commonly used to transmit information over the switched telephone network is limited to a maximum operating rate of between 28.8K bps and 33.6K bps, with the rate achievable dependent upon the quality of the connection and according to the modulation technique employed. In theory, the maximum operating rate of an analog modem that has been designed for use on the switched telephone network is limited by the 4K Hz bandwidth provided by the communications carrier for a switched telephone channel.

In 1924, Nyquist proved, in what is now referred to as the Nyquist theorem, that the maximum signaling rate of a device is limited to twice the available bandwidth; beyond that rate, inter-symbol interference occurs and adversely affects the transmission. As an example, for the 4K Hz telephone channel, this means the maximum signaling rate of a modem used to transmit on that medium is limited to 8000 baud. Baud is a term used to indicate signal changes per second.

The Quadrature Amplitude Modulation Technique

The most commonly used modem modulation technique, quadrature amplitude modulation (QAM), uses a combination of phase and amplitude to convey the settings of a group of bits in one signal change, enabling four bits to be represented by one baud change. This in turn enables an 8000 baud signaling rate to transport data at a rate of 32K bps when QAM is used for modulation.

Due to the 4K Hz telephone channel limitation, however, data transmission rates are limited to approximately 32K bps, with a slightly higher rate of 33.6K bps recently achieved by a few modem vendors using a modified QAM technique. Although the incorporation of data compression into modems provides a potential doubling to quadrupling of modem throughput, to between 67.2K bps and 134.4K bps, the ability of a modem to compress data depends upon the susceptibility of data to the compression algorithm being used. Because that susceptibility varies considerably as a modem user performs different operations, the end result is a variable compression rate; even though it is not noticeable during file transfer operations, that variable rate becomes extremely noticeable during interactive operations. In addition, even with the ability to compress data at a high rate, the resulting information transfer rate of 134.4K bps pales by comparison to the operating rate obtainable through the use of cable modems. It is clear, however, that advances in modem and cabling technology are limited with respect to increasing the performance of modems used to communicate via the switched telephone network.

CABLE MODEMS

The key difference between an analog modem designed for use on the public switched telephone network and a cable modem is in the bandwidth of the channels they are designed to use. Cable TV uses RG-11 cable for the main CATV trunk and RG-59 cable from trunk distribution points into and through residences and offices. Both types of coaxial cable have 75 ohms impedance and support broadband transmission, which means that two or more channels separated by frequency can be simultaneously transported on the cable.

From Unidirectional to Bidirectional Systems

A cable TV broadcasting infrastructure uses 6M Hz channels within the bandwidth of RG-11 and RG-59 cable to transmit a TV channel. Most CATV systems are currently unidirectional, which means that TV signals are broadcast from the CATV system operator without any provision for receiving a return signal. This transmission limitation is gradually being overcome as CATV operators begin to add bidirectional amplifiers to their networks that, when they are installed, will support transmission from subscribers in the reverse direction to conventional TV signal broadcasts. This will enable CATV systems to support the standardized transmit frequency range of 5M Hz to 42M Hz, and receive a frequency range of 54M Hz to 550M Hz, with 6M Hz cable TV channels.

By using one or more 6M Hz cable TV channels, a cable modem obtains the use of a bandwidth that is 1500 times greater (6M Hz/4K Hz) than that provided by a voice channel on the switched telephone network. This

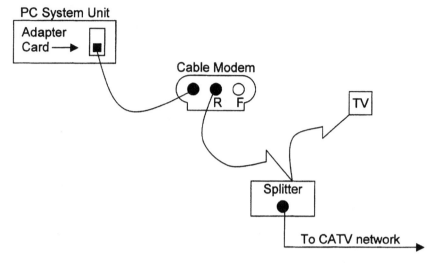

Exhibit 23.1. Cabling for a Zenith network cable modem system.

means that the modem can support a signaling rate of twice the bandwidth, or 12M baud, on one TV channel, based upon the Nyquist theorem, before the occurrence of inter-symbol interference.

The primary difference between cable modems currently being used in field trials is in their use of one or more 6M Hz TV channels within the band of channels carried by a coaxial cable, and their methods of attachment to the CATV network. One cable modem manufactured by Zenith Network Systems, a subsidiary of Zenith Electronics of Glenview, Illinois, operates on 6M Hz channels at 4M bps to the subscriber, using a special filtering technique to prevent data channels from interfering with adjacent information, which can be in the form of either data or video, that would coexist with the data transmission provided by the cable modem. The uplink or return data rate occurs at 500K bps. Modem modulation is biphase shift key (BPSK), which means that two bits (bi) are encoded in each phase change, and the modem's phase changes are shifted in phase from one to another. This modem is also frequency-agile, which means it can be set to operate on any standardized channel on a broadband CATV system.

The Zenith cable modem is actually one portion of a series of components required for a PC to use the modem. A complete transmission system requires the use of a Zenith cable modem, Ethernet 10BASE-T adapter card with a 15-conductor pin connector, and a 15-conductor shielded cable to connect the cable modem to the adapter. Exhibit 23.1 illustrates the cabling required to connect a PC to a CATV network via the use of a Zenith Network Systems cable modem.

When the adapter card is installed in the PC it, in effect, turns the computer into a client workstation. Because the adapter is an Ethernet 10BASE-T card, this means that the channel being used by the cable modem operates as one long CSMA/CD Local Area Network, with each PC user competing with other PC users for access to the channel. Because of this, the CATV operator should segment its cable distribution system to limit the number of cable modems attached to any segment, similar to the manner in which conventional LANs are limited with respect to the maximum number of workstations that can be connected to the LAN.

The connector labeled "R" on the rear of the cable modem is a reverse cable connector designed for networks that use a single coaxial cable. The second connector, labeled "F," represents a forward cable connector that would be used if the modem were connected to a cable system that uses two cables. In such a system, one cable is dedicated to conventional CATV broadcasting through one-way amplifiers, which precludes reverse transmission on the same cable. This type of system also requires the use of a second cable to obtain a transmission capability in the reverse direction.

A High-Speed Cable Modem Architecture

In addition to the previously described cable modem based upon the exclusive use of RF technology and biphase shift key modulation, Zenith Electronics Corporation announced a high-speed cable modem architecture. This architecture is based on the use of 16-VSB (vestigial sideband), a technique developed by Zenith as part of the organization's high-definition research, as well as the 256 quadrature amplitude modulation technology. Through the use of more complex modulation techniques for which more data bits can be represented by one signal change, the Zenith modem architecture can support data rates up to 40M bps on a 6M Hz cable channel.

Recognizing the fact that many cable TV systems will be limited to one-way transmission in the foreseeable future because of the time and cost associated with upgrading the CATV infrastructure, Zenith plans to support a range of options and speeds for upstream data transmission. According to Zenith, both telephone (analog modulation) and RF return path transmission capabilities will be incorporated into different versions of this new family of cable modems. For many cable modem applications, such as Internet operations, the use of the switched network for a return path should provide an acceptable level of performance. The rationale for this is best noted by examining the communications interaction between a potential cable modem user and the cable network as a user searches out and accesses various points on the World Wide Web.

On the Web

When users access a Web page, they transmit a universal resource locator (URL) address that represents the document they wish to view. This address is transported using the HTTP within a packet. The HTTP consists of an address that totals fewer than 100 characters, which are used to frame the address to which the message is being transported, as well as the address of the originator of the request. The destination Web server uses the document address to locate the requested page on the server, retrieves it from disk, and forms a packet using the source address from the incoming packet as the destination address for the outgoing packets. If the requested document contains a full screen of text, the packet contain close to 2000 characters, because a full screen of text consists of 80 columns by 24 rows of data (i.e., 1920 characters). However, because a typical Web page contains one or more graphics, the total amount of data transmitted from the server to the user will be, in actuality, substantially more than 2000 characters. For example, it is assumed that the Web page in question includes a 3 in. x 3 in. photograph, drawing, or schematic diagram that has been scanned using a resolution of 300 dots per inch. Regardless of the color of the image, each square inch of the image requires 11,250 bytes of storage. If the image was scanned using a 256-color resolution, each pixel requires a byte to represent its color, resulting in 90,000 bytes of storage per square inch. Thus, a 3 in. x 3 in. color image requires 270,000 bytes of storage.

Because HTTP breaks large files into small packets for transmission, the image might be carried by a sequence of approximately 100 packets, each roughly 2700 bytes in length, to include packet overhead. Thus, the short, 100-character transmission from a user can result in a response of 280,000 bytes. Because a user connected to the Web typically clicks on hotlinks that represent document addresses to view other documents, most Web operations represent asymmetrical transmission, that is, more transmissions return to the user than the user actually originates. Thus, a high-speed cable channel with a low-speed reverse path occurring over the switched telephone network may actually be sufficient for most data transmission applications.

The previously described asymmetrical transmission operation of users was also recognized by Intel Corporation, which took it into consideration when designing its CablePort cable modem system. That cable modem is designed to provide an average downstream data rate of 27M bps and a 96K bps upstream rate. One interesting difference between Zenith and Intel concerning their cable modem systems is in the type of adapter card required to be used in the PC. Because Intel provides a higher downstream operating rate than what is usable by a 10BASE-T adapter card, the user must install a Fast Ethernet(100M bps) adapter card in the PC to be able to use the Intel cable modem. Although no commercial costs were provided by Zenith or Intel for field trial operations, it is worth noting that a Fast Ethernet adapter has a retail cost of approximately $250, whereas a 10BASE-T adapter can be obtained for less than $50.

A second difference between the Zenith and Intel modems concerns their upstream capability. Although Zenith's new architecture permits support of the switched telephone network for locations where CATV operators cannot provide reverse direction transmission, the Intel system did not offer this capability when this chapter was researched.

RECOMMENDED COURSE OF ACTION

Although the technology of cable modems is in its infancy, the data center manager can still plan for their use. Whereas the type of cable modem offered will depend upon the CATV operators' cable infrastructure (i.e., either unidirectional or bidirectional), as well as the cable modem vendor the data center manager selects, each cable modem requires the use of RG-11 coaxial cable. Thus, if the manager has previously installed such cabling as part of a legacy terminal to mainframe or legacy LAN wiring system and are considering its removal, he may wish to leave the cabling in place. If RG-11 cabling has not been installed, the data center manager may wish to consider contacting the local CATV operator to determine when cable modems will be supported and the type the operator intends to use. If it intends to use bidirectional transmission via RF modulation, the data center manager can develop a wiring plan that requires only the use of RG-11 cable. If the CATV operator says it intends to provide reverse transmission via the public switched telephone network, the wiring plan must be modified to ensure that each cable modem user will have an available telephone jack. By understanding how cable modems operate and planning the organization's wiring infrastructure to use this evolving technology, the data center manager will be prepared for its future use.

Chapter 24
LAN-WAN Interconnection Requirements and Implementation Considerations

Duane E. Sharp

Networkologist: one who professionally practices the art and business of networkology ... an industry mover and shaker ... network technology driver ... one who designs enterprisewide networks and applications, evaluates today's network products and tomorrow's networking technologies; and understands that the network is the application that provides the competitive edge.

Courtesy of *Network World*

THE INTERNET, DOUBLING IN SIZE EVERY YEAR SINCE 1988, is an excellent example of the need to interconnect. Analysts estimate that over 50 million people worldwide are logging on to the Internet, with growth expected to continue exponentially. IDC estimates that by the year 2000, more than 180 million PCs worldwide will be networked via in-building LANs worldwide, a 360 percent increase in just five years. Today, more and more businesses are being interconnected in a networked community of interconnected WANs, as seamless as a LAN workgroup, and interconnectivity among local and wide area networks is one of the fundamental requirements of most network installations.

Standards and Protocols

The International Organization for Standardization (ISO) has defined a Reference Model for internetworking that has become a worldwide standard

0-8493-9824-X/00/$0.00+$.50
© 2000 by CRC Press LLC

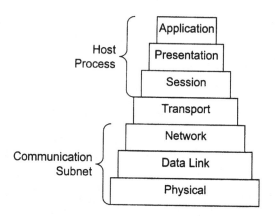

Exhibit 24.1. The open system interconnection (OSI) reference model.

---

or high-level protocol for designers of network products and for network designers. The reference model in Exhibit 24.1 defines the computer communications function in terms of seven distinct layers, and is designed to enable open systems to communicate with one another. In the world of standards, open systems are defined under the OSI reference model as those that comply with protocols for communication with other open systems, protocols which are common to both systems.

Design Issues

There are several significant technological developments and societal phenomena that have impacted the network designer's world over the past few years. PCs have proliferated and LANs have become as common and as essential as telephone networks. A growth rate of 100 to 200 percent per year of workstations per network is not uncommon. Rapid and sometimes instantaneous growth of businesses through acquisitions and mergers has resulted in a dramatic increase in the requirement to interconnect — often among widely dispersed geographical areas.

As a result of these changes in the requirements of businesses to communicate, frequently over considerable distances, today's network designer is usually required to include LAN-WAN interconnectivity in a network design.

LAN-WAN interconnectivity and the type of transmission facility required for a particular application are key design issues in interconnecting networks, as well as being essential components in determining network performance.

Once the functional goals for the internetwork are defined, they can be used as a statement of objectives. The primary features to be considered in designing a LAN-WAN internetwork are not dissimilar to those for a LAN, which are:

- Cost
- Performance
- Maintenance and support
- Reliability
- Redundancy
- Robustness

Robustness is especially critical to the LAN-WAN integration because a robust integration architecture will enable the internetwork to handle periods of heavy usage or peak activity.

Understanding Applications

A number of different networking applications may be required in the internetworking environment — file transfer, electronic messaging, electronic commerce, or multimedia transmission, to name a few. If there are common elements among these applications, the design job will be easier. It is important for enterprise managers to clearly understand the applications that will run on the LAN-WAN internetwork and their requirements in terms of the network characteristics.

Analyzing Network Traffic

This function will require a determination of the internetwork traffic that will flow among various network locations and the performance levels required by users at the remote sites.

Forecasting Traffic Growth

An analysis of the traffic growth over the next year, three years, and five years will ensure that the network capacity and components will be able to handle the increased traffic that will occur as the network matures.

Identifying and Selecting Network Components

The LAN-WAN interconnection will require hardware and software components at every location. The network designer will determine which LAN architecture — Ethernet, Token Ring, Fast Ethernet, FDDI, ATM — is implemented, and then ensure that the LAN-WAN internetwork provides a seamless interface, by appropriate selection of components.

The LAN operating system in existence at each location — Banyan VINES, Novell NetWare, 3COM 3 + Open, Windows NT, for example — will

Exhibit 24.2.   Characteristics of network components.

Router
- Operates at OSI network layer
- Depends on network layer protocol
- Uses network topology
- Separates subnetworks into logical elements
- Internetwork communication applications

Repeater
- Operates at OSI physical layer
- Extends LAN range
- Regenerates/repeates physical signals

Brouter
- Operates at OSI data link and network layers
- Combines the protocol transparency of a bridge with the ability to route certain protocols
- Used for networks with mixed-protocol traffic

Bridge
- Operates at OSI data link layer
- Logically separates network segments
- Independent of higher layer protocols
- Used for LAN traffic management

Gateway
- Operates at OSI higher levels
- Dependent on user application
- Used for application-to-application communication

also be an important consideration in the interconnection process. It is much easier to interconnect operating systems with a degree of common-ality in hardware or software, even if they have different architectures and protocols.

Internetworking Hardware and Software

There are five different types of hardware devices used in internetworking design, as depicted in Exhibit 24.2:

- Routers
- Repeaters
- Brouters
- Bridges
- Gateways

One or more of these devices will be selected by the designer to handle LAN-WAN interconnection requirements involving multimedia, dissimilar LAN architectures, several different protocols, or compatible application programs to be accessed across the network.

Routers. Routers separate network traffic based on the network layer protocol (Exhibit 24.1), and are commonly used for internetwork commu-nications. These devices control network traffic by filtering according to

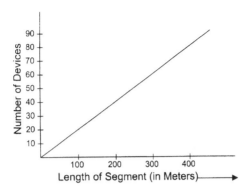

Exhibit 24.3. Ethernet network: devices per meter of cable length.

protocol, dividing networks logically instead of physically. Routers can divide networks into various subnets so that only traffic destined for particular addresses passes between segments. This form of intelligent forwarding and filtering usually results in reduced network speed because the process takes more time than required by a switch or bridge that looks at access to the shared transmission medium.

Repeaters. Repeaters are the building blocks of complex networks and are an important element in LAN-WAN internetworks, extending the physical length of a cable by amplifying signals and allowing additional workstations to be connected in each network segment. For example, in a thin Ethernet/IEEE 802.3 LAN, 30 devices can be supported for each 185-meter segment. Repeaters can be inserted to accommodate more devices per segment or an increase in the length of a segment. All network architectures have constraints that dictate how many devices can be attached per segment. Exhibit 24.3 illustrates these constraints for a typical Ethernet architecture. Other networks — ARCNET, Token Ring, and FDDI — have similar limitations on number of devices and distance between segments.

Repeaters also monitor all connected segments in a network to ensure that the basic characteristics are present for the network to perform correctly. When a network becomes inoperable — for example, when a break occurs — all segments in a network may become inoperable. Repeaters limit the effect of these problems to the faulty section of cable by segmenting the network, disconnecting the problem segment, and allowing unaffected segments to function normally.

Bridge. A bridge is a "traffic manager" used to divide the network into logical subsets, and to direct traffic away from workstations that frequently communicate on a common LAN. Most bridges are multiport devices that connect one network to another, using store-and-forward filtering techniques and handling potential bridging loops between networks. Bridges enable redundancy to be built into a network by providing multiple pathways between network segments.

Brouters. Brouters are hybrids of the bridge and router, are also referred to as routing bridges, and are designed to provide the processing speed of a bridge with the internetworking capabilities of a router. They are protocol-independent devices that direct traffic based on the OSI data link access (Exhibit 24.1). However, they are more sophisticated devices, designed to logically segment the network based on the routing algorithm, higher layer protocol, or the WAN architecture that has been implemented.

Gateways. Gateways are devices that have been designed to handle specific applications, such as the interconnection between different classes of hardware or network architectures — mainframes, Token Rings, workstations, or midrange systems. They may operate at all seven OSI layers (Exhibit 24.1) and are often used to interconnect incompatible e-mail systems, to convert and transfer files from one system to another, or to enable interoperability between dissimilar operating systems.

BUILDING NETWORKED COMMUNITIES WITH NETWARE

Over the years, Novell, Inc. has played a leading role in perfecting the foundation technology resulting in networked communities of PC users and business workgroups. Workgroup networks enable individuals to share documents and expensive hardware resources such as printers and disk drives.

These workgroup networks can be expanded to support communication and collaboration in enterprisewide WANs, leading to a variety of LAN-WAN interconnection options. Novell and other networking companies anticipated that the original concept of building communities of PC users by connecting workgroups into enterprise networks was the way of the future (Exhibit 24.4).

The latest version of Novell's network operating system provides the full range of distributed services required to enable networking enterprisewide WANs. NetWare products now run on more than 2.5 million networks; therefore, a sound knowledge of Novell's networking products is important for the network designer.

FUNDAMENTAL PRINCIPLES OF LAN-WAN INTERNETWORKING

Novell's strategy for forging the future of networking provides a guideline for network designers, and rests on three basic principles: smart networks; anytime, anywhere access; and network heterogeneity.

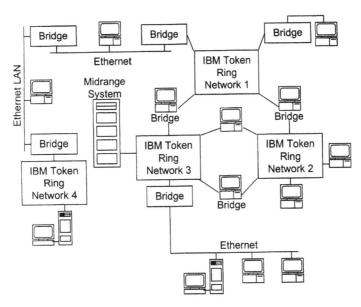

Exhibit 24.4.   Typical bridge interconnections among multiple LANs.

The Smart Network

The first principle maintains that making networks smarter can relieve users of the arcane world of operating systems, applications, and tools. Without a smart network that identifies the user, knows what information is required, and how to provide it to the user, connections to a global network will be a difficult task.

Network Access: Anytime, Anywhere

This principle is based on the premise that a simple, single log-in procedure will enable access to these smart networks anytime, from anywhere, by anyone. Such access would, among other things, transform work from a place into an activity. For many, the concept of the virtual office is already here, and with it, enormous new demands for accessing information, resources, and other people. In the current thinking on networks, "the network has become the computer."

The Heterogeneous Network

The final principle recognizes that the network will always be heterogeneous, with several different operating systems and many different applications and services, designed with a variety of tools, and capable of being accessed from a wide variety of intelligent devices.

Interweaving disparate business units of international organizations, located at different physical sites into a single network presents real issues of hardware and software compatibility. On a global scale, the complexities of integration increase exponentially. Network designers need to establish corporate computing standards that will remain in effect with changes in business requirements and applications. Through each stage of the evolution of networking — first building workgroup communities of PC users, then building enterprise communities of workgroups and a single community linking them all together — the challenge is for the network to present a simple homogeneous view of its entire heterogeneous resources for users, administrators, and developers.

TRANSMISSION ALTERNATIVES IN LAN-WAN NETWORKS: SEEKING A PATH THROUGH A WAN TECHNOLOGY JUNGLE

The choices available to users today in the selection of a LAN-WAN interconnection are wide ranging. While previous services usually offered minimal bandwidth and were unreliable and overpriced, they did the job. WAN services available today are cheaper, offer greater bandwidth, and are far more reliable.

These services are available in a variety of shapes and sizes, as standard telephone lines, digital communications lines, switched or permanent links, and packet- or circuit-switched connections, depending on the particular needs of the network.

For an existing LAN, the LAN characteristics will have been previously determined. If the LAN is in the design stages, the WAN media can be selected once the LAN specifications have been defined.

The following considerations will assist in determining which media to select.

- Will the network connections be used for LAN connections and to connect telecommuters to the corporate information system?
- What level of traffic will the WAN handle? And how often?
- What are the forecast traffic patterns for the LAN-WAN internetwork? Constant bit rate video, file transfer, or multimedia?
- Will the traffic cross regional, national, or global boundaries, requiring special considerations for regulatory provisions?
- What level of reliability is needed? Is a backup required?
- What level of service will WAN communications require? Round-the-clock? Intermittent?

Answers to these questions will provide direction to the network designer in determining which transmission technologies will fit the specification for the LAN-WAN interconnection. The following paragraphs provide some of the pros and cons of the various common transmission technologies available to the network designer:

POTS (Plain Old Telephone System)

The traditional telephone system (Plain Old Telephone System, or POTS) is useful in situations where only a limited amount of bandwidth (up to 28.8Kbps) is required for periodic connections. Telecommuting applications and low backup of WAN links fall into this category, where the analog connection provided by the POTS is of sufficient bandwidth.

However, POTS cannot meet the requirements of high bandwidth applications, such a multimedia transmissions, or other high-performance requirements of most modern networks.

The key to using this medium is to understand its limitations in terms of long-distance reliability, and to use it mainly for local connections to minimize the costs incurred by distance-sensitive pricing.

ISDN

One of the communication technologies that has gained prominence and will prove useful in many LAN-WAN internetworks, is ISDN (Integrated Services Digital Networks). This technology is an evolution of POTS, enabling faster, more reliable digital connections on existing telephony infrastructures.

The increased speed, low latency, and reliability extends the range of applications to which ISDN can be applied, to the extent that it is useful for constant bit-rate applications such as videoconferencing. Like POTS, it is useful for telecommuting applications, and at much higher speeds, as well as such applications as direct or backup LAN-to-LAN connectivity.

A major aspect of ISDN that will undoubtedly ensure a long life for this technology is that in North America, ISDN is widely deployed and available in most dialing areas. By comparison, other technologies such as ASDL (Asymmetric Digital Subscriber Line) and cable have relatively sparse geographical coverage. On the other hand, although it is capable of much higher speed connections (between 128Kbps and 2.048Mbps) than POTS, its cost effectiveness is limited to intermittent local transmissions, due to its distance and usage-sensitive tariffs.

Leased Lines

Leased lines have been the foundation of corporate internetworks in North America, although their permanence limits their use to LAN-to-LAN connections. In terms of performance for corporate communications, they can provide suitable network solutions because they offer a range of speeds from 19.2Kbps and T3, and provide 99.99 percent uptime (in North America). They are dedicated permanent links; however, they are more secure than other WAN alternatives and suitable for a variety of different types of network traffic (including video).

A disadvantage of leased lines is their cost. Leased line connections are costly because pricing is distance sensitive, an important consideration in evaluating leased lines over equivalent-bandwidth alternatives.

X.25

Packet-switched networks are an alternative to direct connections, with X.25 as the most advanced, established international protocol. With packet-switched services, a communications link is a virtual connection that does not exist physically.

An advantage of X.25 services is that the protocol is available on a universal basis, offering bandwidths ranging from 9.2Kbps to 256Kbps. The service is so well established that it supports a number of access technologies, including POTS, ISDN, and leased line connections. This capability makes X.25 ideally suited for global LAN-WAN internetworks.

However, X.25 is not suited for high-bandwidth applications (such as video), which cannot tolerate the latency introduced by a packet-switched network.

Frame Relay

Frame Relay is a packet-switched service that will replace leased lines. Dial-up access into Frame Relay networks via POTS and ISDN has made this a viable remote user solution in many network environments. It is a simplified version of the X.25 protocol, without the error correction facilities that guarantee reliable data delivery. The cost of Frame Relay is usually less than an equivalent-bandwidth leased line, with the price differential growing as the distance between sites increases.

One downside to Frame Relay is that it is only available where digital communications facilities are in place. Further maturation of this technology should provide Frame Relay with the same degree of flexibility as X.25.

ATM

Asynchronous Transfer Mode (ATM), the most sophisticated of transmission technologies, is a cell-switching, multiplexing technology that combines the features of circuit switching (constant transmission delay and guaranteed capacity) with those of packet switching (flexibility and efficiency for intermittent traffic). It is particularly suitable for the simultaneous transmission of voice, video, and data, and is finding wide application in multimedia environments.

The ATM Forum, a standards organization with over 700 members formed in the early 1990s to promote ATM interoperability, has developed a range of standards for ATM to meet a variety of network management, interface, and transmission requirements, while product vendors have been developing products to meet these standards.

ATM was originally developed as a WAN technology for broadband ISDN. Using ATM as a WAN aggregate link extends of the use of ATM as a backbone in a campus environment and to larger LAN-WAN environments, where design decisions are influenced by the progress of tariffs and service rollouts by carriers.

ATM is a natural successor to FDDI at the enterprise level, offering scalability and fault tolerance, as well as providing an integration point for other networking technologies such as Ethernet, Token Ring, and Frame Relay. Over the past few years, ATM has grown in popularity in those applications where multimedia capability is a fundamental requirement and where cost and complexity are not inhibiting factors.

The basic transmission unit in ATM is defined to be a fixed-length cell with the following characteristics:

- Switching is performed in silicon, providing much lower switch latencies and much higher switch throughputs.
- Fixed length cells allow the switch to operate isochronously with fixed and predictable delays.

ATM is asynchronous in nature — there are no fixed arrival rates of cells — and operates in a constant bit rate mode for video or voice applications because it is carried electronically on an asynchronous transport system. ATM is tightly coupled with this underlying transmission media.

For LAN-WAN internetworking, the potential applications of ATM are:

- As a replacement for broadcast LAN media (Ethernet, Token Ring, or FDDI)
- As a LAN backbone technology in a campus or metropolitan area environment
- As a WAN aggregate link technology

For a LAN backbone, ATM has been described as better than FDDI architecture. ATM backbones scale well because the technology is non-broadcast, providing dedicated, nonblocking, 155Mbps, bidirectional, point-to-point virtual circuits between routers. This means that there is no contention for bandwidth as there is in FDDI, thus allowing for more devices to be added to the backbone without compromising effective throughput of existing devices. This important characteristic of ATM makes it a key transmission architecture for consideration in LAN-WAN internetworks where it can meet the required specifications.

Unfortunately for the network designer, current ATM offerings do not provide a viable means to emulate the broadcast nature of LAN media. In many network environments, ATM is used primarily as a permanent virtual circuit.

While ATM is gradually evolving into a standard building block for network backbones, its growth in some networking environments has been inhibited by three factors:

- Relative complexity of implementation compared to other protocols
- The high cost of interface products for desktop applications
- Limited availability of ATM products for various computer types

Addressing and dynamic signaling are two issues with ATM that need to be resolved. For example, a network administrator needs to do significant network configuration analysis to perform simple network modifications, such as adding a new user to an ATM LAN.

Current assessments of ATM, the most advanced of the transmission technologies available today, indicate that it will be at least another year before this technology penetrates the WAN market significantly, and it will be two or more years before it makes a significant impact on the LAN environment.

SUMMARY

Each of the LAN-WAN internetworking transmission media described has certain strengths and weaknesses that make them best suited to specific applications. Some industry forecasters predict that Ethernet will continue to be the technology of choice for most corporations, in both LAN and LAN-WAN environments, for several reasons: its pervasiveness in current networks; the wide availability of products; the relatively painless growth for bandwidth; and price.

However, the technologies available for interconnecting LANs and WANs — hardware, software, network operating systems, transmission media — are rapidly evolving, along with standards for implementation and reduced costs. It is important that the network designer retains flexibility within the network architecture, continually assessing vendor offerings, to take advantage of new, proven technologies that will enhance network performance.

Chapter 25
Enterprise Deployment: Building an IP PBX Telephony Network

John Fiske

INTERNET TELEPHONY HAS BEEN INCREASINGLY EXPLORED and implemented as a viable communication tool in large corporations. A main component of enterprise IP voice is the IP PBX, which functions the way a traditional PBX does. It allows calls to be transferred throughout the organization, it allows easy intra-enterprise calls, and it operates automatically.

An IP PBX is different in almost every other respect. Not only is it easier and less costly to operate and maintain, it operates with different technology. The IP PBX has paid off for the corporations using it through reduced manpower and by eliminating an entire (telephone) network. This chapter provides other payoff ideas and an explanation of the technology behind the IP PBX.

THE PBX

Yesterday's PBX fulfilled a simple need: it allowed users to talk together, and also allowed users to talk out to the PSTN (public switched telephone network). PBX (premise branch exchange) manufacturers fulfilled this need by installing a mainframe computer into the enterprise and connecting a proprietary line card interface to either analog phones or proprietary digital phones. The connection out to the PSTN was established through a trunk interface card.

Today's PC-based PBX similarly fulfills a need. Phones on the enterprise side and the PSTN on the outside can be connected together. The approach with a PC-based PBX is fundamentally the same as the mainframe PBX architecture. The big difference is the use of relatively inexpensive PCs instead of hefty mainframe computers.

The third generation, tomorrow's PBX, is the IP-based (Internet Protocol) PBX. Again, it fulfills a by-now well-known need, but with a lot of other benefits. Instead of using a line interface card and circuit-switched card, it uses the TCP/IP network switching voice packets through an Ethernet, ATM, Frame Relay, ISDN, or whatever satisfactorily carries TCP/IP.

THE IP-PBX

Full PBX capabilities over IP LAN/WAN networks promise to substitute and replace traditional enterprise PBXs, and are an important step toward full voice and data convergence. In the IP PBX, voice traffic is digitized and compressed, placed into data packets, and transmitted across the packet network directly between the stations or WAN interfaces. End stations communicate with a call control server only when a call processing function, such as transferring a call, creating a conference call, or sending a call to voice mail, is required or requested.

Standards and the IP PBX

An IP PBX operates within the ITU (International Telecommunications Union) Standards (H.323 and T.120) that define how data equipment works in a data environment and define the signaling, call control, and audio compression for packet delivery of voice and video communications on IP networks. Without these standards in place and strictly followed, interoperability would not be possible.

Components

An IP PBX requires three components: the desktop telephone, call manager software, and a WAN/IP gateway. These three components are attached to existing LAN/WAN infrastructure.

The Desktop Telephone. Users have two desktop phone choices:

1. An IP Ethernet phone that plugs directly into an Ethernet jack.
2. Handsets or headsets that plug into their PC.

The IP Ethernet telephone resembles a normal digital PBX set, but instead of connecting to a proprietary PBX port, it plugs into a standard Ethernet LAN jack. An IP telephone delivers audio quality comparable to that of a PBX telephone and is easy to use with single-button access to line appearances and features. The IP telephone can operate as a standard IP device with its own IP address. A fully H.323-compatible IP phone can talk to any other H.323 device. The following are key characteristics of the IP telephone:

- Connects directly to any 10 Base-T Ethernet (RJ45) network.
- Programmable buttons for features, speed dialing, or line appearances.
- IP address and signaling (TCP/IP) to call manager.
- H.323 standards.
- Built-in compression: G.711; G.723 (ITU standards), on a call and feature basis.
- IP address assignment and configuration with DHCP keypad or BootP.
- Administration and button configuration through a Web browser.
- Built-in encryption for privacy protection during voice conversation.
- Third-pair or phantom powered to permit power backup in the event of building power failure.
- One-button collaboration (T.120) with PC and NetMeeting for features such as application sharing, video, chat, and whiteboarding.
- Built-in repeater port for cascading Ethernet devices.

The Call Manager. The call manager provides the network intelligence to enable simple-to-use and feature-rich IP communications. Call manager software is designed to work seamlessly with existing telephony systems (PBX or Centrex) or can provide full PBX functionality on its own. It can be deployed as a single IP PBX in a single office, or as a single IP PBX with multiple geographically dispersed users. With total switch and network independence, administrators can create a truly virtual campus environment utilizing a common Web browser.

By installing the call manager software on a Windows NT server in the IP network, features such as call, hold, call transfer, call forward, call park, caller identification, and multiple line appearances are provided to the IP phone. The SMDI interface on the call manager provides connectivity to various voice mail and IVR systems along with CDR reporting for call accounting and billing.

The call manager provides the call processing functionality for the IP PBX. It manages the resources of the IP PBX by signaling and coordinating call control activities. The call manager sets up a call by instructing the calling party to set up an RTP audio stream to the other device, either telephone or gateway. Once an audio stream is set up between two devices, the call manager is idle until a new request (such as transfer or disconnect) is made. In the event the call manager fails during a call, the two parties stay connected and can complete their call. Various signaling protocols, such as Q.931 for ISDN WAN control and H.225/H.245 for IP packet control, are managed and controlled by the call manager.

The call manager also manages calling zones to ensure efficient bandwidth performance at the maximum audio quality. When a call is routed over a low-bandwidth IP pipe, the call manager will instruct the IP phone to use a lower bit rate audio compression, such as G.723. For calls toward the

PSTN, the call manager will have the phones use G.711, which is the compression required for PSTN calling.

The call manager offers a standard directory service that allows other applications on the network to access the call directory. It can be overseen via a Web browser and provides remote management for diagnostics and maintenance from anywhere in the world. The browser provides an intuitive interface for administrators and users. Upon administrator approval, users can access and configure their own phones. Call records are kept in a standard CDR database for billing and tracking activity.

The Gateway. IP-based telephony systems today need to connect to the PSTN and the existing PBX. Gateways are specifically designed to convert voice from the packet domain to the circuit-switched domain.

The gateway converts packetized voice to a format that can be accepted by the PSTN. Since the digitized format for voice on the packet network is often different than on the PSTN, the gateway will provide a type of conversion called transcoding. Gateways also pass signaling information.

Based on the various PSTN interfaces, there is a need for both a digital and analog trunk version. Gateways must all support supplementary services, such as call transfer and hold across subnets in the IP network and should be easily configured using the Web browser. Support for supplemental services is in the H.323 Standard and allows for the RTP audio stream to be redirected to different IP ports.

Configurations and Applications

The IP PBX is not defined by physical hardware limitations, as is a traditional PBX or even the newer "un-PBX" systems. Traditional PBXs or un-PBXs have constraints that limit scaling the system. For example, the circuit switch matrix that defines how many connections can be made at one time is based on the specific model of the PBX that has been installed. Once the limit has been reached, the entire PBX usually must be replaced.

Another limitation is the hardware line cards required for every telephone device or trunk interface. These cards fit into cabinets and when the growth of the system requires more cards than cabinet space the entire system again must be replaced.

IP PBXs are very different in their architecture. Instead of a circuit switch matrix to make connections, the IP PBX uses LAN bandwidth to make voice connections. For telephone calls, the voice traffic does not pass through a central server or call manager. The call manager only performs signaling to set up and manage call states. Therefore, it can handle a large number of calls with fewer restrictions or limitations.

In addition, because of the scalability of LAN architectures, the IP PBX can scale linearly from one port to thousands of ports. When more ports are needed, additional hubs and switches can be added to grow the system without replacing the current investment.

IP Telephony Off an Existing PBX. This configuration extends the existing PBX within the campus using the IP network as transport. The IP PBX connects to the PBX using either an analog or digital gateway, depending on the expectations of voice traffic and the number of users. The call manager software runs on an NT server in the data center.

This application allows a business, enterprise, university, or other large organization to extend normal telephony services using the existing IP LAN. The call manager provides feature functionality to the IP telephones, with features such as transfer, secretarial call coverage, and parallel dial plan used by the PBX. With the gateway interface to the PBX, users can call users with PBX telephones or call to the PSTN with the same privileges and restraints set by the enterprise administrator.

Remote Offices Over an IP Network. This application is simply an extension of the previous configuration with the inclusion of IP WAN connectivity to remote sites. The same basic rules apply for the IP PBX, just as they would for a single-site deployment. The call manager can remain on the central site, or a secondary call manager can be deployed at the remote location.

This configuration is a common initial application for the IP PBX product line. Companies with multiple sites can now easily install full telephony systems while leveraging the IP data network already in place. This saves costs for long-distance calling, as well as eliminates the cost to install a second network at each remote location. This option also enhances flexibility for growing or shrinking locations based on business conditions and making changes.

Using the analog access gateway at the remote site, the remote workers have local calling. Long-distance calling can be muted over the IP WAN link and consolidated from the central site to maximize long-distance calling costs and administration. With the IP PBX capability to configure audio compression based on call routing, calls destined to the main location would use a lower bit rate compression to conserve bandwidth.

Network Deployment

The configuration of an IP PBX as a network-based service (such as an ISP) has characteristics similar to the previous configurations, except the call manager and the gateway are located in the WAN. On premise would be IP phones and possibly a smaller analog gateway for local calling and backup, in case the IP link to the network is unavailable.

In addition to local and long-distance calling, the network provider can also provide traditional services like voice mail and call center services with the applications residing either at the remote location or in the network. The provider can also provide billing and management services for the customer: a range of telecommunications services in addition to long-distance routing and Internet access. The configuration options are based on the flexibility and power of IP networking.

PRACTICAL ADVANTAGES OF THE IP PBX

The IP PBX is expected to offer significant advantages in large-scale telephony. The earliest advantages pertain to cost. The benefits multiply, however, and include:

- *Cost.* Using the existing datacom network for voice transport, there is no need for the circuit-switched card or line interface card, and those expenses are avoided.
- *Total cost of ownership.* When one moves a phone on a circuit-switched PBX, one must call a PBX administrator, who makes an entry in a database that moves the phone from one physical port to another. It is logistical agony. IP phones are simpler and less costly in every way.
- *Maintenance.* One can plug in an IP phone directly out of the box. It automatically configures with a call management server, and it gets a directory number. Maintenance and configuration are simpler and easier.
- *Support.* There is no need for external support from field technicians from a proprietary PBX manufacturer. Additionally, there is a vast hiring pool of people who know Windows NT, TAPI, and TCP/IP — much greater than the number of people who know a particular vendor's circuit-switched PBX.
- *Extensible.* On a distributed campus with a unified dial plan and unified feature management, one can browse into the call processing server and manage the database from any point on the network.
- *Availability.* It is not necessary to pay for the extra availability the PBX vendors design into the system. One can pay a lot of money for very good PBX design work. But with an IP PBX, one does not pay for the extra capacity if it is not needed.
- *Capacity.* Using a dual Pentium Pro 300MHz server, one can run 500 to 600 phones. With the advent of inter-server signaling, it will be theoretically possible to scale the system up to 100,000 lines, or larger.

Payoffs

There are several ways an IP PBX will save a company money.

- *Long-distance charge savings.* In many international markets, especially highly regulated ones, communications carriers have artificially high tariffs, as compared to carriers in deregulated markets. Additionally, these carriers have lower tariffs for data connections. There is short-term opportunity to exploit these differences ... until carriers close the gap between voice and data costs. Longer-term cost savings will come from consolidation and management of all WAN connections, the Internet, local calling, and long distance through a single gateway/router device.
- *Data and voice convergence.* Data and voice conversion will facilitate new business practices, enabling people to work more effectively. This technology will release customers from barriers imposed by proprietary solutions, allowing organizations to develop.
- *Cutting acquisition and operating costs.* In 1997, the capital cost of building a LAN PBX system was slightly higher than the cost of building a traditional PBX. The changing marketplace has changed this model, however. The cost of swiftly evolving LAN equipment has fallen below the also declining cost of traditional PBX equipment.
- *Administration costs.* This is the single largest opportunity to reduce costs. One will manage a single network instead of two parallel networks. Today's PBX requires a full-time staffer to manage the PBX database. In the traditional PBX, it costs $60 to $80 to move a phone. With the IP PBX, this cost is eliminated. It is also easier and cheaper to add a phone extension. General management of the IP PBX is identical to that of the IP network, which means that the same people with the same knowledge can be used in both arenas.

CONCLUSION

Corporate IP networks are becoming increasingly pervasive and essential. Consequently, the business LAN no longer occupies a niche department. Those departments are always looking for ways to improve the network's capabilities. Rapid improvement in technology and standards is driving these efforts. It was not long ago that companies started trials for IP telephony with gateways between their PBXs and the IP networks. Now they are moving to the next step by integrating telephony services and IP telephones controlled by call manager server software. The revolution has begun, and the momentum to converge voice and data networks reveals a new value paradigm. For many companies, the real value comes not from lower (or eliminated) long distance charges, but from the reduced cost of operating and managing a separate voice network.

The IP PBX is a pillar in this revolution. Connectivity spells efficiency and productivity. The traditional PBX provided the connectivity, but the IP PBX is cheaper to acquire and easier to operate and maintain. The IP PBX, evolving still, suggests a new way for businesses to communicate. As this latest communications revolution sweeps across the land, one may want to join it.

Section V
Desktop Computing

THIS CHAPTER INTRODUCES ANOTHER NEW TOPIC not included in last year's edition of handbook — desktop computing. IT operations managers must understand the user's desktop configuration in order to effectively provide enterprise-wide computing services to all PCs connected to central computers through local area and wide area networks. In addition, IT managers are typically responsible for centrally managing user desktop software configurations through network management tools. In this section, you will be introduced to a wide range of desktop computing technology solutions that will help manage this important investment.

Chapter 26, "A Quick Overview of Linux," provides a quick overview of Linux, listing the features and drawbacks of Linux, and providing sources for additional information. Linux is a UNIX-type operating system, originally created by Linus Torvalds in 1991, which has been enhanced by developers around the world. Enterprise IT managers should take a serious look at Linux to determine if it will meet their desktop operating system requirements. The software is free, or close to free, and it has all the functions of an operating system required by the enterprise, yet it also has some drawbacks.

The ability to enable remote users to share resources on NT workstations and servers represents one of the major benefits of using the NT operating system, as explored in Chapter 27, "Evaluating the Performance of NT-Based Systems." By enabling employees in an organization to share access to drives, folders, and files, you obtain the ability to significantly enhance productivity. However, you also provide the potential for other persons with access to your organization's network to either intentionally, or unintentionally, read or modify existing data, as well as store new files whose contents could have an adverse effect upon the operation of your organization. Thus, IT managers must understand the importance of the options associated with Windows NT resource sharing as they control access to shares, as well as govern the level of security associated with network-based resources.

In Chapter 28, "Configuring TCP/IP on a Windows NT Workstation," the configuration of Transmission Control Protocol/Internet Protocol (TCP/IP) on a Windows NT workstation is discussed. With the widespread acceptance and use of TCP/IP in the industry today, IT managers must continue to increase their understanding of how TCP/IP can be leveraged to increase performance and productivity in their environment. Windows NT, which is already used extensively in the industry as a server operating system, is expected to soon also be the predominant desktop operating system. As TCP/IP begins to replace the older Internet Packet Exchange/Sequential Packet Exchange (IPX/SPX) protocol, IT managers need understand how TCP/IP should be configured with Windows NT.

As indicated in the chapters above, the desktop interface is the user's window to any system. Although standard screen structure, the use of icons and color, and sharper screen quality have all contributed to improvements in the way systems are presented to a wide audience of users, an interface encompasses far more than screen format. In Chapter 29, "More Productive User Interfaces," the general desktop interface is explored. Although flexible user interfaces help people accomplish subordinate tasks more efficiently, gains in efficiency must be balanced against the need to meet overall system goals. By identifying users and their characteristics, collecting detailed information on user tasks and goals, and involving users continuously in an iterative design process, IT managers and designers will build interfaces which are productive, as well as flexible.

The last two chapters in this section address the issue of graphical user interfaces (GUIs). IT operations managers need to understand how these interfaces impact the way end users access and use IT resources across networks within an enterprise environment. In Chapter 30, "Creating GUIs Users Can Use: Usability Analysis," you will learn how to determine user requirements for the development of highly usable interfaces. In Chapter 31, "Building GUIs Users Can Use: Usability Development," you will learn how to take those requirements and translate them into a workable design.

Chapter 26
A Quick Overview of Linux

Raj Rajagopal

LINUX IS A UNIX-TYPE OPERATING SYSTEM, originally created by Linus Torvalds in 1991, that has been enhanced by developers around the world. Linux is an independent POSIX implementation and is compliant with X/Open and POSIX standards. Linux is developed and distributed under the GNU General Public License. The GNU license specifies that the source code for Linux plus any Linux enhancements should be freely available to everyone. Vendors are free to charge for distributing Linux, and the availability of source code does not apply to applications developed on top of Linux. Linux features includes true multi-tasking, multi-user support, virtual memory, shared libraries, demand loading, proper memory management, TCP/IP networking, shell, file structure, utilities, and applications that are common in many UNIX implementations. A complete list of features is included in Exhibit 26.1. Linux is a candidate operating system to be evaluated by enterprise and data center managers who have any flavor of (or are considering acquiring) UNIX or Windows NT.

Sudden Surge of Interest in Linux

For an operating system invented in 1991, the interest in Linux has only recently surged. Like many other computer- and Internet-related phenomena, Linux has again proved that there is strength in numbers. Linux has reached the critical mass of users where vendors have started taking an interest in the operating system. Exhibit 26.2 shows the number of Linux users from 1993 to 1997. These numbers are estimates from Red Hat Software, one of the distributors of Linux.

The biggest customers for Linux include Internet service providers that use Linux along with the free APACHE Web server, universities, and Web developers. While Exhibit 26.2 shows cumulative numbers, analysts expected Red Hat to ship about 400,000 CDs the same year. By contrast,

Exhibit 26.1. Linux features.

Feature	Description
Virtual memory	Possible to add swapping areas during runtime. Up to 16 swapping areas each of which can hold 128MB and can be used for a total of 2GB swap space.
Development languages	Supports most common languages including C, C++, Java, Ada95, Pascal, FORTRAN, etc.
UNIX commands, tools supported	Commands include ls, tr, sed, awk, etc. Tools include gcc, gdb, make, bison, flex, perl, rcs, cvs, and prof.
UNIX source/binary compatibility	Compatible with most POSIX, System V, and BSD at the source level. Through iBCS2-compliant emulation, compatible with many SCO, SVR3, and SVR4 at the binary level.
Graphical environments	X11R5 and X11R6. Motif is available separately.
Shells	All three common shells.
Editors	GNU Emacs, Xemacs, MicroEmacs; jove; ez; epoch; elvis; GNU vi; vim; vile; joe; pico; and jed.
Internationalization	Supports many localized and customized keyboards.
LAN support	Supports Appletalk server and NetWare client and server.
Internet communications	Supports TCP/IP networking including FTP, Telnet, etc.
File systems	Linux file system supports file systems of up to 4TB and names up to 255 characters long. Also supports NFS and System V. Transparent access to MS-DOS FAT partitions via a separate file system. Partition looks like a normal UNIX file system.
CD-ROM	CD-ROM file system reads all standard CD-ROM formats.
Y2K compliancy	Compliant. Linux's 32-bit data representation should handle dates until the year 2038.

Microsoft Corporation is estimated to have sold more than 100 million copies of Windows that same year.

Vendor Support for Linux

The growth in users has resulted in renewed interest in Linux from many vendors. Intel Corporation and Netscape Communications Corporation have announced an investment in Red Hat Software. Two venture capital firms, Benchmark Capital of Menlo Park, CA, and Boston-based Greylock, have also made investments in Red Hat.

Besides financial support, vendors have also started providing product support. Major vendors, including Sybase, Oracle, Netscape, Informix, Computer Associates, Interbase, and Corel, have announced versions for Linux. Some of the popular applications available for Linux are summarized in Exhibit 26.3.

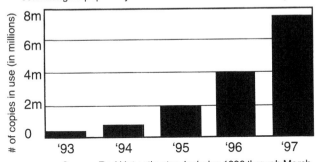

How large is Linux?

Since Linux can freely be downloaded from the Internet, estimating its popularity is difficult. Here's Red Hot's best guess

Source: Red Hot estimates. Includes 1996 through March.

Exhibit 26.2.   Linux user base.

Exhibit 26.3.   Applications available for Linux.

Application Category	Popular Products
Office applications	Star Office, Applixware, WordPerfect, XessL:ite4 spreadsheet
PDF support	Adobe Acrobat Reader
Backup	Backup/9000, BRU 2000
Video player	MpegTV Player
Database support	Sybase Enterprise Adaptive Server, Oracle DBMS, InterBase, Informix-SE
Web software	Apache Web Server, Netscape Communicator, Red Hat Web Server

Linux Customers

Linux is used extensively at universities and by ISPs as Web servers. Linux is also used in research and development environments and in government. The visual effects company Digital Domain used Linux in creating visual effects for the movie "Titanic." The U.S. Department of Defense uses Linux for DNS platforms and SMTP mail relays.

OPERATING REQUIREMENTS FOR LINUX

Most Linux versions run on most Intel-based machines, although other platforms are also supported (see Exhibit 26.4). Besides the Web pages of specific Linux distributors, the Web pages http://www.linux.org and http://sunsite.unc.edu/mdw/HOWTO/INFO-SHEET.html provide more detailed lists of hardware, video cards, disk controllers, etc.

Exhibit 26.4. Linux operating requirements.

Component	Comments
Processor	Most Intel-based machines. Some implementations support multi-processor such as SMP. Other processors supported include Sun SPARC, Alpha, PowerPC, RS/6000, MIPS, and Macintosh.
Memory	4MB required to install most distributions; 5MB to 10MB for minimal setup; 8MB to 16MB required to run X. Requires swap partitions.
Hard disk	Hard drive required. 8MB to 16MB for swap partition. 24MB for basic installation with no X, development tools, or TeX. Most installations require 40MB to 80MB minimum, including free space. Complete systems need 60MB to 200MB.
Bus	Supports 386/486/Pentium machines with ISA, EISA, PCI, and VLB buses. VESA local bus and PCI are supported. SCSI support is available in some implementations.
Coexistence with other operating systems	Linux will coexist with DOS, MS-Windows, and OS/2 on the hard drive. Partitioning the hard disk is required for each operating system.

LINUX SOURCES

Linux is freely available on the Internet (see Linux-related FTP sites) along with the source. Linux is also available through distributors. There are many different Linux versions, or distributions. A distribution is the compiled Linux software and source code usually combined with extra features such as configuration, installation, Web, and other applications for the specific version. Most importantly, however, distributors provide support for their version. Some distributions are available for download at no charge, while others are available at prices typically in the range of $50 to $100 on CD-ROM from Linux distributors/vendors/retailers.html worldwide. Keep in mind that some of the distributors offer multiple distributions, which differ in price and features. When picking distributions, enterprise and data center managers need to consider the features and other applications besides evaluating the operating system itself.

Other options include purchasing Linux preinstalled on a computer, or purchasing a book that includes a complimentary CD-ROM (see Exhibit 26.5).

Linux-Related Web and FTP Sites

There are a number of Web and FTP sites that provide the Linux code, as well as applications for Linux. Some of the popular ones are shown in Exhibit 26.6.

Exhibit 26.5.   Linux distributors.

Organization	Product	Web Address	Features and Comments
Caldera	OpenLinux	www.caldera.com	Includes a new graphical desktop called K Desktop Environment (KDE), Sybase Enterprise Adaptive Server.
Work Group Solutions	Linux Pro	www.wgs.com	The Linus Pro Plus package includes a 7 CD-ROM set, a Linux Encyclopedia, a 1600+ page reference manual, etc. Linux Pro is aimed at the professional developer.
S.u.S.E. LLC	S.u.S.E. Linux	www.suse.com	S.u.S.E. Linux package includes 4 CD-ROMs, a reference book, and about 800 preconfigured, compiled packages. It features a menu-driven installation, hypertext help, a X11R6.3-based graphical interface, and source code.
Red Hat Software	Red Hat Linux	www.redhat.com	The Red Hat Linux Operating System, which has won many awards, can be used as a Web server, e-mail server, DNS server, or a news server for multiple sites, with virtual hosting. The package includes the Apache Web server, sendmail, publishing, calendars, Internet tools, X Window system, Netscape Navigator, and Netscape Communicator. The operating system includes disk partitioning with Disk Druid, autodetection of hardware, configuration for multiple window managers, graphical tools, and sound support.
Debian	Debian Linux	www.debian.org	Debian is not a company. Debian Linux is produced by volunteers and the primary focus is Intel-based machines. Although it is only supported through e-mail/third parties, support from the volunteers is normally very quick. Compared to other sources, the software is probably the cheapest (less than U.S. $5 for 2 CDs, or download for free).

Exhibit 26.6. Linux-related Web and FTP sites.

Site	Comments
sunsite.unc.edu	Free Linux implementation at /pub/linux
tsx-11.mit.edu	Free Linux implementation at /pub/linux
ftp.ncsa.uiuc.edu	Mosaic Web browser and Web server software for Linux
ftp2.netscape.com	Netscape Web Browser for Linux
ftp.blackdown.org	Sun's Java Development Kit for Linux
sunsite.unc.com/mdw/linux.html	Linux Documentation Project Web page

LINUX DRAWBACKS

Popular products such as Microsoft Office and some common databases will not run on Linux. Unless the Linux distribution is from a reputable vendor, support for Linux can sometimes be hard to come by. The support situation may be changing, at least for some major players. At a recent Comdex show, Red Hat Software announced 24-hour enterprise support for its Linux users starting in 1999. A similar service was also due in 1999 from another Linux distributor, Pacific HiTech. Installations planning to use Linux should be prepared to hire technically adept Linux pros to ensure that problems can be handled in a timely manner. While there are a lot of enthusiastic programmers working on the operating system itself, the situation is different when it comes to peripheral device support. Peripherals typically need drivers, and details of the peripheral necessary to write the drivers are not commonly available. It is up to the peripheral vendors to come up with the drivers for the different platforms. Peripheral vendors do not always make a Linux version and, even when they do, it may require some effort to make the configuration work in an installation. Users accustomed to the Windows GUI may feel that the user interfaces available for Linux are not that user friendly. While Linux is UNIX-like and follows X/Open and POSIX standards, it has not been formally branded as UNIX 98 compliant. This is due, in part, to the fact that Linux is unlike a traditional UNIX offering from one manufacturer that is responsible for paying for the development and certification.

IMPLICATIONS OF LINUX

Windows NT has been able to make significant inroads into the low-end server market because it is typically priced lower than many UNIX offerings and is, in general, easier to use. Although Linux is UNIX-like in terms of ease of use, it does offer significant price advantages. This should appeal to cost-conscious customers, particularly those who do not mind the potential drawbacks listed above. While the ability of Linux to make significant inroads into the NT market is debatable, Linux is certainly bound to prove a very strong challenger to low-end UNIX solutions that are priced significantly higher than Linux.

Exhibit 26.7. Linux usage guidance.

Situations for Which Linux Is a Good Candidate	Situations for Which Linux Is Not a Good Candidate
DP environment is very cost-conscious	DP environment requires UNIX branding
DP environment has skills to make things work	Mission-critical applications
Environment that has many UNIX users and programmers	Need a wide array of peripherals
Linux-proven applications and environments such as Web servers, universities, and R&D establishments	Installations that need 24×7 support (this may have changed for some Linux vendors in 1999)

On the high end, applications tend to be more mission critical and customers are typically concerned about reliability, availability, and serviceability as much or more than the price. Hence, Linux may not have as much of an impact on the high end, unless one or more of the distributors establish themselves to the point that customers are comfortable about the support.

GUIDANCE FOR LINUX USAGE

Exhibit 26.7 summarizes Linux usage guidelines for enterprise and data center managers.

LINUX FUTURE OUTLOOK

The money from the venture capital and investments at Red Hat will most likely go toward creating an enterprise server group within Red Hat. Linux will follow the same path as other UNIX operating systems and Windows NT and transition to a 64-bit architecture. Intel has already indicated that the company intends to support a 64-bit version of Linux with their Merced chip and is working on adding to Linux its Wired for Management features, features that are aimed at making Linux easier to install in a corporation. In addition, Intel has also already disclosed details of its universal driver initiative, which aims to make developing Linux applications much easier.

All these developments and the new interest by users and vendors bode well for Linux. The potential downfall is that Linux may face the same problems as UNIX where there are multiple versions and applications are not portable from one version to another.

LINUX RESOURCES

Help on Linux is available through a variety of sources such as newsgroups (see Exhibit 26.8), publications such as the *Linux Journal,* and books. Linux International is a nonprofit consortium of Linux users and vendors.

Exhibit 26.8.   Linux-related newsgroups.

Newsgroup	Description
comp.os.linux.announce	Announcements of Linux developments
comp.os.linux.devlopment.apps	For Linux applications development programmers
comp.os.linux.devlopment.system	For Linux operating system development programmers
comp.os.linux.hardware	Linux hardware specifications
comp.os.linux.admin	System administration questions
comp.os.linux.misc	Miscellaneous questions and issues
comp.os.linux.setup	Installation/setup problems
comp.os.linux.answers	Answers to problems
comp.os.linux.help	Questions and answers for particular problems
comp.os.linux.networking	Linux network-related questions and issues

Books on Linux include:

1. *Linux Unleashed* by Sams. Over 1100 pages and includes a CD. August 1998.
2. *Running Linux* by Matt Welsh and Lar Kaufman. O'Reilly & Associates. 650 pages, 2nd ed., August 1996.
3. *Teach Yourself Linux in 24 Hours* by Bill Ball, Stephen Smoogen, and Ryan K. Stephens. Sams Publishing. 380 pages and includes a CD.

CONCLUSION

Linux is definitely worth a serious evaluation by enterprise and data center managers who are looking for cost-effective solutions. It is a rich operating system that is gaining momentum. It is free and is being used for some specific applications. The support situation is improving. It may not, however, be appropriate for enterprise and data center managers who are considering mission-critical applications, who need a wide array of peripherals, or who need UNIX branding.

Chapter 27
Evaluating the Performance of NT-Based Systems

Gilbert Held

COMPUTER PERFORMANCE REPRESENTS A TOPIC that in one area is very similar to a discussion of the weather — that is, many people can be expected to talk about both topics. However, unlike the weather, which is normally beyond one's control, one does have some latitude when it comes to tailoring the performance of a computer system. By changing hardware components, adding additional memory, swapping a fixed disk for a faster one, and tuning software components, one can usually enhance the performance of a computer. Unfortunately, until recently it was difficult to evaluate the benefits derived from changing hardware or modifying software settings. Fortunately for Microsoft Windows NT users, this operating system includes a built-in performance monitor that can be used to determine the existing level of performance of a computer, as well as for ascertaining the impact of hardware and software changes. Thus, by understanding how to use the Windows NT built-in Performance Monitor utility — either by itself to ascertain the performance of various computer components or in conjunction with hardware and software changes — one obtains the ability to evaluate the performance of an NT computer. In doing so, one might be able to determine that a simple and easy-to-perform operation may be all that is required to eliminate a performance bottleneck, alleviating the necessity to replace or upgrade an existing computer. Thus, in addition to providing a mechanism to examine the level of performance of existing hardware and software, the use of the Windows NT Performance Monitor may enable one to postpone or avoid an expensive equipment upgrade.

OVERVIEW

There are several key components of a Windows NT computer system that can affect its performance. Those components include the amount of

0-8493-9824-X/00/$0.00+$.50
© 2000 by CRC Press LLC

memory installed in the computer, the access time and data transfer rate of hard disks, the type of processor or processors installed on the computer's motherboard, and the type of network adapter card used for a connection to a LAN. In addition to hardware, there are also several software component settings that can have a major effect on the performance of an NT-based computer system. Two of those software settings are the use of virtual memory and the operation of a screen saver. Concerning the latter, one of the most overlooked facts about computers is the fact that the use of a screen saver requires CPU cycles. This means that the simple act of removing a screen saver from a heavily utilized server will enhance its performance.

Unfortunately, the simplicity associated with enabling and disabling the use of a screen saver does not carry over to other hardware and software changes. That is, while the decision to activate or disable a screen saver is a binary decision, the decisions associated with altering hardware or changing system properties are more complex. Thus, in many instances, one will want to consider making an initial hardware or software change and then use the NT Performance Monitor to access the results of the change on computer performance. Recognizing the old adage that "the proof of the pudding is in the eating," one can now focus on the use of virtual memory and its potential effect on the performance of a computer.

VIRTUAL MEMORY

Both Windows NT Workstation and Windows NT Server are similar products, with the key difference between the two being the fact that the server version is optimized to support more users accessing its resources. Thus, although this discussion of virtual memory is applicable to both versions of Windows NT, it is more applicable for Windows NT Server because the use of virtual memory has a greater impact on a computer running multiple applications accessed by many persons than a computer operating multiple applications operated by one or a few persons.

Virtual memory is a term used to reference the use of disk storage as a temporary storage area for program code and other information normally stored in random access memory (RAM). When the RAM storage requirements of applications programs and various NT operating system modules exceed physical RAM, NT will temporarily swap data to virtual memory. When that information is required again, Windows NT will retrieve it from disk and, if necessary, swap other information to virtual memory. Although virtual memory swapping is transparent to the user, it has a significant effect on computer performance.

PERFORMANCE EFFECT

When Windows NT uses its virtual memory capability, it transfers data to and from a special file on the hard disk, referred to as a virtual-memory paging file. This file is also commonly referred to as a swap file. The transfer of information to and from disk occurs at electromechanical speed, with the movement of disk read/write heads over an appropriate disk sector contributing to a major portion of the delay in reading from or writing to a disk. Although modern disk drives are relatively fast devices, they still operate at 1/50th to 1/100th the speed of computer memory in terms of data transfer capability. While paging will always adversely affect the performance of a computer, the size of the paging file on the computer can have a more profound impact. If the size of the paging file is too small for the amount of activity on the server, one can experience a "thrashing" condition, with the operating system repetitively reading and writing small portions of RAM to and from disk.

As this occurs, the performance of the computer will be significantly impacted because additional input/output (I/O) operations are occurring that contribute to delays in processing application data. For example, if operating a database application on the server, the paging operations will delay access to the database. While an individual paging operation will hardly be noticeable, when thrashing occurs, the delays can become significant, especially if the server supports hundreds of employees. Although one could alleviate this condition via the installation of additional RAM, one could also considerably enhance the performance of the server by making an adjustment to the size of the system's virtual memory paging file. How this is done is the focus of the next section.

CHANGING THE PAGING FILE

Since the introduction of Windows NT version 3.5, Microsoft has considerably changed the interface and components of the operating system. However, one component that has retained both its location and general properties is the System Properties dialog box in the NT Control Panel. Through NT version 5.0, one can use the Performance tab in the System Properties dialog box to review the computer's current virtual memory page file settings as well as to change those settings.

Exhibit 27.1 illustrates the screen display of the System Properties dialog box selected from the Control Panel under Windows NT version 5.0. Note that the middle portion of the dialog box displays the current size of the paging file and provides the ability to change the size of that file.

Under Windows NT, a virtual memory paging file is automatically created on the computer when the operating system is installed. The size of the paging file initially created is based on the amount of RAM installed in

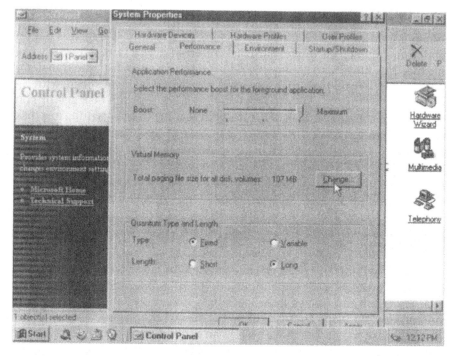

Exhibit 27.1.   View the size of the Windows NT paging file from the performance tab in the system properties dialog box.

the computer, and is typically set by the operating system to equal that amount plus 12 MB. However, the size of the file also depends on the amount of available free space on the hard drive when the paging file is created. Thus, if one installs Windows NT over a prior version of the operating system, or over a different operating system, and then changes the hard drive or removes obsolete files, the size of the paging file may vary from the Microsoft recommendation. In addition, the recommendation is merely a recommendation and may not be suitable for the traffic expected to be supported by the server. Thus, one can now examine how to change the size of the paging file and then observe changes in performance resulting from changing the size of the paging file.

Exhibit 27.2 illustrates the screen display resulting from selecting the button labeled "change" in the Performance tab in the System Properties dialog box. Note that the Virtual Memory dialog box displays the initial size of the paging file, which represents the recommended size of the file and its maximum size. The latter setting permits an area on disk to be reserved to enable the size of the paging file to grow. In this example, the paging file is shown set to 107 MB and can grow to 157 MB.

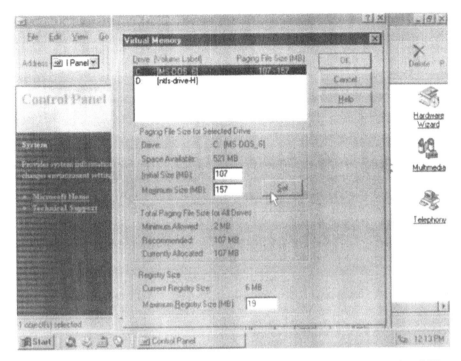

Exhibit 27.2. The Windows NT virtual memory dialog box provides the ability to both view and change the size of a computer's paging file.

Although Microsoft's default settings for the computer's paging file will be sufficient for many users, it is a fact of life that very rarely are two computers used in a similar manner. This means that for some Windows NT users, an adjustment to the size of the paging file may be in order. However, how can one determine if sluggish performance is being caused by an improper allocation of paging file space, the inability of the computer's processor to support current operations, a lack of RAM, or another factor? The answer to this question can be obtained through the use of the Windows NT Performance, Monitor which provides the key for evaluating the performance of an NT computer.

EVALUATING NT PERFORMANCE

Exhibit 27.3 illustrates the initial display of the NT Performance Monitor after the plus sign (+) button in the icon bar across the top of the display was clicked. That action results in the display of the dialog box labeled "Add to Chart," which enables one to display in real time metrics associated with different counters, which are in turn associated with different NT objects. Under Windows NT, an object is a higher layer component, such as a processor or paging file. The counters represent performance elements

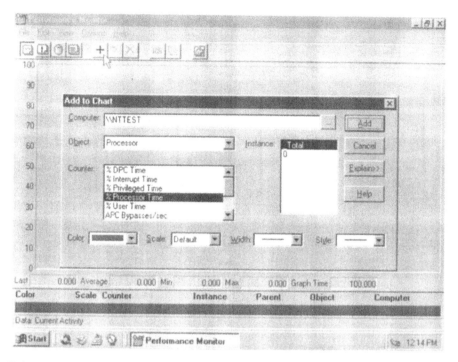

Exhibit 27.3.   Selecting the % processor time counter for display in a line chart.

whose values are tracked. If the computer contains two or more objects, such as a multiprocessor computer with two or more processors installed on the motherboard, each processor will have an instance associated with it. One would then be required to select the instance to identify the particular processor for which one wants a counter to be displayed.

Returning to Exhibit 27.3, note that the counter "% Processor Time" was selected. This will result in the display of the percentage of processor time being used once the "Add" button is clicked. By observing this metric, one would be able to note whether or not the processor was a bottleneck. Also note that if that computer is connected to a network and one has an appropriate account on another NT computer, one can use Performance Monitor on the computer to monitor the performance of a distant computer. Thus, a supervisor or user with a series of appropriate accounts on different computers could periodically monitor the performance of a network of NT computers from one location.

The previous concern about the size of the NT paging file can now be addressed. Exhibit 27.4 illustrates the selection of the "Paging File" object in the Performance Monitor utility program. In examining Exhibit 27.4, note

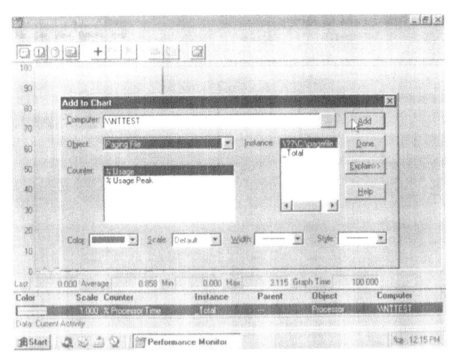

Exhibit 27.4. **Selecting the performance monitor paging file object permits the display of two counters associate with that object.**

that Performance Monitor does not provide a direct indication of the amount of usage associated with the paging file. Instead, one can select the % Usage, % Usage Peak, or both counters to be displayed over a period of time. As one adds counters to be displayed, Performance Monitor will automatically change the color for displaying the counter; however, one can elect to override the default color with a specific color. Similarly, one can change the scale linewidth used for the display of a specific counter and the style of the line. Although those options provide the ability to customize the display of a series of counters on a common screen display, they do not alter the ability to display any counter, as all counters are built into the program and must be used as-is. If one requires an explanation of the use of a counter, one can click on the "Explain" button, which will result in a brief explanation of the use of a counter being displayed at the bottom of the screen. Once the selection of counters is complete, pressing the "Done" button results in the display of those counters.

Exhibit 27.5 illustrates the display of the % Processor Time, % Usage and % Usage Peak, the latter two counters being associated with the paging file object. A careful examination of the colors of the lines plotted would indicate

293

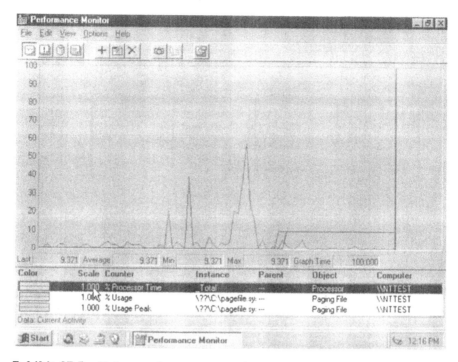

Exhibit 27.5. **Using performance monitor to display the values of three counters.**

that the % Processor Time periodically spiked to 40 and 60 percent, while the percent usage and % Usage Peak associated with the paging file never exceeded 10 percent. If you were running a mixture of typical applications and monitored performance during the busy hour (which represents the hour of the day with the highest amount of server activity), this would indicate that one can safely reduce the size of the paging file. This could be valuable information that translates into the bottom line of an organization if it is low on available disk space and wishes to defer the downtime associated with the installation of a new drive.

As indicated in this article, Performance Monitor provides one with the ability to view the use of different hardware and software components. By using Performance Monitor, one can observe the existing performance of hardware and software as a mechanism for the adjustment of computer components. Then one can reuse Performance Monitor to evaluate the effect of those changes, as well as to periodically monitor the performance of the computer. In doing so, one may be able to note potential problems before they occur and initiate corrective action prior to the user community experiencing the effect of performance bottlenecks.

Chapter 28
Configuring TCP/IP on a Windows NT Computer

Gilbert Held

DUE TO THE MIGRATION OF MANY CORPORATE NETWORKS to the TCP/IP protocol suite, it is important to understand how to appropriately configure workstations and servers to support this suite. In addition, due to the rapid growth in the use of Windows NT, which now accounts for over 60 percent of the corporate networking server market, it is also important to understand how to configure the TCP/IP protocol suite for operation on Microsoft's NT platforms. Thus, the focus of this article covers the key address that must be used to configure TCP/IP on any operating system while using the Windows NT platform to specifically illustrate how to configure this protocol suite on this popular operating system.

OVERVIEW

There are two basic methods to consider when configuring the TCP/IP protocol suite. The first method involves installing a Dynamic Host Configuration Protocol (DHCP) server that dynamically issues Internet Protocol (IP) addresses to clients that can be both workstations and servers. Most organizations that use a DHCP server do so because they may have hundreds or thousands of workstations and issuing, configuring, and maintaining IP addresses could become an administrative burden. If an organization decides to use DHCP, each workstation and server that receives an IP address from the DHCP server will still require a small degree of customization. Specifically, users or a LAN administrator will still have to manually configure each workstation to use DHCP, as well as to specify the host name and domain name (which is noted later in this chapter).

The second method associated with configuring the TCP/IP protocol is to assign IP addresses and several additional pieces of information to each station on the network. This chapter primarily focuses on this latter method, illustrating the addresses and data that must be supplied to configure the TCP/IP protocol suite on a Windows NT platform. Because both Windows NT Workstation and Windows NT Server use the same method to configure the TCP/IP protocol suite, the example here is limited to configuring TCP/IP on a Windows NT server.

WINDOWS NT CONFIGURATION

From the Start menu, select Settings>Control Panel. Once the Control panel is displayed, double-click on the Network icon to display the Network dialog box. If the TCP/IP is not installed, one can do so by selecting the Protocols tab in the Network dialog box and then selecting the Add button. Once the TCP/IP protocol suite is added to the computer, the Network dialog box appears similar to the one shown in Exhibit 28.1.

The computer system used by this author was configured to support four protocols to include TCP/IP. To configure TCP/IP, first click on the network protocol entry of TCP/IP Protocol. Then click on the button labeled Properties, which the arrow cursor is located on in Exhibit 28.1.

IP ADDRESS REQUIREMENTS

Selecting the button labeled Properties shown in Exhibit 28.1 results in the display of a new dialog box labeled Microsoft TCP/IP Properties. Exhibit 28.2 shows the dialog box that has its IP Address tab illustrated. By initially focusing attention on the selectable items on the IP Address tab, note the difference between using DHCP to provide IP addresses and manually configuring workstations to support a specific IP address.

Under TCP/IP, each interface must have a unique IP address. Because a network adapter provides the interface to a network for workstations and servers, the IP Address tab shown in Exhibit 28.2 provides Windows NT users with the ability to configure an IP address for each adapter installed in a computer. If only one adapter is installed in the computer, one only has to configure an IP address or select the DHCP option discussed next. Otherwise, configure an IP address or select the use of DHCP for each adapter installed in the computer that one wants to support the TCP/IP protocol suite. Although one could theoretically configure one adapter card to obtain an IP address from a DHCP server and another adapter to be configured manually with a static IP address, this is not normally done. This is because that action would defeat the purpose of using a DHCP server because its use is designed to reduce the administrative burden associated with having to individually configure a large number of computers.

The area under the rectangular box labeled Adapter in Exhibit 28.2 provides the ability to either specify the use of a DHCP server for IP address assignments, or manually specify an IP address and other addressing

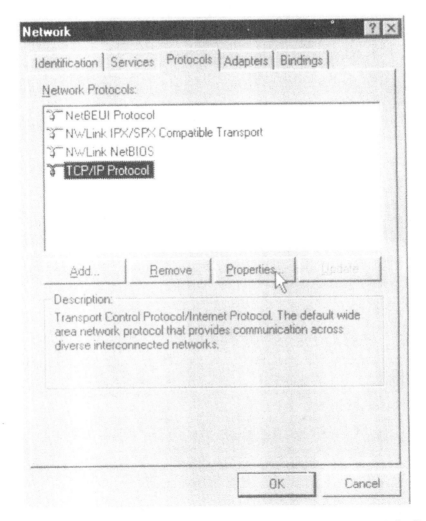

Exhibit 28.1. Configure TCP/IP on a Windows NT workstation or server by first selecting the Protocols tab from the Network dialog box. Then select the Properties button.

information required to correctly configure the computer. Selecting the first button labeled "Obtain an IP address from a DHCP server," in effect configures the computer to obtain a dynamic IP address issued by a DHCP server. Doing so simplifies IP address management as one would not have to complete the IP addressing information required if the IP address had been manually specified. Thus, one of the key reasons for the use of a DHCP server is IP address administration. A second reason behind the use of a DHCP server concerns the movement of workstations and servers. For a

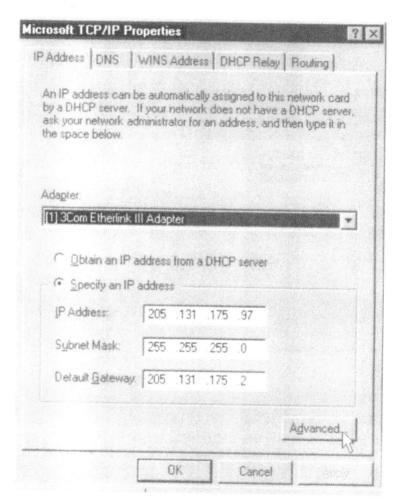

Exhibit 28.2. The IP Address tab in the Microsoft TCP/IP Properties dialog box provides the ability to select an IP address from a DHCP server or manually specifying an IP address.

large network with many subnets and periodical movement of workstations and servers from one segment to another, one would have to reconfigure each computer's IP address when it is moved. Because network
operations can be adversely affected by duplicate IP addresses, the network manager or LAN administrator must carefully document all network
changes, which creates an administrative burden that can also be allevi-
ated by the use of a DHCP server. However, the preceding benefits are not
without cost. The use of a DHCP server requires a network manager or LAN
administrator to set up a DHCP server to lease addresses for predefined

periods of time. This results in the DHCP server periodically querying network devices after each device has leased an IP address for a specific period of time. As the life of the lease approaches termination, the server will communicate with the network device to extend the lease, resulting in additional network traffic. Due to the preceding, most organizations with a few hundred or less devices typically elect to use a manual IP address configuration method that results in the assignment of a static IP address for each device. The remainder of this chapter focuses on this method of IP address assignment by examining the data elements that must be specified when one selects the Specify an IP address button as shown in Exhibit 28.2.

In examining the lower portion of Exhibit 28.2, note that three addresses must be entered in the IP Address tab when the Specify an IP address button is selected. Those addresses are the specific IP address assigned to the selected adapter card, a subnet mask, and the address of the default gateway. Each is discussed below.

IP Address

The IP address represents a unique 32-bit address assigned to the interface connected to a network. As previously discussed, because the adapter card provides the interface to the network, one can view the IP address as being assigned to the adapter card. The 32-bit IP address represents four 8-bit bytes. Because each 8-bit byte can vary in value from decimal 0 to decimal 255, an alternate method used to represent the binary value of a 32-bit IP address is through the use of four decimal digits, commonly referred to as dotted decimal notation because a decimal point is used to separate the decimal value of one 8-bit byte from another. Thus, the IP address shown in Exhibit 28.2 that has the value 205.131.175.97 actually represents a 32-bit binary number. However, because it is rather awkward to work with 32-bit binary numbers, the Internet Assigned Numbers Authority (IANA) assigns IP address space using dotted decimal numbers, which are also used by hardware and software developers to configure equipment.

Under IP Version 4 — the current version of the Internet Protocol — there are three types of IP addresses that are assigned to organizations. Those addresses are referred to as Class A, Class B, and Class C addresses. Each type of address consists of a network portion and a host portion. The network portion of the address indicates a specific network, while the host portion of the address indicates a specific host on the network. Exhibit 28.3 provides a summary of the number of bytes used to denote the network and host identifiers for Class A, B, and C addresses.

In examining the entries in Exhibit 28.3, one unanswered question concerns how one address class is differentiated from another. The answer to this question is the composition of the first byte of each address. A Class A

Address Class	Network Portion (Bytes)	Host Portion (Bytes)
A	1	3
B	2	2
C	3	1

Exhibit 28.3. Network/host assignments.

address begins with a value of binary 0 in bit 8 of the first byte. In comparison, a Class B address begins with a value of binary 10 in bit positions 8 and 7 in the first byte, while a Class C address begins with a value of binary 11 in bit positions 8 and 7 in the first byte. This results in a Class A address ranging from 0 to 127, while a Class B address ranges from 128 to 191. A Class C address then falls in the range 192 through 255. Thus, the IP address shown entered in Exhibit 28.2 represents a Class C address.

From Exhibit 28.3, a Class C address consists of a 3-byte network portion and a 1-byte host portion. Thus, the IP address shown in Exhibit 28.2 represents host 97 on the network 205.131.175.0.

As a further review of IP addresses, it should be noted that there are two host addresses one cannot use for each address class. Those addresses are 0, which represents "this network," and a value of 255 for each host byte, which represents a broadcast address. Thus, for a Class C address, the permitted host values would range from 1 to 254, resulting in a maximum of 254 distinct interfaces being capable of being supported on a Class C network.

Subnet Mask

If one subdivides a network into two or more segments but retains one IP address for both segments, then one would use an appropriate value in the subnet mask to enable the device being configured to recognize data transmitted to the device. When one subdivides an IP network, two or more subnets are created. When this occurs, the network portion of the IP address is extended internally to the network while simultaneously reducing the host portion of the address. The extended network address represents the subnet that is used to identify a specific subnet on which a host resides.

The subnet mask represents a sequence of set bits that is logically ANDed with the IP address to determine the extended network address. Because the first or first two bit positions of an IP address indicates the type of address, it also indicates the length of the network portion of the address prior to subnetting. By subtracting the length of the IP address from the ANDed length, the device can determine the length of the subnet portion of the address and the value in the subnet portion. For example, the subnet mask of 255.255.255.0 shown in Exhibit 28.2 when ANDed with the IP address of 205.131.175.97 results in a 24-bit address. However, because the network address of 205.131.175.0 represents a Class C address that consists of a 3-byte network address and 1-byte host address, this indicates that no subnetting occurred. Thus, a subnet mask of 255.255.255.0 represents a nonsubnetted Class C address. Similarly, a subnet mask of 255.255.0.0 would indicate a nonsubnetted Class B address, while a subnet mask of 255.0.0.0 would represent a nonsubnetted Class A network address.

Default Gateway

The third IP address one must enter in the IP Address tab shown in Exhibit 28.2 is the address of the default gateway. In actuality, this address represents the address of a router. However, when TCP/IP was originally developed, the term "gateway" was used to reference a device that routed information between networks. Thus, the term "gateway" represents antiquated terminology that most hardware and software vendors elect to continue to use although the term "router" would be more accurate as the new millennium approaches.

Although one can correctly configure a network device to use the TCP/IP protocol suite by entering an IP address, subnet mask, and default gateway address, it may be desirable to enter some additional addresses. Those addresses are entered by clicking on the button labeled Advanced and selecting the tab labeled DNS. Thus, in concluding this examination of configuring TCP/IP to operate on a Windows NT-based computer platform, one can now focus attention on each additional configuration area.

ADVANCED IP ADDRESSING

By clicking on the button labeled Advanced previously shown in Exhibit 28.2, one obtains the ability to modify or remove a previous gateway address assignment or to enter additional gateway addresses. Microsoft's implementation of the TCP/IP protocol suite enables users to specify up to three gateway addresses. Exhibit 28.4 illustrates the Advanced IP Addressing dialog box, indicating the result from clicking on an Add box that is obscured by a pop-up dialog box labeled TCP/IP Gateway Address. By clicking on the Add button, one can add up to three gateway addresses that will be tried in the order they are entered.

THE DNS TAB

The second optional series of IP addressing entries is reflected by the use of the DNS tab shown in Exhibit 28.5. DNS, a mnemonic for Domain Name System, represents the translation service between near-English host and domain names and IP addresses. When users surf the World Wide Web,

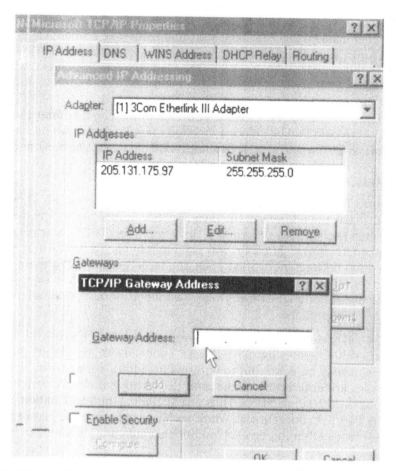

Exhibit 28.4. Through the use of the Advanced IP Addressing dialog box, one can enter up to three gateway addresses that will be tried in the order they are entered.

access an FTP server, or perform another TCP/IP application that requires a destination address, they typically specify a near-English mnemonic and represent the destination and not an IP address. This is because it is much easier to remember addresses in terms of near-English mnemonics. This also means that a translation process is required to convert those near-English mnemonics to IP addresses because routing and address recognition are based on IP addresses.

If one wants employees on a private TCP/IP network or persons on the Internet to be able to access a computer through the use of a near-English mnemonic, one would use the DNS tab shown in Exhibit 28.4, to specify a

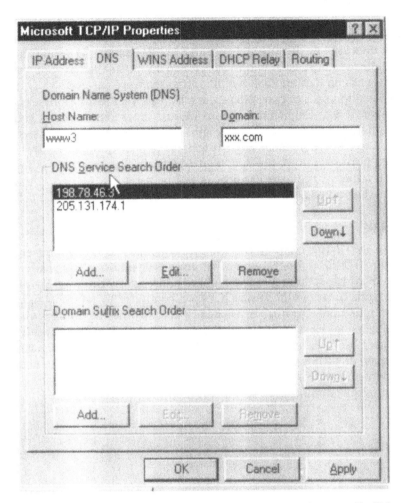

Exhibit 28.5. The DNS tab provides the opportunity to specify a near-English mnemonic to reference a computer as well as one or more addresses of DNS servers to resolve near-English mnemonic addresses entered to access other computers.

host name and domain name. In the example shown at the top of Exhibit 28.4 the host name WWW3 and domain xxx.com is shown entered. Thus, other persons can refer to the computer being configured as www.xxx.com instead of its IP address of 205.131.175.97.

If one intends to use a computer to access other computers and to only specify IP addresses, one does not have to specify any additional information. However, if one wants to use that computer to access other computers by specifying their near-English mnemonic address, then one must specify one or more DNS service addresses. Those addresses can represent the address of DNS servers operated by one's organization or a DNS server operated by the Internet Service Provider. Similar to permitting multiple gateway addresses, Windows NT also supports the entry of multiple DNS servers. In Exhibit 28.4, two IP addresses were entered, which represents the addresses of two DNS servers. If an address resolution is required to convert a near-English mnemonic address entered to access a Web site or another TCP/IP application, the first DNS IP address will be used in an attempt to resolve the near English address to an IP address. If, after a predefined period of time, the specified address does not resolve the near-English address, the next IP address will be used in a second attempt to resolve the address.

SUMMARY

As indicated in this chapter, there are three IP addresses one must enter to configure TCP/IP to operate on a Windows NT platform. Those addresses are an IP address, subnet mask, and the address of a gateway. However, if one intends to have other users access a computer by referencing a near-English mnemonic address or wishes to access other computers via their near-English address, then one must also configure the computer through the use of the DNS tab shown in Exhibit 28.4. By carefully configuring the computer, ensuring there are no duplicate IP addresses on the network, and following addressing rules, if one subnets the network, then one can configure the computers to support the TCP/IP protocol suite.

Chapter 29
More Productive User Interfaces

Paul Nisenbaum
Robert E. Umbaugh

THE INTERFACE IS THE USER'S WINDOW to any system. Although standard screen structure, the use of icons and color, and sharper screen quality have all contributed to improvements in the way systems are presented to a wide audience of users, an interface encompasses far more than screen format.

As a mechanism that lets people customize a user interface to their needs, a flexible user interface relates to the total hardware and software system. Most computer hardware and software, either purchased or developed in-house, provides some degree of flexible user interface that allows users to control their computing system. For example, users can adjust the contrast on a display monitor, assign synonyms to commands, create macros, and split the screen for multiple windows.

These and other components of a flexible interface have become expected standard features. Most people probably do not even think about whether the interface is flexible, but if they did not have the ability to customize function keys or set the time to military or AM/PM format, they would no doubt notice its absence.

PC users demand the ability to easily control hardware and software. Even minicomputer and mainframe vendors now offer personal computer-like interfaces. The implementation of client/server systems that let PC users access mainframe information also signifies that people want to control their computers on their own terms. Without a doubt, people want the ability to tailor their computing systems.

Yet, although a system may have a flexible, efficient, and intuitive user interface, the interface may be counterproductive unless it enables users to complete goals, not just subordinate tasks. It is the responsibility of the IS manager and system designer to ensure that gains in efficiency also contribute to the achievement of overall system goals.

NEED FOR GOAL-ALIGNED INTERFACES

The following example illustrates the importance of aligning flexible user interfaces with system goals. An inventory control clerk has the ability to customize the online data entry application and workplace environment in the following ways:

- Designating abbreviations, so that by typing fewer characters and pressing one function key, whole phrases or paragraphs are displayed.
- Changing and intermixing type fonts.
- Changing colors and highlights.
- Rearranging an online form to make entering both data and text easier.
- Adjusting the keyboard and monitor to reduce fatigue and prevent carpal tunnel syndrome.

If the goal is to quickly and accurately itemize the inventory, however, a portable bar code system could be a better solution. Understanding the overall goal, working with the user and others to precisely define what tasks need to be accomplished, and restructuring work steps would have been a better approach to defining the right process and the subsequent system interfaces.

EXAMPLES OF NONPRODUCTIVE FLEXIBILITY

Merely defining a goal first does not guarantee an efficient way of reaching it. Consider the following example of the data center goal of monitoring a workload such as the payroll system:

Workload Monitoring

In this example, monitoring software can display four workload states: not scheduled to run, running on schedule, running behind schedule, and unable to complete on schedule.

To provide maximum user flexibility, hardware and software could be provided that would allow each staff member on each shift to highlight these states with a choice of 1000 colors. Although this might be beneficial for a single user, each time another person approached the console, the new user would have to determine which color represented a particular state. This user in turn might spend time reconfiguring the colors to his or her liking. The situation may then be repeated when yet another person approaches the console.

Instead of accruing time lost in terms of users figuring out the color scheme and customizing the highlighting, a more efficient solution would be to limit either the color choices or the customization privileges, or to limit a combination of the two with default settings. Although the user interface with 1000 color choices may be easy to use and flexible, it does not necessarily help meet the overall goal of monitoring the workload.

Navigating from One Panel to Another

Flexible interfaces also let users customize the subordinate task of navigating from one panel to another. Variations of this example can be seen in microcomputer, minicomputer, and mainframe systems. The user can choose from among the following ways to select the name of the destination panel:

- Selecting panel destination choices from a sequence of menus.
- Selecting a labeled push button.
- Typing the destination panel name on the command line.
- Typing the destination panel abbreviation name on the command line.
- Typing a user-created synonym for the destination panel name on the command line.
- Selecting the destination panel from a help panel.
- Selecting an icon (either system provided or user created) representing the destination panel.
- Selecting the destination panel from an index.

Knowing which approach is best in a given situation results from careful analysis and consultation with users. Providing all of these options would probably be overkill.

In both user interface examples described — assigning colors to objects and navigating between panels — an appropriate balance must be reached between too little and too much flexibility. Are the many color selections and the navigation techniques helpful in satisfying the varied desires and needs of users? Do they help users reach stated goals and improve productivity, or do they simply carry a flexible interface to an extreme? If the user has to spend too much time deciding which way to do something or learning a multitude of techniques, productivity may suffer.

CREATING USABLE AND PRODUCTIVE SYSTEMS

Three steps are key to developing systems with beneficial flexible user interfaces:

1. Identifying the users and their characteristics.
2. Identifying user tasks.
3. Involving users continuously.

IDENTIFYING USERS AND THEIR CHARACTERISTICS

The first step in design is to determine who will be using the completed system. Collecting information about these people in an organized fashion helps ensure that fewer items fall through the cracks and that similarities and differences among users become apparent. The system can then be designed to accommodate various user characteristics.

Helpful information includes current and previous job titles or levels, formal and informal education, and experience with various computer systems. Less tangible, but equally important, may be the user's motivation for learning and using new systems.

Collecting User Information

Whether to poll all users or only a representative sample depends on the number of potential users. If ten people will be using the system, then it probably makes sense to question all of them. For 2000 users, a sample would be sufficient.

For best results, the sample should include users with various skill levels and job classifications who will actually use the system. It is a mistake to design an interface for the most skilled or most knowledgeable user. A more effective approach is to design a system with the needs of less gifted users in mind and provide enough flexibility for the more advanced users to build their own shortcuts and techniques.

For example, if the payroll manager and IS manager agree on building a new payroll application, they will no doubt have definite ideas about the design. Once the application is up and running, however, they may have only peripheral involvement with it. Within the payroll department, the application administrator and others may be interested in customization and various bells and whistles. But the primary users of the application, the data entry staff, might not have the skill, time, nor desire to explore computer applications. It is therefore essential that the everyday data entry users, as well as the more experienced and the less frequent users, be included in the collection sample.

Exhibit 29.1 provides a sample form for collecting information on user characteristics; it can assist the designer and be tailored or used as is. For increased efficiency, it may make sense to combine the step of gathering user characteristics with the next step: identifying current goals and user tasks.

IDENTIFYING USER TASKS

The importance of identifying user tasks should not be underestimated in the development of systems and user interfaces. Special attention needs to be given to collecting this information. User tasks can be as broad as getting the payroll out and as narrow as deleting a looping transaction with one keystroke. It is crucial to identify goals and their subordinate tasks.

Examples of Goals and Subordinate Tasks

The system designer needs to determine the level of detail to be gathered. The first visit to a user may be to gather the higher level tasks, with subsequent visits used to focus on fine details. For example, if the goal is to restore an accidentally deleted file, the tasks are to phone the data center and ask to have the file restored, locate the tape on which the file resides, and request a tape mount.

If the goal is to print the monthly problem management report, the tasks are: collect the daily and weekly reports from remote machines by uploading to the mainframe, run the job to create the monthly report, set up the printer with preprinted forms, and submit the print job.

Understanding Users' Human Nature

As with other endeavors involving people, things may not always be as they seem. For reasons that are both conscious and subconscious, people may not be as forthcoming, direct, or honest as might be expected. Personal agendas and corporate politics transcend even the most seemingly cut-and-dried situation.

When approached with questions, some people feel they are being judged and must give a correct answer. Because they do not want to appear ignorant to the observer or their peers or supervisors, their answers may not accurately reflect their job. Other people may not speak candidly for fear of retribution, no matter how much assurance to the contrary they are given. They may have been reprimanded in the past or know of others who have had a similar negative experience. Still other users may emphasize only a small part of their job because that is the area in which they feel most competent. Gaining a more balanced view of some users may necessitate several visits over a few days or weeks.

Many approaches for gathering information about user goals and tasks can be concurrently employed to cover a wide variety of users and their settings. The recommended approaches in the following sections can be adapted or expanded to the particular needs of the designers.

Remaining open to surprises. Acute observation of a user without preconceived notions can lead to startling revelations for both the designer and the user. Keeping an open mind early in the design phase avoids costly and time-consuming work later on.

Observing the user or users on several occasions. Personal observation by the designer is the best way to begin to gather information about the user interface. Having personal knowledge of the details of the application is helpful but not absolutely necessary to the experienced observer. Because

309

Part 1: User Characteristics	
For project	
Date(s)	
Department	
Observer	
Name	
Job title	
Job level	(entry-level, senior)
Department	
Education	
Degrees	
Additional courses, seminars	
Experience	
Previous job titles	
Current job	(years)
Subject area	(years)
Microcomputer	(years)
Minicomputer	(years)
Mainframe	(years)
Use computer on current job	(daily, quarterly)
Motivation	(reluctant, eager)

Part 2: Current Hardware	
Mainframe or minicomputer terminal type	(monochrome, four color)
Personal computer	(display: monochrome—amber or green, VGA, SVGA; sound; RAM; hard drive; LAN or host emulator cards)
Data entry	(Keyboard, mouse, touch screen, voice)
Printer	(Local, remote, paper type, speed duplex, multiform)
Modem	(Internal, external, baud rate, LAN-connected)
Miscellaneous	(Swivel monitor stand, printer stand, adjustable chair or desk, lighting)

Exhibit 29.1. Sample form for collecting user information.

Part 3: Current Software Applications		
Application, Brand, and Version	**Frequency Used (Hourly/Quarterly)**	**Expertise (Novice/Expert)**
CAD/CAM		
CASE tools		
Customer support		
Data base		
Desktop publishing		
E-mail		
Financial planning		
Graphic presentation		
Help desk		
Human resources		
Inventory		
Operating system		
Payroll		
Printer management		
Problem management		
Programming (languages)		
Service-level management		
Spreadsheet		
Statistics		
System administrator (name system)		
Tape management		
Utilities Word processing		

Exhibit 29.1. (continued)

making a single observation is risky, the designer should try to schedule observations at different times of the day and on different days of the week. In some cases, the system may be suffering from slow response time, the user may be doing nontypical tasks, or personal issues may be affecting the user's performance. When an interface is being designed for a task for the first time, the designer will have to make observations on the manual tasks and use judgment and experience to design a pilot interface for the user to try.

Asking users why they do tasks in a certain way. Designers should listen carefully to what users say about why they perform tasks in a specific way and ask users if they are satisfied with the current way of doing things. If they are not, the designer should ask why or how tasks could be performed differently. Could they be combined or eliminated? And how often are they performed?

To stimulate the user's thinking about options, the designer may opt to describe typical options or demonstrate optional interfaces in a technology demonstration lab. The expense of such labs hinders most companies from using them, but those that do report high levels of success in designing user interfaces that are productive and goal aligned.

Meeting with a single user at a time. Many people are reluctant to speak up when they are part of a group, especially when talking about new technology or new ways of doing things. Meeting with single users often lets the designer probe more deeply into tasks and goals and broadens understanding.

Meeting with a group of coworkers who share common responsibilities.
Although there are distinct advantages in meeting with single users, meeting in groups yields valuable information, as well. Users stimulate ideas in each other and, perhaps more important, group discussions often indicate areas of disagreement or conflict that the designer should follow up on later.

Meeting with coworkers of an employee to gather information on the tasks and goals of other jobs. Although this technique is not always as productive as meeting with the users themselves, it occasionally provides revealing information that can make the difference between success and failure. The designer needs to be a skilled interviewer who can differentiate between comments related to the task and those that reflect personal observations about the person doing the job.

Meeting with customers — in-house and out. Meeting with customers is especially critical if the proposed or existing system involves electronic document interchange or is expected to at some point in its life.

Asking if the task is essential to complete the specific goal. In all meetings with users it is important that the designer repeatedly probe whether all

312

the tasks being systematized are necessary to achieving the overall goal. This is especially true when going from manual to computerized tasks for the first time. The older the company the more likely it is that the task is being done because "that's the way we have always done it."

Meeting with vendors. There are many reasons to meet with vendors, both software and hardware, when considering alternative user interfaces. Vendors are often a good source of information regarding new technology, and they can constructively critique the designers' ideas for proposed interfaces. The IS management team should never allow the vendor to design or dictate the interface, however, unless the vendor is under contract to do so and has special expertise in this area.

Asking the user's supervisor about the goals and tasks of the job. It is not uncommon for IS staff to design and build a system based on what they think is good input from users only to find that a supervisor or higher management do not like it or, worse yet, were about to restructure jobs and thereby invalidate all or some of the system elements. Checking up the ladder makes good sense.

INVOLVING USERS CONTINUOUSLY

Including users in an iterative design process helps ensure that the final product allows users to meet their overall goals and provides appropriate facilities for users to customize the user interface. The iterative process includes demonstrations of work in progress to users at various developmental stages. Paper and online prototypes can be used initially, with the actual product demonstrated as it evolves. Sessions can be held both for individuals and for groups, with hands-on sessions scheduled when appropriate. The designer needs to constantly monitor user input and adjust the product accordingly.

A usability lab can provide a no-risk opportunity for users to try out a system during the latter stages of development. At the same time, it has the potential to give system builders insight into exactly how users will exercise the system once it goes into production. The usability lab is also often used to stress parts of the system during development in order to identify areas of weakness, missing features, or inappropriate interfaces. The labs can be located in-house or contracted out, and they vary greatly in complexity and cost.

First Iteration

When the designer initially sorts through the collected user characteristics, goals, and tasks, and other information, the overall goals will probably appear fairly obvious. A high-level design based on these goals must be presented to users. Without a confirmation of this system view, the entire project may face an uphill battle. The designer needs to demonstrate that the system is a tool to make the users' jobs more productive.

Continuing the Cycle of User Feedback

As the design evolves, care should be taken to incorporate common areas of concern noted during the examination of the user input. When the users view the next level of design, they should express confidence in their new tool. Designers who listen to and incorporate feedback from users into the next design iteration not only make the users feel like part of the process, but give them a stake in the eventual adoption and use of the system.

This cyclical process needs to progress quickly so the users do not lose interest. Using rapid prototyping techniques can maximize effort and feedback. Actual scenarios give life to the design, and users can participate by asking specific questions, such as "What if I selected this field?" or "What happens on the last Friday of the quarter if it is part of a three-day holiday?" Eventually, live data should be used in the user review sessions to help test the system and generate enthusiasm. Once again, feedback about the use of the system needs to be carefully evaluated and, if appropriate, incorporated into the next iteration. Here again, a usability lab may provide an effective and productive tool.

BALANCING FLEXIBILITY AND PRODUCTIVITY

As is the case with almost anything related to systems development, the decision of how much flexibility and how many options to give users involves tradeoffs. Users accustomed to using systems based on dumb terminals — so-called green screens — will find almost any degree of flexibility an improvement. But the step from green screens to intelligent terminals is usually so great that both designers and users can get carried away if some reasonable limitations are not applied.

Improvements that make a user's job go faster and smoother with less strain are easy to justify in most cases because of the inherent power and flexibility already built into most intelligent terminals. It is when further systems development work that results in significant investment of project time and money is needed that some form of cost/benefit analysis is necessary, however informal it might be. Today's emphasis on worker eye strain and injuries to the wrist and arms may make it prudent to provide as much flexibility as the project budget will allow.

The soundest approach, therefore, may be to allow good judgment and common sense to prevail. The final test is that user management be satisfied that their money is being well spent and that the flexibility provided will pay a return either in direct or indirect benefit to the enterprise.

CONCLUSION

Although the participation of users in the systems development process can clearly lead to better systems, their involvement needs to be carefully managed. It bears repeating that the designer should always remember that people sometimes bring personal agendas into the workplace that may have a negative influence on a seemingly impartial opinion. When involving users in design, designers should work to maintain a positive environment.

One rule to remember is that users may expect their input to be visible in the product. If they do not see their requests in the design, they may reject further participation, become hostile to the project, and discourage others. If they are paying customers, they may even begin buying from other vendors.

Users may become defensive when the tasks they have been doing a certain way turn out to be inefficient or unnecessary. They may contradict or seek to invalidate the statements of others because of office politics. All this is part of the process of designing productive systems, and designers and IS managers must learn how to manage it.

Chapter 30
Creating GUIs Users Can Use: Usability Analysis

Luke Hohmann

INFORMATION SYSTEMS ARE SUPPOSED TO HELP, but very often end users regard a new system as more of a hindrance than a help. There are many explanations why users would find an information system an obstacle in getting their work done. One is that the system does not perform the tasks users must do to accomplish their work. Another common reason is that the systems are just too difficult to use. Usability is the answer for such end-user complaints.

GUIs are the part of an information system that users work with. Often, when users refer to a system, they are actually referring to the GUI. Because of its importance to users, users may reject a system if they object to its GUI. Thus, creating a usable GUI is key to the success of any information system. This chapter gives systems development managers a firm understanding of what usability is, how to manage interface development when usability is a goal, and how to perform usability analysis so that developers know what users look for in an interface they can actually use.

WHAT IS USABILITY?

Usability refers to the quality of the user interface as perceived by the user. Unfortunately, both "usability" and "quality" can be nebulous terms, so human-computer interaction (HCI) professionals have used the following to more completely describe usability:

- A highly usable GUI allows the user to accomplish one or more specific tasks easily, efficiently, and with a minimum number of errors. Extremely usable interfaces fade over time and enable the user to concentrate completely on the task at hand. This is referred to as transparency. An extreme example of transparency in action is a child playing a video game.

- A highly usable GUI is easy to learn and, once learned, is easy to remember.
- The use and arrangement of controls, the colors and layout of both large and small details, and the ability to customize the user interface all contribute to a sense of satisfaction, enjoyment, and accomplishment.

Usability cannot be determined without an understanding of users and the context in which they work. For example, a highly usable GUI for a chemical engineer performing experiments is quite different than a highly usable interface for an airline reservations clerk. Developing a clear understanding of the users for each domain is a central aspect of the design process and will be discussed in greater detail later in this article.

The term *usability* addresses both quantitative and qualitative dimensions of the user interface. Depending on the specific user population, a development effort should focus its efforts on maximizing appropriate variables. For example, a data entry application should place more emphasis on such things as lowering error rates and efficiency of data entry, while a decision support system for senior executives might place more emphasis on learnability. Sometimes, such goals are explicitly stated in requirements documents. Other times, these goals must be inferred from an understanding of the development environment. In both cases, the specific performance requirements with respect to usability should be discussed and agreed to by relevant groups.

Benefits of Usability

The importance of usability in a product can be described in economic terms. A large amount of compelling economic data indicates that usability is an investment that pays for itself quickly over the life of the product. Whereas a detailed summary of the economic impact of usability is beyond the scope of this article, imagine the impact of reducing the number of calls to the technical support organization by 20 to 50 percent because the application is easier to use. Or, imagine the impact of increasing customer satisfaction. Other benefits that commonly results in projects emphasizing usability include the following:

- Reduced training costs
- Reduced support and service costs
- Reduced error costs
- Increased productivity of users
- Increased customer satisfaction
- Increased maintainability

It is generally not possible to simultaneously achieve every possible benefit of usability. A system that is easy to learn for novices is likely to be far too slow for experts. Because of this, it is best to review the project requirements and determine the most important usability goals that will guide the development process. A subsequent section will provide greater detail on establishing usability goals.

Usability in Large Corporations

When one goes to the store to purchase a piece of software for personal use, one has the right to refuse any application that does not appear to meet one's needs — including subjective preferences. This effect of market forces continues to drive the designers of shrink-wrapped software to create projects that are truly easy to use.

Unfortunately, designers of software applications in large corporations are usually not driven by market forces. Instead, they attend to other forces — typically the needs of senior management. As a result, the usability of most applications in large corporations is abysmal. If you are a manager working on an internal application in a large application concentrate on those ways you can introduce the usability-enhancing activities described below. While you may not be driven by the same market forces as managers creating shrink-wrapped applications, the benefits of usability are as applicable within the corporation as they are in the external marketplace.

COMPONENTS OF A USABILITY DEVELOPMENT PROCESS

Building highly usable software systems centers around four key components, which are detailed in the following sections:

Understanding Users. The cornerstone of building highly usable GUIs is based on an intimate understanding of the users, their needs, and the tasks that must be accomplished. The outcome of this understanding results in a description of the users' mental model. A mental model is the internal representation of the problem the user has formed as he accomplishes tasks. Understanding this internal representation enables designers to create a system model that supplements and supports users. Understanding the users and involving them in the design process is such an important part of building highly usable systems that it is often referred to user-centered design.

Progression from Lo-Fidelity to Hi-Fidelity Systems. Building usable systems is based on a gradual progression from "lo-fidelity" paper-and-pencil-based prototypes to "hi-fidelity" working systems. Such an approach encourages exploration through low-cost tools and efficient processes until the basic structure of the user interface has been established. This basic structure can then be validated through working systems. This approach is most effective when users are actively involved throughout the entire process from the earliest phases of the project.

Adherence to Proven Design Principles. Through extensive empirical studies, HCI professionals have published several principles to guide the decisions made by designers. These simple and effective principles transcend any single platform and dramatically contribute to usability. The utilization of design principles is strengthened through the use of usability specifications, quantifiable statements used to formally test the usability of the system. Usability specifications (i.e., the application must load within 40 seconds) are the quantifiable expressions of the usability benefits desired from the project.

Usability Testing. Each outcome produced during development is tested — and retested — with users and iteratively refined. Testing provides the critical feedback necessary to ensure designers are meeting user needs. An added benefit of testing is that it involves users throughout the development effort. When testing is properly integrated, it encourages users to think of the system as something they own, increasing system acceptance.

The following sections of this chapter focus on the first component of the usability development process: understanding users.

Development Process Roadmap

The components of usability described above can be incorporated into an overall roadmap that describes the development processes, along with the outcomes associated with each process. In Exhibit 30.1, traditional activities associated with project are shown to the left, while the activities associated with usability are displayed to the right.

Traditional activities associated with systems development include product specification; system analysis, including data and process modeling; system design; system architecture; detailed module design; and implementation. It is important to note that these activities are shown in a simplistic, waterfall-inspired development process. The author does not advocate the use of a waterfall process and instead prefers that systems be constructed iteratively.

The usability activities, depicted on the right-hand side of Exhibit 30.1, constitute the main activities associated with the usability aspects of the project. These include establishing usability specifications, user and task analysis, two distinct design phases, and the implementation of the design.

Traditional
Development

Usability
Development

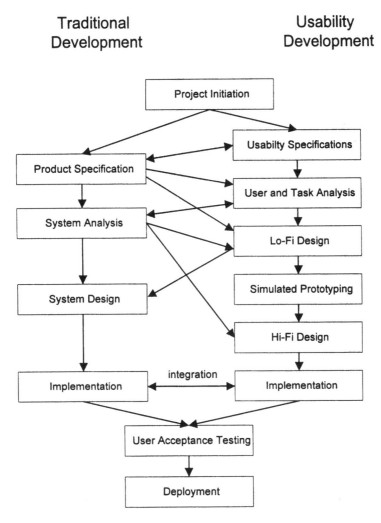

Exhibit 30.1. A comparison of activities in traditional systems development
and usability-based development.

Importance of Prototyping

Prototyping seems to be getting a bad name. Developers are often scared
to show naïve managers a prototype, fearful that their manager will do one
of two hideous acts. First, the manager will prevent the development staff
from making the inevitable modifications that are needed for the final version of any system before it moves into production. The second reason,
which is unfortunately both more common and more damaging, is that
developers fear their managers will expect a fully functioning system after

being shown just a prototype. Users are also highly susceptible to this second problem, and can easily expect delivery of a system far too quickly. Because of this, prototyping is sometimes avoided altogether. Refusing to prototype at all is not the solution. Prototyping, in the form of lo-fi and hi-fi window design, is absolutely essential in any GUI development effort.

Users are quite poor at defining exactly what they want the system to do in advance. In other words, it is far easier to demonstrate what is wrong with a proposed user interface than to sit down and describe the ideal solution. This is why the first step of the design process is the creation of simple, paper-and-pencil, lo-fi window prototypes. I expect my users to make changes to my initial proposals. I want them to propose such changes, for unless they own the process, I am not likely to be successful.

A prototype can be used to answer a difficult question without putting the project at risk or wasting valuable resources. For example, suppose I want to try a different report format. Instead of writing a complex query, I would simply write down the information on a piece of paper and show it to a user. Then, we would extend the design of the report together. Following this, I would mock-up the report using my word processor to make certain it provided the required information. Only when this was signed off would I write any code.

Now, what about the first two problems: the need for modifications and the need to avoid mistaking a prototype for a production system? As a manager, one is indeed responsible for making certain that the final system as created by development staff closely adheres to the prototype approved by the customer. Thus, the manager needs to manage changes to the prototype just like any other set of changes to the project. Depending on the scope and complexity of the project, this means that changes to the user interface may be under the control of a formal change control board.

The second issue is just a matter of plain common sense: do not expect developers to turn a prototype, no matter how slick, into a working, production-quality system overnight. Expecting this will produce ulcers, divorces, and burnout — not highly usable systems.

USABILITY SPECIFICATIONS

A software project is initiated with one or more specific objectives. Embedded in these objectives are both quantitative and qualitative aspects of usability. By writing such specifications in a concrete manner, the project can ensure that these objectives are realized. A usability specification consists of specific attributes, ways to measure attributes, and a description of acceptable ranges.

Common usability attributes that impact the development of the system include the following:

- Ease of installation.
- Learnability.
- Ability to locate specific (advanced) features.
- Overall acceptability.
- Degree of internationalization.

Measuring techniques include:

- Time to complete task.
- Number or percentage of errors.
- Percentage of tasks completed in a given time.
- Time spent in errors and recovery.
- Number of commands/actions to perform task(s).
- Frequency of help and documentation use.
- Number of times users expressed frustration or happiness.

Examples of acceptable ranges include:

- The system must boot in less than 90 seconds; more than 120 seconds requires a redesign.
- A user with 3 weeks constant use of the system must retain 85 percent of core skills (as measured by the standard competency test) after 3 to 5 weeks of disuse; less than 85 percent retention indicates a need for reducing the conceptual load.

Be careful of the degree of detail in the usability specification. Many authors advocate establishing extremely formal usability specifications. The problem is that such specifications must be tested. Extremely formal approaches substantially increase the duration and effort of the testing effort. Of course, extremely precise specifications are appropriate if there is an economic or moral justification (i.e., a chemotherapy dispensing unit must be designed to be used with an absolute minimum number of errors), but most shrink-wrapped and corporate development efforts can produce quite acceptable levels of usability without such precise specifications. A common way of documenting formal specifications is shown in Exhibit 30.2.

An alternative, and less formal, way to think about usability specifications is to think of usability in terms of well-documented priorities. By sharing these priorities with the development staff, design decisions and future test plans can be made according to a shared set of priorities.

USER AND TASK ANALYSIS

The purpose of user and task analysis is to develop an understanding of the users, their tasks, and the context in which they conduct their required

Exhibit 30.2. A way for documenting formal specifications.

Attribute	Measuring Concept	Unacceptable	Planned	Best Case
Overall satisfaction	User selects a rating from 1 to 7 where 1 means "extremely dissatisfied" and 7 means "extremely satisfied"	<3	5	7

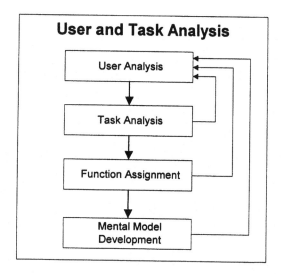

Exhibit 30.3. Activities in user and task analysis.

work. Once these are complete, a function assignment can be performed to clearly identify the distribution of tasks between the user and the system. These activities are displayed in Exhibit 30.3.

User Analysis

The purpose of a user analysis is to clearly define who the intended user of the system really is through a series of context-free, open-ended questions. Such questions explore user experience, context, and expectations. They might include:

- Experience:
    - What are your ideas about computers and GUIs?
    - When do they perform the task?
    - How do they perform the task?

- How frequently do they perform the task?
- What can you tell me about good ways of communicating with the user?
- Does the user use any special language?
- Context:
  - What is the working environment?
  - Tell me about the different groups of people who perform the work. Is work done alone or in a group? Is work shared?
  - Who interacts with the system in other ways?
  - For example, who installs/maintains/administers the system?
  - Tell me about the culture in which this system will be used — the places, the people, anything else?
- Expectations:
  - Can I talk with some users about what they would like to have happen?
  - What features do they want? (If users have difficulty answering this question, propose specific features and ask if the user would like or dislike the specific feature.)
  - How will the current work environment change when the system is introduced? How will it remain the same? (Designers may have to propose specific changes; ask if these changes would be considered desirable.)

Asking these questions usually takes no more than a few hours, but the data the answers provide is invaluable to the success of the project.

Task Analysis

Task analysis seeks to answer two very simple questions. First, what tasks are the users doing now that the system will augment, change, enhance, modify, or replace? Second, what tasks will the user perform in the new system?

The first part of task analysis is to develop a clear understanding of how the system is currently being used. It proceeds as shown in Exhibit 30.4. The fourth step shown in Exhibit 30.4, creating an overall roadmap, is especially important for projects involved with replacing an existing user interface with a redesigned user interface. One common example of this is the decision to upgrade an older, 3270-style mainframe system with a state-of-the-art GUI. Navigating older systems to accomplish even simple tasks can be extraordinarily complex, and without an overall roadmap of how the system currently works, developers cannot be entirely certain that the new system provides all the capabilities of the old system.

Use Cases. The second aspect of task analysis, that of describing how the new system will work, is often done through use cases. A use case is a structured prose document that describes the sequence of events between

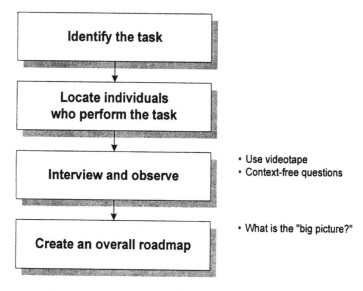

Exhibit 30.4. Initial steps in task analysis.

Exhibit 30.5. Sample use case.

Use case:	Searching a patent database to find all patents invented by a given person.
	Context/Motivation: Identify key employees within the organization.
	Description: This use case begins when a human resources associate searches a patent data base to find all patents invented by a given person. The associate enters the name of the person into the patent management system, which returns all patents in the current data base that match the name of that person. The system will optionally print a report of all such patents as requested by the user.

one or more actors, and the system as one of the actors (typically, the user) attempts to accomplish some task.

Use cases come in several flavors, some appropriate for the initial stages of task analysis, and some appropriate for later stages. A high-level use case is preferred in the early stages of the project, for it allows the interactions between the user and the system to be described in a manner that is completely independent of any specific user interface. This point is especially important: it is a mistake to settle on a given user interface when the basic tasks being undertaken by the user are not well known. An example of a high-level use case is given in Exhibit 30.5.

It is a mistake to get hung up on the specific format of a use case. Instead, concentrate on describing tasks in a format suitable for the development organization. A use case can be expanded into a more detailed format as needed later in the development process. For example, the use case above does not illustrate the specific format and contents of the report, nor does it show the content and format of the results of the query. Both of these items can be expanded during later stages of development. More importantly, use cases are not generated once and then placed on the shelf. Rather, they are used in conjunction with specific design techniques over the life of the project and are augmented with even more detail prior to implementation.

Function Assignment

As users and tasks are identified, the specific functions detailed in the requirements spring to life. At this stage, it is often appropriate to ask if the identified tasks should be performed by the user, performed by the system automatically on behalf of the user, or initiated by the user but performed by the system. This step is called function assignment, and can be absolutely essential in systems whose goals are to automate existing business processes.

To illustrate, consider an electronic mail system. Most users automatically place incoming mail into a specific location, often an "in-box." As a user of the system, did you explicitly *tell* the mail system to place mail there? No; it did this on your behalf, usually as part of its default configuration. Placing mail automatically in an in-box is an example of a required task that is performed automatically by the user.

While most systems can benefit from a function assignment, it is an optional step in the overall development effort.

Mental Model Development

The final step of user and task analysis is to propose various mental models of how the users think about and approach their tasks. Mental models are not documented in any formal manner. Instead, they are informal observations about how designers think users approach their tasks. For example, a designer creating a new project planning tool discovered after several interviews that managers think of dependencies within the project as a web or maze, instead of a GANTT or PERT chart. This provided insight into creative new ways of organizing tasks, displaying information, or providing notification of critical path dependencies.

User and Task Analysis in the Real World

In practice, user analysis, task analysis, and function assignment proceed in an iterative manner, as decisions made in one activity can affect prior decisions made in another. For example, the real user of the system is not always the user identified in the requirements.

In one project, a group of designers was asked to design a GUI for a new bookstore management system. The primary user identified in the requirements was the clerk, who would be using the bookstore to perform such tasks such as searching the online catalog for books and placing special orders for books not currently within the inventory.

In attempting to understand the tasks performed by the clerk, the designers realized that one important user not explicitly listed in the requirement was the customer, who would much prefer to search for books on his own without the assistance of the clerk. Perhaps even more importantly, the clerks were glad to assist in the design of a system that would offload what they considered to be a mundane task.

In the long run, the system was able to effectively serve both classes of users. Customers could perform simple searches on their own, while clerks used more sophisticated searching techniques to help customers track down hard-to-find or ill-defined items. Such results are not surprising when designers are given a chance to interact with the intended users of the system during task analysis.

RECOMMENDED COURSE OF ACTION

A highly usable GUI is simply a GUI that lets end users work more efficiently and effectively with a system. To create a usable GUI, systems developers must understand their users, the context in which users work, and what users need to get their work done. The two major steps to arriving at an understanding of users are: gather usability specifications, and user and task analysis. Following are checklists systems developers can use to ensure they have completed these two steps:

Usability Specifications Checklist

- ❏ No more than two primary usability benefits have been identified for the development effort and published throughout the development organization.
- ❏ A competent usability professional has been identified to assist with economic calculations should management require cost justification of this new approach to systems development.
- ❏ Each desired benefit has been associated with an appropriate user group, as defined on the next page.

❑ The usability specifications have been shared with the designers. The designers agree that the specifications are achievable.

User and Task Analysis Checklist

❑ A target population of representative users has been identified.

❑ An overall roadmap of the *tasks* of current users has been identified.

  ❑ If redesigning a current system, developers have made screen snapshots of *every* screen and have annotated each screen with a description of the task(s) it supports.

  ❑ If redesigning a current system, each task has a set of screen snapshots that describe, in detail, how the user engages the system to accomplish the task.

❑ A set of high-level use cases documents the current understanding of the system. These are specified without regard to any specific user interface that might be developed over the life of the project.

❑ A list of users has been reviewed.

❑ Users have reviewed the list of use cases.

❑ All requirements are covered by the use cases.

❑ No use case introduces a new requirement.

❑ A description of the mental model of the users summarizes findings.

❑ A functional assignment has been performed (Optional).

Recommended Reading

The field of GUI design, and books that purport to tell managers and developers how to do it better, is growing every day. Fortunately, the following timeless classics provide real value if the reader wishes to find more information about a specific topic.

Gause G., and G. Weinberg. *Exploring Requirements Quality Before Design*. New York: Dorset House, 1989. Managing requirements is at the heart of effective software development. Unfortunately, most projects do a surprisingly poor job of this! This book is appropriate for all levels of managers and developers, and is arguably *the single,* most *practical* and *effective* book ever written on how to improve your software development practices.

Gould, J. D. "How to Design Usable Systems," in *Handbook of Human-Computer Interaction*, M. Helander (Ed.) Elsevier Science Publishers B.V., New York (1988). This article is one of the most important articles ever written on the topic of designing usable systems. Gould provides his own set of checklists, along with numerous examples to support his claims.

Nielsen, J. Usability Engineering. New York: Harcourt Brace & Company, 1993. This book provides a more in-depth view of usability engineering. It includes a concise executive overview and a detailed list of testing techniques. It is suitable for technical leads and senior architects who want to be aware of the issues without expending the energy to create an in-depth understanding of design.

Collins, Dave. *Designing Object-Oriented User Interfaces,* Redwood City, CA: The Benjamin/Cummings Publishing Company, Inc. 1995. This book should be required reading for any developer given primary responsibility for the design of the user interface. Collins addresses the proper construction of the system model and shows how it should be implemented.

Microsoft Press. *The Windows Guidelines for GUI Design.* Chances are good your applications will have to run on Microsoft Windows platforms. Why not make certain it adheres to the standard?

Chapter 31
Building GUIs
Users Can Use:
Usability Development

Luke Hohmann

BEGINNING WITH THE CHAPTERS "Creating GUIs Users Can Use: Usability Analysis" and "Designing Usable User Interfaces," which examined how usability affects the front-end stages of development, these chapters on usability and graphical user interfaces (GUIs) conclude by explaining how usability is incorporated into the actual development of GUIs. Usability stresses the importance of end users' experiences with an interface, which is a goal different from that of other development approaches. To reach that goal, developers must change their attitudes towards developing GUIs and how they perform. This work is also different from other types of development.

The World Wide Web's reach has even affected GUI development. Web-based interfaces (e.g., browsers) have certain limitations and characteristics that affect usability development. This chapter concludes with an explanation of how to adapt usability techniques for developing browser interfaces.

USABILITY DEVELOPMENT PROCESS

It is impossible to engage in a detailed discussion of systems development planning in a chapter of this length — the variables, constraints, and forces are too complex. Disclaimers aside, it is important to understand just how a focus on usability affects development plans.

Exhibit 31.1 shows that many, but not all, of the activities associated with developing highly usable systems can be conducted in parallel with traditional development activities. The following sections describe the specific planning considerations for each activity:

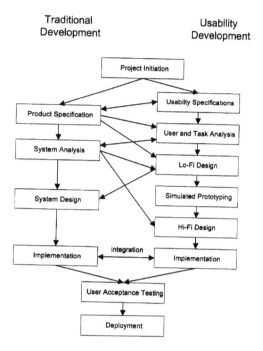

Exhibit 31.1. **Activities in traditional systems development and usability-based development.**

Usability Specifications

Usability specifications are most effective when developed in concert with the product specification. They should be considered as part of the product specification. The usability specification often affects system analysis by sensitizing the development team to aspects of the system that require special attention.

User and Task Analysis

Although the product specification (or associated marketing literature) should identify broad classes of target users, the information contained in these documents are not detailed enough for the development of a highly usable system. Thus, the product specification feeds the user and task analysis. Once the broad classes of users have been identified, user and task analysis can be conducted in parallel with other systems development and analysis activities. Finally, the user and task analysis will coevolve with the system analysis.

Lo-Fi Design

Once systems development management has made the commitment to the usability approach chapters, developers are often eager to begin lo-fi design as quickly as possible. Allowing developers to begin lo-fi design before product specification is complete is a mistake — they are likely to waste effort in designing a user interface that fails to match the true needs of the user. However, lo-fi design can be initiated immediately upon completion of user and task analysis, even if the rest of the traditional analysis is not yet complete. If the plan calls for the development of a lo-fi prototype in parallel with traditional analysis, periodic reviews of both the lo-fi prototype and the data or class models should be conducted to make certain the system can support the lo-fi design.

Simulated Prototyping and Hi-Fi Design

The motivation for simulated prototyping is to ensure that the basic structure of the system as specified in the lo-fi prototype meets the needs of users. It is in the transition of lo-fi design to simulated prototyping that the development plan can begin to exhibit high degrees of parallelism. Specifically, while the user interface design team is testing and enhancing the lo-fi prototype, the remainder of the development team can be engaged in the design and implementation of the system.

Implementation

Several specific implementation activities can be done at this time. First, the development team should concentrate building of a core set of functions that must be provided independently of the user interface. Second, the development should focus on the creation of appropriate test plans to ensure the correct operation of the system. Third, the development team must make certain the database model of the system is correct. All of these core activities, and several additional ones, can be conducted in parallel with the final design of the user interface.

The final stage of development is the integration of the user interface with the remainder of the system. It is best to perform integration in a series of cycles that incrementally increase the functionality of the system. For example, the first cycle might consist of integrating the sign on screen and one or two of the features provided in the main menu. Subsequent cycles would increase overall functionality by interconnecting additional screens with the underlying implementation as guided by the most important use cases.

CHANGING DEVELOPERS' ATTITUDES

The degree to which a development organization changes its traditional planning practices to incorporate usability sends a strong signal to the development team regarding how important the organization considers usable systems. Quite literally, if there is no time devoted to the creation of lo-fi prototypes, there will be no passion in the team for usability.

The previous paragraph was written with the subtle implication that management does not want to practice usability engineering. Although this can be true, most managers enthusiastically support the development of highly usable systems once they realize the clear and direct financial benefits of this approach. Specifically, developing usable systems is good for the bottom line.

But what happens when developers are reluctant to try this approach? For example, developers of a successful shrink-wrapped software application are asked to redesign their system to support new features. Problems occur when the user interface must undergo radical transformation to support these new features.

Because these developers have been successful without a usability approach, they may feel that they do not need to use the techniques described in this chapter for the redesign. This is a serious mistake for at least three reasons. First, changing an existing system can alienate users unless they are certain that learning the new system will provide the necessary benefits. Second, the business goals almost always include expanding the application into new market domains. Thus, while the development team may have obtained a great deal of knowledge about their current users, it is usually the case that very little is known about new users. More dangerous, unless the team takes the time to learn about these new users, they are likely to make design decisions on incorrect knowledge, seriously detracting from overall usability for all users. Third, the development team often has an overly inflated view of the true usability of their application. There are very few applications that cannot be substantially improved through the application of usability principles.

What is the appropriate managerial response in this case? First, developers should know that the development plan specifically includes the activities described in this chapter. Second, the development effort must continue until the appropriate deliverables associated with each activity are completed. If the development team knows management is serious about this approach, they will quickly adopt the same attitude.

DEVELOPERS AND ROLES

Complex systems are created by multifaceted teams: developers work in conjunction with technical writers, marketers, salespeople, and a host of others with specialized skills. This section addresses the roles and personnel needed in the development of highly usable systems, and assumes the development effort is focused on creating a system for a corporate environment. Such systems range from decision support systems to financial accounting systems, as well as a wide variety of internal corporate systems such as human resource systems. Excluded from this category are such application categories as games, virtual reality systems, and Web sites devoted to entertainment content.

Senior Architect

The senior architect is the person (or small team of up to three people) responsible for the creation of the system architecture. The system architecture defines the basic "structure" of the system (e.g., the high-level modules comprising the major functions of the system, the management and distribution of data, the kind and style of its user interface, what platform(s) will it run on, and so forth). A well-defined system architecture is absolutely essential if any of the discrete development activities are to be conducted in parallel.

Software Developers

Software developers perform the bulk of the work associated with the development of the system, ranging from requirements analysis to implementation and testing. Unfortunately, most development projects also ask their developers to design the user interface without giving them the necessary training. Most developers can design adequate user interfaces if given the proper training, such as a three- or five-day class in human factors or usability engineering.

Graphic Designers/Usability Engineers

Ideally, a project will have access to graphic designers to assist in the creation of the user interface and usability engineers to assist in the design and evaluation of the system. Can a development project succeed without individuals? Certainly. However, as the sophistication of the user interface increases (i.e., a greater emphasis on graphics or specialized interaction mechanisms such as drag and drop), the greater the risk to the project if the skills of such professionals are not retained.

The key point in selecting roles for the team is to ensure that the roles in the project efficiently and explicitly support the system architecture and overall usability goals of the project.

DEVELOPING USABLE INTERFACES FOR WEB SYSTEMS

Although the basic principles of usability and the managerial approach for achieving it described in this chapter are the same for the Web as for any other application, there are some important usability considerations for Web-based applications. The first concerns the capabilities and limitations of Web browsers and Java. The second deals with important aspects of usability.

Capabilities and Limitations of HTML

As a mark-up language, HTML can perform a wide range of useful tasks. HTML can:

- Show a variety of fonts, embedded graphics, and tables.
- Present forms containing input fields, radio buttons, and check boxes.

HTML forms are used to gather input from the user, which is then sent to the server. Once the data is received, the server executes a program and returns the result.

Three essential aspects of usability and several aspects of implementation are affected by this approach. First, HTML forms have no "state." Thus, a designer cannot dynamically disable or enable a button based on a field value, a technique common in non-HTML GUI applications. Similarly, if an HTML input field requires a numeric value and the user enters a character string, only the server can detect and respond to the error. Second, there is no guarantee that what a designer creates is what the user sees because the user has ultimate control of the representation of the page. For example, if a designer uses graphics to enhance the usability of the application, the user may never see them. Third, HTML provides hyperlinking, which means one part of a page can directly access or "jump" to another page (or identified section of a page). The advantage is the ability to cross-reference vast amounts of information. The disadvantage is the ease with which a user can become lost in hyperspace.

From an implementation perspective, the server is responsible for processing forms and dynamically generating HTML-based responses. Based on the complexity of this response, the programming required to do this can be fairly time consuming. Another common alternative is to use "helper" applications. A helper application is stored on the client and is used to process data coming from the server. For example, a company might place employee manuals in Adobe Acrobat format. When an employee wishes to learn more about a specific policy, the server would download the manual. The browser would then invoke the Adobe Acrobat reader to display the information. The most important aspect to remember is that HTML is not a programming language.

Java

Java is a fully featured, object-oriented programming language designed to facilitate application development and deployment on the Internet. Although an in-depth discussion of Java is beyond the scope of this chapter, the relevant aspects from the perspective of building highly usable Web-based applications are discussed.

Java is platform independent. Specifically, a Java application (usually referred to as an applet) is downloaded from the server to the client browser. The browser then executes this program, usually as a separate thread in the client. Because Java is a programming language, the appearance of the application is under control of the developer. Graphics can be dynamic, controls can enable or disable other controls, validate input, and so forth. New objects can be created on the fly.

One concern with Java and usability involves the potential for damage if a user downloads a potentially hostile applet. The designers of Java considered this undesirable effect and created a robust security model. The model is not perfect — a handful of researchers have been able to break it — but is steadily improving. By the time this book is published, these problems should be fixed.

From an implementation perspective, Java is similar in syntax and structure to C++. Fortunately, Java is simpler and more robust, and many of the problems that plague C++ (such as templates and poor memory management) do not exist in Java.

CONCLUSION

Ultimately, creating highly usable systems is based on a more robust and healthy dialog between the development team and the users. The processes of user and task analysis, lo-fi design, simulated prototyping, and hi-fi design (with testing) all serve to increase the interaction between the development team and the user. This interaction is completely focused on the needs of the user as supported by the system in a manner that ensures all parties benefit: users will enjoy their systems more, developers can take more pride in their work, and management can take the savings directly to the bottom line.

Section VI
Equipment Asset Management

ANOTHER NEW TOPIC NOT INCLUDED IN LAST YEAR'S EDITION OF THE HANDBOOK, equipment asset management, is presented in this section. IT operations managers are responsible for the acquisition and maintenance of assets under their control. These assets include both IT hardware and software, ranging from PCs and printers, to mainframes and large, enterprise-wide purchased applications. To remain competitive, organizations must acquire and use information-technology resources effectively. With the introduction of new decision-support- and systems-development tools — including prototyping methods — and end users' growing computer literacy and independence, serious attention must be given not only to receiving financial return on investment, but also to acquiring quality products from multiple vendors who are reliable.

In the first chapter of this section, the IT operations manager is provided with valuable solutions on how to provide network management support, including such routine tasks as providing user support and troubleshooting, adding users to the network, changing users' access rights, and keeping track of hardware and software. As explained in "Reducing the Cost of PC Connectivity," networks, and the needs of the users attached to them, are constantly changing. Keeping up with these changes is a labor-intensive and costly proposition. Unfortunately, many of the costs associated with keeping a network running are hard to quantify. This chapter helps identify some of the hidden costs of PC connectivity, and shows how to estimate the potential savings that can be reaped by carefully selecting PC-connectivity products.

The IT operations manager should also be skilled in conducting an economic analysis of equipment, including mechanisms for allocating values to both mandatory and desirable features, as well as assessing vendor bids and negotiating wisely with vendors. Chapter 33, "Evaluating Equipment: A Methodology for Success," addresses these issues and provides a sample worksheet useful in evaluating vendor bids. In today's era of technological complexity, many computer and communications hardware products are incorporating an increasing number of features. Whereas the addition of features generally makes products more difficult to configure and use, these features also make equipment more difficult to evaluate. This chapter describes a procedure that, if set up as a predefined routine, can be used to compare and contrast the economic value of features associated with different vendor products, thus providing the IT operations manager with a methodology to successfully evaluate equipment.

Chapter 34, "Understanding the Desktop Management Interface," describes the desktop management interface (DMI) specification which defines hardware and software interfaces, as well as data files which enable a computer to determine and report information about its components. The DMI simplifies the management and operation of computers; therefore, IT operations managers involved with the acquisition of hardware and software must understand how the DMI operates, as well as the benefits that can be derived from its use. The investment in the acquisition of DMI-compliant hardware and software products should be viewed as a long-term investment that can provide considerable benefits associated with the cost of owning, configuring, troubleshooting, and managing a computer system, by simplifying the support and administration of desktop computers.

The management of information technology is no longer a self-contained operation within IT. In the early years of automation, acquisition of information technology was placed completely in the hands of the IT staff. Information-systems professionals identified the basic applications and solicited assistance and bids from selective vendors. IT designed the database, acquired the computers, developed or bought the software, and implemented systems. Chapter 35, "Managing the IT Procurement Process," suggests practical strategies for procurement and use of computer resources, which include input from many departments within an organization, including IT, end users, and business management. This chapter emphasizes computer resource planning with an integrated procurement process, from assessment through allocation.

Chapter 36, "An IT Asset Management Toolkit," presents basic considerations for better controlling costs and managing the deployment of, and migration to, new technologies. Because an organization's ability to compete is based directly on its ability to assess its current technological state, and to migrate to a more competitive one, asset management is a dynamic, integrated mandate of sophisticated IT organizations. A comprehensive asset management toolkit comprising process, tools, and effective management, can realize substantial savings in the purchasing; deployment; and sale of the goods, techniques, and know-how in a company's competitive arsenal.

The last decade has brought huge changes in organizations which have long-term involvement in both purchasing and leasing acquisitions. After years of accepting almost anything a vendor proposed, the IT industry has learned that it can save millions of dollars with wise procurement practices. Chapter 37, "How to do Better Deals in Leasing," takes a look at this turnaround, and at the fundamental tenet upon which it is based. There are significant advantages for the lessee who selects the right leasing source and maximizes competition among the contenders. The expenditure of time and resources necessary to properly evaluate leasing sources should be viewed as a mandatory and valuable part of the acquisition process. It is the "legwork" that is critical to selecting the leasing company with the best qualifications for a given transaction.

Chapter 32
Reducing the Cost of PC Connectivity

Salvatore Salamone

NETWORK MANAGEMENT HAS ALWAYS BEEN A VERY LABOR-INTENSIVE PROPOSITION. Routine tasks, such as providing user support and troubleshooting, adding users to the network, changing users' access rights, and keeping track of hardware and software, have typically been performed manually.

For many years, the true costs of managing networks were unknown. This gap in information was due to the nature of the costs; many are hidden, hard-to-quantify support costs. Consequently, companies seldom, if ever, had a sense of what budget resources were needed to keep their networks up and running.

Compounding the difficulty of measuring support costs was the fact that local area network management was decentralized. The recurring labor charges for network staffers to provide user support were often absorbed in many different operating budgets. As LAN management functions became centralized, however, companies could begin to assess the magnitude of the situation.

THE HIDDEN COSTS OF HARDWARE

Whereas quantifying the costs of networking still presents difficulties, progress has been made in the last year or two, thanks to several studies by market research firms. Though each uses different metrics, all of these studies have come to the same conclusion: the costs to perform routine management tasks on a network are staggering.

For example, NetWare LAN support costs $778 per user, per year, according to a survey of 180 large user organizations conducted by Business Research Group, Newton, MA. A study of LAN support costs by Forrester Research Inc., Cambridge, MA, found that for a 5000-user network, supporting users on a PC LAN costs three times as much as supporting an equal number of users on an SNA network. Another study estimates that, on average, the support costs per node in a LAN environment come to about $1200 per year. For a modest-sized network of 250 users, that totals $300,000 a year just to keep the network up and running.

The cost to handle other administrative tasks, such as user moves, adds, or changes, is just as astonishing. Annually, American businesses spend about $1.3 billion moving, adding, and changing users' access rights on networks, according to the consultancy Datapro, based in Delran, NJ.

Basically, what these studies as a whole point out is that during a three- to five-year life cycle, the support costs of connecting a PC to a network can easily exceed the money spent on the equipment itself. Today, for example, a 60M Hz Pentium-based PC, with 8M bytes of RAM, 730M-byte hard disk drive, a CD-ROM, 32-bit PCI graphics accelerator board with 1M byte of DRAM, a 15-inch color monitor, bundled with MS-DOS 6.22, Windows for Workgroups 3.11, and Microsoft Office, costs about $2000. Another $250 adds a 10Base T adapter card, which makes for a very decent desktop system for $2250. In contrast, using the most conservative estimate, which is the Business Research Group's $778 per node annually for a NetWare LAN, support costs will exceed the price of the desktop system in less than three years.

THE HIDDEN COSTS OF SOFTWARE

The recurring costs of using networked computers can easily surpass the purchase price of the products themselves. Whereas this is certainly the case with hardware, it is even more true with software.

Software licensing fees account for only 14 percent of the total cost of using software, according to a study by the Gartner Group, Stamford CT. In fact, user support is the largest portion of the total cost of ownership, amounting to an incredible 45 percent. Administrative tasks, such as ensuring that concurrent licensing agreements are being properly enforced, account for another 13 percent of the total cost. In addition, just to distribute and install software costs more than the actual purchase price. The Gartner Group study found that software installation and distribution accounts for about 17 percent of a company's total software costs (see Exhibit 32.1).

Reducing the cost of software ownership is achievable and starts with making intelligent purchasing decisions. In many organizations, software purchases are made on a one-node, one-license basis. That approach works well, but only if all software acquisitions are made as a centralized function. In most organizations, however, departments buy software as they need it. This decentralization of purchasing, combined with a lack of up-to-date information about what is on every desktop, has led many organizations to buy more software than is necessary. The Personal Computer Asset Management Institute, an organization of end-user companies and

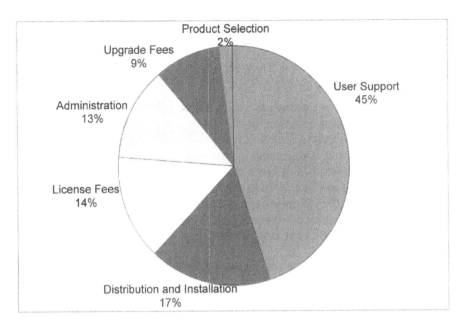

Exhibit 32.1.   The costs of software ownership.

vendors that is dedicated to looking at the costs of managing network assets, estimates that in 1994, U.S. companies, government, and military organizations spent as much as $2 billion on software they already owned.

Situations of this kind can be avoided when a data center manager or network administrator is aware of which software is sitting on the network and the local drives. This is information that an effective connectivity package can help with. For example, with this information, a data center or network administrator could easily size up the situation and reduce the number of licenses. The savings that result can be substantial. For example, if 10 percent of the desktops in a 1000-node network already have Microsoft Office, a company could save the purchase price of those licenses. That amounts to a savings of about $48,000, based on a retail price of $480 for Microsoft Office.

Many companies still rely on annual inventories that require a network staffer to physically travel from PC to PC performing audits. Such inventories are expensive, taking, on average, about a half hour per PC. For a modest-sized network with 250 PCs, the total inventory would take 125 hours, or the equivalent of three networking staffers working solely on inventory for one full week. As another example, that means completing the inventory for an organization with 1000 PCs would take three people four solid weeks.

Most organizations are not able to dedicate staffers to such tasks. Even if they could, the inventory information is quickly outdated. Yet knowing exactly what is on the network is one way to cut the lifetime ownership costs associated with network connectivity and reduce the cost of gaining access to information.

Another way to save money is to buy software that reduces distribution and installation costs. Specifically, the data center manager can select connectivity software that is installed from the server. To cut the administrative costs associated with managing software licenses, the manager could also select a vendor that offers a blanket licensing agreement for all the organization's connectivity needs. That eliminates any worry that comes from having to juggle different types of licensing agreements for each part of the company's connectivity solution. The manager needs only to consider the number of PCs the organization has.

THE HIDDEN COSTS OF PC-TO-HOST CONNECTIVITY

Because recurring end-user support costs form the largest portion of the total cost of connecting a PC to a network, this is an important area to check for cost savings. Typically, nonstandard desktop configurations have stymied the efforts of data center or network managers trying to reduce support costs. Some managers estimate that nonstandard configurations can triple the help desk workload.

Unfortunately, nonstandard configurations are common. When companies try to give their users access to data on host computers, they often use a protocol stack from one vendor and a terminal emulator from another. When the same users need access to an additional host, yet another vendor's terminal emulator may be used. Selecting products in this manner can lead to problems. There may be conflicts that prohibit the products from working together. And using a mix of products on a single desktop may require rebooting the computer when switching between the products.

Choosing a single vendor for all connectivity needs simplifies administrative tasks and cuts costs in several ways. First, it eliminates conflicts so that a company can save time troubleshooting problems. When a problem arises, having selected a single vendor also eliminates vendor finger pointing; for example, when the stack vendor blames the terminal emulation vendor, and vice versa.

A second advantage of the single-vendor connectivity approach is that it reduces end-user training costs, because all the products from one vendor use the same interface for connectivity. If a user is accessing an IBM host and needs to connect to a Digital host, he or she is presented with the same look and feel on the screen. A common user interface is a key in many organizations. After all, the goal is to give end users access to data, not to teach them how to use multiple connectivity software packages.

A third way to cut administrative costs is to choose intelligent connectivity software. Namely, the data center manager should look for software that can identify what is already installed and automatically make the best network connection to a particular host. Some connectivity software even has enough built-in intelligence to alert the user, data center, or network manager to potential trouble spots, thus avoiding conflicts. For the most part, the manager should look for software that is smart enough not to create new connectivity problems.

Diagnostics

In addition to looking for software that will not cause problems, the manager should also look for software that facilitates diagnosing problems when they do occur. Built-in features aid help desk staffers, who, in order to deliver support, need up-to-the-minute information about the programs and files residing on hard disks throughout the organization. For example, users might call the help desk because they are having trouble connecting to a particular host. They connected yesterday, but for some reason they are not able to today. With all of the moves, adds, and changes that take place on a network on a daily basis, this is a common problem. The help desk needs to know what users have running on their machines when they call for help. By quickly identifying that a caller is running an old version of a networking module, a help desk technician can save a lot of time.

That is just one example of a benefit derived from using effective connectivity software. Typically, an organization using intelligent connectivity software can reap other benefits. For example, some connectivity software allows the help desk technician to view a user's settings and configuration. This can be quite helpful if the user has changed the configurations from a standard setting. By being able to quickly identify such a change, a help desk staffer can easily rectify the situation.

To reduce this type of problem even further, the data center or network administrator might want to select connectivity software that lets him, if he so chooses, prevent users from changing their configurations at all.

Some connectivity software products help reduce recurring labor costs by virtue of their advanced troubleshooting and management tools. Additionally, use of such connectivity software can help reduce the cost to distribute and install other software; perform administrative tasks, such as software management, handling access rights, and mapping applications to drives; and diagnose problems on the network. The appropriate connectivity software helps in all of these areas. It frees up network staffers' time so that they can concentrate on more urgent tasks, such as troubleshooting network problems.

Having access to information about each PC on a network can actually help an organization become more proactive — thus further reducing support costs by alerting the data center manager or network manager to a potential problem before it has an impact on the users attached to the network. In this proactive mode of operation, a data center or network administrator can identify a problem in the making and correct the situation before users are bothered. This allows network staffs to operate more efficiently, because they can turn their attention to preventing problems rather than spending all of their time putting out fires.

COST SAVINGS BY PARTNERING WITH ONE CONNECTIVITY VENDOR

Selecting one vendor for all the organization's PC connectivity needs saves both time and money, because there are far fewer conflicts to resolve. That means users are able to quickly get up and running on the network. In addition, it means an organization can save money because staffers do not waste time resolving conflicts.

Data center and network administrators can estimate how much they will save when partnering with a single PC connectivity vendor by using the following formula:

Cost of multivendor approach = Direct labor costs to resolve conflicts
+ Lost productivity of workers affected by conflict
+ Lost revenues that people would have generated if there had been no conflicts

Direct Labor Costs. The direct labor costs can be derived by multiplying the hourly wage of the network staffer solving the conflict by the number of hours used to troubleshoot the conflict. That is the cost to take care of one PC. The administrator will need to multiply that figure by the number of PCs experiencing different conflicts.

The salary of a technical support person often varies within the organization. The data center manager should keep in mind that a fairly sophisticated level of technical expertise is required to resolve a conflict between, for example, one vendor's protocol stack and another vendor's terminal emulation program. That means the manager must dedicate one of the staff's more highly skilled — and highly paid — staffers to the problem.

Exhibit 32.2. The cost to resolve multivendor program conflicts.

Number of PCs in the Organization	PCs Affected: 5%	PCs Affected: 10%	PCs Affected: 15%
200	$1,200	$2,400	$6,000
500	$3,000	$6,000	$15,000
1,000	$6,000	$12,000	$30,000
2,000	$12,000	$24,000	$60,000

Note: Figures are based on six hours to resolve each conflict and a labor cost of $20 per hour, the approximate hourly rate for a staffer making $40,000 per year.

Exhibit 32.3. The cost of productivity lost through program conflicts.

Number of PCs in the Organization	PCs Affected: 5%	PCs Affected: 10%	PCs Affected: 15%
200	$600	$1,200	$3,000
500	$1,500	$3,000	$7,500
1,000	$3,000	$6,000	$15,000
2,000	$6,000	$12,000	$30,000

Note: Figures are based on six hours to resolve each conflict and an average hourly of $10 per hour, the approximate hourly rate for an employee making $20,000 per year, for all employees affected by the outage

Exhibit 32.4. The total cost of a network connectivity problem.

Number of PCs in the Organization	PCs Affected: 5%	PCs Affected: 10%	PCs Affected: 15%
200	$1,800	$3,600	$9,000
500	$4,500	$9,000	$22,500
1,000	$9,000	$18,000	$45,000
2,000	$18,000	$36,000	$90,000

For example, an organization's mid- to upper-level technical staffers make between $40,000 and $50,000 per year. That breaks down to about $20 to $25 per hour. If it takes six hours to troubleshoot and resolve a connectivity problem, that means the company spends $120 to $150 per PC. If 5 percent of a company's PCs have conflicts of various natures, the cost to resolve conflicts between different vendors' products will be between $1500 to $1875 in an organization with 250 PCs, and between $6000 and $7500 in an organization with 1000 PCs.

Exhibit 32.2, Exhibit 32.3, and Exhibit 32.4 can be used to quickly calculate the direct labor costs for various hourly wages, hours to resolve each conflict, and number of PCs affected.

Lost productivity due to network downtime when there are program conflicts can also be estimated in the same manner. The data center manager simply multiplies the average hourly salary of the employees affected by the number of PCs involved. That number is multiplied by the number of hours it takes to resolve the problem. Exhibit 32.3 gives some examples of the costs of lost productivity.

The total cost of a network connectivity problem due to incompatibility between different vendors' products would be the sum of the network staffer's time to resolve the problem, plus the lost productivity due to the problem. For the examples given above, that total cost is demonstrated in Exhibit 32.4.

Estimating the Less-Tangible Losses

It is easy to get a handle on the direct labor charges that an organization incurs to resolve problems resulting from the use of products from multiple PC connectivity vendors. It is more difficult to calculate the cost due to lost productivity and lost revenues.

For example, it may take six hours of a network staffer's time to resolve a conflict, but that period may be spread over several days. Most conflicts will require calls to at least two vendors. There is often finger pointing between the vendors, each placing blame on the other. Even if it takes only one vendor to resolve the problem, it is not uncommon to wait two days to get a return call.

It could be that a person whose PC is having a connectivity problem might not be able to access for two days a database residing on a networked host. That means this person cannot perform one aspect of his or her job for that period of time. That is a loss of productivity. In addition, if the person's job involves any form of customer service, billing, or handling invoices, the inability of this person to do the job can quickly translate into lost revenues for the company.

The data center manager should take these factors into account when selecting PC connectivity software. The rule of thumb is to find a single vendor with a reputation for timely support.

CONCLUSION

In addition to considering the technical advantages of using one vendor's connectivity software offerings over another's, there are several other issues to think about before selecting a product. The data center manager should:

- Look for a vendor that can provide help desk training for the organization's staffers, as well as make on-site network troubleshooting visits.
- Look at the vendor's total connectivity line. Selecting a vendor that offers all the pieces of the connectivity puzzle that are needed, or may be needed in the future, is essential. The organization may need only one type of connectivity today, but with corporate acquisitions happening all the time, the data center manager may tomorrow find himself or herself face-to-face with vastly different host connectivity needs. The careful manager must take all of the hidden cost issues into account before purchasing products.

Such unpredictability about future connectivity needs makes it imperative to consider the long-term costs of using any product. The manager should not waste vast amounts of technical resources resolving continual conflicts between different products every time the organization adds another division or business unit.

Because networks are such dynamic environments, the data center manager must take all of the hidden cost issues into account before purchasing products. Choosing the ones that will help reduce the total cost of ownership when it comes to PC connectivity is an achievable goal.

Chapter 33
Evaluating Equipment: A Methodology for Success

Gilbert Held

To SATISFY ANY ORGANIZATION'S BASIC OPERATIONAL REQUIREMENTS, the data center manager needs to be able to distinguish mandatory computer and communications hardware features from those that are desirable. Once minimum mandatory requirements are determined, the manager should have a step in the evaluation process to associate value for each desirable feature and weigh the costs against the perceived value.

Conducting an economic analysis of equipment should include mechanisms for allocating values to both mandatory and desirable features, and a sound methodology enables the data center manager to assess vendor bids and negotiate with vendors wisely. This chapter addresses issues involved in invitations to bid — and provides a sample worksheet useful in determining each bid's economic value to the organization.

THE EVALUATION PROCESS

The first stage or step in the equipment evaluation process is to define equipment requirements. Because any detailed discussion of equipment evaluation is considerably enhanced by relating the discussion to an actual product, this chapter uses a World Wide Web server as the hardware platform for assessment purposes.

The term *World Wide Web server* represents a range of hardware platforms, from a personal computer (PC) that operates the public-domain LINUS UNIX-emulator operating system to a multimillion-dollar minicomputer operating UNIX. Although many organizations acquire equipment on a brand-name or equivalent basis, another popular method to delineate equipment requirements is to list the mandatory operating characteristics of hardware to be acquired.

Minimum hardware requirements for a Web server might include, for example, a processor speed of 24 Millions of Instructions Per Second (MIPS), 32M-byte memory, 4G-bytes of disk storage, a VGA video display console, and communications devices that include a 100 base-T local area network and 24 RS-232 ports that supply dial-in capabilities. For the purpose of this chapter, this set of requirements is the minimum that an organization should anticipate acquiring. In developing these minimum hardware requirements, however, the data center manager must distinguish between mandatory and desirable features.

DEFINING MANDATORY AND DESIRABLE FEATURES

A mandatory feature represents a feature necessary to achieve an operational state to satisfy organizational requirements. If a vendor cannot provide the capability or the performance level required for a mandatory feature, it is excluded from the acquisition process. In comparison, a desirable feature represents a characteristic or level of performance associated with a feature that, if not offered, does not adversely affect the ability of a vendor's product to satisfy the organization's basic operational requirements. The inability of a vendor to offer a desirable feature does not exclude the vendor from consideration.

An example of a desirable feature is a vendor's disk storage units which are manufactured as 3G-byte drives. To satisfy the minimum hardware requirement of 4G-bytes of disk storage specified earlier in this chapter, the vendor must bid two drives, with a combined data storage capacity of 6G-bytes. In this case, 4G-bytes of disk storage represents a mandatory feature, whereas the two additional gigabytes of disk storage represent a desirable feature. Whether or not the data center manager wishes to assign a value to the two additional gigabytes of data storage, as well as how he would assign values to desirable features, represent the second and third stages of the evaluation process.

The second stage of the evaluation process is to determine whether any desirable features are associated with equipment the organization has decided to acquire and, if so, associate a value for each feature. For example, if the organization believes that the addition of images to Web home pages will eventually require additional disk storage beyond the mandatory requirement of 4G-bytes, the data center manager could list additional disk storage as a desirable feature. As an example of the use of a desirable feature, the manager might modify the organization disk storage requirements so that 4G-bytes represent mandatory disk storage and up to four additional gigabytes are desirable. Thus, vendors would have to bid a hardware configuration with a minimum of 4G-bytes of disk storage, whereas up to 8G-bytes of storage representing mandatory and desirable storage would be evaluated. In this scenario, in a vendor bid of more than 8G-bytes of data storage capacity, only the first eight would be considered. The actual manner by which the data center manager would evaluate the mandatory and desirable features associated with different vendor hardware configurations is based on a technique known as cost-value evaluation. Because this technique requires a value to be assigned to any desirable features, this chapter first develops a set of desirable features and assigns a value to each desirable feature, by way of illustration.

CONSIDERING DESIRABLE FEATURES

The engineering design associated with various computer platforms results in product features than can vary considerably between vendor products. In addition to previously discussed differences in disk drive storage capacity, other common computer feature differences the data center manager should include are the amount of random access memory (RAM); processor power expressed in Millions of Instructions Per Second that can be executed; communications support; and video display capability.

Although establishing a minimum set of mandatory requirements is important, those requirements should not be expressed as absolutes, because doing so could exclude one or more vendors from consideration. For example, consider the Video Display Console, which was established as being VGA. Today, many computer manufacturers include an extended VGA (EVGA) capability that provides support for VGA, as well as for resolutions beyond the 640 by 350 pixel resolution of the VGA standard. Thus, if the data center manager had specified an absolute VGA support, the EVGA capability of a vendor could theoretically disqualify a vendor from being considered. This is, in fact, another argument in favor of specifying mandatory and desirable features.

To illustrate how requirements can be specified as mandatory and desirable features, this chapter uses the minimum hardware features previously listed (i.e., a processor speed of 24, 32M-byte memory, 4G-Bytes of disk storage, a VGA video display console, and communications devices that include a 100 base-T local area network and 24 RS-232 ports that supply dial-in capabilities as a foundation). Because these features represent the minimum hardware features necessary to satisfy organizational requirements, they are specified as mandatory features. Functionality that exceeds these minimum capabilities are considered desirable features.

Exhibit 33.1 provides an example of how the minimum hardware requirements previously listed could be rewritten to indicate mandatory and

Exhibit 33.1.   Minimum mandatory and desirable hardware features.

Feature	Mandatory	Desirable
Processor Speed	24	30
Memory (in Megabytes)	32	64
Disk Storage (in Gigabytes)	4	8
Video Display	VGA	EVGA
Local Area Network	100BASE-2	N/A
Dial-in Ports	24 RS 232	N/A

desirable hardware features. In examining the entries in Exhibit 33.1, it should be noted that the lack of an entry in the column labeled "Desirable" indicates that the mandatory feature is an absolute requirement.

DETERMINING DESIRABLE FEATURE VALUE

To understand why the data center manager must consider assigning a value to each desirable feature value associated with equipment he anticipates acquiring, the manager must consider the possible sources where each feature can be obtained. For example, consider the additional 32M bytes of memory listed in Exhibit 33.1 that, as a desirable feature, results in 64M bytes of total memory. If one vendor bids a system with 32M bytes of memory and another vendor bids a system with 64M bytes of memory, it would be neither fair nor equitable to directly compare the cost of the two computer systems. Instead, the data center manager must consider the value of the additional 32M bytes that could be added to the cost of the 32M-byte system. Doing so would then provide a fair and equitable method for the evaluation of different hardware configurations.

In determining the bids for a system with 64M bytes of memory, it would be neither fair nor equitable to directly compare the cost of the two computer systems. Instead, the data center manager must consider the value of the additional 32M bytes of memory that could be added to the cost of the 32M-byte system. Doing so would then provide a fair and equitable method for the evaluation of different hardware configurations.

In determining the value of a desirable feature, the data center manager must consider the fact that the modular design of computer systems provides the ability to acquire components from numerous third-party sources, as well as from the manufacturer. Thus, the manager must consider whether a desirable feature can be obtained from a third party and, if so, its cost.

If the cost of the desirable feature from a third party is less than the cost bid by the manufacturer, the data center manager would then use the third-party cost as the value to be associated with the desirable feature.

To illustrate this concept, this chapter assumes that Vendor A's response to the request-to-bid specification simply meets the organization's mandatory requirement to include 32M bytes of system memory, whereas Vendor B's proposal includes the ability to expand system RAM by 32M bytes at a cost of $1800. If the manager could purchase 32M bytes of RAM from a third party for $1600, the value of this desirable feature would be $1600 instead of $1800, because the manager could purchase it from a third party instead of the equipment manufacturer.

Once requirements are defined and bids are received based on the mandatory and desirable equipment features, a value can be assigned to each desirable feature. After this step is completed, the data center manager is ready to evaluate equipment using the cost-value technique. The next step is to examine the cost-value evaluation technique and use it to obtain an economic analysis of World Wide Web server hardware bids from several vendors.

THE COST-VALUE EVALUATION TECHNIQUE

The cost-value evaluation technique represents a methodology for conducting an economic analysis of equipment that may have the minimum set of features, but can differ in functionality beyond that set. Because it is quite common for processor speeds, disk storage capacity, and similar operational features to differ among vendor products, a methodology for obtaining a mechanism to evaluate those differences becomes necessary.

The cost-value evaluation technique provides that mechanism, as it enables the data center manager to allocate a value to desirable features that, when added to the basic cost of mandatory features, provide a mechanism for performing a cost evaluation of mandatory and desirable features.

The cost-value evaluation process requires the manager to first separate the cost of mandatory features from the cost of desirable features. Next, a value is assigned to each desirable feature. This value assignment results in using either the cost of the desirable feature bid by a vendor or its cost when obtainable from a third party, whichever is lower. If, for some reason, the desirable feature has no value to the organization, a cost of zero would be assigned to that feature, because it would not be bought.

Once a value has been assigned to each desirable feature, the manager adds the equipment cost and desirable-feature values to obtain a total cost for each vendor product. Then, the lowest total cost would represent the best economic value.

Exhibit 33.2. Mandatory and desirable hardware features for a World Wide Web server.

Feature	Mandatory	Desirable
Processor Speed	24	30
Memory (in Megabytes)	32	64
Disk Storage (in Gigabytes)	4	8
Video Display	VGA	EVGA
Local Area Network	100BASE-2	N/A
Dial-in Ports	24 RS 232	N/A

A Practical Application of the Cost-Value Evaluation Technique

This chapter prepares hypothetical bids from two vendors to illustrate the use of the cost-value evaluation technique to obtain a basis for comparing desirable features that can differ between vendor products or even within the product line of one vendor. To illustrate the application of the cost-value evaluation technique, this chapter assumes that the organization issued an Invitation to Bid document, which listed the mandatory and desirable hardware features for a World Wide Web server as shown in Exhibit 33.2.

It is also assumed that two vendors respond to the document. Vendor A bids $86,000 to supply hardware that meets the organization's mandatory features; Vendor B bids $87,500. Each vendor provides a bid for each desirable feature listed in Exhibit 33.2, and an investigation of hardware component compatibility indicates that some desirable features for each vendor server could be obtained from third-party sources. Therefore, the cost evaluation worksheet might be constructed as shown in Exhibit 33.3.

In examining the completed cost-value evaluation worksheet, it should be noted that the cost of the mandatory features are first separated from the cost of the desirable features. Next, each desirable feature is listed to include the cost bid by each vendor for the feature and, if applicable, its third-party cost. Then, the lower of the applicable vendor or third-party costs is entered for the cost of the desirable feature in the appropriate vendor column. To illustrate this concept, this chapter examines and discusses each of the four desirable feature entries in Exhibit 33.3. Because it is assumed that an upgraded processor cannot be obtained from a third-party source, the cost bid by each vendor is entered into the appropriate vendor column. Concerning the upgraded-memory desirable feature, in this example, it is assumed that Vendor A bid $1850 and Vendor B bid $1750, whereas compatible memory was available from a third party for $1600. Thus, $1600 was entered in each vendor column for the cost evaluation of memory.

The additional disk storage capacity was assumed to cost $4000 if acquired from Vendor A and $3800 if acquired from Vendor B, whereas a

Exhibit 33.3. Cost evaluation worksheet.

Mandatory Features				Vendor A $86,000	Vendor B $87,500

Desirable Features

Feature	Vendor A Cost	Vendor B Cost	Third-Party Cost		
Processor	$2,500	$2,200	N/A	$2,500	$2,200
Memory	$1,800	$1,750	$1,600	$1,600	$1,600
Disk Storage	$4,000	$3,800	$2,500	$2,500	$2,500
Video	Included	$200	$350	$0	$200
Total Cost				**$92,600**	**$94,000**

third party could provide compatible storage for $2500. Thus, the lower cost of $2500 was entered in each vendor column for cost evaluation purposes.

The fourth desirable feature was an extended video display capability. In this example, it was assumed that this capability was included as standard in Vendor A's hardware. Thus, no additional cost is associated with Vendor A for this desirable feature. Because Vendor B's cost was $200 for the video desirable feature and its third-party cost was determined to be $350, $200 was placed in the Vendor B column.

Once a cost is associated to each vendor for each desirable feature, these costs are then added to the cost of the mandatory features. In the example, this results in a total cost of $92,600 for Vendor A and $94,000 for Vendor B. Therefore, Vendor A would be considered to provide the best economic value when considering the cost of mandatory and desirable features to include the cost of the latter from third-party sources.

RECOMMENDED COURSE OF ACTION

The cost-value evaluation technique provides an easy-to-implement mechanism to compare the cost of mandatory and desirable features. Concerning the latter, this technique enables the data center manager to evaluate the value of desirable features across different vendor product lines, as well as consider the cost of desirable features from third-party sources. As such, it provides an important tool to obtain a comprehensive economic analysis for evaluating the cost of equipment, including a mechanism for considering both vendor and third-party sources when acquiring equipment. Not only does this technique consider the cost of third-party equipment, it also considers the value of built-in features one vendor may offer that another vendor may only provide as an option. Thus, the application of the cost-value evaluation technique provides a comprehensive economic analysis tool that can be used to provide management with information vital for the planning and decision-making processes.

Chapter 34
Understanding the Desktop Management Interface

Gilbert Held

THE DESKTOP MANAGEMENT INTERFACE (DMI) represents a specification developed by the Desktop Management Task Force (DMTF), a consortium of hardware and software manufacturers and developers that included AST Research, Compaq, Dell Computer, IBM, Microsoft, and Lotus. The DMI specification defines software and hardware interfaces as well as data files that enable a computer to determine and report information about its components.

COMPONENTS

The three key components of Desktop Management Interface are the management interface, service layer, and component interface. The management interface provides a service-layer interface, by which management applications access component information without having to access specific, individual component interfaces. The service layer manages a data base that contains the management information format (MIF) of files that contain information about the status of a component and its configuration. The third portion of DMI is the component interface that enables component information and commands to be exchanged with the service layer.

A management application can operate on the same computer as the DMI components, or on a computer separate from the one with the DMI components. If on a remote computer, the management application accesses the DMI via the DMI's management interface. The service layer provides access to the MIF data base, which contains such information as the manufacturer of the computer, its product name, serial number, system BIOS, BIOS manufacturer, processor, and hundreds of additional hardware characteristics. The MIF data base information is extremely valuable in automatically generating a detailed inventory of computers, as well as in

0-8493-9824-X/00/$0.00+$.50
© 2000 by CRC Press LLC

determining incompatibilities between hardware and software components or isolating other problems. For example, some Intel 80486 and Pentium-based computer systems have been manufactured with over 20 different versions of BIOS. Some management application programs have been programmed to compare BIOS versions against the versions of other hardware and software components in the system and to automatically check for known incompatibilities. The feature saves end users and help-desk personnel tens of hours of effort to determine the cause of computer problems.

The service layer of DMI resides on computers manufactured to support the DMI specification. The service layer consists of a binary executable file and is inactive until the desktop user invokes its operation. The manual installation of the DMI Service Layer under DOS results in the following screen:

```
C:\DMI\DOS\BIN>s1
DOS DMI Service Layer.
Copyright(C) 1992-1994 Intel Corporation.
DOS SL Version 1.1
Installing components—please wait a moment.
SYSTEM.MIF installed
The DOS DMI Service Layer has been loaded. Desktop Management
   Interface Specification DMI 1.0
```

Currently, there are DMI Service Layers available for several desktop computer operating systems including MS-DOS, Microsoft Windows, Microsoft Windows for Workgroups, Microsoft Windows 95, and IBM's OS/2.

Although the DMI service layer can be installed manually, as demonstrated earlier, most users more than likely use an entry in their AUTOEXEC.BAT file to automatically install the service layer whenever their computers are powered on or a system reset operation is performed. Because the DMIs depend on the installation of their service layer on each computer to be managed, most, if not all, data center managers and LAN administrators can be expected to insist on the automatic loading of the Desktop Management Interface service layer on all DMI-compliant desktop computers. This allows a management application program on a LAN to automatically communicate through the management interface to the service layer, thereby managing each computer's MIF data base and desktop components. The components include peripheral devices and operating software modules, and data center managers receive up-to-date information about the configuration and operation of hardware and software on each DMI-compliant computer.

THE MIF

The core component of the Desktop Management Interface is the MIF data base. In actuality, the MIF represents a language with a specific grammar and syntax, which specify the manageable attributes of each managed device. The MIF consists of a series of group definitions. Each group consists of a name, class, identification, and description, as well as one or more attributes and similar information for the attribute. An attribute can have a single value, or it can be part of a table and be linked by an index key.

Currently, the Desktop Management Task Force has defined MIFs for the basic desktop computer to include its processor, memory, operating system, disk drivers, and computer ports, and are developing MIFs for printers, network adapters, and multimedia components — including CD-ROM and audio cards.

THE PROCESSOR GROUP

The processor group in the MIF resides on the author's Pentium desktop computer. This group consists of three attributes: the processor index, which contains an index to the processor table, the processor type, and the processor family. The processor group looks like this:

```
Start Group
   Name = "Processor"
   Class= "DMTF/Processor/001"
   ID = 6
   Description= "This group defines the attributes for each and
      every process
   Key = 1
   Start Attribute
      Name = "Processor Index"
      ID = 1
      Description = "An index into the processor table."
      Type = Integer
      Access = Read-Only
      Storage = Common
      Value = * "DellInst"
   End Attribute
   Start Attribute
      Name = "Processor Type"
      ID= 2
      Description = "The type of processor currently in the system."
      Type = Start Enum
         0x01 = "Other"
         0x02= "Unknown"
         0x03 = "Central Processor"
         0x04 = "Math Processor"
         0x05= "DSP Processor"
         0x06 = "Video Processor"
      End Enum
   Access = Read-Only
   Storage = Common
   Value = * "DellInst"
   End Attribute
```

```
Start Attribute
   Name = "Processor Family"
   ID = 3
   Description = "The family of processors to which this processor
      belongs."
   Type = Start ENUM
      0x01= "Other"
      0x02 = "Unknown"
      0x03 = "8086"
      0x04= "80286"
   Storage = Specific
   Value = * "DellInst"
End Attribute
End Group
```

A management application, which could be a local or remote program, interrogates the processor group and retrieves information concerning the type of processor and its family. Because access to each attribute is read-only, a management application cannot change the value of any attribute in the processor group in the MIF. However, other groups in an MIF can contain attributes with read-write access capability, which enables a manager to reset the value of an attribute as a mechanism to fix an improper configuration or to change a configuration to correspond to a change in the hardware or software installed on a computer.

DMI BENEFITS

In addition to being able to determine and report information concerning the hardware and software components in a desktop computer, Desktop Management Interface provides benefits that include automatic execution of asset management and smoother communications with technical support specialists concerning information required to troubleshoot a computer and expedite its configuration.

Disaster Recovery

Through the use of a management application manager on a LAN, the data center manager can query each workstation and automatically obtain an inventory of the components of each computer. This information can be extremely valuable during times when disaster recovery procedures are essential. Managers can, for example, assist users who must reprogram CMOS after a battery failure; they can also obtain the information required to reestablish network operations in the event of a fire, flood, or other type of disaster. Concerning its use as a disaster recovery mechanism, managers should always place a copy of the asset management report at an offsite location so that the critical information is available. The information in the asset management report is of considerable assistance in extreme cases if, for example, an organization has to reconstruct a LAN at another building, or in a smaller replacement scenario if the organization simply has to replace a few computers that became inoperative due to a sprinkler malfunction or workstations that have been destroyed because of an electrical fire.

Reducing Downtime

When modern computers lock up, the cause of the problem can range from hardware and software incompatibilities to problems in hardware and software bugs. Through the use of a DMI management application, the data center manager can initiate the self testing of hardware components and retrieve information about configuration parameters and BIOS levels, information that can be extremely useful to help desk personnel attempting to troubleshoot desktop problems. Thus, the use of Desktop Management Interface-compatible computers provides organizations with the potential to reduce the costs associated with owning, operating, and managing desktop computers due to the advantages associated with their ability to facilitate configuration and troubleshooting operations.

LIMITATIONS

Although Desktop Management Interface represents a significant step toward improving the operation, use, and management of desktop computers, it is an emerging technology, and only over the coming years will its advantages become clear. Most organizations will need to replace the installed base of non-DMI-compliant desktop computers with DMI computers over a number of years — even a decade or more. In addition, MIF file specifications for printers, CD-ROMs, and sound cards — although scheduled to be released in 1996 — will require time for vendors manufacturing those components to support the MIF specifications. Therefore, the advantages associated with the use of DMI-compliant computers and peripherals will be obtained gradually over a period of time.

Data center managers should consider the acquisition of DMI-compliant computers and management application programs as a long-term investment. Management application programs, for example, can be used to redirect information from each desktop to such network management programs as Hewlett-Packard's OpenView for Windows and Intel's LANDesk Manager; this expands considerably the capability of those and other management programs to manage the desktop, as well as to provide information about network resources.

DMI SUPPORT

Obtaining the benefits of Desktop Management Interface will be an evolutionary process; therefore, data center managers need to consider several procedures when acquiring desktop peripherals. First, because such devices are replaced more rapidly than desktop computers, users should consider acquiring DMI-compliant peripherals rather than non-compliant peripherals. Second, users should note that peripherals that were not designed to be compliant with the DMI specifications can be used with Desktop Management Interface-compliant computers; however, if non-compliant peripherals are used, the manager will not be able to retrieve DMI information from those peripherals, perform diagnostic tests using the Desktop Management Interface manager, or perform confirmation operations on the peripheral device with the DMI manager.

CONCLUSION

The ability to manage the desktop can provide a considerable degree of assistance in configuring devices, troubleshooting problems, and performing asset management functions. Desktop Management Interface is a relatively recent standard whose specifications for many desktop peripheral devices are in the process of being formulated; therefore, an investment in the acquisition of DMI-compliant hardware and software products should be viewed as a long-term investment that can provide considerable benefits associated with the cost of owning, configuring, troubleshooting, and managing a computer system by simplifying the support and administration of desktop computers. The first step in desktop management — acquiring DMI-compliant products as the organization purchases new computers and peripheral devices — increases the organization's ability to manage its computer assets; provides information to help desk personnel that enables them to execute troubleshooting operations; and facilitates the examination of computer configurations and the resetting of configuration elements when required. This, in turn, eventually results in a reduction in the lifetime cost of ownership of desktop computers.

Chapter 35
Managing the IT Procurement Process

Robert Heckman

AN IT PROCUREMENT PROCESS, FORMAL OR INFORMAL, exists in every organization that acquires information technology. As users of information systems increasingly find themselves in roles as customer of multiple technology vendors, this IT procurement process assumes greater management significance. In addition to hardware, operating system software, and telecommunications equipment and services — information resources traditionally acquired in the marketplace — organizations now turn to outside providers for many components of their application systems, application development and integration, and a broad variety of system management services. Yet despite this trend, there has to date been little, if any, research investigating the IT procurement process. While IS development activities are represented by at least 120 keywords in the keyword classification scheme for IS research literature (Barki et al., 1993), market-oriented strategies for information resource acquisition are represented by a single key phrase — "Outsourcing of IS."

Several studies of IT procurement issues have recently been commissioned by the Society for Information Management (SIM) Working Group on IT Procurement. These studies are an attempt to begin a systematic investigation of critical IT procurement issues. This chapter presents a model of the IT procurement process which was developed by the SIM Working Group to provide a framework for studying IT procurement. This model has provided the conceptual context for the Working Group's empirical research projects, and a framework for organizing key issues and questions. The model represents IT procurement as consisting of six major processes. Contained within each major process is a series of sub-processes and a set of key questions.

Section 2 presents background material which provides a context for the development of the model. Section 3 describes the process used by the Working Group in developing the model. Section 4 describes the model in detail, and Section 5 presents an analysis of key IT procurement management issues identified by the Working Group. The discussion in Section 6 includes recommendations and an example of how the model might be used to improve the management of the IT procurement function.

BACKGROUND

IT procurement is an interdisciplinary process, typically involving staff members from the IS organization, purchasing, legal, financial/treasury, and end users from all departments throughout the firm. This complex organization structure, the great number of different products and services available, and the speed with which new products are introduced to the marketplace make IT procurement an extremely intricate and volatile process.

Two relatively recent trends suggest that a disciplined, process-oriented framework might be needed to help us better understand and manage the complex IT procurement activity. The first trend is the *evolution of the information resource acquisition process* from an internal, unstructured, craft-like activity to a more structured, market-oriented discipline. The second trend is the recent expanded focus on *business process analysis and design*.

Evolution of the Information Resource Acquisition Process

Heckman and Sawyer (1996) have described an information resource (IR) acquisition model which characterizes the acquisition process using two dimensions: *source* and *process*. Exhibit 35.1 shows the model, which illustrates that an IR can be acquired from an internal (hierarchy) or external (market) source, and the acquisition process can be either structured or unstructured. Exhibit 35.1 also shows how the model can be used to illustrate the evolution of information resource acquisition in organizations over time.

The exhibit suggests that in the early years of computing, organizations developed many of their systems internally, using relatively unstructured processes. As experience with system development grew, more structured methods of analysis, design and programming were developed, and software construction began to evolve from a craft-like activity to an engineering discipline. As information technology price performance dramatically improved and microcomputers became available, the era of end-user computing began. In this era, organizations tended to turn outward to the market to meet more of their information resource needs, but they did so with relatively little structure or discipline in the process. Finally, in the current era, organizations are recognizing the need to bring more order to their IR acquisition activities. As client server architectures become more complex and interconnected, the need for more disciplined management of the

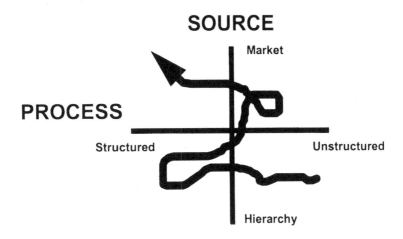

Exhibit 35.1. **Information resource acquisition model: the evolution of IT acquisition.**

procurement process will also grow. The IS literature has begun to indirectly address this need in debates about the appropriate management of IT outsourcing relationships (Lacity et al., 1995; McFarlan and Nolan, 1995).

One way to impose discipline or structure on a process is to develop a framework which allows the process to be analyzed and managed in a systematic way. An example of such a framework is the traditional systems development life cycle (SDLC). The SDLC framework allowed discipline to be introduced to the process of systems analysis and design, and laid the groundwork for the development of methodologies intended to improve reliability and productivity (Reifer, 1994; Thayer, 1988; Rook, 1986; Vaughn and Parkinson, 1994). It enabled not only the creation of structured analysis and design tools, but also made possible systems development approaches which transcend the traditional SDLC. It can be argued that the SDLC was an essential evolutionary step which made possible the more advanced approaches of rapid prototyping, object-oriented analysis, joint application development (JAD), etc. The IT procurement process framework might provide a similar evolutionary function.

Business Process Analysis and Design

Business process analysis and redesign has become an important management tool for both American and global businesses. Davenport and Short define a business process as *a set of logically related tasks performed to achieve a defined business outcome.* Business processes are generally

369

independent of organizational structure, and this attribute has led to great interest in business process redesign (BPR). In BPR, important business processes are decomposed and reassembled in ways that are intended to be more efficient and effective. Techniques and principles for the analysis and design of business processes have been widely promulgated (e.g., Hammer 1990, Davenport and Short, 1990, Teng et al. 1994, Sampler and Short, 1994), however all have in common the necessity to identify, understand, and measure the components or sub-processes which comprise a critical business process.

The process framework described below attempts to accomplish this objective in the IT procurement domain. It provides a comprehensive description of the processes and sub-processes which are involved in procuring IT products and services. By identifying and describing the process in detail, efforts to analyze measure and redesign IT procurement activities can begin from a firm foundation.

DEVELOPMENT OF THE FRAMEWORK

In January 1994, the Society for Information Management (SIM) Working Group on Information Technology Procurement was formed to exchange information on managing IT procurement and to foster collaboration among the different professions participating in the IT procurement process. The IT Procurement Process Framework was developed by a twelve-member subgroup comprised of senior IT procurement executives from large North American companies.

The task of developing the framework took place over the course of several meetings and lasted approximately one year. A modified nominal group process was used, in which individual members independently developed frameworks which described the IT procurement process as they understood it. In a series of several work sessions, these individual models were synthesized and combined to produce the six-process framework presented below. Once the six major procurement processes had been identified, a modified nominal group process was once again followed to elicit the subprocesses to be included under each major process. Finally, a nominal group process was once again used to elicit a set of key issues which the group felt presented managerial challenges in each of the six processes. The key issues were conceived of as the critical questions which must be successfully addressed to effectively manage each process. Thus, they represent the most important issues faced by those executives responsible for the management of the IT procurement function.

The process framework and key issues were reviewed by the Working Group approximately one year later (summer, 1996), and modifications to definitions, sub-processes, and key issues were made at that time. The key

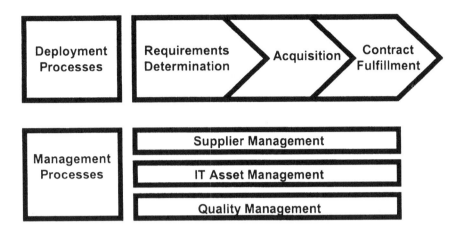

Exhibit 35.2.   The IT procurement process.

issue content analysis described below was conducted following the Working Group review in early 1997.

THE IT PROCUREMENT FRAMEWORK: PROCESSES, SUB-PROCESSES, AND KEY ISSUES

The IT Procurement Process Framework provides a vehicle to systematically describe the processes and sub-processes involved in IT procurement. Exhibit 35.2 illustrates six major processes in IT procurement activities. Each of these major processes consists of a number of sub-processes. Exhibits 35.3 through 35.8 list the sub-process included in each of the major processes. These tables also include the key issues identified by the Working Group.

Procurement activities can be divided into two distinct types of processes: *deployment processes* and *management processes.*

Deployment processes consist of activities that are performed (to a greater or lesser extent) each time an IT product or service is acquired. Each individual procurement can be thought of in terms of a life cycle which begins with requirements determination, proceeds through activities involved in the actual acquisition of a product or service, and is completed as the terms specified in the contract are fulfilled. Each IT product or service that is acquired has its own individual iteration of this deployment life cycle.

Requirements determination is the process of determining the business justification, requirements, specifications, and approvals to proceed

371

Definition

The process of determining the business justification, requirements, specifications, and approvals to proceed with the procurement process.

Subprocesses

- Identify need
- Put together cross functional team and identify roles and responsibilities
- Continuously refine requirements and specifications in accordance with user needs
- Gather information regarding alternative solutions
- Perform cost-benefit analysis or other analytic technique to justify expenditure
- Evaluate alternative solutions (including build/buy, in-house/outsource, etc.) and associated risk and benefits
- Develop procurement plans which are integrated with project plans
- Gain approval for the expenditure.
- Develop preliminary negotiation strategies

Key Issues

- What are the important components of an appropriate procurement plan? [S]
- How much planning (front-end loading) is appropriate or necessary for different types of acquisitions (e.g., commodity purchases vs. complex, unique acquisitions)? [S]
- How should project teams be configured for different types of acquisitions (appropriate internal and/or external resources, project leader, etc.)? [IR]
- How should changes in scope, and changes in orders be handled? [P]
- What are the important cost vs. budget considerations? [F]
- What are the most effective methods of obtaining executive commitment? [E]
- Can requirements be separated from wants? [P]
- Should performance specifications and other outputs be captured for use in later phases such as quality management? [P]

Exhibit 35.3.   Requirements determination.

---

with the procurement process. It includes sub-processes such as organizing project teams, using cost-benefit or other analytic techniques to justify investments, defining alternatives, assessing relative risks and benefits defining specifications, and obtaining necessary approvals to proceed with the procurement process. (Exhibit 35.3.)

Definition

The process of evaluating and selecting appropriate suppliers and completing procurement arrangements for the required products and services.

Subprocesses

- Develop sourcing strategy including the short list of suitable suppliers
- Generate appropriate communication to suppliers (RFP, RFQ, etc.) including financing alternatives
- Analyze and evaluate supplier responses and proposals
- Plan formal negotiation strategy
- Negotiate contract
- Review contract terms and conditions
- Award contract and execute documents
- Identify value added from the negotiation using appropriate metrics

Key Issues

- Is there support of corporate purchasing programs, policies, and guidelines (which can be based on technology, financing, accounting, competitive impacts, social impacts, etc.)? [E]
- What tools optimize the procurement process? [P]
  —EDI?
  —Autofax?
  —Procurement Cards?
- What processes in acquisition phase can be eliminated, automated or minimized? [P]
- Is it wise to be outsourcing all or part of the procurement process? [IR]
- What are the appropriate roles of users, legal, purchasing, and IS in the procurement process? [IR]

Exhibit 35.4. Acquisition.

Acquisition is the process of evaluating and selecting appropriate suppliers and completing procurement arrangements for the required products and services. It includes identification of sourcing alternatives, generating communications (such as RFPs and RFQs) to suppliers, evaluating supplier proposals, and negotiating contracts with suppliers. (Exhibit 35.4.)

Contract fulfillment is the process of managing and coordinating all activities involved in fulfilling contract requirements. It includes expediting of orders, acceptance of products or services, installation of systems, contract administration, management of post-installation services such as warranty and maintenance, and disposal of obsolete assets. (Exhibit 35.5.)

Definition

The process of managing and coordinating all activities involved in fulfilling contract requirements.

Subprocesses

- Expedite orders and facilitate required changes
- Receive material and supplies, update databases, and reconcile discrepancies
- Acceptance of hardware, software, or services
- Deliver materials and services as required, either direct or to drop-off points
- Handle returns
- Installation of hardware, software, or services
- Contract administration
- Process invoices and issue payment to suppliers
- Resolve payment problems
- Manage post-installation services (e.g., warranty, maintenance, etc.)
- Resolve financial status and physical disposal of excess or obsolete assets
- Maintain quality records

Key Issues

- What are some provisions for early termination and/or renewals? [L]
- What are the best methods for assessing vendor strategies for ongoing maintenance costs? [ER]
- What interaction between various internal departments aids the processes? [IR]

Exhibit 35.5. Contract fulfillment.

Management processes consist of those activities involved in the overall governance of IT procurement. These activities are not specific to any particular procurement event, but rather are generalized across all such events. Three general classes of IT procurement management processes are Supplier Management, Asset Management, and Quality Management.

Supplier management is the process of optimizing customer-supplier relationships to add value to the business. It includes activities such as development of a supplier portfolio strategy, development of relationship strategies for key suppliers, assessing and influencing supplier performance, and managing communication with suppliers. (Exhibit 35.6.)

Definition

The process of optimizing customer-supplier relationships to add value to the business.

Subprocesses

- Categorize suppliers by value to the organization (e.g., volume, sole source, commodity, strategic alliance). Allocate resources to most important (key) suppliers.
- Develop and maintain a relationship strategy for each category of supplier.
- Establish and communicate performance expectations that are realistic and measurable.
- Monitor, measure, and assess vendor performance.
- Provide vendor feedback on performance metrics.
- Work with suppliers to continuously improve performance. Know when to say when.
- Continuously assess supplier qualifications against your requirements (existing and potential suppliers).
- Ensure that relationship roles and responsibilities are well defined.
- Participate in industry/technology information sharing with key suppliers.

Key Issues

- How do you distinguish between transactional/tactical and strategic relationships? [ER]
- How can expectations on both sides be most effectively managed? Should relationships be based on people-to-people understandings or solely upon the contractual agreement (get it in writing)? What is the right balance? [ER]
- How can discretionary collaborative behavior — cooperation above and beyond the letter of the contract — be encouraged? Are true partnerships with vendors possible, or does it take too long? What defines a partnership? [ER]
- How should multiple vendor relationships be managed? [ER]
- How should communication networks (both internal and external) be structured to optimize effective information exchange? Where are the most important roles and contact points? [IR]
- How formal should a measurement system be? What kind of report card is effective? What are appropriate metrics for delivery and quality? [M]
- What is the best way to continuously assess the ability of a vendor to go forward with new technologies? [M]

Exhibit 35.6   Supplier management.

Key Issues (continued)

- What legal aspects of the relationship are of most concern (e.g., nondisclosure, affirmative action, intellectual property, etc.)? [L]
- What is the best way to keep current with IT vendor practices and trends? What role does maintaining "market knowledge" play in supplier management? [M]
- What is the optimal supplier-management strategy for a given environment? [S]
- How important is the development of master contract language? [L]
- In some sectors there is an increasing number of suppliers and technologies, while in others vendor consolidation is occurring. In what circumstances should the number of relationships be expanded or reduced? [ER]
- What are the best ways to get suppliers to buy into master agreements? [L]
- What are the best ways to continuously judge vendor financial stability? [M]
- Where is the supplier positioned in the product life cycle? [M]
- How should suppliers be categorized (e.g., strategic, key, new, etc.) in order to allow for prioritization of efforts? [M]
- What are the opportunities and concerns to watch for when one IT supplier is acquired by another? [M]

Exhibit 35.6. (continued)

Asset management is the process of optimizing the utilization of all IT assets throughout their entire life cycle in order to meet the needs of the business. It includes activities such as development of asset management strategies and policies, development and maintenance of asset management information systems, evaluation of the life cycle cost of IT asset ownership, and management of asset redeployment and disposal policies. (Exhibit 35.7.)

Quality management is the process of assuring continuous improvement in the IT procurement process and in all products and services acquired for IT purposes in an organization. It includes activities such as product testing, statistical process control, acceptance testing, quality reviews with suppliers and facility audits. (Exhibit 35.8.)

KEY IT PROCUREMENT MANAGEMENT ISSUES

Exhibits 35.3 through 35.8 contain 76 key IT procurement management issues identified by the members of the Working Group. These issues represent the

Definition

The process of optimizing the utilization of all IT assets throughout their entire life cycle in order to meet the needs of the business.

Subprocesses

- Develop and maintain asset management strategies and policies. Identify and determine which assets to track. May include hardware, software licenses, and related services.
- Implement and maintain appropriate asset management databases, systems and tools.
- Develop a disciplined process to track and control inventory to facilitate such things as budgeting, help desk, life-cycle management, software release distribution, capital accounting, compliance monitoring, configuration planning, procurement leverage, redeployment planning, change management, disaster recovery planning, software maintenance, warranty coverage, lease management, and agreement management.
- Identify the factors that make up the total life cycle cost of ownership:
- Communicate software license compliance policy throughout the organization.

Key Issues

- What assets are included in IT asset management (e.g., data, human resources, consumables, courseware)? [F]
- How can legal department holdups be reduced? [P]
- What is the best way to communicate corporate-wide agreements? [IR]
- How should small ticket assets be handled? [P]
- How do you move from reactive to proactive contracting? [S]
- Are there ways of dealing with licenses that require counts of users? [L]
- What are the best ways of managing concurrent software licensing? [L]
- Can we be contracting for efficiency using national contracts for purchase, servicing, licensing?[P]
- How can we manage and track software as an asset? [F]
- How can the workload in software contracting be reduced? [P]
- Are there ways to encourage contract administration to be handled by the vendor? [P]
- Is it possible to simultaneously manage all three life cycles: technical, functional, and economical? [S]
- How do we become proactive in risk management? [S]
- What is the appropriate assignment of internal responsibilities (e.g., compliance)? [IR]
- Do you need to track all items? [P]

Exhibit 35.7.   Asset management.

Key Issues (continued)

- How much control (a) can you afford? (b) do you need? (c) do you want? [F]
- What are the critical success factors for effective asset management? [S]
- What practices are most effective for the redeployment of assets? [P]
- Are there adequate systems available to track both hard and soft assets? Are there any integrated solutions (support, tracking, and contract management)? [P]
- What are the best ways to handle the rapid increase in volume and rapid changes in technology? [P]
- What is the appropriate reaction to dwindling centralized control of the desktop with non-conformance to guidelines and procedures? [IR]
- Is there a true business understanding of the total cost of ownership over the entire life cycle of an asset? [F]
- What are the impacts on organizational structure? [IR]
- What kind of reporting is most effective? [P]
- How can one manage tax issues — indemnification, payments, insurance issues ? [F]
- What issues should be considered in end-of-lease processes? [P]

Exhibit 35.7. (continued)

Definition

The process of assuring continuous improvement in all elements of the IT procurement framework.

Subprocesses

- Define and track meaningful process metrics on an ongoing basis.
- Conduct periodic quality reviews with suppliers.
  - — Provide formal feedback to vendors on their performance.
  - — Facilitate open and honest communication in the process.

- Collect and prioritize ideas for process improvement.
- Use formal quality improvement efforts involving the appropriate people.
  - — Participants may include both internal resources and vendor personnel.
- Recognize and reward quality improvement results on an ongoing basis.
  - — Recognize non-performance/unsatisfactory results
- Audit vendors' facilities and capabilities.
- Conduct ongoing performance tests against agreed upon standards;
  - — e.g., acceptance test, stress test, regression test, etc.
- Utilize appropriate industry standards (e.g., ISO 900, SEI Capability Maturity)
- Periodically review vendors' statistical process control data.

Exhibit 35.8.   Quality management.

Key Issues

- What is the best way to drive supplier quality management systems? [ER]
- What is the appropriate mix of audits (supplier/site/regional, etc.) for quality and procedural conformance?[M]
- What is the importance of relating this process to the earliest stages of the requirement determination process? [P]
- What corrective actions are effective? [P]
- When and how is it appropriate to audit a supplier's financials? [M]
- What is an effective way to audit material or services received? [M]
- What is the best way to build quality assurance into the process, as opposed to inspecting for quality after the fact? [P]
- What metrics are the most meaningful quantitative measures? [M]
- How to best measure qualitative information, such as client satisfaction? [M]
- When should you use surveys, and how can they be designed effectively? [M]
- How often should measurements be done? [M]
- How do you ensure that the data you collect is valid, current, and relevant? [M]
- What is the best medium and format to deliver the data to those who need it? [P]
- What are useful performance and quality metrics for the IT procurement function? [M]
- How to effectively recognize and reward quality improvement? [ER]
- When is it time to reengineer a process rather than just improve it? [P]
- How much communication between vendor and customer is needed to be effective? [ER]

Exhibit 35.8. (continued)

---

beliefs of these domain experts concerning the most serious challenges facing managers of the IT procurement function. In order to better understand the key issues, a content analysis was performed to determine if there were a few main themes underlying these questions. The content analysis identified eight themes, which are shown in Exhibit 35.9, ranked according to the number of times each theme occurred in the key issue list. (Each theme in Exhibit 35.9 is labeled by a one- or two-letter code. These codes also appear in Exhibits 35.3 through 35.8 to indicate how each key issue was categorized.) The following themes were those which the rankings in Exhibit 35.9 suggest are most important to the senior procurement managers in the SIM Working Group:

Rank	[Code]	Theme	# Key Issues Containing This Theme
1.	[P]	Process management, design, and efficiency	21
2.	[M]	Meassurement, assessment, evaluation (of vendor and self)	16
3.	[ER]	External relationships (with suppliers)	9
4.	[IR]	Internal relationships (internal teams, roles, communication)	9
5.	[S]	Strategy and planning	7
6.	[L]	Legal issues	6
7.	[F]	Financial, total cost of ownership(TCO) issues	6
8.	[E]	Executive support for procurement function	2

Exhibit 35.9. Ranked themes in key issues.

Process management, design, and efficiency. Practicing IT procurement managers are most concerned with the issue of how to make the procurement process more efficient. The questions that reflect this theme address the use of automated tools such as EDI and procurement cards, reducing cycle time in contracting processes, development and use of asset tracking systems and other reporting systems, and the integration of subprocesses at early and later stages of the procurement life cycle. The emergence of process efficiency as the leading issue may indicate that procurement managers are under pressure to demonstrate the economic value of their organizational contribution, and thus follow the last decade's broad management trend of rigorously managing costs.

Measurement, assessment, evaluation. The second most important theme concerns the search for reliable and valid ways to evaluate and assess performance. This search for useful assessment methods and measures is directed both at external suppliers and at the internal procurement process itself. The latter focus is consistent with the notion that procurement managers are looking for objective ways to assess and demonstrate their contribution. The focus on supplier assessment reflects an understanding that successful supplier relationships must be built on a foundation of high quality supplier performance.

Internal and external relationships. The third and fourth most frequently cited themes deal with the issue of creating effective working relationships. The importance of such relationships is an outgrowth of the cross-functional nature of the IT procurement process within organizations, and the general transition from internal to external sources for information resource (IR) acquisition. Venkatraman and Loh (1994) characterize the IR acquisition process as having evolved from managing a portfolio of technologies to managing a portfolio of relationships, and the results of this analysis suggest that practicing managers agree.

Other themes. The other issues which concern senior procurement managers are planning to develop an effective procurement strategy, legal problems, financial and total cost of ownership (TCO) concerns, and obtaining executive support for their activities.

DISCUSSION: A MANAGEMENT AGENDA FOR THE IT PROCUREMENT PROCESS

The process framework and key issues identified by the SIM IT Procurement Working Group suggest an agenda for future efforts to improve the management of the IT procurement process. The agenda contains five action items that may best be carried out through a collaboration between practicing IT procurement managers and academic researchers. The action items are:

1. Develop IT procurement performance metrics and use them to benchmark the IT procurement process.
2. Clarify roles in the procurement process in order to build effective internal and external relationships.
3. Use the procurement process framework as a tool to assist in re-engineering the IT procurement process.
4. Use the framework as a guide for future research.
5. Use the framework to structure IT procurement training and education.

1. Develop IT procurement performance metrics and use them to benchmark the IT procurement process. Disciplined management of any process requires appropriate performance metrics, and members of the Working Group have noted that good metrics for the IT procurement process are in short supply. The process framework is currently providing structure to an effort by the Working Group to collect a rich set of performance metrics which can be used to raise the level of IT procurement management. In this effort, four classes of performance metrics have been identified:

1. Effectiveness metrics
2. Efficiency metrics
3. Quality metrics
4. Cycle time metrics

Closely related to the metrics development issue is the need felt by many procurement professionals to benchmark critical procurement processes. The framework provides a guide to the process selection activity in the benchmarking planning stage. For example, the framework has been used by several companies to identify supplier management and asset management sub-processes for benchmarking.

2. Clarify roles in the procurement process in order to build effective internal and external relationships. IT procurement will continue to be a cross-functional process which depends on the effective collaboration of many different organizational actors for success. Inside the customer organization, representatives of IS, legal, purchasing, finance, and user departments must work together to buy, install, and use IT products and services. Partnerships and alliances with suppliers and other organizations outside the boundaries of one's own firm are more necessary than ever as long-term outsourcing and consortia arrangements become more common. The key question is how these multifaceted relationships should be structured and managed.

Internally, organizational structures, roles, standards, policies, and procedures must be developed which facilitate effective cooperation. Externally, contracts must be crafted which clarify expectations and responsibilities between the parties. Recent research, however, suggests that formal mechanisms are not always the best means to stimulate collaboration. The most useful forms of collaboration are often discretionary — that is, they may be contributed or withheld without concern for formal reward or sanction (Heckman and Guskey, 1997). Formal job descriptions, procedures, and contracts will never cover all the eventualities which may arise in complex relationships. Therefore, managers must find the cultural and other mechanisms which create environments that elicit discretionary collaboration both internally and externally.

3. Use the procurement process framework as a tool to assist in reengineering the IT procurement process. Another exciting use for the framework is to serve as the foundation for efforts to reengineer procurement processes. One firm analyzed the sub-processes involved in the requirements analysis and acquisition stages of the procurement life cycle in order to reduce procurement and contracting cycle time. Instead of looking at the deployment sub-processes as a linear sequence of activities, this innovative company used the framework to analyze and develop a compression strategy to reduce the cycle time in its IT contracting process by performing a number of sub-processes in parallel.

4. Use the framework as a guide for future research. The framework has been used by the SIM IT Procurement Working Group to identify topics of greatest interest for empirical research. For example, survey research investigating ACQUISITION (software contracting practices and contracting efficiency,), ASSET MANAGEMENT (total life cycle cost of ownership and asset tracking systems), and SUPPLIER MANAGEMENT (supplier evaluation) has been recently completed. The key issues identified in the current paper can likewise be used to frame a research agenda that will have practical relevance to practitioners.

5. Use the framework to structure IT procurement training and education.

The framework has been used to provide the underlying structure for a university course covering IT procurement. It also provides the basis for shorter practitioner workshops and can be used by companies developing in-house training in IT procurement for users, technologists, and procurement specialists.

This five-item agenda provides a foundation for the professionalization of the IT procurement discipline. As the acquisition of information resources becomes more market oriented and less a function of internal development, the role of the IT professional will necessarily change. The IT professional of the future will need fewer technology skills because these skills will be provided by external vendors that specialize in supplying them. The skills that will be critical to the IT organization of the future are those marketplace skills that will be found in IT procurement organizations. The management agenda described in this chapter provides a first step toward the effective leadership of such organizations.

References

Barki, H., Rivard, S., and Talbot, J. "A Keyword Classification Scheme for IS Research Literature: An Update," *MIS Quarterly*, 17:2, June 1993, 209–226.

Davenport, T. and Short, J. "The New Industrial Engineering: Information Technology and Business Process Redesign," *Sloan Management Review*, Summer 1990, 11–27.

Heckman, R. and Guskey, A. "The Relationship Between University and Alumni: Toward a Theory of Discretionary Collaborative Behavior," *Journal of Marketing Theory and Practice*, in press.

Heckman, R. and Sawyer, S. "A Model of Information Resource Acquisition," *Proceedings of the Second Annual Americas Conference on Information Systems*, Phoenix, AZ, 1996.

Hammer, M. "Reengineering Work: Don't Automate, Obliterate," *Harvard Business Review*, July/August 1990, 104–112.

Lacity, M. C., Willcocks, L. P., and Feeny, D. F., "IT Outsourcing: Maximize Flexibility and Control," *Harvard Business Review*, May-June 1995, 84–93.

McFarlan, F. W. and Nolan, R. L., "How to Manage an IT Outsourcing Alliance," *Sloan Management Review*, 36:2, Winter 1995, 9–23.

Reifer, D. *Software Management*, IEEE Press, Los Alamitos, CA, 1994.

Rook, P. "Controlling Software Projects," *Software Engineering Journal*, 1986, 79–87.

Sampler, J. and Short, J. "An Examination of Information Technology's Impact on the Value of Information and Expertise: Implications for Organizational Change," *Journal of Management Information Systems*, 11:2, Fall 1994, 59–73.

Teng, J., Grover, V., and Fiedler, K. "Business Process Reengineering: Charting a Strategic Path for the Information Age," *California Management Review*, Spring 1994, 9–31.

Thayer, R. "Software Engineering Project Management: A Top-Down View," in R. Thayer, ed., *IEEE Proceedings on Project Management*, IEEE Press, Los Alimitos CA, 1988, 15–53.

Vaughn, M. and Parkinson, G. *Development Effectiveness*, John Wiley & Sons, New York, 1994.

Venkatraman, N. and Loh, L. "The Shifting Logic of the IS Organization: from Technical Portfolio to Relationship Portfolio," *Information Strategy: The Executive's Journal*, Winter 1994, 5–11.

Chapter 36
An IT Asset Management Toolkit

Martin F. Medeiros II

THE TERM ASSET MANAGEMENT is used to describe, in general, the method of accounting for the goods, techniques, and know-how in a company's competitive arsenal. Such a method is designed to maximize the competitive potential of these assets by controlling the costs of their purchasing, deployment, and sale. What are these technology assets? The category includes software, both proprietary and third-party; hardware, owned outright or leased; and various intellectual property, such as trademarks, copyrights, and patents. Excluded are physical plant components such as elevator controls and security cameras; although technologically driven, they have to do with the noninformational systems of a company and hence are outside the scope of this discussion.

Because an organization's ability to compete is based directly on its ability to assess its current technological state and migrate to a more competitive one, stakes are high in the asset management game. Consider these examples:

- An investment banker describes the target of a buyout, asking what should concern him or her from a technological aspect. After an inquiry into the target's technological infrastructure and its Year 2000 compliance efforts, the target drops its asking price by over $7 million, because it cannot get a handle on the current state of its assets.
- Contrary to the belief of the Software Publisher's Association, practically no firms actively pirate software; in fact, the overwhelming majority buy many more licenses than they need or can use in the current architecture. More than one Fortune 500 company is over-licensed to the tune of more than $5 million.

- The CIO of an international mortgage company claims that a new discovery tool deployed throughout all the machines in a 4000-node client/server environment with over 750 North American locations gives him a good handle on the company's assets, but after being asked a few questions, he realizes that he has no grasp of their full extent.

This chapter presents basic considerations for better controlling costs and managing the deployment of and migration to new technologies. Here, the term cost is used in the broad sense: it encompasses the so-called fully loaded or total cost of ownership models that look not just to the initial outlay but to the cost over the life of the asset. Asset management — involving the successful development of that ubiquitous triad of process, tools, and management — is a dynamic, integrated mandate of sophisticated IT organizations.

ASSET MANAGEMENT PROCESSES

The Front End: Building Information Technology

The most valuable assets any organization manages are the copyrights, trademarks, patents, and work product it creates to remain competitive. Unlikely as it may seem, many organizations play fast and loose with these assets, even start-ups, who have the most to lose, because those assets may be the only ones they have.

Here, vigilant protection is of primary importance. It is vital to know what the organization's intellectual property assets are and what they cost. These assets need to be defended against theft and misuse and protected with written procedures that are effectively and continually communicated to all employees.

Effective management also includes a technology exit strategy: if the technology becomes commonplace in the industry and is available off the shelf, what would it cost to continue developing the proprietary system and how much would it cost to migrate off that system to a commercially available system? Every company must decide whether to buy or build. In the past, this was primarily a cost-driven decision, but it is evolving into a security issue as corporate espionage increases. Keeping in-house development close is eclipsing the pure cost model.

For those organizations with proprietary systems, there are three key questions:

1. Where is it?
2. Who is managing it?
3. How is it classified (e.g., mission critical or revenue generator)?

A frequent occurrence in IT management is the failure to assign stable employee or department ownership of critical proprietary systems. Companies reorganize frequently and, more often than one might think, the company jewels are neglected. The next executive put in charge has to pay a king's ransom for the savvy consultant who has managed the system through the upheaval to keep it up and running. It is important to avoid having a third party act as the only repository of knowledge.

The solution to potential loss of intellectual property assets is an intellectual property audit. A team of managers, executives, and intellectual property attorneys identify and review the company's assets, then define and map out an intellectual property protection strategy. Organizations reluctant to make their assets public by filing patents or copyrights may look to trade secret law for protection. The importance of intellectual property protection must be communicated to the entire organization. Executives and managers cannot assume; they must inform. And no one should be left out of the loop.

The Front End: Buying Information Technology

A great deal of the IT budget is spent on external resources — usually more than 50 percent. The best way to track assets is information capture on the front-end of the transaction. Many organizations are great at knowing how much they paid for something — they run a 2- to 5-year straight-line depreciation. While this is necessary for tax and accounting purposes, it is of no help in figuring deployment costs, contract compliance, or invoice resolution processes. Book value, value to the business, and cost of migration are three separate values that mature organizations monitor continually. This is where the buying process comes in.

If you are one of the few organizations left on the planet with decentralized IT purchasing, asset management is the least of your problems. If there are multiple doors and more exceptions than rules, you can rest assured that you are losing millions of dollars every month on an IT budget of $60 million or greater. At a minimum, an organization must have:

1. A centralized IT purchasing group with a professional staff of experienced procurement professionals, attorneys, and negotiators who initiate, negotiate, and record all contracts, whether national or international.
2. A defined process on how to document requirements prior to entering the marketplace.
3. A suite of contracts with enforceable terms and conditions reflecting the organization's particular business, legal, and technological requirements.

4. A cross-functional team approach when negotiating deals, including representatives from legal, engineering, business customer, and finance.

5. A repository of contract data that allows for invoice resolution and for configuration information. This last tool is essential for ensuring that the organization is on the winning side of a leasing agreement.

Without a centralized IT purchasing organization, it is impossible to effectively control assets. Purchasing must be controlled before the assets can be managed.

Architectural Standards

"You cannot lose your job by going with [insert monopolist vendor name here]" — but you can lose a lot of money and, then, possibly your job. The 1990s were filled with major near-monopolists releasing technologies with serious flaws: most notably, basic functionality on shrink-wrap software with install bases in excess of a million seats. These problems are compounded by highly distributed networks running heterogeneous technologies. For these reasons, the technology vendor (provided, of course, it is reliable) is not as important as the standard chosen.

Once standards have been chosen, the process for changing them must be documented. The following basic questions should be answered:

1. What is the baseline technology?
2. How often will the organization review refurbishment cycles?
3. What is the organization's policy for upgrades, service packs, and patches?

ASSET MANAGEMENT TOOLS

Know Contracts

The first tool is contractual language. No company can have uniform terms for every transaction, but consistency is a necessary and admirable goal. A suite of standard contract forms that supplies consistent terms with fall-back positions for typical provisions should be adopted. For example: How far in advance must lease termination notice be generated? What is the term for so-called technology refresh cycles? Are software licenses enterprise, MIPS based, per seat, or concurrent use?

It is important to engage competent counsel who knows not only the legal side of the transaction, but also the business side. Terms may vary greatly depending on whether the organization is the buyer or seller of technology. The drop-dead issues should be known and memorialized in good forms.

Record Contracts

Contracts need to be memorialized in some sort of database. There are many products on the market, but the best ones have alarms indicating contract termination dates or when deliverables should be met. These products also may have links to the actual scanned images of contracts.

Leasing Contracts

Many vendors immediately claim they have an asset management solution — leasing. (The second thing they will tell you is that you need a discovery tool; this will be discussed later.) By now it should be clear that no large company will win with leasing unless it has its asset management act together. If an organization is undertaking leasing and signing the vendor's contract as is, it is a foregone conclusion that the organization is getting the short end of the deal.

To date, every vendor lease agreement the author has reviewed has been draconian. Most Fortune 500 lessees will end up in breach by the end of the lease term because of the picayune requirements embodied in these contracts. On the other hand, there are leasing companies that offer great value. They work closely with their customers and know that a good leasing relationship requires commitment on both sides.

These leasing companies are the exception to the rule, which is that most lessors count on their customers not having the processes, tools, and management in place to reap advantage from leasing. Many organizations operate in a haze, allowing the lessor to maximize benefit on their side. Leases also require a great deal of care and feeding because assets are sold, bundled, and unbundled seemingly as often as mortgage-backed securities. Leasing companies are also susceptible to macro-economic forces. One need only pick up the *Wall Street Journal* to read about capital company X restructuring and selling off its portfolio to capital company Y. This thickens the fog. Strong notice language in the contract is the best way to mitigate such problems.

Asset Discovery Software

The second thing vendors claim is the need for asset discovery software. An asset discovery tool is generally LAN-based software installed on the server with a self-distribution tool that goes to the client and lets an administrator know how many copies are needed of software, hard-disk space, processor type, serial number, and in some cases, peripheral type. There are more than 100 products on the market; less than ten are highly sophisticated integrated packages and, in this group, the discovery agent is but one part of the solution. Those packages that cater to the telecommunications and data communications networks employ strategies that can run effectively on the WAN.

More sophisticated vendors assert that most asset discovery tools can track from 60 to 70 percent of the assets on a network. Discovery tools designed especially for network hubs, routers, and switches can have an even higher discovery rate.

Here again, it is important to remain alert: these claims are accurate for only a handful of vendors. Very robust systems exist that will account for even glass-house operations, including printing and the DASD form. But remember, no single tool does everything well. The more distributed the environment, the more customized the implementation has to be and, consequently, the data-capture error rate will also be proportionately higher.

It is wise to negotiate terms with several vendors and to lock in price at the trial stage. Software should be rolled out to headquarters and then to field offices. For a universe of 10,000 personal computers and a data center, it will cost around $2 million for packages that include discovery agent, software distribution, a contract compliance feature, and data conversion of a 2000-record scaleable contract database. An RFP should be issued for these larger implementations.

Financial Software

The overwhelming majority of accounting packages include a fixed asset component for tax depreciation purposes. This function is absolutely necessary for any organization. These packages include many other holistic approaches to the enterprise solution from a financial perspective, ranging from human resource reporting to accounts payable.

Few, if any, of these packages, however, will provide the information an IT manager needs for the component-level decisions an IT organization has to make. For example, if one wants to know how much it will cost to upgrade to the newest desktop tool suite, one will not get the hard-disk size information from a financial package. One may not even get it from the contracts database. The asset discovery tool would be most effective for this operation. Some discovery tools even resolve contractual configuration information from a purchase order with what the discovery agent finds on one's network. At the date of this writing, no major software vendors seem to tie the financial side with the discovery agent or contract side of asset management. If these systems fed each other in a reliable, consistent manner, the power of this tool would be formidable and would surely capture the largest market share.

The largest gap in the financial software industry is the lack of a sophisticated method of tracking the value of intellectual property assets. Much of this has been thrown into the ubiquitous good will or other asset entry, but this is an extremely unsophisticated way of handling know-how at this point in the information age. The accurate reporting and accounting of these assets are critical to the proper valuation of an organization. For security purposes, code names should be used for intellectual property assets on database entries.

Physical Inventory

Every effective asset management project begins with a process for controlling the assets. Now that one knows the discovery tool will help, at best, 70 percent of the inventory, what about the rest? The baseline physical inventory is one element of the process. Physical inventories are expensive and become obsolete if a day goes by when assets come into the environment and are not verified with the other asset-tracking tool and processes. Thus, asset management is a dynamic process, not a static one. That said, the physical inventory should be part of the solution — not *the* solution.

MANAGING THE PROCESS

Executive Support

No Fortune 1000 company can accurately predict the future. Each of the author's Fortune 500 clients has gone through a major reorganization during the engagement. Several have gone through as many as four in one year. Executives are not always aware of the cost savings generated by an integrated approach to asset management. The sophisticated ones do, but are too busy to tackle it. If the senior executives cannot keep their eyes on asset management, then who will?

Ownership at the managerial level — paired with communication — is critical. The individual who has accepted the asset management challenge must interface with executives to show the direction and value of the process to the organization. The old adage is true: if you are the asset management revolutionary in your organization, chances are you are not an executive — but as the revolutionary, you have to provide the executives with compelling arguments for change.

The manager or process owner must be able to concentrate actual head count on the process. This cannot be done by a drive-by consultant. *In situ* management of the team that involves procurement, finance, and engineering/architecture is paramount.

Procurement Management

Because asset management begins with intake, when the asset comes in the door, the procurement manager must embrace the asset management vision. The individual must be trustworthy, intelligent, cooperative, and able to get the job done. In addition to the resume, he must relentlessly use metrics to give data to the others on the asset management team. All decision criteria must be objective, and conflict-of-interest issues must be monitored and resolved by a clear, well-communicated policy.

Outsourcers and Integrators

One potential danger with close business contractors results from the "fox guarding the chicken coop" situation. Outsourcers and integrators have a bias for new products. As microprocessor speeds keep up with Moore's Law (doubling in transistor capacity every 12 to 18 months), the burn rate of these acquisition cycles can be astronomical. Integrators are famous for selling the Ferrari desktop when the Chevy pickup is requested, and name-brand outsourcers are not known to be cost-conscious.

For these reasons, IT managers must ensure that all processes involving integrators and outsourcers are audited and keep a direct hand in the process. Assets above the architectural baseline should be redeployed and all others quickly sold to save warehouse fees. Remember, asset management begins well before the integrator puts an organization's bar-coded label on the machine.

Attorney Roles

Attorneys play a critical role in the procurement process on the contract side. Organizations need full-time attorneys sitting in on this process. These individuals will have a good handle on performance and, because they are attuned to working closely with business clients, they understand the typical cycle of an asset — only when they know usage rates can they effectively record these requirements in a contract. The attorneys require a good understanding of technology matters that most affect asset management, including leasing, software licensing, personal computer provisioning, mainframe technologies, and intellectual property.

CONCLUSION

Now that distributed heterogeneous technology networks are mature, asset management is critical for maximizing shareholder value. Asset management is not an event. It is a process, requiring constant oversight. For this reason, just acquiring the toolkit is not sufficient; without effective management, a tool is useless. With it, a company can easily realize savings that are huge by Fortune 500 standards. Critical success factors include a robust process, management ownership, and full executive support. Organizations best able to play the asset management game have a professional world-class procurement organization and a sophisticated view of intellectual property.

Chapter 37
How to Do Better Deals in Leasing

Joe Auer

Those with long-term involvements in acquisitions — either purchasing or leasing — have seen some huge changes in the last decade. During that period, there has been an evolution in techniques: buyers, who used to be ill-prepared, often uninformed, and sometimes desperate, have matured into sophisticated and savvy procurement professionals. After years of accepting almost anything a vendor proposed, the high-tech industry has learned that it can save millions of dollars with wise procurement practices. This chapter takes a look at that turnaround and the fundamental tenet upon which it is based.

In any competition — which high-tech acquisition has certainly become — a major contributing factor to winning is to know one's opponent. And, thanks to ICN and other consulting groups, clients today know (and understand the motivation of) their suppliers. A great deal of a client's acquisition strategy is based on that knowledge. It follows, then, that the lessor stands a greater chance of winning business when it understands, perhaps even anticipates, a lessee's requirements. To the benefit of both lessees and lessors, here then are the important factors for a lessee to consider in doing a better lease deal.

WHAT DOES THE LESSEE LOOK FOR?

Lessees have learned that selecting a leasing company is as difficult and as critical as selecting the equipment itself. (In ICN's Leasing Negotiations Workshop, from which the following information is excerpted, ICN trains lessees to evaluate a number of points when selecting a lessor.) A partial list of items that must be evaluated before committing to a leasing company includes:

- Financial strength
- Life expectancy
- Experience and expertise

- Business philosophy and compatibility
- Broker involvement

The informed lessee will examine all of these areas.

Financial Strength

The leasing company should have either the capital for the system or the proven ability to raise the capital promptly through committed investors and/or lenders. If the lease is to be leveraged with debt, the leasing company must have the necessary contacts and expertise to obtain debt financing at an acceptable interest rate and within the desired time frame. Although the lessee's credit rating is a big factor, the financial standing and experience of the leasing company are also important.

Regardless of the attractiveness of the deal from a financial standpoint, the lessee will have nothing but trouble (and, perhaps, ultimately have its equipment repossessed) if the lessor is unable to obtain the necessary financing on a timely basis. A worst-case scenario can occur when the lessor is unable to arrange financing to pay for the equipment, yet it has been shipped to and installed by the lessee. At such times, the lessee finds itself faced with having to make payments under an unconditional payment obligation, standard on lessor leases, nicknamed a "hell or high water" provision. However, in addition, the lessee has to pay the purchase price to the manufacturer to avoid loss of the equipment. Indeed, enlightened lessees do not allow their lease terms to begin until the equipment is accepted and the lessor pays for the equipment.

Life Expectancy

Minimally, the financial stability of the potential leasing company should be such that there is no question that it will remain in business for at least the term of the lease, including the renewal period. The lessor's ability to perform during the lease term can be very important. If the lessor goes out of business, any generous upgrade and trade-in provisions in the lease may become meaningless. Other lease obligations imposed on the lessor may also become unenforceable. Without backup support for a lessor's performance obligations, the lessee can find itself in difficulty. In the event the lessor can assign the lease, it is important to make sure none of its obligations can be assigned.

Probably the best measures of the lessor's financial stability are its earnings history and management expertise. To be sure, negotiating with a lessor that enjoys almost unconscionable profit levels may be somewhat challenging, but an extremely profitable lessor is most likely a sound contractual partner, assuming that the profits were honestly earned. Notwithstanding the lessor's profitability, the lessee must be able to negotiate a favorable transaction. On the other hand, an overly aggressive leasing company that readily gives out deals that are "too good to be true" may not have a particularly long life expectancy and, as a result, the deal that seemed too good to be true may end up being exactly that.

The prudent lessee will ask for copies of the lessor's financial statements and appropriate bank references. When large, publicly held leasing companies are involved, the lessee should obtain copies of the firm's annual and quarterly reports to shareholders, and Form 10-K and 10-Q reports to the Securities and Exchange Commission. Management quality should also be analyzed, using these reports and individual resumes as source material.

Experience and Expertise

The principals and representatives of the leasing company should have the expertise necessary to deal with the lessee's specific business and financial needs. For example, a lessor with a fine track record on small transactions may or may not be able to handle a large transaction involving multiple systems and sites. The small firm, however, may be able to furnish more customized service and advice on a large or small acquisition. Nonetheless, the complexities and financial requirements of the transaction may mandate the use of a large, sophisticated lessor.

Some leasing firms may offer special expertise in dealing with the practical and regulatory problems involved in the lessee's business. Other firms may have little experience with the lessee's business but, alternatively, may have superior abilities to package and optimize the financial side of the transaction. One group of companies may specialize in simplifying the transaction for the lessee that has little or no experience in leasing, a one-stop shopping deal. Other firms may handle only the most complex transactions.

The key is to objectively select a lessor that meets the lessee's special interests and needs. Note the word *objectively*. This selection criterion requires an impartial assessment of the lessor's credentials and special abilities, not a biased prejudgment based on gut reaction and the warmth of the relationship with a salesman. The best protection in this area is to obtain a client list from the potential lessor. Although the lessor will tend to give out favorable references, each reference should be contacted — not merely to obtain a general favorable/unfavorable reaction, but also to receive comments on the lessor's strengths and weaknesses in areas that are particularly important to the prospective lessee. When possible, the lessee should make special efforts to obtain comments from other users in the same industry who have acquired similar systems through comparable transactions by using trade association contacts, the Internet, outside consulting firms (like ICN) who specialize in assisting lessees, and any other source of lessor-specific experiences.

Business Philosophy and Compatibility

The lessor must be willing to do business in a manner that will enhance the lessee's management objectives and operating needs. For example, some lessors will not offer competitive 1- or 2-year leases. Quite clearly, the lessee who requires this type of lease should not waste time negotiating with firms that offer only 3-, 4-, or 5-year leases. Other lessors specialize in larger systems. If the lessee even conceptually anticipates adding or swapping out components during the lease term, it should not seriously consider leasing from a lessor that finds such small additions and deletions to be an unprofitable annoyance. On the other hand, a lessee that does not require that type of flexibility may save money by engaging a lessor with more restrictive standards.

The leasing company should also be willing and able to design a lease agreement and payment stream that will meet the lessee's specific requirements. A lessor that does not have the ability to offer a number of payment alternatives, including step payment programs and the like, may not be capable of meeting the lessee's income and financial statement goals. Perhaps more important, the lessor's inability to offer this type of flexibility may be indicative of other deficiencies in expertise or innovation.

The lessor should be willing to negotiate appropriate changes in its standard lease form. Virtually without exception, standard lessor and lender lease financing forms are drafted to maximize the protection afforded to those parties and, as a result, the protection afforded to the lessee is minimized. This type of drafting is a perfectly acceptable legal practice, assuming the lessee is able to make the changes necessary to equalize the transaction and protect its interests. Most form documents, particularly leases, need to be tailored to the individual transaction in order to reflect the agreements involved and protect the interests of all the parties.

In most situations, a lessee should refuse to do business with a leasing company that insists on using its standard documents and no others. Any exceptions to this decision should be made only after detailed review of the lessor's documents by the lessee's attorneys, accountants, and operations executives. In fairness, it should be noted that the financing required for most leases mandates that the lease documents be acceptable to any lending institution involved. Although less flexibility may be available with respect to certain forms and provisions that are critical to protect the lender's interest, even here negotiations are possible and may be advisable to protect the lessee's interest.

Broker Involvement

The lessee should determine at the outset whether it will be dealing directly with the leasing company as a principal or with a broker. In many situations, the prospective entity offering to put the lease financing together may look like a principal lessor; that is, it may be called the "XYZ Leasing Company," but in actuality, it may be a broker. In other words, the XYZ Leasing Company may intend to merely locate a true leasing company or other interested party to purchase the desired equipment and lease it to the lessee. Depending on circumstances, the insinuation of an independent broker between the lessee and the actual lessor may only add to the cost and the negotiating problems involved in the transaction. An independent broker may add indirect fees and expenses to the proposal, increase the possibility for misunderstandings, and create time delays. Then, too, the broker has little incentive to provide assistance once the lease is signed and its fee is paid. On the other hand, a competent independent broker may provide valuable technical or financial assistance and free the lessee's executives for other responsibilities. The broker also may be able to locate necessary equipment that cannot be made available through any other source.

When the services of a broker are desired, the lessee should also consider whether the assistance could be better provided by the leasing company itself. Some lessors maintain significant in-house inventories and offer full-service broker/dealer/lessor programs. Other lessors offer brokerage activities but do not maintain equipment inventories. Still other lessors avoid both broker and dealer services and rely almost entirely on established brokers, dealers, and manufacturers as equipment sources. Additionally, there are a number of equipment manufacturers that have their own captive leasing entities. As suggested previously, the lessee should select the type of lessor most capable of meeting the lessee's special needs in a given transaction.

STRUCTURING A MUTUALLY ADVANTAGEOUS TRANSACTION

There are significant advantages to the lessee that selects the right leasing source and maximizes competition among the contenders. During the evaluation process, the various sources will quote a variety of interest or lease rates; terminating discussions with those quoting higher rates is tempting. Nevertheless, the lessee must avoid allowing such tentative rates to influence the selection of potential lessors. In many instances, the overall quality and financial stability of the leasing company and the substance of the transaction will be more critical to the lessee in the long run than a minor savings in interest rate. More importantly, interest or lease rates quoted early in the proceedings often change rather substantially before the deal closes. Unfortunately, whether quoted as firm or tentative, particularly low rates often increase significantly as the competition with higher rates is eliminated from consideration. On the other hand, initial high rates sometimes decline as the various leasing sources attempt to best the competition. And always keep in mind, changing economic conditions can influence rates as negotiations progress.

The ideal position for a lessee is to present all the potential lessors with a competently drafted Lessee Form Lease Document. The lessors should respond to each provision in the lessee lease as a bid requirement. This gives the lessee a strong evaluation tool, one which allows the comparison of "apples to apples."

There is no doubt that dealing with a number of leasing sources can be a time-consuming and frustrating task for the lessee's executives, lawyers, and accountants. However, the expenditure of time and resources necessary to properly evaluate the available leasing sources should be viewed as a mandatory and valuable part of the acquisition process. It is the "legwork" critical to selecting the leasing company with the best qualifications for a given transaction.

Section VII
Customer Support Operations

THE RESPONSIBILITY FOR PROVIDING CUSTOMER SUPPORT for the use of technology deployed by the organization's IT department has grown dramatically over the last 10 years. Within most organizations, this responsibility is typically placed directly on the shoulders of IT operations management. "Customer Support Operations," another new section in this year's handbook, addresses the issues IT managers face in providing to end users this valuable service. To meet this challenge, IT departments are establishing customer-support help desks; providing liaisons into the organization's user departments; assisting end users with their development of client/server applications; providing consultation through user-feedback sessions, and delegating access and control of systems directly to end-user groups. The IT operations manager must understand the best practices in providing these highly visible and critical services.

Chapter 38, "Managing the User Interface," provides practical advice to both IT departments and consultants for developing a relationship with end users that will ensure the success of a project, as well as customer satisfaction. Most well-run organizations have shifted responsibility for processing of mainframe-based application system reporting to end users. With this shift, the time required to develop custom software, eliminate backlogged projects, and to respond to user complaints should decrease, but because of increasing user demands, this is not always the case. In addition, many end users have insatiable appetites for more and newer technology. In response, some organizations have moved IT professionals into user organizations to create a department technical staff resource. This chapter focuses on this response, as well as other alternatives, for meeting the needs of the customer and fine-tuning the relationship between IT and end users.

Systems development management's role is also changing, especially in its interactions with corporate end users within the organization. The user community is increasing the pressure on systems development managers to provide them with increasing control over organizational data processing power. Chapter 39, "Managing End-User Development," explores the issues associated with the development, maintenance, operation, and support of client/server-based systems. Enterprise operations IT managers must understand these issues so that they can best support end users who depend on the IT back-office infrastructure that supports these systems.

One of the best ways to help end users is to provide them directly with the tools and processes needed to be self-supporting. In Chapter 40, "Helping Users Help Themselves," alternatives for IT self-support are discussed, including their advantages and disadvantages. This shift to self-supporting user groups has contributed to the formation of end-user computing (EUC) departments. To manage an increasing work load, hold down costs, and keep service high, end-user computing departments must adopt a consultative approach to providing support. Chapter 41, "The Consultative Approach to Client Support," provides guidelines for moving to a customer-focused, consultative approach that allows support groups to explore alternative ways of providing service to end-user customers. Discussed in this chapter are steps for conducting end-user feedback sessions and an outline of the skills needed to implement a successful consultative approach to providing support.

With the increase in end-user self-sufficiency in IT computing and support comes the need for security and control guidelines. Chapter 42, "End-User Computing Control Guidelines," examines security within the context of an architecture based on quality. Providing effective security in an end-user computing environment is a challenge. Security must first be defined, and then the services required to meet management's expectations concerning security must be established. The IT operations manager must understand these end-user controls, primarily because they are granted to end users from the IT department.

The final chapter in the section, "Reviewing End-User Applications," provides an overview of the requirements for reviewing end-user applications and suggests guidelines for preparing for such a review. Reviewing end-user application improves the quality of end-user computing, protects the investment in end-user computing, and points out potential problems with user-developed applications that could damage the organization's business.

Chapter 38
Managing the User Interface

Ann S. Angel

MOST WELL-RUN ORGANIZATIONS have turned their mainframe into a data repository and given the tools to the business units to query and report in any format they choose. The time it takes to custom develop software, eliminate backlogged projects, and respond to customer complaints should be decreasing, but because of increasing user demands, this is not always the case. Many clients have an insatiable appetite for more and newer technology. In some cases, users are as sophisticated in their use of generic software as the IS professional is about languages and logic.

The technology gap is closing between IS and their clients, but the communication gap is not. The IS professional who has spent a lifetime building programs on the mainframe with COBOL or FORTRAN is now confronted with clients talking in terms of macros built in Visual Basic and Object Linking and Embedding (OLE). In some cases, the role is reversing and the client wants IS to move in technical circles where they are not necessarily skilled. Most IS managers are working hard to move their technology base to the newer products and hardware, but keeping up with the changes and maintaining a normal work load is a serious challenge.

Some companies have moved systems analysts into the business unit to create a departmental technical staff person. This person is the interface between IS and the less-technical department management. A major insurance company changed the job title of systems development manager to customer service manager several years ago, which implies a totally different function. Thinking of users as customers or clients is at the heart of establishing a new relationship between IS and users.

This chapter focuses on fine-tuning the relationship between IS and users, sometimes referred to as clients. The techniques presented were developed by an IS consultant and can be successfully used by either in-house IS departments or contractors.

0-8493-9824-X/00/$0.00+$.50
© 2000 by CRC Press LLC

FOCUS		Process	Satisfaction	Care
Consumer	Focus	Transactions	Customer	Relationship
⇓	Goal	Speed and Accuracy	Meet Expectations	Exceed Expectations
⇓	Strategy	Reduce Time	Convenience	Value
Client	Viewpoint	Consumer	Customer	Client

Exhibit 38.1.   Moving from end user as consumer to end user as client.

THE CLIENT-ORIENTED ORGANIZATION

There are options for making IS more in tune with the clients, more proactive in meeting their needs, and in the long run, better able to establish a win-win relationship. The chart in Exhibit 38.1 shows the changes in the focus, goals, and strategy when IS moves along the continuum from treating the end user as the consumer of products and services to the client.

In a client-oriented organization, the IS department looks for opportunities to improve the working relationship between the service deliverer and the client. IS looks for chances to "identify and take away their pain" — that is, to create new products and services that will make them more efficient, reduce costs, and increase profits.

Clients want:

- Reliable products and services.
- Responsiveness to their individual needs.
- Assurances or guarantees that a solution will work.
- Empathy for their point of view.
- Tangible results.

The Reality about Complaints. Many IS managers are under the impression that if there are no calls of complaint, there are no problems. This is not necessarily so. Research validates that only 5 percent of people complain to management, 45 percent complain to the front-line person, and 50 percent never complain at all. These no-complaint people in an open marketplace simply take their business elsewhere. Complaints, therefore, have little bearing on whether clients are happy with services. Among other reasons, clients choose not to complain because they:

- Have the perception that it is not worth the time and trouble.
- Believe that no one really cares and that it will do no good.
- Have no formal channels for filing a complaint.

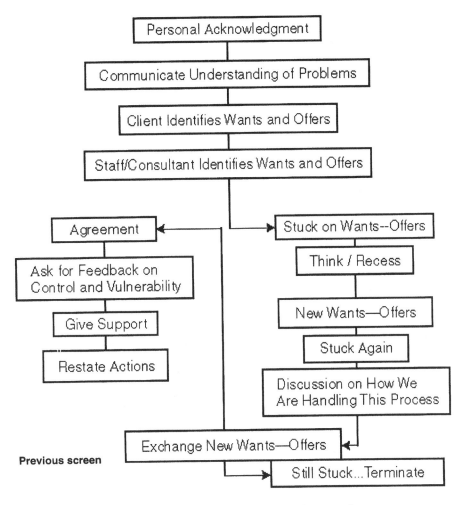

Exhibit 38.2. Navigating the contracting meeting.

Many IS trainers solicit feedback from their students, or customers, in the form of course evaluations. Consultants as well as in-house IS departments can benefit from frequently checking with their clients (the end users) to find out how expectations and requirements are being met. This is also an opportunity to ask about new projects or organizational changes that may be on the horizon. It is foremost a chance to strengthen the partnership between IS and the client.

COMMUNICATION IS THE KEY

Establishing a line of communication and keeping it open, even in the face of possible conflict, is the critical key to a successful client relationship.

Every business unit, including IS, has its own jargon. Some simple ground rules may be used to ensure clear communication.

Rules for Establishing a Common Vocabulary

The end-user support staffer should be an active listener. Listening involves achieving a common understanding with the speaker regarding the intentions, feelings, and beliefs the speaker is attempting to communicate. An active listener must also be willing to give frequent feedback and can help the speaker by:

- Stopping the conversation to ask for clarification of a term. Each person should understand the importance and impact of the terminology.
- Asking the client to develop a list of definitions common to that business unit that may have different meanings from the common usage of the words.
- Developing a dictionary to clarify computer terms that may be confusing to the client.
- Communicating the technology in terms that can be understood by non-technical people and giving them plenty of opportunities to ask for explanations.
- Setting up "dialog demos." Clients could arrange to have a tour of the systems department, including operations. IS could explain the systems development cycle and how IS professionals do their work. The client department could return the favor for the IS support team.

THE PHASES OF CONSULTING

When a consultant or in-house IS employee approaches a department or company for the first time to determine their requirements for new systems development, there must be a process to ensure success. Just as IS would not think of sitting down to write a program without some clear idea of what the end result needs to be, IS cannot define a client need without fully following the process.

When setting out to complete a project for a client, many consultants and IS departments follow a process that includes: contracting, diagnosing the problem, and providing feedback.

Contracting

Negotiating 'Wants.' The client may know what is needed to improve workflow and efficiency, but may not have a clear idea of the cost of programming or systems development. It is the job of the IS representative (whether in-house or consultant) to help clients determine what they can afford, what they can eliminate from their wish list and still meet the ultimate goals, and when they can use an alternative resource like a generic

PC-based product. Exhibit 38.2 provides a diagram for navigating the initial client meeting.

Coping with Mixed Motivation. Office politics sometimes cloud people's perspectives. The IS consultant should help the client to see the big picture or the corporate perspective; this is a way for them to measure their individual needs against the whole. It is important to be diplomatic when informing a client that their needs are a lower priority than those of people in another department.

If a situation arises in which IS is used as pawn between disputing parties in departmental politics, the IS employee or consultant should approach IS management and discuss possible solutions to the resolve the problem. It may also be necessary to involve the management of the client department.

Dealing with Concerns of Exposure and Loss of Control. When PCs and local networks first became practical tools of office automation, there was a great deal of concern about loss of data integrity and security. Time has proved that departmental processing is the most efficient, effective way to run the organization's business. PC software has broadened the scope of user productivity and lessened the demands on mainframes and development staff. The original concern resulted from a fear of loss of control and power, which is only natural. Many clients will express such fears when IS begins to change things.

Involving Users in Planning. Systems development should involve the primary users in the planning stage. All the users who are stakeholders should be involved in planning. This may include other departments that will rely heavily on the output of the current or planned system. It may be front-line users as well as management. All of the stakeholders should be in consensus before any decisions are finalized.

Diagnosing the Problem

Analysis. A thorough analysis of the workflow and processing requirements should be performed before any project is started. To do otherwise may result in a situation where IS recommends a solution, programs and implements the system, and finds that the staff is not using it because it did not do what they wanted it to do.

Resisting the Urge for Complete Data. Defining the scope of a project and staying inside the parameters are critical to project completion. However, it is helpful to consider opportunities for future developments while the system is being designed. This makes future additions and modifications easier.

Making the Diagnosis Process Client Centered. The IS employee or consultant should interview the clients in a department to find out why things are done the way they are, and then help the client see a different perspective and a better way of doing things, if necessary. Following are ways to make an interview client centered:

- Concentrate on current workflow and task identification.
- Ask questions to clarify what is being done and in what sequence.
- Ask questions regarding duplication of work or record keeping.
- Without criticizing, determine if there are legitimate reasons for duplication of work; if not, try to get a buy-in for eliminating the duplicated task.
- Teach streamlining procedures and tasks before automating.
- Never assume that the client staff will eliminate a step in the task just because the computer system does not include it. The steps in a task should be fully explained to the clients.
- Do not make decisions about processing requirements without fully discussing the issues with management and staff, especially the primary users.

Providing Feedback

Funneling Data. After the analysis, IS should be able to give the client feedback about the systems they have requested, including costs and resource availability. Often during the diagnosis, IS will uncover facts and figures that might surprise the client. A feedback meeting, as early as possible in the life of the project, is the best time to bring all surprises to the table.

Identifying and Dealing with Resistance. IS may encounter resistance from some users to the change management is requesting. It is not impossible to change people's perceptions so that they accept the new ideas and systems, but management needs to be aware of the resistance so a strategy for dealing with it can be developed. IS may be unaware of certain reasons for resistance within a department — management may be able to shed light on user prejudices or preconceived ideas about the way things are done.

Decision Making. It is helpful for a consultant or in-house IS employee to learn the skills of getting people to reach a consensus in a group meeting. Once clients have heard IS feedback, everyone must reach a final decision about a project. All important parties should be in this meeting, otherwise the absent parties may try to unseat the decision later.

Focusing on Here-and-Now Choices. Clients should realize that they may need to choose the most critical pieces of the project for implementation in the beginning and wait on others until budget funds or resources are available. If they can see the plan for meeting critical needs now and eventually getting most of the less important requirements addressed as well, they are more likely to accept the initial offerings.

Not Taking Things Personally. It is difficult for a presenter to remain completely objective when pitching a plan for project completion. However, decisions are based on business, and the IS staff member or consultant cannot afford to take it as a personal affront if the client decides not to implement the recommendations. This is a critical time to keep a positive attitude for the sake of preserving any future relationship with the clients.

CONCLUSION

Following are tips for applying the principles discussed in this chapter to real-life situations:

- Teach the user how to streamline procedures by:
  - Analyzing current processes.
  - Being objective.
  - Eliminating any unnecessary steps and redundant record keeping.
- Get the client involved in the analysis and decision-making process by:
  - Defining the automation objectives.
  - Agreeing on what problems need to be solved.
  - Determining internal and external pressures.
  - Defining the tasks that need to be automated and setting priorities.
- Select appropriate off-the-shelf software by:
  - Setting standards for generic packages while remaining flexible.
  - Selecting packages that have a been on the market a long time and have an extensive user and support base.
  - Choosing packages written in languages that can be modified and supported locally, and where source code is available.
  - Choosing the product with the most training and support available.
- Define hardware platforms and requirements by:
  - Avoiding bias toward the mainframe. If the clients believe the consultant or IS employee's knowledge is only on one platform, they may not trust suggestions.
- Ensure productivity gains by:
  - Making recommendations to the client that will ensure that their systems investments are being used correctly and efficiently. They should also understand the requirements for training.
  - Arranging training for the client management team.
  - Encouraging users to learn more about their software and to use the upper-end functionality. Some outside costs can be eliminated simply by using equipment and software already in place.
  - Training and cross-training all users. A department should not be reliant on one person's expertise.

Chapter 39
Managing End-User Development

John Windsor
Leon A. Kappelman
Carl Stephen Guynes

CLIENT/SERVER COMPUTING IS GROWING IN POPULARITY, driven by two major factors. Top management believes client/server technology saves them money, and users believe that in an environment in which the information systems department is not responsive enough, client/server computing can solve all of their needs. Unfortunately, neither case is necessarily true. In fact, client/server-based End-User Computing is a two-edged sword — with both edges cutting the IS department.

The major problem with client/server technology is that neither top management nor end users fully understand all that is involved in providing an organizationwide computing infrastructure. Top management can easily understand that the hardware for a client/server system costs less than a mainframe, but they have a very difficult time understanding multi-platform software costs, the costs of controls to protect data integrity, or why support costs rise. For their part, end users have little or no understanding of why they cannot upload their local data to the organizational database. Often, end users want significant access to the organizational database, and such concepts as controls and data integrity have little meaning for them — until problems actually occur.

IS MANAGER'S ROLE

As cheaper workstation technologies increase the drive for direct exploitation of available information, IS managers need to change their approach to end-user development. That is, rather than opposing or resisting the migration, they need to keep in sharp focus the lasting business benefits that end-user development can bring; no longer can they position themselves between the end user and the technology.

The goal of end-user development is to allocate responsibility and facilitate the information system (IS) construction process. Although traditionally IS has been responsible for IS construction in a client/server environment, today the end users often take on this responsibility, and development is possible only when end users understand the technology and process. Therefore, a partnership of end users and IS is an effective means for establishing the appropriate control and support measures needed for systems implementation.

The leadership for implementing an end-user developed system can be placed with a user, but that position must be guided and supported by the IS department. All the knowledge gained from years of handling problems in standardization, documentation, testing, maintenance, and performance should be shared with the rest of the organization.

In matters of security, too, IS is in an excellent position to play a strong role in protecting the systems and data that are the lifeblood of the organization, because historically it has been charged with helping to maintain the integrity of the organizational data base and have established extensive controls to protect that data. Going forward, IS should be concerned with where organizational data is being downloaded and with the stability and security of the networking systems that are installed throughout the organization.

MANAGING END-USER COMPUTING

IS managers can reduce the risks of end-user development by developing an effective strategy for controls, which must both foster organizational efficiency in using limited information resources and provide support to maintain high-quality systems. Key areas of control include vendor selection, software and hardware selection, and data security; two primary dimensions to a control strategy are levels of control and mechanisms of control. Examples of levels of control are high control (i.e., IS controls all development), moderate control (i.e., IS approves development activities), and low control (i.e., IS maintains a hands-off policy). Examples of mechanisms of control are standards, policies, and procedures.

Each area requiring control should be evaluated and the appropriate level and mechanisms of control applied. Balance is important, because too much control restrains the benefits of end-user computing, and too little control allows all the risks associated with end-user computing to flourish. A fine line, of course, exists between support and controls, and some of the best support mechanisms also provide control benefits.

Depending on how much they know and how well they can communicate, end users require varying levels of assistance, including help with product evaluation, purchasing, training, application development, testing services, application consulting, software and training libraries, user groups, and backup facilities. Simultaneously, IS needs to demonstrate to end users why controls are needed.

User-Developed Systems: Disadvantages

The sense of ownership that can be such a positive factor for user involvement in application development may also create major problems. Systems may be viewed as "belonging to" the user departments, creating situations in which hardware and software purchases introduce products that are incompatible with the existing system. Users may even develop the attitude that the system must be modified to meet their design decisions, rather than the users adhering to company standards.

Data. The ownership problem can extend to user-developed data and data bases, which, in fact, must be viewed as organizationwide resources that must be used effectively. As data becomes associated with a particular user department, the development of private data bases can be a major problem. In addition, the rest of an organization depends on timely data. However, as a department develops private data bases, the importance of updates to the organizational data base diminishes, in their eyes, and they may not see to the task with as much diligence as is necessary. Consequently, the data used for decision making by the rest of the organization becomes out of date.

Software. The ownership of software creates a similar problem. As a department develops software that provides enhanced decision-making capabilities, department users' willingness to share the software may well decline. In addition, the private software bank creates situations in which other users are forced to develop the same tools on their own, wasting precious organizational resources.

User ability to identify correct and complete requirements for an application is limited. Users know their own needs, but that does not make them good analysts. Often the user needs the assistance of an IS professional. On their own, users may:

- Apply incorrect formulas or models.
- Use incomplete or outdated information, or both.
- Develop applications that already exist.
- Select untested or inappropriate software.
- Lack adequate knowledge of the importance of quality-assurance procedures.
- Overpay for hardware, software, and support.

Other activities normally performed by IS can be neglected by end users. They may fail to:

- Follow organizational standards or guidelines.
- Test assumptions or models.
- Train other users adequately.
- Document an application adequately.
- Maintain an accurate inventory of software, hardware, and data.
- Maintain security.
- Provide for backup and recovery.
- Follow software licensing agreements properly.

User-Developed Systems: Advantages

Potential benefits for user-developed client/server systems do exist. Client/server systems can speed up the application development process, because projects do not have to compete for scarce mainframe or programmer resources. Fewer bottlenecks lead to faster response time and may have an impact on reducing the systems development backlogs found in most organizations. In addition, powerful desktop workstations can run applications that are impractical to run on the mainframe. Central processing unit-intensive applications, such as graphics and data analysis, often require client/server computing's distributed processing and shared data to be efficient. This is because the server, regardless of the hardware platform, can be freed up to process other applications when such intensive applications are run on desktop workstations.

User development can also relieve a shortage of system development personnel. Better systems can sometimes be developed by knowledgeable users who know the needs of their jobs and the organization. Although users sometimes need some assistance from IS, the user-developed system minimizes the necessity for a middleman.

Ultimately, end-user-developed systems provide more control to the users. Users usually get systems quickly by developing the systems themselves, and they turn out to be more satisfied and committed to them.

TECHNICAL PROBLEMS IN CLIENT/SERVER ENVIRONMENTS

By nature, client/server-based end-user computing creates a diverse environment. Multiple platforms, vendors, and technologies require a variety of support that is not otherwise necessary, and IS managers can play a pivotal role in juggling them all.

The Effects of Diversity

For example, client/server-based end-user computing requires more diverse technical support than mainframe-based systems, as it allows an organization to use hardware and software from many different vendors. Support contracts may be required with each of these vendors, so to minimize the difficulties of having multiple vendors, a company must establish internal hardware and software standards.

Client/server systems require more technical experts because of the diversity of technologies that must be brought together to create an effective system. For example, most developers understand either the mainframe system or the microcomputer, but not both. Because an organization may have a shortage of skilled and experienced developers, creating client/server applications involves more trial and error than does developing older, well-understood mainframe applications. Developers may need to go through extensive training to learn the new technology. Therefore, in addition to retraining current employees, a company may have to consider hiring specialists in local area network (LAN) administration, DBA, application development, project management, and technical support for users.

A Lack of Standards

As with most developing technology, client/server computing does not have agreed-upon industry standards. Currently, no standard exists for retrieving, manipulating, and maintaining complex data, such as graphics, text, and images, and standards must be established before combining products from different vendors becomes a reality in client/server technology.

In the communications arena, structured query language (SQL) is a standardized data-access language that enables communications among various PCs and an organization's data bases; however, each data base management system (DBMS) vendor has its own SQL dialect. This adds to the complexity of building transparent links between front-end tools and back-end data base servers.

Additional problems arise when an organization is to take advantage of its investment in existing computing resources — typically a mainframe — while moving into a client/server environment. The ability to communicate with the mainframe as if it were a server is available through several protocols, most typically, TCP/IP. However, client software is mostly based on other protocols. The network hardware needed to include the mainframe in the client/server system is an additional expenditure, generally not included in the prices quoted by software vendors. Finally, most client/server software that is compatible with the mainframe links only to specific software on the mainframe. The company must either have current versions of that software or maintain both platforms at compatible levels.

A Scarcity of Tools

Serious security and access control issues also must be considered. Right now, the lack of automatic backup and recovery tools is a big deterrent for organizations considering moving to a client/server environment.

Backup and recovery procedures have been improving, but logging procedures are still inadequate. Until these tools are developed, organizations cannot place mission-critical applications on client/server platforms.

Because the server is usually the central location for critical data, adequate physical security and operational security measures need to be taken to ensure data safety. A large number of tools perform security and control functions on mainframe systems, which have been dealing with data security for many years. All of these mainframe tools can help with the client/server effort, but they are not designed specifically for client/server environments.

Today, there is still a lack of client/server-oriented communications, diagnostic, and applications tools. These troubleshooting tools are more powerful than they were several years ago, but they are less robust than those readily available for mainframes.

There is also a lack of good tools for converting existing applications to client/server routines. This forces client/server users to either write new client/server applications from scratch or use the existing applications on the mainframe. Most organizations have invested in millions of lines of mainframe code that cannot be easily converted to client/server use, so mainframes will be required for many more years.

TECHNICAL BENEFITS IN CLIENT/SERVER ENVIRONMENTS

In a client/server-based end-user computing environment, users begin to feel direct involvement with the software, data, hardware, and the system's performance. They define their critical needs and allocate the resources they are willing to spend on those needs. Such involvement is the foundation for building a sense of ownership, which has long been a corporate objective, because ownership results in numerous benefits. In fact, research has shown that a key to the success of any new development project is user involvement in the process of developing and implementing their own information systems.

If installed properly, client/server systems should reduce IS department operating costs, because the hardware typically uses replicated configurations, thereby allowing a greater coverage of the sophisticated support environment. In addition, client/server systems provide a better return on technology investments, because they allow niche or specialized technology to be configured as "common resources," which are widely available within the computing environment. If the proper controls are in place, client/server computing should allow greater access to organizational data and information while providing for appropriate data security.

Traffic Reduction

In the client/server environment, the workstation controls the user interface. Most commonly, the user interface commands are processed on the client (e.g., the workstation). This frees the server to do other types of computing. Because the server is free of user interface and other types of computations performed by the client, it is able to devote more resources to specific computing tasks, such as intensive number crunching or large data base searches. Also, controlling the user interface at the client keeps each keystroke off the network.

Full data files do not need to be sent to another workstation for processing, as in networked microcomputer-based environments; only answers to requests from the clients are sent. Because the client receives only the data requested, network traffic is reduced and performance is improved. Access is also easier because resources are transparent to users. The reduction in both file and keystroke traffic dramatically cuts network use and cost.

Improved Performance

Client/server systems allow organizations to put applications on less expensive workstations, using them instead of expensive mainframe and midrange systems as clients or servers. Existing mainframes can be used as enterprise data management and storage systems, while most daily activity is moved to lower-cost networked platforms. Server performance is also cheaper than equivalent mainframe performance. Microcomputer MIPS (e.g., millions of instructions per second, a performance measurement) can provide a cost advantage of several hundred to one, compared with mainframe MIPS. Another cost advantage is that client/server data base management systems are less expensive than mainframe DBMSs. Moreover, the client/server model provides faster performance for CPU-intensive applications, because much of the processing is done locally, and the applications do not have to compete for mainframe central processing unit time.

Data base servers centralize the data and enable remote access. Client/server computing allows multiuser access to shared data bases. With client/server computing, users can tap into both the data that was stored in their departments in the past and any other organizational data that they need to access. In addition to access to more data, users have broader access to expensive resources, use data and applications on systems purchased from different vendors, and tap the power of larger systems. With client/server computing, users have access to large data bases, printers, and high-speed processors, all of which improve user productivity and quality.

Client/server computing allows organizations to extend the lifespan of existing computer equipment. The existing mainframes can be retained to perform as servers and to process some of the existing applications that cannot be converted to client/server applications. Client/server computing is flexible in that either the client or the server platform can be independently upgraded at any time. As processing needs change, servers can be upgraded or downgraded without having to develop new front-end applications. As the number of users increases, client machines can be added without affecting the other clients or the servers.

CONCLUSION

The successful implementation of client/server-based, end-user developed systems requires involvement by top management, representatives from user groups, and IS management, because only with all three can a balanced approach take place. For example, it is possible for IS to become so involved with the decision and selection process that it ignores the organization's strategic concerns. For their part, the end users may not see the value of careful and reasoned selection and end up with a solution that, at the beginning, may seem to meet their requirements but in the long run may not solve their real business needs.

The major issues to be considered would include ways that the system could improve efficiency, minimize costs, provide a competitive advantage, and reduce cycle time. Developers should build a model of the organization's work flow and data flow, which helps in designing networks and in determining how data should be distributed. The tools that are selected are determined by the data and systems requirements and require a great deal of investigation before a decision is made on which application is appropriate for the system's particular needs.

The users must be made aware of the client/server technology and the benefits that it can provide. A knowledge of the proposed client/server solution should be disseminated to all concerned groups. This knowledge is key to the proper use of the technology, as the users are in a better position to evaluate the technology. If the users can use the system and it solves the business problem, the chance for systems success is high.

Chapter 40
Helping Users Help Themselves

James A. Larson
Carol L. Larson

PCs ARE AN INDISPENSABLE TOOL for most office workers and are an integral part of critical business activities by providing applications for word processing, financial analysis, data base management, e-mail, and Web browsing. Annually, business enterprises spend thousands of dollars in support for each PC used by employees.

PCs are more complex than they were just a few years ago because:

- **Software developers are creating more complex applications.** To remain competitive, software vendors are adding more functions to their applications. For example, basic word processors have been extended to include spell checkers, grammar checkers, layout and formatting capabilities, and illustration and graphics capabilities. New versions of existing software appear almost annually.
- **Software developers are creating new applications.** New general-purpose applications are appearing, including desktop conferencing, document management, and simulation. New vertical applications are also appearing, providing new features and functions useful for specialized businesses.
- **Operating systems are more complex.** More functions common to multiple applications are finding their way into the PC operating system.

Because of the rapid evolution of PC environments and the lack of cooperation among software vendors, PCs frequently suffer failures because of software inefficiency, incompatibility, and instability. These failures result in increased calls to the help desk. In addition, more PCs are being sold than ever before, so there is a larger population of users to support. New multimedia capabilities, as well as other enhancements, have helped to make PCs more complex. This adds up to record numbers of technical support calls requiring more technical expertise. Most enterprises have help desk operations in which technical support agents answer users' questions and help with difficult tasks.

HELP DESKS AND TECHNICAL SUPPORT AGENTS

A typical help desk operation consists of one or more technical support agents who respond to telephone calls from PC users requesting help. For each request, a technical support agent creates a "trouble ticket," which is an entry in a "trouble log" that describes who requested help, the nature of the problem, and the location and configuration of the user's PC. After helping the user, the technical support agent records the diagnosis and the action taken to repair the problem and "closes" the trouble ticket. Help desk agents may examine the trouble ticket log to analyze the types of help being requested by users and to generate suggestions and responses to frequently asked questions, which are then made available to users.

Exhibit 40.1 illustrates three levels of help that can be made available to users. If users frequently experience delays when telephoning for help and are often placed on hold while the technical support agents help other users, the help desk function can be improved by providing:

- **Local PC help.** This reduces help calls by using the PC to detect and resolve its own problems locally, often before the user is even aware of them.
- **Automated help.** This reduces help calls by using intranet Web servers to provide help information directly to the user.
- **Personal help from technical support agents.** This type of help should be the user's last resort. Personal help is still an integral part of the help desk function, however, and should still be performed regardless of other methods of help available.

Using PC Software to Reduce Help Desk Calls

The ideal place to tackle PC problems is at their source, before the problems result in technical support calls. With the appropriate amount of information and intelligence, the PC can detect and resolve many problems itself before the user is aware of them.

The following three types of technology supply a PC with intelligence:

1. **Wizards.** These software devices help novice users by applying intelligence in the form of carefully crafted sequences of steps to perform difficult operations.
2. **Expert systems.** These systems apply rules discovered by the technical support staff from the trouble log. The rules detect and

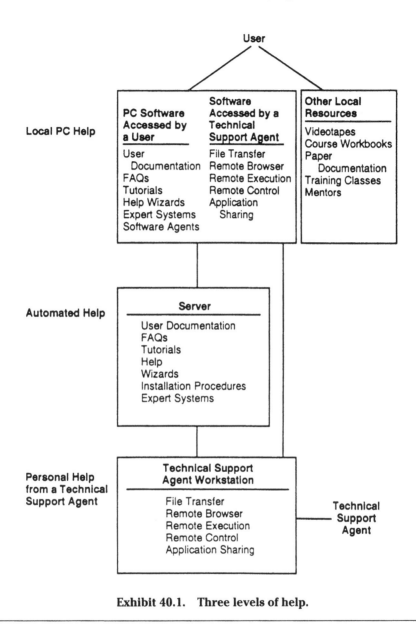

Exhibit 40.1.   Three levels of help.

resolve frequent PC problems. Call centers can build expert systems using case-based-reasoning inference engines.

3. **Software agents.**   These agents monitor the PC to detect and automatically resolve PC problems. Included in this category are applications that scan memory and detect viruses, examine memory utilization and make the appropriate adjustments, test the hardware,

and reconfigure the system automatically. Software applications that "tune up" a PC are beginning to appear on the market. Tune-up applications examine and optimize environmental parameters so the PC works faster. An example of this is the adjustment of memory allocation.

Reducing Help Desk Calls with an Intranet Web Server

Another way to reduce help calls is to make help information easily accessible to users. Many call centers use intranet Web servers to store helpful information that users can access directly. Following are examples of automated help:

- Online user documentation, installation instructions, frequently asked questions (FAQs), and other advice that helps users solve their own problems.
- Installation files and software upgrades that users can download and install automatically onto their PCs.
- Expert systems that contain rules that may be more up-to-date than the rules in the expert system on the user's PC. When a local expert system cannot solve a particular problem, it is passed to the expert system on the Web server for resolution.

New Tools for Diagnosing and Resolving PC Problems

Certain tools enable technical support agents to remotely diagnose and repair software without having to travel to the user's site and work directly on the user's PC. These tools include file transfer, remote browsers, remote execution, remote control, and application sharing.

File transfer. Technical support agents can use any of several file transfer applications to upload and review such user files as AUTOEXEC.BAT, SYS.INI, and CONFIG.SYS. The support agent edits the uploaded files and then downloads the updated files and device drivers back onto the user's PC. The technical support agent can also download new applications and updates to existing applications and install them remotely.

Remote browsers. Remote browsers allow technical support agents to scan configuration and registry files in a PC directly from the help desk. The agents examine critical parameter values to diagnose problems on the user's PC. Most remote browsers also let technical support agents update parameter values on the user's PC.

Remote execution. Technical support agents write scripts for downloading to the user's PC with the file transfer capability. Once the scripts are downloaded, the technical support agent can execute the script remotely to change the parameters and configurations on the user's PC. The remote execution capability is especially useful after downloading new software and the associated installation procedure. The technical support agent remotely initiates the installation procedure and verifies that it has been completed successfully.

Remote control and application sharing. Remote control applications allow a technical support agent to remotely initiate and control the user's PC. The support agent sees the user's entire display and uses the mouse and keyboard on their own PC to drive the application executing on the user's PC. Application sharing allows a technical support agent to share the windows of an application executing on the user's PC — a user can thus demonstrate a problem to the agent, who in turn can demonstrate how to resolve the problem.

Examples of remote control and application sharing tools include:

- CoSession http://www.cosession.com/triton/co-win.htm.
- CarbonCopy http://www.micro.com/cc/cc.htm.
- ReachOut http://www.stac.com/soft/rocont.htm.
- Norton pcAnywhere http://www.symantec.com/product/index.htm (choose pcAnywhere).
- LapLink http://www.travsoft.com.

TOOLS FOR AUTOMATING PC SUPPORT

A typical application life cycle consists of software installation, user training, troubleshooting and maintenance, and replacement. Help desk operations attempt to minimize support costs by applying tools that automate many of these tasks.

Installing Software

Installing a new software package on hundreds of PCs can be a time-consuming process, especially if a technician must personally locate and install the software on every PC in the enterprise. By leveraging the connectivity provided by local area networks (LANs), this task can be minimized.

Initially, a new application is installed on a server. From their individual PCs, users can remotely invoke the application on the server and download the results back to their PCs for review. When users begin to execute the application more frequently, they may download the application directly to their PCs and use automated installation procedures to install the application.

User Training

After the new application is made available, users will most likely be anxious to learn when and how to use it. Most enterprises use at least two traditional techniques for user training — classes and mentoring.

Training classes. Users attend scheduled sessions where an instructor explains when and how to use the application. However, it may be difficult to schedule training sessions convenient for all users. Instructors may also vary in their teaching effectiveness.

Mentoring. A knowledgeable user mentors a novice user in the operation of the application. However, this close working arrangement with the user may distract the mentor from other tasks, so novice users may have limited access to the mentor.

Some enterprises find it cost effective to place more of the responsibility for training onto the user by enabling the user to self-train, if and when the user finds training necessary. Several self-training techniques, such as videotapes and course workbooks, online tutorials, online wizards, online help, user documentation, and FAQs, are useful.

Videotapes and course workbooks. A professional instructor prepares a videotape for novice users to watch at their convenience. The workbook focuses the user on critical concepts and actions. However, novice users may find sections of the videotape boring or out of date.

Online tutorials. The novice user watches an online tutorial demonstrating when and how to use the application. Some online tutorials have interactive tasks for the novice to perform that reinforce critical concepts and actions. Users experienced with similar applications can bypass the online tutorial and focus on a "what's new and different" section instead.

Online wizards. Novice users can invoke an online wizard that leads them through a series of steps and assists them in making choices and decisions to accomplish a high-level task. At the same time, the user learns how to perform the high-level task.

Online help. The user requests assistance from a help system to perform a specific task. However, the user may be unable to locate the answer to their specific question if the help system designer failed to anticipate the user's particular question.

User documentation. The user examines the help manual for instructions about the use of the application. However, paper documentation may be bulky, can be misplaced, can intimidate the user, and may be incomplete or out of date. Paper documentation can be avoided by distributing the documentation to the user via e-mail. More organizations are starting to place documentation on an HTML server so users can access it from any computer with an HTML browser. A single, centralized source of documentation has the advantage of providing one location where it can be updated.

Frequently asked questions (FAQs). Documenting and publishing frequently asked questions and their answers allows users to learn new techniques and solutions to common problems. FAQs should be incorporated into the online documentation as quickly as possible.

PROCTORING NEW OR DIFFICULT OPERATIONS

Even with the use of online tutorials, wizards, documentation, and FAQs, it is sometimes necessary for a user to seek help from a technical support agent. Through a sequence of verbal questions and answers, the agent solicits a description of the problem, diagnoses the problem, and leads the user through the steps to fix a problem. However, these telephone dialogs may be time consuming, especially with novice users who may not be able to articulate precisely what the problem is or perform the necessary steps to correct the problem.

Application sharing and remote control enable both the user and the technical support agent to view the execution of a single application executing on the user's machine. The user demonstrates the problem to the technical support agent, who performs the appropriate operations to correct the problem. Alternatively, the agent demonstrates the appropriate steps to the user to correct the problem so the user learns how to correct the problem should it reoccur. Application sharing and remote control are powerful tools, especially when a technical support agent is also available to answer questions over the phone.

MONITORING USER ACTIVITY

Technical support agents may use LAN management software to remotely monitor possible trouble spots and resolve them before users notice the problems. LAN management suites such as Intel's LANDesk (see http://www.intel.com/com-net/sns/showcase/index.htm) include tools to monitor and resolve problems in the following components of an enterprise LAN:

- Network communication loads.
- Print queues.
- Printer availability.
- Server access.
- User computer software and hardware errors.

Monitors detect bottlenecks and broken components. Rule-based expert systems attempt to resolve problems by adjusting environmental parameters, such as queue lengths and active processes.

SUPPORT FOR TELECOMMUTERS

Many employees perform work-related activities on their home or portable PCs while on the road for their job. If the PC is able to connect to the enterprise's LAN via a modem, technical support agents may use file transfer, remote execution, browsing, remote control, and application sharing tools to diagnose and repair the PCs. If the user has access to a second telephone line, then the technical support agent and user may discuss the problem verbally while the support agent uses remote browsers, remote execution, remote control, and application sharing tools to resolve the user's problem. If the user's modem supports both data and voice transfer using protocols such as digital simultaneous voice and data (DSVD), then the user and the agent can talk through the problem while the technical support agent diagnoses and repairs it.

CONCLUSION

An enterprise should institute three levels of user help and assistance — local PC help, automated help from a server, and personal help from technical support agents. This gives users several lines of defense to turn to before their problem results in a trouble ticket.

Providing users with more sources of support allows the end-user computing staff to be more productive. The support staff can focus more energy on rolling out new software, troubleshooting, and training; the user can spend more time working because of reduced trouble-related downtime; and the entire enterprise can save money.

Chapter 41

The Consultative Approach to Client Support

Kate Nasser

In this age of technology, cost containment, fluid information-based organizations, and cuts in training budgets, productivity is key; embracing a productive customer philosophy is well worth the effort. The IT department's biggest hurdle in implementing this philosophy is a lack of customer trust. To earn it, support staff members must understand their end-user customers' business needs and expectations and, just as important, exhibit that understanding. Awareness is not enough; trust is built first by listening and then by visibly and audibly illustrating understanding. Without first building a base of trust, end-user computing (EUC) support groups cannot implement a productive customer philosophy.

This philosophy does not sanction discourteous or patronizing behavior that is sure to make the customer unhappy. The manner in which the problem is solved or the request is filled remains important with the productive customer philosophy. The difference is that the problem solvers using a happy-customer philosophy do not always use their expertise to find the solution that will make the customer productive. Instead, they yield to the customers' definition of what will make the customer happy. The staff members using a productive-customer philosophy start with the customers' trust in them and their respect for the customers' business needs. From there, customers and staff work in partnership to find the best solution.

To bring customer service excellence to end-user computing, the IT manager must exemplify to the support staff the customer service philosophy they need to communicate to and use with end users. Defining a customer service philosophy is the first essential move toward service excellence. If technology support groups overlook this phase, miscommunication with end users is likely to follow, resulting in an antagonistic and uncooperative working relationship.

Defining the philosophy involves knowing whether the support group's primary customer service goal is to have happy end-user customers or productive end-user customers. Although having both would certainly be ideal, it is not always feasible. For example, an end user might call and request a word processor that is different form the standard everyone else in the organization is using. The happy-customer philosophy that says the customer is always right would lead the support group to automatically submit a purchase order for a new word processor. The productive-customer philosophy would lead the support staff manager to ask the customer a series of questions about his or her technology needs. (In requesting a new word processor, the customer has not articulated a need but has described his or her proposed solution to it.) This needs analysis must be done in a timely, action-oriented manner so the end-user customer knows that the questions are not just another IT bureaucratic stall.

HISTORY OF CLIENT SUPPORT

The prevalence of a happy-customer philosophy has its roots in the history of end-user computing. The introduction of microcomputers came at a time when non-IT staff (e.g., end users) had reached their limit on long IT backlogs and slow responses to requests. IT at that point was focusing neither on happiness nor on productivity.

Even as IT and end-user customers were both approving large numbers of microcomputer purchases, IT did not analyze the total support needs and infrastructure demands of using those computers. IS allowed end users to do whatever they wanted until they had a problem. The stage was set for a reactive troubleshooting approach to end-user computing and a happy-customer philosophy.

Because IT did not take microcomputers seriously or see the financial and business impact of computing without standards, procedures, or expert input, it established a precedent of nonpartnership with end users. In fact, end-user computing support groups were not even part of IT in the early years. The EUC philosophy was to be responsive by giving customers what they wanted — as quickly as possible. Their goal was to distinguish themselves from the slow-moving, unresponsive IT departments by focusing primarily on customer happiness.

MAKING THE TRANSITION

Organizations have changed dramatically since the introduction of personal computing. Networks alone have brought legitimacy to standards for the desktop. Client servers now hold and run critical applications. Access to information highways is becoming a strong factor to competitive advantage. Compatibility and accessibility among applications, functions, and departments are tacit if not explicit end-user customer expectations. Customers expect their end-user support groups to provide expert guidance — even though these same customers may complain if the answer is not what they initially wanted to hear. The stage is now set for a consultative approach to end-user computing, a shift from the historically reactive setup.

Making the transition to a consultative approach to client support requires the IT manager to learn and understand the differences among needs, expectations, problems, and solutions and then train the support staff to make the same distinctions. The following case study illustrates these differences.

An end-user customer, Pat, is a marketing manager with responsibility for key product launches. Her department is a fast-moving unit that needs a lot of support. Pat is dissatisfied with IT service and is meeting with senior IT staff members who support marketing. She complains, "My department has problems using the company's systems and technology. When a crunch hits, the technology seems either to break down or my department cannot make it do what is needed."

IT responds that its training courses explain how to use the technology and systems. Pat answers that her department does not always have time to refer to the training manuals and follow them step by step, especially right before a product launch, and these launches are central to the company's business. IT replies that it is understaffed and cannot always respond immediately to Pat's department's requests. The discussion continues with no resolution, and the marketing department eventually goes outside the company for technical guidance and support.

This case study did not have to have an unhappy ending, however. IT could have adopted a consultative approach. If, during discussions with Pat, IT managers had asked themselves the following questions, the encounter would have gone much differently:

- What are Pat's needs?
- What are the marketing department's needs regarding technology?
- What problems is marketing facing?
- What are marketing's expectations and how can IT best address those expectations?
- What are the solutions to marketing's needs and problems?

In the previous case study, the managers were looking for the end user to define the problem and maybe even the solution. Because IT was exploring very little and listening even less, customer service during this discussion was very poor. Without effective questioning and objective listening, IT cannot solve Pat's problems, nor will Pat feel that the department has provided excellent customer service.

By using a productive-customer philosophy, the IT staff could be much more consultative in discussions with end users. A consultative dialogue would enable support people to determine needs, problems, expectations, and solutions. In the previous case study, IT established a position based on what it thought marketing was requesting. If the staff had listened effectively, the conversation would have gone something like this. Pat would have said, "We have problems in using the systems and technology we already have. When the crunch hits, the technology either breaks down or we cannot figure out how to get it to do what we need."

IT would have responded, "We have some logs with us from the calls your group has made for help. Could we discuss a few of these calls?"

Pat might have replied, "Good. This first one noted here was two days before our launch. We were gearing up and producing slides for our key customer campaign. The graphics package would not let us change style backgrounds from one slide to the next. The technology would not do what we needed, and we could not stop at that point to take a training course."

IT might have answered, "We understand your frustration. Certainly, a training course at that point is not appropriate. One of your people did take the training course last year. Evidently you are still experiencing some difficulties?"

At this point, Pat would probably say, "Yes, but can't your staff give us help when we need it?" IT would reply that it certainly wants to help marketing and it has a few ideas. Does marketing have a schedule for its launches — those crunch periods? If IT could plan for these periods, it might be able to put a staff member on call for marketing's after-hours requests.

In addition, IT might offer to meet with marketing before the launch to understand the functions it would be trying on the system. A staff member could coach marketing staff on how to perform those functions. If marketing needs hands-on support, IT could explain these needs to a contractor and provide figures on how much a contractor would cost.

The differences between the two versions of this meeting are striking. Both happen every day in organizations throughout the country. The first scenario is plagued with assumptions, disclaimers, and traditional claims about being too busy to provide the service requested. The second version is exploratory and searches to define needs and expectations before deciding on solutions. The IS group neither refuses Pat's solution to just send someone down when they need help nor accedes to it without comment. The IT manager negotiates for a proactive solution to gain information about launch support needs. In addition, the manager mentions that if hands-on support is essential, the support group can coordinate and oversee contract help. The staff members are providing value because they understand the marketing department's real need.

The answer to the first question (What are Pat's needs during the discussion?) is simple. Pat needs to see the technical staff involved and committed to making things better. Furthermore, Pat will be more likely to explore solution alternatives if IT shows more interest in finding workable outcomes.

The answer to the second question (What are marketing's needs regarding technology?) is that they need technology that helps them have a successful launch or at the very least does not hinder a successful launch. The problem marketing is facing is using the technology during crunch times — when it is critical that they be able to use the technology. Marketing's expectations are that the IT support group will help them use the technology they procured for them.

The best way for the IT department to address marketing's expectations and find a solution to marketing's problems and needs is to realize that help does not have to be hands-on during a crisis. In fact, the most effective help prevents the crisis in the first place. The IT manager can offer a proactive solution during a tense meeting in which Pat, the customer, is focusing on the next expected crisis. The happy-customer philosophy would give Pat whatever Pat suggested. The productive-customer philosophy allows the experts to offer other solutions to meet the customer's needs and prevent crises. Knowing the difference between a need, a problem, an expectation, and a solution is key to excellence in customer service.

Addressing all aspects of marketing's needs is another key factor in service excellence. The meeting just outlined could have lasted much longer and investigated issues of business challenges, technology training, and other outside solutions. In this case, IT will bring focus to marketing's business challenges during the next meeting and beyond.

IT will build rapport, credibility, and trust by using a consultative approach in such meetings and by delivering expert, timely solutions.

To achieve a consistent reputation of customer service excellence, IT must address other business units in the same manner. At no time should IT act as if its purpose for existence is technology. Customer-focused end-user support, the productive-customer philosophy, is the future of IT.

MARKETING AND IMPLEMENTING CUSTOMER-FOCUSED SUPPORT

Step 1: Understanding Customer Needs and Expectations

Customer-focused support begins with IT working to understand customer needs and expectations. End-user feedback sessions, which are a special type of focus group, help do this in two ways. First, by their very design, these in-person sessions focus on customers and communicate the IT manager's interest in providing excellent service. Second, the sessions allow for much clearer understanding of end-user customers' needs and expectations than paper or electronic surveys. For example, an end-user customer statement such as "We need immediate support for all the in-house application systems" is vague. What does the term *immediate* mean? Does the word *all* mean all the ones they use, all the ones ever coded, or all the ones they see as critical to the business? In-person feedback sessions allow for immediate clarification of end-user requests. Such clarifying questions eventually help dispel the myths that end-user customers are unreasonable and want the moon for no cost. Consultation, partnership, influence, and negotiation seem real and feasible during and after successful feedback sessions. Planning, structure, and expert facilitation are critical to the success of these sessions.

The planning starts with the IT manager and key staff brainstorming about how they believe end-user customer departments view current service and support. This step generates possible caution signs to consider in running the sessions. It also allows the IT manager and staff to sense which end-user customer departments are their allies and which oppose them.

At this point in the planning, the IT manager should formulate three open-ended questions to pose in every feedback session. Standard questions from which to work include:

- What current support services does the end user find valuable?
- What current services are not valuable?
- What services does the department need that IT is not providing or procuring?

The important components of the session are timing, notetaking, and communication. A 75-minute session with 25 participants usually works well, and assigning two scribes to take notes on the proceedings ensures more accurate capture of the feedback. One notetaker should work either from a flip chart or computer projection to make the notetaking visible to the participants so they will know IT is listening. The IT support group can review these summaries later. The second notetaker should be typing details directly into a computer.

The session needs rules about communication; otherwise it can deteriorate into an endless voicing of complaints that serves only as a therapy session for venting dissatisfactions. The meeting leader, who may be a specialized facilitator or the IT manager, opens the meeting with purpose, goals, exit outcomes, and suggested communication formats. A wish-list format requires participants to pose their opinions in action-oriented suggestions for IT rather than in broad accusations.

IT support staff members should attend the session to listen and to understand end-user customers, and they must follow these guidelines. The guidelines should be covered in a separate preparation session held for IT members before the feedback sessions. The main rule is that IT support group members should not participate verbally except to ask clarifying questions or respond to non rhetorical questions from participants.

These guidelines prevent IT staff from becoming defensive during the feedback sessions and taking time with attempts to explain why they cannot fulfill individual requests.

When running multiple feedback sessions, the IT manager and support staff — as well as the outside facilitator if one is used — should debrief each other between sessions. Staff need a chance to vent any frustrations they felt but did not voice during the previous session. Having done this, they are more prepared to listen during the next session. In such feedback sessions, IT support staff who are used to hearing mostly negative feedback are typically amazed at the amount of positive reactions they receive. These sessions give end users a chance to verbalize their needs and hear what other end-user customers need. Fears that hearing other end users' needs would escalate all end users' expectations are typically unrealized. Instead, the sessions show users the true scope of demands the IT support department is juggling and attempting to meet. More realistic expectations are likely to follow.

Step 2: Analyzing the Data

Whether these feedback sessions or some other method are used to help support groups understand current and near-term customer expectations, analyzing and acting on the data is crucial. End users assume and expect changes to follow such inquiries about their expectations. If the IT department does not intend to explore new strategies for delivering service and support, it should not perform any kind of inquiry. Surveying needs and expectations with no visible attempts at change will simply solidify end users' views of IT as a nonresponsive bureaucracy. It may also reduce the customer response rate on future inquiries and surveys.

As the support group analyzes the data collected, it should consider the following points:

- There are many contributing factors to each response.
- Cause-and-effect deductions cannot be made from response data alone.
- Low-frequency responses are not automatically unimportant. They may be critical to the business of the organization.
- The responses should be scrutinized for misdefinitions and the differences between needs and solutions.
- The customer trends that indicate high dissatisfaction and high satisfaction should be carefully charted. Emotional components to these responses provide opportunities for early change and marketing of strengths.
- The organizational factors that contributed to these points of high dissatisfaction and high satisfaction should be listed. A short, targeted meeting to create this list produces the best results. After the list has been created, it should be put aside for two to three days and then revisited in the first of IT's changing strategy meetings (which are discussed in the following section).

Step 3: Thinking Creatively in Client Support Strategy Sessions

Many IT professionals argue that if they could change the way they are providing services, they already would have. It is difficult to transform the way people think about technology service and support; however, it is not impossible. Changes in attitudes and thinking almost always occur when something or someone helps people see the particular situation from a different perspective.

Feedback sessions are one mechanism for reaching this new insight. Customers' discussion, examples, and frustrations may help the support group envision that different way of providing service. Assigning IT staff members to rotating stints in end-user customer departments frequently helps as well. Yet, a more concentrated effort may be necessary after the feedback sessions are over. Within six months of the feedback sessions, participants will want to see some change — however small.

Creative thinking and problem-solving techniques in a series of strategy meetings can bring IT staff to the new insight that is required. Many exercises have been designed to help support personnel break through mental blocks and status quo thinking. The IT manager may find that an expert facilitator can help create momentum and initiate creative thought in the first few meetings. Expert facilitators can be found in an organization's human resources department or outside the organization. Facilitators need to be impartial and unaffected by the decisions that are made in the meeting. End-user customers and IT support staff members are often too close to the issues to be objective facilitators.

The following practices are useful in running a strategy session:

- Questioning what has always been assumed to be fact.
- If IT support staff total six or more, breaking into pairs or trios for five-minute creative bursts and then sharing the results as a total group.
- As a whole group, expanding on the ideas from the creative bursts.
- Noting any comments on roadblocks to each idea.
- Having pairs argue in favor of ideas they believe will not work. This forces people to see the ideas from a different angle.
- Structuring each strategy session to allow time for introduction, creative bursts, discussion, and closure on at least two ideas. Each session should be a step closer to building the new customer-focused strategy.
- Resisting the tendency to analyze and discuss without coming to closure. IT divisions often make this mistake. It may be the analytical personalities, the belief that a perfect solution exists, or a basic resistance to change that produces this detrimental behavior. In any case, the objective facilitator can help IT move past endless discussions and toward action.
- Visibly posting the reasons for changing or transforming the IT support group during every strategy session along with the question: What about the customer? Support staff members can look to these visual cues to avoid slipping into status quo thinking.

Communicating the new strategy. At the end of the strategy sessions, IT will have a new mission statement that reflects its primary purpose for existence and its customer service philosophy. From that statement should flow new or revised processes, procedures, and service-level agreements. Once these changes have been drafted, a pilot to test the new strategy should be undertaken to determine how well it works.

If the new mission statement accurately reflects the overall business technology needs of the end-user departments, a trial implementation of the new service strategy is all that is needed to determine necessary modifications. Endless analysis, discussion, and planning do not test the efficacy of new procedures and processes.

For a pilot program to be effective, the support department must make sure end users are aware that the new strategy is in a pilot phase. This does not mean, however, that the program should be implemented in a lackluster manner. IT must be confident about its new strategy and simultaneously open to end-user feedback on the new strategy. In fact, the IT manager must solicit feedback at regular intervals to determine needed changes along the way.

The timing of a pilot is also important. Many departments want to stress test their new service strategy during peak periods of customer use. Although stress testing is an excellent idea, it should not be the first thing IT does in a pilot. End users need time to adjust to changes, and IT support needs an initial test of its understanding of business technology needs before it conducts a stress test.

An initial test requires introducing a new service strategy six weeks before an expected peak period. This provides time to modify processes and an adequate window to motivate end users to work with the support group in the short term to minimize the potential for crises during the peak period. If new technology platforms or systems for customer use are part of the new strategy, the timing of the initial test must be adjusted according to technical demands.

Communicating the changes to end users is critical to a new strategy's success. IT managers must be creative to catch the attention of jaded end users and to signal that changes really are in the works. The manager should improve the standard communication mechanism in place in the organization.

An option is to conduct kickoff sessions that end users attend during lunch or before work. Attending this event enables customers to meet the IS support staff, see the new technology they have been requesting, or attend a software package clinic. During the kickoff, the support staff can distribute information highlighting the new service strategy and processes. These highlights can be outlined in repeated 10- to 15-minute briefings. This event can also be customized for each end-user department and presented in each unit's area. Above all, the support group must reach out and market changes in the best possible light by showing confidence and enthusiasm.

Step 5: Phasing in the Final Plan

The pilot is a short, concentrated period to test the new strategy and changes in processes and procedures. During the pilot, the support group should collect end-user feedback, monitor its own assessments, and work to remain open to potential changes to the initial plan. IT support staff members may be tempted to rationalize the design of the new strategy and resist modifications because they experience creative ownership. The consultative approach, however, requires that support personnel create a strategy in partnership with end-user customer knowledge and input. The pilot phase is a partnership opportunity.

After revising the service strategy and processes as needed, the IT manager must finalize the plan and phase it in throughout the organization. Often a pilot period tests a plan with key end-user representatives. The final plan is phased in to eventually service all end users with the new processes and procedures. If IT does not phase in the services, end-user customers will expect 100 percent availability of all promised services the first time they make a request.

SKILLS FOR THE CONSULTATIVE APPROACH

The consultative approach to client support service, based on the productive customer philosophy, involves much more than technical acumen. The IT department's specialized technical analysts may not have the consulting skills needed for such an approach. The IT manager must therefore assess staff skills and provide appropriate training where necessary. The IT manager may also need to implement training to help support staff members shift from a focus on solving technical problems to a focus on addressing business technology challenges.

In assessing staff skills, the IT manager should look for:

- *Telephone skills.* These are required for gathering customer feedback and diagnosing and solving problems, especially at remote sites. This is not purely the domain of a front-line help desk.
- *Consultative communication skills.* Techniques include asking open-ended questions, assessing customer priorities, and opening exploratory discussions.
- *Interpersonal skills.* The key interpersonal skills are assessing personal space requirements, reading body language, estimating personality types and social styles, and adjusting behavior as needed.
- *Time management and organizational skills.* IT staff must juggle many priorities, keep communication flowing on status, market as they go, and of course, solve technical problems. This presents quite a challenge to IT management and staff, especially to IT members who were previously assigned only to long-term projects.
- *Negotiation skills.* Win-win negotiation skills do not come naturally to everyone. Yet all IT staff members can and should learn this valuable skill set. The productive customer philosophy requires IT staff to negotiate with end users whenever various options to solve service problems and meet service needs are explored.
- *Listening skills.* Listening is the most important skill for consultative service. Success in this endeavor is not possible without hearing end users' viewpoints.

This list is meant to guide an overall staff development effort. The organization's human resources department may be able to help assess these skills and then search for specific training and mechanisms to teach support personnel in unskilled areas. Customized courses are the most valuable because staff can spend the training time applying skills to the IT department's environment. Generalized customer service training courses provide overall principles and leave IT to translate them to their environment after the course.

IT managers need the same skills as the support staff. Moreover, managers must exemplify to the staff the attitudes and philosophy they want the staff to exhibit to end-user customers. For example, an IT manager who wants the support staff to listen to end users can teach by example by listening carefully to staff members. The manager must outline the vision and strategy and then exemplify it to staff.

If IT managers want to encourage teamwork and participation with end users — both key aspects of a consultative service environment — they must develop the support group into its own team. A group rarely begins as an empowered team that is able to make strategic decisions without guidance.

CONCLUSION

The consultative approach to customer service is the basis for IT department service excellence. In everyday terms, it means anticipating and understanding the end users' immediate needs and expectations, exploring options to meet their broader strategic needs, following through on details, communicating throughout the process, and delivering what is promised.

When dining out at a restaurant, for example, patrons evaluate the service according to these same criteria. Excellent service includes all of these elements. People are drawn to go back to similar experiences because they meet their needs and expectations without hassle. Even when mix-ups in service occur, the diner trusts that the service provider will aptly handle the mix-up.

IT department customers respond in the same way if the support group has built that base of trust. Small steps that show the group is changing for the better help gain that trust. Thinking and planning alone do not.

Chapter 42
End-User Computing Control Guidelines

Ron Hale

THIS CHAPTER EXAMINES END-USER COMPUTING CONTROL within the context of an architecture based on quality. As end-user computing systems have advanced, many of the security and management issues have been addressed. A central administration capability and an effective level of access authorization and authentication generally exist for current systems that are connected to networks. In prior architectures, the network was only a transport mechanism. In many of the systems that are being designed and implemented today, however, the network is the system and provides many of the controls that had been available on the mainframe. For example, many workstations now provide power-on passwords; storage capacity has expanded sufficiently so that workers are not required to maintain diskette files; and control over access to system functions and to data is protected not only through physical means but also through logical security, encryption, and other techniques.

ARCHITECTURAL APPROACHES TO INFORMATION PROTECTION

Although tools are becoming available (i.e., from hardware providers, security product developers, and network vendors) that can be used to solve many of the confidentiality and integrity problems common in end-user computing, the approach to implementing control is often not as straightforward as is common in centralized processing environments. The goals of worker empowerment, increased functionality and utility, and the ability of end-users to control their environment must be guarded. In many organizations, end-users have the political strength and independence to resist efforts that are seen as restrictive or costly. In addition, networks, remote access, distributed data servers, Internet tools, and the other components that have become part of the end-user environment have made control a difficult task.

To address the complexity of end-user computing, an architectural approach is required; it helps to ensure that an organization's control strategy and technical strategy are mutually supportive. The components of an information protection architecture include management, confidentiality and integrity controls, and continuity controls.

MANAGEMENT STRUCTURE

Perhaps the best and most expedient means of bringing stability to the end-user platform is to develop an effective management structure.

Distributed Management

Because end-user computing is highly distributed, and because local personnel and managers are responsible for controlling the business environment where end-user solutions are implemented, it is appropriate that control responsibilities are also distributed. Centralized administration and management of security in a highly decentralized environment cannot work without a great deal of effort and a large staff. When authority for managing control is distributed within the organization, management can expect a higher degree of voluntary compliance; in particular, where adherence to policies and procedures is included in personnel evaluation criteria. If distributed responsibility is properly implemented, ensuring that the goals of the program are consistent with the requirements and goals of the business unit is more likely to be successful.

Distributing security responsibilities may mean that traditional information protection roles need to be redefined. In many centralized organizations, security specialists are responsible for implementing and managing access control. In a distributed end-user environment, this is not practical. There are too many systems and users for the security organization to manage access control. Even with the availability of network and other tools, it may not be appropriate for security personnel to be responsible for access administration. In many distributed environments where advanced networks have been implemented, access controls may best be managed by network administrators. In a similar manner, server, UNIX, and any other system security may best be managed by personnel responsible for that environment.

With many technologies that are used in distributed and end-user computing environments, no special classes of administration are defined for security. Administrators have access to root or operate at the operating system level with all rights and privileges. In such cases, it is not appropriate for security personnel to take an active role in managing access security. Their role should be more consultative in nature. They could also be involved with monitoring and risk management planning, which are potentially more beneficial to the organization and more in line with management responsibilities.

Security Management Committee

Because security in end-user computing environments is distributive, greater acceptance of policies and procedures can be expected if the organization as a whole is involved with defining the environment. To achieve this, a security management committee can be created that represents some of the largest or most influential information technology users and technology groups. This committee should be responsible for recommending the security policy and for developing the procedures and standards that will be in force throughout the enterprise.

Representation on the committee by the internal audit department is often beneficial, and their support and insight can be important in developing an effective security management structure. However, consideration must be given to the control responsibilities of audit and the need to separate their responsibility for monitoring compliance with controls and for developing controls as part of the security committee. In some enterprises, this is not a major issue because internal audit takes a more consultative position. If maintaining the independence of audit is important, then audit can participate as an observer.

Senior Executive Support

The internal audit department traditionally had an advantage over the security organization because of its reporting relationship. Internal auditors in most organizations report to senior executives, which enables them to discuss significant control concerns and to get management acceptance of actions that need to be taken to resolve issues. Security has traditionally reported to IS management and has not had the executive exposure unless there has been a security compromise or other incident. In a distributed environment, it may be beneficial to have the security department and the security management committee report to a senior executive who will be a champion and who has sufficient authority within the enterprise to promote information protection as an important and necessary part of managing the business. Such a reporting relationship will also remove security from the purely technical environment of information systems and place it in a more business-focused environment.

POLICY AND STRATEGY

The ability to communicate strategy and requirements is essential in an end-user computing environment. This communication generally takes the form of enterprisewide policy statements and is supported by procedures, standards, and guidelines that can be targeted to specific business functions, technology platforms, or information sources.

The Information Protection Policy Statement

An information protection policy statement should define management expectations for information protection, the responsibilities of individuals and groups for protecting information, and the organizational structure that will assist management in implementing protection approaches that are consistent with the business strategy. Because the statement will be widely distributed and is meant to clearly communicate management's and users' responsibilities, it should not take the form of a legal document. The effectiveness of the information protection policy depends in large part on its effective communication.

Classification of Information

To protect information, users and managers need to have a consistent definition of what information is important and what protective measures are appropriate. In any organization, local management will be inclined to feel that their information is more sensitive and critical than other information within the organization. From an organizational standpoint, this may not be the case. To ensure that the organization protects only to the appropriate level the information that has the highest value or is the most sensitive, a classification method must be in place.

In the mainframe environment, all information was protected essentially to the same level by default. In a distributed and end-user computing environment, such levels of protection are not practical and represent a significant cost in terms of organizational efficiency. The information protection policy should clearly identify the criteria that should be used in classification, the labels that are to be used to communicate classification decisions, and the nature of controls that are appropriate for each class of information.

Classifying information is a difficult task. There is a tendency to view variations in the nature of information or in its use as separate information classes. However, the fewer the classes of information that an enterprise defines, the easier it is to classify the information and to understand what needs to be done to protect it. In many organizations, information is classified only according to its sensitivity and criticality. Classes of sensitivity can be: highly sensitive, sensitive, proprietary, and public. Classes of criticality can be defined in terms of the period within which information needs to be made available following a business disruption.

440

Monitoring and Control

A method of monitoring the control system and correcting disruptive variances must be established. Such monitoring can include traditional audit and system reports, but because the system is distributed and addresses all information, total reliance on traditional approaches may not be effective.

In an end-user computing environment, relying on business management to call security personnel when they need help is unrealistic. Security needs to be proactive. By periodically meeting with business managers or their representatives and discussing their security issues and concerns, security personnel can determine the difficulties that are being experienced and can detect changes in risk due to new technology, the application of technology, or business processes. By increasing dialogue and promoting the awareness that security wants to improve performance, not to block progress, these meetings can help ensure that business management will seek security assistance when a problem arises.

Standards, Procedures, and Guidelines

The other elements of effective management — standards, procedures, and guidelines — define in terms of technology and business processes precisely how controls are to be implemented. Standards could be developed for documenting end-user applications and spreadsheets, access controls and access paths, system implementation and design specifications, and other elements that need to be consistent across an enterprise. Procedures define how something is done, such as testing applications, managing change in end-user environments, and gaining approval for access to information and systems. Guidelines provide a suggested approach to security when differences in organizations make consistency difficult or when local processes need to be defined. Policies, procedures, standards, and guidelines are each a significant component in the information protection architecture.

CONFIDENTIALITY AND INTEGRITY CONTROLS

Confidentiality and integrity controls are intended to operate on physical, logical, and procedural levels. Because end-user computing is primarily business and user focused, security solutions need to be tightly integrated into the way the business is managed and how work is done.

Physical Controls

In early end-user computing solutions, physical security was the only available control to ensure the protection of the hardware, software, and information. This control helped to ensure the availability of the system as well as to prevent unauthorized access to information and functions.

With the spread of distributed computing and local networks, physical controls still maintain a certain significance. Devices such as data, application, and security servers need to be protected from unauthorized access, and continuity of service needs to be ensured. For example, the integrity of the system must be protected in cases where local users have been given access to servers and have installed programs or made modifications that resulted in service interruptions. Contract maintenance personnel should be prevented from running diagnostics or performing other procedures unless they are escorted and supervised. System code should be protected from unauthorized modifications. Vendor personnel should be monitored to ensure that any modifications or diagnostic routines will not compromise system integrity or provide unknown or unauthorized access paths.

The network represents a critical element of end-user computing solutions. Network devices, including the transmission path, need to be protected from unauthorized access. Protection of the path is important to ensure the continuity of network traffic and to prevent unauthorized monitoring of the traffic.

Last, media used with end-user systems need to be protected. As with mainframe systems, files on user workstations and servers need to be backed up regularly. Backup copies need to be taken off-site to ensure that they will be available in the event of a disaster. During transit and in storage, media need to be protected from unauthorized access or modification. Media that are used with the local workstation may also need to be protected. Users may produce magnetic output to store intermediate work products, to provide local backup of strategic files, or to take home to work with. These media, and all media associated with end-user systems, need to be protected to the highest level of classification of the information contained therein.

System Controls

System security in end-user computing solutions is as significant as mainframe security is in centralized architectures. The difference lies in the tools and techniques that are available in the distributed world, which are often not as all-encompassing or as effective as are mainframe tools, and in the types of vulnerabilities.

Tools. In the mainframe world, one tool can be used to identify and to protect all data as well as system resources. For each device in the distributed environment, there may be an associated internal security capability and tool. Tools are often not consistent across platforms and are not complementary. They do not allow for a single point of administration and provide little efficiency from an enterprise standpoint. To gain this efficiency, additional security products need to be installed.

Even when a multiplicity of security tools is used, a decision needs to be made about where to place the locus of control. In some central management solutions, the mainframe becomes the center of access control and authentication. However, this may not be appropriate in organizations that have made the decision to move away from a mainframe. Distributed security management solutions may be practical for some of the many systems used in an environment, but may not address security in all environments.

Another approach to implementing a consistent access control system across all environments is to use tools such as Kerberos. Because considerable effort may be required to link existing mainframe applications and users with end users, such an approach requires a strong commitment from the organization.

Vulnerablilties. In some systems used to support end-user computing, problems in the design of the operating system or with the tools and functions that are bundled with the system have resulted in security vulnerabilities. For example, UNIX administrators have reported compromises of system integrity due to bugs in system software such as editors and main programs. These compromises have been well publicized and exploited by system crackers.

The lack of experience in effective system management has introduced other vulnerabilities. Distributed, open systems may be easier to break because they are open. UNIX source code is available, and high schools and universities teach classes on how to work with UNIX. Persons intent on breaking UNIX systems have these systems available to practice on, the ready documentation to learn a great deal about the system, and a cracker underground that can mentor their activities and provide additional insights. MVS systems, on the contrary, are not open, available, or easy to break. Although UNIX is frequently pointed to as a security problem, similar vulnerabilities can be found in many systems typically used in the end-user or distributed system environment.

The task of security then is to identify areas of risk or technical compromise and to find ways to mitigate the risk or to detect attempts to compromise the integrity of the system. The risk of outsiders penetrating system security should not be management's only concern. Insiders represent a substantial risk, because they not only have all of the knowledge that is available to the cracker community, but also understand the security environment, have increased availability to systems, and have potentially more time to attempt to break the system. Thus, an internal compromise may be more significant than an attack from outside of the organization.

Data base controls. Access to the data base represents another area of risk in a distributed environment. In mainframe systems, access paths to data are limited, and the security system can be used to control both the data and the paths. In distributed and end-user systems, data can be distributed across an enterprise. In many instances, the path to the data is expected to be controlled through the application. However, users frequently are given other software tools that can provide access through an alternate, unprotected path. For example, user access to data may be defined within client software provided on their systems. Controls may be menu driven or table driven. At the same time, users may be provided with interactive SQL products that can be used to define SELECTS and other data base operations. If the data base is implemented on top of the system level, and if access is provided through a listener port that will acquiesce to any request, users may have the ability to access, modify, and write anything to the data base.

Network and Communications Controls

Access path controls also need to be implemented at the network level. In many environments, various access paths are used, each with different security characteristics and levels of control. One path may be intended for after-hour employee access. Another may be developed to provide system manager access for trouble shooting and testing. Vendors and support personnel may have an entirely different path. In addition, individual users may implement their own access path through internal modems using remote communication software such as PC Anywhere.

Multiple and inconsistent paths can create an opportunity for system compromise. Some paths might not be effectively monitored, so if a compromise were to occur, security and system management might not be aware of the condition.

Access path controls. To help ensure the integrity of the network, it is best to provide only limited access points. This helps both in detecting unauthorized access attempts and in correcting problems. Different levels of access may require different levels of security. Because system support personnel will be operating at the system level, they may require the use of one-time passwords. Individual users may be given multiple-use passwords if their access is not considered to be a significant security risk and if monitoring and detection controls are effective.

Access path schematic. If multiple access paths are provided, the cost of security may not be consistent with the risks or the risks may not be effectively controlled to support business protection requirements. To identify where control reliance is placed and the consistency of controls across an environment, an access path schematic should be used. This schematic depicts users; the path that they take to system resources, including data; control points; and the extent of reliance on controls. Often, it shows control points where major reliance is placed or where the control is inappropriate and the level of reliance is inconsistent with the general security architecture.

Some users (e.g., network support) may employ several diverse access paths, including dial-in access, Internet access, or private network access, depending on the type of maintenance or diagnostic activities that are required. For system and application access, reliance is placed at the control level on the use of shared identifiers and passwords. Routers that are accessed by network support may have two levels of access provided, one that permits modification of router tables and another that permits only read access to this information. This could represent a significant security vulnerability, in particular when certain routers are used as firewalls between the Internet and the internal network.

External users are provided with dial-back access to the network. At each level of access through the application, they are required to enter individual user identifiers and passwords, user authentication is performed, and an access decision is made. This may be a burden for the users and could provide ineffective security, in particular when password format and change interval requirements are not consistent. An excessive number of passwords, frequent changes, and a perception on the part of users that security is too restrictive may lead to writing passwords down, selecting trivial passwords, or using other measures that weaken the level of security.

Application and Process Controls

The last component of confidentiality and integrity controls is involved with applications and processes. Because end-user computing is generally highly integrated into the management of a business function, security solutions need to address not only the technology but also the process. Application development controls need to be consistent with the type and extent of development activity within the end-user area. At a minimum, spreadsheets and other business tools should be documented and the master preserved in a secure location. It may be appropriate to take master copies off-site to ensure their integrity and recovery.

Work flow management software can be used to protect the integrity of processes. This software is generally a middleware system that allows management to develop rules that define what is expected or the limits imposed on a process, as well as to create graphical images that define the process flow. For example, work flow rules can be developed that establish the organization's purchase authorization limits. If a purchase order exceeds the defined limit, the process flow will control what happens to the transaction and will automatically route it to the user with the appropriate signature authority. Through work flow management software, processes can be controlled, end-user solutions can be tightly integrated into business functions, and effective integrity controls can be ensured throughout the process.

CONTINUITY CONTROLS

Because much of the data and processing capability is distributed in end-user computing environments, continuity controls need to be distributed across an organization if systems are to be adequately protected. Centralized solutions for continuity may not be acceptable. Servers may be backed up by a centralized administration group, but this may not adequately protect work in progress or work that is completed on the user's workstation.

In some instances, network backup strategies have been developed to periodically back up the user's workstation. This can be a costly undertaking given the number of workstations and the size of local disk drives. However, with the availability of higher bandwidth networks, compression algorithms, and a strategy of periodically backing up only modified files, a centrally controlled process may be effective in such cases.

In many organizations, the risk of business disruption is not in the mainframe environment but in the systems that have been distributed across an enterprise. End-user computing systems need to be considered when the recovery and continuity strategy for an enterprise, and in particular the business function, is developed. Plans need to be developed to address the criticality of end-user systems to each business function and to determine the best approach to recovering these systems as defined by their importance to the overall enterprise.

CONCLUSION

End-user computing represents a significant departure from traditional data processing. It also represents a unique opportunity to integrate confidentiality, integrity, and continuity with business processes and with the use of information within business units. The following are the confidentiality, integrity, and continuity efforts that should be considered in the context of end-user computing:

- *Establish an enterprisewide information protection policy.* Because information and technology are distributed, responsibility for protecting information also needs to be distributed. A policy should define individual and organizational responsibility for protecting information, the classes of information that need to be protected, and the nature of the protection controls that are required. In addition, the policy should express management's concern for information protection and should provide the basic structure for achieving its goals.

- *Develop a management structure for information protection.* The role of traditional security organizations needs to change to support end-user computing environments. Security needs to be less involved with directly administering access control and more involved with designing controls. Protection management may need to be supported by an enterprisewide committee to represent technical groups as well as users' organizations. The security committee should be chaired by the security manager and should be responsible for managing changes to the protection policy and its implementation throughout the enterprise.

- *Develop appropriate technical components.* An appropriate technical architecture needs to be developed to support the distinct protection requirements of end-user computing. The use of new technologies, increased dependence on networks, easy access to data, and the challenge of protecting end-user-developed applications must be addressed. From a network standpoint, external access points need to be consolidated for better manageability and increased control. Authentication and monitoring controls need to be implemented at the boundary point between the external and internal networks. Access paths to data need to be identified, and all access paths should be secured to the same level. Application development and change control processes need to be adjusted to reduce integrity and continuity risks. Within the end-user environment, controls must be implemented to ensure that access is authorized, that users can be authenticated, and that responsibility for individual actions can be assigned. Auditability controls, to help ensure that unauthorized actions can be detected, also need to be in place. New software solutions, including workforce management middleware solutions, may be used to help ensure that sensitive business processes are effectively controlled.

- *Provide an execution and feedback mechanism.* The end-user computing environment is characterized by rapid and frequent change. The systems that users have available, the software that can be used, and the utilities that can be purchased change daily. To manage change and to provide consistency and control, a means needs to be developed to detect changes either in business processes or requirements or in the technology or its use within an enterprise. To be effective, confidentiality, integrity, and continuity need to be considered in advance of change and throughout the life cycle.

Chapter 43
Reviewing End-User Applications

Steven M. Williford

IN MOST ORGANIZATIONS, sophisticated end users are building their own applications. This trend began with computer-literate end users developing simple applications to increase their personal productivity. End-user applications development has since evolved to include complex applications developed by groups of users and shared across departmental boundaries throughout the organization. Data from these applications is used by decision makers at all levels of the company.

It is obvious to most end-user computing and IS managers that applications with such organizationwide implications deserve careful scrutiny. However, they are not always familiar with an effective mechanism for evaluating these applications. The method for reviewing end-user-developed applications discussed in this chapter can provide information not only for improving application quality but for determining the effectiveness of end-user computing (and end-user computing support) in general.

A review of user-developed applications can indicate the need for changes in the end-user computing support department and its services as well as in its system of controls. In addition, such a review can provide direction for strategic planning within the organization and is a valuable and helpful step in measuring the effectiveness of end-user computing support department policies and procedures. Auditors might also initiate an audit of end-user applications as part of a continuous improvement or total quality management program being undertaken in their organization.

End-user computing or IS managers should also consider performing a review of end-user applications as a proactive step toward being able to justify the existence of the end-user computing support department. For example, a review may reveal that some end-user applications contribute heavily to increased productivity in the workplace. In an era marked by budget cuts and downsizing, it is always wise to be able to point out such triumphs.

DEFINITIONS AND CHARACTERISTICS

Each organization may use a different set of definitions to describe various aspects of end-user computing support, and it is important to have a common understanding of the terms to be used. The following definitions are used in this chapter.

- *Application.* An application is a set of computer programs, data, and procedures that is used to resolve a business-specific problem. For example, the accounting department may develop and implement an application that generates profit-and-loss statements.
- *Product.* Products are the software used to develop or assist in the development of computer systems. Examples are spreadsheets, word processors, fourth-generation languages (4GLs), CASE tools, or graphics packages. Tools is another common term for product.
- *System.* A system is a combination of computer applications, processes, and deliverables. During a review of end-user applications, it is important to determine the fit of the application within the system. An example is a budget system in which individual managers collect data from individuals using a manual process (e.g., paper forms), transfer the data to spreadsheets, and then electronically transmit the information to the accounting department, which consolidates the information and uses a budget forecasting application to create reports for senior management.
- *Work group.* This is a group that performs a common business function, independent of organizational boundaries, and is tied together by a system or process. The managers who collect data for the budget system make up a work group; they may all report to different managers in different departments, and each person is probably in more than one work group. Other work groups include project development and training.
- *Work unit.* This term is used for such organizational units as departments, divisions, or sections (e.g., accounting, human resources, and engineering). An application typically resides in a work unit (i.e., is run by that unit) but affects other units throughout the organization.

It is also important to review the unique characteristics of the end-user computing environment as they relate to user-developed applications:

- *Point of control.* In an end-user computing environment, the person using the application has either developed the application or is typically closer to the developer organizationally.
- *The critical nature of applications.* End-user applications tend to be valued less and are often not developed under the strict guidelines of traditional IS applications. Because of this, the impact of the application's

being in error or not working at all is often not considered until it is too late.

- *Range of measuring criticality and value.* End-user applications may range from trivial to mission critical. Applications created by IS have a much narrower range but are concentrated toward the critical end of the scale.
- *Development.* In an end-user computing environment, the people who handle any one application may be scattered organizationally; the applications may also be scattered over time and across products. For example, an application may originally be developed on a word processing package. If the math requirements for the application become too complicated, the application would be transferred to a spreadsheet product. Finally, the application may be converted to a data base product to handle complex reporting requirements.
- *Quantity of applications.* There are more applications developed by end users than by the IS department, but they are usually smaller in scope and more tuned to individual productivity.
- *Type of products.* End-user development products usually provide a group of standard functions (e.g., Lotus 1-2-3 provides built-in functions). Creating a complex application using these products may require a high degree of knowledge about the development product or may necessitate using several development products to create a single application.

OVERCOMING MISCONCEPTIONS

In some organizations, senior IS management initiates a review on behalf of user managers who may be concerned that their applications are getting away from them. In these cases, the end-user computing support department managers may be asked to help sell the idea to corporate managers. In most organizations, gaining any management commitment to reviewing end-user applications requires overcoming several obstacles. The following sections discuss common management objections to reviewing end-user applications and ways to overcome this mind-set.

End-user applications are not significant. This is a typical misconception on the part of either corporate managers or senior IS managers. End-user applications may be perceived as transient, disposable, and not production oriented — therefore, not significant. Traditional applications that are run by the IS department and cannot be tampered with in any way by anyone other than a technical expert are viewed as much more substantial, stable, and worthwhile. Senior management may be unwilling to approve an investment in reviewing what they perceive to be insignificant applications. To change this viewpoint and bring them up to date, end-user computing managers should make the effort to point out particular end-user-developed applications that are currently providing critical data or contributing more concretely to improved productivity and increased bottom-line benefits.

Ease of use results in effective applications. This is another common misconception of senior management and IS management. They may believe that the ease of use of end-user applications development products would prevent users from creating anything but the most effective applications. Again, managers would be reluctant to spend resources on reviewing applications that they feel are typically well created. This misconception has been amplified by sales promotions that vigorously emphasize the ease of use of these products. IS managers should point out to senior managers that development products have limitations and that ease of use not only cannot guarantee that applications do what they were intended to do but can contribute to end users creating unnecessary applications and duplicating effort.

The end users will not cooperate with the review. This is a common objection of user management and their employees. IS managers should promote the concept of an informal reviewing method (e.g., an inventory or statistics review, both of which are discussed in a later section) that would be less of an imposition on end users and, therefore, less of a threat to those users who are very protective of their current work processes.

In some organizations, end users react to a review of their applications in much the same way they would react to an audit of their personal finances by the IRS — that is, they view it as a hassle and something they would like to avoid at all costs, regardless of whether they feel they have anything to hide (e.g., pirated software). If this is the case, the IS department might want to consider setting up self-audit guidelines with the cooperation of the users, or have them participate in the first central review. Review guidelines explain what the review team will be looking for. When end users know what to expect and have a chance to evaluate their own applications using the same criteria the reviewers will be using, they are typically far more willing to cooperate with the actual review. In addition, involving them in the review can alleviate an us-versus-them attitude.

PREPARING FOR THE REVIEW

The reviewing process follows a life cycle similar to that of any other project. The steps discussed in this chapter cover preparation for a review; they provide the background necessary to begin a review. These steps are designed as a general guideline. Not all companies may need all the steps, and early reviews (undertaken when end-user development is still relatively new to the organization) will usually not follow all the steps. Preparing for a review requires:

- Defining the review objectives.
- Defining the review method.
- Defining the scope and content of the review.

Each of these is discussed in the following sections and summarized as follows:

Define Review Objectives. The audit may be designed to:

- Determine, identify, or resolve end-user applications problems.
- Evaluate end-user computing support group services.
- Respond to financial issues.
- Collect specific information.
- Provide input to strategic or long-range planning.

Define the Review Method. Four of the most effective methods are:

- Formal audit.
- Inventory.
- Statistical review.
- Best guess review.

Define the Scope and Content of the Review. Determining the scope and content helps:

- Define what the end-user computing department will consider as end-user computing.
- Define which environments a particular review will evaluate.

Defining Review Objectives. Review objectives help determine the results and essentially guide the process by defining the intent of the review. IS and user managers should define and agree to the objectives before proceeding. In general, reviews are more successful if they focus on a particular objective. For example:

Once it has been established that a review of end-user applications would be helpful or even necessary in a particular organization, careful preparation for conducting the review should begin. Although some more informal reviews may not require all the steps discussed in this chapter, for the most part, each step is an important and necessary component of a successful review (i.e., one that provides useful and valuable information). The following is a checklist of these steps:

Define Review Objectives

The audit may be designed to:

- Determine, identify, or resolve end-user applications problems.
- Evaluate end-user computing support group services.
- Respond to financial issues.
- Collect specific information.
- Provide input to strategic or long-range planning.

Define the Review Method

Four of the most effective methods are:

- Formal audit.
- Inventory.
- Statistical review.
- Best-guess review.

Define the Scope and Content of the Review

Determining the scope and content helps:

- Define what the end-user computing department will consider as end-user computing.
- Define which environments a particular review will evaluate.

Exhibit 43.1. Steps to prepare for end-user computing audit.

- *Determine, identify, or resolve end-user applications problems.* This common objective ensures that the review will provide answers to such questions as:
  - Is there a problem with end-user applications (i.e., are particular applications proving to be error-prone, duplicating effort, or providing inaccurate data)?
  - What is the exact problem with a particular application (i.e., why is the application providing inaccurate data)?
  - How can this problem be solved? For example, what can be done to make this application more effective, or should a better set of checks and balances be implemented to validate end-user applications? A better set of checks and balances might involve comparing the results of an end-user application that reports sales volume by region to the results of a traditional IS application that tracks the same information.
  - What are the consequences of ignoring the flaws in this application?
  - Who should fix this application?

— Is it worth the cost to fix the application, or should use of the application be discontinued? For example, end users might create an application that automates the extraction and compilation of sales data from a larger system. The cost of maintaining or repairing such a system could be prohibitive if the data from the larger system could just as easily be compiled using a calculator.

- *Evaluate end-user computing support group services.* When there are complaints from the user areas (i.e., users may feel that they are not getting enough support to develop effective applications) or when the end-user computing department takes on new levels of support, it may consider a review of end-user applications to help them evaluate current services. For example, such a review can reveal a large number of error-prone or ineffective applications, which would indicate a need for more development support. The review might reveal that a number of users are duplicating applications development efforts or are sharing inaccurate data from one application. Users may have developed applications that are inappropriate or inadequate for solving the problems they were designed to address. Any of these scenarios would indicate an increased need for support of end-user applications development. Typical questions to be answered with this objective are:
  — Can the services be improved?
  — Should new services be added?
  — Should services be moved to or from another group of end users?
  — Are resources being allocated effectively (i.e., is the marketing department the only user group without any productivity-increasing applications)?

- *Respond to financial issues.* This objective can provide pertinent information if budget cuts or competition within IS for resources threatens the end-user computing support department. A review of user-developed applications may lend credence to the need for end-user computing support of the development and implementation of valuable computer applications by pointing out an application that may be saving a great deal of time and money in a particular user area. A review with this objective provides information similar to the answers provided when evaluating services in the objective; however, the information is then used to answer such questions as:
  — Can the end-user computing support group be reduced or eliminated?
  — Can the services to user-developers be reduced?
  — Can some budgetary efficiencies be gained in supporting end-user applications development?

- *Collect specific information.* Corporate or IS management may request information about end-user applications, especially if they receive data from them on a regular basis or if (as in applications run in the payroll department) many people would be affected by an inaccurate application. It is also not unlikely that user management would request an investigation of end-user applications in their area. Both of these cases are more common in companies that are committed to a continuous improvement or total quality program.

- *Provide input to strategic or long-range planning.* A review with this objective would highlight much of the same information found in a review to evaluate services or respond to financial issues but would add a more strategic element to the process. For example, this objective would answer such questions as:
  — Do end-user applications contribute to accomplishing corporate goals?
  — Are there end-user applications that might create strategic opportunities if implemented on a broader scale?
  — Are resources adequate to initiate or foster development of end-user applications that might eventually contribute to achieving strategic goals?

Defining the Review Method

The methods of collecting data should be determined by the political climate, the people who will act on the results of the audit, and the resources available to perform the work. The following sections discuss five of the most common and effective methods for reviewing end-user applications and examine the most appropriate instances for using each of them.

Formal audit. This method for auditing end-user applications is usually selected if the audit is requested by corporate management. They may be concerned about applications that are built to provide financial information or about the possibility of misconduct associated with user applications. Because most organizations are audited in a financial sense, corporate and user management are familiar with the process and the results of a less formal method. However, a formal audit is more expensive and often more upsetting to the participants (e.g., the end users).

Inventory. Taking an inventory of end-user applications involves gathering information about the products and applications on each workstation. Although an inventory is a less formal variation of an audit and may be perceived by corporate and senior IS management as less significant than a formal audit, it provides much of the same information as a formal audit. An inventory can be useful when the information will be used for improving the user environment, preparing for later, more formal audits, or providing feedback to management. The end-user computing support department may initiate this type of review for purely informational purposes to increase support staff awareness of end-user applications development (i.e., the objective may simply be to determine the number of end-user applications or to evaluate their sophistication). Inventories can be done in less time and are less expensive than formal audits. In addition, they can easily be done by the IS department without the consultation of a professional auditor. An inventory is more low-key than a formal audit, and taking an inventory of applications is far less threatening to end users.

Statistical review. Statistical reviewing involves collecting raw data from the help desk, support logs, computer transactions, or similar sources. This method of auditing is useful only if the support department generates a statistically significant amount of readily available data. This implies a large number of applications, a large number of users, and centralized support or centrally controlled computing resources (e.g., mainframes and local area networks). A statistical review is most appropriate when minor tuning of end-user computing services is the objective. This is an extensive process that provides enough information to confirm or deny perceptions or indicate the need to change; it has a product focus, which can tell how many people are using Lotus 1-2-3 or how many are using WordPerfect. These statistics often come from LANs as users go through the network to access the product. This product focus does not provide much useful information for deciding how to change.

Best-guess review. This is the most informal type of review. When time is a critical element, a best-guess review can be performed on the basis of the existing knowledge of the end-user computing support staff. This can even be classified as a review of the IS department's impression of end-user applications. Corporate or senior IS management may request a report on end-user applications within the organization. Such a review can be useful if support people and users are centralized and the support people are familiar with the users and their applications. The IS staff can also use the results to make changes within their limits of authority. Although a best-guess review does not gather significant unbiased data, it can be surprisingly useful just to get end-user computing staff impressions down on paper.

Defining the Scope and Content of the Review

The scope defines the extent of the review and should also state specific limits of the review — that is, what is and is not to be accomplished. In most organizations and with most types of review, it may be helpful to involve users from a broad range of areas to participate in defining the scope. Knowledge of the review and involvement in the definition of the review scope by the users can be valuable in promoting their buy-in to the results.

The review may be limited to particular products, environments, a type of user, a work unit, or a specific application or system. Determining the scope and content focuses on the appropriate applications. As part of defining the scope and content of the application it is necessary to determine the types of end-user environments to be audited. This definition of environment is used to:

- Define what the IS department considers end-user computing, that is, to determine whether a particular application will actually be considered a user-developed application. For example, in some organizations a programmer's use of an end-user product to create an application would be considered end-user computing and the application would be included in a review of end-user applications. In most companies, however, applications that should be included in a review of end-user applications come from the point-of-origin, shared work unit, and work group environments. Applications in a turnover environment can also be included because, although development may be done by another group, end users work with the application on a daily basis. Each of these environment classifications is discussed at the end of this section.
- Define which environments a particular review will evaluate. For example, the application developed by the programmer using an end-user development tool would fit in the distributed environment, which is also discussed at the end of this section. However, the review might be designed to investigate only applications developed in a point-of-origin environment.

In each organization, end-user computing may consist of several environments. Each environment is defined by products, support, and resources. Although there may be a few exceptions or hybrids, an end-user computing environment can usually fit into one of the general categories discussed in the following sections.

Point-of-origin environment. In this environment, all functions are performed by the person who needs the application. This is how end-user computing began and is often the image management still has of it. These applications are generally developed to improve personal productivity. They are typically considered to be disposable — that is, instead of performing any significant maintenance, the applications are simply redeveloped. Redevelopment makes sense because new techniques or products can often make the applications more useful.

Shared environment. In a shared environment, original development of the application is performed by a person who needs the application. However, the application is then shared with other people within a work unit or work group. If any maintenance is done to the application, the new version is also distributed to the other users in the unit.

Work unit environment. In this environment, applications development and maintenance are performed by people within an organizational unit to meet a need of or increase the productivity of the work unit as a whole (unlike point-of-origin and shared applications, which are developed for the individual). The applications are usually more sophisticated and designed to be more easily maintained. They may also be developed by someone whose job responsibilities include applications development.

Work group environment. In a work group environment, applications development and maintenance are performed by people within a work group for use by others in the work group. The developer is someone who has the time and ability to create an application that fulfills an informally identified need of the work group. In most cases, the application solves problems of duration (e.g., expediting the process) not effort (i.e., productivity).

Turnover environment. In this type of environment, applications are developed by one group and turned over to another group for maintenance and maybe to a third group for actual use. There are many combinations, but some common examples are:

- The application is developed by the end-user computing support group and turned over to a work unit for maintenance and use. This combination is popular during end-user computing start-up phases and during the implementation of new product or technology.
- The application is developed and used by the end user but turned over to end-user computing support for maintenance.

Distributed environment. In a distributed environment, applications are developed and maintained by a work unit for use by others. The developing work unit is responsible for development and maintenance only. They may report to a user group or indirectly to central IS. The development products may be traditional programming products or end-user computing products. Although this is not typically considered an end-user computing environment, in some organizations the work unit is the end-user computing support group.

Centralized development and support environment. In this environment, a programming group under the direct control of central information systems develops and maintains applications for use by end users. Although centralized programming groups in some organizations may use end-user computing products for applications development, in general, applications developed in this environment are not reviewed with other end-user applications.

Reseeded environment. A common hybrid of environments occurs when a point-of-origin application becomes shared. In these instances, the people receiving the application typically fine tune it for their particular jobs using their own product knowledge. This causes several versions of the original application to exist, tuned to each user's expertise and needs. Maintenance of the original application is driven by having the expertise and time available to make alterations rather than by the need for such alterations. This reseeded application grows into another application that should be grouped and reviewed with point-of-origin applications. However, these applications should be reviewed to ensure that they are not duplicating effort. Fifteen to twenty applications may grow out of a single application. In many cases, one application customized for each user would suffice.

Determining the Application Environment

During preparation for the review, the scope and content phase helps determine which end-user environments should be included. For example, the IS staff may decide that only point-of-origin applications will be included in a particular review. The first step in actually performing the review is to identify the environment to which particular applications belong. To do this, it is necessary to isolate who performed the functions associated with the life cycle of the individual application. These functions are:

- *Needs identification.* Who decided something needed to be done, and what were the basic objectives of the application created to do that something?
- *Design.* Who designed the processes, procedures, and appearance of the application?
- *Creation.* Who created the technical parts of the application (e.g., spreadsheets, macros, programs, or data)?
- *Implementation.* Who decided when and how the implementations would proceed?
- *Use.* Who actually uses the application?
- *Training.* Who developed and implemented the training and education for the application? Typically, this is an informal and undocumented process — tutoring is the most common training method.
- *Maintenance.* Who maintains the application? Who handles problem resolution, tunes the application, makes improvements to the application, connects the application to other applications, rewrites the application using different products, or clones the application into new applications?
- *Ongoing decision making.* Who makes decisions about enhancements or replacements?

The matrix in Exhibit 43.1 matches answers to these questions with the different environments.

Evaluating Applications Development Controls

This step in performing the review provides information about the controls in effect concerning end-user applications. It should address the following questions:

- Who controls the development of the application?
- Are there controls in place to decide what types of applications users can develop?
- Are the controls enforced? Can they be enforced?

Determining Application Criticality

This checklist helps determine the critical level of specific applications:

- Does the application create reports for anyone at or above the vice-presidential level?
- Does the application handle money? Issue an invoice? Issue refunds? Collect or record payments? Transfer bank funds?
- Does the application make financial decisions about stock investments or the timing of deposits or withdrawals?
- Does the application participate in a production process; that is, does it:
  — Issue a policy, loan, or prescription?
  — Update inventory information?
  — Control distribution channels?
- What is the size of the application? The larger the application (or group of applications that form a system), the more difficult it is to manage.

Determining the Level of Security

This set of questions can help determine not only the level of security that already exists concerning end-user applications but the level of security that is most appropriate to the particular applications being reviewed. The following questions pertain to physical security:

- Are devices, work areas, and data media locked?
- Is there public access to these areas during the day?
- Is the room locked at night?
- Is access to the area monitored?
- Is there a policy or some way to determine the level of security necessary?

ENVIRONMENT \ FUNCTION	Needs Identification	Design	Creation	Implementation	Use	Training	Maintenance	Ongoing Decision Making
Point of Origin	User	User	User	User	User only	User	User	User
Shared	Original User	Original user	Original user	Original user	Original user and users with similar needs	Original user or subsequent users	Original user and subsequent users	Original user
Work Unit	Work unit expert or manager	Work unit analyst and product expert	Work unit expert	Work unit expert	Someone other than the developer	Initially by work unit expert—later by user	Work unit expert	Work unit management
Work Group	Work group	Analyst and product expert	Work group expert	Work group	Work group	Initially by work group expert—later by user	Work group expert	Work group users
Turnover	User or work unit	Developing group	Developing group	Developing group and user	User	Developer	Developing group	Work unit management
Distributed	Work unit	Developing group	Developing group	Developing group and work unit	Portion of the work unit	Developing group, work unit expert	Developing group	Work unit management
Centralized	Work unit	Developing group	Developing group	Developing group and work unit	Portion of the work unit	Developing group, work unit expert	Developing group	Work unit management

Exhibit 43.2. Environment-function matrix.

The following questions relate to the security of data, programs, and input/output and to general security:

- How is data secured? By user? By work unit? By work area? By device?
- Is the data secured within the application?
- Who has access to the data?
- Is use of the programs controlled?
- Are data entry forms, reports, or graphs controlled, filed, or shredded?
- Is there some way to identify sensitive items?

Reviewing the Use and Availability of the Product

Creating complex applications using an end-user development product often requires more product knowledge than creating them using a comparable programming language. The end-user developer may go to great lengths to get around end-user product limitations when the application could probably be created more easily using traditional programming or a different tool. The questions in the following checklist help evaluate the appropriateness of the development products in use to create specific applications:

- Are products being used appropriately? To answer this question, it is necessary to match user application needs to the tool used to create the application. This can help indicate the inappropriate use of development products (e.g., use of a spreadsheet as a word processor or a word processor as a data base).
- Is the user applying the product functions appropriately for the applications being developed or used? For example, a row and column function would not be the most effective function for an application designed to generate 10 or 15 reports using the same data but different layouts.

As part of this step, the availability of end-user applications development products should be assessed. The following questions address this issue:

- Which products are available to this user?
- Which of the available products are employed by this user?
- Are these products targeted to this user?

Reviewing User Capabilities and Development Product Knowledge

This step in conducting a review of end-user applications focuses on the end user's ability to develop applications using a particular product and to select an appropriate development product for the application being created. The questions to answer are:

- Is the user adequately trained in the use of the development product he is currently creating applications with? Is additional training necessary or available?
- Does the end user understand the development aspects of the product?
- Is the end user familiar with the process for developing applications? With development methodologies? With applications testing and maintenance guidelines?
- Has the end user determined and initiated or requested an appropriate level of support and backup for this application?
- Is the end user aware of the potential impact of failure of the application?
- Are the development products being used by this end user appropriate for the applications being developed?
- If the user is maintaining the application, does that user possess sufficient knowledge of the product to perform maintenance?

Reviewing User Management of Data

Because the data collected using end-user applications is increasingly used to make high-level decisions within the organization, careful scrutiny of end-user management of that data is essential. The following questions address this important issue:

- Is redundant data controlled?
- Is data sharing possible with this application?
- Who creates or alters the data from this application?
- Is data from traditional IS or mainframe systems — often called production data — updated by end-user applications or processes? If so, is the data controlled or verified?
- If data is transformed from product to product (e.g., from spreadsheet to data base), from type to type (e.g., HEX to ASCII), or from paper to electronic media, is it verified by a balancing procedure?
- Are data dictionaries, common field names, data lengths, field descriptions, and definitions used?
- Are numeric fields of different lengths passed from one application to another?

Reviewing the Applications

This is obviously an important step in a review of end-user applications. The following questions focus on an evaluation of the applications themselves and assess problem resolution, backup, documentation, links, and audit trails associated with these applications:

- Problem resolution:
  — Is there a mechanism in place to recognize whether an application has a problem?
  — Is there an established procedure for reporting application problems?
  — Is there a formal process in place to determine what that problem may be or to resolve or correct the problem?
  — Are these procedures being followed?

- Backup:
  — Is the application backed up?
  — Is the data backed up?
  — Are the reports backed up?
  — Is there a backup person capable of performing the activities on the application?
  — Are backup procedures in effect for support, development, and maintenance of the application?

- Documentation:
  — What documentation is required for the application? Is the application critical enough to require extensive documentation? Is the application somewhat critical and therefore deserving of at least some documentation? Is the application a personal productivity enhancer for a small task and therefore deserving of only informal or no documentation?
  — If documentation guidelines are in place, are they being followed?
  — How is the documentation maintained, stored, and updated?

- Links:
  — How are the data, programs, processes, input, output, and people associated with this application connected?
  — What is received by the application?
  — Where does the application send data, information, knowledge, and decisions?
  — Are these links documented?
- Audit trail:
  — Are the results of this application verified or cross-checked with other results?
  — Who is notified if the results of the application cannot be verified by other results?

GUIDELINES FOR IMPROVING END-USER APPLICATIONS DEVELOPMENT

Reviewing end-user applications requires that some resources (e.g., time and money) be spent. In most companies, these resources are scarce; what resources are available are often sought after by more than one group. A review of end-user applications is often low on senior management's priority list. Reducing the time it takes to collect information can greatly improve the IS department's chances of gaining approval for the review. However, reducing the need to collect information can decrease the need to conduct a review at all. This can be done by setting up and enforcing adherence to end-user applications development guidelines. It is a cost-effective way to improve the end-user applications development environment and help conserve limited resources.

To begin, general guidelines should be created and distributed before a planned review is started. The effectiveness of the guidelines can then be evaluated. The following checklist outlines some areas in which guidelines established by the IS department can improve end- user applications development:

- *Use of end-user development products.* Users should be provided with a set of hypothetical examples of appropriate and inappropriate uses of development products (i.e., which products should be used to develop which types of applications).
- *Documentation.* A checklist or matrix of situations and the appropriate documentation for each should be developed. This could also include who will review an application and whether review of the application is required or optional.
- *Support for design and development.* A quick-reference card of functions or types of problems supported by various groups can be distributed to end-user developers.
- *Responsibility and authority.* A list of responsibilities should be distributed that clearly states who owns the application, who owns the data, and who owns problem resolution.
- *Corporate computing policy.* Corporate policies regarding illegal software, freeware or shareware, and security issues should be made available to end-user developers.

One tactic to improve the quality of end-user applications development, while avoiding some of the costs in time and money of a full-fledged review, is to set up work group auditors. These people may report to a corporate auditing group or to the IS department on a regular basis concerning end-user applications development. This is particularly effective with remote users.

CONCLUSION

The increase in the number of end users developing complex applications and the corresponding reliance of decision makers at all levels of the organization on the data produced by these applications make a careful evaluation of the applications a necessary endeavor. In the current end-user environment, a failed application can seriously damage the business of the organization. To ensure that a review meets the objectives set out for it, IS managers must carefully plan the details of each aspect of the review. This chapter outlines the steps that should be taken before and during an actual review of end-user applications.

Section VIII
Quality Control and Computer Security

THE PRIMARY GOAL OF QUALITY AND SECURITY CONTROLS is to provide for an error-free, efficiently operated, and restricted-access environment for computer and network systems. The IT operations manager is responsible for providing a framework and the tools necessary to ensure an efficiently run and well-secured environment. System reliability and integrity require that enterprise systems are secured from unauthorized attack, both from within and outside the organization. The responsibility of the enterprise operations manager extends well beyond the boundaries of the IT department into the distributed computing environment that exists today.

The primary goals of a computer system and data network security program are to prevent unauthorized access to computer systems and facilities and, should unauthorized access occur, to prevent the misuse of — or damage to — computer and network assets. Chapter 44, "The Basics of Computer System and Data Network Security," discusses the security functions: avoidance, deterrence, prevention, detection, recovery, and correction, and provides examples of preventive measures in each area of risk. Complete security against unauthorized computer access, misuse, and damage is, by all practical measures, not economically feasible. Reducing and limiting such breaches, however, is achievable.

IT operations managers must also be concerned with achieving quality from IT systems and resources. IT managers must view improvement of quality as an economic necessity, because end users increasingly demand improved value in the products and services they purchase. Chapter 45, "Achieving Quality in Data Center Operations," examines how operations management can use the Malcolm Baldridge National Quality Award (MBNQA) framework to implement and execute a quality program to maximize data center productivity. The quality of data center operations is key to maximizing the effectiveness of the IT function. The MBNQA provides a framework for assessing the quality of a business function.

An important element in the quest to achieve total quality is determining the balance between the cost of investment in the product or service vs.

the cost of downtime. Chapter 46, "Evaluating Platform Reliability and Measuring Its Dollar Value," provides common definitions, dispels misconceptions, and offers tools for determining costs of downtime. Recognizing the growing importance of reliability to business, platform vendors have begun to make claims about reliability. Being able to speak the same language as the vendor is critical as the IT operations manager assesses his or her organization's computing needs and then matches these requirements to products and services offered. This is especially true with platform reliability, as continuing computer operations are critical to the organization's competitiveness.

An area where quality and security must be equally focused is computer virus protection. During the past few years, more than 4000 distinct types of computer viruses have been identified. Armed with a basic understanding of how viruses work, the IT manager can more easily identify symptoms of a virus's presence and can initiate corrective action. Chapter 47, "Understanding the Virus Threat," discusses how viruses can enter and infect the computer, symptoms associated with viruses, as well as preventive measures that minimize the threat. Computer viruses are a threat to critical corporate data and even business operations. They strike networked computers, software downloaded from bulletin boards, and data copied to diskettes.

The most publicized IT application regarding security and privacy is e-mail. As e-mail communication continues to grow by leaps and bounds, users' concerns for privacy grow by equal measure. Chapter 48, "E-mail Security and Privacy," addresses the security concerns that all organizations using e-mail should be aware of, the leading organizations setting e-mail security standards, as well as effective firewall and encryption solutions. The IT operations manager must lead the organization to adopt a strategy of strong security controls for e-mail involving the creation of firewalls for internal systems and the network, as well as incorporating detailed authentication approaches, such as passwords that expire after each use.

Threats of attack from the Internet are further explored in Chapter 49, "Internet Security and Firewall Policies." As networks become larger, expanding beyond the desktop — even beyond the walls of the organization to support telecommuters and other traveling employees — the reliability and availability of those networks and their attached systems becomes paramount. IT operations managers must implement firewall security systems to protect their organizations from external attack.

The final chapter in this section, "Improving Quality With Software Metrics," addresses the quality issues in software development and maintenance. The chapter discusses a representative sample of the available models, identifies the major life cycle models; and describes the activities, inputs, and outputs for each of these phases. This chapter also recommends several appropriate software metrics, classified as process metrics versus product metrics, to quantitatively measure and control the overall process and phase of the software life cycle.

Chapter 44
The Basics of Computer System and Data Network Security

C. Warren Axelrod

ONE PRIMARY GOAL OF A COMPUTER SYSTEM AND DATA NETWORK SECURITY PROGRAM is to prevent unauthorized access to computer systems and facilities. Another goal, should unauthorized access occur, is to prevent the misuse of, or damage to, computer and network assets. If, despite security precautions, an incident of such unauthorized access causes damage, the data security department should act immediately to recover from the intrusion and to prevent recurrence.

The complete protection of computer systems and data networks has become increasingly complex, expensive, and restrictive as computer systems move from centralized mainframes and minicomputers to distributed client-server architectures and as data networks provide broader access to an exploding population of end users. Consequently, complete protection is seldom economically justifiable. Data center and data network managers must accept some trade-offs and compromises. Although absolute protection is not feasible, the occurrences of breaches of security and damage to assets can be reduced through careful evaluation of risks and implementation of preventive measures. This chapter brings together fundamental security concepts to provide data center managers and data network managers with an overview of the data security function. Examples of preventive measures are provided for each area of risk discussed.

BASIC SECURITY FUNCTIONS

There are six basic data security functions. The first three — avoidance, deterrence, and prevention — address the organization's need to control the level of access and limit the distribution of access authority. The last three — detection, recovery, and correction — respond to unauthorized intrusions or destruction of assets.

Avoidance is the elimination of a threat to assets or the removal of assets from potential danger. Deterrence is the discouragement of behavior that threatens computer assets. Prevention is the implementation of measures to protect assets in the event of an attempted security breach.

In response to an attempted or actual security breach, detection is the deployment of means to recognize intrusion or damage and to raise an alarm during the breach. Recovery includes determining the extent of the damage and returning the system to operating condition. Correction is the introduction of new measures or the improvement of existing measures to avoid similar security breaches in the future.

SECURITY VIOLATIONS

Computer systems and data networks must be secured against three types of violations: unauthorized access, misuse, and damage.

Unauthorized access is the gaining of illicit entry — physically or electronically — to the computer facility, the system software, or the data. Misuse is the manipulation of computer and network assets against the interests of the organization, whether or not any damage results. Damage is the adverse modification or destruction of physical or electronic computer and network assets. Damage is essentially an extreme form of misuse, and whether an attempt to misuse a system results in damage is often a matter of chance. Some forms of misuse may leave a computer system or network physically and logically intact, but can cause irreparable financial damage to an organization.

Exhibit 44.1 indicates the type of violation addressed by each security measure. These measures are arranged according to the six basic security functions. The major areas of risk are discussed in the following sections.

AVOIDANCE

Avoidance is a strategy that prevents unauthorized access, misuse, and damage. The strengths and weaknesses of avoidance methods are discussed in the following sections.

Avoiding Unauthorized Access

The top row of Exhibit 44.1 illustrates how abusive access to a system or facility can be avoided by keeping potential abusers and target systems as far apart as possible. An organization should be particularly careful in its screening of individuals, such as those under consideration for employment, who might be given access to the system. Potential employees should be subject to intensive background investigations to ensure that all statements with regard to previous experience and education are accurate

Exhibit 44.1.   Security functions by type of breach.

Security Function	Avoidance	Deterrence
Unauthorized Access	• Screen employees before hiring and assigning to computer and network functions. • Locate computer and network facilities in remote or nondescript buildings. • Do not advertise locations or means of access to computer and network facilities. • Limit the number of systems accessible to users.	• Install highly visible access controls (e.g., guards and cameras). • Implement search procedures for mail, especially packages. • Implement well-monitored sign-in and sign-out procedures for facilities. • Take strong action in the event of attempted unauthorized access. • Do not disclose known weaknesses in access control.
Misuse	• Restrict availability of data, programs, and documentation. • Limit the number of copies of data programs and documentation. • Limit the number of staff members with access to systems, networks, and facilities. • Limit physical access to essential areas only. Limit knowledge on a need-to-know basis. • Limit use of systems to essential use only. • Reduce overlap of applications.	• Install very apparent measures for monitoring use of systems and networks (e.g., security software to report each use by person and type of use). • Question even small deviations from expected use patterns. • Take strong, well-publicized action for even minor infringements.
Damage	• Disperse computer and network facilities — both long-range and short-range — so that damage to one component cannot affect others. • Design software architecture and network topology with independent modules so that damage to one does not affect others. • Minimize procedural linkages to reduce the domino effect. • Expand knowledge of critical systems and networks beyond one individual.	• Use the same measures as for misuse with even stronger actions and sanctions for attempted or successful destructive activities, be they willful or negligent. • Accidental damage with no evidence of negligence should be dealt with sternly.

and complete. Several specialized firms perform independent checks and can verify statements regarding education, employment history, and criminal records. Character references should be obtained and verified. Personal impressions are also valuable; it is advisable to have several staff members meet with job candidates to obtain their impressions.

Screening Non-Employees. In addition, the screening process should extend to all non-employees who are granted access (e.g., consultants, vendor staff, service personnel and, increasingly, customers), though not to the same degree as potential employees.

In cases of personnel working for other firms, it is more reasonable to perform a check on the organization providing the service staff and to ensure, through contractual language, that the service organization takes full responsibility for its own staff. Checks on a service organization should include an investigation of that company's employee screening procedures and a review of references from companies with which the service organization has recently conducted business. It is also important to ensure that suitable confidentiality and vendor liability clauses are included in consulting and service agreements.

When customers are granted direct access to the organization's computer systems via the company's or a third party's data network, the usual credit checks and business viability verifications need to be performed. In addition, due diligence examinations to uncover any previous fraudulent customer activities should be conducted. The extent of such checks should be based on an evaluation of the magnitude of the assets at risk, the probability of recovering such assets if stolen, and an assessment of the probability that a customer would risk reputation and possible legal action if caught.

A standard security policy is that anyone who has not been screened should not be given system access. For example, frequent deliveries or pickups should be conducted in nonsensitive areas in all cases in which delivery personnel have not been screened. In addition, information regarding the location and nature of computer installations should be restricted whenever possible. Limiting the number of persons who know the systems' location and function also limits the risk of unauthorized access.

Maintaining a Low Profile. Although it is not practical to provide the kind of stringent security necessary for sensitive military facilities, it is reasonable to encourage low profiles for computer facilities and data networks. Large signs indicating the company name or the nature of the facility should certainly be avoided in all cases. Inside buildings, the organization should avoid using signs indicating the location of the data center, or can instead use signs with non-descriptive language (e.g., facilities management). The slight inconvenience caused to authorized persons is more than compensated for by the barrier put before unwelcome visitors.

Another desirable, but not always practical, approach to avoiding unauthorized access is to limit the number of computer systems and potential points of access. This reduces the number of targets and simplifies the task of protecting them. Concentrating resources in this manner, however, can increase the magnitude of a potential loss if unauthorized access were to be obtained.

From a marketing perspective, it may be desirable to advertise easy customer access to services offered on organizations' computer systems. However, the specific whereabouts of computer and network facilities should be restricted information.

Distributed Environments. Organizations have increasingly begun to distribute their computing facilities throughout the organization, sometimes situating the facilities externally, with other firms, or with individuals outside the organization (e.g., customers and business partners). This distribution limits the amount of protection that a centralized IS function can provide to the organization's computer resources. In such a distributed environment, security measures must extend to terminals, workstations, and other remote devices that are connected to the organization's central facilities, because these remote facilities are often not within the direct physical control of the organization itself. Security measures should also be applied to the links among systems and devices — not only to private and public networks, but also to network equipment and facilities.

The methods that should be used to control access to remote facilities and networks are an extension of those used for a central facility; however, the measures are more difficult to implement and manage. The difficulty of protecting physically isolated equipment is caused by the equipment's remote location — which, ironically, was originally intended to facilitate access to users.

The screening process is much more critical in a distributed environment because the number and variety of individuals with authorized access is generally much larger than for centralized systems. Not only are the users scattered around the organization, they may be employees of other firms, such as service providers and business partners, or private individuals, as with retail customers. Nevertheless, it is necessary to ensure that users who can gain authorized access to any device or network are rigorously screened. As with centralized facilities, the persons given access to remote and networked facilities should be restricted to essential uses only.

Obvious designations as to the existence and purpose of remote devices and network equipment should be avoided. Authorized users should be advised not to make any documentation available to or accessible by others with access to the physical area. In addition, they should not leave their terminals or workstations in an operating condition that would allow someone else to gain access easily.

477

Avoiding Misuse

Basically, system misuse can be avoided by restricting the activities of those who have gained or are allowed access to the system, network, or facilities. The fundamental premise of avoiding misuse is that, if the system, network, or facilities are difficult to access, some potential acts of misuse cannot occur. If the organization severely limits the number of people who can enter facilities or gain access to systems and networks and limits authorized users to necessary functions and features, they reduce the occurrences of misuse. This concept applies whether the systems are centrally located or widely dispersed. The data network exposure becomes more significant for dispersed systems.

The trend is toward much broader access to an organization's computer systems. Examples are students and staff having direct access to college computer systems, customers and suppliers connecting into companies' systems, and private citizens accessing government data. Again, the organization might be able to be somewhat selective in determining who gets access privileges, but it would appear that such restrictions are becoming less viable. The real key to avoidance of misuse is the building of impenetrable firewalls between what is available to general users and those components of the system which, if misused, do not affect the underlying systems.

Limiting the availability and accessibility of software copies, information about related systems, and overlapping application programs restricts the end users' environments to those processes in which end users have direct interest. Strict adherence to separation-of-duties policies and restricting applications by discrete functional areas also help organizations avoid the misuse of computer and network assets and facilities.

Avoiding Damage

As shown in Exhibit 44.1, some of the recommendations for avoiding damage conflict with those for avoiding access and misuse. For example, avoidance of access favors limiting the number of facilities, thereby reducing the number of targets that have to be protected. But if more systems are placed in a single facility, the probable extent of any damage is increased. IS functions, therefore, must strike a balance between the two conflicting principles. A compromise would be to operate as few facilities as is feasible, and to ensure that they are sufficiently dispersed, so that an extensive disaster (e.g., an earthquake) or regional electrical or telephone power failure is less likely to affect a number of critical facilities.

Another conflict is between limiting the employees' knowledge of systems to avoid misuse and informing employees sufficiently about the system so that one individual cannot alter the software or data to the organization's disadvantage without another being able to recognize and remedy the alteration. The avoidance of damage will reduce the potential spread of a damaging event. Consequently, data center managers and network managers should aim for as much physical, logical, and procedural separation of systems and data networks as possible, so that any damage would be contained.

DETERRENCE

The advantages and disadvantages of deterrence — the discouragement of behavior that threatens computer assets — are discussed in the following sections.

Deterring Unauthorized Access

The deterrence of attempts at unauthorized access can be achieved through a combination of highly visible warnings and well-publicized consequences. Warning notices provide obvious indications that all attempts to access a facility, system, or network will encounter the organization's rigorous screening methods. Publicized consequences let potential intruders know that any perpetrators who are apprehended will be penalized according to company policy or prosecuted to the full extent of the law.

Deterring Misuse and Damage

Controls that monitor actual use of systems after access has been gained are effective deterrents of illicit and unauthorized actions, because they increase the probability of detecting potential misusers. Monitoring actual use is complex, however, because the range of possible damaging activities is very large, whereas controlling access involves monitoring a single activity, namely, gaining entry. The actions taken against those caught attempting misuse or damage should be sufficiently severe to deter individuals contemplating similar activities.

PREVENTION

Preventing unauthorized access, misuse, and damage takes various forms. The advantages and drawbacks to each are discussed in the following sections.

Preventing Unauthorized Access

The standard method for preventing unauthorized logical access to a computer system or data network is the password sign-on procedure. This method, which is the most common and well known, is vulnerable to a knowledgeable violator, but is extremely effective against novice intruders. Although the visibility of access controls can be an effective deterrent, it is usually less effective in preventing unauthorized access. The most effective preventive measures are generally those that are hidden, as they are much more difficult to identify and break.

Increasingly, the trend is to extend access to more and more end users, many of whom — such as customers — are not under the direct control of the organization responsible for the systems. The major online services (such as America Online, Compuserve, and Prodigy) and Internet Access Providers are only too eager to grant ready access to expand their customer base, and service providers are falling over themselves to offer their wares over these services. In such a situation, the goal must be to control access rather than to prevent it. In the past, banks sent out millions of unsolicited credit cards without careful analysis of potential customers' credit-worthiness, and bad debts skyrocketed. To some extent, the online services and access providers are doing much the same by blanketing the population with disks and offers of free service. In reality, the risk is not of the same order as with credit cards, but there is the potential for fraud and worse. The service providers have come up with methods to limit their potential exposure; for example, by obtaining a credit card number in advance so that services can be billed with relative assurance that they will be paid for.

It is when money transactions begin to take place over these networks that the real need for security and control comes to the fore, and significant efforts are being made to ensure secure and fraud-free money transactions. Realistically, such transactions are not much different from the millions of transactions that take place each day over telephone lines, except that, as the human element is replaced by computer-based services, there is a greater need to have systems and procedures to protect against unauthorized transactions.

Completely preventing unauthorized access to communications networks can be particularly difficult to achieve technically. Networks using dedicated private lines are the most readily protected because at least the end equipment can be guarded physically, and dedicated lines provide less opportunity for an unauthorized person to gain access. Public telephone lines are the most vulnerable because essentially anyone can attempt to dial in. Some techniques (e.g., callback systems, which break the connection and dial back the end user at a specific number) provide somewhat greater security, but are complex and relatively costly. Most of these techniques are highly restrictive of computer facilities' normal operations and therefore are often undesirable. Nevertheless, many of the most highly publicized computer break-ins have been accomplished over public networks, which suggests that some technical measures should be taken to restrict access and to ensure that only authorized users are allowed to use the systems.

In addition, it is advisable to limit both the physical and logical points of access. This not only allows better monitoring and control, but can greatly reduce the cost of protection. Whatever access controls are in place, provisions should be made for backup in the event that one method fails as a result of staff unavailability, power or equipment failure, or negligence.

Preventing Misuse and Damage

Preventing misuse of and damage to a computer system or data network after an intruder has gained access depends on the system's or network's ability to isolate and control potentially damaging functions. Such prevention measures include security software that allows only authorized personnel to access, change, or copy specific data and programs.

Networks are particularly vulnerable to misuse and damage because they present difficulty in protecting components and communications media from access. One way to prevent misuse of the data carried on a network is to use encryption. The computer industry has devoted a great deal of work to encryption techniques, which code the messages transmitted through the network. The encrypted messages can be understood only when decoded with a key; while encrypted, the data is meaningless to those lacking the key. Access to the key must be restricted to authorized persons. There has been considerable controversy surrounding encryption, as the U.S. government has been advocating a method using the so-called "Clipper" chip, whereby government agencies can have access to the keys for all public and private communications.

Aside from physical damage, network equipment can be rendered useless if the switch settings are changed or, as such devices become more sophisticated and software controlled, if the programs are deleted or modified. In some cases, the same types of security access measures that are available for computer systems are also available for high-end communications devices.

Logical security measures should be backed up to guard against accidental or deliberate destruction of the primary system, and they should be installed on backup systems to ensure security if a disaster backup plan is invoked.

DETECTION

Detection methods have their strengths and weaknesses, as discussed in the following sections.

Detecting Unauthorized Access

Access controls are not foolproof. Given that breaches do occur, misuse or damage to the system can be prevented if intrusions are detected. A variety of techniques can be employed for detecting physical or logical access.

Physical Access. Common detection systems for physical access to facilities include video cameras connected to television monitors and videocassette records at guards' desks. Such systems are common in banks, offices, metropolitan apartment buildings, and stores selling valuable products or located in dangerous areas. The very presence of such systems may be a deterrent to potential intruders because it is clear that offenders could be identified through the videotape. In darkened areas, where standard video cameras may not work, other technologies (e.g., infrared or ultrasonic cameras and sensors) can record or detect intrusions.

Logical Access. Remote or local logical access to a computer system or data network can be detected and sometimes traced using the various software packages that check and record all attempts to gain logical access to systems and networks and warn of any unauthorized or atypical attempts. Security programs are available separately or as options with other software from computer and communications equipment manufacturers and software vendors.

Detecting Misuse

System misuse can be difficult to detect because perpetrators may not leave any easily detected evidence, especially if they have changed nothing (i.e., databases may be accessed, read, and copied, but not modified). Because of this detection problem, a category of EDP audit software has been designed to monitor attempted system misuse. Such software can detect and report unauthorized attempts to access programs and data, as well as determine whether the system has been used in unauthorized ways. Audit software has traditionally been available for mainframes and large networks and is now available for local area networks connecting microcomputers, workstations, and network and file servers.

Previously, organizations expressed little interest in acquiring software to detect unauthorized access to, and misuse of, microcomputer-based systems. It was believed that physical controls (e.g., locks and keys) and logical controls (e.g., passwords) were adequate. Highly publicized computer virus attacks, however, have raised organizations' awareness that, even when physical access is prevented, a virus can be introduced into a system from a diskette or communications line. Several available software packages are designed to detect such misuse and remove its cause.

Detecting Damage

Software can also help determine whether misuse of the system has caused damage to programs or data. In general, such programs and procedures are invoked when an access attempt is known to have been made or when there is a suspicion that someone has been tampering with the programs or data.

Routine software checks should ensure that updated versions of the programs have not been installed after the last official installation date, that unauthorized programs or versions of programs are not present, and that no programs are missing which should have been installed. If any of these situations occur, all production programs should be reloaded from a protected source as soon as possible. Copies of earlier versions of all production programs should be retained in a secure place for restoration purposes.

These procedures, however, often do not detect computer viruses, which can remain dormant and, therefore, undiscovered until they are triggered into action. There is also a real danger that earlier versions of programs contain viruses. Unless a virus announces its existence, damage (e.g., lost data) may be blamed on such other causes as hardware failure or operator error. If an incident of damage cannot be fully explained, the data center manager or data network manager should be aware of the possibility that viruses may be present and should seek to remove them.

Mechanisms within the application programs should check the integrity of the data on a continuing basis. For example, such mechanisms should determine whether any change in the number of items or bytes in a data file or database is consistent with the number added or subtracted by any process. There should be a check to ensure that, if a file or database has been closed and then opened some time later, the number of items in the file or database has not changed during an inactive interim period. Although these are relatively simple tests, they can be effective in detecting damage. A more complete test of each system component is extremely time-consuming and expensive and is usually reserved for instances in which personnel are relatively certain that damage has occurred. In such cases, the intent of the process is to determine the nature and extent of the damage rather than its occurrence.

Frequently, damage to programs or data is detected only by chance, such as when a previously stable process does not complete successfully or when users discover that some information produced by the system is incorrect or inconsistent. In such cases, it is necessary to quickly determine whether the aberration is due to error, misinterpretation, or damage.

For the physical protection of facilities, a range of detection devices is available for smoke, fire, flooding, and other physical threats. Such devices, however, only signal the presence of an active, readily detectable, damaging agent. In general, they do not detect preliminary damage that might lead to fires or flooding (i.e., the slow deterioration of materials or structural decay). Such damage can be detected early only through a program of regular inspections and tests by experts.

RECOVERY

Should the worst happen and damage occurs, a data center's ability to recover is of critical importance.

Recovering from Unauthorized Access

If the access security controls are damaged during an attempted breach — whether or not the attempt succeeds — it is vital to reinstitute security control quickly. For example, if a door lock is destroyed during a break-in, it must be quickly replaced to eliminate the vulnerability resulting from an unlockable door. At the very least, the previous access controls should be restored. If the break-in indicates deficiencies in the previous mechanisms, however, they should be modified, as described in the section on correcting access-control deficiencies.

Recovery from Misuse and Damage

A recovery process should bring the misused or damaged system back to its condition before the event occurred that caused the damage. If the misuse or damage continues, measures must be instituted immediately to halt the abuse, even if they are only interim measures. A contingency plan should be written, tested, and periodically reviewed before any damaging event ever takes place, so that the organization is fully equipped to enact effective recovery procedures.

CORRECTION

There are several issues concerning corrections measures.

Correcting Access-Control Deficiencies

If unauthorized access occurs, the controls in place are either inadequate or inadequately enforced. In such cases, changes must be made to the access controls or procedures to ensure that the same type of unauthorized access can be prevented in the future.

To some extent this is "closing the barnyard door after the horse has fled." However, it may also be construed as recognition of the fact that the competition is ongoing between security methods and those motivated to break them. No sooner is a more sophisticated security method created than someone is working on a method to break it. This results in a continuous escalation of security measures. Often, an organization does not realize that its security measures have been outwitted until an actual break-in occurs.

RECOMMENDED COURSE OF ACTION

Among the options available to data center and network managers, preventive security measures are the most effective. They may prevent access by unauthorized users or prevent authorized users from causing damage through negligence. An effective overall security program should include controls and procedures for handling all phases of a potential security breach.

When initiating a security program for a particular system or network, data center and network managers should define the system security according to the estimated value of resources to be protected, the most vulnerable routes for access or damage to resources, and the feasibility of protecting those routes without severely compromising the primary functions of the system. This chapter defines all possible areas in which security can be implemented to prevent damage. The guidelines defined here should be modified and implemented according to the requirements of a particular system.

Chapter 45
Achieving Quality in Data Center Operations
Jeff Murrell

IMPROVING QUALITY IS AN ECONOMIC NECESSITY, because customers increasingly demand improved value in the products and services they purchase. In addition, corporate profitability demands 100 percent productivity for every dollar the corporation spends. Improving quality is free, because it reduces the costs of rework, service, and replacement. High quality results in improved customer perception of value, which also reduces costs.

Corporations need effective information services to compete, and data center managers are feeling the brunt of today's competitive environment. Data center management is competing with outsourcers, who are winning over the data center function. Only through high-quality operations can the advances of the outsourcers be staved off.

Both internal and external data center customers are becoming increasingly computer literate. As a result, they are increasing demands for availability, capability, cost effectiveness, and quality. To satisfy these requirements, the data center, its suppliers, and its customers must develop a partnership.

Individual data center staff members also feel the need to improve quality. In general, staff members need to feel a level of personal satisfaction from their work and the quality of service they provide to customers. They also know that their professional success and security depends in large part on the ability of their organization to remain competitive.

This chapter examines how these needs for improving the quality of data center operations can be met through the MBNQA framework. Established in 1987 to foster quality in U.S. industry, the award was named after the former secretary of the commerce department, Malcolm Baldridge. It is

Exhibit 45.1. Malcolm Baldridge Quality Award evaluation categories.

	Points
Leadership	90
Information and Analysis	75
Strategic Quality Planning	55
Human Resource Development and Management	140
Process Management	140
Business Results	250
Customer Focus and Satisfaction	250
Total	1000

administered by the NIST and the American Society for Quality Control and is awarded each year by the president.

THE MALCOLM BALDRIDGE QUALITY AWARD

The award was created to promote awareness and understanding of total quality, to foster improvement in performance, and to promote the sharing of quality practices among businesses. Any company having more than 50 percent of its employees or assets, or both, in the U.S., or any division of such a company that makes more than 50 percent of its revenue from outside customers, can compete for the award. Every year, the award is given to no more than two winners in each of the following categories:

- Manufacturing
- Service
- Small Business

The award is won by companies that have exceeded a certain benchmark level of quality. The award committee examines not only how a contestant plans for quality, but also how the contestant implements a total quality plan and the plan's results. Contestants are evaluated in 24 areas addressed in the seven categories listed in Exhibit 45.1. A contestant may be awarded up to 1000 points, and the largest share of points can be won in the customer focus and satisfaction category. This point system underscores the fact that a satisfied customer is the proof of a contestant's commitment to total quality.

Award winners can use the award in their marketing strategy. In winning the award, however, they are required to share their techniques with others. This chapter examines how techniques used by previous winners for achieving total quality can be applied to data center operations. One technique that all winners have in common is that they continuously look for new areas for improvement. The next time they apply for the award, they will be expected to improve on their previous winning score.

THE ROLE OF THE DATA CENTER MANAGER

Data center management must set the overall climate for quality. One way to establish this climate is to promote the following:

- *Customer focus.* Everyone in the data center has a customer, and it is the customer who, by defining the requirements to be met, defines total quality. The data center manager should promote customer awareness by actively encouraging contact with customers in order to understand requirements and to communicate the results of quality improvement.
- *Continuous improvement.* Quality is not attained by being satisfied with the status quo. For example, 99 percent systems availability or two-second response time are no longer adequate. These may be acceptable milestones in a quality improvement program, but the ultimate goal must be 100 percent quality as defined by the customer.
- *Involving all staff members.* Management must ensure that all employees have the opportunity to express their suggestions and ideas for achieving quality.

Data center operations managers must look at quality as a discipline and keep current with changes in this discipline. They can accomplish this by attending trade conferences, reading relevant literature, and networking with colleagues to share and learn quality practices.

Managers must also implement a program that defines metrics by which data center operations can be measured and reported. Once measurements are obtained, they can be compared to other companies to establish areas for special focus. This process is known as benchmarking and is discussed in a later section of this chapter.

Data center operations managers should also promote total quality outside the organization. The MBNQA committee examines how the top management of contestant companies promote quality beyond their own organizations. Data center managers can be ambassadors of quality to their suppliers and customers. It is equally important for data center managers to communicate the message of quality to senior management and let it be known that achieving quality is a goal of the data center.

ASSESSING QUALITY

Assessing quality is one step in the MBNQA framework. When assessing data center performance, data center managers must measure quality and not quantity. For example, a given data center contains 500 MIPS (million instructions per second) of computing power and 2T bytes of direct access storage, processes a million transactions a day, and prints 10 million pages of laser output a month. These quantitative metrics gauge the size of the center's operations and could be used to select a comparison group for benchmarking. However, these metrics do not assess the quality of the operations.

Such metrics as percent availability, cycle time, and price provide a qualitative view. It is important that data center managers use metrics that their customers can understand. It may be useful to measure systems availability, for instance, but it is more valuable to be able to measure availability of an application to its end users. Such a metric might include not only systems availability, but also the availability of the applications database, of the network connection to the customer, and of the terminal used to access the application. Price is also a valid qualitative metric if it is cost-based and stated in terms the customer can understand. For example, cost per accounts-payable-invoice-processed relates more to business value than a cost in terms of inquiry task time and I/O.

After a set of metrics has been chosen and the quality of the center's operations has been measured, the measurements should be compared. A comparison to customer expectations will yield information that can be used to decide if the appropriate set of metrics has been chosen and if performance is approaching requirements. A formal customer survey may be conducted, or simple one-to-one interviews with key customer representatives can be used as a general guide.

Comparisons to other organizations often provide the impetus for improvement and can identify areas that should be improved. Comparison with peers and MBNQA winners is valuable, but can be arduous in terms of arranging schedules and ensuring that the same categories are being compared. Competitions held by publishers and other industry groups allow a unique opportunity for comparison. The most authoritative assessment, however, comes from a formal benchmarking effort.

Assessment Tools

Several tools aid in presenting information in a clear and concise way, and these tools should be used in the quality assessment. These tools include:

- *Bar graphs.* These are often used to make comparisons. They can also be used effectively in dealing with suppliers to compare performance against the competition.
- *Pie charts.* These are useful in presenting a point-in-time analysis (e.g., an analysis of which applications are creating console message traffic, or of the breakdown of tape-library activity).
- *Line graphs.* These are effective for showing results over a period of time.
- *Pareto charts.* Named after their inventor, Vilfredo Pareto, these charts are effective for showing the causes of a problem in descending order of their frequency. Pareto postulated that the top 20 percent of causes usually account for 80 percent of a problem. Exhibit 45.2 presents a sample Pareto chart.

Help Desk Calls			Batch Abends	
Subject	**Percentage**	**Code**	**Reason**	**Percentage**
Security	10	SOFF	Dataset Missing	5
PWS Software	9	SOC7	Data Exception	5
Datacom	6	SOFF	Unable to Allocate	4
LAN	5	U1500	DB on/off Condition	4
EDI	5	U0888	Tape/Disk Error	4
Voice	4	S04E	DB2	4
Help Desk	4	S322	Time-Out	4
Consulting	3	S004	BDT, EDI	4
PWS Order	3	SB37	Disk Space	3
Other	20	SD37	File Full	2

Exhibit 45.2. Sample Pareto chart.

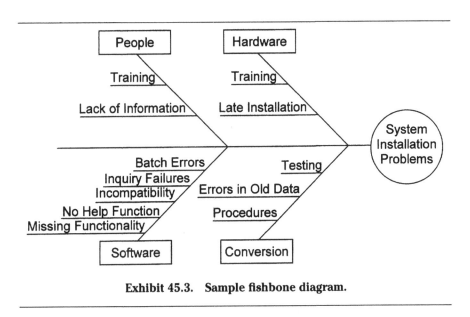

Exhibit 45.3. Sample fishbone diagram.

- *Fishbone diagrams.* These can be used by quality teams to understand and categorize causes of low quality to identify areas that require more focused attention. Exhibit 45.3 shows a sample fishbone diagram.

BENCHMARKING

Companies such as Real Decisions Inc., Compass Corp., and Nolan Norton conduct benchmarking studies of data center operations and compare the results of the studies to those of other customers. If a data center participates in a formal benchmark study, the following guidelines should be followed:

491

- *Allocating sufficient time.* Gathering input for the study is a dedicated effort that may require days or weeks. It is important to spend quality time.
- *Working with the benchmarker.* Data center managers should work with those conducting the study to ensure that the data they provide for the study is the same type of data stored in the benchmark database. For example, when counting disk storage, one data center might include data sets migrated to tape and another might not.
- *Conducting benchmark studies frequently and regularly.* Maintaining quality requires continuous improvement, and a point-in-time assessment cannot meet the demands of quality. However, a frequency higher than once per year is probably not going to show demonstrable improvement.
- *Studying leaders.* After the benchmark results are known, data center managers should study the examples set by quality leaders.
- *Using the results for internal public relations.* The results of the benchmark study should be shown to customers and senior management to prove that the data center's operations are competitive, and to highlight the areas targeted for improvement. Outsourcers remain in business by focusing on areas where they can be more efficient, but data center managers can stave off outsourcers by focusing on areas that need improvement.

The following should be avoided when participating in a benchmark study:

- *Limiting the analysis solely to the company's industry.* Data center managers can learn much from data centers whose companies are involved in unrelated industries.
- *Accepting nebulous, generic results.* The benchmarker should be able to provide explicit and detailed results, as well as to meaningfully interpret these results. The benchmarker should not be allowed to give observations and recommendations that could be given by anyone reading the trade press. Data center managers should be wary of form reports in which only the company name has been changed.
- *Rationalizing.* Data center managers should not allow themselves to rationalize a poor performance comparison. Instead, they should find out how the data centers which did well in certain categories achieved those results.

PLANNING CONSIDERATIONS

In planning for a total quality environment in the data center, it is important that all data center staff understand that quality is part of their job, and not the responsibility of a quality control department. It is very helpful to charter one individual with articulating and promoting the message of quality.

This person can also be the spokesperson to external parties interested in the data center's quality process. This individual can also arrange training programs, team meetings, and reviews that are part of an ongoing quality program.

Quality must be regarded as a journey, and not a destination. Achieving quality is a multiyear investment — not the program of the year — and must be integrated with everyday operations. Aggressive goals must be set, and higher goals should be set once the original ones have been attained. Setting goals in terms of a percentage is recommended for the data center embarking on a quality program. Once the goal of 99 percent performance has been reached, however, goals should be set in terms of parts-per-million, which is more meaningful in this case. Such companies as Motorola, IBM, and Texas Instruments have as their quality standard six sigma, which equates to a failure rate of 3.4 parts per million.

INVOLVING STAFF

In addition to data center management, the data center staff is key in realizing quality. Data center management must provide an environment that facilitates the full participation of each staff member in realizing quality. A professional-development infrastructure should become part of the data center's budget to ensure that training is available. At least ten days of technical training per person, per year should be budgeted. This amount should not be cut, because keeping the staff's technical skills current is crucial to quality performance. Career counseling should also be provided to ensure that the staff can realize their fullest potential. Employees should be given feedback on their performance, and good performance should be rewarded.

Not only are individual contributions important, but teams play an important part in realizing quality. Teams can often accomplish what one individual cannot. Although empowerment is currently a buzzword, giving personnel the feeling of empowerment can be advantageous if they feel empowered to act on behalf of the customer without having to check with their superiors. Customers also appreciate this.

QUALITY ASSURANCE

Quality is ensured when customers are involved in designing the solution to their needs. The service-level agreement states customer expectations for the service to be provided by the data center. By providing service at or above the agreement level, the data center's role is ensured in the customer's operations. The service-level agreement also allows actual performance to be compared to expected performance, which can be used to determine areas for improvement.

The data center manager can internally assess processes to identify areas for improvement. For example, analysis of the contributions to cycle time in correcting a system outage or in addressing a help desk call could cause the elimination of steps that add no value to the result. Supplier involvement is also key to quality success. Contracts should stipulate specific quality-performance measures. Competitive assessments should include cost, quality issues, and total cost of ownership. To provide quality, suppliers should be part of a partnership with the data center.

MEASURING RESULTS

Such metrics as IS cost as a percentage of corporate revenue; IS headcount as a percentage of the corporate total; and comparison to competitors' product prices demonstrate over time quality performance and continuous improvement. The data center's contributions to the organization's operations are measured in terms of systems availability, on-time completion of production processing, and abend frequency for both online processing and batch processing.

Metrics about staff also indicate the quality of the organization. The rate of employee turnover, percentage of staff contributing suggestions for improvement, average number of training days, and favorable attitude survey scores are such people metrics. The current trend toward organizational flattening makes the contributor-to-supervisor ratio a measure of employee empowerment. This metric should be used with care, because some argue that there is a limit to the effectiveness with which a flat organization can operate. The ideal contributor-to-supervisor ratio is probably in the range of 10:1; however, this ratio varies by function.

Measuring and reporting results of a quality improvement program is a powerful tool for promoting the effectiveness of data center operations to senior management. Goals can be set at the corporate level and progress toward these goals can be reported over time.

On the operational level, daily performance can be tracked using various logging mechanisms, and a sophisticated performance tracking system can automatically notify key personnel when performance boundaries are exceeded. Availability tracking systems can be fed by automated operations tools, so that an entry is made automatically when an application or server is out of service. The operator is prompted for descriptive information and is saved the tedium of logging time down, time up, and elapsed time.

An extremely sophisticated system for tracking quality can be used by individual business entities to set their performance goals. Actual performance data is automatically fed into a database by various tracking systems. Executive reports can be generated using an executive information system interface.

THE IMPORTANCE OF CUSTOMER SATISFACTION

Customer satisfaction is central to quality. Data center managers may think they understand what constitutes quality, but their customers know quality. Using advisory boards, teams, or simple one-on-one meetings, data center managers can work with customers to establish the priorities for service-level achievement and the metrics by which quality is measured.

Every staff member in the data center must be aware that she or he has a customer. The console operator's customer may be a technical support staff member who needs a change installed, the tape library operator's customer is the owner of the batch job, and the help desk is a key customer contact area.

The help desk is often where the customer's opinion of the data center is formed. Therefore, the help desk is a prime area for focusing on quality. Tracking such metrics as call-abandon rate, average hold time, and percentage of first-time resolutions measures the performance of the desk. However, a deeper understanding of this area's performance can be obtained by having customers rate its service and by measuring cycle time.

Complaint management is an interesting area for measuring customer satisfaction. Many organizations treat a complaint as a nuisance, but each complaint is an opportunity to improve quality if the cause of the complaint is found. For every person calling the help desk, there may be ten other customers with the same problem, and correcting the problem for the caller does not help the other ten who did not call. When the help desk receives a call from a customer with a complaint, the help desk should do more than find the solution to the problem. Follow-up calls should be made to ensure that the customer is satisfied. To obtain a higher level of customer satisfaction, the customers can be rewarded with free service for reporting a quality problem.

When striving to maintain a high level of customer satisfaction, data center managers should be aware that customers always demand increasingly higher levels of satisfaction. What customers consider to be a high performance level today, they will eventually consider to be a standard level of performance.

Surveys

Surveys are an effective way to solicit customer feedback on satisfaction levels. When using surveys, data center management should:

- *Carefully select the survey population.* Different groups of customers exist and their interests are different. For example, system developers may expect sub-second response time, but end users might be satisfied with a slower response.

- *Ensure relevant sample size.* Data center managers must ensure that the survey does not sample less than a statistically significant part of the customer population.
- *Conduct the survey regularly.* To ensure that performance is improving, the survey should be conducted regularly.
- *Share survey results with the customer.* If customers are informed about the results and what the data center will do to improve performance, they will be more inclined to fill out the next survey.

When using surveys to measure customer satisfaction, data center managers should avoid:

- *Leading survey participants.* A survey should not contain questions that lead the customer to a given answer. For example, when asked if they would like better response time, most customers will answer yes.
- *Asking obvious questions.* One such question is to ask customers if they would be willing to pay for better response time.
- *Asking irrelevant questions.* The survey should contain only questions that contribute to understanding customer satisfaction.
- *Using a scale for giving responses.* If survey participants are asked to give their answers according to a scale from 1 to 5, the overall answer will often be between 3.5 and 4.0, which tells nothing.
- *Rationalizing results.* Data center managers should not rationalize survey results. An example of such rationalizing is to think that a result is attributable to the customers' inability to understand the question.

CONCLUSION

Customer satisfaction is key to providing quality, and every data center staff member has a customer who determines requirements and defines what constitutes quality. To implement a successful quality-improvement program for data center operations, the following steps, as outlined in the MBNQA framework, should be followed:

- Performance should be assessed using metrics that can measure quality.
- Results of the assessment should be compared with other data centers.
- The data center's operations should be benchmarked.
- A quality-improvement plan should be developed, based on the benchmark study.
- All staff members must be involved in the pursuit of quality.
- Customer satisfaction should be used as the basis of any quality improvement program.

When embarking on a quality-improvement program, data center managers must also remember that the pursuit of quality is an ongoing process rather than the attainment of a fixed set of goals; quality is a journey, not a destination.

Chapter 46
Evaluating Platform Reliability and Measuring Its Dollar Value

Chris Rooke

AS BUSINESSES OFFER MORE OF THEIR PRODUCTS AND SERVICES ONLINE, reliability of computer-based services is becoming increasingly central to competitiveness. If a company markets its products on the World Wide Web, for example, and the network or the application becomes unavailable, potential buyers simply will order from another Web site.

Recognizing the growing importance of reliability to business, platform vendors have begun to make claims about reliability. It is difficult to make meaningful comparisons, however, because different vendors describe it in different ways, and various myths have found their way into data center vocabulary.

MYTHS ABOUT RELIABILITY

Following are 10 of the many misconceptions about computer system reliability:

Myth 1: A Million-Hour Mean Time Between Failure Is Enough.

To calculate mean time between failure (MTBF), vendors divide the number of operating hours by the number of failures. There are 8,760 hours in one year, so:

$$\text{MTBF} = \frac{\text{Number of devices * 8,760}}{\text{Number of failures}}$$

The MTBF does not describe how long a device will last. Rather, it defines the reliability of a large device population during the "useful life" of the product, typically 5 to 10 years. For example, if the device MTBF is a million hours (114 years), and a company has 1000 devices operating for a year, nearly nine devices will fail every year, even though the device is operating as specified.

The MTBF of a device should not be confused with the MTBF of a system. Million-hour MTBF apply to individual devices, such as disks or power supplies. In the case of a mainframe manufacturer with an installed base of 30,000 mainframes, however, the vendor can rightly claim 99.9 percent hardware reliability with a MTBF of 10,000 hours (417 days). The business can still expect 26,280 mainframe crashes per year, or one crash every 20 minutes, from hardware errors alone. In addition, the 10,000-hour figure also assumes that design, manufacturing, installation, and service processes are perfect.

The MTBF is just one element of availability. Another statistic to discuss with vendors is Mean Time To Repair, which includes the time not only to repair hardware, but also to recover large databases, check them for corruption, and ensure that no transactions were lost. A platform with a lengthy mean time to repair (MTTR) can result in long downtimes, even though failures are infrequent. Given the importance of the MTTR, a more accurate way to predict availability is:

$$availability = \frac{MTBF + MTTR}{MTBF}$$

where:

$MTBF$ and $MTTR$ are expressed in hours

Myth 2: Fault Tolerance Applies to Hardware Only

The business justification for eliminating outages is their cost in lost revenue, reputation, disenchanted customers, or productivity. The cause of an outage — in a workstation, server, application, or network — is totally irrelevant to end users. The end users take a simplistic view of fault tolerance: is the application available when they want to use it?

When evaluating fault-tolerant platforms, the data center manager should ask whether the vendor provides fault-tolerant software, as well as hardware.

Myth 3: Fault Tolerance Is Expensive

Fault tolerance is often assumed to imply redundant hardware and is therefore assumed to be expensive. The myth is perpetuated because some vendors offer fault-tolerant "pair and spare" architectures at a considerable price premium.

In the most effective fault-tolerant architectures, however, the most expensive units — the processors — do not use "hot stand-by" techniques. Instead, each processor is performing useful application processing even as it is available to take over the immediate work of a failed unit. In the event of a failure, work can be dynamically balanced across remaining processing units.

To evaluate the price/performance of fault-tolerant servers, data center managers can consult the industry-standard Transaction Performance Processing Council TPC-C Benchmark, which is independently audited. The TPC-C Benchmark considers the five-year cost of ownership rather than simple purchase price. This benchmark cannot accurately predict an individual company's precise costs, but it does illustrate the relative costs of different platforms.

The TPC-C Benchmark does not factor in the costs of downtime; data center managers can calculate these costs using the model, "Calculating the Business Costs of Downtime," presented later in this chapter.

Myth 4: Failover Systems Reduce Downtime to a Few Minutes a Year

A failover system links two conventional systems, enabling them to recover as quickly as possible from a system failure. There is no disagreement that failover systems suffer more downtime than fault-tolerant systems: they have little additional technology to prevent failures. When failures do occur, the best recovery time claims range from 5 minutes to 15 minutes, compared with the instantaneous recovery of a fault-tolerant system. Failover systems also introduce new causes of downtime, such as faulty scripts and false failovers.

Vendors of failover systems assert that almost everyone can live with a few minutes of downtime per year. This may be true for some businesses, but downtime in failover systems is actually much longer than a few minutes. Tandem Computers has developed a client/server availability model that can be used to predict downtime. It is available on the World Wide Web: http://www.tandem.com/prod/nsa/. The model uses a representative client/server environment containing 1000 clients, 20 hubs, 6 routers, 40 database servers, and 1 network management server. For non-fault-tolerant systems, the predicted annual downtime is approximately 12,000 minutes, or 200 hours per client, which translates to 97.7 percent availability. For configurations of fault-tolerant systems and networks, the predicted annual downtime is 59 hours per client, or 99.3 percent availability. Fifty-nine hours for each client is significantly more than "a few minutes."

Myth 5: Planned Downtime Is Both Acceptable and Necessary

Scheduled or planned downtime is usually accepted as necessary, occurring not only because of such massive reconfigurations as major operating system, hardware, or application program upgrades, but also for more mundane reasons, such as backing up files, reorganizing the database, or general maintenance. The aggregate downtime from these frequent, smaller activities is significant and is becoming more so as databases grow and windows for maintenance shrink because of demands for 24 x 7 online access. The non-fault-tolerant version of the predictive client/server model reveals that reconfiguration and planned downtime are responsible for 32 percent of all outages (or about 64 hours per client per year). Of this 32 percent, some 20 percent, or about 40 hours per client per year, occur in the server.

The technology exists to largely eliminate planned downtime. One example is online reorganization; the other is online database management operations, such as moving and merging partitions, splitting partitions, and adding disks. Another example is shared-disk technology, which enables massive reconfigurations, such as complete system upgrades, to be performed with downtime of only a few minutes. Therefore, data center managers do not have to accept planned downtime as unavoidable. When evaluating new systems, managers should ask for demos or references of the time needed to perform complete system upgrades and other required maintenance functions.

Myth 6: All Systems Provide the Same Level of Data Integrity

Data integrity means that data is checked for accuracy at all critical junctures, so that if something fails, the data is kept complete and free from flaws and does not suffer irrecoverable corruption. Data integrity is a key requirement for nearly all applications.

Full data integrity requires that all hardware and software components and all elements in the data path — from source of input, through the processor and memory, to the storage media and all databases — contain some form of checking.

To keep the prices of their products as low as possible, many vendors leave out most of this data-integrity technology. Some workstation vendors, intending to sell their workstations for serious business applications, are beginning to realize the need for better hardware data integrity. However, a server or workstation that includes only data-integrity checks on memory, by way of error correction codes, still has many unchecked elements on the data path between the processor and storage media in which corruption would not be detected. Transient errors, for example, occur whenever a PC or workstation freezes. If data integrity features are not designed into the hardware and software, transient errors can cause data corruption in the processor; in memory; in the storage media itself; or on any data path between these components; and errors can result in that corrupt data being written to storage media. Unfortunately, the people most likely to discover data corruption are customers.

It is critical to ask vendors where data integrity checks are performed on the data path between the processor and storage media.

Myth 7: Availability Is Scalable

Processing power is scalable in parallel systems; businesses can gain more processing power simply by adding new processors. Availability, however, is not scalable.

The availability of a small network of users can be quite high, but the availability achieved does not scale upward with size and complexity. Rather, if the data center puts 10,000 PCs in a distributed network with all the routers, LANs, bridges, and Network Operating System in place, the probability of all the pieces working at any given time is zero. That does not mean all the pieces need to be up and running at a given time, but how does the data center manager determine which subsets are need to run a critical application, and how does the manager dynamically reconfigure to support that subset? The move to put critical business applications into large client/server LAN environments creates a tremendous new requirement for reliable computing — a requirement that can be met only by pushing fault tolerance out into the network and to the desktop.

Similarly, if availability is not designed into the operating system, database, and application software, the business is inhibited in its ability to deliver new 24 x 7 services. Therefore, the data center manager must ask vendors about the availability of not only their hardware, but also their software.

Myth 8: Reliability Can Be Added On

Reliability comprises both availability and data integrity.

Availability. Increasing availability in products not designed for availability is expensive and difficult to manage. Availability involves both hardware and software. The ability to update a database while it is being backed up to tape, for example, is crucial for businesses with 24 x 7 operations. If this capability is not designed into the database, an upgrade may cost the business many years and research dollars. Similarly, redesigning an operating system to tolerate transient errors is costly; it is far more economical to purchase an operating system designed from the outset with this capability.

Data Integrity. Data integrity results when mechanisms are in place to verify data accuracy at critical junctures, to prevent irrecoverable corruption when a system component fails. The complex task of designing systems with data integrity starts at the chip level, extends through memory to the processor, down the data paths, and all the way out to the storage media. Many vendors, however, leave out most of this data-integrity technology. For example, a server or workstation that includes only data-integrity checks on the processor, by using two microprocessors in lockstep, still has many unchecked elements on the data path between the processor and storage media where corruption would not be detected.

Adding data integrity to systems not designed for reliability requires extensive, costly product redesign.

Myth 9: Checklists Are a Valid Basis for Comparing Availability

Issues of availability and data integrity defy meaningful reductions to a final score. One recent study contained 66 features divided into 9 sections but omitted considerations of database availability because of the increased complexity to the checklist, even though the role of database management utilities has become critical in meeting the challenge of 24 x 7 availability.

The other difficulties with checklists are tradeoffs among availability, cost, performance, and even application profile. For example, redundant array of independent disks (RAID) 5 capability is frequently listed as a requirement in availability checklists, yet disk mirroring is an alternative for achieving DASD fault tolerance. RAID 5 is a very price-competitive solution for databases with low levels of access; mirrored disks are more price competitive for high-volume access and fast-response-time requirements.

Myth 10: Clusters Have No Single Point of Failure

Many consultants assert that clusters have no single point of failure. This is a mistake, resulting from the concept that single points of failure are eliminated when no hardware or software component exists in the cluster without a backup component.

The real question is whether a single point of failure, whether hardware or software, causes denial of service or loss or duplication of data. The first definition looks at the technology; the second considers the end-user view of availability.

Some consultants see no contradiction in reporting that level-3 failover (e.g., the automatic re-submission of in-flight transactions) requires failover-specific application code. This means that in-flight transactions are lost without the use of expertly written application code. This clearly violates the concept of no loss of data. Moreover, clusters using level-3 capabilities depend on failover scripts. Designed fault tolerance eliminates the drawbacks of failover scripts, which include skilled and costly programmers, application dependency, non-portability, and a tendency for false failovers. By the cluster vendors' own admission, recovery takes at least 5 minutes to 15 minutes. Whether this constitutes denial of service is clearly a judgment to be made by the end user, but with the average cost-per-outage minute running at $1300, the cost of downtime for a cluster is about $13,000 per outage or approximately $117,000 per year, every year.

A LEXICON FOR ASSESSING RELIABILITY

With the preponderance of these myths, there clearly is a need to define precisely the terms used to discuss and measure reliability.

Outages: Inability to Deliver Services

An outage is planned or unplanned time during which the computing environment cannot deliver services, whether because of unavailability of the hardware, system software, application, network, or client. Measuring availability in terms of outage minutes that the end user experiences gives the most complete and accurate picture of downtime in the entire computing environment. End-user outage minutes are simply outage minutes multiplied by the number of end users affected by the outage.

The data center manager should include planned outages in the outage measurement. This enables him or her to track efforts to reduce the downtime that results from a daily or weekly planned downtime window. A service provider with a goal of delivering a service 16 hours a day, 7 days a week, has 8 hours of planned outage each day. The availability goal for this service can be stated as "no more than 480 outage minutes each day," or 172,200 outage minutes per year. Another service provider, committed to providing 24 x 7 availability, may have a service-level agreement that says "no more than 500 outage minutes per year."

Classifications of Outages

The following five categories are generally accepted to represent all failures in the computing environment.

- *Physical.* Physical faults are failures in the hardware. All hardware components break eventually, no matter how high the MTBF. Transient hardware failures, those that do not recur when the hardware is restarted, are not reduced as MTBF increases. Studies have shown that 80 percent of all hardware failures are caused by transient hardware faults. Without adequate protection, these failures can lead to corrupt data within the processor, or between the processor and the disk, and therefore lead to corrupt data on the disk.

- *Design.* Coding errors or faulty design can cause failures of software components. Good software engineering practices can eliminate most of the software errors before code goes to production, but a few design and coding errors will still exist. Studies have shown that 85 percent to 99 percent of all software failures in production are due to transient software failures.
- *Operations.* Errors caused by operations personnel include accidents, inexperience, or malice.
- *Environmental.* Intentional or accidental failures are caused by power, cooling, network connection, and natural disasters (e.g., hurricanes, earthquakes, and floods).
- *Reconfiguration.* Planned downtime for maintenance is required for software upgrades, file reorganization or database restructuring, migrations to new hardware, and such configuration changes as adding disks or client devices.

Assessing reliability requires consideration of all five classes of outages. To help managers determine whether a specific platform meets their companies' specifics, Tandem Computers provides a list of detailed questions, available at http://www.tandem.com/prod/nsa/ on the World Wide Web.

Reliability: A Continuum of Availability with Data Integrity at the Base

As stated earlier, reliable computing is a continuum of availability, with data integrity as the foundation across the continuum. Definitions of the levels of availability help data center managers evaluate the information available in the marketplace.

- *Standard.* Standard servers have no availability enhancements. Recovery from failures can be take hours or days.
- *High Availability.* High-availability systems can tolerate outages caused by physical or design failures affecting disks and power supplies. They include some redundant components, such as mirrored disks, extra power supplies, and fans. High-availability systems recover from disruptions faster than standard systems. However, recovery time is measured in minutes or even hours, so downtime is very noticeable to users. Transactions are lost and have to be reentered, resulting in lost productivity and lost business.
- *Fault Tolerance.* Fault-tolerant systems are able to tolerate physical and design failures for all the hardware components of the system. This includes board-level fault tolerance, multiple processors, mirrored disks or RAID, dual-ported controllers, and redundant power supplies and cooling. Some vendors refer to this as "no single point of failure."
- *Continuous Availability.* Continuous-availability systems add to the availability provided by fault-tolerant systems by tolerating both operating

system software failures and planned outages caused by changes to the system hardware or operating system software.

- *Permanent Availability.* Permanent availability is the ability to tolerate outages in all outage classes in all parts of the system.

CALCULATING THE BUSINESS COSTS OF DOWNTIME

The myths and definitions about reliability are important, yet they are peripheral to the main issue: the real costs of the lack of reliability to the organization. Accurate estimates can help justify purchases. A spreadsheet model for calculating the costs of downtime is available on Tandem's Web site: www.tandem.com/INFOCTR/HTML/BROCHURE/ECONAVBR.html. The spreadsheet facilitates estimating the minutes of each type of outage for each element of the computer system, focusing on those that cause the most downtime.

CONCLUSION

Reliability can cost little to obtain and much to ignore. Downtime and lack of data integrity are expensive — and are becoming more so as businesses conduct more business online. At the same time, a reputation for superior availability can actually increase revenues by ensuring the loyalty of existing customers and attracting new ones.

To accurately assess the reliability of new computer systems considered for purchase, data center professionals must consider:

- The validity of measures of reliability; for example, the need to consider Mean Time To Repair as well as MTBF.
- Software as well as hardware reliability.
- Whether planned downtime is truly necessary.
- Data integrity.

Chapter 47
Understanding the Virus Threat

Gilbert Held

DURING THE PAST FEW YEARS, more than 4000 distinct types of computer viruses have been identified. It is beyond the scope of any chapter to cover more than a handful of viruses; however, this chapter focuses on the operating characteristics of viruses. Armed with a basic understanding of how viruses work, the data center manager can more easily identify symptoms of a virus's presence and initiate corrective action. This chapter also discusses why updating a virus protection program is critical and, if not maintained, how that program can provide a very false indication of protection. Because the design of most types of attack software are structured to operate on the logical organization of data stored on disk, this chapter begins with a tutorial concerning data storage.

DISK STORAGE

The ability to place data on a disk or diskette requires the media to be formatted. The formatting process includes physical formatting, by which the sector addresses of each sector are written as a header or preamble to the location where sector data will be stored. During the physical formatting process, synchronization bytes and gap bytes are added to the media to assist the disk controller in read and write operations. Synchronization bytes prefix sector headers and function as a mechanism to alert the controller to the fact that they will shortly be placed over a sector address; gap bytes provide a timing tolerance enabling the controller to read across multiple sectors.

Logical formatting involves the organization of a disk into directories and the creation of an index area that contains pointers to locations where files are stored. During the logical format process a disk is organized into four main storage areas: a boot sector, File Allocation Table, root directory, and data storage area, where the contents of files are actually stored.

0-8493-9824-X/00/$0.00+$.50
© 2000 by CRC Press LLC

Today, just about all hard disks are manufactured with physical or low-level formatting performed on the media. The ability of a virus developer to initiate physical formatting of a hard drive requires appropriate low-level controller coding. In contrast, the logical formatting of floppy disks is standardized and can be performed regardless of the controller used in a particular computer; therefore, disks represent a more inviting target for the virus developer. The familiar Disk Operating System FORMAT command actually performs a logical format of a hard drive and both a physical and logical format of a diskette.

BOOT SECTOR

The boot sector contains a short program commonly referred to as a bootstrap loader, which occupies the first sector of the first track on the top side of a disk. That location is technically referred to as sector 1, track 0, side 0. The program placed in that location loads the rest of the operating system, as well as information concerning how data is stored on the disk. Critical information necessary to correctly load the rest of the operating system is included in the boot sector, such as the number of bytes per sector, number of tracks, number of sectors per track, number of platters, and similar media definition descriptions.

Because of the important role the boot sector plays in governing the operation of the computer, it is a frequent target of virus developers. In fact, the category of viruses developed to attack the boot sector of a disk are collectively referred to as boot-sector viruses.

Some boot-sector viruses place false information into the boot sector. In such cases, the user completes his or her PC operations and turns off the computer; the next day, the user turns on the computer and is led to believe that the hard drive is no longer recognizable. Other boot-sector viruses simply replicate themselves each time the user turns on the PC or performs a system reset; each time, the process takes a few sectors of the hard disk until, after a period of time, the available storage capacity is considerably diminished or even eliminated.

FILE ALLOCATION TABLE

The FAT stores the status of disk storage units. For a diskette, the File Allocation Table records the status of sectors, while a hard-disk FAT records the status of a grouping of logically consecutive sectors, referred to as a cluster.

During the logical format process, addressing information is placed into each sector header and the byte hex F6 is continuously written into each data area. By reading the previously written bytes, Disk Operating System can note bad sectors and mark them accordingly. Exhibit 47.1 lists the possible FAT entries and includes their hex values and the meaning of each entry.

508

Exhibit 47.1. Possible FAT entries.

Hex Value	Meaning
0000	Available Cluster
0002-FFFEF	Cluster Used for File Storage
FFFO-FF6	Reserved for Future Use
FFF7	Bad Cluster
FFF8-FFFF	Last Cluster in a File

A few of the entries in Exhibit 47.1 warrant elaboration. The term *cluster* is applicable to both disk and diskette and, when used with a diskette, represents a grouping of precisely one sector. As data is recorded onto a disk and requires more than one cluster of storage, a value between hex 02 and hex FFEF indicates that the cluster not only provides file storage, but functions as a pointer to the location of the next cluster used by a multicluster spanning file.

Because of the importance of the FAT, a particular series of viruses, called FAT infectors, commonly attack that disk location. For example, a FAT infector virus might swap the hex values of two FAT entries between hex 02 and hex FFEF, causing files to become discombobulated. Another insidious trick performed by some FAT infector viruses is to terminate a multicluster file prematurely by entering a hex value from FFF8 to FFFF in place of a pointer value and then marking the remaining clusters as either available or as bad clusters.

ROOT DIRECTORY

The third part of system information stored on a disk is the root directory. On a hard drive, the root directory can contain up to 512 entries of 32 bytes each that reference either subdirectories or files.

Exhibit 47.2 lists the directory entry fields to include the size in bytes of each field. Similar to the File Allocation Table, Disk Operating System uses special codes to indicate the status of files. Those codes are placed in the first byte of the file-name field. A zero (0) in the first byte of a file name indicates an unused directory entry, while a hex E5 is placed in the first byte of a file name to indicate that a file was erased. The hex E5 in the first byte of a file name explains why the use of the DOS UNDELETE command or a utility program from a third-party vendor designed to recover erased files prompts the user to enter the first letter of the file to be undeleted. That is, when the user erases a file, DOS does not actually erase the contents of the file. Instead, it simply places a hex E5 in the first byte of the file-name field, which indicates the file was erased, overwriting the first character of the actual file name.

Exhibit 47.2. Directory entry fields.

Field	Size (in Bytes)
File Name	8B
Extension	3B
Attributes	1B
Reserved	10B
Time	2B
Date	2B
Starting FAT Entry	2B
File Size	4B

The importance of directory entries is recognized by virus developers, who design another class of viruses to operate upon those entries. Referred to as directory infectors, some such viruses may set the attribute field's hidden bit position for all directory entries, making all the files disappear from view. Other common methods of attack include jumbling file names and changing the starting FAT entry value. Concerning FAT entry values, since that is the first location where the actual file begins its change, this represents a destructive action that turns the harmless prank nature of some virus developers into a destructive mechanism, which proves that good and frequent backups represent a practical method to recover from attack software.

GENERAL CATEGORIES OF ATTACK SOFTWARE

In actuality, a virus represents only one category or type of a larger category, called attack software. Other common types of attack software include logic bombs, worms, and trojans.

A logic bomb is a program that remains dormant until triggered by some extended event, such as the execution of a valid program. A worm is a program that replicates itself in a nondestructive manner, simply eating away at disk space or memory, or both, until the user's ability to perform productive operations is adversely affected. In fact, the Internet Morris virus was actually a worm. The last category of attack software is the trojan, named after the large, hollow wooden horse that housed Greek soldiers and entered the walls of Troy. The trojan is a program that functions as a delivery vehicle for typically destructive codes. One common method for creating a trojan uses the name of a Disk Operating System executable program file, but uses the extension .COM instead of the extension .EXE. When DOS encounters two files with the same names, but with the extensions .COM and .EXE, DOS attempts to load and execute the file with the extension .COM. A .COM file contains an exact image of how a file appears in memory and is faster to load and more compact than an .EXE file. However, a .COM file is restricted to 64K bytes and can freeze the computer.

The original definition of an attack software is a program that reproduces its own code, placing the code onto other programs so that when those programs are executed the attack software spreads. That definition, still essentially correct, makes no mention of the software's effect which, in essence, results from the type of attack software, as well as the manner in which it was coded. A logic bomb simply displays a message, such as X Shopping Days Til Christmas, and is relatively benign until its frequency of occurrence increases to the point that it is no longer an amusement. A trojan becomes active and reproduces itself each time a program is activated.

SOFTWARE ATTACK PREVENTION

Recognizing the harm that can result from attack software, data center managers can take the first line of defense: to recognize potential entry points and use a detection anti-virus program to scan software loaded onto computers from diskette or files obtained via a communications facility. Currently, over 50 programs do this, including the Microsoft Anti-Virus program (included in most versions of Windows and, in actuality, licensed from Central Point Software), utility programs available from other commercial sources, and freeware and shareware programs available from CompuServe, America Online, and other information utilities. For illustrative purposes, this chapter uses the Microsoft Anti-Virus program.

Exhibit 47.3 shows the initial Microsoft Anti-Virus window, which displays a summary of accessible drives that includes network drives. No drive has been selected in this window.

The key to the use of the anti-virus program is the Scan menu. The options for that menu are illustrated in Exhibit 47.4.

The Detect option in the Scan menu is only applicable for finding or locating viruses. Selecting that menu option or pressing the Detect button results in the program scanning the selected drive, examining files to determine whether recognizable virus characteristics are present, and if they are, to note the presence of a potential virus. Important to note is that virus development is a continuing process. Thus, if the data center does not obtain frequent updates to an anti-virus program, the probability increases that new viruses will not be detected.

The Clean option both finds and cleans, or removes, found viruses. The Delete CHKLIST files option references a file named CHKLIST.MS, which is created when the program is run and contains information about each disk file, including its size, date of creation, attributes, and a check sum to verify that the file was not altered. Thus, the CHKLIST.MS file is used by the program to alert the user to changes made to a file since a previous Detect or Clean operation.

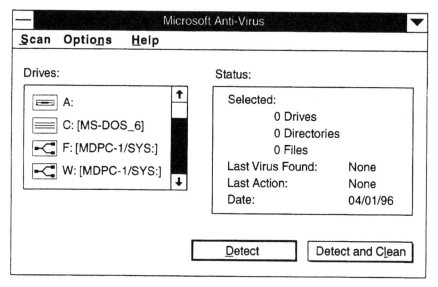

Exhibit 47.3.   The Microsoft Anti-Virus window.

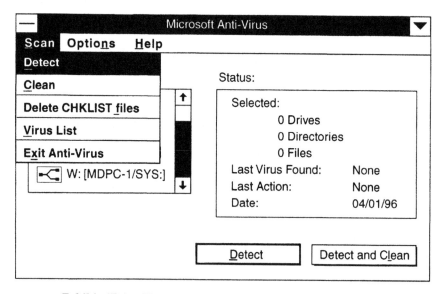

Exhibit 47.4.   The Microsoft Anti-Virus scan menu options.

Exhibit 47.5 illustrates the scanning process display window, which is similar in appearance for both Detect and Clean operations. During either operation, the files being scanned and their directory locations are displayed, and the selected numeric values reduce by increments as the scanning process progresses. Exhibit 47.6 illustrates the summary Statistics displayed by the Microsoft Anti-Virus program. Included is the Scan Time, which can be useful if the user is considering whether to run the program as a start-up operation or selectively. Some organizations make it a policy to require employees to use an anti-virus scanner automatically each day, either with an AUTOEXEC.BAT command or by the placement of a program icon in the Windows Start-Up Group. Scanning is a useful practice if disk scan time is relatively short, and the program is frequently updated; however, the scan of a 1G-byte disk can require 20 minutes to 30 minutes. A much better solution is to scan the contents of diskettes before placing files onto the hard drive. Doing so is not only speedier, but limits the scan to one of two possible viral points of entry. Concerning the other point of entry, which is communications, the data center manager may wish to consider placing all downloaded files in a specific directory. Then, the user could use an anti-virus program that supports the scanning of files in specified directories to both reduce scanning time, as well as to focus the scanning effort on new files. Then, if a virus is identified, the user should scan the entire drive as a protection mechanism to ensure that the virus has not spread beyond the directory.

The Virus List entry in the Scan menu (in Exhibit 47.4) can be considered to represent a learning tool concerning the effect of many viruses. Exhibit 47.7 illustrates the Virus List window displayed by selecting the Virus List entry in the Scan menu. This window displays the names of viruses known to the program, their type, size, and the number of variants. By selecting a virus, the user can display additional information about a virus. Exhibit 47.8 illustrates the Information About Virus window display after the Ada Virus was selected from the Virus List window. This new window provides a summary concerning the effect of that the virus and what it infects.

RECOMMENDED COURSE OF ACTION

Although an understanding of how viruses operate is important in recognizing their systems, it is also important to be prepared. To do so, the data center manager should scan important files and most importantly, keep a backup of all data. In addition, when using a virus-scanning program, users should make sure that it is frequently upgraded to the latest release supported by the developer, because only the latest release of a virus-scanning program may recognize a newly developed virus; the use of an older release may provide a false sense of security.

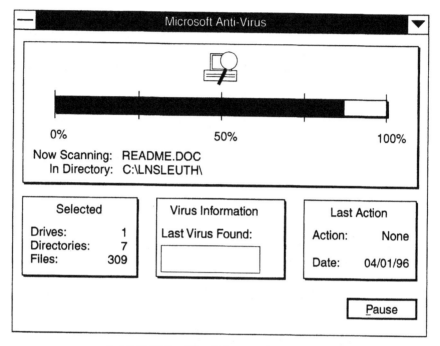

Exhibit 47.5.   The disk-scanning process.

	Scanned	Infected	Cleaned
Hard Disks	1	0	0
Floppy Disks	0	0	0
Total Disks	1	0	0
COM Files	64	0	0
EXE Files	410	0	0
Other Files	2436	0	0
Total Files	2910	0	0
Scan Time	**00:03:19**		

Exhibit 47.6.   Summary statistics.

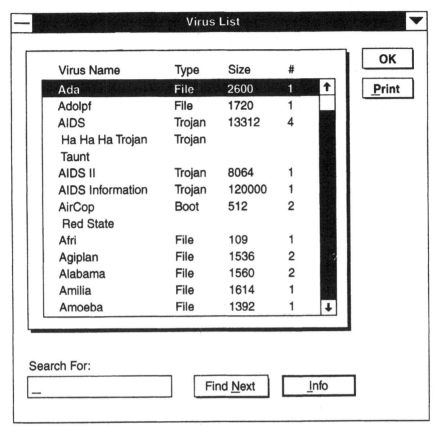

Exhibit 47.7. The virus list window.

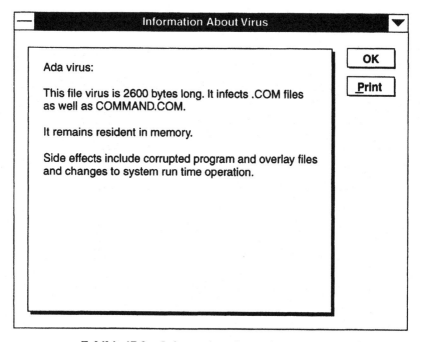

Exhibit 47.8.   Information about virus window.

Chapter 48
E-Mail Security and Privacy

Stewart S. Miller

THE MAJORITY OF ELECTRONIC MAIL, or e-mail, is not a private form of communication. E-mail is often less secure than sending personal or business messages on a postcard. Many businesses monitor employee computer files, e-mail, or voice mail. Some corporations monitor e-mail to ensure that trade secrets are not being communicated to the outside world. Because e-mail often travels through many computers, it is easy to intercept messages.

Bulletin board systems, college campus networks, commercial information services, and the Internet are mainly open information systems where hackers can easily tamper with e-mail. Whenever mail is sent over the Internet, the message first arrives at the Internet service provider's (ISP) outgoing mail server. Once there, anyone using that provider can read the mail as it goes out to its destination.

Passwords do not protect e-mail. Most major e-mail and groupware products that combine messaging, file management, and scheduling allow the network administrator to change passwords at any time and read, delete, or alter any messages on the server. Network monitoring programs, including AG Group's LocalPeek, Farallon Computing's Traffic Watch II, and Neon Software's NetMinder allow network managers to read files sent over the Internet. In fact, these products mimic tools specifically designed for surveillance used primarily on mainframe systems. Encryption is a key element in secure communications over the Internet. Pretty Good Privacy software encrypts e-mail-attached computer files, making them unreadable to most hackers. PGP is a worldwide standard for e-mail security. Anonymous remailers allow users to send e-mail to network newsgroups or directly to recipients so that they cannot tell the sender's real name or e-mail address. For business communications, one of the motivations behind the use of PGP is to prevent the sale of company business plans or customer-list information to competitors.

ESTABLISHING SECURE E-MAIL STANDARDS

Secure Multipurpose Internet Mail Extension (SMIME) is a standard for secure e-mail communications that will soon be built into most e-mail products. A secure e-mail standard allows users to communicate safely between separate or unknown mail platforms. SMIME guarantees security end to end using digital signature technology. SMIME can be used for applications such as processing business transactions between trading partners over the Internet. SMIME is one of the only ways to prove that users sent what they claim to have sent.

The SMIME specification was developed to allow interoperability between various e-mail platforms using Rivest-Shamir-Adleman (RSA) encryption. This standard permits various encryption schemes, various key lengths, and digital signatures. SMIME also supports VeriSign's digital certificates, which is a form of identification used in electronic commerce.

Verification of e-mail services is a key component in preventing fraudulent messages. Netscape Navigator supports VeriSign's Digital IDs and SMIME. Qualcomm, the manufacturer of Eudora, plans to include an API layer to SMIME in Version 3.0 of its e-mail program. In addition to encryption, SMIME modules link into the Eudora translator and offer PGP. WorldTalk, a manufacturer of gateway mail software, is building SMIME support into its network application router to permit cross-communications throughout disparate e-mail packages, in addition to centralized mail management and Internet access.

When a gateway supports SMIME, businesses can audit files as they enter and leave the company. SMIME can replace software based on PGP code. The difference between the two security technologies is that SMIME uses a structured certificate hierarchy; PGP is more limited because it relies on precertification of clients and servers for authentication.

Businesses are working closely with agencies such as the Internet Engineering Task Force (IETF) to achieve effective security for e-mail on the Internet. The lack of a common e-mail security standard is a hurdle to electronic commerce efforts. The Internet has failed to achieve its full potential because of the lack of secure transmission standards. However, standards are continually being proposed at meetings such as the E-Mail World conference, at which businesses work toward ensuring interoperability between e-mail vendors' implementations.

Secure Directories

Many companies are developing directories of businesses on the Internet. Banyan Systems Inc. has released Switchboard, a highly scalable directory that allows Internet users to locate electronic addresses and other information for businesses worldwide. Switchboard appears to be the biggest Internet address directory in existence. This system also offers safeguards to protect privacy and permit secure communication.

When Internet e-mail users express concerns over privacy, Switchboard implements a feature much like Caller ID that alerts a listed person whenever anyone asks for the person's address. The recipient, who will be given information about whomever is seeking the address, can then decide whether to allow access.

Privacy Enhanced Mail (PEM)

The IETF is working to establish a standard for encrypting data in e-mail, designed to be a stable specification on which vendors can build products that can work together. Once the specifications have been clarified, the proposed standard is adopted as a final standard. The IETF standard for encryption includes PEM technology.

PEM encrypts e-mail into the Multipurpose Internet Mail Extension (MIME),which is the standard for attaching files to an e-mail message. PEM provides a utility called nonrepudiation, in which an e-mail message is automatically signed by the sender. Therefore, privacy is assured so that the author is unable to deny at a later point in time that he sent the message. PEM uses the Digital Encryption Standard (DES) and public key encryption technology to ensure that messages are easy for legitimate users to decrypt, yet difficult for hackers to decode.

PGP uses the RSA algorithm along with an enhanced idea encryption algorithm. Although the draft standards for PEM are not yet widely supported, they will probably gain acceptance as the language of the draft is clarified to remove ambiguity regarding the manner in which users are named and certified.

LEADING E-MAIL COALITIONS

Internet Mail Consortium (IMC)

The IMC is a new union of users and vendors interested in developing e-mail standards for the Internet. The group formed because its members feel that present organizations have not acted quickly enough to adopt standards for the Internet. The IMC acts as a link between e-mail users, vendors, and the IETF.

The IMC plans to build consensus on conflicting Internet mail security protocols by holding informative workshops. This group's goal is to establish one unifying system that will ensure privacy in e-mail communications. The IMC's four founding members are Clorox Co., First Virtual Holdings Inc., Innosoft International Inc., and Qualcomm Inc.

For the IMC to attain its goal, it needs users and vendors to come together to discuss Internet mail issues. The IMC will most likely have even more influence than the Electronic Messaging Association on technical and business issues involving e-mail and the Internet.

Electronic Messaging Association (EMA)

The EMA is one source for users to consult if they have problems with their e-mail. The EMA's primary purpose to assign standards to e-mail-message attachments. In the EMA's efforts to regulate e-mail, security issues have been most prevalent regarding Internet communication. The EMA is making strides toward secure file transfers, thanks to the advent of PGP's success with encryption of e-mail file attachments.

The EMA is comprised of corporate users and vendors of e-mail and messaging products. The EMA focuses heavily on the X.400 standard and has recently established a work group to research interoperability between Simple Mail Transfer Protocol (SMTP) and X.400 systems.

The EMA formed a Message Attachment Working Group in 1993 whose purpose was to develop a standard for identifying file attachments transmitted from one vendor's e-mail system to another. The group was set up to use the IETF's MIME and the X.400 File Transfer Body Part (FTBP) as the method for identifying different attachment types. The FTBP defines an attachment by the application that created it. The EMA formed tests that were considered successful if the attachment was received without experiencing data loss.

Attachment transfers are simple when done from within one vendor's mail system, but difficult when performed across systems. File attachments from Microsoft, Lotus, and WordPerfect were used to make certain that the specification developed was capable of transferring attachments.

The next step is integrating MIME and SMIME support into future e-mail packages. It is typical for X.400 to be used as a backbone system for e-mail connectivity. There is a high degree of interest in developing secure methods of transmitting attachments in SMIME. MIME is the current standard for Internet file attachments, and SMIME is well on its way to becoming the secure standard for e-mail communications.

CORPORATE SECURITY: PROBLEMS AND SOLUTIONS

One of the biggest security problems an organization faces involves how to implement a secure server yet allow access to the applications and resources from the corporate intranet. If an organization's Web or mail server is not protected by a firewall or kept on a secured part of the network, then data is open to hacker attacks. In terms of commercial transactions on the

Internet, such a security breach can have lasting repercussions that could make customers lose faith in a company. A hacker could easily alter shipping data, create bogus orders, or simply steal money or products directly from a company's online site.

Security is a full-time job — e-mail is vulnerable to eavesdropping, address spoofing, and wiretapping. A security breach can be anything from unauthorized access by an employee to a hacker break-in. Attacks are not always conducted in a piecemeal fashion. Sometimes they occur on the entire system and focus on stealing or destroying the total assets of a company. Security breaches have resulted in corporate losses ranging from several hundred to several million dollars.

Many organizations are not even aware that security breaches occur many times. A hacker can enter and exit a system undetected. Only when data or e-mail becomes lost, stolen, or tampered with do companies start to realize how much money an organization can actually lose in the process.

Internal Precautions

The first step toward preventing data loss is to take internal precautions. Defunct user accounts should be deleted right away, users should not log on at unauthorized or non-business hours, and, of course, users should be warned against posting their passwords in easily accessible places.

Employees should be up to date concerning corporate security measures. Internal attacks can sometimes be thwarted simply by alerting all users that there are stringent security measures in place. Also, many workers do not realize the value of the data they have access to. Users can be encouraged to be more vigilant if they are made aware of potential losses due to breaches in security.

Firewalls

Firewalls provide an excellent means of keeping data integrity safe. They have the power to block entry points into the system — if an intruder does not have an account name or password, then access is denied. When configured correctly, firewalls reduce the number of accounts that are accessible from outside the network, and as a result, make the system much less vulnerable.

Firewalls are an excellent method of keeping attacks from spreading from one point in the network to another. Firewalls restrict users to one controlled location in the network — access is granted (or denied) at one highly guarded point. Firewalls stop hackers from getting close to security defenses and offer the best protection when placed near a point where the internal network or intranet connects to the larger Internet. Any network traffic that comes from, or goes out to, the Internet must go through the firewall, which then approves each transmission and deems it acceptable or unacceptable.

Preventing E-mail Flooding and Denial of Service

Corporations sometimes fall prey to e-mail "bombs," which essentially flood an e-mail account with several hundred or several thousand messages. This overwhelms the entire system and disrupts network services so that other messages cannot get through.

One solution some vendors provide is an e-mail filter. If the e-mail bombs are originating from one domain or a few domains, the recipient can simply input those domains into the filter to be screened and deleted before cluttering up an e-mail account.

While an e-mail flood is interrupting service, a hacker can entirely disable or reroute services. These attacks can be combated by programming the system to shut out connections or questionable domains that repeatedly try to log into the system unsuccessfully. Attackers are, therefore, prevented from inputting multiple passwords in an attempt to gain access and shut down service. However, if repeated attempts on each user account result in shutting the account down, a hacker can effectively deny service to multiple people in an organization by simply trying to access all of the user accounts unsuccessfully. This would effectively deny service to most of the users.

When a security breach is successful, the hacker gains complete access to a user account, and assets are in jeopardy. One effective method of preventing an attack is to run a secure gateway such as Netscape's Commerce Server, which makes it very difficult for hackers to breach Internet security.

Encryption

Most Internet e-mail security measures are accomplished using encryption and authentication methods. The Internet Privacy Enhanced Mail standard is the method of encrypting e-mail recommended by the IETF.

Another way to secure e-mail contents is the digital signature method, which identifies, stores, and verifies handwritten signatures electronically. This process is accomplished when users sign their names using a digitized pen on a computer. The service can record the specific signature metrics, the speed at which the signature is written, and the order of the unique handwritten strokes. The information is used as a basis to match with any computerized document signed by the same individual again. The comparison can determine the identity of the sender for submitting online payments or securing confidential data.

Administrators often encrypt data across wide area networks in addition to using digital signatures in e-mail packages to determine a user's true identity. The combination of encryption and digital signatures helps slow hacker attempts at gaining network access. However, companies still need to guard against the many methods of hacking, including phone tampering and remote access authentication.

The good news is that encryption is becoming universally accepted on the Internet. In some cases, users do not even realize that the latest Netscape Navigator Web browser employs encryption to secure both documents and e-mail messages. It uses the secure socket layer (SSL) protocol, supported by all of the major Web browsers and servers, to accomplish this goal and provide a safer means of communication.

Unlisted Sites

One method of protecting an e-mail site is to take the unlisted approach. This is an effective security model that works only if no one knows that a particular site exists. If no one knows the site is there, no one will try to hack it. Unfortunately, this model is only good as long as the site remains a secret, and because the Internet is an open system with multiple search engines, the site will probably not remain secret for long.

An Integrated Strategy

An organization concerned with network security may want to control access at each host and for all network services, which is more effective than the piecemeal approach of securing each service individually. This solution can involve the creation of firewalls for internal systems and the network, as well as incorporating detailed authentication approaches, such as a password that expires after each use. Encryption can also be implemented on various levels to protect important data as it travels throughout the network.

SECURING THE FUTURE

The Internet evolved as an open system; however, it is this very openness that makes this venue of communicating so risky. The expansion of the Internet has promoted the growth of e-mail as a relatively quick, low-cost, easy-to-use method of communication. However, the irrefutable fact is that information is power, which makes this particular form of communicating an attractive target for thieves. This chapter has dealt with the problems surrounding e-mail privacy and has proposed a few practical, easy-to-implement solutions.

Chapter 49
Internet Security and Firewall Policies

William Hugh Murray

ANY ATTEMPT TO DESCRIBE ANYTHING AS DYNAMIC, not to say unstable, as the Internet, is likely to make one look foolish. Describing the Internet can be likened to five blind men trying to describe an elephant. However, the elephant remains an elephant, it does not change during the examination and discussion. On the other hand, descriptions of the Internet that are only a few years old are already so out of date as to be inaccurate, if not dangerously misleading.

The Internet is already the most complex artifact in history. It may turn out to be important or it may not. On the chance that it is or will be important, it makes sense to try to understand it, no matter how difficult and uncertain an explanation is likely to be.

THE CHARACTERISTICS OF THE INTERNET

The Internet can be defined and described, in part, in terms of its characteristics. Although it is possible for a network to have some of these characteristics without having them all, they are related in subtle ways.

Public and Open

Perhaps one of the most important characteristics of the Internet, at least from a security point of view, is that it is essentially public and open. It is public in the sense that, like the phone system, anyone can use it. One may have to go to a pay phone, a kiosk, or the public library, but anyone can use it. Libraries have been known to hand out user IDs with the same frequency as library cards. No requirements exist to be able to use the Internet, i.e., anyone can use it. In addition, as in broadcast TV, radio, or magazine advertising, most of the traffic is public. Its value increases with the number of people who see it. Although it has not always been so, most of the servers and services available on the Internet do not know or care who their users are. No user identification or authentication is required. The serv-

0-8493-9824-X/00/$0.00+$.50

ers may count the accesses and they might like to know the demographics of those who visit, but otherwise, the greater number of visits, the more successful the site is considered.

Similar to it being public, the Internet is open. Like the postal system, for the price of a postage stamp, anyone can send a message. For the price of an accommodation address, anyone can receive a message. Although there may be an agreement to pay, no other permission is required and, as a rule, payment in advance is not required. The Internet is also open in the sense that with a minimum of notice to or cooperation of others a connection can be made. A node at the edge of a network can be added easily and unilaterally, creating a new connection between networks. Therefore, it is difficult, nearly impossible, to know what the network looks like.

Although only a small percentage of the traffic on the Internet is sensitive to disclosure and most applications and services are free, almost all traffic is sensitive to contamination and most services are sensitive to interference. Moreover, although many who offer public information on the Internet want many people to see it, they want it to get through intact; they do not want it modified, they do not want it broken, and they do not want to be responsible for what they did not say. The public and open nature of the Internet makes this more difficult to achieve. It also makes it more difficult to achieve confidentiality and accountability for that traffic and those applications that require them.

Inclusive Network of Networks

By definition, an internetwork is a network that connects networks. Therefore, the Internet is a network of networks. It is one collection of all networks, and the economic advantage of a connection is so great as to be irresistible. Moreover, although isolated networks may exist in the short term, in the long term, the internetwork will be one. Isolated networks that persist will be so sparse, small, and temporary as not to be significant.

Mesh Topology

The Internet has a mesh topology, which means that, except at the edges, most nodes are connected to two or more other nodes. In addition, there are multiple paths between any two points on the network, because the topology maximizes the potential that a message will get through and maximizes the total message carrying potential (e.g., bandwidth) of the network. On the other hand, at least by default, users do not know what path their traffic will follow or what nodes and links their messages will traverse.

Flat

Ideally, the Internet is flat, as opposed to hierarchical. Information flows directly from the origin to the destination rather than to a central switching point and then back out to the destination. Therefore, the cost to send a message between any two points on the network is the same as between any other two points. The time required for a message to move between any two points is roughly the same as for any other two points chosen at random. Finally, the bandwidth between any two points is roughly the same as for any other two points.

As expected, messages flow more quickly between nodes that are close together. However, it is possible for a part of a message to circle the globe, even when addressed to a nearby node. So, at least on average, across all randomly chosen pairs of nodes, the Internet is flat.

Broadcast

A node that desires to send a message to another node broadcasts that message to the remainder of the network. Depending on the routing algorithm used, the originating node may prefer nodes that it thinks are in the direction of the destination. However, it is possible for a message to traverse the globe even when addressed to a nearby node. Other nodes that receive the message look at the destination address in the message and forward it in the general direction of that destination. This is similar to a point-to-point network in which the path between two points is determined in advance and dedicated, at least for the instant, to carrying that message. Although every packet does not pass every node and it is possible for users to influence the path that their traffic follows, few users have the necessary special knowledge to take advantage of this capability. They do not know how to exercise the control or to distinguish one path from another. Such control, if used, would limit the paths and bandwidth available to the traffic and be achieved at the cost of a reduction in the chances that the traffic would get through quickly.

Different Types of Internet Connections

Three kinds of connections are available on the Internet:

1. *Packet-Switched.* Related to the idea of broadcast is that of packet-switched. A message is broken into packets, each packet is labelled as to its origin and destination and then is broadcast onto the network. Other nodes forward the packet in the general direction of the destination. It is possible that adjacent packets in a message will follow different paths to the destination. This is the opposite of circuit-switched networks, such as the voice network, in which a circuit or path is determined in advance and all parts of the message follow the same path. In a packet-switched network, an intervening node may see only a part of a message. On the other hand, it increases the number of nodes that may see a part of it.

2. *Peer-Connected.* Nodes on the Internet are "peer connected." No node dominates or controls another. Thus, by default, all nodes behave as if they trust all other nodes as themselves. The implication is that the level of trust is equal to that of the least trusted node.

3. *Any-to-Any Connection.* Like the postal system, and except as otherwise restricted, any device connected to the Internet can send a message to any other device. There is no requirement for an answer but, at a minimum, the destination device must recognize the message and make a decision about it.

Increasing Interoperability

If connectivity is the ability to send a message to any node, interoperability is the ability to get a meaningful answer back. Already, the Internet is better at answering questions than most individuals are at asking questions. The Internet can provide a report of freeway traffic in Los Angeles, hotel availability in London, or the schedule of every opera house in the world for the next two years. It can also locate all the bed and breakfast lodgings in most places in the world, and get an index to the treasures of the Vatican Library or of the British Museum. Individuals can locate and download graphics, moving images, and general and specialized software. A query on "Mona Lisa" returns references to both 1000 different prints of Da Vinci's "La Gioconda" and a sound clip of the Nat King Cole song. If the necessary software is unavailable to interoperate with another system at a particular layer, softfware can be downloaded at another.

As protocols and interfaces become more standard, they become more useful. As the use of a standard increases, so does the propensity to comply with it. The less standard an interface, the more it must include information about its intended or productive use.

No Central Authority

Although there are authorities such as the Internet Activities Board (IAB)and the Internet Engineering Task Force (IETF), which make architectural and design decisions for the Internet, no one is obliged to follow them. The individual networks are independently owned and operated. There is no central authority that is responsible for the operation of the entire network. Because the network is global, it is not even subject to the authority of any single nation state.

INTERNET PROTOCOLS

The Internet can also be defined and described in terms of the communication protocols that it employs. One somewhat pure definition is that the Internet is that collection of interconnected networks that employ the transmission control protocol and Internet protocol and transmission control protocol/Internet protocol (TCP/IP) suite of protocols. A more practical definition is that the Internet is that set plus those networks connected to it by appropriate gateways. (For purposes of this definition, a gateway is a node that translates traffic from one protocol to another.)

The Internet Protocol

The fundamental protocol of the Internet is IP, the Internet protocol. IP is the network layer protocol for the TCP/IP Protocol Suite. It is fundamental in the sense that all other protocols are built on it. It is connectionless, best-effort, packet-switched, and unchecked. "Best effort" means that the network will do its best to deliver the packet, but there are no guarantees. "Unchecked" means that there is no redundancy in the protocol to enable either the sender or the receiver to know whether the packet was received correctly. There is no acknowledgment of the receipt of the message. The receiver cannot be sure that the message comes from where the origin address of the packet says that it comes from.

IP is to the Internet as the postcard is to the postal system: limited in capacity, function, and intent. However, just as a message of any length can be sent by using multiple postcards, or by using one postcard to acknowledge or to check on another, IP packets can be composed in such a way as to compensate for all of these limitations. These compositions make up the higher level protocols.

The Transmission Control Protocol

The transmission control protocol (TCP), is the standard Internet protocol (IP) for the transfer layer. It defines how IP packets are sent back and forth between a sender and a receiver to provide many of the things that IP does not. However, even TCP does not provide security nor the reliability of origin and destination. Both the sender and the receiver know that they are talking to someone that is orderly and well behaved, but they do not know for sure that it is their intended party, and they do not know if any one is listening in.

The Oldest and Most Widely Used Protocols

The following are among the oldest and most widely used protocols on the Internet:

- **Telnet.** This was originally intended for connecting host-dependent terminals to remote systems or applications. Today, it is used by terminal emulator programs on workstations.

- **File Transfer Protocol.** FTP is used to move files from one system to another.
- **Simple Mail Transfer Protocol.** SMTP is used for e-mail.

The applications of these protocols are discussed in subsequent sections.

Other Common Protocols

In addition to those protocols previously discussed are the following:

- **Serial Line Internet Protocol.** The serial line Internet protocol (SLIP) is used to exchange IP traffic with a device, usually a workstation, that is running the proper protocols but without a separate address. It is used to connect workstations to hosts or to Internet service providers through the dial-switched network. It is analogous to an extension cord or a remote.
- **Point-to-Point Protocol.** The point-to-point protocol (PPP) is similar to Serial Line Internet Protocol, but is associated with leased lines. It is usually used to connect a single system to a boundary or "edge" node.
- **Network Time Protocol.** The network time protocol (NTP) is used to set and synchronize the system clocks of Internet nodes. It is able to synchronize all systems in a network to within milliseconds of each other, i.e., to within the accuracy and precision of the system clocks themselves.
- **Secure Protocols.** Recently, secure versions of these protocols have been specified, and reference implementations of these protocols are available for Unix systems.

INTERNET APPLICATIONS

Recall the analogy that describing the Internet can be likened to five blind men trying to describe an elephant. For most of the blind men, the Internet elephant looks like its applications. The Internet is open as to its applications. No real limit to the number of applications exists, and new ones are added every day. However, some applications are significant enough that a description of those applications describes how the net looks to most users.

E-mail

The most widely used application on the Internet is e-mail. E-mail rivals television, copiers, and facsimile machines in its rate of growth. Moreover, as was the case with copiers and facsimiles, it is becoming difficult to remember how business was conducted before e-mail.

Internet e-mail uses the simple mail transfer protocol (SMTP), and the multipurpose Internet mail exchange (MIME) protocol. MIME runs on top of SMTP to permit the exchange of files, programs, sounds, images, and moving images. E-mail is the most interconnected and interoperable application. Even those networks that have resisted connection to the Internet at other levels are connected at the e-mail layer.

In addition, e-mail is the most ubiquitous application in the Internet; it interoperates with many of the others. Several servers are on the Internet that accept mail messages, convert them into requests for other services, convert the answers to those mail messages, and send them back to the requestor. Thus, a user who has access to e-mail functionality has access to all of the information on the network (e.g., Internet).

Logging on to a Remote System

One of the earliest and most obvious of Internet applications was to create a session between a terminal on one system and an application on a remote system. This kind of application used a client process on the origin system, the telnet client. It is initiated by entering the command, telnet, on the originating system. The parameters of the command specify the target system and any nondefault characteristics of the connection request. The request is responded to by the telnet server, a started process (a daemon in Unix parlance) on the target system. The protocol is also called telnet. The user on the origin system sees a prompt from the answering server process — for example, the operating system or an application — on the target system. The user is usually expected to logon, that is, send a user identifier (e.g., user ID) and authenticating data (e.g., a password) to the target system. However, for the target system, the user identifier and password are optional.

File Transfer

The File Transfer Protocol (FTP) is used to exchange file system objects between systems. It is symmetric and works in either direction. Either system may initiate a transfer in either direction. The FTP process (daemon in Unix parlance) must have access to the file system. That is, in systems with closed file systems, the process or the user on whose behalf it is operating must possess the necessary access rights (e.g., read, write, or create) to the file object or directory on which it wants to operate.

A convention called, "anonymous FTP," permits the protocol to be used for public applications. The user can logon to the system with a user ID of anonymous, which requires no password. By convention, users are requested to put their origin system and user ID in the password field. However, the value in this field is not checked or validated in any way; a blank will work as well as the truth.

VULNERABILITIES ON THE INTERNET

The vulnerabilities on the Internet are closely related to its characteristics, its protocols, its uses, and its history. In addition, because the Internet is a broadcast network, messages are vulnerable to disclosure, replay, and interference.

The large number of components on the Internet makes it vulnerable to flaws in the implementation of those components. Because there may be many instances of a flaw, elimination of them is extremely difficult.

Many components in systems peer connected to the Internet contain "escape" mechanisms. These are invoked by an otherwise unlikely character sequence to cause what follows this escape sequence to be handled, not by the component itself, but by the environment in which it runs, often with the privilege of the "escaped from" component. A famous escape mechanism, exploited by the infamous "All Souls" worm, was the debug feature of the sendmail mail handler. This option was invoked by an escape sequence in a message that caused what followed it to be passed through to Unix to be executed as a command. The worm used this feature, among others, to copy and execute itself.

Because nodes are peer connected and trust each other, compromise of one may result in compromise of many, perhaps all. In a peer-connected network, the level of trust in the network is equal to that of the least trusted node or link.

Many of the vulerabilities described in the preceding paragraphs are features rather than flaws. In other words, they are desired and valued by some users and managers. Because of their value, their total elimination is unlikely.

Every node on the Internet has a system manager or privileged user. This user is not subject to any controls intended to ensure that users and their systems are orderly and well behaved. In single-user systems, the only user is a peer of the privileged user in the multi-user system. That user is assumed to have the same motivation, training, and supervision as the manager of a multi-user system. The vast number of such users ensures that at least some of them will be disorderly and unreliable. Because they are all peers and because the systems are peer connected, it makes little difference which of them are trustworthy.

The Internet is so large and complex that no one — not the designers, not the implementers, not the operators, and not the users — fully apprehends it, much less comprehends it. All of them are the blind men. Nonetheless, its immense scope and size make it unlikely that it will ever be perfect. Attackers look on it as a "target rich" environment. Although most nodes on the network are implemented, configured, and operated so as to resist attack, the great number of them ensures that there will always be some that are vulnerable to attack.

Finally, two of the vulnerabilities on the Internet — insecure links and insecure nodes — are fundamental. In other words, they are inherent to the Internet nature, use, intent, or at least its history. Contrary to popular belief, they are not the result of errors, flaws, or failures on the parts of the designers, implementers, or operators of the network. Rather, these insecure links and nodes are the result of attempts to have the greatest chance of getting a message from point *A* to point *B* in the least amount of time. They are never going to go away — it is not simply a matter of time. Indeed, at least for the next five years, they are likely to get worse. That is, vulnerabilities will increase faster than the ability to fix them. Moreover, the number of insecure links and nodes in the network are both growing at a much faster rate than the number of secure ones. This vulnerability is certain and extremely resistant to change.

ATTACKS ON THE INTERNET

The conditions for a successful attack include necessary access, special knowledge, work, and time. Because of its nature, all of these things are somewhat more available on the Internet than on other networks. Because the Internet is open, almost anyone can gain access. Most of the special knowledge in the world is recorded, encapsulated, and available on the Internet, mostly for the taking; although every now and then, permission is required. Even much of the necessary work to launch a successful attack has been encapsulated in computer programs. Thus, they can be perpetrated by those who lack skill and special knowledge and who are not prepared to do the work themselves.

Eavesdropping

As packets move through the net, they can be observed by privileged users of the nodes or by using special equipment to listen in on the links. These attacks are easily automated.

Packet and Password Grabbers

A packet grabber is an automated eavesdropping attack, a program that copies packets as they move through an intermediate node (e.g., a node between the origin and destination). A password grabber is a special case of a packet grabber that identifies and stores for later use user IDs and passwords as they pass through an intermediate node. Because, at least as a general rule, unprivileged processes cannot look at traffic in transit, password grabbers must be installed by privileged users. However, recent experience suggests that they are often placed in penetrated systems. Writing password grabbers requires special knowledge and work. However, so many copies of those programs now exist that the attack can be used even by those without the knowledge and not prepared to do the work. The Internet has so may password grabbers that passwords in the clear are not sufficiently reliable for commercial or other sensitive applications, so the problem moves from the category of an attack to that of a pervasive problem.

Address Spoofing

The origin address on the IP packet is not reliable. The sending system can set this address to any value that it wishes. Nonetheless, by convention and for convenience, many systems rely on this address to determine where a packet came from and to decide how to treat it. Packets carrying the origin address of recognized systems may be treated as though they had originated on a trusted system. Again, with sufficient work and knowledge, it is possible to write a program to exploit this trust. Toolkits for building this kind of attack have been written and distributed within the hacker community.

Trojan Horses

A Trojan Horse attack is in one in which a hostile entity (for example, armed warriors) is concealed inside a benign or trusted one (such as a gift horse) to get it through a protective barrier or perimeter; in the original case, it was the walls of the city of Troy. In computer science, it usually refers to a malicious program included in another program or even in data. Although most systems are vulnerable to this kind of attack to some degree and it has always been a concern, until the proliferation of desktop computers and viruses, it was not a problem.

As previously discussed, both node-to-node connectivity and trust and open file systems make the Internet particularly vulnerable. Trojan Horses can and do travel over any of the popular protocols and in any of the popular object types. For example, they can travel in files over FTP, as documents over MIME, or in arbitrary objects called by HTML scripts fetched from World Wide Web (WWW) servers by browsers. Although some browsers and interpreters (e.g., HotJava) are designed to resist such attacks, most are not. Even in situations in which the browser or interpreter is resistant, it is always possible to dupe some users in a large population.

Trojan Horses are easily executed because they have attractive names or descriptions or the names of frequently used programs. They may require a minimum of user cooperation. For example, the PRANK (virus) was implemented as a MS Word macro and could spread in any Word document. Simply asking Word to open an infected document would contaminate that copy of Word and any document that it subsequently opened. If an infected document were attached to an e-mail message, an act as simple as double clicking the icon for the document would be sufficient to execute the macro. Because such a macro can contain and call an arbitrary program, there is no limit to the sophistication of the program or the contamination it can cause.

Trojan Horse attacks are of special concern on the Internet because they compromise trust of end-point nodes, of the net, and of applications on the net.

Browsing

Browsing means going through the network to look at available, public, accidentally and erroneously available data in search of something of value. Specifically, in an attack sense, this search method looks for special data that will reduce the cost of an attack against other nodes. For example, many systems implement or provide directory services. These directory services return the names of enrolled users, e.g., user identifiers. The information returned by these public services is used by the attacker to identify targets and thereby reduce the cost of attack. Attackers also use browsing to identify and download attack programs.

Exhaustion

When confronted with good security and when all other attacks fail, an attacker can always fall back on trying all possible combinations of data (e.g., user identifiers and passwords) until he or she finds one that gets through. Traditional systems resisted such attacks by disconnecting disorderly devices (i.e., devices that failed to successfully logon). Because the Internet is a broadcast network, there is no connection to break. A system must look at every packet addressed to it and make a determination as to what to do with it. It is possible to spread the attack over time or across addresses so as to disguise the attack as errors or noise.

Denial of Service

Denial of service attacks are those that cause failures by overloading or consuming all available resources. On the Internet, this class of attack includes "spamming" or overloading a target with unwanted traffic. Although the target is not damaged in any permanent way, it may be unable to provide critical services to those intended to use it.

DEFENDING AGAINST ATTACKS ON THE INTERNET

A vast number of options exist that the implementers, operators, and users of the net can use to limit these vulnerabilities and the attacks against them. However, in considering them, keep in mind that these vulnerabilities are fundamental to the nature of the Internet. The only way to eliminate all of the risk is to either eliminate the Internet or alter it so fundamentally that it will lose its identity. Clearly, neither of these options is viable. Rather, the defenses should be balanced against the vulnerablities so as to preserve essential trust. Discussions of some broad categories of defense mechanisms follow.

Isolation and Compartmentation

Of course, the most obvious defense against network attacks is simply not to attach, connect, or participate in a network. Not only is this defense effective, it is also demonstrable to the satisfaction of third parties. However, the value of the security obtained rarely compensates for the lost value of connecting or participating in a network. Moreover, it has often been said that sensitive defense systems are safe because they are not connected to public networks.

Because the value of connecting to a network is high and because the cost of that connection is low, isolation is difficult to maintain. Even a very small system or a single desktop workstation can form a connection between networks.

Policies

In the presence of known connections, people can provide protection. They can recognize attacks and take timely and appropriate action. However, for this to be effective, it must be planned and pervasive. If management wishes to rely on individuals, it must tell them in advance what action to take. A policy is an expression of management's intention. It should contain a recapitulation of the user behavior that management relies on. It should also clearly delineate the responsibilities of employees and managers. Finally, it should specifically address the responsibility to report anomalies.

Bastions

Bastions are "projecting" fortifications. They are strong systems that can be seen from the outside (e.g., the public network), but which are designed to resist attack (i.e., by recognizing only a very limited repertoire of application specific commands). Bastions normally hide the generality and flexibility of their operating systems from the network. A full-function gateway system that can be seen from the public network is called a bastion host. Such a gateway must be able to protect itself from its traffic. Finally, because most protective mechanisms can be bypassed or circumvented, all applications and services that can be seen from the network should be able to resist their traffic.

Filters

Filters are processes that pass some traffic while rejecting some other traffic. The intent is to pass safe traffic and to resist attack traffic. Filters may operate on headers or content. Many filters operate on the basis of the origin address in the header. They pass traffic that appears to have originated on recognized or trusted systems. They may also operate on a combination of origin, protocol, and destination. For example, they may pass mail traffic from unknown origins to the mail port on the post office machine and reject outside traffic addressed to the telnet port on the same machine. Filters are important. For further information see the subsequent section.

Wrappers

Wrappers are proxy programs or processes. They can be viewed as traffic filtering programs. They are designed to protect the target from unintended traffic, known attacks, or to compensate for known weaknesses. They often assume the name of the process that they are intended to protect (e.g., common functions or known targets). For example, suppose that a privileged program is known to have a flaw or an escape mechanism that can be exploited by a packet or a message. A wrapper can be given the name of that program, placed ahead of it in the search order, and used to protect against messages of the dangerous form. After eliminating all messages of the dangerous form, the remainder are passed to the "wrapped" program as normal.

Using a wrapper is a preferrable alternative to patching or replacing the vulnerable program and it presents a lower risk to cure a vulnerability. They have been employed to great advantage in Unix systems where it is often easier to use the wrapper than to find out whether the particular version of Unix or one of its subsystems that is being used has a particular problem. The most famous wrappers are a collection known as COPS. These are used to protect Unix systems from a set of known attacks and vulnerabilities.

FILTERS: THE MOST POPULAR DEFENSE

Filters are the most popular defense to ward off network attacks. The intent is to pass normal traffic while rejecting all attack traffic. Of course, the difficulty is in being able to recognize the difference between the two. Filters are normally based on the origin, the destination, and the kind of traffic. Traffic is permitted to flow from trusted or known sources to safe or intended destinations. Of course, most destinations will ignore traffic that is not addressed to them but will certainly listen to attack traffic that is addressed to them. Filtering on destination address can protect the system from seeing attack traffic at the expense of protecting it from all traffic.

Filters Implemented by Using Routers

In part, because networks are usually connected to each other through routers, routers are a favorite place to filter traffic. The same logic that is used by the router to decide where to send traffic can be used to reject traffic (i.e., to decide to send it to the "bit bucket"). For example, only those packets that appear to have originated on systems whose addresses are recognized (i.e., on a list of known systems) may be accepted.

Packets by Address: IP Address and Port

A filter must have criteria by which to decide which traffic to pass and which to reject. The criteria must appear in the packet. The most frequently used criteria are the IP origin and destination addresses. Typically, this is expressed as an address pair. In other words, traffic appearing to originate at *A* and addressed to *B* may pass this router. Although it could say all traffic originating at *A* may pass or all traffic intended for *B* may pass, this is significantly less rigorous or secure.

The origin and destination are usually expressed as IP addresses and may be further qualified by port. That is, traffic originating on the mail port of *A* may pass to the mail port on *B*, but to no other port.

Protocols

The protocol is also visible in the packet and is useful for routing and security purposes. For example, the filter may pass traffic in the SMTP protocol to pass to the mail server, while not allowing other IP traffic addressed to the same service to pass. Because the intent of the traffic is more obvious in the higher level protocols, filtering by protocol can be very effective and useful.

Firewalls

It is beyond the scope of this chapter to provide instruction on how to build or even to operate a firewall. Within the allotted space, it is difficult to simply convey an understanding of their nature and use. A basic definition and discussion follows:

The *American Heritage Dictionary* defines a firewall as "a fireproof wall used as a barrier to prevent the spread of a fire." By analogy, a network firewall is a traffic-proof barrier used to prevent the spread of disorderly or malicious traffic. More specifically, a firewall is a special collection of hardware and software that connects two networks and that is used to protect each with regard to which side of the firewall a fire will start on.

Like most analogies, this one is instructive even at the extremes where it begins to break down. In the analogy, a firewall is assumed to resist fire equally in both directions. It is symmetric; it does not have to treat fire on one side of the wall differently from fire on the other. It must resist fire, but it must pass people. However, it is easy to distinguish people from fire, and all people and all fire, on either side of the wall, are treated the same. The task of the network firewall is to distinguish between threatening and non-threatening traffic and to do so differently depending on which side the traffic originates. In the presence of fire, a firewall need not pass people; resisting fire is more important than passing people. However, the network firewall will rarely be permitted to reject all traffic in the name of rejecting all attack traffic. It will usually be required to pass legitimate traffic, even in the presence of known attack traffic.

Moreover, a firewall is not is a box; it is not a product that can be purchased off the shelf. At time of this writing, more than 40 vendors offer products that are described, at least in part, as firewalls. Although similarities among them exist, there are also fundamental differences in their approaches. Even given a complete understanding of company requirements and security policy, gaining sufficient knowledge about tens of products to decide which one is most appropriate is a major challenge.

Firewall Policy Positions

Four fundamental policy positions are available to network operators. The firewall policy will be the result of these postures and of the applications on the network.

Paranoid. The first of these positions is called paranoid. It is motivated by extreme caution and probably fear, and characterized by the absence of a connection to the Internet.

Prudent. The second position is called prudent or restrictive. It, too, is motivated by caution, but also by a recognition of the value of connection to the Internet. It is characterized by the fact that everything that is not explicitly allowed is implicitly forbidden. For example, a private Internet user would have to be explicitly authorized to telnet to a system on the public Internet.

Permissive. The permissive posture is the opposite of the restrictive policy. Under this policy, everything that is not explicitly forbidden is implicitly allowed. Obviously, it is the intent of this policy to forbid the necessary conditions for all known attacks. This policy is intended to provide a level of protection with a minimum of interference with applications. This is the policy most likely to be used when applying a firewall to an existing connection. It is particularly useful if little is known about the applications and if there is a strong desire not to interfere with or break those applications. It is the policy most likely to be recommended by Internet service providers who are motivated to maximize the value of the connection.

Promiscuous. The promiscuous policy is that anything goes. Under this policy, there are multiple connections and any legitimate packet can flow from any source to any destination.

Choosing a Firewall Policy

An interesting question is: why would anyone want to be in positions one or four? Remarkably, position one is the default position for business. Most businesses have not yet connected to the Internet. Position four is the default policy for the Internet; all connections and traffic are tolerated in the name of maximizing the bandwidth and the potential for getting messages through.

If an Internet service provider is asked for guidance on a firewall policy, it will likely recommend that the position should be on the promiscuous side of permissive. The service provider will supply a list of restrictions to address all of the attacks that it knows about. However, this permits exposure to a large set of fundamental vulnerabilities. This is, in part, because the Internet service provider believes in the value of the net and does not wish to deny its clients any benefits without necessity.

In most cases, reason dictates a position on the paranoid side of prudent or restrictive. In other words, permit only that traffic that is associated with a particular value for which the net is being used. The flow of all other traffic should be resisted.

A Conservative Firewall Policy

A conservative firewall policy is intended to position an institution or network on the paranoid side of restrictive. The intent is to protect not only against known and expected attacks, but also against those that have not been invented yet. It is driven by fundamental vulnerabilities rather than by known threats and attacks. It attempts to take only those risks that are necessary to accomodate the intended applications.

In addition, no information about the private network should be available on the public net. Private net addresses should never appear on the public net; they should be replaced or aliased to an address that the firewall owns. Addresses on packets and messages should be re-encoded at the firewall. Similarly, users' internal e-mail addresses should not appear on the public net. These private addresses should be replaced with the name of the site or enterprise at the firewall on the way out and replaced on the way in.

Protocols should not traverse the firewall. Traffic should be decoded and re-encoded at the firewall. For example, a SMTP carrying a message should be decoded into a message and then re-encoded into another SMTP for transmission at the firewall.

Reusable passwords should not traverse the firewall in either direction. Incoming passwords may be replays and are not reliable evidence of the identity of the user. Outgoing passwords may be similar to those used by users on the inside, and their use across the firewall may compromise internal systems. A preference for Secure telnet or FTP should be made. These protocols provide end-to-encryption for all traffic, including the password. Alternatively, one-time passwords (e.g., SecureID or s-key) could be used. Although these do not protect all traffic, they protect against replays.

Proxies should represent the public net to the private net. For example, when a user of the private net wishes to access a World Wide Web (WWW) server on the public net, he or she should be transparently routed through the WWW proxy on the firewall. This proxy should hide the user's address from the public net, and protects both nets and the user. The user cannot misrepresent his or her address to the public net, and a process on the public net can directly attack only the proxy, not the user.

Only a limited set of limited applications should be permitted. Under this policy, such a limited application as e-mail is permitted, and such a very general application as telnet is discouraged. Telnet is very general and flexible, and its intent is not obvious. It is vulnerable as a target and useful for attack.

Only those public applications that are intended for use on the public net should be placed on the public net. The public should not be permitted to traverse a firewall simply for the purpose of gaining access to public applications.

Applications on the public net should be implemented on dedicated and isolated servers. The server should be dedicated to a single use; it should not rely on the operating system to protect the application. Public servers should not know about the private net. Any connection to the private net should be to an application and over a trusted path. Privileged access to such servers should require strong authentication.

The public should not be granted read-and-write access to the same resource. For example, if the public can read a web page, they should not be able to write to it. The ability to write to it would permit them to alter or contaminate the data in a manner that could prove embarrassing. If a directory is provided to which the public can send files, they should not be able to read from that directory. If they can both read and write to the directory,

Application	Encryption
E-mail	PGP, SecureXchange, PEM, S-MIME
File	PGP, RSA Secure, Entrust
Application	DES, IDEA, stelnet, sftp
Client/Server	Secure Socket Layer (SSL)
Gateway-to-gateway	Digital, IBM, TIS
World Wide Web	s-http
Secure IP	S/WAN

Exhibit 49.1.   Encryption on the Internet.

they may use it simply as storage in lieu of their own. They may also use it to store contraband data that they would not want on their own systems and which might also prove embarrassing.

ENCRYPTION

Encryption is the application and use of secret, as opposed to public, codes. It is a powerful defense that can deal with many of the problems related to vulnerable links and even some of those related to insecure nodes. It is inexpensive and effective. In addition, multiple implementations are available. However, it is limited as to the open node problems that it can deal with and may require some management infrastructure. Exhibit 49.1 displays some of the encryption choices available for selected applications on the Internet.

Encryption is used for two fundamental purposes on the net. The first is to preserve necessary confidentiality on the net, which is the traditional use of cryptography. The second is to enable some confidence about with whom one is talking. In other words, if conversation is in a language that can only be spoken by one other, the correct parties are speaking to one another.

Encryption can also be used to resist password grabbers and other eavesdropping attacks.

USING THE INTERNET IN A RELATIVELY SAFE ENVIRONMENT

The following are recommendations for using the Internet in a relatively safe way. Although few will follow all of these recommendations, there is risk involved in any deviation from the recommendations. Moreover, although complete adherence to these recommendations will not eliminate all vulnerabilities, it will address many of them. Finally, although complete adherence will not eliminate all risks, following these recommendations provides a reasonable balance between risk and other values.

- **Do not rely on the secrecy or authenticity of any information traversing the Internet in public codes.** Names and addresses, credit card numbers, passwords, and other data received from the public net may be replays rather than originals. Amounts and account numbers may have been tampered with.
- **Choose a single point of connection to the Internet.** Although the Internet is inherently mesh connected, and more than one connection may be necessary to avoid single points of failure, the more connections, and the more points of attack, the more difficult it is to maintain consistent controls. The fewer the number of points of connection, the fewer the potential points of attack and the easier to maintain control.
- **Connect to the Internet only with equipment dedicated to that purpose.** When computers were expensive, it was economical to put as many applications as possible on the costly hardware. Communication software was added to connect existing multi-use, multi-user systems to the net. Attacks exploited this gratuitous generality. Because of less expensive hardware, hardware connected to the net should be dedicated to that use. All other applications should be run on other systems.
- **Choose application-only connections.** Many of the compromises of the Internet have resulted from the fact that the components were connected at the system layer and that attacks have succeeded in escaping the application to the more general and flexible system layer. If in an attack encounters the e-mail service, it should see nothing else. If it escapes the e-mail application, it should see nothing. Under no circumstances, should it see the prompt of an operating system that knows about any other system. In other words, the operating system should be hidden from the public net.
- **Limit the use of telnet.** Telnet, particularly to the operating system, is a very general and flexible capability. It can be both used for attack and is vulnerable to attacks. Most of its functions and capabilities can be accomplished with safer alternatives.
- **Use end-to-end encryption for commercial applications on the net.** Although most of the applications and traffic on the public net are public, commercial and other private applications on the public net must be conducted in secret codes.
- **Require strong authentication.** Users of private applications on the public net or of the public net for commercial applications must use strong authentication. Two independent kinds of evidence should be employed to determine the identity of a user, and the authentication data must be protected from capture and replay.
- **Log, monitor, and meter events and traffic.** Given enough time, almost any attack can succeed. It is important to be able to recognize attack traffic and correct for it early. Attacks can usually be recognized

by a change — often a sudden increase — from normal traffic patterns. It is useful to know what normal traffic looks like to be able to recognize variances on a timely basis, and to communicate the condition of those variances to managers who can take timely corrective action.

CONCLUSION

The Internet is as ubiquitous as the telephone and for similar reasons. It gives users such an economic advantage over nonusers that the nonusers are forced to become users. Pundits are fond of saying that no one is making money on the Internet. This position is fatuous and suggests that tens of thousands of enterprises are behaving irrationally. What is meant is that no one is conducting commerce on the Internet, at least not in the sense that they are selling, distributing, billing, and being paid over the Internet. Of course, many firms are doing one or more of these. Many others are making money, mostly by reducing costs. Many companies are using the Internet because it is the most efficient way to support customers.

The Internet holds out the promise to empower, enrich, and perhaps even ennoble. A minimum level of public trust and confidence must be maintained if that promise becomes a reality. That trust is both fragile and irreparable.

Because fundamental vulnerabilities on the network exist and because all possible attacks cannot be anticipated, a conservative policy and a responsive posture are required.

Chapter 50
Improving Quality with Software Metrics

Ian S. Hayes

T O SUCCESSFULLY MANAGE INFORMATION SYSTEMS in these cost-conscious times, IS managers must become more effective in delivering their services. They should be able to identify and replicate practices that result in higher productivity, lower costs, and higher quality, and correct or eliminate ineffective practices. This process requires a continuous flow of information to determine the quality of the IS activities being managed. Subjective guesses are not accurate enough and are open to dispute. Solid, objective measurements are required.

This chapter discusses how to use software metrics as a basis for making management decisions. It describes the sources and methods of collection for the data presented and demonstrates how cost and frequency-of-change information can be used with technical metrics to provide comparisons of cost for quality and productivity. The chapter also uses historical data collected from over 12,000 programs in more than 65 companies to illustrate the current state of IS software and conversely to identify the desirable characteristics in a program or system. Programming standards are recommended, based on the metrics described, and steps for implementing a software measurement program are outlined.

WHY MEASURE?

Most IS departments do not have formal methods for measuring their programming and maintenance activities. As a result, the management of these departments would be hard pressed to answer questions such as:

- Has quality or productivity improved or declined in the last five years? By how much?
- Which programs or systems require a disproportionate amount of programming resources to maintain?
- What are the desirable characteristics in a program or system?

- Does a new software tool or development technique actually improve quality or productivity?
- Does increased quality actually lead to decreased cost?

All these questions, and more, could be answered through the implementation of a formal measurement program.

A comprehensive measurement program would combine software quality metrics, frequency, and quantity of change information with cost or effort information to provide an accurate picture of current programming practices. This information would be used to:

- *Define Quality.* Which practices are effective? What are their characteristics? The answers to these questions provide a real-world definition of quality. For example, small programs cost far less to maintain than large programs. Therefore, small is beneficial in programming.
- *Quantify Quality.* Once a definition of quality has been identified, the IS environment can be measured to determine the volume of characteristics. For instance, how many of the programs in a general ledger application are too large to maintain effectively?
- *Set a Baseline.* Each compilation of measurement information provides a baseline of comparison for future runs. This baseline can be used for identifying trends, setting improvement objectives, and for measuring progress against those objectives. Continuing the example, after one year of improvement activities, what percentage of the general ledger programs are still too large?

Combining cost and effort data with software quality metrics is particularly valuable for management decision making. It enables IS managers to determine relative productivity rates and to make cost-quality comparisons. Productivity rate information helps identify productivity bottlenecks and provides a foundation for accurate task estimation. Cost and quality information provides a basis for cost justifying quality improvement activities.

Maintaining a historical data base of key measurement data enables long-term validation of the decisions made from the measurement data. Quality and productivity trends can be determined, and the use and collection of the metrics information can be fine tuned if necessary. The benefits can be periodically reanalyzed to ensure that they are matching their cost-justification projections. Finally, as the base of historic data grows, it becomes more valuable for verifying task estimates.

METHODS USED IN THIS STUDY

There are three major categories of data used in this chapter: technical quality data, cost and effort data, and frequency-of-change data. This data is gathered through a variety of automated and manual methods. Much of the data presented here was gathered from Keane, Inc.'s reengineering consulting practice. Keane's analysis combines its ADW/INSPECTOR metrics with other statistics, such as programmer cost, maintenance effort by task, frequency of change, and failure rates, to assist IS management in making strategic decisions about its application portfolio.

Technical Quality

The software metrics data presented in this chapter is a combination of statistics that have been gathered over five years by both Language Technology, Inc. (now a part of KnowledgeWare) and Keane, Inc. The software quality statistics are derived primarily from a data base of more than 150 software metrics collected using an automated COBOL analysis tool. This data base was originally developed by Language Technology from data contributed by more than 65 customers. The data base encompasses well beyond 12,000 COBOL programs consisting of 23 million lines of code.

Cost and Effort

Cost and effort data are essentially equivalent. For example, effort can be converted to cost by multiplying the number of hours expended by the average cost rate for the programmers. Gathering this data varies widely from company to company. Common sources are time-accounting systems, budgets, or task-tracking systems. Ideally, programmer time is charged to specific projects and is broken down by type of task. This is rarely available, so in most cases, specific cost allocations have to be extrapolated from available information.

Frequency of Change

Determining productivity rates and isolating the most volatile and, hence, high-payback areas of an application system require the availability of frequency and volume-of-change information. This type of information can take many forms, depending on the company's practices. For example, if the company measures function points, volume of change is the number of function points added, deleted, or modified over a period of time. Another method is to track user change requests. These methods are less accurate from a programmer's point of view, but they have the advantage of having more meaning to the business areas. More commonly, however, this data is derived from the company's library management system. If set up properly, the library management system can provide reports on the number of changes made for each module contained within it, and often it can state the size, in lines of code, for each of those changes.

METRICS AND COST

Many companies are content with using only technical metrics to evaluate their programming and maintenance practices. Although this gives them the ability to evaluate the quality of their practices, it does not allow the correlation of quality to cost. This correlation provides a wide range of information that is invaluable to IS management. Some key examples of analyses that are accomplished in conjunction with cost are:

- Productivity measurement.
- Comparison of applications by effectiveness.
- Establishing the value of quality.
- Isolation of areas of high cost and high payback.
- Task estimate validation.
- Cost justification.

Examples of these analyses are illustrated in the following sections.

Productivity Measurement

Productivity measurement is a sensitive topic among those who are to be measured. Given the level of accuracy of the numbers available in most companies, productivity comparisons are best done at the application level rather than at the individual level. The basis for measuring productivity is effort per unit of work. Using cost in place of effort is equally valid. Potential units of measure include function points, statements, lines of code, change requests, or any other unit of work routinely measured by the company. Each has its own strengths and weaknesses, but any unit works for gross measures. The best unit that is easily available should be used because 80 percent of the value can be derived with the first 20 percent of the effort. A typical unit used by Keane is the number of lines of code changed per year. *Changed,* in this case, is defined as added, modified, or deleted. This number has the advantage of being relatively easy to obtain through ADW/INSPECTOR and a library management tool.

Taking the overall cost or effort expended on maintenance for a given application and dividing it by the volume of changes leads to a productivity factor. For example, application A may have a productivity factor of $10 per line of code changed. Improvements in productivity are reflected as a corresponding drop in the per-unit cost.

Comparison of Applications by Effectiveness

As Exhibit 50.1 illustrates, the productivity factor may be used to compare applications against each other. Five applications that were measured during a portfolio analysis are ranked against each other by their relative productivity factors. This relative ranking provides a challenge to management to determine why productivity is better for one application than

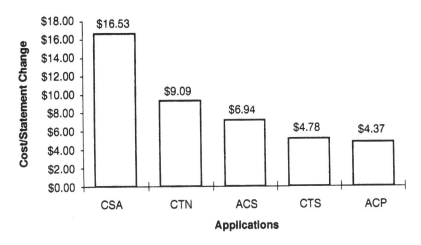

Exhibit 50.1.   Comparison of applications by effectiveness.

another. Is it due to technical quality, personnel, or maintenance records? Answering these questions has inestimable value. If the factors causing low costs on ACP could be duplicated on CSA, there would be an almost four-fold increase in productivity.

Establishing the Value of Quality

Exhibit 50.2 is a combination of the productivity statistics in Exhibit 50.1 and average application quality statistics. The quality is measured by the average ADW/INSPECTOR composite score for all the programs within the application. This metric will be explained in more detail later in this chapter; in short, the score ranges from 0 to 100, with 100 being ideal.

The combination of cost and quality data as illustrated in Exhibit 50.2 demonstrates the strong correlation between application quality and the cost of maintenance. Even small increases in average quality generally result in measurable reductions in the cost of maintenance. This correlation between application quality and the cost of maintenance is typical when multiple applications within a company are measured. Performing this type of correlation is valuable for developing actual dollar benefit estimates for quality improvement efforts.

Isolation of Areas of High Cost and High Payback

Some programs within an application consume a much higher proportion of maintenance resources than other programs. These programs may be isolated by distributing the cost and change data down to the individual program level. Whereas programmers can generally identify the top one or

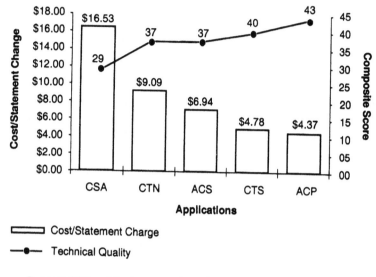

Exhibit 50.2. The impact of quality on maintenance costs.

two programs requiring the most maintenance effort, the overall distribution of maintenance cost and effort is often surprising. Interestingly, between 3 and 5 percent of the programs in a given application account for 50 to 80 percent of the overall maintenance effort. Those numbers are remarkably consistent across many companies. Exhibit 50.3 illustrates this cost distribution for the five applications used in the previous examples. Twenty programs, or approximately 3 percent of the total number of programs, account for 50 percent of the overall cost of maintenance.

To develop this graph, yearly maintenance costs were allocated to each program within the applications. The programs were sorted by cost, and the graph line charts the accumulation of these costs (i.e., from the left, point 1 is the percentage cost of the most expensive program; point 2 is the sum of the two most expensive programs). Knowing where effort is actually expended allows improvement activities to be targeted to those programs in which the value would be the highest. Of the programs in this example, 28 percent had no maintenance effort expended on them at all. Consequently, they would have no payback if improved.

Task Estimate Validation

Keeping cost statistics and, in particular, developing a productivity factor is valuable for use in estimating the effort and cost of maintenance changes. Once the approximate size of a maintenance change is known, it can be multiplied against the productivity factor to provide an approximate

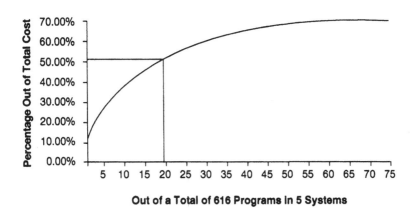

Out of a Total of 616 Programs In 5 Systems

Exhibit 50.3.   Distribution of cost by program.

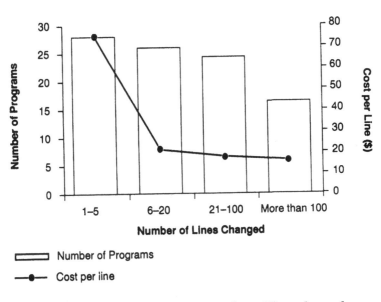

Exhibit 50.4.   Cost per line vs. number of lines changed.

scope of effort. This may be used directly or as a validation for other estimation methodologies. If cost or effort data is correlated against other factors, such as size or technical quality, these factors can be used as modifiers when estimating. For example, Exhibit 50.4 illustrates the cost per statement changed based on the number of statements changed in a particular modification for a client.

As would be expected, maintenance modifications that encompass only a few lines of code are more expensive per statement changed than larger modifications. This reflects the overhead for finding, inserting, testing, and placing the modification into production. The overhead factors are generally uniform relative to the size of the modification. Knowing this curve allows the calculation of an adjustment factor that can be applied to estimates for small changes.

Cost Justification

Using methods similar to the estimation technique described above, cost and productivity factors can be used for developing cost/benefit analyses for justifying new productivity tools or methodologies. For instance, the comparison of the five applications in Exhibit 50.2 can easily be used to justify quality improvement efforts. The only additional piece of necessary information is the total volume of changes. In the case of application CTN, this volume is about 114,000 statements per year. This application costs $9.09 per statement maintained, whereas application ACP costs $4.37. If the quality of CTN could be improved to meet or exceed that of ACP, one would expect that its cost of maintenance would be similar to ACP. Thus, if the improvement activities resulted in a per-statement drop in cost of $4.72 ($9.09 – $4.37), the anticipated benefit would be about $538,000 per year (114,000 x $4.72), Comparing this benefit to the cost of making the necessary improvements would provide the cost justification.

METRICS AND QUALITY

Cost metrics describe the value of a particular activity, whereas technical metrics evaluate the quality of its implementation. This industry has over 30 years of experience in the effectiveness of programming practices, yet practitioners still argue about the merits of such advances as GO TO-less programming. The metrics in the Language Technology data base confirm most theories on effective programming. This data should be used to define the standards by which programming is performed. Even though the data is based on COBOL programs and programmers, the insights are not limited to that environment. Human abilities for handling complexity, for example, are not language, or even programming, dependent.

Background

Some important definitions are necessary before embarking on a discussion of the metrics and their meanings. Perhaps the most important definition is that of the ADW/INSPECTOR composite score. As its name implies, this metric is a composite of a number of other measures. A 0-to-100 scale is used to provide a quick ranking of programs by quality. This metric has a consistently high correlation with other measures of quality and it is an accurate predictor of relative maintenance effort and, therefore, cost between programs. The composite score is calculated as follows:

- Degree of structure (based on McCabe's essential complexity): 25 percent.
- Degree of complexity (based on McCabe's cyclomatic complexity): 25 percent.
- Number of ALTER verbs: 10 percent.
- Number of GO TO (e.g., non-exit) verbs: 10 percent.
- Number of fall throughs (e.g., to non-exit statements): 10 percent.
- Number of active procedure exits: 10 percent.
- Number of recursive procedures: 10 percent.

A perfect program receives 100 points (totally structured, not complex, and no ALTERs or GO TOs).

Other important definitions are:

- *Active Procedure Exits.* These result when a PERFORMed procedure within a COBOL program is exited by a GO TO while still active from a PERFORM. Unpredictable program behavior can result when these procedures are reached via another control path in the program.
- *Recursive Procedures.* These are the result of a PERFORMed procedure being re-PERFORMed before completing a previous PERFORM. It too can cause unpredictable behavior.
- *McCabe Metrics.* These will be discussed in the following sections.
- *Lines of Code.* These are the specific number of lines of 80 column COBOL text in a program. Statements are the count of COBOL procedural verbs, such as MOVEs or ADDs.

Industry Averages

A major advantage of having a large multicompany data base of metrics is the ability to compare a specific company's application software with the rest of the industry. This provides a relative measure for that software against its "average" peers.

Exhibit 50.5 contains the characteristics for the average COBOL program. The characteristics of the average program may surprise many programmers: it is small in size and its quality is high. These effects are the result of mixing older COBOL programs with more newly developed code. As with averages in general, this obscures the very different characteristics of these two distinct categories.

This distinction between new and old code is illuminated when the programs within the data base are distributed by composite score. This distribution is shown in Exhibit 50.6.

Metric	Industry Average
Composite Score	60
Unstructured	43%
Complex	47%
Lines of Code	1902
Statements	666
GO TOs	52
Fall Throughs	23
Recursion	3
Active Exits	12

Exhibit 50.5. Characteristics for the average COBOL program.

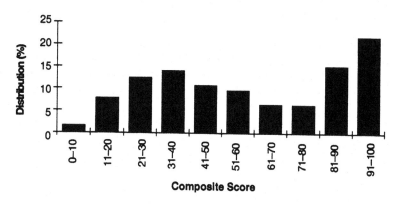

Exhibit 50.6. Characteristics for the average COBOL program.

The score distribution in Exhibit 50.6 is bimodal (i.e., there are two separate peaks). The peak at the far left is that of the average old application; its average program is in the 35-point range for the composite score. The peak at the far right mostly represents newer programs. Many new programs are created in conformance with rigorous structured programming standards and tend to be high in quality.

Over time, however, this quality tends to degrade through the effects of multiple coding changes unless specific quality efforts are in place. This decline is made apparent by the number of programs in the 81-to-90-point range.

The differentiation between the newer code and the older code becomes even more clear when the data is categorized by structure and complexity.

Exhibit 50.7 divides programs into four quadrants using unstructured percentages and complex percentages. The newer programs tend to be

	Noncomplex	Complex
Unstructured	678 Programs 5% of Total 347,083 Lines 1% of Total 89,864 Statements 1% Total	6,285 Programs 50% of Total 16,867,023 Lines 71% of Total 6,131,621 Statements 74% Total
Structured	3,769 Programs 30% of Total 3,070,197 Lines 13% of Total 906,110 Statements 11% Total	1,772 Programs 14% of Total 3,501,542 Lines 15% of Total 1,200,590 Statements 14% Total

25% (left of Unstructured/Structured rows)

Noncomplex   25%   Complex

Exhibit 50.7.   Categorizing code by structure and complexity.

concentrated in the lower left quadrant. They are structured (i.e., under 25 percent unstructured), and not complex (under 25 percent complex). Whereas 30 percent of the programs fall into this desirable category, they make up only 11 percent of the total number of COBOL statements, the measure of actual code content.

Conversely, the older programs tend to be concentrated in the upper right quadrant and are both unstructured and complex. The upper right quadrant contains the worst 50 percent of the programs. Using statements as the measure, those programs make up 74 percent of the physical volume of COBOL code.

Even more instructive is selecting the average program from each quadrant. These averages are illustrated in Exhibit 50.8. In this exhibit, overlaps are the same as active procedure exits, and procedure size is the number of lines of code in the COBOL program's procedure division.

Structured/noncomplex. As mentioned earlier, these are the desirable programs. They have a very high average composite score of 93 points and a very low unstructured percentage and complex percentage. This is particularly interesting given the 25 percent cutoff for unstructured percentage and complex percentage; the low numbers are well below the expected average of about 12.5 percent for an even distribution. Size is an important factor in the quality of these programs. Desirability in programs is achieved through the combination of small size, high structure, and no GO TOs. Despite the single GO TO in the average, the majority of the programs in this category have no GO TOs at all.

Unstructured/noncomplex. These are the rarest programs in the data base sample due to the difficulty of creating an unstructured program without

Metric	Structured Noncomplex	Unstructured Noncomplex	Structured Complex	Unstructured Complex
Composite Score:	93	63	78	34
Unstructured %:	1	66	4	77
Complex %:	3	1	50	78
Size in Location:	815	512	1976	2684
Statements:	240	133	678	976
Procedure Size:	451	236	1227	1565
Go Tos:	1	9	5	100
Fall Throughs:	1	5	3	43
Recursion:	0	0	0	5
OverLaps:	0	1	0	14
Deadcode:	6	10	9	36

Exhibit 50.8.   Average programs per structure and complexity.

measurably increasing its complexity. This is generally possible in only very small programs, which is demonstrated by the fact that these programs make up 5 percent of the total in number but only 1 percent of the physical volume in statements.

These programs are surprisingly unstructured given their very small size. This lack of structure is caused by the increase in the average number of GO TOs and fall throughs. The drop in quality reflected in this quadrant results in an increase in the number of lines of dead code. Dead or inexecutable code is generally introduced accidentally when a poorly understood program is modified. These programs could easily be improved by simply running them through a structuring tool.

Structured/complex. This quadrant contains programs that are highly complex despite being structured. Some of these programs are necessarily complex due to the nature of the tasks they are performing; others are needlessly complex because of poor design. In either case, studies have shown that both error rates and testing effort increase as complexity increases. Complexity is highly correlated to program size. This is demonstrated by the significantly larger size of these programs as compared to the programs in the noncomplex categories. The presence of additional numbers of GO TOs and fall throughs also results in an increased complexity. The best method for reducing complexity in a structured program is to subdivide complex portions of that program into smaller noncomplex portions whenever

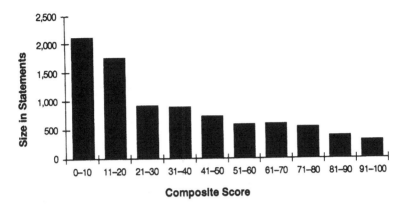

Exhibit 50.9. Distribution by size.

possible. Breaking larger programs into multiple smaller modules also reduces complexity.

Unstructured/complex. The programs in this quadrant are the classic old COBOL programs. The composite score drops dramatically as the result of increased complexity and decreased structure. Size has increased significantly, making these programs even more difficult to understand. Particularly alarming is the massive increase in poor coding practices, such as GO TOs, fall throughs, and recursion. These are averages, however; there are programs that are considerably worse in this category. This major drop in quality results in programs that are very hard to maintain and have significantly higher failure rates. This is reflected in the increased number of lines of dead code. Programs in this category are candidates for reengineering improvement activities to lower the cost and effort of maintenance.

Program Size Factors

Perhaps the most critical determinate of a program's quality and maintainability is its size. It is theoretically possible to produce a large, well-structured, noncomplex program; however, analysis of the statistics in the metrics data base show that this is an extremely rare occurrence. In fact, size in statements has a strong correlation with every negative programming practice. Size is not a component of the composite score, but as Exhibit 50.9 illustrates, the composite score increases as the size decreases.

In fact, programs in the ideal composite score range of 93 to 100 points average only 240 statements in size. This size appears to be a boundary in program understanding. It appears consistently in the analysis results from

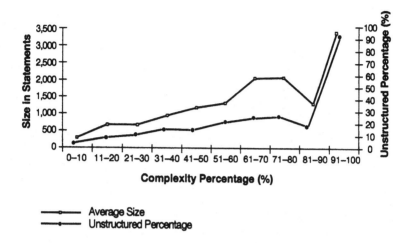

Exhibit 50.10. Size and structure compared to complexity percentage.

company to company. In one client engagement, multiple years of ADW/INSPECTOR metrics were available, allowing the comparison of the effects of maintenance changes over time. When compared by composite score, programs under 240 statements in size either retained their score through multiple maintenance changes or actually improved in score. Conversely, programs over 240 statements generally declined in composite score. This effect appears to be caused by the relationship of complexity and size. Exhibit 50.10 is a graph of size, structure, and complexity correlation.

Again, although structure and complexity should be independent of size, they are highly related in practice. The sheer size of large programs makes them difficult to understand fully and often forces programmers to make localized program modifications that actually increase complexity and degrade structure. This tendency accelerates over time until the large program becomes unmaintainable.

As would be expected, size is related to the cost of maintenance. The graph in Exhibit 50.11 is from another Keane portfolio analysis engagement. The bars represent the number of programs in each size category. The graph line shows the total maintenance expenditure in dollars for all the programs in each respective column.

The highest expenditure of dollars is on the smallest number of programs, those with over 1,000 statements in size. The second-highest total expenditure is for the programs in the under-250-statement category; however, as the bar indicates, they make up a disproportionate number of the

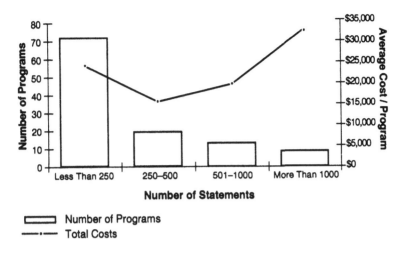

Exhibit 50.11.   Distribution of expenditures by program size.

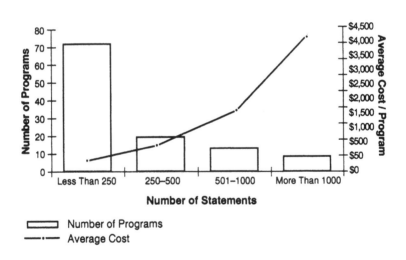

Exhibit 50.12.   Distribution of programs and costs by program size.

programs. This data is more dramatic when the average maintenance cost per program is graphed in Exhibit 50.12.

McCabe Metrics

The metrics of T. J. McCabe are widely used to measure the complexity and structure of programs. Numerous studies have shown that these metrics are

Exhibit 50.13. Distribution by number of statements per paragraph.

accurate predictors of program defect rates and program understandability. There are two separate metrics: cyclomatic complexity and essential complexity. Both metrics are based on measuring single-entry, single-exit blocks of code. In a structured COBOL program, these blocks of code are individual paragraphs. In a convoluted, unstructured program, the entire program may be one single-entry, single-exit block.

Cyclomatic complexity. This is the measure of the number of test paths within a given single-entry, single-exit block of code. The number of defects in a block of code greatly increases when the number of test paths in that block exceeds 9. This is based on the theory that the average person can assimilate 7 plus or minus 2 (e.g., 7 +/–2) pieces of detail at a time in short-term memory. In COBOL programs, the number of test paths can be estimated by counting the number of IF statements in the block of code being measured. Adding 1 to this number gives the total number of unique test paths in that block of code. Therefore, as long as there are no more than 9 IF statements in each single-entry, single-exit block of code, it will meet the McCabe standards.

The 7 +/–2 levels of detail principle represented by cyclomatic complexity comes through in Exhibit 50.13. This graph from the metrics data base shows the distribution of the number of statements per paragraph across the entire data base.

The standard deviation in this graph is 8 +/–4, showing that programmers naturally tend to limit themselves to the McCabe cyclomatic constraints.

Essential Complexity

Essential complexity measures the degree of structure in a block of code. Essential complexity is measured by reducing all structured constructs (e.g., conditions, sequence, and loops) out of a given block of code, then measuring the remaining complexity. If no complexity remains, the piece of code is structured. Any remaining complexity is unessential (i.e., it could be removed by structuring that piece of code). Unstructured percentage is the sum of the number of unstructured paths divided by the total number of paths in the program. Essential complexity is used to measure if a particular program is in compliance with structured standards. It also predicts the ease with which a program can be modularized. Exhibit 50.14 illustrates this principle in an unstructured program.

The program in the real life portion of the illustration is primarily unstructured. The first two and last two paragraphs are single-entry, single-exit, but the entire middle section of the program is so interwoven with control flow that it is effectively one large block. The structure chart represents a view of the program if it were imported into a CASE tool. The middle block in the structure chart, shown as paragraph Initial-Read, actually contains all the code from the convoluted middle section, as shown in Behind the Scenes. If this program were to be modularized for reusability, this large block of code could not be easily subdivided unless it was structured first. Ideal programs should be totally structured as measured by McCabe's essential complexity.

GO TOS AND GO TO EXITS

Despite the advent and supposed acceptance of structured programming, GO TOs are still used. ADW/INSPECTOR can differentiate between GO TOs and GO TO EXITs, which allows them to be examined separately. GO TO EXITs can theoretically be structured, so they are not penalized in the composite score. When GO TO non-exits are used within a program, they greatly increase its complexity. This is shown in Exhibit 50.15.

This complexity increases disproportionately as the number of GO TOs increases. Exhibit 50.16 shows the effect of GO TOs on the Composite Score.

The number of GO TO nonexits accounts for 10 points of the composite score. As can be seen from this graph, their effect on program quality is far beyond those 10 points.

Many programmers argue in favor of the use of GO TO EXITs. This construct was originally used to reduce nesting of IF statements within paragraphs. This is no longer necessary in structured programming. Structuring tools can be used to automatically control nesting levels, and the use of structured CASE constructs eliminates much of the complexity involved in the nesting of related conditions. If implemented correctly, GO TO EXITs should have no effect on structure and complexity. In practice, this is not true. Exhibit 50.17 shows the number of GO TO EXITs graphed against complexity.

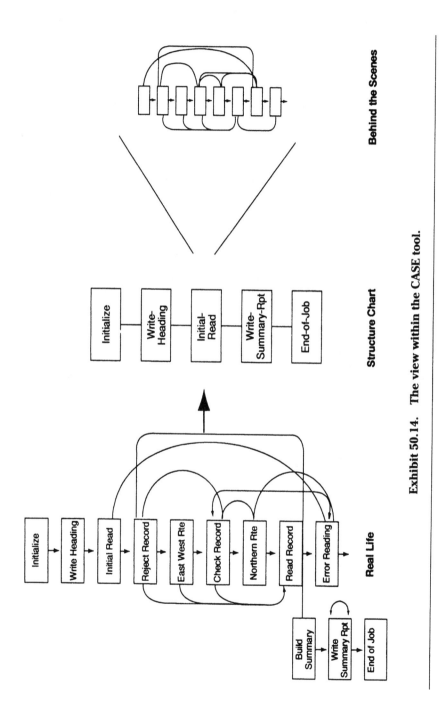

Exhibit 50.14. The view within the CASE tool.

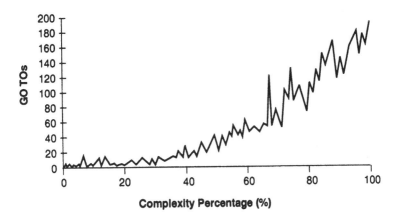

Exhibit 50.15. The effect of GO TOs on complexity.

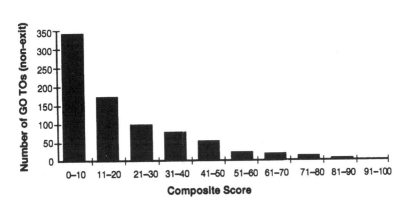

Exhibit 50.16. GO TOs by composite score.

Although the correlation is not as strong with GO TO non-exits, GO TO EXITs increase program complexity. This appears to be the result of two factors. First, GO TO EXITs are legitimate as long as they go to the correct exit. Unfortunately, their very existence invites accidental misuse. Second, the presence of any GO TOs tends to beget other GO TOs. For these reasons, it makes the most sense to avoid the use of any GO TOs when programming.

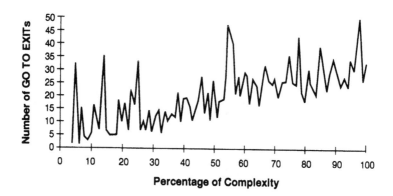

Exhibit 50.17.   The effect of GO TO EXITs on complexity.

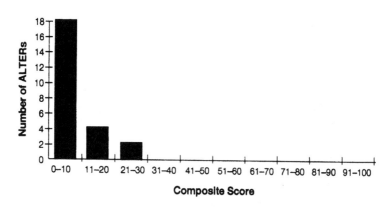

Exhibit 50.18.   ALTERs by composite score.

ALTERS

The ALTER verb is rarely seen in COBOL nowadays. A vestige from the assembly programming days, it appears only in some of the oldest programs. When ALTERs are present, their negative effect on quality amply justifies their removal. This may be done manually or automatically with a structuring tool. As with GO TOs, ALTERs comprise 10 points of the composite score. Again, however, their effect extends far beyond those 10 points. This is shown in Exhibit 50.18.

The presence of any ALTERs within a program tends to push it below 30 points in the composite score. ALTERs also greatly increase the number of test paths within the program. The worst example in the data base was a

1,500-line program that contained 508 ALTER statements. It had 4,718 separate test paths as measured by McCabe's cyclomatic complexity.

METRICS AND STANDARDS

With more than 30 years of industry experience in COBOL programming, one would expect that the characteristics that make one program easier to maintain than another would be well known and incorporated into IS practices. Unfortunately, that has not been the case, in part because of the lack of agreement about what makes a desirable program. The data presented in this chapter should shed some light on some of the most important characteristics.

The maintainability of COBOL programs can be greatly enhanced, thereby lowering the cost and effort of maintenance, by following a few simple standards. The key to excellence in COBOL programs is understandability. If a program can be easily understood, it can be modified quickly, can be tested more thoroughly, and will be less likely to contain defects.

When all the data is analyzed, the three crucial characteristics that lead to understandability are size, structure, and modularity.

- *Size.* Once a program exceeds a certain size, it becomes difficult to understand and maintain just due to sheer mass. Changes are made to large programs without understanding the context of the whole program. This introduces poor coding practices and increases complexity. Large programs tend to contain many functions. Modifications to any of these functions require analysis and testing of the entire program, further increasing maintenance effort. Thus, small is better in programming. As the data in this chapter indicates, the ideal size limit appears to be 240 or fewer COBOL statements.
- *Structure.* Programs consisting of well-organized, single-function paragraphs are the easiest to understand and maintain. Strictly following the dictates of structured programming helps ensure that programs meet these standards. Further, if a program is structured, by definition it does not contain any poor coding constructs, such as GO TOs, fall throughs, or recursion.
- *Modularity.* Each paragraph in the program should consist of a single business function, and it should have only one entry and one exit. Further, the business functions must be modularized such that each paragraph consists of 8±4 COBOL statements. If the program is structured, this rule ensures that the program is not complex by the McCabe standard. This simplifies testing, enables the location and reuse of business functions, and enhances the value of importing the program into a CASE environment.

Metric	Recommended
Standard Composite Score	93–100
Unstructured	0%
Complex	Less than 25%
Lines of Code	750 or Less
Statements	240 or Less
Statements per paragraph*	8–12
GO TOs	0
Fall Throughs	0
Recursion	0
Active Exits	0

*Average standards per paragraph is calculated by dividing the total number of procedure statements in the program by the total number of paragraphs.

Exhibit 50.19. Optimum metric values for measuring COBOL compliance

Each of the three characteristics described above should be incorporated into IS coding standards for both new development and maintenance. Adherence to these standards can be easily measured with an analysis tool like ADW/INSPECTOR using the metrics discussed in this chapter. Exhibit 50.19 contains the optimum metric values for measuring compliance with these recommended COBOL programming standards.

For new development, these standards can be directly applied as acceptance criteria for newly written programs. Following these standards ensures that these new programs are easy to modify in the future.

For maintenance and enhancement projects, these standards become targets. At the very minimum, programs should be measured after each modification to ensure that quality is maintained. Ideally, programmers can attempt to slowly improve programs to get closer to these standards each time they make a maintenance change.

Finally, these standards are a goal for reengineering or other improvement activities to existing code. These efforts should be targeted at only the most highly maintained 3 to 5 percent of the programs to ensure payback. Attempting to reengineer all code to this standard would be cost prohibitive, and it would not provide any benefits on rarely maintained programs.

CONCLUSION

A software measurement program can provide IS managers with valuable insights on how to best manage their scarce resources. As the examples in this chapter demonstrate, metrics can be used to identify specific standards and methods that save money and resources. They can pinpoint when to apply most effectively that knowledge. They can be used to estimate the effort for programming tasks and to quantify the benefits of improvement tasks.

Gaining these benefits requires implementing a software measurement program. Some basic steps are:

Defining objectives. Define why a measurement program is needed and what the specific types of questions to be answered are. This identifies what type of data is needed and the scope of the effort.

Identifying data sources. A check should be made of the existing data. Is the data complete as required? What data can be collected automatically? What data must be collected manually? Some examples of each type of data should be collected to check its ease of collection, accuracy, and completeness.

Obtaining tools. If the company does not already have an analysis tool, it is time to get one. Some tools, such as project tracking and library management software, may be in house but may require specific option settings to collect the necessary data.

Defining reports. Copies of the reports and graphs that will be used as output of the measurement program should be mocked up. Distribution frequency should be decided on. Displaying these examples is a key to getting buy-in on the project.

Pilot testing. Results from the preceding steps should be tested on a pilot set of applications. It is best to use two or three diverse types of applications to ensure that any potential problems are caught. Training requirements should be identified for those involved in the project.

Tuning the results. Any of the collection methods, metrics, and reports should be fine tuned, using the results of the pilot test. This information should be used to estimate effort for the final roll out.

Developing a roll-out plan. A plan should be developed to roll out the measurement program across the organization, making sure to include sufficient training.

Implement. The process is put in place. Data should be reexamined periodically and tuned accordingly as new information is received. Results should be saved in a data base to allow for comparisons over time.

Section IX
Contingency Planning

WHEN IT SYSTEMS ARE THREATENED by either an outside attack or by a natural disaster resulting in complete system failure, the IT operations manager must have a plan in place to recover computer processing capability through some alternative approach — a contingency plan. This last section of the handbook addresses the important issues associated with disaster recovery or contingency planning. A data center recovery plan consists of documented plans and procedures that will be employed by key data center personnel following a disaster for the express purpose of resuming data center operations in an organized and timely manner.

Chapter 51, "Introduction to Data Center Recovery Planning," introduces data center recovery planning concepts and begins a three-part series on data recovery planning which continues in Chapters 52 and 53, "Developing a Data Center Recovery Plan: Part I" and "Developing a Data Center Recovery Plan: Part II." These three chapters provide a comprehensive approach for developing a contingency plan for your organization. You will learn the definition and history of data center recovery planning; plan-development assumptions; selecting a plan-development committee; establishing the plan's scope; establishing its objects; determining the premise of the plan; establishing the level of detail for the plan; establishing the plan's format; and determining recovery logistics.

Because of the real-time, on-line nature of computing today, data centers have become nerve centers for organizations. If the data center goes down, so does the rest of an organization. In addition to the pressing business case for data center recovery planning, there may be a regulatory need for having a recovery plan in place. Chapter 51 introduces the concepts behind this important planning aspect that every IT operations manager must master.

Chapters 52 and 53 examine a seven-step process that IT operations managers can use to develop a recovery plan for their data centers. Because data centers comprise a variety of systems, planning for recovery from a disaster in a data center is a complex process. Chapter 52 shows how to begin this difficult process by spelling out the preliminary steps of developing a disaster plan and illustrating these steps with sample plan documents. IT managers must also ensure that the plan consists of the right balance of detailed information. The plan will not be useful if it skimps on necessary details or if it is so detailed that no one will ever be able to follow it. Chapter 53 teaches how IT managers can give a recovery plan the correct level of detail and format so that it can be carried out when disaster strikes.

The growth in the use of LANs has resulted in vital corporate information moving onto the LAN. However, instead of being regulated to servers, important information necessary for an organization to resume operations in the event of a disaster resides on both servers and workstations. Because of this, the IT operations manager must consider incorporating both client and server information into the corporate disaster recovery plan. Practical techniques need to be considered for integrating the backup of client and server databases onto a minicomputer or mainframe. Doing so saves both time and money, because IT managers can to use existing disaster recovery plans with only slight modification. Chapter 54, "Integrating LANs Into the Disaster Recovery Plan," considers methods of integrating client and server data into the corporate disaster recovery plan.

In Chapter 55, "The Legal Issues of Disaster Recovery Planning," we shift the focus to the legal issues in corporate contingency planning, which are some of the most misunderstood and confusing aspects of the entire process of creating a disaster recovery plan. IT managers often must assume the role of disaster recovery planners; however, they are not expected to be as knowledgeable as lawyers in this role. As a result, IT managers can be encumbered with the responsibility of understanding the minutiae of existing regulatory guidelines and the legal consequences of their organizations' failure to implement an effective disaster recovery plan. No specific laws state categorically that an organization must have a disaster recovery plan, but there is a body of legal precedents which can be used to hold companies responsible to those affected by a company's inability to cope with, or recover from, a disaster. Chapter 55 outlines those precedents and suggests precautions to take to minimize this legal risk.

With just about all activities of the modern corporation now residing on mainframe, minicomputer, or microcomputer-based servers, most organizations recognize the value of performing backups on a regularly scheduled basis. Although backups provide a mechanism to recover from the adverse effect of a hard disk crash or a similar hardware problem, they do not protect an organization from more catastrophic failures resulting from fire, flood, or an explosion similar to the terrorist bombing at the World

Trade Center. Chapter 56, "Using Televaulting and Hot and Cold Sites for Disaster Recovery," explores disaster-recovery alternatives for certain types of disasters that require one to consider moving the data off-site, as well as providing for a mechanism for using that data in the event current facilities cannot be used. These alternatives are televaulting, hot sites, and cold sites.

Security is also an important consideration that must be addressed during a disaster-recovery operation. During disasters, when all IT and communications staff are focused on system recovery and repair, computer and communications facilities and information and network resources are critically vulnerable. Security procedures are often ignored, and security controls are often not in place. Chapter 57, "Data Processing and Communications Security During Recovery and Repair," presents guidelines for the data security administrator, who must ensure that the security and integrity of data and facilities are not further compromised during the recovery and repair of systems and communications networks.

Chapter 51
Introduction to Data Center Recovery Planning

Edward S. Devlin
Cole H. Emerson
Leo A. Wrobel, Jr.

THIS CHAPTER INTRODUCES DATA CENTER RECOVERY planning concepts and begins a three-part series on data center recovery planning (see also Chapters 52 and 53, "Developing a Data Center Recovery Plan: Parts I and II"). This chapter introduces:

- The definition of data center recovery planning and how it differs from business resumption planning.
- The history of data center recovery planning.
- Development assumptions.

DEFINITION OF A DATA CENTER RECOVERY PLAN

A data center recovery plan (DCRP) consists of documented plans and procedures that will be employed by key data center personnel following a disaster for the express purpose of resuming data center operations in an organized and timely manner. The DCRP lists the documented recovery responsibilities. These resources include recovery plan procedures, checklist, and forms.

Disaster

Although a disaster is defined in the dictionary as a sudden, calamitous event bringing great damage, loss, or destruction, a disaster will be defined in the DCRP as any extended interruption to data center operations. The interruption can be from physical damage to the building or the data center contents, but it does not have to be. The term *disaster* will be used to indicate any situation in which computer services have suffered an interruption that may extend beyond an acceptable time frame. The following are examples of disasters:

- A hardware failure causes data center operations to be interrupted over an extended period of time.
- A power company suffers a disaster on its premises, causing an interruption of its services and resulting in a data center outage.
- A telephone company suffers a disaster on its premises, causing an interruption of services and resulting in a data center outage.

Acceptable Time Frame

The definition of an "acceptable time frame" varies among companies. To one company, the acceptable time frame may be one day; to another, it may be five days. Each recovery planner must identify the acceptable time frame for the specific company.

The DCRP contains the recovery responsibilities for data center personnel primarily, but it also includes information as to the support roles of both the executive management and the staff departments.

Executive Management Committee

The executive management committee is the group of senior executives that deals with all the major crises that face the company. Although they are not directly involved in the data center recovery operation, they need to be kept informed of its progress throughout. The committee intervenes only when the situation warrants it.

Staff Departments

The staff departments include corporate security, building services/engineering, public relations, human resources, insurance, legal, and purchasing. They are directly involved in assisting the data center during the recovery operation. The DCRP identifies who in each staff department should be notified if there is a disaster and what support they will provide. The DCRP does not document how they will provide support; that information is included in the companywide business resumption plan.

The Difference Between Data Center Recovery Plan and Business Resumption Planning

The business resumption plan (BRP) consists of documented plans and procedures that will be employed by key company personnel following a disaster for the express purpose of resuming business operation in a timely manner. The BRP contains documented business resumption responsibilities for all departments in the company (i.e., the revenue-generating department,

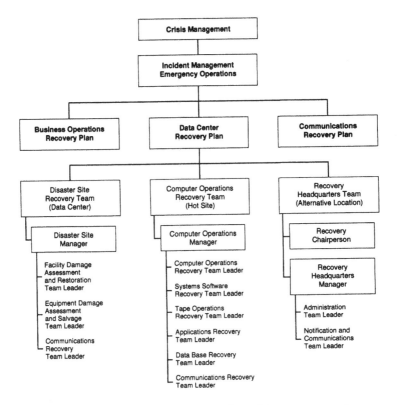

Exhibit 51.1. Plan components for crisis management.

the staff departments, and the executive management committee). The DCRP is just one component of the overall plan for crisis management. (See Exhibit 51.1.)

THE DATA CENTER RECOVERY PLAN MODEL

The data center is one of the divisions of the information systems (IS) department. The responsibilities of the IS department include the data center, as well as communications, personal computers, and networks. There is no single IS department organization common to all companies. The organization model that is used in this chapter assumes that the IS department comprises five divisions:

- Systems programming
- Data center operations
- Applications programming
- Database
- Communications

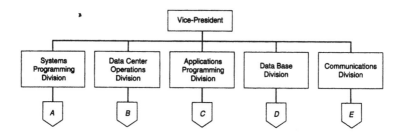

Exhibit 51.2. Information systems department.

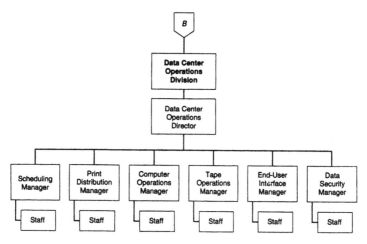

Exhibit 51.3. Data center operations division.

The vice president of information systems manages the department; each of the five divisions is managed by a director. (See Exhibit 51.2.)

The systems programming division consists of a director and the teams responsible for each of the major operating systems; each team is supervised by a manager. The data center operations division consists of a director and various teams, each supervised by a manager. (See Exhibit 51.3.)

The applications programming division consists of a director and teams for each major application systems (e.g., a financial systems team). The database division consists of a director and a staff of database specialists. Last, the communications division consists of a director and two teams — the data communications team and the voice communications team — each supervised by a manager. This model IS department is the subject of the DCRP that is discussed in this series of chapters.

HISTORY OF DATA CENTER RECOVERY PLANNING

Data centers throughout the United States started documenting formal recovery plans in 1973. Before 1973, certain segments of the plan were developed, but not complete DCRPs. For example, the data center division of an IS department typically documented its role in a data center recovery operation, but the systems and the applications programming divisions did not. As these divisions began to prepare recovery plans, they often failed to synchronize them with the other divisions' plans. This situation created the demand for documented, formal plans so that all divisions could establish a uniform set of recovery objectives.

The data center was the focal point for the development of the disaster recovery plans during the 1970s, because the revenue-generating departments of most companies needed to provide information to or obtain information from the data center to accomplish their business objectives. Because the data center was responsible for the processing of information, it had to develop plans to minimize the length of time the computer would be unable to provide access to this information.

The Evolution of Data Center Recovery Planning: 1970s through 1990s

There are several differences between the DCRPs of the 1970s and the 1990s. First, if a data center was disabled by disaster in the early 1970s, it would not have prevented the company from performing its essential business functions. Because the computer typically acted as an after-the-fact bookkeeper, the business functions would still have been performed; the company could have delivered its product or services, although it would suffer from late billing of customers and late receipt or receivables. Today, the disabling of the data center can prevent a company from completing many of its essential business functions. The impact of the interruption could result in a significant loss of revenue, profits, and company credibility.

A second difference is that today's computer environments are much more complex than they were during the 1970s. During the 1970s, data centers operated in a batch environment. The end users' work was carried into the data entry area, where it was keyed; the keyed input was then sent to the schedulers, who submitted it for processing. After the completion of processing, it was sent to quality control, where it was balanced to the control figures. The output would then be picked up by or delivered to the end user.

If there was disaster, the end users' work could be taken to another data entry location for keying. (If there were no other data entry locations available, it could be taken to a data entry service bureau or to the computer backup site.) The keyed input would be sent to schedulers at the computer backup site, where it would be submitted for processing. After processing, it would be sent to quality control, either at the computer backup site or recovery headquarters, where it could be balanced to the controls. The output would then be delivered to the end user.

Today's data centers operate in an online environment. End users work directly on workstations; the data is sent to the data center electronically. The end user can call up programs remotely to process the input. After processing, the output is sent back to the end user electronically. Such online environments require that complex technical issues be addressed and implemented before a disaster occurs. When a disaster causes an interruption to the data center's processing, the applications must move to a computer backup site. Such an environment requires several technical issues to be addressed, including ensuring that:

- The backup site has compatible hardware, processors, disk drives, and tape drives.
- There is sufficient disk space to bring up the operating systems and utilities and run the application.
- The operating systems and utilities can be loaded.
- Application data files can be loaded onto to the disk space provided by the backup site.
- Application data files can be reconstructed from the time of backup to the off-premises tapes to the time of the disaster.
- Data processed earlier in the day but destroyed before it could be backed up and sent off premises can be reentered.
- End-user workstation data communications lines can be switched into the backup site.
- The security concerns of critical data in a dial-up network environment are addressed.

The good news is there are now more resources available to help deal with these complex issues. First, there are commercial hot sites. Although such hot sites can meet the needs of most companies today, they cannot meet the disk space and communications requirements of the largest data centers.

Second, testing procedures can help ensure that there is sufficient disk space at the backup hot site for loading of operating systems, utilities, and application data files. During such testing, the reconstruction of data files can also be verified. Third, electronic vaulting can be used to send current transactions off premises immediately after they are received by the data center.

The final difference in recovery planning between the 1970s and the 1990s is that the recovery plans of the 1970s did not address end users, staff departments, and executive management. Data center personnel felt that if a disaster did strike, they would be the only group in the company prepared to respond. (They often complained that they would be up and running, but they would not have anything to process because they were the only group in the company that had done any planning.) Today's DCRPs include planning sessions with end users, staff departments that will support the recovery operation, and members of the executive management team that will oversee operation. These planning sessions help the rest of the organization in preparing its overall resumption plan.

Importance of a Data Center Today

With increased use of PC-based LANs, the question of the importance of today's data center is often raised. There is no doubt that local area networks had an impact on the role of the data center in the organization. As local area networks become entwined in wide area networks, however, they often communicate with each other through the data center's mainframe. In many respects, the data center remains the heart of the organization, sending information that allows the company head to make decisions and offices and factories to perform specific functions.

REASONS FOR DEVELOPING A DCRP

There are four potential catalysts that generates a company's need to develop a DCRP:

- There is a regulatory requirement for the company to have a DCRP.
- The company believes that it could be held liable by its clients or customers for not having one.
- The company is aware of a recent disaster to a company in the same geographic area or industry.
- The company believes that the impact from an extended business outage to the data center is too risky.

Regulatory Requirements

First, companies develop the DCRP to be in compliance with regulations governing their industry. For example, the banking industry has had regulations requiring the documentation of a DCRP since May 1983, when BC-177 was issued by the Comptroller of the Currency, requiring all national banks to have a DCRP. This regulation may have been the result of a fire that extensively damaged the headquarters building of Norwest Bank in Minneapolis in November 1982.

The initial version of the BC-177 regulation indicated that the DCRP was needed for any areas of the bank that contained computers. A later version added any areas of the bank that had such electronic equipment as terminals that connect to a mainframe or minicomputer. Currently, this requirement covers any essential business operations of the bank regardless of whether there are any computers.

Liability

Companies have also indicated that a DCRP can help them defend against litigation from customers or clients, even if the plan did not work.

Recent Disaster

Many companies begin a DCRP project just after a disaster occurs in their area or to a company in their business. For example, several insurance companies developed or strengthened their DCRP after the Penn Mutual Insurance Company fire in Philadelphia on May 30, 1989. (A contributing factor might have been the public acknowledgment that the fire was caused by an arsonist who was able to gain access to an area restricted by an access control system.)

Impact Analysis

Many companies have analyzed what the business impact would be if the data center were not operational for an extended period of time. This is the most common reason executive management is willing to provide a budget for this process. The results of a comprehensive business impact analysis and a data center application impact analysis often prompt the executive committee to require the development of a data recovery plan. The business impact analysis analyzes the impact on the company if any of the business functions suffer an extended interruption. The application impact analysis analyzes the impact on the application owner, or any end user, if the data center cannot process a specific computer application for an extended period of time. Typically, other high-profile areas of the company are also required to develop a plan shortly after the data center is.

CONCLUSION

This chapter introduced the basics of a data center recovery planning: what it is; how it has evolved over the past decades; why it is important. Its companion Chapters 52, "Developing a Data Recovery Plan: Part I and Chapter 53, "Developing a Data Center Recovery Plan: Part II" discuss seven steps involved in developing a disaster recovery plan. The following section examines the assumptions that are made in developing a plan in those two chapters.

RECOVERY PLAN DEVELOPMENT ASSUMPTIONS

Because potential recovery issues are related to the size of a company, the size of its data center, the type of disaster, and the level of damage caused by the disaster, the following parameters have been used to structure a DCRP in this series of chapters.

- The location of the data center is in a separate building from the corporate headquarters.
- The corporate headquarters house the executive, the staff departments, and the data center end users. The executive personnel are the key officers of the company that have final decision-making authority. The staff department personnel manage departments that are responsible for such functions as corporate security, human resources, public relations, insurance, legal, purchasing, and transportation. These are departments that contribute to the successful operation of the company but do not generate revenue for the company. The data center end users are departments that use the data center mainframe to process information that is used in generating revenue and is essential to their day-to-day operations.
- If the computer center is in the same building as the corporate headquarters, the company must consider the companywide planning elements.
- The data center organization that the DCRP is being developed for is as presented in this series of chapters. It is large enough to staff the different teams that make up a data center. For small companies, it may be necessary to combine the responsibilities of two or more teams into one team. If a suggested team is not needed, it can be eliminated.
- The disaster scenario for the DCRP that is covered in this series of chapters is as follows:
  - A disaster has occurred causing physical damage to the computer and data communications network equipment, resulting in the inability to use the computer center to support business operations.
  - The disaster is isolated in the building housing the data center and communications network. (Regional or local disaster logistics are discussed as exceptions.)
  - The data center is inaccessible following the disaster and may remain inaccessible for an extended period of time.
  - The data files, supplies, and forms located inside the data center have been damaged or destroyed.
  - Key data center personnel have not been injured in the disaster and are available to perform the required recovery actions.

Chapter 52
Developing a Data Center Recovery Plan: Part 1

Edward S. Devlin
Cole H. Emerson
Leo A. Wrobel, Jr.

CHAPTER 51 INTRODUCED DATA CENTER RECOVERY PLANNING CONCEPTS. This chapter examines the first part of a seven-step process that data center managers can use to develop a recovery plan for their centers. This chapter discusses steps one through four:

1. Selecting a plan development committee.
2. Establishing the plan's scope.
3. Establishing its objects.
4. Determining the premise of the plan (i.e., making assumptions about the readiness of the plan and the types of disaster that may occur).

The examination of this seven-step process concludes in Chapter 53, "Developing a Data Recovery Plan: Part II."

STEP 1: SELECT MEMBERS OF THE DEVELOPMENT COMMITTEE

The first step in developing the DCRP is selecting the development committee. (See Exhibit 52.1.) The development committee is composed of the personnel that have been selected to work on the development and documentation of the DCRP.

The selection of who will be on the committee is important, because this team participates in the development, documentation, implementation, and testing phases of the DCRP project. This group decides on the recovery

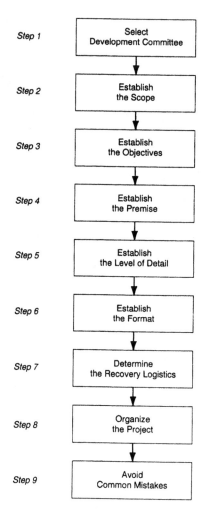

Step 1 — Select Development Committee

Step 2 — Establish the Scope

Step 3 — Establish the Objectives

Step 4 — Establish the Premise

Step 5 — Establish the Level of Detail

Step 6 — Establish the Format

Step 7 — Determine the Recovery Logistics

Step 8 — Organize the Project

Step 9 — Avoid Common Mistakes

Exhibit 52.1.   The DCRP development steps.

strategies, the resources, and the procedures that will be used in the recovery program.

The DCRP can be thought of as a chain made up of strong links (the recovery team) connected to one another. The recovery teams work together to provide a strong resource during a recovery operation, just like the links work together to form a strong chain.

If the person selected to be the representative for a particular division on the development committee is too busy to give the project sufficient time, that team's section of the plan may be a weak link, and a chain is only as strong as its weakest link. Unless all links in the recovery plan are strong, the chain will be likely to break, resulting in a recovery operation that is neither organized nor timely.

The DCRP coordinator initiates the process of selecting the development committee. The DCRP coordinator is the representative of the IS department head who has been given the primary responsibility and authority for carrying out the recovery planning project.

The DCRP coordinator should first obtain an organization chart of the IS department. The DCRP coordinator then meets with the head of the IS department and the directors of the divisions to determine who should represent each division on the development committee and what recovery teams will be drawn from each division. The directors are from systems programming, data center operations, application programming, database, and communications divisions.

After the directors have designated their choices for the development committee and selected the recovery teams from each division, they should identify which personnel will be the recovery team leaders — those with primary recovery team leader responsibilities — and those who will be their alternates or backups. An overview of the major recovery teams is presented in Exhibit 52.2.

The DCRP coordinator and the development committee will meet with the recovery team leaders and their alternates several times during the development phase of the project — for example, during the formal kickoff meeting, during individual recovery team meetings, and during any multiple team meetings. The DCRP coordinator should then meet with the development committee representatives to establish the scope, objectives, premise, level of detail, format, and logistics that will be used in the DCRP.

STEP 2: ESTABLISH THE SCOPE FOR THE DCRP

One of the first steps the development committee takes is to establish the scope of the DCRP. In the DCRP project, the term *scope* refers to establishing the range of operation the DCRP will cover. The DCRP consists of documented plans and procedures that will be employed by key IS personnel following a disaster for the express purpose of resuming data center operations in an organized and timely manner. The critical word is *following,* as opposed to before or during. Those elements that deal with plans and procedures to be employed before and during are parts of other corporate plans. For example, building evacuation procedures may be used during a disaster.

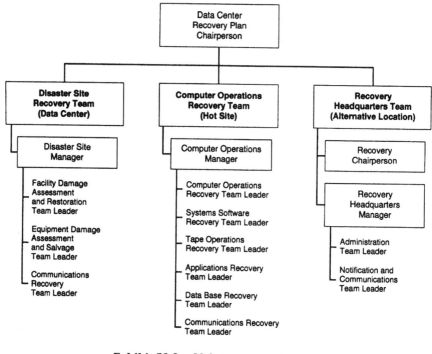

Exhibit 52.2. Major recovery teams.

Areas Covered by the DCRP Scope

The scope of the DCRP addresses the responsibilities of data center personnel from the time they are notified of the disaster to the time the data center returns to a normal environment and the DCRP is terminated. These responsibilities are defined by the initial disaster alert procedure, disaster site recovery logistics, backup site operations logistics, and recovery headquarters logistics. The term *logistics* as used in the DCRP means the preplanning for the procurement of recovery resources and material and for the transportation of personnel and resources.

How to Identify the Scope

To identify the elements in the scope, for the DCRP coordinator and the development committee should start with the groups that make up the IS department. Each of these groups has a role in preparing the recovery of their area should a disaster strike the department.

For example, the development committee should determine from the data center operations director whether there are any computers housed inside the computer center that are controlled (owned or leased) by other departments. If so, who is responsible for their recovery following a disaster? If they are controlled by the departments that own or lease them, and not by the data center, they should be covered by the business resumption plan (BRP) for that department. If they are controlled by the data center, their repair or replacement is the responsibility of the data center. Another key concern in this type of situation is identifying who is responsible for backing up and protecting the data on these computers: in some cases, it is the department that owns or leases the computer; in others, it is the data center. This should be clarified and clearly documented in the scope.

Areas Not Covered by the DCRP Scope

It is also important for the scope to identify any means that will not be included in the range of operations covered by the DCRP. The following are some examples of areas not usually addressed within the scope of the DCRP:

- The plans and procedures dealing with situations before a disaster occurs that are intended to minimize the potential for a disaster to occur. This is usually the day-to-day responsibility of the corporate security and corporate building's services department. These departments are responsible for minimizing exposures and implementing plans and procedures to accomplish this.
- The policies and procedures that deal with situations during a disaster — for example, attempting to extinguish fire; evacuating a building; searching for a bomb following a bomb threat; and evacuation to a center of a building during a tornado. These procedures are established as part of emergency response plans. The person responsible for the emergency response plans is either the corporate safety officer or the head of the human resources department. They are the management representatives who have the responsibility to establish the corporate policies on what they should do if they are at work when a disaster occurs and policies on what they should do if they are not at work at the time of an areawide disaster. (e.g., earthquake or hurricane).
- Computers installed outside the data center.
- Data centers in other countries.
- The way in which end-user departments react to a disaster that has affected the data center. All end users should have documented how they will temporarily perform their business functions in the BRP.
- The way in which end-user departments resume their business operations if the disaster strikes their department. The end users' procedures to address how the department will continue their business operations is part of the BRP, not the DCRP.

A benefit of clearly documenting the scope is that it clarifies for executive management which areas are covered in the DCRP and which are not.

THE DATA CENTER RECOVERY PLAN SCOPE

The data center recovery plan (DCRP) is designed to respond to a disaster that affects the data center located at [data center address]. The plan documents the data center recovery responsibilities, procedures, checklists, and forms that will be used to manage and control the recovery of essential computer operations following a disaster.

The plans included in the DCRP provide for the recovery of the [company name] critical applications and includes detailed recovery procedures for the following data center areas:

- Sytems programming division.
- Data center operations division.
- Applications programming division.
- Database division.
- Communications division.

The data center recovery plan does not address or provide recovery strategies for:

- Computers installed at any [company name] locations outside the control of the data center, including:
  -- Midrange computers installed in other departments.
  -- Personal computers and LANs installed in other departments.
- End-user department operations, including:
  -- The business operations of end users of the data center services. (They are addressed in their departments' plans in the business resumption program.)
- [Company name] data center locations in other countries. (They are addressed in that country's data center recovery plan.)

Exhibit 52.3.   Scope statement.

This can eliminate the problem of executive management assuming that the DCRP will be used to recover a department other than the data center. An example of the DCRP scope is provided in Exhibit 52.3.

STEP 3: ESTABLISH THE OBJECTIVES FOR THE DCRP

The next step the development committee should take is to establish the objectives of the DCRP. The term *objective* as used in the DCRP project means the goals toward which the DCRP are directed.

There are two types of objectives. The first are the company's objectives. The company's objectives are documented in the DCRP. The second type of objectives are those participants — for example, objectives of the data center operations director, data center's end users, and executive management. The participants' objectives help determine the strategies and procedures that will be incorporated in the DCRP.

The Company's Objectives

The company's objectives of the DCRP are usually to:

- Limit the magnitude of any loss by minimizing the duration of the interruption of processing to the critical applications.
- Assess damage to the data center facilities and equipment and repair the damage.
- Recover data center information critical to the operation of the company.
- Manage the recovery operation in an organized and timely manner.
- Prepare data center personnel to respond effectively in a recovery situation.
- Prepare the staff departments to provide support during a data center recovery operation.

Limit the Magnitude of Any Loss. To limit the magnitude of any loss, the DCRP should have a section that minimizes the duration of the interruption of processing critical applications. This can be accomplished by including a computer backup site strategy in the DCRP that allows the data center to resume the processing of critical applications quickly.

Assess Damage to the Data Center. To assess damage to the data center facilities and equipment and repair the damage, the DCRP should have a section that identifies how data center personnel will assess damage to the facilities and equipment and how they will arrange for repairing the damage.

Recover Data Center Information. To recover data center information critical to the operation of the company, the DCRP should have a section that identifies how backups of critical information are protected, where they are protected, how they will be retrieved, and how they will be reprocessed and reconstructed.

Manage the Recovery Operation. To manage the recovery operation in an organized and timely manner, the DCRP should have a section that identifies what has to be done during the recovery operation, who should do it, and how they should do it.

Prepare Data Center Personnel to Respond. To prepare the data center personnel to respond effectively in a recovery, they need to be adequately trained and given the opportunity to exercise their recovery responsibilities on a periodic basis.

Prepare the Staff Departments. To prepare the staff departments to provide support during a data center recovery operation, they should be trained adequately and should participate in periodic exercises.

The Participants' Objectives

When asked what objective the DCRP should meet, the data center end users have one answer in mind, executive management another, and the data center director yet another. End users typically want the DCRP to provide a means to return the data center to processing end-user applications within hours of the time the interruption occurred. The data center operations director wants the DCRP to provide a means to return the data center to processing quickly by using the best backup site strategy available — for example, a duplicate computer with the same configuration down to the disk and tapes drives. Although this may be a perfect technical solution, it is usually the most costly. The executive management committee also wants the DCRP to provide a means to have the data center return to processing quickly but is concerned with using the most cost-effective backup site strategy.

Reaching Agreement on the Objectives

Despite this seeming impasse, companies are able to resolve the differences through negotiation.

Executive Negotiation. Presenting executives with the results of the applications impact analysis may help them realize that the least expensive solution for a computer backup site may not be in the best interest of the company if it results in the company losing money, credibility, and customers. They are then more open to alternatives. For example, the reciprocal backup site agreement is generally considered the most cost-effective solution; an alternative is the commercial hot site. Although a commercial hot site costs more than the reciprocal agreement, it costs less than a duplicate or near-duplicate in-house site.

Data Center Operations Director Negotiation. Presented with the need to have the most cost-effective backup site strategy (e.g., a reciprocal backup site agreement), the data center director may respond that this solution will not meet the end users' objectives because it does not allow the data center to process many of the end users' applications. But they may then be more willing to consider another alternative (e.g., a commercial hot site) to the more expensive ideal technical solution. The commercial hot site may not have all of the resources the data center director would like, but it is a better solution than the reciprocal agreement.

The Data Center Recovery Plan Objectives

The data center group is responsible for responding to any disruption of computer services (short or long term). By activating the data center recovery plan, data center personnel can restore the critical applications in a timely and organized manner consistent with the resources approved by executive management.

The DCRP has been developed to accomplish the DCRP following objectives:

- Limit the magnitude of any loss minimizing the duration of the interruption to the critical application services.
- Assess damage to the data center facilities and equipment, repair damage, and activate the repaired computer center.
- Recover data center data and information critical to the operation of the company.
- Manage the recovery operation in an organized and effective manner.
- Prepare the data center personnel to respond effectively in a recovery situation.
- Prepare the staff departments that will provide support during a data center recovery operation.

To accomplish these objectives, the data center team will depend on support from executive management, end users, and staff departments. These support personnel have been identified and included in the DCRP manual.

Exhibit 52.4. Objectives statement.

Once the objectives have been agreed on, the DCRP coordinator and the development committee can determine the resources and options that allow the data center to meet its objectives. This will enable the DCRP coordinator to meet the participants' objective, which is to have a DCRP that will manage any recovery operation in an organized and effective manner. An example of the DCRP objectives is provided in Exhibit 52.4.

STEP 4: ESTABLISH THE DISASTER PREMISE FOR THE DCRP

The next step the development committee should undertake is to establish the premise for the DCRP. The term *premise* as used in the DCRP refers to the assumptions made about the readiness of the DCRP at the time of the disaster. Therefore, the premise contains the assumptions regarding the readiness of the DCRP as well as the disaster scenario on which the DCRP has been developed.

The feasibility of the DCRP depends on the compliance with the premise of the plan. If the items in the premise are not complied with, the DCRP may not be able to meet the objectives for which it was developed.

Assumptions

Some of the key assumptions of the premise are that:

- All personnel with recovery responsibilities have been adequately trained and tested.
- A computer backup site is in place.
- A communications network backup strategy is in place.
- Data protection procedures are in place.
- Systems programming and application data backups are being protected.
- Procedures are in place for reconstructing the application files and database files.
- Essential documentation and material are available from an off-premises storage location.

Personnel Trained and Tested. This element of the premise assumes either that all recovery personnel have participated in the writing of the responsibilites and the preparation of the procedures or that their role has been thoroughly explained to them. It also assumes that they have taken part in at least one test in which they actually performed the responsibilities and used the procedures.

Computer Backup Site in Place. This element of the premise assumes that a backup site agreement or contract does exist, that the backup site will meet the needs of the DCRP, and that the backup site has been tested to ensure that it will work.

Data Protection Procedures in Place. This element of the premise assumes that essential data is being backed up frequently and is being rotated to an off-premises, or off-site, storage location. Off premises indicates that the essential backup data has been moved outside of the building housing the data center. If a company moves essential data out of the computer room or the tape library and stores it in another part of the same building, this does not provide off-premises or off-site protection. For example, if a disaster rendered the building inaccessible for several days, the backup data would be useless because it could not be retrieved.

Systems Programming and Application Data Backups Protected. This element of the premise assumes that all of the necessary data has been identified and is being rotated off premises. This is not always the case. There are a number of reasons why companies have partial data recovery capability using their off-premises storage location.

Reconstruction Procedures in Place. This element of the premise assumes that the technical people have analyzed the conditions in which they would be required to recover data center files and information using only the backups stored in the off-premises storage locations. As part of this element, it is assumed that the DCRP contains documented procedures on how to reconstruct the files based on the generation of files that will be retrieved from the off-premises location.

Essential Documentation/Material Available from Off Premises. This element of the premise assumes that all documentation, supplies, and any other resources needed for the recovery of the data center have been identified and are available from an off-premises storage location. An example of the DCRP premise is provided in Exhibit 52.5.

Types of Disasters

The DCRP coordinator should determine the types of disasters that could strike the data center. Generally, disasters can be broken into three categories: acts of nature, accidents, and intentional acts. The acts of nature include earthquakes, hurricanes, tornadoes, and floods. Accidents include explosions and fires, internal flooding, loss of power, and loss of communications. Intentional acts include vandalism, sabotage, terrorism, and arson (see Exhibit 52.6).

Disaster Scenarios of the Premise

Some of the key elements that relate to the disaster scenario of the premise for which the DCRP has been developed are: the types of disasters that could strike the data center, the type of damage the disaster could cause, and the areas of the data center that could be affected.

Types of Disaster Scenarios. Two types of disaster scenarios can be addressed: the single, isolated disaster or a wide-area, regional disaster. A single, isolated disaster affects only the building housing the data center. There may be other companies in the building, but only one building is affected by the disaster. A wide-area, regional disaster affects the building housing the data center and additional buildings, as well. This happens most often following an earthquake, a flood, or a hurricane.

Levels of Damage. Two levels of damage are evaluated: the best-case situation and the worst-case situation. In the best-case situation, it is assumed that data center personnel will be able to gain access to the site of the disaster quickly and will be able to retrieve all of the resources they would need to move the processing to a computer backup site. It is also assumed that there is a minimum amount of damage to data center equipment and to the building housing the data center, allowing the DRCP personnel to repair the facility rapidly and return the processing from the backup site quickly. An example of a single, isolated, best-case scenario is provided in Exhibit 52.7.

CONTINGENCY PLANNING

The feasibility of the data center recovery plan depends on compliance with the premise plan.

The premise for the DCRP is:

- All trained personnel with recovery responsibilities have been adequately trained and tested on their assigned roles.
- A computer backup site strategy has been approved by executive management and is in place. This backup site strategy has been tested and will meet the objectives of the DCRP.
- Data protection procedures (backup and rotation) have been approved by executive management and are in place.
- Essential system and application data has been identified and is being protected.
- The procedures to be used to reconstruct the applications using the backup copies of application data stored in the off-premises location have been documented and tested.
- To ensure proper data is still protected following changes to an application or database, change control standards and methods are in place. The responsibility for the identification and protection of data has been assigned.
- Essential documentation, materials, and resources are stored off premises.
- The DCRP is reviewed on a regular basis to ensure that it remains current and correct.
- An ongoing DCRP awareness and training program is in place.
- The plan is exercised frequently during the course of the year.

The premise is based on the following disaster scenario:

- A disaster has occurred, causing physical damage to the computer equipment and resulting in the inability to use the data center to support business operations.
- The data center is inaccessible following the disaster and may remain inaccessible for an extended period of time.
- The data, supplies, and forms located inside the data center have been damaged or destroyed.
- Key data center personnel have not been injured in the disaster and are available to perform the required recovery action (either primary or alternate).

If the items in the premise are not complied with, the feasibility of the DCRP and its ability to meet the objectives for which it was developed are in doubt.

Exhibit 52.5.   Premise statement.

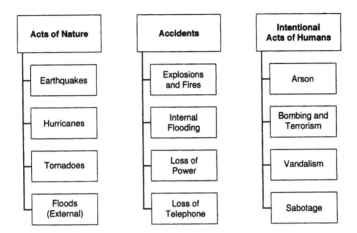

Exhibit 52.6.   Types of disasters.

The Data Center Recovery Plan

Single, Isolated, Best-Case Disaster Scenario

There has been a disaster in the building housing the data center.

The building is accessible within hours of the disaster:

- The building has not suffered any major structural damage.
- There are no toxic-or hazardous-material problems.

There is no damage to the data center or its contents:

- The equipment has not suffered any major damage.
- The data on storage media has not been damaged.
- The voice and data communications were interrupted for a few hours but are now working again.

Employees will be able to resume their business operations at their regular locations tomorrow.

Exhibit 52.7.   Single isolated, best-case disaster scenario.

<u>The Data Center Recovery Plan</u>

<u>Single, Isolated, Worst-Case Disaster Scenario</u>

There has been a fire in the building housing the data center.

The building will be inaccessible for days:

- The building has suffered major structural damage. Local authorities have condemned the building because they deem it unsafe.
- The Environmental Protection Agency has found toxins in the air; it considers the building to have a hazardous-materials problem.

The building has suffered extensive damage and will require a minimum of six months to repair.

Some of the equipment in the data center has been destroyed, and the remaining equipment has been damaged and needs repair.

Much of the information stored in the storage media in the data center has been destroyed, and the remaining information has been damaged and needs repair. The voice and data communications are damaged and may not be operational in this location for an extended period of time.

Employees will not be able to resume their business operations at their regular locations.

Exhibit 52.8. Single isolated, worst-case disaster scenario.

In the worst-case situation, it is assumed that the data center personnel will be unable to gain access to the building for at least several days. There will be no retrieval of the resources from the building. The data center recovery operation will depend on the resources located outside the building (i.e., from the off-premises locations or other offices of the company). In the worst case, it is also assumed that equipment and all other data are destroyed. Employees will have to resume their operations at temporary locations, where they may need to stay for months before the disaster site can be repaired. An example of a single, isolated, worst-case disaster scenario is provided in Exhibit 52.8.

In a wide-area, regional disaster, it is assumed that the buildings will be inaccessible for an extended period of time and that the equipment and contents have been destroyed. It is also assumed that vendors will be forced to respond to the problem using a priority-based response plan; for example, support for government locations first, other high-profile industries next, and routine installations last. An example of a wide-area, regional disaster scenario is provided in Exhibit 52.9.

<u>The Data Recovery Plan</u>

<u>Wide-Area, Regional Disaster Scenario</u>

A wide-area (regional) disaster has occurred (e.g., earthquake, hurricane, tornado, or flood).

The building housing the data center has been damaged by the disaster. It will not be accessible until local authorities have certified that it is safe to reenter.

There has been some damage to the contents located inside the data center:

- Some computer equipment has been destroyed, and the remaining equipment has been damaged and needs repair.
- Some data and voice communications equipment and lines have been destroyed, and the remaining equipment has been damaged and needs repair.
- Some data and records have been destroyed and needs to be restored.

Employees have suffered personal losses:

- Employees and family members have been injured:
  -- Some while inside the data center.
  -- Some while they were at home.
  -- There have been some fatalities.
- Homes and their personal property have been damaged or destroyed.

The disaster zone has lost a significant amount of its infrastructure:

- Bridges, overpasses, and roads have been damaged and are unusable.
- Parking areas have been damaged or water has been contaminated and is not available.
- Food is not available in the disaster zone.

Exhibit 52.9. Wide-area, regional disaster scenario

Selecting the Scenario. In the initial development phase, the DCRP should use a single, isolated, worst-case disaster scenario. Some members of the development committee may prefer to develop the DCRP using a best-case scenario, because the best-case scenario is much easier to deal with and does not require the same amount of effort and time. However, if this type of scenario is selected, the DCRP will not be usable in the event of a worst-case disaster. On the other hand, a DCRP developed for the worst-case disaster can handle a best-case disaster.

Other development committee members may prefer to develop a DCRP using a wide-area, regional disaster scenario. The problem with using the wide-area scenario in the initial stage of the development phase is that it presents a number of logistical issues that require policies to be established or support to be committed above and beyond the needs of a single, isolated disaster scenario. For example, a wide-area scenario might require policies to be set stating that personnel may be expected to travel to the data center to participate in one of the disaster site recovery teams, to the computer backup site, or to the recovery headquarters. A policy on requiring personnel to travel in disaster situations that might be construed to be unsafe is not the responsibility of the DCRP coordinator or the development committee; that authority rests with the corporate safety officer or the human resources department.

The wide-area disaster scenario affects not only the company's facilities but many other companies, as well. Recovery service vendors will be forced to respond on the basis of industry classification, with government and life support given first priority. This would invalidate assumptions of vendor commitment based on a single, isolated disaster.

The wide-area scenario must also address the difficult issues of potential injury or death of employees or family members. The issue of injuries to personnel is brought up often during the development of the DCRP. How would the recovery responsibilities be carried out if both the person assigned to the primary role and the alternate were injured in the disaster? Although there have not been many instances in which data center personnel have been injured by a disaster, the development committee does have to consider this in its planning. For example, some companies have assigned to a third person the responsibility of carrying out recovery activities if both the primary and the alternate are injured at the same time.

In short, there is no question that the wide-area scenario must be considered, but not until the logistics that deal with the single, isolated, worst-case disaster scenario are finalized.

CONCLUSION

This chapter took data center managers through the first four steps on the way to developing a recovery plan for their data centers. Most importantly, it showed how to establish the scope of a plan so that the plan covers all appropriate operations needed to recover a data center's activities. The concluding chapter in this series, "Developing a Data Center Recovery Plan: Part II" takes data center managers through the final steps of developing a recovery plan and focuses on the format and level of detail to be used in the plan.

Chapter 53
Developing a Data Center Recovery Plan: Part II

Edward S. Devlin
Cole H. Emerson
Leo A. Wrobel, Jr.

CHAPTER 51 INTRODUCED DATA CENTER RECOVERY PLANNING CONCEPTS, and Chapter 52, "Developing a Data Center Recovery Plan: Part I" explained the following, which are the first steps of a seven-step process data center managers can use to develop a recovery plan for their centers:

1. Selecting a plan development committee.
2. Establishing the plan's scope.
3. Establishing its objects.
4. Determining the premise of the plan (i.e., making assumptions about the readiness of the plan and type of disasters that may occur).

This chapter covers the next three steps in this process:

5. Establishing the level of detail for the plan.
6. Establishing the plan's format.
7. Determining recovery logistics.

STEP 5: ESTABLISH THE LEVEL OF DETAIL FOR THE DCRP

The development committee also needs to establish the level of detail that will be used in the DCRP. The level of detail refers to the depth of information documented in the DCRP manual.

Two Levels of Detail

There are two levels of detail that can be used in the DCRP. The first is designed to keep it simple, easy to develop, and easy to maintain. This is

THE DATA CENTER RECOVERY PLAN

LEVEL OF DETAIL: SIMPLE METHOD

RECOVERY HEADQUARTERS MANAGER

Primary: _____ Alternate: _____

1. Manage the recovery headquarters communication efforts:
   • Notification to department personnel.
   • Management of incoming telephone call control functions.

2. Coordinate staff department activities.

3. Direct recovery headquarters activities throughout the recovery operation, to include:
   • 24-hour personnel coverage.
   • Administrative and clerical activities.
   • Recovery status and expense report preparation.

4. Maintain the personnel location control information throughout the recovery operation.

Exhibit 53.1. Level of detail — simple method.

referred to as the simple method. The second is designed to include the details on how the recovery teams will perform their recovery responsibilities. This is referred to as the detailed method.

The Simple Method. This method includes identifying of recovery responsibilities that have to be performed and the recovery teams that will perform those responsibilities. The documentation in this level of detail does not include how the recovery teams will perform their responsibilities.

The strength of this level of detail is in its ease in development and maintenance. If the development committee is under a severe time constraint to complete the DCRP, it may make a decision to use the simple method for the initial version of the plan. More detail can be added as the plan is updated. The weakness in this level of detail is that it requires that knowledgeable technical people familiar with the company's data center be available to perform the responsibilities. If such knowledgeable people are not available, the person who will step in as the alternate may not completely understand how to perform the responsibilities and in fact may know just enough to be dangerous. An example of DCRP level of detail documentation using the simple method is shown in Exhibit 53.1.

The Detailed Method. This method is considerably more complex, because it includes the technical aspects of performing the recovery responsibilities and requires more effort during the development phase and the maintenance phase. The value of the detailed method is that:

- It gives the primary team leader all the information needed to carry out the responsibilities.
- It gives the alternate all of the information needed to carry out the responsibilities. This is important because in most cases the alternate is not as knowledgeable about the data center functions as the primary leader.
- It gives other data center employees or vendor representatives the documented procedures and checklists on how to carry out recovery responsibilities in case the persons assigned the primary and alternate responsibilities are unable to perform their assigned responsibilities.

The weakness of this level of detail is that it is somewhat more difficult to develop and maintain. The strength of this level of detail is that it is not people dependent; it provides how-to information that the alternate leader or another knowledgeable data center person can use to perform the recovery responsibilities. An example of DCRP level of detail documentation using the detailed method is shown in Exhibit 53.2.

STEP 6: ESTABLISH THE FORMAT FOR DOCUMENTING THE DCRP

The development committee should establish the format to be used in documenting the DCRP. The term *format* as used in the DCRP refers to the organization of the documentation for a recovery team. The format consists of the recovery procedure overview, the initial response actions, the recovery actions, and the administrative actions.

Recovery Procedure Overview. This segment explains the general responsibilities of the team leader, the recovery procedures, the recovery checklists in the recovery team's documentation, and the recovery preparedness tasks of the team leader. An example of the recovery procedure overview format is provided in Exhibit 53.3.

Initial Response Actions. This segment explains the actions the team leader should take after the initial notification that a disaster has occurred. It details where to report, whom to meet with, and how to plan the staffing of the team during the recovery operation. This procedure reminds the team leader that the objectives of the recovery operation will dictate the need for timing and the responsibilities to be activated. The team leader should read the entire recovery team section before performing any assignments. An example of the initial response actions format is provided in Exhibit 53.4.

CONTINGENCY PLANNING

Primary: _____ Alternate: _____

RECOVERY ACTIONS:

1. Manage the recovery headquarters voice and communications efforts.
   Meet with the data center internal communication team leader:

   a. Authorize that department personnel be notified:

      1. Record the location and telephone number of the recovery
         headquarters on the personnel notification procedure (Workpaper
         II4.17). Make copies of this procedure and distribute to all
         personnel carrying out the department notification. This procedure
         has been developed to limit the potential of prematurely alarming
         families of employees who may have been injured by disaster.
      2. Provide the personnel notification information checklist
         (Workpaper II4.18).
      3. Review the priority assigned by the recovery management team to
         identify those individuals who should be called immediately.
      4. Review the instructions for calling personnel believed to have
         been working during the disaster and potentially injured.
      5. Collect the completed personnel notification status reports and
         provide information to recovery managers and responsible staff
         departments.

   b. Manage the incoming telephone call control functions:

      1. Ensure that specific telephone numbers have been assigned to be
         used for incoming calls.
      2. Ensure that personnel have been assigned to monitor the
         telephones designated for incoming calls.
      3. Provide copies of the incoming telephone call procedures and form
         (Workpaper II4.21) to assist in handling all incoming calls
         correctly.
      4. Inform the company telephone operators to direct all return calls
         to the assigned extension at the recovery headquarters.

   c. Ensure that accurate personnel location control information is
      being maintained for all recovery personnel.

2. Coordinate staff department support with recovery managers during the
   recovery operation. Complete a personnel location control form
   (Workpaper II4.13), identifying who is authorized to access the
   recovery headquarters, off-premises storage, disaster recovery backup
   site, and any other location used for recovery.

Exhibit 53.2.   Level of detail — detailed method.

3. Meet with the security representative to review the need to assign security personnel to secure the disaster site and the recovery operation sites. Depending on the nature of the disaster (e.g., bombing, suspicious fire), tighter-than-usual security may be required:

   a. Arrange for the issuance of appropriate security badges and access cards. Meet with personnel from security administration to assist in the identification of appropriate security clearance levels.
   b. Provide a completed personnel location control form (Workpaper II4.13) to security personnel.
   c. Request that admittance be restricted to only authorized personnel who have proper identification.

4. Meet with the data center end-user interface team leader. (The data center end-user interface team leader will act as the focal point for all internal end users and all regional office bureaus and customers.) Direct customer interface activities throughout the recovery operation:

   a. Assist with the development of any statements that will be used during initial contacts with internal end users and external customers.
   b. Ensure that user interface team personnel provide end users and customers with continued current status information on the following:

      1. Recovery of critical applications.
      2. Availability of backup network facilities.
      3. Changes in system processing schedules.

   c. Ensure that adequate user interface team personnel are available to support end-user and customer interface activities throughout the recovery operation. Provide personnel staffing on a 24-hour-a-day basis, if required.

5. Identify equipment requirements and arrange for purchasing to provide copy machines and other office equipment and supplies as required.

6. Manage all administrative and clerical support activities throughout the recovery operation. Meet with the administrative and clerical team leader to coordinate:

   a. Travel requirements.
   b. Cash advance and expense requirements.
   c. Recovery status information.
   d. Recovery team meeting arrangements.

7. Schedule recovery headquarters operations so that 24-hour coverage is provided. Around-the-clock coverage of recovery headquarters telephones will be required.

Exhibit 53.2. Level of detail — detailed method *(continued)*.

```
                    THE DATA CENTER RECOVERY PLAN
                    RECOVERY PROCEDURE OVERVIEW
                 NOTIFICATION AND COMMUNICATIONS TEAM

Primary: _____ Alternate: _____

The responsibilities of the notification and communications team leader
during the recovery operation are to:

•  Coordinate data processing personnel, alert and notification
   activities.
•  Control all incoming telephone calls.
•  Maintain the personnel location control information throughout the
   recovery operation.

The procedures and checklists required to perform these recovery tasks
are:

    Procedure Checklist                    Workpaper
    Recovery Procedure                     II4.22
    Reserved Telephone Numbers List        II4.20

Recovery preparedness tasks include:

•  Conducting periodic recovery plan review sessions with personnel who
   would participate in the recovery operation.
•  Maintaining the recovery plan section and checklists in a current up-
   to-date condition.
•  Keeping a copy of the recovery procedures at home.
```

Exhibit 53.3   Recovery procedure overview.

Recovery Actions. This segment explains the recovery actions the team could take, depending on the objectives of the recovery operation. It deals with such issues as the need to organize a team area at the recovery headquarters, the need to notify vendors that their support is needed, the need to travel to the disaster site or the recovery backup site, and other specific recovery actions documented for the team. An example of the recovery actions format is provided in Exhibit 53.5.

Administrative Actions. This segment explains the administrative actions the team leader is responsible for throughout the recovery operation — for example, maintaining accurate written documentation of changes or modifications, maintaining a record of all personal expenses incurred, and submitting periodic recovery status reports. An example of the administrative actions format is provided in Exhibit 53.6.

THE DATA CENTER RECOVERY PLAN

INITIAL RESPONSE ACTIONS

NOTIFICATION AND COMMUNICATIONS TEAM

Primary: _____ Alternate: _____

Recovery procedures follow. Read the entire section before performing any assignments. The recovery objectives will dictate the need for and timing of all assignments.

1. Report to the recovery headquarters following the initial recovery team alert. Ensure that you bring your off-premises copy of your data center recovery plan, your proximity access card, and your building security badge.

2. Meet with the recovery headquarters manager to review recovery objectives and to receive direction on specific actions to be taken on the basis of the disaster situation.

3. Use the team staffing requirements to assign personnel to the notification and communication team.

4. Complete the personnel location control form (Workpaper II4.13) by identifying the work location and contact phone number of each team member. Retain the completed form for the master recovery file in your area.

Exhibit 53.4. Initial response actions.

STEP 7: DETERMINE THE RECOVERY LOGISTICS

The development committee must also determine the recovery logistics to be used in documenting the DCRP. Broadly speaking, determining the recovery logistics involves identifying what recovery actions should be included in the plan, who should be assigned responsibility for performing these actions, and how the responsibilities should be carried out. These actions include damage assessment, notification, equipment replacement, procurement of recovery materials and facilities, recovery of data, and transportation of personnel and equipment to the backup sites after a disaster.

The following sections provide examples of recovery logistics for the disaster site recovery team, computer operations recovery team, and recovery headquarters team. The examples suggest the types of functions that should be performed by each team. The development committee should consult with key team members to modify this basic set of recovery logistics to meet the specific requirements in the organization.

```
            THE DATA CENTER RECOVERY PLAN
                 RECOVERY ACTIONS
        NOTIFICATION AND COMMUNICATIONS TEAM

Primary: _____ Alternate: _____

1. Review recovery actions for each phase of the recovery effort.

2. Reserve specific telephone numbers to be used for outgoing and
   incoming calls. Indicate the phone extension, whether it is an
   incoming or outgoing line, and who is assigned to monitor the line.

3. Coordinate the department personnel notification activities:

 a. Work with the recovery headquarters manager to assign personnel to
    perform the department personnel notifications:

   1. Recording the location and telephone number of the recovery
      headquarters on the personnel notification procedure (Workpaper
      II4.17). Make copies of this procedure and distribute to all
      individuals performing the department notifications.
   2. Reviewing the instructions for calling personnel believed to have
      been working during the disaster and potentially injured. Refer
      to the personnel notification procedure (Workpaper II4.17). This
      procedure has been developed to limit the possibility of
      prematurely alarming families of employees who may have been
      injured by the disaster.
   3. Reviewing the priority assigned by the recovery management team
      to identify those individuals who should be called immediately.
   4. Providing the individuals with the personnel notification
      checklist (Workpaper II4.18).
   5. Obtaining authorization from the recovery headquarters manager to
      begin department personnel notification activities.
```

Exhibit 53.5.   Recovery actions.

Recovery Logistics for Three Teams

Disaster Site Recovery Team. The disaster site recovery team is responsible for the following logistics:

1. Determining the extent of damage to:
   – Electrical services
   – Air conditioning and heating systems
   – Water and plumbing systems
2. Controlling all building utility repair activities at the disaster site.

THE DATA CENTER RECOVERY PLAN

ADMINISTRATIVE ACTIONS

NOTIFICATION AND COMMUNICATIONS TEAM

Primary: _____ Alternate: _____

1. Maintain the personnel location control form (Workpaper II4.13). Retain the completed forms for the master recovery file in your area.

2. Maintain accurate written documentation of any changes or modifications to standard operating procedures. Make sure temporary changes or modifications do not carry over to normal operations following the recovery operation shutdown.

3. Maintain a record of all personal expenses incurred during the recovery operation (receipts should be attached).

4. Submit periodic written recovery status reports and expense reports to the recovery headquarters manager.

5. Collect disaster recovery time sheets (Workpaper II4.16) from all team members and submit to the administrative and clerical team leader on a weekly basis.

Exhibit 53.6. Administrative actions.

---

3. Determining the extent of damage to:
   – Equipment
   – Data
   – Documentation
   – Supplies
   – Work in Process
4. Ordering replacement equipment.
5. Installing and testing repaired or replacement equipment.
6. If a temporary location is required, identifying, selecting, and preparing a location.
7. Controlling the movement of personnel, equipment, and materials to the prepared site and the disaster recovery backup site.

The disaster site recovery team is responsible for all activities related to damage assessment, salvage, repair, and replacement at the site of the disaster. This team consists of the following members:

- The disaster site manager.
- The facility damage assessment and restoration team leader.
- The equipment damage assessment and restoration team leader.
- The communications recovery team leader.

Computer Operations Recovery Team. The computer operations recovery team is responsible for the following logistics:

1. Initiating the backup site disaster alert.
2. Controlling the retrieval of backup data and documentation from the off-premises tape vault.
3. Managing the loading and initiation of operating systems, libraries, and utilities.
4. Loading and restoring disk data.
5. Reloading and recovering database data and files.
6. Processing systems and jobs according to the approved processing schedule.
7. Enforcing data backup and rotation procedures during the recovery operation.

The computer operations recovery team is responsible for all activities related to restoring the computer services to data center end users. This includes organizing the move to a backup site and the move to the data center after it is repaired. The computer operations recovery team consists of the following members:

- The computer operations manager
- The computer operations team leader
- The systems software team leader
- The tape operations team leader
- The applications recovery team leader
- The communications recovery team leader.

Recovery Headquarters Team. The recovery headquarters team is responsible for the following logistics:

1. Managing the IS department personnel notification activities.
2. Notifying executive and senior management of the disaster situation and recovery plan activation activities.
3. Notifying staff department representatives of the recovery plan activation.
4. Controlling all incoming telephone calls.
5. Providing administrative and clerical support to all recovery personnel throughout the recovery operation.
6. Collecting and processing all expense reports.
7. Collecting, summarizing, and distributing recovery status reports.

The recovery headquarters team is responsible for all activities related to the management of the recovery operation and support of the disaster site recovery team and the computer operations recovery team. The recovery headquarters team consists of the following members:

- Recovery chairperson
- Recovery headquarters manager
- Administrative team leader
- Notification team leader

For an overview of the three major teams and subteams responsible for DCRP recovery logistics, see Exhibit 52.2 in Chapter 52, "Developing a Data Center Recovery Plan: Part I."

CONCLUSION

This chapter took data center managers through the final three steps on the way to developing a recovery plan for their data centers. It showed how to establish the appropriate level of detail and format for these plans. It concluded by discussing what types of recovery actions should be covered in the plan, as well as the team responsible for these actions.

Chapter 54
Integrating LANs into the Disaster Recovery Plan

Gilbert Held

UNTIL RECENTLY, THE CORPORATE MAINFRAME OR MINICOMPUTER was the principal repository of important corporate data. This resulted in the design of corporate disaster recovery plans to safeguard mainframe or minicomputer information, as well as to provide mechanisms to recover data in the event of a disaster.

The growth in the use of local area networks (LANs) resulted in vital corporate information moving onto the LAN. However, instead of being relegated to servers, important information necessary for an organization to resume operations in the event of a disaster resides on both servers and workstations. Because of this, the data center manager must consider incorporating both client and server information into the corporate disaster recovery plan.

This chapter focuses on practical methods and techniques to consider to integrate the backup of client and server databases onto a minicomputer or mainframe. Once this has been accomplished, the data center manager can use the previously developed disaster recovery plan as a foundation for such functions as moving client and server data off-site and retrieving that data. This is because once client and server data are moved onto the mainframe or minicomputer, such data can be treated as another data set within the series of data sets that make up the corporate database. Therefore, an organization's previously developed technique to move backup tapes/cartridges or televault data to an off-site storage location may be able to continue as planned — or with only slight modifications to accommodate the increase in data to be backed up.

0-8493-9824-X/00/$0.00+$.50
© 2000 by CRC Press LLC

DATA TRANSFER

Perhaps the best method to consider when integrating client and server data into the corporate disaster recovery plan is an upward migration data-transfer methodology. That is, workstation data is transferred to a server while server data is transferred to the mainframe or minicomputer. Because this method of data flow places workstation data on appropriate servers, backing up server data to the corporate mainframe or minicomputer also results in the backup of client data. Although this process sounds simple, one key factor must be considered, or the backup of client data could result in a considerable — and unnecessary — expenditure for additional storage capacity. That key factor is the criticality of information stored on client workstations.

WORKSTATION DATA

Although servers can be considered as the central repository of LAN data, not all vital information is stored there. Most workstation users maintain a number of databases of critical information on their workstations. Information can range in scope from Rolodex files used by a pop-up, terminate-and-stay-resident (TSR) program to data files used by electronic spreadsheets operating on the workstation, such as Lotus 1-2-3, Excel, and similar products.

If data center managers attempt to back up all data on each workstation to an appropriate LAN server, they can soon run out of data storage capabilities on their servers. For example, a LAN has 100 workstations served by two servers; if each workstation has a 250M byte disk, the maximum data storage capacity of all workstations on the network is 25G bytes (i.e., 100 * 250M bytes). In comparison, most LAN servers typically have a data storage capacity of between 5G bytes and 10G bytes. Thus, the backup of data stored on each workstation onto the two servers on the LAN could use all available storage on each server, as well as require an additional server or the upgrade of the storage capacity on the existing servers. Therefore, most organizations should consider the selective backup of data from client to server.

SELECTIVE CLIENT BACKUP

The selective backup of client data onto an appropriate server can be a tedious process, if done manually. Fortunately, most LAN operating systems include a login script capability. This capability permits data center managers to create program statements in a script file that are automatically executed when a user accesses the network. For example, NetWare has System, Profile (under NetWare 4.X), and User scripts.

The System script is created by the administrator and is automatically executed whenever any user logs into the network. The primary use of the System script is to create uniform network drive mappings and to display information appropriate to all network users or groups of users, which is accomplished by first examining the user group associated with the new user and comparing that group to one or more groups included in the script. Upon the occurrence of a match, a display statement displays the appropriate message relevant to the group associated with the user.

The Profile script, which is only supported by NetWare 4.X, recognizes the necessity to group users into departments. Although the Profile script is optional, it provides a mechanism to initiate functions based on the affiliation of a network user with an organizational department. Profile scripts are executed after System scripts.

The last script supported by NetWare is the User script. This script is executed last. The User script can be created by the end user or data center manager; however, as a matter of policy, many network administrators restrict the ability of the end user to modify the User script.

Because the User script is always executed upon user login, it represents a mechanism to tailor backup activity to the requirements of each network user. This considerably reduces the amount of data to be moved from clients to server, minimizing not only the amount of data storage required on the server for workstation backup, but also the effect of client-to-server data transfer upon network performance.

The key to the use of a NetWare login script for client backup operations is the # (e.g., the execute command), which enables the execution of any external to the script executable file, such as a Disk Operating System command or a commercial program. For example, the program statement #COPY C:\LOTUS*.WKS F:\%USER_NAME\BACKUP results in the transmission of every file with the extension .KWS in the directory LOTUS on the user's C drives each time he or she logs into the network. Those files are transferred to the directory BACKUP under the directory of the user's %USER_NAME on drive F. %USER_NAME is a NetWare script replaceable variable, which is replaced by the actual user name of the user. For example, if the user name were FWARD, the files would be stored on drive F, which is assigned to the first network drive, in the path F:\FWARD\BACKUP.

Through the use of the %USER_NAME replaceable variable, separate directories can be created for each user and a common target statement can be used to move information to the appropriate server directory location. Therefore, the second portion of the statement #COPY C:\LOTUS*.WKS F:\%USER_NAME\BACKUP results in files being moved to the directory BACKUP under the directory with the user's name on network drive F. Exhibit 54.1 is an illustration of how this common portion of the

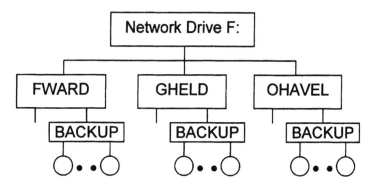

Exhibit 54.1.   Creating a uniform backup structure on a server.

#script statement results in the uniform placement of backup client data on a server when three user names are FWARD, GHELD, and OHAVEL. Exhibit 54.1 illustrates the physical location of files in each BACKUP directory for the three network users. Note that the use of a uniform method to store backed-up data also provides a mechanism to locate data easily when a restoral operation is required. Therefore, a mechanism that places backed-up client data in a predefined server directory structure is an important consideration when tailoring the disaster and recovery plan to include client and server data.

BACKUP OPTIONS

Another effective copying method is the XCOPY statement, which can be used to copy all files or specified files from the current directory and all subdirectories. In comparison, the COPY statement is limited to transferring all files or specified files from the current directory. Therefore, one XCOPY command may be able to replace a series of COPY commands.

The use of COPY and XCOPY moves data as is. In doing so, those statements do not take advantage of the redundancy inherent in data; to do that, the data center manager must use either a commercial or shareware program developed to compress data.

COMPRESSING DATA

In addition to reducing data storage requirements, the use of a compression-performing program can significantly reduce the effect of backup operations upon LAN performance. This is because compressing data before transmitting it to the server results in a lesser quantity of data having to be transmitted.

```
COPY CON: KEYFILE
C:\PAYROLL\*.DAT
C:\LOTUS\*.WKS
C:\QB45\*.DAT
C:\WGRAPH\*.GPH ^Z
```

Exhibit 54.2.   Creating a PKZIP list file.

One of the most popular compression and archiving programs is PKZIP from PKWare, Inc. Although this program is primarily used as a mechanism by computer users to compress data before uploading or downloading files, it also provides a mechanism to facilitate the backup of client information on appropriate servers. For example, the manager can place one copy of PKZIP or a similar archiving and compression-performing program on each server. Then, the user could use the # (execute) command in each user login script to execute PKZIP. This takes advantage of the support of list files by PKZIP, a facility that permits tailoring the operation of the program against a predefined list of files.

A list file contains one or more file names. Once a list file is created, the use of the name of the list file prefixed by an @ results in PKZIP operating upon the file names in the list file instead of command line entries. Because a large number of file names can be placed in a list file, but only a few file names can be placed in a command line entry, the user of a list file can replace a large number of command line entries. Exhibit 54.2 illustrates an example of the creation of a list file containing four entries.

As shown in Exhibit 54.2, the DOS COPY command can be used to create a list file. This example has the list file named KEYFILE and uses the COPY command to copy information from the console into the file. After entering four file paths, the list file was terminated by entering a Control-Z, illustrated by the sequence ^Z on the last line of the referenced exhibit. An alternative to using the COPY command is the use of any word processor capable of saving data in American Standard Code for Information Interchange format. Once the list file has been created, it could be used in a PKZIP command line entry. For the purposes of this chapter, it is used in a script file; therefore, the # prefix would be used in front of the PKZIP entry.

The following login script entry would cause PKZIP on the file server to be executed when a user logs into a NetWare network. In the example, PKZIP would process each file listed in the list file named KEYFILE, creating a compressed, archived file on drive F named BACKUP.ZIP. The backup file is placed in the subdirectory BACKUP under the directory %USER_NAME, in which the actual user name replaces the replaceable variable on the server: #F:\PKZIP@KEYFILE F:\%USER_NAME\BACKUP\BACKUP.ZIP. In this example, the file BACKUP.ZIP represents a compressed file that consists of the contents of each file previously listed in Exhibit 54.2 when the list file was created. Using PKZIP commands instead of Disk Operating System COPY or XCOPY commands significantly reduces the file server storage required for storing client backup data. Typically PKZIP provides a compression ratio averaging 3 to 1, resulting in one-third of the data storage required by the non-compressed files. In addition, the time required to transfer files from client to workstation is reduced by approximately 66 percent, significantly reducing the effects of client backups on network performance. This section has described an effective mechanism for effective transference of information onto servers; the next section discusses server backup operations.

SERVER BACKUP

Although there is a large number of server backup products available, almost all products treat LAN servers as separate entities. A few vendors, however, have recognized that large organizations that operate mainframes or minicomputers also operate LANs. Because organizations that operate mainframes and minicomputers normally have a well-defined disaster backup and recovery plan, the integration of LAN data into the mainframe or minicomputer backup scheme could be very advantageous. First, it would enable the existing tape-rotation scheme, by which mainframe or minicomputer data is moved to an off-site location, to continue. Second, the additional expense associated with adding LAN data to mainframe or minicomputer data would result in a minimal additional cost, especially when compared with the cost of establishing a separate disaster backup and recovery mechanism solely for LAN data. Third, and perhaps most important, the integration of LAN data into an existing disaster backup-and-recovery plan results in the treatment of corporate information as an entity, permitting decisions concerning such key areas as the frequency of backups, backup rotation schedules, backed-up information testing, and recovery operations to be considered from the viewpoint of the entire organization.

RECOMMENDED COURSE OF ACTION

Within the past two years, IBM and two third-party software developers have announced products that integrate LAN data into mainframe and AS/400 system databases. Those programs provide the data center manager with the ability to move LAN data from servers to mainframe and minicomputer storage. Because these programs include the ability to set up scripts to execute at predefined times, managers can use the existing network during evenings and weekends to perform full server saves onto the mainframe, minimizing the effects of transferring gigabyte of data upon network performance.

Integrating client and server information into the corporate disaster recovery plan ensures that client and server data are backed up on a pre-defined schedule and moved to an off-site location. This can be extremely important in the face of disaster, because it ensures that vital LAN information is not only saved, but that as part of the disaster recovery plan, information can be restored and made available for use by organizational personnel. Thus, the integration of LANs into the disaster recovery plan is an item that should not be overlooked.

Chapter 55
The Legal Issues of Disaster Recovery Planning

Tari Schreider

DESPITE THE WIDESPREAD REPORTING IN THE MEDIA of disasters and their effects, many companies, corporate directors, and officers remain apathetic toward implementing a disaster recovery plan. Companies are generally unwilling to commit the finances and resources to implement a plan unless they are forced to do so. However, implementing a proper disaster recovery plan is a strategic, moral, and legal obligation to one's company.

If the billions of dollars spent annually on technology to maintain a competitive edge is an indication of how reliant society is on technology, then failing to implement a disaster recovery plan is an indication of corporate negligence. Standards of care and due diligence are required of all corporations, public or private. Not having a disaster recovery plan violates that fiduciary standard of care.

The legal issues involved in corporate contingency planning are some of the most misunderstood and confusing aspects of the entire process of creating a disaster recovery plan. Disaster recovery planners are not expected to be lawyers; however, they are encumbered with the responsibility of understanding the minutiae and vagueness of existing regulatory guidelines and the legal consequences of their companies' failures to implement an effective disaster recovery plan. Although no specific laws state categorically that an organization must have a disaster recovery plan, there is a body of legal precedents that can be used to hold companies and individuals responsible to those affected by a company's inability to cope with or recover from a disaster.

The entire basis of law relating to the development of disaster recovery plans is found in civil statutes and an interpretation of applicability to disaster recovery planning. These legal precedents form the basis of this chapter.

One of the precedents that can be used against companies that fail to plan for a disaster is drawn from the case of *FJS Electronics v. Fidelity Bank.* In this 1981 case, FJS Electronics sued Fidelity Bank over a failure to stop payment on a check. Although the failure to stop payment of the check was more procedural in nature, the court ruled that Fidelity Bank assumed and, therefore, was responsible for the risk that the system would fail to stop a check. FJS was able to prove that safeguards should have been in place and, therefore, was awarded damages.

This case shows that the use of a computer system in business does not change or lessen an organization's duty of reasonable care in its daily operations. The court ruled that the bank's failure to install a more flexible, error-tolerant system inevitably led to problems. As a result, information technology professionals will be held to a standard of reasonable care. They can breach that duty to maintain reasonable care by not diligently pursuing the development of a disaster recovery plan.

CATEGORIES OF APPLICABLE STATUTES

To help make the data center manager aware of the areas in which disaster recovery planning and the law intersect, Contingency Planning Research, Inc., a White Plains, NY-based management consulting firm, has categorized the applicable statutes and illustrated each with an example. Each area is described; however, this discussion is not intended to present a comprehensive list.

Categories of statutes include but are not limited to the following:

- *Contingency Planning Statutes.* These apply to the development of plans to ensure the recoverability of critical systems. An example is the Federal Financial Institutions Examination Council (FFIEC) guidelines, which replaced previously issued Banking Circulars BC-177 and BC-226.
- *Liability Statutes.* These statutes establish levels of liability under the "Prudent Man Laws" for directors and officers of a corporation. An example is the Foreign Corrupt Practices Act (FCPA).
- *Life/Safety Statutes.* These set out specific ordinances for ensuring the protection of employees in the workplace. Examples include the National Fire Protection Association (NFPA) and the Occupational Safety & Health Administration (OSHA).
- *Risk-Reduction Statutes.* These stipulate areas of risk management required to reduce or mitigate (or both) the effects of a disaster. Examples include Office of the Comptroller of the Currency (OCC) Circular 235 and Thrift Bulletin 30.

- *Security Statutes.* These cover areas of computer fraud, abuse, and mis-appropriation of computerized assets. An example is the Federal Computer Security Act.
- *Vital Records Management Statutes.* These include specifications for the retention and disposition of corporate electronic and hard-copy (e.g., paper) records. An example is the body of IRS Records Retention requirements.

STATUTORY EXAMPLES

When the time comes for the data center manager to defend his company against a civil or criminal lawsuit resulting from damages caused by the company's failure to meet a standard of care, the manager needs more than an "Act of God" defense. When no direct law or statute exists for a specific industry, the courts look instead to other industries for guidelines and legal precedents. The following three statutes represent the areas in which a court will most likely seek a legal precedent:

The Foreign Corrupt Practices Act (FCPA)

The Foreign Corrupt Practices Act (FCPA) of 1977 was originally designed to eliminate bribery and to make illegal the destruction of corporate documents to cover up a crime. To accomplish this, the FCPA requires corporations to "make and keep books, records, and accounts, which, in reasonable detail, accurately and fairly reflect the transactions and dispositions of the assets..." The section of this act that keeps it at the forefront of disaster recovery liability is the "standard of care" wording, whereby management can be judged on their mismanagement of corporate assets.

The FCPA is unique in that it holds corporate managers personally liable for protecting corporate assets. Failure to comply with the FCPA exposes individuals as well as companies to the following penalties:

- Personal fines up to $10,000.
- Corporate fines up to $1,000,000.
- Prison terms up to five years.

The Federal Financial Institutions Examinations Council

The comptroller of the currency has issued various circulars dating back to 1983 (e.g., Banking Circular BC-177) regarding the need for financial institutions to implement disaster recovery plans. However, in 1989, a joint-agency circular was issued on behalf of the following five agencies:

- The Board of Governors of the Federal Reserve System (FRB).
- FDIC.
- The National Credit Union Administration (NCUA).

- The Office of the Comptroller of the Currency (OCC).
- The Office of Thrift Supervision (OTS).

The circular states, "The loss or extended interruption of business operations, including central computing processing, end-user computing, local-area networking, and nationwide telecommunications, poses substantial risk of financial loss and could lead to failure of an institution. As a result, contingency planning now requires an institution-wide emphasis..."

The Federal Financial Institutions Examinations Council guidelines relating to contingency planning are actually contained within ten technology-related Supervisory Policy Statements. These policies are revised every two years and can be acquired through any of the five agencies listed earlier in this section.

The Consumer Credit Protection Act

On November 10, 1992, the 95th Congress, 2nd Session, amended section 2001 of the Consumer Credit Protection Act (15 U.S.C. 1601 et seq.) "TITLE IX-Electronic Funds Transfers." The purpose of this amendment was to remove any ambiguity the previous statute had in identifying the rights and liabilities of consumers, financial institutions, and intermediaries in "Electronic Funds Transfers." This act covers a wide variety of industries, specifically those involved in electronic transactions originating from point-of-sale transfers, automated teller machines, direct deposits or withdrawals of funds, and fund transfers initiated by telephone. The act further states that any company which facilitates electronic payment requests that ultimately result in a debit or credit to a consumer account must comply with the provisions of the act.

Failure to comply with the provisions of this act exposes a company and its employees to the following liabilities:

- Any actual damage sustained by the consumer.
- Amounts of not less than $100 and not greater than $1000 for each act.
- Amounts of $500,000 or greater in class action suits.
- All costs of the court action and reasonable attorneys' fees.

Companies covered under this act are subject to all the liabilities and all the resulting damages approximately caused by the failure to make an electronic funds transfer. The act states that a company may not be liable under the act if that company can demonstrate a certain set of circumstances. The company must show by a "preponderance of evidence" that its actions or failure to act were caused by "...an Act of God or other circumstances beyond its control, that it expressed reasonable care to prevent such an occurrence, and that it expressed such diligence as the circumstances required..."

Standard of Care. Each of the three statutes mentioned in this section is based on the precept of standard of care, which is described by the legal publication entitled *Corpus Juris Secundum,* Volume 19, Section 491. The definition is that "... directors and officers owe a duty to the corporation to be vigilant and to exercise ordinary or reasonable care and diligence and the utmost good faith and fidelity to conserve the corporate property; and, if a loss or depletion of assets results from their willful or negligent failure to perform their duties, or to a willful or fraudulent abuse of their trust, they are liable, provided such losses were the natural and necessary consequences of omission on their part..."

DETERMINING LIABILITY

Courts determine liability by weighing the probability of the loss occurring compared to the magnitude of harm, balanced against the cost of protection. This baseline compels companies to implement a reasonable approach to disaster recovery in which the cost of implementation is in direct correlation to the expected loss. In other words, if a company stands to lose millions of dollars as a result of an interruption to its computerized processing, the courts would take a dim view of a recovery plan which lacked the capability to restore the computer systems in a timely manner.

Another precedent-setting case, referred to as the Hooper Doctrine, can be cited when courts are looking to determine a company's liability. This doctrine establishes that even though many companies do not have a disaster recovery plan, there are "precautions so imperative that even their universal disregard does not excuse their omission." Simply put, a company cannot use, as a defense, the fact that there are no specific requirements to have a disaster recovery plan and that many other companies do not have one.

Liability is not just related to corporations, but extends to individuals who develop disaster recovery plans, as well. In 1989, in *Diversified Graphics v. Ernst & Whinney,* the United States Eighth Circuit Court of Appeals handed down a decision finding a computer specialist guilty of professional negligence. In this case, professional negligence was defined as a failure to act reasonably in light of special knowledge, skills, and abilities.

If the directors and officers of a corporation can be held accountable for not having a disaster recovery plan, then this case provides the precedent for individuals who are certified disaster recovery planners to be held personally accountable for their company's disaster recovery plan.

INSURANCE AS A DEFENSE

Directors and officers (D&O) of companies have a fiduciary responsibility to ensure that any and all reasonable efforts are made to protect their companies. D&O insurance does exist, but it only protects officers if they used good judgment and their decisions resulted in harm to their company or employees, or both. D&O insurance does not cover, however, a company officer who fails to exercise good judgment (i.e., by not implementing a disaster recovery plan).

Errors and omissions (E&O) insurance covers consequential damages that result from errors, omissions, or negligent acts committed in the course of business, or from all of these together. In a 1984 precedent-setting case heard in the District Court of Ohio, the court ruled, "Negligence is a failure to exercise the degree of care that a reasonably prudent person would exercise under the same circumstance." With regard to a trade, practice, or profession, the court added that "the degree of care and skill required is that skill and knowledge normally possessed by members of that profession in good standing in similar communities." Liability insurance does not prevent the organization from being brought to court, but it will pay toward the litigation and penalties incurred as a result.

Disaster recovery practitioners possess a unique expertise and subsequently could be held accountable for their actions and advice in the development of a disaster recovery plan. A word of caution here is that if the data center manager passes himself off as an expert, he should expect to be held accountable as an expert.

CONCLUSION

Courts assess liability by determining the probability of loss, multiplying it by the magnitude of the harm, and balancing them against the cost of prevention. Ostensibly, should the data center manager's company end up in court, the burden of proof would be on the company to prove that all reasonable measures had been taken to mitigate the harm caused by the disaster. There are clearly enough legal precedents for the courts to draw on in determining if a standard of care was taken or if due diligence was exercised in mitigating the effects of the disaster on the company's critical business operations. Every business is governed by laws that dictate how it must conduct itself in the normal course of business. By researching these laws and statutes, the data center manager will eventually find where penalties for non-performance are stipulated. These penalties become the demarcation point for reverse engineering the business operations, thus finding the points of failure that could affect the company's ability to perform under the statutes that specifically govern the company's business.

Chapter 56
Using Televaulting and Hot and Cold Sites for Disaster Recovery

Gilbert Held

TELEVAULTING IS A TERM REPRESENTING telecommunications (tele) and security (vault). When combined, the term defines the transmission of critical information to a secure location. That location can be across the street or thousands of miles away.

The use of televaulting provides a real-time solution to an organization's backup requirements combined with the movement of backup data to an off-site location. In comparison, conventional tape backup requires the physical movement of tapes to an off-site storage location.

Advantages and Disadvantages

There are several advantages and disadvantages associated with televaulting that deserve careful consideration. These advantages and disadvantages normally are compared to conventional tape backup operations and the physical movement of backup tapes to an off-site location.

The primary advantage obtained from the use of televaulting is the ability to perform backups and the delivery of backed up data in real time. For example, consider a car rental or airline reservation system. If backups occur once a day, one could lose tens of thousands of records if a fire, flood, or explosion occurred before the next scheduled backup. In comparison, if televaulting is employed, at most, an organization might lose one or a few records that were being processed when the equipment failure, Act of God, or terrorist incident occurred. Although the ability to minimize the loss of data is the major advantage associated with the use of televaulting, another advantage is the fact that its use automatically moves backup data to an off-site location. Thus, the two primary advantages associated with the use of televaulting are the ability to minimize data loss in the event an equipment failure, terrorist act, or Act of God occurs and the ability to move data automatically to an off-site location.

The primary disadvantages associated with televaulting are in the areas of cost, transmission time, and security. Concerning cost, televaulting relies upon the use of a transmission facility to connect an organization's data center to the backup site. Although the transmission facility can be a dial-up analog or digital connection, in all likelihood it will be a leased line or a frame relay connection. The reason for this is the fact that televaulting results in the transmission of either individual records as they are altered or a small batch of altered records. Typically, the end user has the option of configuring a televaulting software program to define the number of altered records that will serve as a trigger for the transmission of a group of altered records to the backup site. Dial-up transmission occurs too frequently if records are changed in significant volume during the work day. Thus, if the backup site is not within the general vicinity of the data center, each call would represent a toll charge, and the frequent number of toll charges throughout the day more than likely would result in the cost of dial-up communications exceeding the cost of a leased line or the use of a permanent frame relay connection.

A second cost factor associated with televaulting that requires consideration is the software required to perform televaulting operations. In addition to having to obtain a televaulting software module that is compatible with an organization's mainframe, minicomputer, or microcomputer server's operating system, one also must obtain a second module that will operate on a stand-alone computer at an organization's backup site.

Investigating Televaulting Viability

Before implementing televaulting, it is important to determine if this technique represents a viable solution to an organization's backup requirements. To do so, first examine or estimate the number and size of record changes that will occur to the organization's database during the busy hour. Here, the term "busy hour" means the one-hour period with the largest number of updated records. Next, examine the transmission capacity of 56 Kbps and T1 1.544 Mbps circuits against the number of records changed during the busy hour to determine if televaulting can keep pace with changes to the organization's database in real or near real time. For example, assume that 30,000 500-byte records are expected to be changed during the busy hour. This equates to requiring the transmission of 30,000 * 500 bytes, or 15,000,000 bytes, per busy hour. Because there are eight bits per byte and 3600 seconds in an hour, without considering the overhead of the transmission protocol the transmission rate required to transport the busy hour changes in real time becomes:

15,000,000 bytes * 8 bits/byte = 33,333.3 bps

3600 seconds

Because a transmission protocol typically adds 20 percent overhead, multiply the previously computed result by 1.2 and obtain a transmission rate of approximately 40,000 bps. Thus, in this situation a 56 kbps transmission facility easily could accommodate the busy hour traffic.

Now assume 3,000,000 records per hour were estimated to be changed, and each record is 5,000 bytes in length. A total of 3,000,000 * 5,000 bytes/records then must be transmitted to maintain pace with record changes. Thus, during the busy hour, 15,000,000,000 bytes would have to be transmitted. This means that the transmission rate required to transmit busy hour record changes in real time to include the consideration of protocol overhead becomes:

15,000,000,000 bytes * 8 bits/byte * 1.2 = 40,000,000 bps

3600 seconds

In this example, the only way televaulting could be used to keep up with record changes would be through the use of a T3 transmission facility that operates at approximately 45 Mbps. Due to the extremely high cost of T3 transmission lines, which can result in a monthly mileage charge between $50 and $100, plus $5000 or more for each local loop to the building and the off-site location, one carefully must examine the potential advantages of televaulting against the extremely high cost of very high-speed transmission lines.

For example, the monthly cost of a T3 line to provide a televaulting capability between locations in suburban Washington, D.C. and Atlanta easily could exceed $75,000 per month to include the cost of access lines. In addition, it is important to note that the second example would be unsuitable even for batching records for transmission on a T1 line because it would require approximately 26 hours to transmit the busy hour changes at 1.544 Mbps. Thus, it is extremely important to determine the ability of transmission capacity to keep pace with record changes prior to implementing a televaulting solution for disaster recovery.

Security

A third area associated with televaulting that also requires careful consideration is security. Because televaulting results in the transmission of corporate data, one may need to consider the use of encryption to protect the contents of data from inadvertent or intentional snooping. Some televaulting programs include an encryption option, typically including a digital encryption standard (DES) module that can be used on both ends of the data link to protect data in transit. Other programs that do not contain an encryption option should not be eliminated from consideration if an organization requires encryption. This is because one can consider the use of stand-alone hardware encryption devices at each end of the transmission facility that could be used to protect transmitted data.

Not Just for Mainframes

One of the more popular misconceptions concerning televaulting is that many persons consider this backup technique as only being applicable for large, mainframe-centric-type organizations. Although televaulting originally was developed as a solution to the real-time backup requirements of mainframe users, today one can obtain software that provides a televaulting capability for minicomputers and microcomputers, with support for several versions of UNIX, Sun Microcomputer's Solaris, Novell's NetWare, and Microsoft's Windows NT. This means that the data center manager, as well as the network manager and LAN administrator, now have the ability to use televaulting to backup in realtime the contents of LAN servers, as well as to move their contents off site.

HOT AND COLD SITES

There are two types of disaster recovery sites one should consider to counteract the potential effect of natural and manmade disasters. Those sites commonly are referred to as hot sites and cold sites.

A hot site represents a location where an organization or a third party installs hardware and software that will enable the organization to continue its data-processing functions in the event a man-made or natural disaster destroys or renders inaccessible the primary data center location. In comparison, a cold site represents a location available for use in the event of an emergency that does not have the necessary hardware and software to allow personnel to immediately begin backup and recovery operations.

The selection of a hot site or cold site as a disaster recovery location primarily depends upon three items — the critical nature of recovery operations, the time required to purchase and install required hardware and software in the event the primary data center becomes inaccessible, and economics.

Time Issues

If an organization processes credit card bills or performs money transfer operations or similar financial processing, it is highly likely that, in the event of a natural or man-made disaster that renders a data-processing center inaccessible, one will not be able to wait for rapidly ordered equipment to be delivered and installed. Instead, the organization more than likely will want to consider the use of a hot site.

There are two types of hot sites to consider — self-established and third-party. Concerning the latter, there are several vendors, including comdisco and IBM, that will initiate contracts to provide an organization with a predefined data-processing capability to include mainframe, LAN servers, and workstations. Such contracts typically are signed to provide up to 30 or 60 days support because it is expected that an organization would be ordering and installing appropriate hardware and software at another location at the same time your employees are transferred temporarily to the hot site location.

Two of the major problems associated with the use of a hot site include the cost of the contract and having the hot site keep up with hardware and software changes occurring at the organization. Concerning the cost of a third-party hot site, it normally is billed using two elements. The first element is a monthly fee that can range between $5000 and $25,000, which is paid to the vendor to provide the organization with the ability to declare a disaster situation for which the vendor agrees to provide the contracted hardware and software for use. The second part or billing element is associated with the occurrence of a disaster and can result in a bill of $5000 to $25,000 per day, depending upon the data center support required, for the use of the hot site. Because the third-party vendor has a contractual arrangement to provide disaster recovery for many vendors, they typically do not allow one to use their facilities for more than 30 or 60 days. Thus, the organization eventually would have to arrange for another location to continue processing, as well as for the required hardware and software.

Recovery Time

If an organization outsources payroll, accounts payable, and accounts receivable, and uses internal processing for administrative functions, it becomes possible to consider the use of a cold site for disaster recovery operations. As previously discussed, a cold site represents a location that one may lease or own and can use in the event of a disaster, but which does not contain the necessary equipment to resume processing. If an organization uses standard commodity-type computer and network equipment, it may be possible to order such equipment and have the necessary hardware installed within a short period of time after employees relocate to the cold site, or even possibly as they arrive. Then, if the organization either used backup tapes that were transferred to a cold site or televaulted backups to the cold site, one will be able to restore computer operations once the equipment is installed.

The Cold-Hot Site Option

One option that deserves mentioning is referred to by this author as the cold–hot site option. Under this option, one would attempt to locate another organization that performs data processing similar to that performed by the organization, but is not a direct competitor to the organization. Each organization would then agree to serve as a temporary hot site for the other organization. This agreement would be negotiated between organizations concerning the number of employees that could use the other organization's facilities and processing priorities and the duration of the use of the data-processing facilities during an emergency. If an emergency occurs that requires the use of another organization's data-processing facilities, then the organization initially affected could locate an appropriate cold site location and order and install appropriate hardware and software, converting the cold site into a hot site prior to the expiration of the time allowed to use the other organization's facilities. Due to the significant potential savings from the use of a cold–hot site option, it deserves consideration along with the use of conventional hot and cold sites.

RECOMMENDED COURSE OF ACTION

Today, most organizations are highly dependent upon their computational facilities. That degree of dependence can range from not being able to tolerate the loss of more than a few records of data to the ability to lose one or more days worth of transactions. If an organization is more representative of the former, its managers will more than likely want to consider televaulting. Regardless of whether or not an organization is a candidate for televaulting, it is important to consider the ability to resume operations at another location in the event the primary location becomes unusable. In such situations, one should then consider the use of a hot or cold site or a cold–hot site to obtain the ability to resume processing in the event that this happens.

Chapter 57
Data Processing and Communications Security During Recovery and Repair

C. Warren Axelrod

MANY ORGANIZATIONS ASSIGN RESOURCES to primary security controls and contingency planning, but few plan beyond the initial recovery process. As data processing (DP) systems become larger, more dispersed, and increasingly linked together over local-area and wide-area networks (LANs and WANs) and such public networks as the Internet, they become not only more critical to organizations but also more vulnerable to abuse. The occurrences of abuse and disaster are becoming more frequent and are having greater impact as system size, distribution, and interconnections increase. As a result, secondary backup measures and further protection during the recovery process are becoming more critical as well as more complex. Yet, data security during system backup and disaster recovery is not usually addressed by most corporate contingency plans.

Computer systems and communications networks are most vulnerable to breaches in security during backup and disaster recovery activities, in particular. In addition, standard backup measures, such as creating multiple copies of data, programs, passwords, encryption keys, and procedures, and storing these copies at a second location, expose systems to even greater risk of information leaks and security breaches.

Security systems traditionally focus on controlling access to secured facilities, computer software, data, and communications networks. Very little attention is paid to recovering, repairing, and preventing further damage to the security system itself. In some circumstances, fixing a damaged security system first, thereby preventing continuing damage, may be more important than recovering systems and data that remain vulnerable to further damage. After all, restoring a system and network makes little sense when the source of the initial breach is still active. However, circumstances do exist in which the systems and networks are so critical that they must be restored as quickly as possible despite the risk of subsequent breaches.

In this chapter, both the backup of security systems and security procedures during backup and recovery are discussed.

SECURITY AND RECOVERY BASICS

Computers and communications networks can be protected by applying the following six basic security functions: avoidance, deterrence, prevention, detection, recovery, and correction. The first three functions address the need to restrict access and limit the authority to have access; the last three are responses to unauthorized intrusions, abuse, or destruction of assets.

These security functions can be defined as follows:

- *Avoidance.* Removal or elimination of any threat to assets, the protection or removal of threatened assets from actual or potential danger, and not creating surplus vulnerable assets.
- *Deterrence.* Discouragement of action that threatens system security. Publicizing disciplinary actions previously taken or that will be taken if such actions are discovered.
- *Prevention.* Implementation of measures to protect assets from security breaches and from intentional or accidental misuse.
- *Detection.* Implementation of means to recognize potential threats to asset. Monitoring the computer and network environment to determine whether such a threat is imminent, is in process, or has already breached the preventative measures. Detection can include raising an alarm in the event of a security breach.
- *Recovery.* Effort to return the system and networks to an operating condition.
- *Correction.* Introduction of new measures or improvement of existing measures to avoid, deter, or to prevent recurrences of security breaches and misuse of or damage to the computer systems and communications networks.

Data security systems should protect the following three major areas of vulnerability: access, misuse, and damage. Each area can be briefly described as follows:

- *Access.* The gaining of entry, physically or electronically, to computer resources, including software, data, the DP facility, or the communications network.

- *Misuse.* The manipulation of computer and network assets in a manner outside of or detrimental to the interests of the organization, whether or not any specific damage resulted.
- *Damage.* The modification or destruction of physical or logical computer and network assets.

In summary, the goal of computer and network security systems is to prevent unauthorized access to DP and communications systems and facilities. If such access does occur, misuse of or damage to the computer and communications assets must be prevented. If, despite such precautions, access is gained and damage occurs, it is necessary to recover the systems and networks from the intrusion and violation of assets and to take action to prevent recurrence.

Control of Access, Misuse, or Damage

Some security functions relate specifically to access control and are directed at preventing unauthorized intrusion. However, misuse and damage can result from a variety of causes, each of which may require different preventative measures and recovery procedures. Misuse or damage can be caused by intentional misbehavior, negligence, or accident. Based on the six-stage breakdown of security functions previously outlined, Exhibit 57.1 shows which security functions are effective for controlling access and which work to limit misuse and damage.

As shown in Exhibit 57.1, the only security function that can be used to control authorized access is detection. That is, no preventative measures are taken if access is detected and observed to be legitimate. However, for unauthorized access, all available security control should be applied. If unauthorized access is detected, backup security should be implemented to prevent the potential recurrence of similar unauthorized access. As a simple example, if current security access codes, such as passwords, are used by someone not authorized to use the system, the codes should be changed immediately, and authorized users should be informed of the change. If users are responsible for changing their own passwords, they should be notified to make immediate changes.

It should be noted that in Exhibit 57.1 an additional step, repair, has been added to the sequence of security functions. When unauthorized access is detected, after invoking security measures to prevent further similar intrusions, an attempt should be made to recover from the intrusion and to repair or replace damaged or compromised security controls. As an extreme example, if attempted physical access results in an injured guard and a damaged door, it is necessary to replace the guard and repair the door to restore access security. Correction, as shown in Exhibit 57.1, is different from

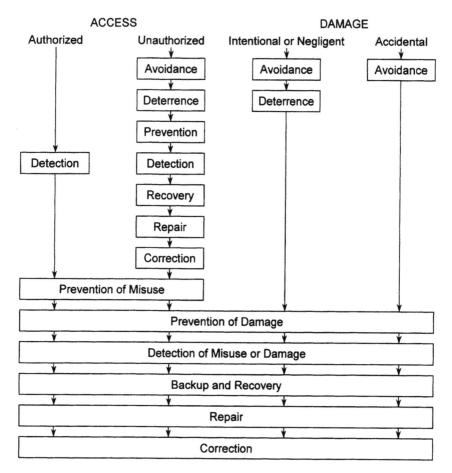

Exhibit 57.1. Measures for controlling access, misuse, and damage.

repair in that it involves changing preventative measures to make them more effective rather than fixing existing measures.

Avoidance and deterrence of damage refers to cases in which the damage is caused by an event other than access, such as a fire in the electrical wiring, a burst pipe causing a flood, or an earthquake. Securing a facility against such damage involves such activities as equipment and facility inspections and worker training. To secure a system against intentional damage or accidental damage caused by negligence, all the avoidance measures should be taken. In addition, it is important to deter any actions that might result in physical damage.

Once access has been gained, whether authorized or not, misuse must be prevented. If misuse is not prevented, it must be at least limited so that it does not cause serious damage. Similarly, potential system abusers should be aware of disciplinary actions, and nonconformance to security guidelines should be noted and eliminated. Preventive measures against misuse and damage generally include access restrictions to systems, networks, and facilities, restrictions on potentially damaging activities (e.g., smoking or keeping open flames), the use of nonflammable and waterproof materials, the locating of computers and network equipment in secured areas, and the installation of protective devices (e.g., surge protection devices and automatic cut-off valves). It should be noted that, in cases of system and network recovery, the deadline requirements for returning the systems and networks to operation may dictate that recovery is only feasible if backup systems, networks, or facilities are available.

SECURITY DURING BACKUP

Once access, misuse, or damage is detected and the organization begins backup, recovery, and repair, security procedures should be followed to:

- Prevent further access, misuse, and damage due to continuance of the initial intrusion or cause of damage.
- Prevent access, misuse, and damage during the vulnerable backup and recovery processes.
- Prevent access, misuse, and damage during the repair process.
- Ensure that security controls do not unduly hinder the backup, recovery, and repair processes.

PREVENTION DURING RECOVERY

After the detection of unauthorized access, misuse, or damage, the highest priority of the data security administrator should be stemming further violations or abuses of the computer systems and networks, with the proviso that human safety should not be compromised. For example, if a fire is detected, the first consideration should be the evacuation of personnel to safety. Immediately after personnel safety is ensured, an attempt should be made to extinguish the fire, but only if the persons doing so are not at risk or are authorized fire fighters.

In the case of detecting unauthorized access to a system or network, the first step is to disconnect unauthorized users from the system, unless apprehension of the perpetrators would be hindered or more harm would be caused to the organization than by allowing continued access. More harm would be caused, for example, if the entire system or network were shut down to stop further unauthorized access — depriving authorized users from performing their work.

The data security administrator should determine whether prevention of further intrusion and abuse is more harmful than continuation of the adverse practice. Because a decision made under such immediate pressure could easily be the wrong one, the rules of action should be carefully specified in advance and strictly enforced during an event. Because it is frequently during the initial moments of an emergency that decisions are most critical, rehearsals, simulations, and other training techniques are a crucial part of such contingency planning.

SECURITY DURING RECOVERY

When the source of abuse has been halted and the situation has been stabilized, recovering the system and facility begins. This may be achieved either on site or at off-site backup facilities.

Physical Access

Because backup and recovery frequently involve non-employees (e.g., fire fighters, messengers, or service engineers), the data security administrator should ensure surveillance of such persons while they are on the premises or handling confidential information. Alternatively, security may be achieved if only authorized persons are allowed access to sensitive areas of information. This may be done by designating emergency personnel in advance. Ironically, emergency surveillance is often conducted by temporarily employing unknown security guards who are unfamiliar with the environment.

Transfer of Data

Transferring confidential, valuable information (e.g., magnetic tapes, reports, or disk packs) to backup sites and returning these media, plus any new information created at the backup site, presents many opportunities for corruption or theft of information. Backup and recovery often necessitate the use of more vulnerable public communications networks, rather than more secure, private data communications networks so that exposures have to be anticipated and the preventative actions taken.

Examples of various approaches to achieving security during backup and recovery are listed in Exhibit 57.2 and are discussed in detail in the following sections.

Physical Access Control

Physical access at the primary and backup sites and access to information and materials in transit can be controlled by retaining reliable security guard service. Temporary security services should be selected in advance, and their references should be checked carefully to avoid hurried, reactive

Exhibit 57.2. Backup and recovery security procedures.

Security Control	Backup and Recovery Procedure
Physical Access	
Guards, On Site	Contract for guard service in advance and preassign employees to guard duty.
Guards, In Transit	Contract in advance with secured transportation service for relocating media and equipment.
Electronic Card Entry System	Provide emergency battery backup for security systems dependent on electricity and provide for manual override system invoked by authorized personnel. Set up contingency access procedures in advance.
Voice and Data Communications Networks	Provide security on contingency lines and equipment equivalent, if possible, to primary networks.
Logical Access	
Passwords	Ensure that existing system passwords can be used on backup systems or issue special contingency passwords. Ensure that changes to the primary system are reflected in the contingency system.
Security Software	Provide comparable and compatible security software and contingency systems.
Dial-up Procedures	Provide contingency dial-up numbers for authorized personnel Pre-specify contingency call-back numbers if the system is designed to hang up and call the user back. Set up equipment and software and specify telephone numbers in advance.
Network Security	Ensure that network security measures (e.g., encryption for data, scrambling for voice) are compatible with the backup systems and that changes to the primary system are reflected in the contingency system.

decisions. Unreliable guard service can negate many of the security controls of backup and recovery. At the same time, contingency access procedures should be developed at both primary and backup sites and for primary and backup communications network facilities, and authorized employees and the guard service should be familiar with these procedures. If electronic entry systems are employed, an alternative method for gaining access should be provided in case the electronic systems are disabled.

Communications Security

Backup communications networks should be armed with security controls. Securing of backup networks is often more difficult than for primary networks, because backup communications lines are often public. Communications backup procedures should accommodate the need to inform users of new changes in dial-up procedures, encryption keys, and communications log-on procedures, when appropriate, and other necessary contact information.

Securing data over public communications carriers can include encryption, error detection codes, positive acknowledgment, or echoplexing. These methods verify message integrity but do not control access. The retention of encryption capability is an issue, particularly during the recovery process, because it means making the required encryption keys available at multiple locations and ensuring that the mechanisms are in place to transfer host or client locations without compromising the security effected by encryption.

Logical Access Controls

It is imperative either to update access passwords and procedures on the backup copies of the system or to have a means of informing users of their backup passwords in case the backup system is activated. Backup passwords should be distributed in the same secure manner as primary passwords. In addition, the security software for the backup system must be continually updated. It would compound a disaster if, after a successful move to a backup site, users were unable to gain access to the system because the security software was not compatible with the primary system or had not been updated to reflect changes in the primary systems and networks.

In summary, specific security measures to ensure continuing system integrity should be appended to every recovery procedure.

Special Security Provisions

The efficiency and effectiveness of the recovery process can be compromised if the same security measures designed to protect the systems and networks under normal operation are implemented during recovery. Security measures must be designed specifically for contingency situations. These security controls must allow for the unusual and urgent requirements of a recovery environment yet still offer protection during a very vulnerable situation.

The most fundamental and significant aspects of security during the recovery phase are that security controls appropriate in normal situations do not work best during disaster recovery and that special provisions must be made in the security procedures to account for such differences. As a simple example, many data centers do not allow system programmers to gain physical access to the computers and prevent applications programmers from having access to production systems. However, during a disaster, a programmer may be critical to effecting a specific recovery. The security procedures must allow for certain individuals to have, in emergency situations, controlled privileged access that may not be available to them under normal operating conditions.

SECURITY DURING REPAIR AND CORRECTION

Frequently, when a disaster has passed and the risk to systems and networks has been reduced, there is a tendency to relax security and repair procedures. Repair and reconstruction often proceeds without the diligence and concentration afforded the recovery process; however, major dangers can result from such relaxation.

First, if another damaging event occurs before the completion of the repair and correction process, the organization may be left without backup or primary systems and networks. Whereas it is improbable that two independent, damaging events will occur in rapid succession, the repair process itself can pose added risk (e.g., welding or high-voltage electrical repair work can increase the risk of fire or further electrical outages). Also, some events have anticipated potential subsequent effects, such as aftershocks from an earthquake or structural damage from a fire or flood resulting in the shifting or collapse of a building.

Second, the repair process usually involves persons (e.g., contractors, electricians, vendors' technicians) who are not familiar with normal, daily operations. The probability of security breaches and abusive or damaging actions increases because of these individuals. A conflict frequently arises between the urgency in repairing damage and the need to carefully plan and control the repair and reconstruction process. Because many types of damage are difficult to predict, setting up contingency plans is impractical or infeasible for any but the most likely incidents. For example, most facilities have procedures for fire prevention and control and for personnel evacuation. Planning for repairs following a fire is often done only after an event when the extent of the damage is known. Much confusion can be eliminated, however, if some simple procedures are followed, such as keeping an up-to-date list of names and telephone numbers for all relevant vendors, contractors, suppliers, and employees. On the other hand, preparation for repair and reconstruction for very rare events, such as a chemical spill, might be handled after the event rather than planned in advance. Basic contingency arrangements should be made such as ensuring that a full set of floor plans and equipment and network layouts is stored at another location.

A reasonable procedure is to make preliminary plans for repairing damage caused by the most likely events, but planning for repairing improbable types of damage does not make sense. Even less justifiable is planning for reconstruction before the event, although names and telephone numbers of contractors and related services should be retained on site. However, special security procedures should be followed during the repair process.

RECOMMENDED COURSE OF ACTION

Risks to computer system and network integrity — through security breaches, misuse, and damage — are amplified considerably after such abuses occur, when the DP and communications environment is in a vulnerable state. Therefore, guarding against further abuses is especially important during the recovery and repair phases following the initial problem. The first line of defense is to ensure that there are fall-back procedures and resources in the event that the primary security system is damaged or otherwise compromised. This helps prevent subsequent breaches. If damage to the computer systems and communications networks occurs despite all precautions, and a recovery and repair process is initiated, security controls, based on those outlined in Exhibit 57.2, should be implemented during the recovery and repair process.

About the Editor

STEVE BLANDING is Regional Director of Technology for Arthur Andersen, based in Houston, Texas. Steve is responsible for directing all internal I/T services, including server and network operations, PC technical services, call-center help-desk services, technology education consulting and training services, data communications, telecommunications, applications development, and technology deployment for the Arthur Andersen offices in Houston, San Antonio, Austin, and New Orleans. He also is responsible for developing and managing the technology capital budget, operating budget, and the technology plan for the region.

Steve has 25 years of experience in the areas of financial auditing, systems auditing, quality assurance, information security, and business-resumption planning for large corporations in the consulting services, financial services, manufacturing, retail electronics, and defense contract industries.

Steve earned a B.S. in Accounting from Virginia Tech and an M.S. in Business Information Systems from Virginia Commonwealth University. He also holds the CIA, CISA, CISSP, CSP, CFE, and CQA certifications. Additionally, he has conducted a number of speaking engagements on various technology topics for the Computer Security Institute, the Information Systems Audit and Control Association, the MIS Training Institute, the FBI Training Academy, and the National Institute on Organized Crime. Steve has also contributed several articles for publication in Auerbach's EDP Auditing Series, the Journal of Accounting and EDP, the *Handbook of Information Security Management,* and EDPACS.

Index

Printed in the United States
By Bookmasters